ISBN: 9781313555142

Published by:
HardPress Publishing
8345 NW 66TH ST #2561
MIAMI FL 33166-2626

Email: info@hardpress.net
Web: http://www.hardpress.net

A HISTORY OF THE UNIVERSITY OF GLASGOW

PUBLISHED BY

JAMES MACLEHOSE AND SONS, GLASGOW,

𝔓ublishers to the 𝔘niversity.

———

MACMILLAN AND CO., LTD., LONDON.

New York, -   *The Macmillan Co.*
Toronto, - -   *The Macmillan Co. of Canada.*
London,   -   *Simpkin, Hamilton and Co.*
Cambridge, - -   *Bowes and Bowes.*
Edinburgh, - -   *Douglas and Foulis.*
Sydney,   -   *Angus and Robertson.*

———

MCMIX

LORD KELVIN, P.C., O.M., G.C.V.O., LL.D., F.R.S.

Professor of Natural Philosophy, 1846-1899. Chancellor of the University, 1904-1907

BORN 1824. DIED 1907

A HISTORY

OF THE

UNIVERSITY OF GLASGOW

From its Foundation in 1451 *to* 1909

BY

JAMES COUTTS, M.A.

FORMERLY REGISTRAR OF THE UNIVERSITY

GLASGOW

JAMES MACLEHOSE AND SONS

PUBLISHERS TO THE UNIVERSITY

1909

T

GLASGOW : PRINTED AT THE UNIVERSITY PRESS
BV ROBERT MACLEHOSE AND CO. LTD.

PREFACE

WHEN in the employment of the University of Glasgow, I was often tempted to wish for a History of that institution, to which one could refer in answering enquiries from the outside, or procuring information needed from time to time by administrators or officials. Besides this interest of a practical nature, I had a keen relish for the story of the University, and I saw that other institutions with no better claims had their Histories, and that the public received them not unkindly. Just before the Paris Exhibition of 1900, I was asked to put together a slight sketch of the University, to accompany some educational exhibits which were to be forwarded. This sketch was translated into French by the late Miss Galloway, but, from some accident or another, it was never sent to the Exhibition. From that time, however, I definitely made up my mind to bring out a History of the University.

It is not for lack of materials that a History has not previously appeared. The *Munimenta* of the Maitland Club embody the main part of the records, charters, and other documents, from the founding of the University to the Royal Commission of 1727, and the Reports of subsequent Commissions add considerably to the stock of information. For the greater part of the time since 1727, the manuscript records are tolerably full, and by the kind permission of the University authorities I have been allowed to peruse them down to about 1860, and to gather from them materials for my History. For a good part of the last half century, a summary of many events and transactions may be obtained from the Abstract of the Proceedings of the University Court, published in successive Calendars; and the Universities (Scotland) Acts of 1858 and 1889, and the Reports of the

Commissions under them, as well as a number of Ordinances made by the University Court, are important in reference to the recent development of the University.

The arrangement of the matter in the University Records, the *Munimenta*, the Reports of Commissions, and kindred sources from which one has to work, give little help in the framing of a narrative, and in many cases the accounts of persons and events require further light before their meaning and relations can be made clear. For the latter purpose I have laid under contribution many books on historical, biographical, and miscellaneous subjects, not only making use of the University Library, but also forming for myself a small collection of books likely to be helpful. From these various sources the framework of a narrative has been slowly put together, and many parts have been written and re-written, and sometimes written over again, before assuming their present form. I desire to add that I alone am responsible for the manner in which the evidence has been interpreted, and for any opinions or estimates expressed in the course of the work.

In the recent period it is natural that events should be more briefly related, and this explains why some aspects of University life noticed before 1858, are afterwards omitted or only mentioned in outline. Having provided a very full Index, I deemed it needless to insert a detailed Table of Contents, and have limited myself to a Plan of the Work, showing the chapters and periods into which it has been divided. There are occasional references to Medicine in the general narrative, but I judged it better to tell the story of the Medical School in a separate chapter. This arrangement obviates the need for too frequent transitions, and gives those interested in the Medical School a continuous and uninterrupted narrative of that department.

I have to record my thanks to the University authorities for permission to inspect the manuscript records during the period mentioned ; to Professor Glaister for some helpful suggestions ; to Professor Moir for information from the records of the Faculty of Procurators regarding the early teaching of Conveyancing ; to Mr. Clapperton, secretary of the University Court, for particulars respecting a number of subjects; to Mr. Galbraith, the Librarian, for the courteous and helpful manner in which access to works in the Library was afforded to me; and to Mr. Craig, Clerk to the General Council, for admitting me to a perusal of the Reports and Minutes of the Council. In a very special degree I have to acknowledge my indebtedness to Mr. Addison, Registrar of the University, for reading the proofs and making many valuable suggestions while the work was passing through the press, and also furnishing information which few others could have supplied, and involving so much care and trouble that few others would have supplied it if they could.

JAMES COUTTS.

PERTH, *30th September,* 1909.

PLAN OF THE WORK

LIST OF ILLUSTRATIONS

to facilitate the working arrangements of the new University, fourteen special deputies were appointed, including the rector, the dean of the faculty of Arts, and one regent in that faculty, to meet once a week at the house of the rector, and consult regarding University affairs, according to their promise given on 19th November, 1451. Thus under the authority and favour of Nicholas V. and James II., with Turnbull as immediate patron and virtual founder, David Cadyow, sub-dean and precentor of the Church of Glasgow, as rector, William Elphinstone, canon of Glasgow, as dean of the faculty of Arts, and Duncan Bunch, William Arthurle, and Alexander Geddas as regents in that faculty, the University began its career.

The early meetings or congregations of the faculty of Arts were held in the Cathedral, or in the Convent of the Friars Preachers, in High Street, but for a short time at the beginning the teaching work of the faculty is said to have been carried on in a building in Rotten Row (*Rattonum via*), called the Old Pedagogy, in which students also had their lodgings. The faculty soon came to teach in other premises, which were also called the Pedagogy and sometimes the College of the faculty of Arts, and the Old Pedagogy by and by passed to other uses, though the name clung to it till, as a time-worn ruin, it was removed within the memory of men still living. In 1453 the faculty held a meeting in the place of the Friars Preachers in High Street, and determined to levy a contribution from the masters ' for the repair of the school in the said place,' and for other purposes. This shows that by 1453 the faculty of Arts were using a school in High Street, and a few years later, in 1460, a most important gift of lands and buildings in the same street was received from James, first Lord Hamilton, who had risen into wealth and power on the ruin of the house of Douglas.

Sir James Hamilton of Cadyow was connected with the Douglases by marriage and descent, and he supported Earl William in his quarrel with the Crown. After Earl William had been slain by the king in Stirling Castle in 1452, Hamilton accompanied Earl James when he rode to Stirling at the head of 600 men, renounced his allegiance, and pillaged and burned the town. After this the king led an army of 30,000 men into the Douglas country and wasted their lands, upon which Douglas and Hamilton submitted. The final trial of strength came in 1455, when the king, having demolished the strong Castle of Inveravon, gathered fresh forces at Glasgow and carried fire and sword into Douglasdale, Avondale, and the lands of Lord Hamilton, and afterwards devastated Ettrick Forest and besieged the Earl's Castle of Abercorn. Douglas had by this time retired to England, leaving his cause in the hands of his brothers and of

Hamilton. The latter, despairing of success, surrendered to the king at Abercorn, and though for a time imprisoned in Roslin Castle, was assured of future favour. The defeat of the Earl's brothers at Arkinholm in May, and the subsequent surrender of the fortress of Threave, completed the ruin of the Douglases, and at a Parliament held in August their estates were either annexed to the Crown or bestowed on nobles friendly to the king, a liberal share falling to Sir James Hamilton of Cadyow, who in 1455 was created first Lord Hamilton.

The Douglas wars and the devastation of their lands and those of Hamilton bore hardly, not only on the districts immediately concerned, but on the neighbouring country, and on the City of Glasgow, from which the forces of the combatants were partly recruited. Much property was destroyed, including crops needful for the subsistence of the people, and trade and industry received a shock from which they could only gradually recover. Destitution followed, the plague broke out in Glasgow in 1455, and wounded and broken men crept back to the city after the war to aggravate the poverty and disease which were witnessed. The University, which had sustained a great loss by the death of Turnbull at Rome towards the end of 1454, felt the pressure of evil times. There was only a small number of incorporations in 1454 and 1455, and, though William Heriss, who was rector for two or three years after this, earned the praise and thanks of the University for his active beneficence, in 1457 the faculty of Arts, on an application by Duncan Bunch and William Arthurle, the regents, ordered six marks to be given them because they were burdened with debts for the rent of the Pedagogy, and in consequence of war, pestilence, and fewness of students. The number of incorporations again improved, and the gift by Lord Hamilton in 1460 of a tenement of buildings with an accompanying area of ground should at least have freed the faculty from the burden of paying rent.

The tenement stood in High Street, between the Place of the Friars Preachers on the south and ground belonging to Thomas Arthurle, chaplain, on the north, and the four contiguous acres of land in Dovehill extended to the Molendinar. The property had some time before been conveyed to the Friars Preachers of Glasgow by Sir Gavin Hamilton, Provost of the Collegiate Church of Bothwell, but in 1455 the Friars resigned their right to it and declared that Sir Gavin and his heirs should be entitled to take back the property into their possession whenever they pleased. The tenement and land thus came into the hands of Lord Hamilton, and in January, 1460, he made a gift of them to Duncan Bunch and the regents of the faculty of Arts, for the use of the regents and students of that faculty, on condition of prayers being said and other religious rites performed for the souls of the founders—Lord Hamilton and his wife, Lady Euphemia, Countess of Douglas and Lady of Bothwell —and of the regents being bound for the future to give faithful counsel in the affairs of the founders and their successors when invited to do so.

Cosmo Innes reviews the evidence on the subject and infers that the tenement bestowed by Lord Hamilton was probably the same which the faculty previously occupied as tenants and for which they paid rent.   As already stated, the faculty were making use of a school in High Street in 1453, and in 1457 one of the burdens which pressed on the regents was the payment of rent for the Pedagogy.   In 1457 the faculty also authorised the expenditure of all the money in their purse on the building of the Pedagogy, and similar outlays on the Pedagogy or College of the faculty of Arts are repeatedly recorded in the following years after the property had been acquired from Hamilton.   The inference drawn by Innes that the successive outlays were applied to the same building is not incompatible with the record, but can hardly be regarded as proved.   The faculty in 1467 ordered the remaining money in the hands of the receptor, Duncan Bunch, to be expended in building a house in the south part of their College, that is, next to the Convent of the Friars Preachers.   Bunch undertook to manage the building, and to return the money in case the house was not built.   The work moved slowly, for at an audit in 1469 Bunch had a balance of twenty pounds, and this sum, along with the receipts of the following year, was ordered to be applied to building the house.

In 1467 Sir Thomas Arthurle, chaplain, who was incorporated as a suppost in 1452, and was doubtless a kinsman of William Arthurle, the regent, conveyed to the latter for the use of the faculty of Arts a tenement in High Street, immediately to the north of Hamilton's, with a strip of land extending to the Molendinar, reserving the tenement to William Arthurle during his life after the donor.   Sir Thomas was dead by 1475, and William Arthurle is last mentioned in 1478, when he had ceased to be a regent, so that probably the tenement had come into the hands of the faculty about that time or soon after.

It will now be appropriate to sketch the organisation of the University and the organisation and work of the faculty of Arts, of all which pretty full records exist, to discuss what organisation existed in other faculties for which separate records do not now exist, and to give a general sketch of the history of the University during the period before the Reformation. Along with the account of the various offices, something will be said of the more notable men who held them.

The chancellor was the most dignified magistrate of the University, holding office, if not by divine right, at least *ex officio* as bishop, and probably, like some other sovereigns, his normal business was rather to reign than to govern.

Though the pope's bull of foundation empowered the successive bishops, as chancellors, to exercise the same authority over doctors, masters, and scholars as the rectors did in the schools of the *studium* of Bologna, they did not exercise this power, but left it to the rectors, on whom also they conferred further jurisdiction. During this period there was no regular and continuous succession of vice-chancellors, though now and again a vice-chancellor exercised the function of conferring degrees, as was done by Duncan Bunch in 1454, the Vicar General in 1456, and Patrick Covyntre in 1494 and 1496. The rector and his four deputies, the bursar, and the promotor, were elected annually at a general congregation held on 25th October (the feast of St. Crispin and St. Crispinian), usually in the chapter house of the Cathedral. All the supposts were entitled to take part in the election, but the voting was not direct. Each nation chose a procurator, the procurators, each in accordance with the mind of his nation, nominated an intrant, and finally the intrants consulted together and elected the rector. This was the full-length procedure as narrated in the most detailed and circumstantial minutes of election, for example, in 1489, 1490, 1512 ; but in the accounts of most of the elections there is no mention of procurators, and the intrants seem to have been elected directly by the nations (1453, 1492, etc.).

In actual practice the rector was the chief ruler and magistrate of the University, who incorporated, or, as we should now say, matriculated new members, summoned and presided over general congregations of the supposts, and, besides the usual periodic business, submitted additional articles for congregation to deal with as occasion arose, special congregations being sometimes convened. He was required to read the University statutes publicly at least once in the year, that the supposts might not profess ignorance of them, and to cause to be recorded all the acts and ' conclusions ' (resolutions) of the University during his time. He was judge in cases affecting members of the University, possessing civil and criminal jurisdiction derived from the bishop, as well as academic jurisdiction. In exercising his judicial functions the rector was enjoined to use the advice of those skilled in law, especially of his four deputies. He appointed the bedellus and the notarius or scribe, the deputies also taking part with him sometimes ; and he was empowered to appoint a person of good reputation, preferably one from the senior beneficed masters, to act as vice-rector in his absence. On ceremonial occasions he was to wear a distinguished costume—a white staff, and, on the greater festivals, a rod of silver being borne before him. On the day of the annual rectorial election the supposts met at the house of the retiring rector, accompanied him to the place of meeting, and, when the election was over, accompanied the new rector back to his house.   On the days of the greater feasts they also met at the house of the rector at the first beat of the bell, and escorted him to the Cathedral and back, while in a similar way they accompanied him to the public University functions.   Perhaps the rector may have felt, like Hamlet, that he was ' most dreadfully attended,' and may have counted it a relief when, in 1490, a statute requiring him to go in procession to church on Sundays and minor feasts was revoked.

David Cadyow, subdean and precentor of the Church of Glasgow, described about ten years later as licentiate in decrees and Canon of Glasgow, was the first rector, probably nominated by the bishop to begin with, though he was appointed by election in 1452, and after an interval was re-elected continuously from 1458 to 1466.   The veteran first regents, Duncan Bunch and William Arthurle, each held the rectorship for a year, in 1468 and 1469 respectively.   In 1474 the electors chose William Elphinstone, master of arts, licentiate in decrees, official-general of Glasgow, and rector of Kirkmichell, afterwards the founder of the University of Aberdeen.   In 1481 Patrick Leich, Canon of Glasgow, was chosen rector, and in the ordinary course he should have presided at the election of his successor next year, but we read that Martin Wan acted as his deputy, Leich being absent ' in the service of our lord the king.'   A scion of the nobility holding a clerical benefice was rector in 1486-7—John Stewart, brother of that great and mighty lord, John, Earl of Lennox, and Lord Dernle (Darnley).   Names of members of the Lennox and Darnley family frequently occur in the early records of the University.   In 1511 the rectorial election was held on Sunday.   In 1513 the record of the election runs : ' *Elegerunt nobilem et illustrem et alti sanguinis virum Magistrum Patricium Graham, fratrem germanum Comitis de Montros, canonicum Glasguensem, in rectorem almae Universitatis Glasguensis pro anno futuro.*'

It was only about six weeks after Flodden, and probably they wished to have a man with strong connections.   Still they were only half satisfied with his performance during the first year, and in 1514 there is a record of a contested election, a thing almost if not quite unique in that early period. Two intrants voted for continuing Patrick Graham in office, while the other two voted for James Stewart, apparently the same who was chosen rector of the University in 1512, when he was described as Canon of Glasgow and rector of Cardross.   In this discord of the intrants it was resolved to decide the election by a majority of votes of the masters, and accordingly they concluded in favour of continuing Graham, and he was again re-elected in

1515 and 1516. There was some difficulty, which is not fully explained, regarding the election of rector in 1497, for it is stated that John Gold-smyth, master of arts, bachelor of decrees, canon of Glasgow, and vicar of Eastwood and Cathcart, was elected rector in absence, by way of com-promise. He deputed Ninian Dawgles, prebendary of Bothwell, to be vice-rector in his absence, and it may be noted that for some years about this time vice-rectors were very frequent. More than once between 1521 and 1526 there was no one present from the northern nation of Alban in the congregation for the rector's election. The same thing happened again in 1537, and gave rise to a strange expedient, for the other nations chose Alexander Logan, a regent, to personate Alban, we can hardly say to represent it.

The four deputies were not intended to act in place of the rector, but were rather deputed on behalf of the nations to form a Council to consult with and advise him in the more important and difficult cases with which he had to deal, as well as in the general administration. They were not appointed by the rector, nor directly by the nations, but were elected by the four intrants as the rector himself was. In the earliest years there is no record of the appointment of deputies, but in 1468, when Duncan Bunch was chosen rector, five persons, not expressly called deputies, were appointed to assist him with their advice ; and next year, when William Arthurle was elected, a doctor of decrees and three canons ' assignati erant deputati ad assistendum rectori.' The practice of appointing deputies on the day of the rectorial election, though not invariably followed, seems to have been firmly established by 1475. They were largely drawn from the clergy ; regents were also frequently appointed (for example, Duncan Bunch, William Arthurle, Patrick Covyntre, and John Doby), and more rarely the dean of the faculty of Arts. When the mode of appointment by intrants is considered, it is curious to note that often two and sometimes three of the intrants were themselves chosen or chose themselves to be deputies. Sometimes special deputies, distinct from the ordinary ones, were appointed to consider particular business remitted to them ; and frequently on the day of the rectorial election two or three masters were appointed to audit, by themselves or along with the rector, the accounts of the bursar (treasurer)—sometimes of two or three bursars.

Usually someone in clerical orders was elected to the office of bursar or treasurer, sometimes a regent was chosen, and in 1521 Matthew Reid, master of the Grammar School. The bursar collected the University dues from those proceeding to graduation, but was not allowed to dispose of the goods of the University without its consent or that of the rector. Some of the graduates were excused, on the ground of poverty, from paying fees, and too many of them were much inclined to excuse themselves. Though the sums to be collected were not large, those who should have paid acted on the motto *festina lente*, and, indeed, the bursar often did likewise in accounting for the fees collected. It must not be supposed that the University bursar dealt with the fees in all departments, for the faculty of Arts had a bursar or receptor of its own, and for a time at least this may have been the case in other faculties. Fees were also payable to various University officers, including the rector, regents, examiners, beadle, and scribe.

The promotor was a kind of sheriff's officer, whose necessary expenses were paid by the University, and whose business it was to recover debts, and to summon before the rector debtors or supposts who had transgressed the statutes, including licentiates who failed to graduate within the time appointed according to their oath. Probably it was not remissness on the part of the promotor, but want of support from the higher powers and obstinacy on the part of debtors that hindered this officer from being effective.

The rector was empowered to appoint the bedellus annually, but the council of deputies usually took part in making the appointment, and in 1519 the vice-rector summoned a general congregation to make the election, and they chose '*Dominum Willelmum Huchesoune, capellanum.*' The bedellus seems to have been frequently graced with a title, for we read of '*Dominus Thomas Crauffurd*' and '*Dominus Jacobus Schaw*' being appointed. In 1460 the bedellus of that time, Archibald M'Nelsone, appears in a list of the incorporated members. The bedellus kept the schools in order, and on the days of public functions arranged the seats of the president, the bishop's chair, the benches of the doctors and nobles, and the places of the supposts. He posted up notices of the public ceremonies, such as graduation and licensing, disputations of the masters, and also of the times of beginning to read books in the course of the teaching. He proclaimed the mass which marked the resumption of lectures, and also proclaimed University holidays and the festivals given to their academic friends by those about to graduate or to be licensed. He administered the oath to licentiates, and himself took oath, on his appointment, to be obedient to the dean and mindful of the welfare of the University, and to intimate to the dean or to any master if he conceived any harm to be impending to one or the other. The bedellus also attended the rector, and on ceremonial occasions bore before him the official mace or rod. The statutes required the bedellus to serve any student of the faculty of Arts who paid him sixpence at the feast of All Saints, but the service for this fee could not have been very exacting. He was also allowed eightpence from each student before admission to trial for the bachelorship in Arts, and eighteen pence from each candidate before he ' determined.' From the rather infrequent notices of the appointment of a bedellus, it seems likely that the same person continued in office for a considerable length of time.

The notarius or scribe was appointed in the same way as the bedellus. He recorded the judicial acts of the rector and the ' conclusions ' (resolutions) of the University meetings, noted the names of members present in the city but absent from meetings of congregation, and wrote out lists of the supposts according to their nations.   One of the statutes provided that each new member incorporated by the rector should pay sixpence of drink-money to the scribe.

The houses and lands bestowed by Hamilton and Arthurle strengthened the faculty of Arts, which alone of the faculties continued in organised working activity during the whole period before the Reformation, and left behind records of its meetings and transactions.   There is, indeed, a gap in the minutes of the faculty from 1509 to 1535, but evidence from other sources shows that its work was actively carried on during this interval, and it was during this time that Major's regency of four or five years gave a fresh stimulus to the life of the University.

The faculty of Arts had a staff of officers similar to those of the University—the dean of the faculty corresponding to the rector of the University, the bursar (or receptor) and the promotor doing similar duties in both cases.   The practice of electing four deputies to form a council for the dean also existed in the faculty of Arts, and their election was provided for by the early statutes, but the custom of electing them, or at least of recording their election, arose rather later (about 1480) than in the case of the rector's deputies.   They advised the dean regarding measures to be proposed to meetings or congregations of the faculty, and regarding the summoning of special meetings, as well as in other matters.   Special deputies were appointed from time to time to audit the accounts of the bursar.   The day for the annual election of the dean and other officials was the 25th of June, the morrow of John the Baptist, and the election was usually held at the altar of St. Nicholas, in the inferior chapter house of the Cathedral, which was the statutory place, but for some time after 1535 elections were held at the altar of the inviolate virgin, though the last four which have been recorded were held in the normal place.   By the statutes masters only were entitled to attend congregations of the faculty, but both masters and students had to attend the mass which was performed before the business of election was entered upon.   Near the end of the period supposts are also mentioned as taking part in the election (1543, 1547, 1552).   The faculty avoided the arbitrary division into nations and the clumsy and intricate voting by means of procurators and intrants which prevailed in University elections.

The dean convened meetings of the faculty in statutory form by an intimation on the doors of the greater church from the dean of the faculty of Arts to all and each of the masters, naming the time, place, and business of the meeting, and summoning them to attend on pain of being fined two shillings.   The fine seems to have been often incurred and seldom exacted, indeed there was a provision that the dean should not proceed to the punishment of perjury against masters failing to attend, but should report the case to the faculty, by whom he should be guided in any further procedure according to the quality of the person and the quantity of the disobedience.   In the business of the congregation the dean was to decide, as far as possible, according to the deliberations of the masters, and was to promote peace in the faculty and execute punishment against transgressors. Duncan Bunch, when acting as regent in 1467, had to deal with an unruly member, William Thomson, vicar of Inverkip, who refused to deliver up certain books to William Arthurle, regent ; and on that occasion Bunch asked the faculty to declare whether a master who felt himself aggrieved by the decision of the dean had a right to appeal to the faculty.   It was declared that, as the dean was head of the body, there could be no such appeal.

No one could be admitted to study for a degree till he had been incorporated as a member (suppost) of the University by the rector, but the subsequent stages of his curriculum were controlled by the dean.   Candidates for the bachelorship were scrutinised by him to see that they had fulfilled the requirements, and after they had been examined, he fixed with the triers (examiners) the date of the candidates' ' determination.'   In the case of candidates for license or for M.A., the dean enquired at the regents what students possessed the qualifications, and examined the certificates of the regents under whom they had studied the ordinary and extraordinary books prescribed, and the triers could admit to examination only the candidates presented by the dean.   License in Arts was not strictly a degree, but a stage on the way to the degree of M.A., and a stage at which candidates were not permitted to rest, for in 1455 the faculty resolved that before admission to license candidates should swear to graduate as M.A. within four months, unless the faculty allowed otherwise for proper cause.

In 1522 the University congregation passed a more stringent regulation.   After strongly reprimanding the bachelors who obtained license and who afterwards, in contempt of the statutes of the University and of the faculty of Arts, and, what was worse, in violation of their own oath, neglected to take the master's degree within the statutory time, the congregation decreed that no bachelor should afterwards be admitted to license till he had deposited suitable caution that within eight days he would appear in the place appointed to receive the degree of master.   The dean kept a record of the results of examinations, and presented for license only those who had satisfied the requirements.   Candidates for the bachelorship were under trial for some time, and afterwards the dean and triers appointed to them a day of ' determination.'   One might interpret this as setting a limit to their probation, but a different interpretation has been given, namely, that the candidates were in use to determine in a continued discourse some question in Logic or Moral Philosophy propounded for the occasion, and were consequently named ' determinants.'

A statute of 1454 enacted that every ' determinant ' before being pronounced a bachelor should pay twelve pence to the dean, and every candidate for license the same sum before being admitted, and that the president should not presume to take the chair till payment was made.   In every general congregation the dean was to have at hand for reference the statutes and book of ' conclusions,' and in order that students might not allege ignorance when they transgressed, the dean or some one of the regents was required to read at least three times a year to a full meeting of students the statutes concerning them.   An official seal for the dean was considered necessary from the earliest times, and in 1455 an order was given to procure one with a hand holding a book engraved in the middle, and a salmon and a bird right and left.

The earliest dean, chosen at the first congregation of the faculty in 1451, was William Elphinstone, Canon of Glasgow, the father of William Elphinstone who was rector in 1474, and afterwards Bishop of Aberdeen. William Sympill, Canon of Glasgow, succeeded Elphinstone as dean in 1453, and he was continued in 1454 and 1455, and re-elected in 1459, 1471, and 1480.   He must have been one of the last survivors of the early University staff, outlasting the veteran regents, Duncan Bunch and William Arthurle, both of whom more than once held office as dean.   John Goldsmyth, bachelor in decrees and master of Arts, vicar of Eastwood and Cathcart, rector of the University in 1490 and 1497, was chosen dean in 1486, 1487, and 1488 ; and Patrick Elphinstone, rector of the University in 1485, 1498, and 1505, was dean in 1489 and 1491.   Thomas Forsyth, master of Arts, Canon of Ross and vicar of Tullynessle, rector of the University in 1501, 1502, and 1503, was chosen dean in 1496, and re-elected continuously till 1500.   Robert Hamilton, rector of Baldernock, was elected dean in 1506, and continued in 1507.

For the next two years the election has not been recorded, and from

1509 to 1535 the faculty minutes are wanting. In February, 1536, William Hamilton was dean, and he was re-elected that year and in 1537. John Stewart, Canon of Glasgow and rector of Moffat, was chosen dean in 1546, and re-elected continuously till 1551. John Layng, Canon of Glasgow, rector of Kirkpatrick, and vicar of Dregarne (Dreghorn), was elected continuously from 1552 to 1555. He was the last of the dynasty of deans before the Reformation of whom we have mention. Now and again a vice-dean was appointed to perform the dean's functions in his absence, as in 1484, when the dean petitioned the faculty for the appointment of a vice-dean, and Walter Lesley, principal regent, was elected, and 1490, when the dean deputed John Doby to be vice-dean.

It has been said that the dean had four deputies to form a council, as the rector had. They were generally canons, rectors, vicars, or prebendaries of the Church, or regents of the College. John Doby and Patrick Covyntre, long-enduring and versatile regents, were deputies as well. In the last quarter of a century of this period the minutes are briefer, and little has been said about deputies.

The bursar, or receptor as he is frequently called, was treasurer, and the office was usually, though not always, held by a regent. Duncan Bunch, ever ready when duties were to be done, was appointed receptor in 1457, and held office for an exceptionally long time, continuing to act as bursar even when also dean ; and the ubiquitous John Doby is mentioned as bursar in 1490. John Houstoun, vicar of Rutherglen, was elected bursar in 1457, and continued for the next three or four years.

The faculty of Arts, as well as the University, elected a promotor—a sort of sheriff's officer—for the recovery of debts and citation of debtors, but in this case also the disappointing frequency with which debts and arrears are mentioned seems to show that the promotor's services were not effective.

The vitality of the faculty of Arts depended mainly on the regents, who seem to have been diligent, and not wanting in ability and learning as these were estimated in their own age and country. Anyone who had received the degree of master was theoretically eligible for the work of teaching, and there was a regulation that after graduation masters should continue two years in the University, but in practice this requirement was generally disregarded. A perusal of the early records leaves no doubt that the teaching which qualified for graduation was carried on, not by masters teaching in virtue of the qualification conferred by their degree, but by certain masters specially chosen and appointed to teach, and known as regents. The appointment seems to have been made by the faculty, though the bishop as chancellor sometimes intervened. At a meeting of the faculty in 1480 John Browne, Canon of Glasgow, who had previously been a regent, was admitted as principal regent in virtue of letters granted to him by the bishop under his seal, and by the dean and faculty under the seal of the faculty.

In 1478 the faculty removed Walter Bunch from the regency, he being then pronounced quite unfit for the office. They then committed the regency to John Goldsmyth and John Doby, with power to them to assume a third regent with consent of the faculty. In 1485 Walter Lesley, principal regent of the pedagogy, petitioned the faculty to provide a suitable regent for the office of principal, alleging that he was no longer able to bear that heavy load. The faculty having considered the matter, urged Lesley to continue in office till next feast of Pentecost, which he freely promised to do. On 18th July, 1488, there was publicly read at a meeting of faculty a letter from the bishop as chancellor, deposing George Crechtone, principal regent, and requiring him to remove from the regency, on pain of ecclesiastical censure. The bishop then enjoined the faculty to provide and choose a fit and learned man to be regent, and they chose John Goldsmyth, vicar of Eastwood and Cathcart. Crechtone must have made his peace with the bishop, for, though no longer principal, he is again mentioned before the close of the year as in the active discharge of a regent's duties.

Usually there were three regents in Arts, but sometimes only two, and it is minuted that on 2nd October, 1481, ' *Magister Joannes Browne, tanquam habens curam collegii artium pro anno futuro, acceptavit onus lecturae per se.*' Rather sweeping deductions have been drawn from this and a few other exceptional entries. The solitary regency of Browne seems to have been brought before the faculty expressly because it was extraordinary, and it lasted only a short time, for on 26th June, 1482, there was elected as one of the deputies on the dean's council Richard Douglas, who is described as one of the regents in Arts, proving that before this time Browne had ceased to be alone in the regency. Even during the last twenty or thirty years of the Catholic period, which were probably less prosperous than the average, frequent evidence occurs of the existence of at least two regents. The regents sat at the same table with students who had sufficient means to lodge and have their meals in the College, and they had to visit the chambers to see that the students were in their places when the College gates were shut at nine in the winter and ten in the summer evenings, but they could take these things by turns, and so enjoy intervals of freedom.

Some rather strict and peremptory regulations, passed in 1532 at a very full congregation of the faculty of Arts, which the rector and the supposts also attended, seem to point to a recent outbreak on the part of the students.   It was ordained that no student, whatever his rank or distinction, should carry arms, as sword, dagger, or other offensive weapon, except in cases where the regents allowed ; and anyone offending against this rule rendered himself liable to expulsion and forfeit of the weapon, unless he corrected himself to the satisfaction of the regents.   A sort of curfew regulation was enacted that no student should be found outside his dormitory when the bell had rung for silence at the time when the regents made their nightly scrutiny.   Another rule was passed that students should not rashly or disrespectfully come in the way of the rector, the dean, or the regents by day or night in the streets, nor play any game, even though a lawful one, in presence of the regents, without obtaining their leave. Punishment for offences against this rule was to be administered *caligis laxatis* in presence of the other students, and repeated offences might be punished by expulsion.   It was further enacted at this time that no student sleeping within the College should bring into or maintain within it a servant or relative who did not understand the scholastic Latin speech, under pain of expulsion of the servant, and even the master if he tried to withstand the will of the regents.

In those old times the regents had—if that was anything—direct association with the nobility, for the young nobles of Scotland frequented the University, and, as is recorded, sometimes made a glorious celebration involving great outlays.   Though there is no evidence of the regents having had academic salaries, the direct and indirect emoluments of office were probably not contemptible for the times.   Regents were frequently beneficed clergy, who drew stipend in that capacity while their ecclesiastical duties were performed by deputy.   Every student entering for the degree of master paid two shillings to his masters (regents), and before license paid twelve pennies to the triers, of whom there were normally four, two being regents.   Students also paid ten shillings to the reader (that is the regent) under whom they heard lectures on the prescribed books.   Further, the College was in those early days not only a place of instruction, but of board and lodgings for students, and for these also payments had to be made to the regents.

The frequency with which regents were chosen to the office of rector (to which some emoluments were attached) and dean, as well as to places on the council of the dean and on committees appointed to revise the statutes or transact other important business, added further weight and consideration to their office.   Apart from their work in the University, hardly any of the regents of this period, except Major and Elphinstone, acquired a fame that has lasted down to the present time ; but if we consider that there were only three regents at a time, and sometimes only two, and that some of them held office for a quarter of a century, we see that the total number in the hundred and nine years was not great, and need not be surprised that after the lapse of four centuries the common lot of oblivion has overtaken them. Who shall say how many of the professors of the present day will live in the memory of the public four hundred years hence!

Duncan Bunch, William Arthurle, and Alexander Geddas, the last a licentiate in theology and a Cistercian monk of Melrose, made the first set of three contemporary regents who began with the beginning of the University. Geddas did not continue long in office, but Arthurle and Bunch, already masters of Arts, were incorporated as members of the University on 23rd September, 1451, and continued together as regents for twenty-two or twenty-three years, while Arthurle held office for two or three years more. He had become a doctor of decrees by 1465 or earlier, and was rector of Hewtone (Hutton). Bunch was vicar of Wistone, and afterwards of Dundonald, and still later canon of Glasgow and prebendary of Renfrew. Both were very active in University affairs, doing duty from time to time as rector of the University, dean of the faculty of Arts, examiner for degrees, intrant, and deputy, besides frequently serving on committees. Probably no members of the University in the four and a half centuries of its existence have rendered it more varied or diligent service. By 1478 Arthurle had ceased to be a regent, for in that year he was appointed one of the non-regent examiners for M.A., and in his later years he seems to have been a sort of trustee on the property left to the College in 1475 by Sir Thomas Arthurle—no doubt a kinsman.

The tenement in High Street, with the lands annexed, conveyed to the College of Arts in 1460 by Lord Hamilton, was vested in Duncan Bunch in the first instance ; and in 1472 he was one of a deputation appointed to remonstrate with James III. against a proposal by the Government to tax members of the University in violation of their privileges. In the last three decades of the fifteenth century Alexander Wemyss, David Gray, John Browne, John Goldsmyth, John Doby, and Patrick Covyntre were the most notable regents, nearly all of them holding office for a considerable time, Covyntre rivalling Bunch and Arthurle in the length and versatility of his service. He continued as principal regent till 1509, when John Spreull was second regent. After 1509 there is a gap in the minutes of the faculty till 1535. John Houstoun, Alexander Hammyltoun, and Alexander Logane are the earliest regents we encounter after the record recommences, and Houstoun continued till the date when the faculty minutes cease in 1555, at which time his colleague in the regency was Robert Cunnynghame. The regency of Major falls within the time when the faculty minutes are wanting, but references to him occur in the University records, and these will afterwards be mentioned.

What the regents taught and the students learned in this early period was mainly the philosophy of Aristotle, not as edited by Tyrannion and Andronicus, but in the diluted versions that were current in the middle ages. In addition, some mathematics were included, while bachelors were also required to read a treatise of Petrus Hispanus. It was laid down that the method of teaching should follow the model of the University of Bologna or of Paris. The statutes required candidates for graduation (*promovendi*) to be instructed and examined in a prescribed set of ordinary and extraordinary books, the faculty having power to dispense with portions of the latter. The ordinary set comprised a book of the *Universals of Porphyry*, and the following works of Aristotle: a book of the *Categories*, two books *On Interpretation*, two books of the *Prior*, and two of the *Later Analytics*, four at least of the *Topics*, namely, the first, second, sixth, and eighth, two books of the *Refutations*, eight books on *Physics*, three *De Coelo et Mundo*, two *On Generation and Corruption*, besides *De Sensu et Sensato*, *De Memoria et Reminiscentia*, *De Somno et Vigilia*, and seven books of *The Metaphysics*. The extraordinary books included the following: the text of *Peter Hispanus* with the *Syncategorematics*, the treatise on *Distributions*, three books of the *Meteorologics*, the treatise *De Spera*, six books of the *Ethics*, if read, and *Principles of Geometry*, if read. It was ordained that the *Vetus Ars* (which apparently included Porphyry's *Universals* and Aristotle's *Predicaments* and *De Interpretatione*) should be read for six weeks, the *Prior* and *Later Analytics* three weeks each, the *Topics* and *Refutations* the same length of time, the eight books of the *Physics* during two months, *On Generation* and *De Coelo et Mundo* for four weeks, *De Anima et Parvis Naturalibus* for six weeks, and the books of *The Metaphysics* for the same length of time. The lecturers, however, were to have a discretion as to the length of time given to the extraordinary books. It is not clear how the various subjects were distributed among the different years of the curriculum.

On the first lawful day after the feast of All Saints a congregation of the faculty of Arts was to be held, when the regents were to present such candidates as had fulfilled the requirements, with a view to their being examined for the degree of bachelor, and those found eligible were to undergo an examination, neither too easy nor too severe, conducted by four masters. The general responsions of candidates were not to be after the feast of St. Valentine, and candidates, attired in cap and furred hood, had to carry on disputations three times a week during Lent, each having previously posted up his questions on the doors of the school. To be eligible, students must have attended in the University at least a year and a half, and they were not allowed to ' determine ' under fifteen years of age, unless in special cases, where the faculty might dispense with one year.   The candidates each paid twelve pence to the dean and triers before examination, and a noble to the faculty, eighteen pence to the bedellus, and fifteen pence to the rector before he ' determined.'   When their trials had been successfully passed the presiding master, by authority of the faculty of Arts, declared that they were henceforth to be reckoned bachelors in Arts there and in all places, in name of the Trinity.

It was also laid down that a general congregation should be held on the third July of each year to ascertain what bachelors were eligible for examination for the degree of master, and the faculty then appointed as triers or examiners two regents and two masters who were not regents. In order to become a master the candidate had first to be admitted to license in Arts.   Within five days of the appointment of triers the examinations began, and until the time of license candidates were not allowed to leave their chambers or lodgings except in the dress worn during examination.   They were required to undergo three general responsions in the schools before license, but two of these might be dispensed with in cases where need, good character, and distinguished scholarship were found in combination.   No one was admitted to the degree of master until he had attained the age of twenty years, nor until he had attended at least three and a half years in the University, a year for graduation purposes including ten months' attendance.   A bachelor from another University who had fulfilled the requirements might, on producing sufficient evidence, be admitted to the higher degree, but was required to pay the same fees as if the earlier degree had been taken at Glasgow.   Every candidate for the master's degree paid eight pence to the bedellus, twelve shillings and eight pence to the faculty, and twelve pence to the triers before license, as also three shillings to the faculty when graduating as master, and an honorarium of two shillings to his regents.

At the time of license those admitted were assigned places in the order of merit or precedence by the triers, and these they were afterwards bound to observe.   Masters at the time of graduation swore to continue their studies in the faculty of Arts for two years unless they procured a legitimate dispensation ; that, to whatever station they might come, they would pay respect and honour to the dean of the faculty ; that they would not repeat elsewhere the degree they had obtained at Glasgow ; and that as far as in them lay they would promote agreement among the four faculties, especially with the faculty of theology.

The rector, chancellor or vice-chancellor, dean of faculty, masters and students assembled at the meeting when license was conferred. It was often called the degree of license (*gradus licentiae*), but it was only a stage on the way to the degree of master, and until that degree had been obtained in due course the licentiate had no right to use it. Those about to be licensed went down on their bended knees, and the chancellor or vice-chancellor, professedly by authority of Almighty God, the apostles Peter and Paul, and the apostolic see, gave them license to read, discuss, and act in the faculty of Arts—again in the name of the Trinity. There is no very detailed account of the ceremony of graduation as master, but we frequently read of licentiates receiving the badges or decorations which belonged to that degree (*insignia magistralia*), and of the putting on of the master's bonnet (*birretum*). At the time of their graduation it was the custom for ' determinants ' and licentiates to give a feast or entertainment to the rector, dean of faculty, regents, and triers, while masters, canons, and beneficed clergy might also be invited by leave of the president. Good cheer seems to have been provided at some of these festivals.

Thus in 1495 we read : ' *Eodem anno processit ad gradum bachallariatus sub Magistro Patricio Covyntre, Alexander Erskyne, filius Domini de eodem, qui et gloriosissimum actum celebravit et solvit ingentes expensas.*' When we remember how many men, presumably of fair means, neglected to pay the fees due to the University and the faculty, it is apt to suggest that they were quite as ready to spend money for convivial purposes as for meeting prosaic obligations.

It is a striking characteristic of this period that at almost every turn in the career of a student he was required to take oath, and the frequency with which oaths were set aside, either by dispensation obtained, or perhaps still oftener by the person who had sworn excusing himself from performance, is hardly less remarkable. The history of this time is sufficient to prove that the mere imposition of oaths is no security for good discipline.

In 1490 a congregation of the faculty had before them the question of dealing with fines incurred by masters who did not continue to study for the prescribed two years, but they seem to have let it drop without coming to a deliverance. Some half dozen years afterwards the faculty were roused to at least a passing mood of earnestness. In July, 1496, Alexander Steward, a bachelor, was, on the entreaty of certain masters, admitted to examination for the master's degree, though he had not fulfilled the statutory requirements, but it was provided that he should continue his studies till Christmas, and that in future no one should prefer such a request, on pain of a fine of five marks.

They seem to have regretted this relaxation, for next year the dean submitted to congregation a number of articles for the advantage and welfare of the faculty.   The first of these articles set forth that, since it was ridiculous and to no purpose to make statutes and neither to keep them nor to demand their performance, it would be expedient and useful to provide for the levying of fines due by masters who did not study for two years after graduation, and to settle the mode of proceeding against those who owed sums for dispensation in such cases.   The faculty were also asked to consider whether, seeing that infringements of the regulations were too easily procured by petitionary vehemence and blandishment, it would be well to provide a statute for the keeping of all the statutes!   The best remedy would doubtless have been, not more statutes but more firmness in the executive ; and to all appearance fines, if they had been exacted, would have been more effective than oaths.   Further matters calling for consideration were the case of masters not obeying the injunctions of the dean, the bringing in by the promotor of all debts due to the faculty, and the salary to be allowed to that official, *quod nullus debet propriis sumptibus militare.*   But after all the faculty do not seem to have got any further than the appointment of four deputies; along with the dean, to come to some finding regarding the subjects in question, and no finding has been recorded.

In December, 1522, a University congregation considered what remedy should be tried against the neglect and disobedience of bachelors who had hitherto received license and who yet, in contempt of the University, the faculty of Arts, and the statutes, and, what was worse, in violation of their own oath, failed to appear within the time limited in order formally to receive the degree of master.   The congregation then laid down a rule of sufficient strictness, so far as words were concerned, that for the future no bachelor should be admitted to license till he had provided suitable caution that he would appear to receive the degree of master within eight days immediately following his admission to license. There was said to be just cause of complaint against some masters, students, and other supposts, who, in despite of the intimations of the rector and the dean duly affixed to the church doors, neglected to attend their congregations, notwithstanding the pains and penalties of perjury and insubordination to which they rendered themselves liable.   A remedy was sought—we might almost say besought—for this evil, ' *quia nisi inferiores superiori, quantumvis etiam infimo, non paruerint, tota policia Universitatis in nichilum redigetur.*'   The meeting decreed that the ancient usage of the University and the statutes should be observed and strictly enforced, but as regards enforcing, they might have added—' *hoc opus, hic labor est.*'

In December, 1517, rules were laid down to check a new evil—or, at all events, one which had not previously been mentioned—the evil of imputing or assuming degrees without due warrant. It was ordained that no one should style a licentiate master on pain of being fined two shillings for each offence ; and that if one who was only a licentiate styled himself master he should be fined twenty shillings as often as he should offend. The official presiding at the licensing ceremony was required to proclaim this enactment, and to explain its effect to the licentiates and others present. The records of the faculty of Arts are wanting in 1517 when this regulation was adopted, but the dean of that faculty is specially mentioned, as well as the rector, as being present in the University congregation which passed the regulation with consent of the rector, the dean of the faculty of Arts, the deputies, and the whole faculty.

Peculiarities of dress—the use of special badges, insignia, and vestments —have long been in favour with academic men, though others, as, for instance, freemasons, have shown a craving more or less akin, and have used strong colours and an infusion of mysticism or symbolism as part of their system. In 1452 the faculty of Arts, in one of their earliest meetings, gave instructions for the purchase of cloth for making a cap. Next year they enacted that candidates who wished to ' determine ' or to enter for general responsions should, three and three among themselves, have a becoming dress, and that each candidate who was rich or beneficed should have a dress of his own, but the rule was soon relaxed if a candidate had a becoming dress, whether his own or borrowed.

Early in 1464 the executors of Patrick Leich delivered to the faculty a hood made of scarlet and furred with ' miniewar,' which he had bequeathed to the faculty. The same day James Hynde was elected keeper of the faculty vestments (*custos habituum*), and it was resolved that in future a keeper of vestments should be elected on the same day as the dean and receiver, and further, that all the money then in the hands of the receiver should be expended on the pedagogy and on dresses for the faculty. In July of the same year Duncan Bunch and Martin Wan were appointed to buy four or six hoods and a master's cap, to be paid from the common purse. For the future those about to be licensed were to pay two shillings, and those about to ' determine ' one shilling, for the repair of the faculty vestments. In 1469 the accounts of the keeper of vestments were audited, and there remained in his hands thirteen shillings and four-pence, which sum the faculty ordered to be expended, along with the receipts of the following year, in buying new hoods and fur.

In 1480 it was noted that the dresses of the faculty needed repair, and instructions were given to ascertain about the sums received for dress and in whose hands they were. From the instructions given from time to time to the promotor regarding the recovery and bringing in of dresses, it would seem that the wearers were by no means careful to return them. In 1490 the faculty instructed John Doby, the bursar, to buy six hoods, sufficiently furred, of proper cloth, and red colour, for the use of the faculty and the students in it. In the same year the University congregation were considering about their cap and hoods, and ordered them, as well as the silver mace, to be repaired.

With the exception of some books and papers, the mace is the oldest article of University property. David Cadyow, the earliest rector, on his re-election in 1460, gave twenty nobles to procure a mace, but this sum proved inadequate, and in 1465 the supposts or members of the University voluntarily submitted to an assessment graduated according to their means, in order that the mace might be completed. The shaft is of silver, but other metals have been used in some of the engraved and ornamental portions. .The upper hexagonal part, which must have been made or modified after the date of the *Nova Erectio*, has a shield on each side, the first of which bears the city arms, the second, a Latin inscription, the third, the arms of the Earl of Morton, the fourth, those of Hamilton, the fifth, the Scottish lion rampant, and the sixth the arms of Turnbull, the virtual founder of the University. On Sundays and minor feasts the silver mace was not used, a white wooden staff being carried before the rector instead. For use in place of this plain wooden staff, Robert Maxwell, rector in 1519, gave a wooden rod ornamented with silver at both ends and in the middle.

In 1453 the University congregation resolved to have a seal with the effigy of St. Kentigern, the patron saint of Glasgow, engraven in the centre, on the right an extended hand holding a book, on the left a fish with a ring, and round the outer border the inscription: *Sigillum Commune Universitatis Glasguensis.* A smaller seal *ad causas* was ordered for the rector, as well as a chest for keeping the private documents (*secreta*) of the University, to be provided with four locks, the keys of which should be in the hands of the deputies. Probably the University seal had been procured without loss of time, but not the seal *ad causas*, for in 1482 it was resolved to procure such a seal, because it was considered hardly becoming that the great seal should be used *in singulis causis.* Upon the seal a rod was to be engraved as well as the inscription: *Sigillum Universitatis Glasguensis ad causas.* Further delay must have occurred, for in 1509 the order for procuring this seal was repeated. In 1455 the congregation of the faculty of Arts ordered a seal with a hand holding a book engraved in the middle and a salmon and a bird to right and left.

Separate records for the other faculties have not been preserved, and in considering them we must put together such references in the early statutes, and in the records of the University and the faculty of Arts, as throw light on the matter.   There can be no question about the comprehensive scope of the University's constitution, but for a long time the other faculties did not develop in the same measure as the faculty of Arts. The pope's bull specifically mentions the faculties of theology, canon law, civil law, and arts, and comprehends within the University any other legitimate faculty whatever.

James II., in his letter of 1453 bestowing privileges on the University, contemplates the existence and organisation of separate faculties, mentioning the deans of faculties among those who are to share in the privileges. The earliest statutes provide that students for a degree in any faculty must be incorporated by the rector ; that graduates in the several faculties must continue to reside and study in the University for the time appointed in the respective faculties ; that those about to graduate in any faculty, but especially in those of arts and canons, should give a feast or entertainment, as the manner was ; that the earlier graduates in any faculty should take precedence on public occasions over later graduates ; and that on the day when degrees were to be conferred in any faculty, lecturing should cease from eight in the morning till noon, and that the students of the particular faculty should gather in good time to the schools to grace the ceremony. Some fragments of statutes concerning the faculty of canons have been preserved.   They relate mostly to fees, but also contain a regulation that no student in this faculty should wear a loose gown without a band. Those about to receive the degree of master of Arts took oath to promote harmony between the four faculties, especially with the faculty of theology.

In numerous cases supposts or office-bearers mentioned in the minutes have degrees in law appended to their names, frequently, though not quite so often, degrees in theology, and once the degree of M.D. occurs.   The degrees in law mentioned are bachelor of laws (*juris utriusque bachallarius*, or *in jure utroque bachallarius*), licentiate in laws (*in legibus licentiatus*, or *in jure utroque licentiatus*), bachelor in decrees (*in decretis bachallarius*), licentiate in decrees (*in decretis licentiatus*), and doctor of decrees (*decretorum doctor*) ; while in theology they are bachelor of theology (*theologiae bachallarius*, or *sacrae theologiae bachallarius*, or *in theologia bachallarius*), licentiate in theology (*in theologia licentiatus*), and doctor of divinity, though this last degree belongs to Major, and he is merely styled *doctor Parisiensis*.[1]   Besides the doctor of medicine or doctor in medicines (*doctor in medicinis*) admitted in 1469, we learn from outside sources that

[1] When incorporated at St. Andrews in 1523 he was styled *Doctor Theologus Parisiensis*.

an English practitioner, who probably had no degree, studied and taught medicine in the University for a short time about 1536. There can be little doubt that many of the degrees mentioned in law and theology had been conferred by the University of Glasgow. In the earlier instances where his name occurs William Arthurle is designated master of Arts only, but a few years later he is styled *decretorum doctor*, and as in the interval he had been continuously engaged as a regent in the faculty of Arts at Glasgow, it is not likely he had obtained the higher degree elsewhere.

There is some positive evidence of graduation and teaching in other faculties than Arts. In 1473 William Elphinstone was made a licentiate in canon law, and next year when elected rector he is styled licentiate in decrees, which makes one conjecture that graduates in decrees belonged to the faculty of canon law. In 1507 it is recorded that Patrick Covyntre, after the previous lectures and disputations had been exacted according to the manner and custom of the University, was pronounced a bachelor of sacred theology by Mr. William Caidyow, professor of theology, presiding in a very full meeting of prelates, lords, and masters. At the beginning of the minute Covyntre, who had long been a regent, is described as ' *ex tunc bachallarius biblicus*,' and sixteen or seventeen years before he is styled bachelor of sacred theology. The case is somewhat peculiar, as they appear to have conferred again a degree Covyntre already possessed. Perhaps his title to the earlier degree had been in some way subjected to question, and they then wished to ' make assurance double sure,' for the minute of 1507 states in much more emphatic terms than usual that the University requirements had been fulfilled, and mentions that the degree was conferred before a large and distinguished meeting. But in whatever way the circumstances are to be explained, the minute is proof of graduation in theology. Some other cases besides that of Caidyow occur in which mention is made of a professor of theology, David Crag of the Friars Preachers, who was incorporated in 1487, being so designated, as also John Major in the later part of his regency, and John Ade (Adamson) in 1521, but we cannot be sure that their title of professor was derived from the University. It may have come to them rather from the Church.

It is recorded that on 29th July, 1460, David Cadyow, precentor of the church of Glasgow and at that time rector of the University, read to the assembled masters and clerics a chapter of the third book *De Vita et Honestate Clericorum*, and continued his reading at the pleasure of his hearers ; that the same day William de Levenax read a chapter of the civil law ; and that on 24th March, 1522, Robert Lile of the Friars Preachers, prior of the convent of Glasgow, began the reading of the fourth book of the *Sentences*, in the monastery of the Friars, in presence of the rector, the dean of faculty, and the other masters, under the presidency of the venerable father and devout man Brother John Ade, professor of sacred theology and provincial of the order of Preachers of the whole kingdom of Scotland.

In 1462 David Cadyow, first rector of the University, set aside an endowment of twelve marks yearly from the revenue of certain lands and tenements in Glasgow for behoof of a clerk in the faculty of canon law reading in the public schools in the city of Glasgow, as the custom was in other Universities, and also celebrating Mass at the altar of the Virgin Mary in the Cathedral for the soul of the donor.

After a time the reading or lecturing had become irregular, but in 1490 the University congregation determined that the holder should be obliged to read according to the terms of the foundation. In 1522, however, when the second regent in arts was appointed to the chaplainry, reference was made to the condition that the chaplain should read in canon law, and it was declared to be impossible in the circumstances then existing to find such a man. For a considerable time the University included schools of canons among its buildings. Attention was called to their being out of repair in 1482, and early next year it was resolved to have them repaired since they were of use to the whole University.

Again in 1502 the University was owing a mark to the rector for a new glass window in the gable of the schools of canons. It was ordered that the repairs in 1483 should be defrayed by the promotor of the University drawing on the funds of the faculty of canons from sums owing by graduates in that faculty. This record is conclusive that in 1483 the faculty of canons was something more than a potentiality, and had an actual existence with some organisation, graduates, and revenue. The statement that the schools of canons were of use to the whole University appears to show that classes in other subjects met there ; but by 1522, when it became impracticable to find a reader to carry out the purposes of Cadyow's foundation, teaching in the faculty of canons seems to have been altogether discontinued.

It is notable that for some considerable time after the foundation of the University the dean of the faculty of Arts is described as dean of that faculty, suggesting that there were then deans of other faculties from whom he was to be distinguished, but afterwards he is called dean of faculty simply, implying that by that time there was only one faculty in fully organised existence. The evidence available leads us to conclude that in the period before the Reformation the University was the scene both of teaching and graduation in the faculties of canons and theology,

THE UNIVERSITY MACE, WITH ITS SHIELDS

though their work may have been intermittent and both faculties had become dormant before the end of the period. Traces of teaching in civil law occur, but here the evidence of any settled or effective organisation is not complete ; and as regards medicine we can hardly say more than that it was treated as worthy of recognition and encouragement within the University.

During this early period a number of endowments, mostly in the form of chaplainries, were conferred, and, though these were of slender amount in individual cases, in the aggregate they may have been of some service. In 1449 James, Lord Hamilton, granted to David Cadyow, afterwards first rector of the University, the chapel of St. Thomas the Martyr in the city of Glasgow. Cadyow made over the rents of this chaplainry for the benefit of a regent in the faculty of Arts. In 1477 Thomas Mungumbre, prebendary of Eglischehame, then rector of the University, David Gray, dean of the faculty of Arts, William Arthurle, Doctor of Decrees, and John Brown were appointed to ride to Ayr, to defend before the abbots of Paisley and Corsreggal the right of the faculty to the chaplainry.

Afterwards the lairds of Halkhead and Mynto complained to the Lords of the Council that their tenants in the lands of Arthurle in Neilston were molested by the faculty of Arts for an annuity from their lands, and that the Bishop of Glasgow and his official were trying the case in the spiritual court. In 1480 the Lords of the Council interdicted the bishop and his official from proceeding with the case, declaring that it was a ' prophane accione ' to be determined by the king's temporal laws, and forbade further molestation of the tenants until it was so determined. Further negotiations took place, and the laird of Halkhead seems to have been brought to pay the rents of the chaplainry, at least occasionally. As already mentioned, Cadyow also bequeathed an annuity of twelve marks from the rent of certain lands and tenements in Glasgow to a clerk in the faculty of canon law reading in the public schools in the city as the custom was in other Universities. Cadyow, who died on 7th March, 1468, further gave twelve marks to found an annuity of ten shillings to the faculty of Arts, for which the faculty agreed to celebrate an obit on the anniversary of his death.

John Restoun, Bachelor in Decrees, perpetual vicar of Dunlop, founded in 1481 a chaplainry in the aisle of St. Michael the Archangel, to be served by a chaplain presented by the rector of the University and his deputies, who were constituted visitors, and attached to it the revenues of certain lands and tenements. In 1487 William Stewart, canon of Glasgow, prebendary of Killearn, and rector of Glassford, founded a chap-lainry in the church of the Friars Preachers of Glasgow, and constituted

c

the rector of the University, the regents in the College of Arts, and the provost and bailies of Glasgow, conservators. In 1506 Sir Archibald Calderwood, vicar of Cadder, gave to the College of the faculty of Arts an annuity of eight shillings for a collation to the dean, regents, masters, and students on the day of celebrating an obit in the convent of the Friars Preachers. Thomas Leiss, subdean of Dunblane and vicar of Dreghorn, gave in 1530, for the benefit of a chaplainry at the altar of St. Michael in the Cathedral, and maintenance of a chaplain in connection with it, three tenements, and annuities amounting to sixty-seven shillings from other tenements and lands—to be administered in terms of a foundation to be made by the rector and dean of faculty of the University. About 1539 James Houstoun, subdean of Glasgow, who founded the collegiate church of St. Mary the Virgin, and St. Anne her mother, appointed the rector of the University and the dean of the faculty of Arts to be visitors of that church, and bequeathed certain funds for annual payments to them, amounting to about twelve shillings in the case of the rector and eight in the case of the dean.

Scotland, which hitherto had no archbishopric, had often been troubled by claims on the part of the Archbishop of York to exercise authority over the Scottish clergy, but in 1473 Patrick Graham, who had succeeded Kennedy as Bishop of St. Andrews, after residing some time in Rome won over the pope to grant a bull raising the see of St. Andrews to an archbishopric. When Graham returned to Scotland he had a very unfavourable reception from the king and the clergy, with whom he seems to have held little, if any, consultation regarding his project. Accusations were showered upon him, and some time afterwards he was displaced from his archbishopric, to which William Sheves, court physician and astrologer, a scheming adventurer who was a special favourite with James III., and took a leading part in attacking Graham, succeeded. But Sheves soon proved as troublesome as if he had been Archbishop of York, and James IV., who had been a canon of Glasgow, procured a bull in 1491 raising its see to an archbishopric, that it might balance and hold in check the see of St. Andrews. The strife was not ended, however, till Parliament silenced the brawling ecclesiastics by threatening to suspend their annual rents unless they respected its authority.

Robert Blackadder held the see of Glasgow at the time when it was raised to an archbishopric, and perhaps it was to mark his sense of promotion in the hierarchy and signalise his quickened zeal for the Church that he summoned about thirty Ayrshire Lollards before the king and his council in 1494, for denying the doctrine of transubstantiation, the efficacy of masses for the dead, the right of the pope to grant absolutions and indulgences, the propriety of worshipping images, relics, and the virgin, and other opinions regarded as heretical. The lairds of Barskimming, Cessnock, Newmilns, and Polkemmet were among the accused, as well as a number of ladies. Blackadder prosecuted, but Barskimming spoke in defence with such wit and good humour that the king, who seems to have had no love for persecution, contrived to bring the trial to a jocular end. For a time we hear little more of protestant doctrines in Scotland, but probably they continued in a more or less latent condition till the Reformation.

The bishops and archbishops were generally favourable to the University, at least in theory, but their good intentions did not always bear fruit. In 1506 Blackadder, with the concurrence of his chapter, declared his intention to annex to the College of his University the vicarages of Cadder, Stobo, Linton, and Killearn, as well as the rectory of Garwald ; and early in 1508 he annexed certain benefices to his College in Glasgow, but the names of the benefices were not specified, and both designs seem to have proved abortive. Gavin Dunbar, who was archbishop from 1525 till his death in 1547, meditated doing something considerable for the University, and in 1537 drew out an instrument for the new foundation of the College, annexing to it the revenues of three vicarages (one of which was the vicarage of Colmonell), with reservation of certain sums to maintain vicars pensioners who should carry on the religious offices of the three benefices.

In actual practice, however, Dunbar's scheme was no more effectual than Blackadder's had been. Before this the University had some hold on Colmonell, for in 1522 David Gibson, the vicar, with consent of the patrons of the benefice and ' of the Rectour and Universite of the Pedagog of Glasgw,' ' to the quhilk Universite the said vicarage is annexit,' granted a lease of the vicarage for nineteen years, at a rent of £20 a year, to Gilbert Kennedy, in consideration of ' certain greit sowmes of money gevin be Maister Gilbert Kennedy, bruther germane to Thomas Kennedy of Bergany, and his freyndis, to the bigging, supportation, help, and reparation of the Universite and Pedagog of Glasgw.' Though this lease speaks of the vicarage as already annexed to the University, the title does not seem to have been secure, for Archbishop Dunbar proposed to annex it in 1537, and in 1558 Archbishop James Beaton, with consent of his chapter, did actually annex it to the University for the benefit of the masters and regents.

Though the prelates of Glasgow were friendly, the interference of some other ecclesiastics caused an occasional ripple on the surface of academic affairs, and among them was the rural dean of Rutherglen. In

1490 the University congregation resolved to present a petition to the bishop as chancellor that he would exempt supposts who were in residence in the University from having to appear in the court of the rural dean of Rutherglen, or of any other rural dean of the diocese of Glasgow. In 1509 the congregation again considered the question of the rural dean's interference, and this time they resolved not to petition, but to retaliate. It was laid down that no master or member should cite another master or member before any other judge than the rector or vice-rector and the deputies. On the question of summoning members who were priests before the rural dean, it was decided, in view of the privileges granted by several bishops and especially by Bishop Turnbull, that the rural dean should be summoned before the rector and admonished for his transgression—all the more because he was himself a master and graduate of the University and sworn to conserve its privileges.

In March, 1522, Sir Peter Alderstoun was accused before a University congregation of executing a citation of the conservator of the privileges of the University of St. Andrews upon Mr. Andrew Smith, in the abode of the religious man Sir David Kyngorne, pensioner of Corsraguell, a suppost of the University. Sir Peter confessed that he had cited the said Mr. Andrew, but declared that he did not in the least understand what letters they were. Mr. Andrew humbly enquired whether it was necessary for him to appear in St. Andrews on the strength of the said citation, or not. After mature consideration it was found that Sir Peter in this thing had wronged the said religious man, Sir David Kyngorne, and the said Mr. Andrew; and it was ordained that Sir Peter should, with uncovered head, ask pardon from the said religious man and from Mr. Andrew, which he did. It was also found that the conservator of St. Andrews was not the judge of Mr. Andrew, and that Mr. Andrew was not bound to appear before him, since the archiepiscopal see of Glasgow was free, both in whole and in part, from the see of St. Andrews.

Notices occur from time to time of repairs on the buildings presented by Hamilton and Arthurle, and there was some extension as well. The building about 1469 of a house in the south part, next to the convent of the Friars Preachers, has already been mentioned, and by 1497 a new hall had been added to the pedagogy and a new kitchen provided. In 1495 John Hugonis was continued as dean in recognition of his great services in building and repairing the College, and in 1507 there is an acknowledgment that the faculty of Arts owed £7 18s. 7d. to Patrick Covyntre, principal regent, which, in addition to the amount derived from College funds, he had expended of his own for the use of the College and for repairs.

In 1502 the University treasury owed the rector, Thomas Forsyth, a mark for a new glass window in the school of canons. Glass was used in public buildings earlier than in dwellings, and in most countries it was not yet common in the latter, but, if we may trust Don Pedro de Ayala, the Spanish Ambassador, glass windows were by this time in general use in Scottish houses. In 1502 there is also a list of utensils delivered by the former provisor to his successor, which it would need an accomplished antiquary to understand, only there is mention of spits, tin disks, and three plates, one of which is ordered for the repair of the other two, as well as of pipes and a hogshead, suggesting that they did not always quench their thirst with water.

From what is recorded regarding the lease of the vicarage of Colmonell granted in 1522 to Gilbert Kennedy, and the great sums of money which he and his friends had contributed to the building, repair, and support of the University, it would appear that considerable improvements were made about that time. As in 1522 Major had been regent for four years, and had drawn an exceptional number of students to the University and enhanced its credit, it was an opportune time for improving the buildings. And if the other edifices had been much improved, it might help to explain a proposal put forward by the rector in 1522 that the University congregation should consider the advisability of letting the tenement called Arthurle Place, then almost ruinous and of little use to the College, to some one able and willing to take it at a certain annual rent. The Arthurle tenement must have been sold or alienated, for we afterwards come upon a record of its being conveyed back to the University.

The printing press, invented towards the close of the middle ages, greatly aided the revival of learning and the Reformation. It is said that before the close of the fifteenth century all the Latin authors were accessible in print, and in the first twenty years of the next century almost all the more valuable Greek authors. About the same time the discoveries of Columbus, Cabot, Vasco Da Gama, and other navigators and explorers who crossed the Atlantic or rounded the Cape of Good Hope, making the old world acquainted with the new, and bringing to light the treasures of the east and the west, not only opened wide and rich territories for trade and commerce, for conquest and colonisation, but the tales which explorers brought back of new lands, new races, new forms of society, awakened the wonder and stimulated the imagination of Europe.

It cannot be said that Scotland was prominent or early in the various departments of this new life and activity, but the new spirit did not leave the country untouched. Orkney and Shetland were added to its territory in the reign of James III., and in the next reign a navy was equipped which for the times might be reckoned considerable. Scotland also made its influence felt at the courts of France and Spain, greatly enlarged its trade with the Netherlands, and improved the general standard of living to such an extent that sumptuary laws were passed to restrain what was considered lavish expenditure on the part of burgesses and others.

Along with material improvement there came a remarkable development of literary and imaginative activity. Dunbar's *Lament for the Makaris* shows that Scotland had become a nest of singers, and their best works bear evidence of classical influence. It is so with Dunbar himself ; with Henrisone, whose chief work dealt with Troilus and Cressida ; and with Gavin Douglas, who gained a lasting fame by translating the *Aeneid* into Scots verse. But these men, as well as Boece and Major, who wrote in prose, were still all or nearly all of the clerical order.

The relations of the clergy and the church to the University were also very close and vital in this early period. The Bishop or Archbishop of Glasgow was its chancellor, and to his influence and patronage the academic body looked for expansion of its equipment or increase of its slender revenues. It was by his permission that the clergy were able to draw stipend for clerical appointments while teaching or studying in the University. The rector and other officers of the University were usually churchmen, and the academic and ecclesiastical institutions were so bound together that the fall of the latter involved the fall of the former. The Church was nearing a catastrophe, for its wealth roused the cupidity of needy and rapacious nobles, while its worldliness and corruption deprived it of public respect and support. Here and there good and able men might be found in the Church, such as Elphinstone, Bishop of Aberdeen, and James Beaton, the last Catholic Bishop of Glasgow before the Reformation, but they were too few to give life and character to the body to which they belonged.

In Scotland the Reformation came a little later than in most other countries, and in Glasgow the great secular and ecclesiastical authority of the archbishop for a time hindered its progress. In 1525 the Scottish Parliament forbade the importation of Lutheran literature, in 1528 Patrick Hamilton, the first Scottish martyr, suffered at St. Andrews, and other victims followed, including Jerome Russell and a young man named Kennedy, condemned at Glasgow by Archbishop Dunbar (who is said to have been inclined to clemency) and a court of inquisitors more ruthless than himself.

Lord Hamilton, the greatest of the early benefactors of the University, acquired exceptional power for himself and his family by marrying as his second wife the Princess Mary, daughter of James II., and widow or divorced wife of Thomas Boyd, a royal favourite who was created first Earl of Arran, but afterwards fell from his high estate and became a degraded outcast. The son of Lord Hamilton and the princess was created Earl of Arran, and their grandson, the second Earl of Arran of the Hamilton line, was chosen regent when James V. died in 1542, leaving his infant daughter Mary to succeed. At first Arran favoured the reformers, and was one of the chief promoters of a resolution passed by Parliament in 1543 opening the Bible in the vulgar tongue to the people, but shortly afterwards he yielded to the ascendancy of his mother's uncle, Cardinal Beaton, and in a half-hearted manner supported the French and Catholic interest. The French king made him Duke of Chatelherault, but he was not a sufficiently ardent partisan, and in 1554 he was ousted from the regency by the queen mother, Mary of Guise.

In 1544 the Castle of Glasgow was seized by Lennox, Glencairn, and others, who had swerved to the English interest when Arran and Beaton were reconciled, but after a siege it was recovered, and eighteen of the defeated party were hanged. But an English army having landed at Leith, the western lords were encouraged to make a fresh diversion ; and John Stewart of Minto, an adherent of Lennox, being provost of Glasgow at the time, his influence and example induced a large number of citizens to swell the ranks of the insurgent army which suffered a heavy defeat on the Gallow Muir.

James Beaton, nephew of the cardinal, was Archbishop of Glasgow from 1552 to 1560. He was friendly to the University, and besides bestowing on it the vicarage of Colmonell as already related, took an interest in the protection of its lands and property in Glasgow. The College lands between the Molendinar and the Muir Butts were measured by his command in 1557, and, instead of extending to four acres as they should have done, were found to contain only three acres, three roods, and one and a quarter fall. It was intended to make the neighbours produce their titles, that it might be ascertained where the fault lay, but this purpose was hindered by the archbishop's journey to France to attend the marriage of Mary Queen of Scots in April, 1558. Before setting out Beaton put himself under the protection of Chatelherault, who had been made bailie of the regality of Glasgow in 1545 when Lennox lost that office on account of his insurrection in the preceding year. The duke bound himself to take the part of the archbishop and his chapter on all necessary occasions, and to assist in expelling heretics from the diocese of Glasgow and punishing heretics within it.

But in September, 1559, the duke's eldest son, who had been obliged to leave France on account of his Protestant leanings, joined the Lords of the Congregation at Stirling, and they proceeded to Hamilton Palace and persuaded the duke himself to espouse their cause.   Near the end of 1559, when the Lords of the Congregation had failed in their attack on Leith, which had been fortified and garrisoned by French troops, they divided into two parties, one of which marched upon Glasgow and the other into Fife.   The western expedition was headed by Chatelherault, Glencairn, Boyd, and Ochiltree.   Heedless of the guarantee of protection to the archbishop and his chapter which he had signed in the beginning of 1558, the duke now purged the Glasgow churches of their idols, seized the castle, and issued proclamations in name of the queen ; but the advance of a detachment of French troops cut short his proceedings.

Overtures had already been made for assistance from England in expelling the French from Leith, and Elizabeth, exasperated at the French sovereign having quartered the arms of England with those of Scotland and France, and dreading the results of a hostile power obtaining a military footing in Scotland, at length made up her mind to act.   Early in 1560 an English fleet blockaded the Firth of Forth against further reinforcements or supplies from France, and in April 9,000 English troops and a slightly more numerous force of Scots sat down before Leith, whose garrison held out stubbornly.   Mary of Guise died on 10th June, and on 6th July a treaty was arranged providing for the withdrawal of the French troops and the demolition of the fortifications of Leith.   In August the Scottish Estates met to sanction a new Confession drawn up by Knox and his brother ministers, to abolish the jurisdiction of the pope, to condemn doctrines and practices inconsistent with the new Confession, and to forbid the celebration of mass on pain of confiscation for the first offence, banishment for the second, and death for the third.

After the proceedings of Chatelherault had been stopped Archbishop Beaton had a short respite, but on the death of the regent Mary of Guise, perceiving that his cause was lost, he retired to France.   The academic records during the latter part of the Catholic period have been written in a brief form, but almost to the end of the period the teaching work of the faculty of Arts seems to have been carried on without much disturbance. The last minute of the faculty, dated in 1555, records the election of two regents and two masters who were not regents to examine three candidates for the degree of Bachelor.   But there can hardly be a doubt that teaching continued for some years longer, for the University minutes record seventeen incorporations in 1557, including the sons of three lairds and the son of the Earl of Glencairn.   Such students would hardly have entered if the College had been in a tottering and confused state.   On 25th October, 1558, the usual meeting was held for the election of rector, and the four

WILLIAM ELPHINSTONE

Sometime Regent in Arts, Rector of the University of Glasgow (1474), afterwards Bishop of Aberdeen

Born circa 1431. Died 1514

From oil painting in the University of Aberdeen

intrants (including John Davidson, principal regent) chose James Balfour, treasurer of the church of Glasgow, to that office. The minute of this meeting is the last of the series in the Catholic period ; and on the fall of the old Church and the flight of Beaton, the academic work was disorganised and for a time suspended.

A professor of Scottish history has said that the University of Glasgow did not meet a real demand in the country, that for more than a hundred years it was permanently on the verge of extinction, and that, while St. Andrews and Aberdeen attained a prosperity fully proportioned to the resources of the country, Glasgow was a failure for the first century of its existence. No doubt the University of Glasgow did in this early period fail to develop a settled equipment and organisation in most of the faculties contemplated in the pope's bull of foundation, and in the main it must be judged by what was done in the faculty of Arts. Even there its teaching staff only reached the modest standard of three regents, sometimes reduced to two, and though there were houses and lands, and there should have been an appreciable income from the fees of students if they had been paid, the settled and direct emoluments were very slender.

When we read of the many thousands of students who at an earlier time thronged the halls of Bologna or Paris or Oxford, the largest muster at Glasgow seems but a handful. But if 30,000 students ever gathered together in the mediaeval Universities, most of them were only following the beaten track of a fashionable academic crusade, and but few drank deeply from the Pierian spring. It may be doubted whether at Glasgow in the most prosperous years before the Reformation more than a hundred students gathered round the teachers in High Street, and the average may not have been much more than a third of that number, but probably most of them did come to apply their minds to what was then considered the higher learning.

It is well when a public institution draws its recruits from all grades of society, but in the present day the aristocracy have withdrawn from the Scottish Universities, and they can be better spared than the democracy. Before the Reformation students were for the most part drawn from the clergy and the families of the nobility and lairds, though even then some students were sprung from the ranks of the burgesses and artisans, and a few are marked as sons of military officers.

The lists of enrolled students include sons of the Earls of Argyle, Lennox, Montrose, Glencairn, Rothes, and Orkney ; of Viscount Rutherglen, Lord Erskine, and Lord Kennedy of Cassilis ; and of numerous lairds, among whom were Maxwell of Caerlaverock, Maxwell of Pollok, and Maxwell of Aikenhead, Wallace of Elderslie, Douglas of Drumlanrig,

Colquhoun of Luss, Houstoun of Houstoun, Maclachlan of Maclachlan, Crichtoun of Sanquhar, Stirling of Glorat, and Hamilton of Haggis. The names of the clergy abound all through the lists, and besides priests, monks, friars, rectors, and vicars, the higher orders are found not unfrequently, as, for example, the Abbots of Kilwinning and Newbattle, the Prior of Blantyre, several priors and the Vicar General of the order of Friars Preachers, and others.   In 1456 and again in 1457 Andrew Stewart, brother of James II., was enrolled, but though he was a Stewart and a brother of the king, it is not clear that he was a royal Stewart.   Shortly after the assassination of James I. his widow married Sir James Stewart, usually known as ' the black knight of Lorne,' and Andrew Stewart was probably a son of her second marriage.

Though there were learned ecclesiastics here and there, the general standard of learning among the clergy in this period was far from satisfactory, and as members of the clerical order formed a great part of the students and graduates, the University surely did good work by raising in some appreciable measure the standard of their education.   That the nobles and lairds needed all the knowledge they had, and that the spread of learning among them was a matter of national importance, is shown by an Act of Parliament passed in 1496, requiring all barons and freeholders of substance to send their eldest sons to the Grammar Schools from the time they were eight or nine years old till they acquired perfect Latin, and afterwards to send them for three years to the Schools of Arts and Law, that they might be qualified to administer law and justice in their various districts.   Though much remained to be done, the University in training so many sons of the aristocracy must have helped in a considerable degree to realise this object of national policy.   And the sprinkling of students sprung from burgesses and members of the industrial order gave promise of the spread of University education in later times so as to reach many of the peasantry and workers.

For about eighty out of the hundred and ten years between 1451 and 1560, lists of incorporated students appear in the *Munimenta,* and for most years a number of graduations appear in the separate records of the faculty of Arts.   Both lists are very incomplete, but the one may be used to show how defective the other is.   For instance, there is a blank in the University list of incorporations for the years 1506, 1507, and 1508, but during that time no fewer than thirty-four graduations have been recorded in the faculty of Arts.[1]   Again, taking the year 1509, in which only eight incorporations have been recorded, we find that the lists of the faculty of Arts

---

[1] The total number is 44, but in some cases the names of the same individuals occur twice in one year, *e.g.* for licence and for M.A.

give twelve additional names which are not included in the list of incorporations.   In the year 1502, where fourteen incorporations have been recorded, eleven separate individuals obtained degrees in Arts, and of these seven are not included in the list of incorporations.   It is therefore quite clear that the number of students must have been much greater than either of the two lists taken by itself would indicate.

For the first year of the University about seventy or eighty incorporations have been entered, which is the highest number recorded.   For the next thirty-four years the incorporations have been more regularly noted than afterwards.   In the time of James IV. tolerably good numbers occur for some years, but with many blanks among them ; yet the records of the faculty of Arts show that the work of teaching and graduating continued in years where no incorporations have been marked.   The advent of Major in 1518 attracted more students than usual, forty-eight incorporations being noted for that year, the highest number recorded for any year except the first.   There is a blank in the records of the faculty of Arts at this time, so that we are unable to check the one list with the other, but the total number of students in attendance had no doubt been greater.   Subsequently till about 1540 the average number of incorporations is tolerably well maintained, but there is some falling off after that.

Universities cannot create great men or men of genius, yet a University would be reckoned unfortunate if it did not from time to time nourish within its halls men whose influence was felt beyond their own immediate circle and after their own lifetime.   St. Andrews, which began forty years earlier, and therefore had a longer period of activity, was more fertile in this respect before the Reformation than Glasgow, yet Glasgow was by no means barren.

One of the most distinguished names on the roll of students, graduates, and office-bearers of the latter University in the early time is that of William Elphinstone.   He was the son of a father of the same name who was a canon of Glasgow and the earliest dean of the faculty of Arts.   It is not always easy to make sure of identifying the proper person in the University records, but from a careful survey of the entries, I should be inclined to infer that the younger and more famous Elphinstone was incorporated in 1457, ' determined ' in 1459, and received the degree of Master of Arts in 1462.   Next year he enjoyed the distinction of being received to the bosom of the faculty.   In 1463 he also became a regent, and a list is given of students who ' determined ' under William Elphinstone, junior, rector of Kirkmichael.   Next year he was still a regent in Arts and rector of Kirkmichael, but by 1465 he had ceased to hold the former office, though he retained the latter for a long time.   He spent several years in academic pursuits in France, and lectured on law at Paris and Orleans. Some time after his return to Scotland he was admitted a licentiate in canon law at Glasgow in 1474, and later in the same year was chosen rector.   In February, 1472, he was one of a deputation sent to remonstrate with the king against levying taxes from members of the University in contravention of their privileges.

In no long time he won the royal favour to such an extent that James III. called him to be a member of the Privy Council, and he was employed in numerous and important embassies in this and the next reign. About 1483 he was appointed Bishop of Aberdeen, and with Aberdeen his name is specially associated.   In 1494 he procured a bull for the foundation of a University there, which actually began its work ten or twelve years later with Hector Boece as principal ; he made additions to the Cathedral, and set about building a stone bridge over the Dee.

Elphinstone was also a master of finance.   He found means for the endowment of King's College and University, and for ample works of public utility and private benevolence, and at his death he left behind him a sum of £10,000 in gold and silver.   It is said that he suggested to James IV. a plan by which the royal treasury might be replenished by calling to account landowners who had neglected conditions of feudal tenure under which the king or some other superior was entitled to manage the revenues of their estates during the minority of heirs, or under which fines or forfeitures might be exacted by the superior.   These laws had long been suffered to remain dormant, but now, when put in force, many were obliged to pay large sums to escape awkward questions about the titles to their estates.   Elphinstone was chiefly instrumental in setting up the earliest printing press in Scotland, that of Chapman and Millar in Edinburgh, and his *Aberdeen Breviary* was one of the notable works issued from it.   As a statesman, diplomatist, lawyer, and churchman his ability and success were conspicuous, while his upright character, high culture, cheerful and winning manners, patronage of learning, and encouragement of good works endeared him to all.   The national disaster at Flodden broke the old man's spirit, the smile vanished from his face, and he died about a year after.

James Beaton, uncle of the Cardinal, was Archbishop of Glasgow for about fifteen years preceding his translation to the see of St. Andrews in 1523, and he was probably instrumental in bringing John Major, the greatest of the pre-Reformation regents, to Glasgow, as he afterwards was in transferring him to St. Andrews.   Major studied at Paris, where he graduated as M.A. in 1496, and in 1508 he was made a Doctor of Divinity of the Sorbonne.   Before his return to Scotland he had acquired a great reputation as a scholar and teacher, had published a number of treatises, and had made considerable progress with his *History*.

When incorporated into the University of Glasgow in November, 1518, he is described as a Doctor of Paris, principal regent of the College and pedagogy of the University, canon of the Chapel Royal, and vicar of Dunlop ; while in 1521 he is styled professor of theology, and next year treasurer of the Chapel Royal of Stirling. He is last mentioned in the Glasgow academic records on 25th October, 1522, but he may probably have continued some time longer at Glasgow, as his incorporation at St. Andrews did not take place till June, 1523. He seems to have been active in the general business of the University as well as in teaching. He is mentioned as an intrant and deputy in the rectorial elections of 1521 and 1522, and in the latter year he was also an auditor of accounts. In 1522 he and James Stewart, who was then rector, procured from James V. and his tutor, John, Duke of Albany, governor of the realm, confirmation of the privileges of the University in its exemption from taxation.

Till recently 1505 was generally accepted as the year in which John Knox was born, but of late a number of investigators have urged the probability of his birth having been about ten years later. The name of John Knox occurs in a list of students who were incorporated at Glasgow in 1522, and since M'Crie's *Life of Knox* appeared, it has been generally assumed that the great reformer was a student at Glasgow. All the ancient accounts agree that Knox studied under Major, but as Major was only four or five years at Glasgow, and a much longer time at St. Andrews, it was long asserted that Knox studied at St. Andrews, though his name is not on the records of that University. M'Crie found the name of Knox in the list of students at Glasgow in Major's time, and, till the recent controversy about the date of the reformer's birth, others have followed M'Crie in assigning Knox as an alumnus of Glasgow. But if the reformer was not born till about 1515, it is clear that he could not have been the John Knox whose name occurs in the incorporation list of 1522. In the present state of the case, however, our verdict must be one of ' not proven.'

Both Knox and Buchanan seem to have imbibed some of their notions as to government and politics from Major, who was their teacher, and was very far from holding the doctrine of the divine right of kings. He held that kings should be dealt with as the welfare of the state required, that the ultimate sovereign power rested with the people, the king's power being ministerial, and that the people might depose a king for his offences, and exclude his family from the throne. Regarding aristocracy his opinion was equally free : ' There is no other nobility but virtue and the practice of it.' Major also denounced the corruptions of the clergy, but though his speculative opinions were advanced, he did not join the reformers.

John Spottiswood, who was afterwards associated with Knox and others in drawing up the *First Book of Discipline*, and who became superintendent of Lothian, was incorporated in 1534, and next year his name appears in a list of bachelors to be examined for license. He was appointed an intrant and deputy at the rectorial election of 1535, and again in 1543.

In his early days David Beaton, afterwards the Cardinal, was educated partly at St. Andrews and partly at Glasgow, being probably drawn to the latter place by the influence of his uncle, James Beaton, Archbishop of Glasgow from 1508 to 1523. He was incorporated as a student at Glasgow in 1511, when about seventeen years of age, and, like many other distinguished Scots of that time, after finishing his academic course in his own country, he repaired to Paris, where he studied theology and law. James V. knew, and probably regretted, the corruptions of the clergy, yet he leaned on the clergy rather than on the nobility, whom he did not manage very skilfully, and so he was led into opposition to the work of the reformers, into a rupture with England, and into the disgraceful rout of Solway Moss. Upon the king's death, Beaton produced what is believed to have been a forged will, appointing himself and three others to the regency, but the nobles put him aside, and for a time he was imprisoned. Yet the Regent Arran was no match for him, and Beaton soon regained his ascendancy, and maintained it till in 1546, shortly after the martyrdom of Wishart, his own assassination followed. Foul as the deed was, it was secretly, if not openly, countenanced and encouraged by the English king and his council.

Though there is no record of James Beaton, nephew of the Cardinal, having studied at Glasgow, he was associated with the University as chancellor and as a benefactor. He was Archbishop of Glasgow from 1552 till 1560, and in 1558 bestowed upon the University the vicarage of Colmonell for the use of the masters and regents teaching within it. He also caused the College lands at Glasgow to be measured, and intended to take action with a view to check the encroachments of neighbours upon them, but the times were against him, and he was obliged to procure a guarantee of protection for himself from the Duke of Chatelherault, who soon afterwards threw in his lot with the reformers, and helped to clear the Glasgow churches of their images.

On the death of the Regent Mary of Guise, and on the very eve of the establishment of the reformed faith, Beaton withdrew to France; yet for about ten years he was permitted to collect the rents of the regality of the see and to grant rights to vassals. He was employed by Queen Mary as ambassador or agent at the court of France, and he acted in the same capacity for her son, James VI. In 1598 a Scottish Act of Parliament restored Beaton to his benefices and dignities—a very anomalous proceeding in view of the establishment of Protestantism. Beaton deposited in the Scots College at Paris part of the records of his see and a number of valuable gold and silver images which had escaped the reforms of Chatelherault, as well as some charters and documents belonging to the University, and there the manuscripts were available for consultation till they were lost or destroyed at the time of the French Revolution. When he died in 1603 he left 80,000 livres to the Scots College, of which he was regarded as the second founder.

William Manderston, incorporated in 1503, and again in 1505, and admitted to the degree of bachelor in 1506, was rector of the University of Paris in 1525. He was a licentiate and afterwards a doctor of medicine of Paris, and by 1530 had returned to Scotland and become rector of the University of St. Andrews. He produced some works in moral philosophy and dialectics, which have long since been forgotten, but in his own generation the author must have been a man of considerable note.

James Bassantin or Bassantoun, son of the laird of Bassendean, as it is now called, in Berwickshire, is said to have studied at Glasgow, though I have not found his name in the very defective lists now available. He was widely known in his own day as a mathematician and astronomer, and not less widely as an astrologer. He travelled extensively on the Continent, settled in France, taught with reputation in the University of Paris, produced a number of works on his favourite subjects, and returning to Scotland about 1562, died in 1568.

On 10th September, 1462, there was incorporated into the University the venerable Master Robert Henrisone, licentiate in arts and bachelor in decrees, who, next to Dunbar, was the greatest Scottish poet of his time. Little is known concerning his life, and we cannot say how long he remained at Glasgow ; but as receiving to the bosom of the University or of the faculty was the customary phrase for an honorary or complimentary admission, and his entry has not been so recorded, it seems likely that his admission was not a mere matter of compliment, and that he had come for study and for fellowship with the intellectual activity and the fresh and hopeful spirit of the new University. He afterwards settled at Dunfermline as a notary, which accords with his degree of bachelor of decrees, and he is generally believed to have been a teacher as well. He is one of the bards whose death is bewailed in Dunbar's *Lament for the Makaris*, published in 1508.

Henrisone in his *Testament of Cresseid* continued Chaucer's *Troilus and Cresseide*, correcting what he deemed to be Chaucer's mistake in leaving unpunished the fickleness and infidelity of the fair Trojan. His *Robene and Makyne*, a ballad of simple and natural grace and pathos in the form of a dialogue between a youth and a maiden, is the earliest of Scottish pastorals. Ready allegorical faculty, sagacity, and quaint humour appear in his rendering of *Æsop's Fables* into Scottish verse, and the tale of the *Uplandis* (country) *Mouse and the Burges* (town) *Mouse*, though differing in many respects, has something of the same spirit as Burns' *Twa Dogs*. Allegorical faculty is also shown in his *Garment of Good Women*, in which, within the compass of half a score of stanzas, he weaves a garment for his mistress ' from the crown to the toe topful ' of virtues and graces. In looking back to the early days of the University, assuredly the ' auld acquaintance ' with Henrisone should not ' be forgot and never brought to mind.'

In 1476 Walter Kennedy, described as a nobleman, was incorporated, and the same year he ' determined,' while two years later he was licensed, admitted to the degree of master, and obtained the further compliment of being received to the bosom of the faculty. He is also mentioned in 1481 as being an examiner of candidates for the bachelorship. There seems to be every reason to believe that this is Walter Kennedy, a son of Lord Kennedy of Cassilis and Dunure, in Ayrshire, afterwards one of the chief poets of his day. Gavin Douglas reckoned him as superior to Dunbar, and the latter, though satirising him mercilessly in the *Flyting of Dunbar and Kennedy*, mentions him very tenderly in the *Lament for the Makaris* :

> ' Gude Maister Walter Kennedy
> In point of death lies verily,
> Great ruth it were that so should be,
> *Timor mortis conturbat me.*'

The *Flyting* reads like a furious bombardment of coarse vituperation, but it seems to have been a piece of sportive gladiatorship with no real enmity behind it. Dunbar liked Kennedy notwithstanding, and felt a keen anxiety when evil seemed to threaten him.

> ' Great ruth it were that so should be.'

Kennedy in his maturer years was rector of Douglas, and while holding that office he again returned to the University in 1511. He is described as ' *canonicus Glasguensis ac rector de Dowglace*,' and his name stands next on the incorporation list to that of David Beaton.

CHAPTER II

FROM THE REFORMATION TO THE REVOLUTION, 1560–1688

I. 1560–1625.

BEFORE the Reformation the University had been dependent on the Church ; and during the period from the Reformation to the Revolution it was still in a great degree subject to ecclesiastical influences. Ministers had to be provided to carry on the work of the new religion all over the country, and their training made a great part of the work of the University at Glasgow as elsewhere. What slender endowments were at first procured for the academic institution came from fragments of the revenues of the old Church ; and when in 1641 Charles I., whose previous revocation of Church and Crown lands alienated since 1542 led the way to a revolution, bestowed additional endowments, they came from the revenues set free by the abolition of Episcopacy, and they were lost when Episcopacy was re-established after the Restoration.

By means of Commissions of Visitation or otherwise the General Assembly sometimes left its mark on the University, and thus chairs of divinity were founded and a chair of medicine suppressed. Covenanting and Royalist Commissions from time to time prescribed religious exercises for the students, the Covenanters recommending archery, golf, and other games as well. And as the various kinds of religious belief or ecclesiastical polity held in turn a somewhat rigorous ascendancy, a number of principals, regents, and professors who did not conform to the wishes of the government of the day had to pay for their independence by resigning their offices or suffering deposition.

The early Scottish reformers had a clear and strong sense of the value of education, and if they had had their way, would have organised a national system on a broad and firm basis, as the *First Book of Discipline* still bears witness. On 29th April, 1560, an order in council commissioned Knox, Winram, Spottiswood, Willock, and Row to draw up a scheme of polity for the Protestant Church, and in the wonderfully short space of twenty-two days they finished their task, and submitted in swift and bold outline a great scheme of organisation for a national Church, a national provision for relief of the poor, and a national system of education. They proposed the establishment of Grammar Schools in every parish, and of Colleges for logic, rhetoric and the tongues in every considerable town, and the remodelling of the organisation of the Universities of St. Andrews, Glasgow, and Aberdeen.   Arts, medicine, law, and theology were to be taught at St. Andrews, but at the other two medicine was to be omitted.   St. Andrews was to have three Colleges, in the first of which arts and medicine were to be taught.   The course in arts was to occupy three years, one year being devoted to dialectic, one to mathematics (including arithmetic, geometry, cosmography, and astronomy), and the third to natural philosophy, and separate readers or professors were to be provided for each of the three departments.

In the same College with arts the reader in medicine was to give his course in that subject extending over five years, and those who passed through it successfully were to be admitted to graduation.   The second College was to train students for graduation in law after a course of one year in ethics, economics, and politics, and four years in municipal law and Roman law, which were to be taught by separate readers.   The third College at St. Andrews was intended to train students for graduation in divinity, after one year devoted to Greek and Hebrew, and five years to the study of the Scriptures under two readers, one of whom was to deal with the Old and the other with the New Testament.   Theology, with its curriculum of six years, was evidently regarded as the crowning faculty, and it is equally evident that the reformers intended graduates in this faculty to be ' mighty in the Scriptures.'   In every College there was to be a principal, managing its property, supervising its teaching, but not himself acting as a teacher, and administering its discipline.   Each College was also to have twenty-four bursars.   Medicine was omitted from the scheme at Glasgow and Aberdeen, and as a consequence the faculties were differently arranged among the two Colleges assigned to each of these cities, but otherwise the teaching and organisation were the same.   The first College at Glasgow and Aberdeen corresponded to the first at St. Andrews, except that it included arts only, and the second included both law and divinity.

The authors of the scheme contemplated that before entering on his University course each student should have had two years of rudimentary teaching, including the Catechism, three or four years at a Grammar School, and four years at a College where Greek, logic, and rhetoric were taught.

When entering the University he would have to produce certificates from the master of the school and the minister of the town where he received his earlier training, and would also have to undergo an examination, in which, if he showed sufficient knowledge of dialectic, he might omit further study in that department, and finish his course in arts in two years. To a great extent University studies were intended to be professional, and even in arts two-thirds of the course were assigned to mathematical and physical science ; but, on the other hand, a considerable amount of literary culture was implied in the Latin of the Grammar School and the tongues of the intermediate College, while logic and rhetoric formed part both of the intermediate and the University course. The provision of Grammar Schools and intermediate Colleges was one of the great merits of the scheme, giving a considerable education to those who could not continue their studies further, and enabling those who entered the University to do so well prepared for its work.

In the scheme of the *Book of Discipline*, as well as afterwards in the municipal foundation and the *Nova Erectio* at Glasgow, prominence is given to College work and the officers and functions of the University, though now and again recognised expressly or by implication, are mostly allowed to fall into the background. The *Book of Discipline* does not speak of a chancellor, but bestows some functions appropriate to a chancellor on the presbyterian superintendent. The rector was to be elected every year by the principals, the regents, and the supposts who had graduated or gone through a certain course of study, and was to make monthly inspections of the Colleges, to act as judge in civil causes between members of the University, and to be an assessor to the city magistrates in trying criminal charges against such members. The superintendent was to be assisted by a procurator, and the rector by two assessors, one a lawyer and the other a theologian ; and all the members, from the rector downwards, were to be exempted from taxation.

It was proposed to give a salary of £200 to each principal of a college and to each reader in Hebrew, Greek, and divinity, while the salary of readers in law and medicine was to be smaller. Each bursar in philosophy, medicine, and law was to receive £20 a year, and each bursar in divinity £24. The total cost of maintaining the three Universities on the basis laid down in the *Book of Discipline* was estimated at the modest sum of £9640 Scots, which in 1560 would correspond to about £2300 sterling.

The Lords of the Congregation perused the *Book of Discipline* many days, and a number signed their approval of it, but the majority rebelled against the provisions which contradicted their selfish longings for Church lands, and spoke derisively of these provisions as 'devout imaginations.' In the circumstances of the time it proved of greater moment to glut the selfish avarice of a few private persons than to provide for the new Church establishment, for the relief of the poor, and for a comprehensive and beneficent plan of national education. By an enactment of the Privy Council in February, 1562, the old Catholic incumbents were left during life in possession of two-thirds of their incomes, the remaining third being divided between the Crown and the protestant clergy. For the rest, except as an ideal, a 'devout imagination,' the reformers' scheme remained a barren one.

In 1562, the year after her return to Scotland, Queen Mary was taking lessons under George Buchanan, and it seems likely that he may have prompted her to do something for the encouragement of learning. At all events the Queen was in Glasgow on the 13th of July, 1563, and issued a letter under the privy seal setting forth the untoward state of the University, part only of its schools and chambers being built, and the provision for poor bursars having ceased, as well as for masters to carry on the work of teaching, so that it looked like the decay of a University rather than an established foundation.

From her zeal for literature and regard for the promotion of virtue the Queen proceeded to found five bursaries for poor children. To provide means for supplying them with food, clothing, and other necessaries she granted to the College the manse and 'kirkroom' of the Friars Preachers within the city, thirteen acres of land, which from other sources we learn to have been the lands of Dovehill, and yearly payments, including ten marks formerly due to the Friars from tenements in the city, twenty marks from Netherton of Hamilton, ten bolls of meal from certain lands in the Lennox, elsewhere stated to be those of Ballagan, and ten marks from the lands and lordship of Avondale. The arrangement was to continue 'ay and quhill ane generall ordoure be takin be ws thairin. At the quhilk tyme we mynd to doit the lands and annuellis forsaidis thairto, and als to mak the said College to be provydit of sic ressonabile leving that tharin the liberale sciences may be planlie techit siclike as the samyn ar in vtheris Collegis of this realme, swa that the College foirsaid salbe reputit Oure Foundatioun in all tyme cuming.' On 31st August of the same year the bailies of Glasgow ordained that four burgesses who had taken a lease of the thirteen acres of land from John Davidson, principal regent of the pedagog of Glasgow, should pay to him an annual rent of twenty-eight bolls of malt.

It will be seen that in 1563 Queen Mary contemplated further regulation and endowment of the University of Glasgow. She never carried out this purpose, but further endowments which she bestowed on the city in 1567 were not long afterwards diverted to the uses of the College. Within five weeks of the murder of Darnley, and possibly as a means of propitiating the Nemesis of public condemnation which that event brought upon her, she granted to the town councils and communities of Edinburgh and Glasgow charters expressed in almost identical terms, and both signed in Edinburgh before the same witnesses, one of whom was Bothwell.

The charter for Edinburgh was signed on the 13th and the other for Glasgow on the 16th of March, 1567. The latter conveyed to the provost, bailies, council and community of Glasgow for the support òf the ministers of the word of God, and for upholding hospitals for poor, maimed, and wretched persons, and orphan and destitute children, the lands and revenues belonging to any chaplainries, altarages, or prebends founded in any church, chapel, or college within the city, together with the place of the Friars Preachers or Black Friars, and Friars Minor or Grey Friars, and the lands and revenues belonging to them, as well as the rents due to any chauntry, altarage, or church within the realm from any lands or houses in Glasgow, or exigible from the provost and bailies of the burgh. The whole of the properties were to be united into one trust to be called Queen Mary's foundation. The charter mentioned the unsettled state of the properties, and pointed out that after the change in religion some prebendaries, chaplains, and friars had fraudulently sold or alienated lands and benefices, while many private persons had laid claim to lands mortified by their ancestors to the Church, and had gained possession through the negligence of town officials and collusion of interested clerics. The Queen rescinded and annulled these alienations and usurpations, but inserted another clause conferring the liferent of their respective benefices on existing prebendaries, chaplains and friars.

As the former holders were thus left in possession during their lives, it seems that the town reaped little benefit, and the proceeds were not sufficient to provide for the ministers without carrying out the other purposes. The Privy Council early in 1562 had enacted that a third part of the fruits and rents of benefices should be paid to collectors appointed by the Crown, the remaining two-thirds being left to the ' auld possessours.' In view of the circumstances at Glasgow, the Regent Moray in 1568 granted to the Magistrates and Council the thirds of the chaplainries and altarages included in Queen Mary's charter òf the preceding year, but shortly after this provision was made for paying the ministers' stipends out of the parsonage teinds. The ministers' stipends being thus secured, the Town Council, with the sanction of Parliament, altered the destination of the endowments conferred by Queen Mary's charter, and bestowed them on the University, which also received a new foundation.

John Davidson has already been mentioned as principal regent before the Reformation. When his name first appears in the incorporation list of 1556, he is described as vicar of Alness, and in connection with the rectorial elections of 1557 and 1558 he is again mentioned and is designated principal regent of the pedagogy of Glasgow. His fifteen years' tenure of the office was a time of eclipse, when the work of teaching, examining, and granting degrees was much interrupted and for a great part of the time probably dormant ; but the deeds which remain show that the University was recognised as a subsisting institution all through the period, and that Davidson was the custodier of its property. He had studied at Paris along with Quintin Kennedy, who became abbot of Crossraguel, and in 1558 issued a polemical treatise on the Catholic side, which was sent to Davidson to be presented to James Beaton, the Archbishop of Glasgow.

Unlike the other office-bearers of the University, Davidson joined the reformers, and in 1563 he published a *Confutation of Kennedy's Papistical Counsels*. Davidson's book is less bitter than most of the controversial works of the time, and he spoke kindly of the fugitive Archbishop ' quha was my guid maister and liberal freind,' and, while combating Kennedy's doctrines, recalled the ' auld Parisiane kyndnes that was betuix us.' Ninian Winzet, in a dedication to Queen Mary, prefixed to a translation of a book in defence of the Catholic faith published towards the end of 1563, eulogises Kennedy's work, and is very severe on Davidson's, characterising it as ' clatteris and I wate nocht quhat.'

Sometime before Winzet's railing comments against Davidson were addressed to the Queen, she had bestowed the manse and ' kirkroom ' of the Friars Preachers with the lands and annuals included in her royal grant of 1563 on Davidson's College, and he lost no time in letting the lands for twenty-eight bolls of malt. In 1564 Arthurle house and garden were restored to Davidson by Robert Lyndsaye of Dunrod, one of the witnesses to the ceremony of delivering earth and stone as symbols of possession being William Donaldson, a servant of the principal regent, which seems to show that the latter was not living in straitened circumstances. A description of the boundaries is given in 1564, and it leaves no doubt that the house was the same which Sir Thomas Arthurle formerly bequeathed to the College, though the small garden, as it is called, may not have included the whole of the ground in Arthurle's bequest.

In a deed of 1569 Davidson, as principal regent and having a right to the chaplainry of St. Michael in the High Church of Glasgow founded in 1481 by John Restoun, and last possessed by the deceased David Gibson, confirmed grants made to Henry Gibson, a burgess, of two tenements in ' Rattonraw' and of lands in Provanside pertaining to the chaplainry ; and granted to Gibson the fruits and rents of the chaplainry for an annual payment of £23. Andrew Hay as rector of the University and patron of the chaplainry concurred in the transaction. On 17th October in the same year Hay presented Davidson to the chaplainry with a view to the funds being used for the maintenance of bursars, and required the regents and any master within the University to aid Davidson in holding the chaplainry and collecting the rents and emoluments ; and this arrangement was confirmed by a letter issued from Stirling on 18th January, 1570, by the Regent Moray, only five days before his assassination. In July following, a decree of the Lords of Council was obtained against the occupiers of lands and tenements pertaining to the chaplainry, ordaining them to make payment to Davidson of the rents and dues. In May, 1570, Davidson as vicar of Colmonell, with consent of the dean and chapter as patrons of that benefice, granted a lease of the vicarage for nineteen years to Gilbert Kennedy, uncle of the laird of Bargany, at a yearly rent of £42 13s. 4d., out of which £16 was to be allowed to the vicar-pensioner. From other sources it appears that Davidson also let the glebe land of Colmonell for an additional sum of £2 annually.

In scholarship Davidson was not a man of any particular mark, and in that respect probably the College did not sustain any irreparable loss when he was appointed minister of Hamilton at some time between 1570 and 1572. But the controversies of the Reformation and the unsettled condition of Church and State for some years after, as well as the battle of Langside near the southern border of the city, and other warlike excursions and alarums, fell within his time ; and it is to his credit that, notwithstanding these commotions, some new endowments were secured, and that he exerted himself with some measure of success to preserve the academic property and revenues.

Still it seems to have been mainly by the efforts of Andrew Hay, parson of Renfrew and vice-superintendent of the West, whom James Melville describes as ' an honest, zealous, frank-hearted gentleman,' that the University was again organised on a settled basis, that its studies began again to flourish, and that it entered with freshness and vigour on a new career of usefulness. By 1569, if not earlier, Hay had become rector of the University, and he continued to hold that office till 1586.

The details of the process by which the Town Council of Glasgow were moved to give a new foundation and further endowments to the University cannot now be traced, but they themselves have put on record that it was by the continual and oft-repeated advice and persuasion of the much respected man Andrew Hay that they took action.   They counted it a loss and detriment to the city that the pedagogy should be tottering for want of means, its studies quenched by poverty, and the youth growing up without training and discipline ; and they desired to restore, endow, and re-erect it, so that from it, as from a Trojan horse, learned and disciplined young men might spring forth to serve all the needs of the country.

The Council's charter of foundation and endowment, dated 8th January, 1573, confirmed by Parliament on the 26th of the same month, transferred to the College or Pedagogy of Glasgow the endowments bestowed on the town by Queen Mary in 1567 for the support of ministers and hospitals.   The funds available from Queen Mary's grant proved inadequate to the support of the ministry, and in 1568 the Regent Moray assigned to the Magistrates and Council for this purpose the thirds of the chaplainries and altarages.   When the funds accruing from Queen Mary's grant were about to be transferred to the College, a further provision for the ministry was needed, and in January, 1572, the Privy Council ordained that the thirds of the parsonage teinds, amounting to about £200 Scots, should be applied to that purpose.   Perhaps it was with a view to save appearances and make some show of compliance with the expressed object of Queen Mary's grant, that the Council appointed the principal publicly to read and expound the Scriptures from the College chair on week days, and the regents in turn to read prayers in Blackfriars Church beside the College, one of the poor students being ordained to ring the bell and summon the other students and the people to the hearing of prayers.

The charter by the Town Council made provision for fifteen persons to reside within the College, where respectable and appropriate maintenance was to be provided for them—a principal or provost, two regents and twelve poor students.   The principal was to hold office for life, and to be appointed by the chancellor, the rector, the dean of faculty, the dean-rector of the church of Hamilton, and the rector of the church of Glasgow, if the two last were preachers of the Word.   The ordinary jurisdiction in matters of discipline concerning the regents and twelve resident students was committed to the principal, and he was to act as professor of theology, and to read and explain the books of Scripture on week days.   He was strictly bound to live within the College—so strictly that if he did otherwise his office was to become vacant.

The regents were to be appointed by the rector, the principal, and the dean of faculty, who also had power to remove them at the end of six years when they had carried two classes through the curriculum, especially if they became sluggish and did not apply themselves to their work. They were to give themselves diligéntly to the teaching of dialectics, physics, ethics, politics, and the whole of philosophy, and were not to undertake other duties to distract them from their academic work, under penalty of deposition by the rector, dean of faculty, and principal. To stimulate the principal and regents to greater diligence in their duties, the founders assigned to the principal forty marks from the vicarage of Colmonell and twenty marks from the College revenue, and from the latter source to each of the two regents twenty marks for dress and extraordinary expenses.

Teachers were allowed to marry, but not to have wives living within the College. Power was reserved to the rector, dean of faculty, principal, and Town Council to establish additional regents and teachers if the state of the College required it. The College and the fifteen foundationers within it, as well as other persons studying there, were declared to be free from all ordinary jurisdiction and from all customs and exactions imposed or to be imposed by the Town Council.

The twelve poor students were to be nominated by the Town Council from sons of burgesses, and though no definite preliminary examination was prescribed, it was laid down that they should be so instructed in grammar as to be fit learners of philosophy. They were to be provided with food and drink and accommodation in the College chambers for the space of three and a half years, which was reckoned the appropriate length of time for obtaining the magisterial laurel—that is, for graduating—in the faculty of arts. It is curious, as showing the connection between secondary and University education, that the Town Council in the deed refounding and endowing the University ordained a certain provision to be made permanently for the master of the Grammar School. Of course it was contemplated that many other students should gather to the revived seminary besides those for whom a living was provided. A religious test, which does not seem to have been of a strict nature, was laid down. No student was to be enrolled till he had made in the presence of the principal and regents the confession of faith and religion recently prescribed by act of Parliament.

It was appointed that twice a year—on 1st March and 1st September —the rector, the dean of faculty, and the bailies of the city should visit the College both in its head and its members, so that if in anything they had gone astray from duty they should be corrected by the visitors. It was also laid down that the visitors should on each of these occasions audit the College accounts, and see that all the expenditure had been in good faith and according to the arrangements enacted, and that there was no fraud in the administration of the preceptors and procurator.

A calculation was to be made whether there was any surplus from the revenue, and if a surplus existed it was to be applied to the most necessary uses of the College and to repairs. The revenues were expected to increase, and if in virtue of the Council's donation to their College the revenues showed an augment beyond what was required for the adequate maintenance of the fifteen founded persons contemplated at the outset, it was to be given to the students and twelve poor scholars or used to institute additional regents and preceptors if the state of the College required it. While the Town Council thus gave a new foundation and further revenues to ' our College,' as they called it, they did not reserve to themselves any great share in the management or patronage. If it had been the Edinburgh Town Council, they would not have missed the opportunity of obtaining authority over the College. The city magistrates of that time whose names appear in the deed of foundation deserve to be honourably remembered among the benefactors of the University. John Stewart of Minto was provost—one of the many lairds of Minto who held office as chief magistrate of Glasgow—and the three bailies were Adam Wallace, Archibald Lyon, and George Elphinstone.

The Town Council were probably some years in maturing their plan which, as we have seen, depended on securing some other provision for the maintenance of the ministry and thus setting free the funds included in Queen Mary's grant of 1567. They appear to have taken up the project in earnest just about the time when Davidson was withdrawing from the position of principal regent ; and from the time of Davidson's withdrawal till the autumn of 1574 when Peter Blackburn entered upon duty as a regent, the work of teaching and study ceased and the College was closed. Blackburn had newly gone through his course of study and graduated at St. Andrews, and he appears to have been a man of industrious and respectable ability. But it was felt that, to put new life into the University after its long depression and eclipse, a man of eminent ability and reputation was needed, and the patrons soon secured the services of one of the most remarkable men who ever taught within its walls.

Andrew Melville was born at Baldovy, near Montrose, in 1545, and his father having fallen at the battle of Pinkie, he early came under the care of his uncle Richard. The uncle was something of a scholar, had travelled on the continent with Erskine of Dun, and studied with him two years at Wittenberg under Melanchthon, both acquiring a leaning towards Protestantism. Erskine, on his return to Scotland, set up a school for Greek at Montrose—a marvellous thing for that time. It was taught by a Frenchman named Pierre de Marsiliers, and under him Andrew Melville, after learning Latin at the Grammar School of Montrose, studied Greek for two years and also made himself proficient in French. When he passed to St. Mary's College, St. Andrews, in 1559, to hear the professors lecture and drill their students from Latin versions of Aristotle, the youth of fourteen astonished his teachers by reading the works of their great oracle in the original Greek. He left St. Andrews in 1564 with the reputation of being the best philosopher, poet, and Grecian of any young master in the land ; and betook himself to further study in Paris, continuing to read Greek, applying himself vigorously to the study of oriental languages, and attending the lectures of Peter Ramus, whose revolutionary ardour in demolishing or attempting to demolish Aristotle made him widely known. Melville also took a course of lectures under Francis Baldwin on civil law.

From Paris he went to be a regent in the College of St. Marceon at Poitiers, where also he studied jurisprudence. But the work of the College was interrupted by a siege of the town in the course of the civil war between Huguenots and Catholics, and when the siege was over he repaired to Geneva, where he was appointed to the chair of humanity in the flourishing and famous Academy founded there ten years before. At Geneva, besides teaching his own subject, Melville was an earnest student of oriental languages and divinity, and lived in friendly fellowship and scholarly emulation with Beza and other learned and famous men. When in 1574 he resolved to return to Scotland, Beza wrote to the General Assembly that the Church of Geneva could not give a stronger proof of affection to the Church of Scotland than by suffering Melville to return that his native country might be enriched with his gifts. His training had indeed fitted him for the arduous work to which he was soon called. The regent Morton offered him a place about court till he could be advanced to some more suitable post when a vacancy occurred ; but Melville was no courtier, and, declining the offer, he proceeded to his brother's house at Baldovy.

The General Assembly which met in August, 1574, being earnestly urged by James Boyd, Archbishop of Glasgow, and Andrew Hay, rector of the University, advised Melville to accept an appointment in that institution. Overtures were also made to secure his services as provost of St. Mary's College, St. Andrews, and he seems to have chosen the western seat of learning because its needs were greater and afforded him a unique opportunity of distinguishing himself by advancing the cause of learning in his native country. After a preliminary visit of inspection and enquiry to Glasgow, he agreed to accept office as principal regent. In the end of October he quitted Baldovy, and on his way south spent two days at Stirling, where he met Buchanan, then engaged in writing his Latin *History of Scotland* and teaching the boy king.   Melville discussed with Buchanan the plan of education to be followed at Glasgow, and was introduced to James VI., who had doubtless been tutored for the occasion, and is said to have discoursed marvellously about knowledge and ignorance while walking up and down led by the hand of old Lady Mar.

Following the system of instruction in use at St. Andrews, where he had been educated, Peter Blackburn, the lately appointed regent, had begun a course at Glasgow, but on the arrival of Melville everything was submitted to his judgment and regulation ; and Melville, like a strong man prodigal of his strength, entered on the work of teaching.   He formed a class of students well versed in Latin, and resolved himself to conduct them through an extended curriculum which he had planned. Having taught them the principles of Greek grammar, he proceeded to the study of logic and rhetoric, using as text-books the *Dialectics* of Ramus and the *Rhetoric* of Talon, a colleague of Ramus.   Concurrently with these studies he read with them in Latin the works of Virgil and Horace, and in Greek those of Homer, Hesiod, Theocritus, Pindar, and Isocrates, pointing out their excellences and drawing from them illustrations of logic and rhetoric.   He then proceeded to teach the *Elements* of Euclid, with the arithmetic and geometry of Ramus, and the geography of Dionysius.   Next he expounded moral philosophy, dealing with the works of Cicero along with the *Ethics* and *Politics* of Aristotle and some of the *Dialogues* of Plato.   In natural philosophy he made use of Fernelius and parts of the writings of Aristotle.   He then gave a view of universal history, supplemented by chronology and the composition of public documents, such as charters, treaties, and the like.

This extraordinary course may be said to have been given *ex gratia*, for it was outside his province as principal regent.   Probably he did not in the earlier sessions take up oriental languages and divinity, the subjects which belonged to his official province, and when he came to deal with these subjects the several regents in arts had begun to teach the various branches assigned to them, thus relieving Melville, at least in great part, from dealing with these branches.   In his proper office as principal regent he taught the Hebrew tongue, first going over the elementary work of Martinius, and then giving a more extended view, accompanied by a praxis on the Psalter and the book of Solomon.   He then introduced his students to Chaldee and Syriac, reading the portions of Ezra and Daniel written in Chaldee, and the Syriac version of the Epistle to the

Galatians.   He also expounded the common heads of divinity in the order of Calvin's Institutes, and lectured on the various books of Scripture.   In addition to all this, he was from 1577 minister of Govan, and throughout the whole time a diligent worker in the affairs of the Church, taking a chief part in drawing up the *Second Book of Discipline*, approved by the General Assembly in 1578, when Melville himself was Moderator.

Few could have carried out this laborious and encyclopaedic course of instruction: few would have done it if they could.   But Melville was eager to raise the academic reputation of his native country, and so vehement and daring a spirit could hardly be untouched with personal ambition.   Urged by both these motives, he threw himself into the work with an ardour and energy almost unbounded.   From the first a fair number of students attended the rejuvenescent University, and in a year or two there was a great increase.   Some who had taken degrees at St. Andrews repaired to Glasgow for further study, and after the interruptions and confusion of the preceding sixteen or eighteen years, degrees were again annually conferred.

There were ten laureations in 1578, six in 1579, five in 1580, eight in 1581, ten in 1582, and eight in 1583.   The record of students enrolled does not begin till 1590, and is rather intermittent for some time, and probably incomplete.   In 1590 there were 35 enrolments ; in 1593, 27 ; in 1598, 67 ; and for the ten years, from 1601 to 1610, the annual average was about 26.   The University may have counted as many students in some of the most prosperous years of the Catholic period as in Melville's time, but it was no light service to raise it again to the same level of prosperity, and after this things continued in a steadier course.   Among the more notable students educated under Melville may be mentioned John Spottiswood, Archbishop of Glasgow, and afterwards of St. Andrews till deposed by the Glasgow General Assembly of 1638, author of a *History of the Church of Scotland* ; Duncan Nairn, the earliest professor in the University of Edinburgh after Principal Rollock, who began the teaching ; Melville's nephew, Patrick, professor of Hebrew at Glasgow, and subsequently at St. Andrews ; and Sir Edward Drummond, Sir Gideon Murray, and Sir James Fullarton, who attained the distinction— not a very noble one—of being courtiers to James VI.

During Melville's career at Glasgow his nephew James, who has left us an interesting and ingenuous biography abounding in curious and useful matter, acted as one of the regents, and another nephew, Patrick, went through the arts curriculum, and graduated in 1578.   While he was principal regent Melville was the light and life of the College, giving a brilliant example of his learning and power as a teacher, and holding good-humoured discussions and disputations with Peter Blackburn and the other regents, as well as with gentlemen of scholarly tastes and accomplishments in the neighbourhood.

Among them were Andrew Hay and Archbishop Boyd, who had been mainly instrumental in bringing him to Glasgow ; Patrick Sharp, master of the Grammar School, who declared he had received more help to the right understanding of the authors he taught there from Melville's easy and entertaining conversation, lit up by flashes of humour and scholarship, than from all the commentators ; Patrick Adamson or Constant, a man of considerable literary ability, but fickle and intriguing ; and Thomas Smeaton, who succeeded Adamson as minister of Paisley, and by and by succeeded Melville himself as principal regent.

In his early days Adamson had been intriguing for a bishopric, but being unsuccessful, he became a zealous preacher against bishops, of whom he gave a satirical classification in the course of a sermon, dividing them into three sorts—My Lord Bishop, being the popish variety ; My Lord's Bishop, the kind then existing in Scotland, where my lord got the benefice, and the bishop merely served to make his title secure ; and the Lord's bishop, who was the true minister of the Gospel.   However, a few years afterwards Adamson was appointed to the see of St. Andrews, and became a bishop of the second class.   Adamson sought the society of Melville, and though the latter had no great faith in the constancy of his new acquaintance, for a time they were on friendly terms.   Before long, however, they came into sharp opposition on questions of church policy, and were estranged from personal friendship.

A man may be famous on account of great ability or learning or inventiveness or research and yet be no great teacher, but even then his ability and reputation usually secure him the respect of his students. But when, as in the case of Melville, an able man is also an able teacher, bringing his whole strength and resources to bear on the work of instructing, encouraging, and helping forward his pupils, he kindles their admiration and awakens in them something of his own ardour and energy in the pursuit of knowledge.   Of course there are always some perverse and erratic students.

In the present day students are sufficiently inclined to be unruly, but three hundred and thirty years ago they were worse inclined, and possessed greater resources of disturbance.   Melville was not strict in small things affecting himself, but he was resolute in maintaining the discipline and credit of the University when occasion arose.

John Maxwell, son of Lord Herries, while a student associated with Andrew Heriot, the prodigal son of a wealthy citizen, neglected his studies, and misbehaved badly. His regent reported the case to Melville, who rebuked him sharply in public. Maxwell was so incensed that he retired into the city, and, along with Heriot, tried to stir up the rabble against the College. Heriot gathered a disorderly crowd, and pursued the masters and students as they were returning from church till they entered the College, Heriot brandishing a sword in the principal's face and showering upon him insulting language. Melville bore it all with patience and composure, and restrained the students, who would fain have retaliated on their assailants. When Lord Herries heard what had happened, he came to Glasgow, greatly commended the forbearance of the principal, and compelled his son to make an apology on the bended knee in the College court.

Another student, Mark Alexander Boyd, destined afterwards to some notability as a soldier of fortune and a writer of Latin verses, occasioned a still greater tumult. He was a youth of good intelligence but wild and quarrelsome temper, who had been troublesome in the Grammar School, and continued to be troublesome in the College, till at length he was chastised by James Melville, his regent, for some offence in the summer of 1580. The youthful culprit pricked his face with his writing instruments, smeared himself with blood, and made his friends believe he had been unmercifully treated by his regent. An investigation by the College authorities exposed the trick, but the lad's kinsmen unwisely supported him in his perversity. Boyd and his cousin, Alexander Cunninghame, a near relation of the Earl of Glencairn, waited for the regent one evening, and prepared to attack him as he was passing through the High Church-yard on his way to the College. Boyd came behind with a baton, but retired when the regent faced him, and Cunninghame, who came on with a drawn sword, was disarmed and detained a prisoner. The rector and the magistrates ordered Cunninghame to appear bareheaded and bare-footed in the place where the assault was committed, and there beg pardon of the University and of the regent he had attacked ; but he disregarded the sentence, and there were rumours and threatenings that the Boyds and Cunninghames would make a violent assault on the University.

Melville procured a summons ordering the offender to appear before the Privy Council, went himself to St. Andrews to support the prosecution, and, in spite of the great influence exerted on the other side, obtained a decree requiring Cunninghame to obey the sentence of the University and Town Council by the 7th of August, or else enter himself a prisoner in the Castle of Blackness within two days afterwards, on pain of being denounced as a rebel and put to the horn. It was feared that Boyd and Glencairn, with their followers, would not suffer their kinsman to go through such a humiliating ordeal, and that bloodshed might ensue. Even the rector, Andrew Hay, advised that the University should not insist on the execution of the decree, but Melville was resolute, and declared that ere it came to this pass ' that we dare not correct our scholars for fear of bangsters and clanned gentlemen, they shall have all the blood of my body first.' On the day appointed for the submission Lord Boyd and the Earl of Glencairn came to Glasgow with four or five hundred followers.

The churchyard, which had been the scene of the assault and was to be the scene of the submission, was filled with armed men, the intention being, without directly refusing the demand of the Privy Council, to overawe the University authorities so that they might let the case go without exacting an apology. Melville, nothing daunted, made his appearance, followed by the rector, regents, and students in their gowns, and the academic procession was allowed to pass forward to the scene of the assault. Cunninghame, bareheaded and barefooted, but richly dressed, and supported by two friends, came jauntily forward, saying he was ready to make his submission if there were any present who would accept it. 'Doubt not of the acceptation ; we are here ready,' replied Melville. And then Cunninghame had to go through his confession and repentance in presence of the four or five hundred gentlemen who had been gathered to save him from that humiliation, and who, having spent three or four hundred marks in the town, went home, as they themselves confessed, greater fools than they came.

About a year after Melville settled at Glasgow, the vicarage of Govan fell vacant by the death of Stephen Beaton, who had possessed it since the days before the Reformation. Not long after Patrick Adamson was moved from Paisley to the court, and became minister to the regent Morton. The regent had been quick to perceive Melville's abilities, and wished to secure him as an adherent and supporter of his policy. But Morton favoured prelacy, and Melville was a firm and steadfast advocate of presbytery, and his daring and independent spirit ill suited him to play the courtier.

Notwithstanding Adamson's satirical sermon against bishops and his having published a translation of Calvin's Catechism in Latin heroic verse, the regent found him willing to reconsider his views of ecclesiastical polity for the sake of benefices and worldly advantages ; and perhaps he still hoped that Melville's constancy might be moved. At all events, the benefice of Govan was offered to him if ' he would be the regent's man and leave off the pursuit of the bishops.' Melville declined the offer, but through the agency of Adamson dealt earnestly with the regent to have the vicarage annexed to the College in order to improve its slender revenues, which could scarcely support two masters without any bursars. No appointment was made for nearly two years, but at length, seeing Melville was not to be moved by personal benefaction, the regent, by the advice of Patrick Adamson, made a new erection of the College, and annexed the vicarage to it, which, says James Melville, ' was the best turn that ever I knew either the regent or Mr. Patrick to do.'

It is generally believed that Melville himself had the chief share in formulating the provisions and regulations of the *Nova Erectio* of 1577. Two years before, he discussed proposed reforms and a new constitution with Alexander Arbuthnot, principal of King's College, Aberdeen, and they agreed on a scheme of reform for the two Universities over which they presided. James VI. was a boy of eleven, and the Earl of Morton, as regent, was the actual chief magistrate of the realm when, in 1577, a charter in their joint names was issued granting to the College or Pedagogy of Glasgow the rectory and vicarage of the parish church of Govan, with its tithes, rents, profits, manses, glebe, and church lands, free from payment of thirds or any other assessment whatever, to be held by the College or Pedagogy, and the principal, masters, regents, bursars, servants, and officials ; and, in addition, confirming the College in the possession of the annual rents, fruits, profits, and emoluments previously bestowed upon it—these also to be held without payment of thirds or any other taxation. The funds were to be applied in the manner set forth in the charter of erection and foundation annexed to the charter which conveyed the Govan benefice and confirmed previous endowments.

This latter charter, usually called the *Nova Erectio*, willed that twelve persons should ordinarily reside within the College and be maintained at its expense, on a scale proportioned to the resources of the revenues, and subject to the discretion of the principal and regents, namely, the principal, three regents, an oeconomus or steward, four poor students, a servant to the principal, a cook, and janitor. They were to live *collegialiter*, and for their maintenance in food and drink twenty-one chalders out of the twenty-four which Govan yielded annually were assigned. If there was anything over after count and reckoning had been made, it was to be applied to the pious uses of the College and in repairing the buildings, according to the decision of the visitors.

The principal was to have the ordinary jurisdiction over the other persons living within the College, and to be professor of divinity and Hebrew and Syriac, giving lectures on theology alternately with instruction in the sacred tongues. In view of the College enjoying the revenues of the church of Govan, the principal was to preach there every Sunday,

E

but not to reside outside the College. He was forbidden to take any extended journey without obtaining the sanction of the rector, dean of faculty, and regents, and if, without having duly obtained leave, he passed three nights outside the College, his office was to become vacant. The appointment of the principal was reserved to the Crown, and notice of the occurrence of a vacancy was to be given by the regents then in office ; but if the Crown did not present within thirty days from the intimation of a vacancy, the right of electing was to pass to the chancellor, the rector, the dean of faculty, and the ministers of Hamilton, Cadder, Monkland, and Renfrew, with other grave and learned men whom the Crown might appoint. It is believed that this curious provision has not been repealed by any subsequent legislation. To the office of principal a salary of 300 marks was attached, with three chalders additional from the revenues of Govan.

It was reckoned enough for the system and convenient working of the College that there should be three regents to instruct the youth and give assistance to the principal. The first regent was appointed to teach the principles of eloquence from the most approved authors, and to be professor of Greek, exercising his students in writing and declaiming, so that they might have equal skill in both Latin and Greek, and become more fitted to receive the doctrines of philosophy. The second was to explain dialectics and logic, and to demonstrate their uses from such authors as Cicero, Plato, and Aristotle, adding the elements of arithmetic and geometry, which were declared to be of no slight moment in fostering erudition and sharpening intellect. Each of these two regents was to have a salary of fifty marks from the old revenues of the College. To the third regent was assigned the teaching of physiology—not what is now understood by that term, but rather physics—and geography, astronomy, and general chronography, which last shed light on other studies as well as on history. Besides teaching, the third regent was to assist in the management of the College in view of the principal being minister of Govan, and to have the care of it during the principal's absence. The election and admission of the regents were committed to the rector, the dean of faculty, and the principal.

The course of instruction in arts, now divided among three regents, was arranged mainly on the model which Melville had himself introduced, but he thought it desirable to alter the practice then prevailing in Universities, and which he himself had at first been obliged to follow, under which a whole class of students was conducted through the various subjects by the same regent, and to fix each regent to a particular subject or group of subjects, which students should take in succession under different regents. Accordingly the *Nova Erectio* declared against the regents changing to a new profession each year as the custom was in other colleges, from which it happened that, while they professed many things, they were skilled in few ; and enjoined them to keep to the same profession.

Superior intelligence, skill in grammar, and want of means on the part of their friends to support them, were laid down as the qualifications of bursars. The presentation of these bursars was reserved to Morton and his heirs, while their admission was committed to the principal, and he was cautioned to see that the rich were not admitted in place of the poor. The bursars were to enter the College on 1st October and remain there during a literary course of three and a half years, ' *quod tempus idoneum judicamus, pro ceterarum Academiarum regni nostri consuetudine, ad stadium philosophicum consummandum et lauream adipiscendam.*' A salary of twenty pounds was assigned to the oeconomus, besides payment of his outlays in collecting the College revenues, one of the most important parts of his duty. Under the direction of the preceptors he was also to provide the things necessary for victuals to the College table, and to give to the principal and preceptors a daily account of the goods bought and brought in. Further, the preceptors themselves, as well as the oeconomus, were bound to render an account of their administration four times a year—on 1st October, 1st February, 1st May, and 1st August—to the rector, the dean of faculty, and the minister of the city of Glasgow, who were constituted visitors and enjoined to see all things administered rightly and in accordance with the intentions of the authors of the *Nova Erectio*, and to reduce affairs to order by their authority.

A hope was expressed that students would gather from all parts of the kingdom, and they were commanded to live peaceably, doing no injury by word or deed to the rector, principal, or regents, but applying themselves diligently to their studies, in order that they might do honour to their parents, service to the Church, and credit to the commonwealth. And because Satan was always trying to seduce the young to the more than Cimmerian darkness of popery, it was ordained that students enrolled in the College should make profession of their faith. The king also willed that the College and Academy of Glasgow should enjoy all the immunities and privileges conferred by his ancestors or himself, or in any other way, on any of the other academies of his kingdom, as freely and peaceably as if they had accrued to it from ancient times beyond the memory of man.

It is curious that the *Nova Erectio* confirmed to the University of Glasgow all the immunities and privileges which had been conferred on any other Scottish University, but did not confirm thei immunities and privileges directly bestowed on itself in past times. This is not explained by saying that it was the era of the Reformation and that the reformers disliked the associations of Universities founded by the pope. For the pope founded the Universities of St. Andrews and Aberdeen, and the *Nova Erectio* confirmed to Glasgow all the privileges contained in these foundations. So far as academic interests were concerned, nothing could be more ample or liberal than the bull of Nicholas V., which established in Glasgow a *studium generale* in the faculties of theology, canon and civil law, arts, and any other legitimate faculty whatsoever, placed its members on a level with his own most distinguished University of Bologna, and conferred on its graduates the most cosmopolitan academic privileges, declaring that without further examination or probation they should be qualified to rule and teach in any other *studium generale*. The privileges granted by King James II.—privileges which had been confirmed by many later kings and regents—were also left out of account in the *Nova Erectio*.

If Morton had really set himself, as he says, to collect the scattered remnants of the University, he might have been expected to produce something considerably different from the *Nova Erectio*, which in the main is concerned with the regulation of a college. The words used in the course of the two charters granting the revenues of the benefice of Govan and setting forth the *Nova Erectio* are *Collegium*, *Pedagogium*, *Gymnasium*, and *Academia*, while the word *Universitas* occurs only once, where it is said of the archbishop, ' *qui est Universitatis Cancellarius.*'

Among the high officers of the institution the rector has all through its history been specially associated with the University, yet he is here called *Rector Academiae*, while the archbishop is *Universitatis Cancellarius*. But the right of granting degrees was recognised, for the charter willed that by the work of the third regent completion should be given to the curriculum in philosophy, and that those who had been capped should hasten the more eagerly to weightier studies—' *ac pileo donatos adolescentes ad graviora studia alacrius contendere.*' Again, the tenure of the bursars was fixed at three years and a half, which was reckoned an adequate time, ' *ad stadium philosophicum consummandum et lauream adipiscendam.*' However anomalous some points in the phraseology of the *Nova Erectio* might be, or however incongruous with the associations of the older University, the restored seminary was still a teaching and a degree granting institution as the pope's *studium generale* had been. From this time the Dean of Faculty came to be regarded as one of the chief University officers, though in its historic development the office belonged to the faculty of arts.

Melville had discussed the question of academic reorganisation with

Arbuthnot, principal of King's College, Aberdeen, and they agreed upon a scheme of reform for their respective institutions.   Contemporaneously with the *Nova Erectio* for Glasgow a *Fundatio Nova* was procured for Aberdeen.   The organisation at Aberdeen was to be similar to that at Glasgow, except that civil law was included as well as theology, while the professorship of canon law and the readership in medicine were abolished. Shortly afterwards, mainly by the agency of Melville with the help of Buchanan and others, a scheme was framed for remodelling St. Andrews. The College of St. Salvator was to have a principal and four regents—the regents doing work similar to that of the faculty of arts at Glasgow, and the principal acting as professor of medicine, while there were to be also a professor of mathematics and one of law.   St. Leonard's was to have the same arrangements as St. Salvator's, but without professors of mathematics and law, and its principal, instead of professing medicine, was to read Plato with his students.   St. Mary's was to be a College of theology, with four professors and a principal, the last of whom was to lecture on systematic theology.

It is curious that of the three nearly contemporary schemes for reconstituting the Scottish Universities, only that for Glasgow remained operative. The scheme for Aberdeen was resisted, and Arbuthnot died in 1583 without seeing it carried out.   It was ratified in Parliament in 1597, but the ratification was halfhearted, and spoke of the scheme as one to be revised.   Revision does not seem to have come, but in 1619 the new foundation for Aberdeen was swept away.   At St. Andrews the plan of reorganisation was only partially carried out, the College of St. Mary's never received the stated number of professors, and in 1621 Parliament repealed its previous ratification and restored the original foundations of the three Colleges at St. Andrews.

It will be seen that of the three schemes the one for Glasgow was narrower than that for Aberdeen, which included law as well as arts and theology, and decidedly narrower than the scheme for St. Andrews, which embraced two Colleges for arts, one of which also included law and medicine, and a third College of theology.   If therefore we take the *Nova Erectio* as indicating Melville's ideal, we must take it as showing only his estimate of what could be done with the means actually available, and not as his ideal of what should be done if adequate resources could be obtained.   In one sense the scheme for Glasgow fared better than the others.   It survived, while they were soon put aside or repealed.

But the *Nova Erectio* did not all survive, for it regulated with too great minuteness details which should have been left to the discretion of the administrators, and the administrators made little scruple about break-

ing through its provisions when it suited them to do so. In this respect
the municipal foundation of 1573 was superior to the *Nova Erectio*, and
many measures which the administrators thought it desirable to adopt,
though they were inconsistent with Morton's foundation, were quite consistent with the municipal foundation. The latter provided for the
institution of additional regents ; the former did not. Yet in three or
four years a fourth regent was added, and by and by a regent or professor
of Latin and a professor of medicine. The *Nova Erectio* declared against
the system of 'regenting.' The municipal foundation left this open, and
in no long time the system of 'regenting' was reintroduced. The *Nova
Erectio* made the principal also minister of Govan, but the duties of the
latter office were declared to be too burdensome for one man to perform
along with those of principal, and the administrators, without more ado,
allowed the principal to contract himself out of his obligations as minister.
The *Nova Erectio* required the goods necessary to furnish the College table
and provide victuals for the twelve founded persons to be bought in by the
oeconomus who collected the College revenues. The administrators by
and by contracted with a burgess of Glasgow—a man who was not
oeconomus and had nothing to do with collecting the College revenues—
to supply victuals for the College table. In itself this might be a very
good arrangement, but it was contrary to the *Nova Erectio*, though quite
legitimate under the municipal foundation. In one respect the municipal
foundation seems to have been of higher authority than the *Nova Erectio*.
The former was ratified by act of parliament ; the latter does not seem
to have been so. It should be remembered, too, that it was under the
municipal foundation that Melville came to Glasgow and taught for the
first three sessions of his tenure, developing the course of instruction to
which the *Nova Erectio* gave its sanction. It was the Town rather than
the Crown or the regent that really restored the University.

The additional revenue from the twenty-four chalders attached to the
Govan benefice has been estimated as worth, at the time when it was
granted, about £400, but this is probably too high. The *Nova Erectio*
states the old revenue of the College at £300 Scots, and one writer after
another has repeated that this was only equal to £25 sterling. It is true
that in the long run Scots money fell to the value of one-twelfth of sterling
money, but at the time of the *Nova Erectio* it was worth much more, and
£300 Scots would then have been equal to about £70 sterling. It also
appears that the £300 mentioned was derived from lands, tenements, and
heritable investments ; but in addition fees were payable for incorporation,
teaching, examination, and other purposes, as well as for board and lodging
within the College in the case of students who lived in that way. The

revenue from other sources than heritable investments must have been considerable for the times, and would be all the more effective because it had not to be divided among many individuals.   Important as the revenue from Govan came to be, it was not realised by the College for some time, as Stephen Beaton, the last Catholic parson of Govan, had in 1574 granted a tack for nineteen years of the parsonage and vicarage to his brother Archibald ; and though the College in 1578 obliged Archibald to take a lease from them for the fifteen years still unexpired, they seem to have gained little immediate advantage except an acknowledgment of their title.

The appointment of the rector, dean of faculty, and minister of Glasgow as visitors to audit the College accounts and control the application of surplus revenue, was in some ways an important step, but in the subsequent history of the institution it did not very often hinder the ordinary administrators from taking their own way.   The authors of the *Nova Erectio* could not foresee the turn events were to take, else they would probably have adopted measures to secure that the same person should not be an ordinary administrator and also a visitor.   In course of time it came to be a very common usage to appoint a professor as dean of faculty, while for more than half a century two successive principals of the University were also ministers of Glasgow.

Peter Blackburn, who had come from St. Andrews and commenced teaching at Glasgow, continued as a regent during the whole of Melville's time and for two years longer, when he was appointed minister at Aberdeen ; but in the earlier years he seems to have been as much employed in the management of the academic property and revenues as in teaching. With the commencement of the session in the autumn of 1575, the principal's nephew, James Melville, then only in his nineteenth year, became a regent, and taught Greek grammar, and portions of Isocrates, Homer, and Hesiod, as well as the *Dialectic* of Ramus and the *Rhetoric* of Talaeus.   This made up the bare minimum of the teaching staff required by the municipal foundation—a principal and two regents.   After Morton had granted the *Nova Erectio* in 1577, Blaise Laurie was appointed a regent, and this completed the teaching staff contemplated by that charter.

In his later sessions at Glasgow, Andrew Melville devoted himself more to the teaching of divinity and oriental languages, being the subjects assigned to the province of the principal, and the arts subjects were left more in the hands of the regents.   Blaise Laurie, as first regent in the sense defined by the *Nova Erectio*, taught Greek and Latin eloquence ; James Melville, as second regent, taught logic, moral philosophy, and some portion of physics ; and Peter Blackburn, as third or highest regent, with a somewhat better salary than the others, taught physics and astronomy.

Besides taking an energetic part in the teaching and discipline of the University, Andrew Melville bestirred himself to secure its property and revenues. In 1577 the Lords of the Council ordered letters to be issued against occupiers of lands and houses owing payments to the College for chaplainries, altarages, and prebends, and against the parishioners of Govan for their teinds, with an exception in favour of the parishioners during the continuance of the tack granted to Archibald Beaton, and another exception regarding the Blackfriars yards in favour of John Graham. Next year the Lords of the Council, at the instance of Melville and Blackburn, found the claim of John Graham, a citizen of Glasgow, to a tenement he occupied, and a number of yards in the neighbourhood of the College, null and void, as resting on two charters, one of which was invalid and the other could not be produced.

In 1579 James VI. may be said to have supplied an omission from the *Nova Erectio.* He issued a letter from Stirling of nearly the same purport as the royal letter which James II. had issued from the same place in 1453. The king took the whole masters, doctors, regents, students, bursars, and supposts of the College, with their lands and property, under his firm peace and protection, and confirmed the exemption of members of the University, prelates only excepted, from all kinds of taxation imposed or to be imposed within the kingdom, as also their exemption from watch and ward.

In 1578 the king by a charter, also dated from Stirling, granted to the masters and regents the lands of Ballagan in Kilmaronock, to be held in mortmain, subject to no further return than the prayers of the masters for the welfare of the granter and his successors. Under Queen Mary's gift of 1563, the College had acquired a right to a payment of ten bolls of meal from these lands, so that King James's gift was more apparent than real. A few months after obtaining the charter, the principal and regents, with consent of Mr. Andrew Hay, parson of Renfrew, rector of the University, and Mr. Thomas Smeaton, dean of faculty, ' for the singular favour that ane honorable man, Maister George Buchannan, teachar of our Souerain Lord in gude lettres, hes borne and shawen at all tymes to our College,' granted a lease for nineteen years of the lands and steading of Ballagan to John Buchanan, who was occupier at that time, the yearly rent to be ' ten bollis gude and sufficient ait meil,' of the measure of the town of Glasgow, delivered at the College at the tenant's expense. George Buchanan had recently presented some books to the University library, and there is an unverified tradition that he was instrumental in procuring the *Nova Erectio*. His name appears as a witness to that charter, and he was a friend of Melville and would be pleased to see measures taken for the advancement of the University, but I have not found evidence that he was actively concerned in drawing up the charter or procuring the royal sanction to it. John Buchanan to whom the lease was granted had doubtless been a kinsman, and from time to time the lease was renewed to members of the clan Buchanan down to 1650. In 1655, however, on the allegation that the lands lay 'neir the Hielands' and at a great distance from the University, but near to the lands of Balloch belonging to Sir John Colquhoun of Luss, the College excambed Ballagan to Sir John for a payment of ten bolls of meal yearly from his lands of Temple of Garscube, which were much nearer, and an annual feu-duty of £12 in addition.

In 1580 an agreement was made with the bailies of Rutherglen regarding the payment of eleven marks due by them to the chaplainry of St. Martin, and an annual of forty shillings to the Vicars' choir of Glasgow; but probably they did not pay very willingly or regularly, and in 1618 a decree was obtained against the provost and bailies for payment of £11 yearly from the burgh rents. In October, 1580, Sir Thomas Eccles, vicar pensioner of Colmonell, from a regard for learning and in return for kindness shown him by the masters of the College, resigned the vicarage in their favour, it having been united to the College of old.

I cannot remember encountering in the period before the Reformation any reference to the existence at that time of bursaries to aid poor students in obtaining a University education, but in the course of Queen Mary's letter of 1563 founding five bursaries in the College and University of Glasgow, the queen mentions among the elements of desolation from which the institution was then suffering—'provisioune for the pouir bursouris and maisters to teche ceissit.' All the Colleges at St. Andrews had bursaries connected with them before the Reformation, but, were it not for her own testimony to their previous existence, Queen Mary might have been reckoned the originator of bursaries at Glasgow. The municipal foundation of 1573 provided for the establishment of twelve bursaries, and the *Nova Erectio* for four more, but besides these foundations of a public character for the benefit of poor students who were to live within the College, the foundation of bursaries by private individuals began in Melville's time with the institution of a bursary by Captain Thomas Craufurd of Jordanhill.

The career of Craufurd, the earliest founder of a bursary from his own private means, was a long and notable one. While still very young he was present at the battle of Pinkie in 1547, and was taken prisoner.

Afterwards he spent some time in military service in France, and returning to Scotland with Queen Mary in 1561, he attended the ill-fated Darnley in his later days, and in 1571, by a skilful and daring night attack, captured the Castle of Dumbarton, which had been held for the exiled queen. He was provost of Glasgow in 1577, and a year before this he mortified to the University an annual of sixteen bolls of oatmeal from the Mill of Partick for the support of a student of philosophy and letters during his course in the College, to be presented by the founder and his heirs when a vacancy occurred, and admitted by the principal and regents after examination, if found worthy and fit to undertake the study of philosophy. Other friends of the student have since followed Captain Craufurd's example, and the bursary system has grown with the growth of the University.

When Melville returned to Scotland in 1574 St. Andrews and Glasgow were bidding against each other for his services, and in 1580 the competition from St. Andrews began again. Melville was zealous for the development of the academic institutions of Scotland, and both as regards reputation and the number of students who attended, St. Andrews was then the foremost of them. Plans for its improvement, including the remodelling of St. Mary's College as a school of divinity, had recently been prepared, and Melville had taken a chief part in framing them and procuring their adoption. He had restored the credit and prosperity of Glasgow University, secured some further endowments, and obtained a royal charter with provisions for its constitution, management, and course of study. His friend Thomas Smeaton, minister of Paisley, who had already been dean of faculty, was proposed as his successor, and he was confident that under Smeaton the University would continue the working arrangements now adopted, and would maintain its credit. And so, not without reluctance, he agreed to become principal of St. Mary's College, St. Andrews. A royal message on the subject was sent to·the General Assembly, and in October, 1580, the Assembly, in spite of earnest opposition from the University of Glasgow, agreed to Melville's translation, and appointed Thomas Smeaton to succeed him. At the end of November, 1580, after six years of strenuous, effective, and brilliant work, Melville quitted Glasgow ' with infinite tears on both sides.'

For some time after this most of those who were appointed to the office of principal held it for only a short period. Smeaton died in three years. Patrick Sharpe, who came next, held office for twenty-eight years—the longest of any principal before the eighteenth century—yet he resigned under constraint. Boyd of Trochrig rendered himself offensive to the court by declining to sign the articles of Perth, and demitted office after about six years of service ; and John Cameron, the next principal, though a most distinguished scholar and obsequious to the court, had hardly completed a single session when he withdrew from his post and retired to France. The Stewart kings were ' too fond to rule alone,' and to regulate affairs in an arbitrary manner without due attention to the feelings and needs of their subjects, and down to the time of the Revolution the want of a good understanding between rulers and people has left its traces in the history of the College as well as of the country.

Thomas Smeaton, who succeeded Melville as principal, was educated at St. Andrews and taught there for some time as a regent in St. Salvator's College, but being then attached to the old religion he withdrew to France at the Reformation. He was some time among the Jesuits in France and afterwards in Rome, and frequently visited the prisons of the Inquisition and conversed with the imprisoned heretics. His opinions began to change, his orthodoxy fell under suspicion, and he was sent back to France, from which he escaped at the time of the massacre of St. Bartholomew, in company with Walsingham, the English ambassador. For a time he taught a school at Colchester, and in 1577 returned to Scotland and accepted appointment as minister of Paisley, chiefly to be near Melville, with whom he continued in close friendship. Next year he was dean of faculty in the University. At Melville's suggestion he wrote an answer to a violent polemical dialogue which had been issued by Archibald Hamilton, a professor at St. Andrews who had withdrawn from his College and returned to the Catholic faith ; and with the approval of the Assembly he translated a work on the method of preaching.

Smeaton was well qualified for the office of principal, but, coming immediately after such a man as Melville and himself dying within about three years, it could not be expected that he would leave a very deep mark on the institution over which he presided. From a deed of his time it appears that the University administrators had some thoughts of removing from the buildings then occupied. In 1581 Michael Littlejohn renounced in favour of the College a tenement and yard on the east side of High Street, adjacent to lands and yards belonging to the Pedagogy on the south and east ; but on the same day the masters, with the consent of the rector and dean of faculty, alienated to Littlejohn and his heirs the three lower yards in the Vicars Alley, formerly belonging to the Vicars of the Choir, for an annual of six shillings and eight pence Scots. It was provided, however, that if the College should remove from the premises then occupied to the place of the Vicars of the Choir or any other site near the Cathedral, Littlejohn and his heirs should be bound to renounce these yards in Vicars Alley in favour of the masters of the College, upon their infefting him in the house and yard adjoining the College which he had quitted in their favour.   In 1581 a decree arbitral was pronounced adjudging Sir James Hamilton to pay to the masters an annual of ten marks formerly due from his lands of Avondale to the Friars Preachers, with £10 in satisfaction of arrears.

In the same year, 1581, Archbishop Boyd shortly before his death mortified to the College 'all and haill our customis of our Troneis of Glasgow, great and small customes, fair or mercat customis or of mett measure or wecht.'   This grant was confirmed by a royal letter, but a few years afterwards Gavin Hamilton of Hill pretended that his father was in possession of the customs of the Tron before the changes and commotions of the Reformation time, and by collusion with the provost and bailies of Glasgow ousted the College from their rights.   In 1586 the Lords of the Council ordered Hill to desist from uplifting the customs and allow the College to resume collecting them and retain possession in all time coming.   Notwithstanding this and further confirmation of the rights of the College in charters by the archbishop and the sovereign, the College did not permanently retain possession.

The University came within the circle of disturbance arising from the appointment of a successor to Archbishop Boyd, who died in 1581.   The king's favourite, Esme Stewart, Earl of Lennox, was allowed to dispose of the see, and though bishops had been forbidden by the General Assembly, he appointed Robert Montgomery, minister of Stirling, a man of little merit or ability, to be Archbishop of Glasgow, on condition that the revenues of the see should be made over to Lennox, Montgomery receiving only a limited stipend.   Prohibited by the Church courts from leaving his ministry at Stirling, refused election by the ministers who constituted the Chapter of Glasgow, and threatened by the General Assembly with deposition and excommunication, Montgomery, though supported by the court, made a solemn promise not to meddle further with the see. But he soon revived his claims to it, and the Presbytery of Glasgow having met to consider the matter, he entered the meeting supported by the magistrates and an armed force, and attempted to stop the proceedings. The Presbytery declined to comply, and their moderator, John Howieson, minister of Cambuslang, who founded a bursary which perpetuates his name in the University, was pulled from the chair by the provost, received a number of blows on the face, and had one of his teeth knocked out, and finally was committed to prison.   The students of the University threatened to retaliate upon those who had assaulted Howieson, and they were dispersed by the guard and several of them wounded.   On account of the opposition of its administrators to the new bishop, the College itself was for a time laid under interdict. In May, 1582, Montgomery and the Presbytery of Glasgow had a controversy over the question who should preach in the Cathedral. On one occasion the nominee of the Presbytery was forcibly ejected from the pulpit by the magistrates, and on another the students indulged in one of those impulsive and irregular adventures into which they sometimes digress. They took possession of the Cathedral and excluded Archbishop Montgomery, Principal Smeaton conducting the services for that day.

Commissioners from the General Assembly appeared at a Convention of Estates held in Perth in July, 1582, and presented a petition to the king setting forth the ' Greiffes of the Kirk.' Among the articles included in it were the following :

' 9. The Ministers, Maisters of Schoolles, and Collage of Glasgw, the verie schollars thairof, in tym of public fast, war, be letters of horning, compellit to leave thair flockes and scholles destitut ; and sensyne, from tym to tym, and place to place, have bein continowit and deleyit ; thairby to consum tham be exorbitant expences, and to wrak the kirks and schoolles whairof they have the charge.

' 10. The Students of the Collage war invadit, and ther bluid crewalie sched, be the Bailyie and commonitie, gatherit thairto be sound of common bell and stroak of drum ; and be certain seditius persones inflambet to have slean them all, and brunt the Collage : and yit na thing don to the authores of the tumult and seditioun.'

In 1574 the Town Council of Glasgow had under consideration the condition of the Cathedral owing to the removal of lead, slates, and other material, and though they were not bound to uphold it, yet they agreed to raise a sum to repair the ' greit monument.' In 1581 Principal Smeaton, Andrew Polwart, dean of faculty, and others representing the kirk, urged the Council again to consider the ruin and decay of the Cathedral with a view to its being repaired. The Council expressed their goodwill to the scheme, and some years later, on a further representation from the minister and kirk session, the needful repairs seem to have been actually carried out.

At the close of Melville's tenure as Principal, Peter Blackburn was regent in physics and astronomy, James Melville in logic and moral philosophy, and Blaise Laurie in Greek. James Melville removed with his uncle to St. Andrews, and another nephew, Patrick Melville, who graduated at Glasgow in 1578, was left to fill the vacancy in logic and moral philosophy. But in a deed of 8th March, 1582, a fourth regent, John Bell, is distinctly mentioned. Some have conjectured that it was Archbishop Boyd's gift of the Tron and other customs that enabled the College to add a fourth regent besides the three for which the *Nova Erectio* pro-

a warrant to convert the College from being a school of theology into a school of philosophy. Part of the winter of 1585-6 Melville spent with his old friend, Andrew Hay, rector of the University of Glasgow, and Hay and others urged Melville to resume the position of principal, now vacant by the death of Smeaton. Melville had still a strong attachment to Glasgow, and if he had consulted his own convenience merely, would probably have accepted the offer. But his College at St. Andrews had fallen on evil days, though it was now emerging a little from the frown of power. Melville was not the man to desert it at such a time, and so he returned, and commenced lecturing there in March, 1586, after an absence of about two years.

The vacancy at Glasgow was at length filled on 10th January, 1586, when King James nominated Patrick Sharpe to succeed Smeaton as principal.[1] Sharpe had been master of the Grammar School, and had there acquired practice in the art of corporal punishment, an accomplishment the memory of which has been handed down to us by the next principal, Boyd of Trochrig. He published *A Short Exposition of Christian Doctrine* in 1599 at Edinburgh, but he was a man of greater knowledge and ability than might be supposed from an estimate of that work. He gave the finishing touches to the education of John Cameron at Glasgow University, and Cameron's scholarship excited astonishment on the Continent when he repaired thither while still a very young man. During the twenty-eight years Sharpe held office the University, though not undergoing any remarkable changes or vicissitudes, held its own and made some progress. We take it as a compliment to the reputation of Glasgow that Napier of Merchiston, the inventor of Logarithms, sent his son to study there in 1594, though himself an alumnus of St. Andrews.

A contract dated in 1608 between the principal and masters and Andrew Herbertson, a burgess of Glasgow, who became purveyor to the masters, bursars, and student boarders, throws light on the manner of living within the College three hundred years ago. Herbertson agreed to take up house in the College on 23rd October, and to furnish the four masters, Archibald Hamilton, Michael Wallace, Walter Whiteford, and Gabriel Maxwell, the eight bursars, and as many boarders as the masters might take in from among the students, ' with meat and drink and all things requisite for honest boarders ' till the first day of May following. The days of the week were divided into flesh days and fish days, the former

[1] So much time having elapsed from the occurrence of the vacancy without the King having made an appointment, the right of electing for this time should have passed to the Chancellor, rector, dean of faculty, and others specified in the *Nova Erectio* as entitled to elect in such a case.

including Sunday, Monday, Tuesday, Wednesday, and Thursday, and the latter Friday and Saturday. Herbertson undertook to provide on the flesh days for the masters and others who paid on the same scale breakfast at nine in the morning, consisting of ' ane soup ' of fine wheat bread, or a portion of cold meat, with some dry bread and drink ; and at twelve noon to lay a covered table in the hall and serve them with broth, ' skink,' the best sodden beef and mutton in the market, roasted mutton or veal, as the seasons might make convenient, with a fowl or some equivalent, an ample supply of good wheat bread, and good stale ale, eight or ten days old, better than the ' haill ' ale in the town. The supper was to be ' siclike.'

On the fish days, Friday and Saturday, he was to provide at breakfast a fresh egg for each, with some cold meat, or milk and bread, also some dry bread and drink ; at noon kail (broth), eggs, herring, and three courses of fish when they could be had, otherwise their equivalent in bread and milk, ' fryouris ' with dry bread as before ; and at supper ' siclike.' Three bursars seem to have messed together, and on the flesh days they had for breakfast ' ane soup of ait bread ' and a drink ; at noon broth with a ' tail ' of fresh beef, with sufficient bread and ale ; at evening a ' tail ' of fresh beef to every mess ; and on fish days bread and drink as on other days, with an egg at breakfast ; at noon eggs, herring, and another course ; in the evening ' siclike.' Herbertson was to provide a skilled cook, and to light a good fire in the hall at noon and in the evening, from the time of his entry till ' Fastreinsevin.'

It was agreed that Herbertson should be paid £30 Scots per quarter for the board of each of the four masters, and £16 13s. 4d. per quarter for each of the eight bursars—the first quarter to be paid in hand, and the rest monthly at the beginning of each month. He was also to receive £30 for providing the fire, and 10 marks as a fee to the cook. If any master or bursar, with the principal's leave, was absent eight days or longer, a deduction was to be made ; and if any outside guests were invited to dinner, or things provided beyond the bill of fare contracted for, Herbertson was to have an additional allowance. Unauthorised persons were forbidden to be present in the hall at the time of dinner or supper, and no food was to be sent to the chambers of students under pretext of sickness, unless by order of the principal and masters, while punishment was denounced against any who should carry away food to others. Student boarders who paid at the same rate as the masters sat at the same table with them, and others who could not afford so much might sit with the bursars and partake of the same fare with them. It will be noted that there was no provision for the principal in this contract, though sitting at the common table was reckoned incumbent upon him, and when the next principal was appointed in 1615 he asked to be excused from doing so.

After having attained to full age, James, in July, 1587, on the plea that the Crown had been impoverished by gifts to the Church before the Reformation, leading to a necessity for undue taxation, procured the sanction of Parliament to the annexation to the Crown of the Church lands, the temporalities of benefices. The lands which had belonged to the old Church were, in fact, used to defeat the policy and objects of the leaders of the new Church, for in no long time James made grants of these to courtiers and royal favourites, and was soon able to sway the nobility and landowners to support his policy. But at the time when Parliament sanctioned the annexation of the Church lands to the Crown, measures were taken to confirm the grants already made to the University. On the 29th July, 1587, the king granted a general charter, which was the same day ratified by Parliament, confirming to the University the rectory and vicarage of Govan, with the annexed teinds and emoluments, being the endowments conveyed by the regent Morton and the king in the charter accompanying the *Nova Erectio* ; the lands, houses, and revenues formerly belonging to any order of friars, or any chaplainry or altarage within the town of Glasgow, the endowments conveyed by the Town Council ; the customs of the Tron granted by the archbishop ; and also the immunity of the College revenues from all taxes and impositions, in accordance with the royal charter of 1579. The confirmation of these revenues and privileges was declared to be ' notwithstanding the annexatioun of the ecclesiasticall landis laitly annexed to the croun of this realme and the generall revocatioun or vther restauratioun quhatsumever,' in which the lands, tenements, annual rents, customs, and teinds mortified to the College were in no way to be comprehended.

On 28th June, 1617, during the single visit made by James VI. to Scotland after he became king of England as well, an act of Parliament was passed annexing the kirks of Kilbride and Renfrew to the College, with their parsonages, vicarages, teinds, and emoluments, but with a reservation against tacks or factories, and a provision that twelve chalders should be paid to the ministers in each case. The act set forth that ' oure Souerane Lord, being maist carefull of the vphalding and intertenement of vniuersities, colledges, and schooles, quhilkis ar the verie trew seminarie of all literature and sciences,' for the training of youth ' to serve his Maiestie in sick places and funchounes of the commounwealthe as they sal happin to be called unto ; and haveing consideratioun of the small prouisioun and meanis of the rentis of the Colledge of Glasgow, quhilkis ar nocht sufficient to interteyne the ordiner memberis of the said Colledge, and to repair the building and fabrick thairoff, quhilk will schortlie cum to ruine and decaye, except the samen be tymouslie helpit: Thairfore his Maiestie, with aduyis and consent of the thrie estaittis of this present Parliament, annexes, vnites, and incorporattis in and to the said Colledge of Glasgow . . . the kirk of Kilbryd, personage and vicarage thairoff . . . togidder with the kirk of Renfrew, personage and vicarage thairoff . . . with the haill maillis, fermes, teindis, teyndschevis, small teyndis, fructis, rentis, proffittis, emolumentis, and dewties quhatsumeuir pertening or belanging to the said kirkis . . . to remayne with the said Colledge, professoures, and memberis of the same, and to be frielie bruikit, joysit, and intromettit with be thame as ane proper pairt of thair patrymonie in all tyme cuming.' Shortly afterwards the Archbishop of Glasgow resigned into the king's hands the right to the kirk of Torrens, regarded as a pendicle to the kirk of Kilbride, and usually served by the Kilbride minister, in order that it might be annexed to the kirk of Kilbride and the united parish made over to the College, and in 1618 this was done.

Tacks of the teinds of Colmonell, Gorbals, Whiteinch Meadow, Little Govan, and Polmadie occur at various intervals from 1587 to 1621. In 1610 James Wylie made over to the College his liferent right to the lands in Glasgow and Culross pertaining to the chaplainry of St. Mungo ; and in 1628 and the following year James King, advocate, lay chaplain of St. Mungo, made over to the University the lands and tenements of the chaplainry in the High Street, between the College on the one side and the churchyard of the Friars Preachers on the other ; while in 1630 Sir John Blackadder of Tulliallan, who was patron of the chaplainry, resigned all right to it, from regard to the College where he and his ancestors had been educated for many ages, the College agreeing to erect a conspicuous tablet to commemorate the benefaction.[1]

In 1610 David Wemyss, who was the first minister at Glasgow after the Reformation, and who must now have reached an advanced age, resigned in favour of the principal and masters his right to all the Vicars' yards on the west side of the alley at the back of the High Kirk, after a decree of removal had been pronounced against him ; and William Wemyss, merchant, the occupier, also renounced his claims and agreed to remove, but stipulated for permission to take away his kail plants. In 1615 John Spottiswood, formerly Archbishop of Glasgow and then newly appointed to be Archbishop of St. Andrews, from his zeal for the advancement of letters and the instruction of youth, and his special goodwill to

---

[1] Before the demolition of the old College buildings in High Street, the tablet was to be seen on the eastern wall of the principal's dwelling house.

the University of Glasgow in which he had been educated, made over to the principal, masters, and regents a tenement of land with a garden, situated between the College and the College gardens, which he had purchased from James Fleming and his spouse. This gift of Spottiswood's must have been a very desirable acquisition, as it would have been very inconvenient to have had strangers owning and using plots of ground within the College possessions.

John Howieson, minister of Cambuslang—who in 1582 had been so rudely dealt with by the forces of the Town Council mustered in support of Archbishop Montgomery—mortified in 1613 a thousand marks for the support of a bursar, and some years later bequeathed a considerable number of books to the library. A remarkable and in some sense prolific bursary fund was destined to the University in 1607 by Michael Wilsone of Eastborne, Sussex, who had been a student in 1585, and afterwards became a classical teacher. He mortified a sum of £500 sterling for repairing the decayed part of the buildings and for supporting a bursar of his own kindred or the son of a burgess of Glasgow.

The money was not readily or promptly paid, and in 1621 the principal and regents, in gratitude to Sir William Alexander of Menstrie, afterwards Earl of Stirling, for recovering to the use of the College the money left by Wilsone, obliged themselves to institute a bursary of which Sir William and his heirs should be patrons. Sir William was a royal favourite, and in 1614 was appointed Master of Requests for Scotland, and in 1626 Secretary of State. His influence in such an affair would be great, but still he does not seem to have been equal to the task single-handed ; for we find that the chancellor, rector, and Senate, from gratitude to James Carmichael of Westraw for services in recovering Wilsone's legacy, agreed to found another bursary and to confer the patronage on Carmichael and his heirs. Two other bursaries sprang from the same source, for in 1640 the Provost and Town Council approved of a proposal by the College that, besides the bursaries already created, two further bursars, to be presented by the Provost, should be maintained from the funds which Wilsone had left. Long before this the Town Council had discontinued the bursaries originated under their foundation of 1573. Under the sanction of an act of Parliament, the magistrates in 1594 altered the application of the funds previously destined to the support of poor students, and applied them to the maintenance of the ministry within the city, declaring that the funds for bursaries had been abused, and applied to the support, not of poor students, but of rich men's sons.

Towards the end of his tenure Principal Sharpe had trouble from royal commissioners appointed to visit the College and reform its alleged abuses, the nature of which is not very clear. However, the commissioners reported to the king that ' the cause of all these abuses was in the principal,' and a further meeting of the commissioners was appointed to be held in August, 1614, to proceed against him. Under the advice of his friends, Sharpe saved himself from deposition by resigning.

The next principal was Robert Boyd of Trochrig, in Ayrshire, son of Archbishop Boyd, who, along with Andrew Hay, had been instrumental in bringing Melville to Glasgow. Educated at the University of Edinburgh, young Boyd afterwards betook himself to France, and after teaching for some time in the schools of Tours and Montauban, was in 1606 appointed a professor in the University of Saumur. He had gained a reputation for learning and capacity, and the king invited him to become principal at Glasgow in succession to Sharpe. He was admitted to office early in 1615, with certain reservations and restrictions, some of which were incompatible with the provisions of the *Nova Erectio*, and probably beyond the power of the administrators to sanction. Boyd said he would make trial of the office for a year, but would not undertake all that the principal was bound to by the foundation, which he considered too much for one individual. Owing to infirm health and small strength, he desired to be freed from taking meals at the common table, and from administering corporal punishment to the students. Sharpe, his predecessor, had administered such punishment, but he had been inured to it as master of the Grammar School before he became principal.

In December, 1621, shortly before Boyd's withdrawal from office, the academic administrators and some others agreed to another measure which, however desirable it might be in itself, was still a contravention of the *Nova Erectio*. The chancellor, rector, dean of faculty, Mr. John Bell, Mr. John Blackburn, ' and divers others ' met in the common hall, along with the principal and regents, and declared that, from long experience and the testimony of Principal Boyd, they found no one could efficiently discharge the office of pastor of Govan and of a doctor in the College ; and they ordained that the principal and his successors should be freed from the ministry of the parish of Govan. They further stated that the people of Govan, who paid their tithes to the College, could not be, as was necessary for their edification, ' attended, instructed, catechised, visited, comforted, governed ' by a principal so closely bound to reside and teach in the College. The minister was allowed a stipend of 500 marks or five chalders of meal, with the proceeds of the small teinds of the parish, and the presentation was vested in the College.

It was one of Boyd's accomplishments that he ' spoke and wrote Latine most natively and fluently,' and on one occasion during his incumbency as principal he was called upon to exercise this accomplishment in presence and praise of the king.   James was in Scotland from 13th May to 4th August, 1617, and towards the end of July spent nearly a week in Glasgow and Paisley.   Boyd was one of the chief men who took part in the reception of the king when he entered Glasgow on 22nd July.   Principal Boyd welcomed the king in a Latin oration and laudatory Latin verses, while David Dickson, one of the regents, recited Greek verses in his honour, and Mr. William Hay of Barro, the commissary, gave utterance to loyal and dutiful sentiments in the vernacular.

Principal Boyd, though the son of a tulchan bishop, was averse to the king's policy of forcing prelacy on Scotland.   Before his accession to the English throne the king had made some progress in undoing the act of 1592, by which all previous legislation in favour of the Reformed Church was ratified and Presbyterianism formally sanctioned ; and after succeeding to the English crown he continued the work of building up prelacy in Scotland by instalments.   An act for the restoration of bishops was passed in 1606, Courts of High Commission were established four years later, and in 1618 the General Assembly which met at Perth was coerced into passing the articles of Perth, as they were called.   These required kneeling at the communion, episcopal confirmation for the young, baptism on the Sunday after birth, private communion for the sick, and the observation of holidays.   Spottiswood, who acted as moderator, informed the Assembly that every minister who did not consent to the articles would be banished or deprived of his ministry, and the Assembly was required to vote on the five articles together and not take them singly.   Though the articles were carried, about fifty voted against them, and a number declined to vote. Many ministers did not adopt the innovations desired by the court, and they had better congregations and more of the public sympathy than those who did so.

Mr. John Livingstone, a minister of some note in the next generation, relates how things went in Glasgow.   'While I was in the Colledge of Glasgow in the year 1619 or 1620, being (as I think) the first year that kneeling at the communion was brought in there, I being with some two or three of the young men of the Colledge sett down among the people at the table, and Mr. James Law, the pretended Bishop of Glasgow, coming to celebrate the communion, he urged all the people to fall down and kneel.   Some did so : we sat still.   He came to us, commanding us to kneel or to depart.   Somewhat I spoke to him, but doe not perfectly remember what I said.   It was to this purpose that there was no warrand for kneeling, and for want of it we ought not to be excommunicated from the table of the Lord. He caused some of the people about us to rise, that we might remove, which we did. The next day the principall, Mr. Robert Boyd, called me to him, and said within two or three weeks he would celebrate the communion at Govan, for he was also minister at Govan, and desired me that any whom I knew to be well affected of the young men in the Colledge I would bring them with me to him. Although he was an man of an soure-like disposition and carriage, I always found him soe kind and familiar as made me wonder. Sometimes he would call me and some other three or four, and lay down books before us, and have us sing setts of musick, wherein he took great delight.'

The articles of Perth gave occasion to Boyd's twice losing the office of principal. At the end of 1621 or early in 1622 he quitted his office at Glasgow rather than sign the obnoxious articles. He was almost immediately appointed principal of the University of Edinburgh, but there too he was threatened with the displeasure of the king unless he would sign, and again he resigned. He was afterwards appointed minister of Paisley, but there fresh troubles awaited him, the worst being a quarrel with the widow of the Earl of Abercorn, the lady having turned Catholic. He died in his forty-ninth year, in January, 1627.

John Cameron, Boyd's successor, was one of the most learned men who ever studied or taught within the University, and it is remarkable that his tenure as principal was one of the shortest on record. He was born in Glasgow, and educated at the University of his native town, where he graduated in arts in 1599, at the age of nineteen or twenty. Having shown extraordinary powers as a student and given promise of future eminence, he was in the same year appointed regent in Greek. He had given the usual undertaking to continue six years in his station as regent, but his restless spirit and relish for new scenes and new enterprises, as well as the example of many of his countrymen who achieved distinction abroad as scholars or soldiers of fortune, urged him to a continental career. He repaired to Bordeaux, where he was welcomed by the two protestant ministers, and his ready and varied scholarship, especially his knowledge and skill in Greek, excited surprise and admiration, and procured for the young adventurer the friendship of the learned veteran Casaubon. Cameron was appointed regent in classics in the newly founded College of Bergerac, and soon afterwards professor of philosophy in the University of Sedan. In two years he quitted this professorship, and after visiting Paris, returned to find a fresh welcome at Bordeaux. He was soon appointed to a scholarship for divinity students maintained at the expense of the French Protestant Church, the conditions of which allowed him to study at any protestant college ; and while holding it he became travelling tutor to the sons of the Chancellor of Navarre, with whom he spent one year at Paris, two at Geneva, and nearly a year at Heidelberg.

In April, 1608, be came prominently into notice by maintaining in the University of Heidelberg a series of theses *De Triplici Dei cum Homine Foedere*. In the same year one of the protestant ministers at Bordeaux having died, Cameron was called to fill the vacancy, his colleague being a Scotsman named Primrose. Protestantism was tolerated, but not very freely or fully tolerated, in Bordeaux ; the protestant ministers some-times met with suspicion and annoyance ; and matters reached a crisis in connection with the case of two protestant captains who had been accused of piracy and sentenced to death, and whose appeal to the parlia-ment of Bordeaux against the justice of the sentence was hastily rejected. Cameron, who had attended them in their last moments, published an account of the fortitude and resignation with which the two doomed men had encountered the ignominious death to which they were sentenced. This tract gave great offence to the authorities, and was burned by the hands of the common executioner. Much against the will of his congre-gation, Cameron was transferred in 1618 to the professorship of divinity in Saumur, where Mark Duncan, another kindly Scot, who had gained a considerable reputation as professor of philosophy and practitioner in physic, was a colleague. Two years later Cameron engaged in an intel-lectual tournament, lasting for four days, with Daniel Tilenus, who had adopted Arminian doctrines and challenged Cameron to public contro-versy. Civil disturbances which broke out in France in 1620 led to the dispersion of the students of Saumur, and Cameron betook himself to London, where he gave lectures privately on theology.

Cameron had now achieved a European reputation as a scholar ; he was strangely obsequious in his views regarding the supremacy of kings ; and he was inclined to favour bishops. It was therefore very natural that James should select him for the office of Principal at Glasgow, to do the work which Boyd had declined, and bring the College to conform to the articles of Perth. He was nominated to the office, and came north in such haste that he outstripped his presentation, which had not even been drafted, for in August, 1622, the Archbishop of Glasgow wrote to Boyd, explaining that Cameron had come hurriedly from the king without a presentation, and asking Boyd to send his, or a copy of it, that a presenta-tion in similar terms might be made out for Cameron. In 1622, when the new principal entered upon office, the temper and circumstances of the College were not such as to make it follow readily in the direction in which he wished to lead. Neither teachers nor students would have failed to show constitutional loyalty to a king who kept within the reasonable bounds of limited monarchy. But there was no relish for James's doctrine of the divine right and absolute power of kings, or for the policy by which he continued to thrust on the people forms of church government and religious ceremonies they did not wish.

Cameron was at a disadvantage in coming to Glasgow to support the unpopular measures of the court, for conscientious objections to which his predecessor had been obliged to give up office. Yet his great learning and his affable and winning manner, broken though it sometimes was by impetuous outbursts, were fitted to make some impression, and Robert Baillie was one of those whom he almost persuaded to approve Episcopacy ; but in the main he seems to have enjoyed little favour with the towns-people, the students, or his academic colleagues. Probably he may have taken counsel with Archbishop Law in concerting his measures. At all events they came before the Senate on 6th January, 1623, with twin proposals which would doubtless be gratifying to the feelings of the sovereign. On the motion of the archbishop, the Senate decreed that in future no one should attain to any dignity or exercise any office in the University without taking the oath of supremacy and allegiance ; and on the motion of Cameron, he himself was empowered to draw up a form of prayer for the king, the prince, the royal family, the nobility, the magistrates, the bishops, and the ministers, to be used every morning and evening in meetings of single classes and in general meetings. The prayer, which Cameron was empowered to give out to the young men to be learned by them, had very little of religion in it, and was more concerned with the earthly than the heavenly king. The opening words prayed God to guard and govern the order of the State and the Church, and the closing sentence prayed for minds reverent and heedful of the civil and ecclesiastical order, seriously reflecting that God himself was the author of all order. The king was acknowledged as before all, and only less than God himself upon earth, and the students were to be grateful to heaven that it was their happy lot to be born while this king was reigning.

Cameron seems to have been impatient that the regents and others did not fall into line with his views and sentiments. Mr. John Livingstone in his account of the life of Robert Blair, who in his early days was a regent in the College, tells us that in the course of the work of the College disputations on theses were being carried on, with the principal in the chair. It fell to the lot of Blair to impugn a thesis, and when he pressed his antagonist rather severely, the principal came to the rescue, and in his haste advanced something that savoured of Arminianism. Blair prosecuted his advantage, and the principal was saved from further trouble for that time by the hour striking for the close of the debate.

When the day arrived for continuing the disputation, Cameron wished Blair to resume, and though he would gladly have avoided any further difference with the principal by allowing someone else to appear against the thesis, the principal insisted that he should proceed. Blair then recapitulated the discussion of the previous day, and offered to prosecute his argument against Cameron's last answer, which provoked some warm words from the principal. On this, Mr. Robert Scott, one of the city ministers, and at that time rector of the University, rose and pointed out that Blair had not transgressed the rules of debate. The principal then cried out, 'There is a faction'; and to avoid further disorder the proceedings were stopped. It is said that after this Cameron, having conceived a desire that Blair should be removed from the College, took rather ungenerous means to aid his purpose. With the help of one of Blair's students he searched the regent's dictates, and found in some passages on Aristotle's *Politics* that Blair gave a preference to elective rather than to hereditary monarchy. Cameron communicated this to the king, who made no great account of the matter, but the principal used his influence with the archbishop and others to such purpose that Blair found it prudent to leave the College.

The records contain no mention of Cameron's resignation, or of the circumstances or even the date of his withdrawal. Probably he found little satisfaction in his position at Glasgow and little prospect of improvement, and in a few months he made up his mind to leave. He had begun teaching at Glasgow in November, 1622, and in July, 1623, he was back in France, so that his great learning and ability can scarcely have been exercised for even one full session in the office of principal. Unfortunately no kindly fate awaited him in France, where the king forbade him to hold any office in the churches or universities.

In 1624 the king relented, and Cameron became professor of divinity at Montauban. Here his doctrines of supremacy for kings and passive obedience for subjects were as little relished as in Scotland. They were distasteful to his friends, and he had some enemies also, by one of whom he was stabbed in the street. He died soon afterwards from the effects of the wound, at the age of forty-six. He was not very prone to write, but when he took up the pen he wrote with readiness and power. Editions of his works were published at Saumur and Geneva. The extraordinary extent of Cameron's reading and the strength of his memory led him to be called ' the walking library '; Bishop Hall counted him the most learned author Scotland had produced ; and Milton in the *Tetrachordon* eulogised him as ' a late writer much applauded ; an ingenious writer and in high esteem.'

II. 1625–1660.

AFTER the withdrawal of Cameron, the office of principal remained vacant for fully two years and a half, and Charles I. had been nearly a year on the throne before it was filled by the admission of John Strang, then minister of Errol. He continued to preside over the University for about a quarter of a century, and, like several of his predecessors, his tenure was ended by an enforced resignation. It was an eventful and troubled quarter of a century in the history of the country, witnessing the king's early and drastic interference with the ownership of land ; the attempt to impose Laud's liturgy and the explosion it occasioned ; the national covenant of 1638, followed by the General Assembly at Glasgow which deposed the bishops, put aside the Book of Canons, the new liturgy, and the articles of Perth, and abolished the High Commission Court ; the first and second 'bishops' wars'; the visit of Charles to Scotland in 1641, after he had come into serious conflict with the parliament of England, when he ratified the acts passed against Episcopacy in 1639, and granted most of the other measures demanded by his Scottish subjects ; and the campaign of Montrose in Scotland, and the civil war in England, followed by the execution of the king and the beginning of the Commonwealth. The earlier policy of Charles regarding the tenure of land in Scotland, but still more the legislation of 1641 abolishing Episcopacy, had important effects on the University revenues derived from church lands.

But amid all the turmoil and tumult in the country, the University underwent a greater development than it had ever done in an equal period of time in its previous history. A movement was set on foot for providing it with new buildings by means of public subscriptions, and in a considerable measure it proved successful ; the revenues were greatly improved by a royal gift, confirmed by parliament, of the feu-duties and teinds of the bishopric of Galloway and the abbeys and priory annexed to it ; a professor or regent of Humanity was added to the faculty of Arts, though this chair was for some time rather unstable ; the faculty of divinity, in which the principal had hitherto been the sole teacher, was reinforced by the appointment of two professors of theology ; and, by the institution of a professorship of medicine, a beginning was made with another faculty destined to attain strength and importance in the future.

Strang's father was minister at Irvine, and there he was born about

1584. Early in life he lost his father, and his mother having soon afterwards married Robert Wilkie, minister of Kilmarnock, Strang received the rudiments of his education there, having Zachary Boyd for a schoolfellow. At a very early age he was sent to St. Leonard's College, St. Andrews, and after a distinguished course of study, graduated as Master of Arts at the precocious age of sixteen. For a number of years he acted as a regent in the College, and in the beginning of 1614 settled as minister of Errol. Lord Errol and his family, who were among his parishioners, had fallen under the influence of a Jesuit bearing their own name of Hay, and had become Catholics ; but Strang made some impression on Errol himself, and succeeded in winning back his son and two daughters to the Protestant faith.

An attempt was made—at the instance of the king and the bishops, it is said—to revive degrees in theology, and when in 1616 the University of St. Andrews conferred the degree of Doctor of Divinity on a number of persons, Strang was one of the recipients. During King James's visit to Scotland next year, Strang acquitted himself with special distinction in the course of an academic disputation held at St. Andrews in the royal presence. He was a member of the General Assembly in which the articles of Perth were passed, and gave his vote against them. Yet those who were striving to advance the interests of Episcopacy seem to have hoped that he might be induced to come over and help them. Apparently through the influence of Spottiswood, the Archbishop of St. Andrews, Strang was nominated as a member of the Court of High Commission, but he never attended its meetings or took part in its proceedings. Strang was appointed to be one of the ministers of Edinburgh in 1620, but firmly declined to accept the call, probably because he foresaw troubled times impending, and thought himself safer from pitfalls and entanglements at Errol than at Edinburgh. It is said that even when he received the king's presentation to be principal of Glasgow University, he was still reluctant to leave the quiet life which he enjoyed at Errol ; and that it was only after a second letter from Court and repeated solicitations from the University and city of Glasgow that he entered upon the office whose tenure had come to a violent end in the case of his three predecessors.

In Strang's time finance was one of the cardinal interests in academic administration. The University was continually striving for ampler means, and obliged carefully to guard the endowments it already possessed. These endowments were mostly derived from grants of the old lands and revenues of the Church and from teinds, and a new and revolutionary settlement regarding this kind of property was made early in the reign of Charles I. After the overthrow of the Catholic religion the reformers wisely but vainly claimed the lands and tithes of the Roman clergy for the maintenance of the ministers, the education of the young, and the support of the poor. In 1562 it was arranged that the surviving Catholic incumbents should be allowed two-thirds of their benefices for life, the other third being parted between the Protestant ministers and the Crown. Under this arrangement ministers got only poor stipends, but matters were somewhat improved when parliament, under the guidance of the Regent Moray, authorised the Church to appoint its own collectors of thirds, making the claim preferential, and declaring that this should continue only till the Church should obtain the teinds—its proper patrimony.

The Regent Morton persuaded the General Assembly to make him collector of thirds, but the ministers did not benefit by the change, and many parishes were left without pastors. As time went on the recovery of church property by the Reformed Church became hopeless. In 1587 James annexed to the crown the lands of all ecclesiastical benefices not already gifted to laymen, but excepting the tithes. This act of annexation was afterwards rescinded in 1606, as it hindered the king's favourite pursuit of restoring Episcopacy, but by that time little was left. Lay commendators had been generally appointed to the abbeys as the Catholic abbots died out. They frequently procured from the king heritable rights to the property ; and by and by the king abandoned the form of appointing commendators, and distributed large grants of church property to nobles and favourites. A number of bishoprics were also assigned to laymen, and they drew the revenues and employed on as thrifty terms as practicable tulchan bishops to perform the clerical functions. The meagre stipends of ministers were paid from the thirds, varying from time to time with the decisions of the modificators, but in 1617 a parliamentary commission ordained that these stipends should be paid, not from a general fund but from the tithes of the parish where each officiated.

Charles I., at the outset of his reign, revoked not only the grants of church lands made by his father, but all the grants of church and crown lands made since the death of James V., when the infant Queen Mary succeeded to the crown. This rash and violent measure affected nearly all the landowners and a very large portion of the lands of the whole country, alienated the nobility from the king, brought them into league with the ministers and the commons against the crown in the national troubles which ensued, and had a powerful influence in bringing about the downfall of Charles. In 1627 the king in pursuance of his design appointed a Commission for Surrenders of Superiorities and Teinds, which was empowered to treat with the Lords of Erection, as the recipients of royal grants of church lands were called, and to settle a composition by which these lands might be transferred to the crown.

The Commission did not, however, settle the terms of surrender, but declared that the Superiorities of Erection should be resigned into the king's hand, and that the owners should accept the composition which he might be pleased to offer. After this the landowners, the clergy, the burghs interested, and the tacksmen and holders of teinds submitted their cases to Charles, who in 1629 issued four sets of ' decreits arbitral ' addressed to the four parties whose interests were involved. For the church lands the crown agreed to pay 1000 marks Scots for each chalder of victual and for each 100 marks of money feu-duty ; and it was laid down that the teinds (generally reckoned as one-fifth of the rental) might be bought by the heritors at nine years' purchase. Commissioners assigned such stipends as they thought fit out of the teinds to the ministers, who henceforth enjoyed better and more secure emoluments. In 1633 parliament sanctioned the arrangements, and sub-commissioners were set to work over the country to value the teinds, but for a long time the heritors were slow to purchase.

These proceedings, though they ended in a kind of settlement, gave rise to much unsettlement in reference to former church property during their course, and no doubt the University authorities watched them with interest blended with anxiety. Towards the end of 1629 the king had pronounced the decrees forming the basis of legislation, and probably it was with a view to remove doubt as to the position of the University in regard to its revenues from former church property that, in June, 1630, there was procured from him a general charter of confirmation under the great seal, confirming all the foundations, rights, and securities previously conferred on the University, especially the rights and revenues of the Friars Preachers, of the Vicars of the Choir of Glasgow, and of various chaplainries and altarages ; the right of patronage of the churches of Govan, Renfrew, Kilbride, Colmonell, and Dalziel, with their teinds ; the Tron and certain other customs leviable within the city of Glasgow ; the privileges, jurisdiction, immunities, and exemption from taxation granted by former sovereigns and by the bishops and archbishops of Glasgow and others. By the same charter he allocated to the principal £1000 Scots yearly (confirming his right to a house, garden, and servant), 400 marks to the first regent, 300 marks to the second, 200 marks to the third, and 100 marks to the fourth, besides the daily victuals and sustentation of the principal and regents within the College according to use and wont ; and also settled that the University should pay twelve chalders yearly to the minister of Renfrew, twelve chalders to the minister of the united parish of Kilbride and Torrance, 500 marks or five chalders to the minister of Govan, and to the minister of Dalziel a stipend out of the teinds of his parish, modified or to be modified according to the laws of the realm.

It seems the University authorities were not without some misgiving respecting the settlement, for, when the king's signature for this charter was presented to the Lords of Exchequer, the rector, the dean of faculty, and the principal appeared and bound themselves to ratify the king's decree, provided it did not prejudice their revenues. However, the charter was, with some reservations, ratified by parliament in 1633, the same year in which the general scheme respecting church lands, teinds, and ministers' stipends received parliamentary sanction.

A number of measures were taken to guard the interests of the College. About 1632 a decree was obtained securing right to the salmon taken from the ' crove ' in the Kelvin, which were held to belong to the vicarage teind of Govan. In 1633 a judgment of the Court of Session sustained the freedom of the masters of the University from taxation, and next year Zachary Boyd, then dean of faculty, took out a suspension against the provost and bailies, who had imposed on him a share of a parliamentary tax. The Lords of the Council in 1634 granted a warrant for general letters against heritors, feuars, and others for the whole revenues of the College ; in 1636 the Commissioners for Surrenders and Teinds ratified an arrangement come to by Lord Belhaven and the College respecting the teinds of Gorbals and Bridgend ; and the same year the Lords of Exchequer gave a decree against the reluctant burgh of Rutherglen for payment of £11 yearly to the College as succeeding to the rights of the Vicars of the Choir of Glasgow.

An agreement was made in 1637 with the minister of Govan as to his stipend and emoluments, which were fixed on a more liberal scale than that laid down in the king's charter, and for some time to come the records are thickly strewn with rentals and valuations of benefices. Limitations in favour of the University were inserted in a number of grants made to the Magistrates and Council about this time. In 1633 parliament ratified all grants by Charles I. or his predecessors to the magistrates and community of Glasgow, in recognition of the great charges and expenses sustained in rendering the Clyde navigable, to the great advantage of adjacent shires for imports and exports ; as well as of outlays for upholding the Cathedral, and for building the Tolbooth and several bridges ; but reserved the rights and privileges of the College, the right of the archbishop to nominate magistrates, and the right of the Duke of Lennox to baliery and justiciary. Again, in 1636 the provost and Council gave a bond that a royal charter then obtained should not prejudice the College or the archbishop.

In 1634 Charles wrote to the Archbishop of Glasgow, recalling the fact that former kings had endowed the College with the tithes of four churches, and stating that he was informed certain persons were to take advantage of some small defect in the College rights.   The king gave instructions that, in the event of anyone purchasing from the crown a presentation to any church or benefice belonging to the College, the archbishop should not give collation till the presentee had granted security not to disturb the possession or right of the College.   The question naturally occurs whether the king might not have secured the object directly and efficaciously by taking the security before granting the presentation.

Next year the king sent a letter to the Lord Advocate, informing him that the rights of the College to the teinds of Govan, Kilbride, and Renfrew were to be questioned, and commanding him to plead in defence of these rights before any judge or judicatory in the realm.   In 1634 the king, who had been in Scotland in the preceding year, wrote to the archbishop: ' We have upon occasion of our late being in Scotland observed some things we think fit to put in better order.'   And then he instructed the archbishop that members of the College in their gowns should in a body attend the morning and evening services in the Cathedral on Sundays and church holidays, and should also wear their academic habits in the University and in the streets.   The archbishop was required to give an account by letter that this practice had begun, and afterwards at least once a year regarding its continuance.   Such matters as these, one would think, need hardly have called for the high intervention of royalty.

Emboldened by the better provision made in 1633 for the ministers of the church, the administrators of the College two or three years afterwards petitioned the king for aid, and perhaps there is a trace of exaggeration in their statements.   They represented that, in consequence of the smallness of their revenues, decay of learning was likely to ensue ; and that those who attained to any charge in the College usually abandoned it before they had sufficient time to improve their own knowledge or to benefit others ; or if they remained they were reduced to necessities that bred contempt of their condition of life, and discouraged them from following their charge and studies.

In April, 1636, Charles replied to the petition in a letter, which Principal Strang on 22nd June following presented to the Commissioners for Surrenders and Teinds.   In this letter the king declared that, as he had formerly been careful to endow the Church with competent means, so he was willing that some expedient should be found whereby the seminaries from which religion and learning flowed should be ' provydit with necessarie pleasour ' ; and he instructed the Commissioners to take into their serious consideration the state of the revenue of the College, and, so far as they could, to prescribe some way in which it might be helped. The Commissioners requested Strang to report on the revenues and condition of the College, and the number of masters, students, officers, and servants requiring to be entertained within it, and, with the help and advice of the remaining masters, to suggest such expedients as might be devised for increasing the income. In October, 1636, the king commissioned Spottiswood, the Archbishop of St. Andrews, his son, Sir Robert Spottiswood, president of the Court of Session, the Archbishop of Glasgow, the Earl of Traquair, Lord Treasurer, the Earl of Haddington, Lord Privy Seal, the Earl of Stirling, ' our secreter,' the Earls of Wintoun, Roxburgh, Lauderdale, and Southesk, the bishops of Edinburgh, Ross, Galloway, Aberdeen, Brechin, and Dunblane, and other members of the Privy Council to enquire into the revenues of the Universities of Scotland and the causes that had impaired them, and to take such measures as they deemed fit for bettering their estates and reforming their abuses. By way of encouragement Charles added: ' For your better doing quheroff we will, upon your advertisement, be assisting in anything quherin yow sall give us your advyse which lawfullie and convenientlie can be done by us ; so we doe expect from yow ane exact report off your proceedings heerin as off a service quherof we will tak speciall notice, and quheroff the good succes will be verie acceptable to us.'

Early in 1637 the Lords of the Council requested the rector, principal, and regents of Glasgow University to send commissioners to inform them regarding the revenues, the founded persons within the College, the foundations new and old, the order of teaching, and the visitations made from time to time ; and also to give advice regarding the best way of helping the patrimony of the College and removing any abuses. The principal was appointed to appear before the Council and give the desired information.

A statement prepared in 1637 of the revenue and expenditure has been preserved. The total yearly revenue is set down at £4416 3s. 11d. Scots, £2443 being from rental in victual (chalders, bolls, etc.), and £1973 3s. 11d. from rental in money. The ordinary expenditure is stated as £4848 16s. 8d. in money and two chalders in victual. The expenditure and certain necessary deductions from revenue together make £5103 11s. 9d., and when this is balanced against the revenue, it leaves a deficit of £687 7s. 10d. Scots. The yearly expenditure includes the stipend of the principal, £1000 ; of the four regents, 1000 marks ; the minister of Govan, two chalders victual and 600 marks ; the reader of

Govan, 20 marks ; the choir of Govan, £4 ; the poor beyond the bridge and in St. Nicholas Hospital, £7 10s.; agents, advocates, etc., in Edinburgh, 50 marks ; messengers-at-arms, £20 ; clerks, writers, and procurators in Glasgow, £24 ; sheriff-officers, town-officers, etc., £8 ; stipend of collector, 200 marks ; travelling expenses on College business, £120 ; the provisor, 100 marks ; the cook and his servants, £10 ; the porter, 40 marks ; board of the principal and four regents, £800 ; board of 14 bursars, principal's servant, porter, provisor, and cook, 1800 marks ; supplying napery, etc., £40 ; washing napery, £12 ; extras at College table at time of promotions, electing rector, etc., £60 ; cleaning, £10 ; coals and peats, £80 ; maintaining buildings, £100.

The College authorities urged the decay of the buildings, parts of which near the inner close were dilapidated, the liability to legal expenses, and the probability of the College incurring great charges in trying the state of the benefices and leading witnesses ; and pointed out that, while the king's foundation provided for the board of twelve founded persons, there were now many more to be maintained. They recommended that the stipends of the existing masters should be increased, and that more professors of Divinity and other liberal sciences should be established ; but could make no suggestion regarding the best way to augment the revenue, leaving that to the bounty and liberality of His Majesty, to whom the Lords of the Council could best give advice.

Help for the University revenues was at hand, but it did not come from the Commissioners for Surrenders and Teinds or from the Privy Council, nor could the form in which it came be very grateful to the archbishops and bishops, who made so large a part of the body whom the king in the second place invited to deal with the question of academic finance. The same year in which the administrators of the University submitted their statement to the Privy Council public affairs in Scotland were brought to a crisis by an attempt to impose on the Church the service book known as ' Laud's liturgy.'

The ministers and the people had long been alienated by the royal policy regarding the Church ; and the hasty and violent interference of Charles with the tenure of Scottish land, as well as the ostentatious favour and the high civil offices which he bestowed on the bishops, roused the dislike and opposition of the nobility and landowners, and produced a coalition between them and the ministers and people which proved more than a match for the power of the crown. 1638 was the year of the National Covenant and the memorable General Assembly held at Glasgow, which deposed the bishops and overthrew the ecclesiastical system that had been slowly and painfully reared by Charles and his father. Next year witnessed the first ' Bishops' War,' in which a Scottish army of 20,000 men under Leslie marched to Dunse Law, near the border, while the army of Charles, nearly equal in number, but inferior in discipline, equipment, and earnestness of purpose, encamped two or three miles south of Berwick. The king, having little reason to expect success from warfare, entered into negotiations, and by the Pacification of Berwick agreed to call a General Assembly and Parliament to settle the national affairs.

The Assembly and the Parliament met, and in the main they re-enacted what the Glasgow Assembly had done, but the king delayed to ratify their measures, and in the second ' Bishops' War ' a Scottish army in 1640 crossed the border and took possession of Newcastle. Charles mustered a second army, but again he was unequal to the task of doing battle with the Scots, and again the leaders resorted to negotiations, which this time were much more protracted. The king had wearied out the patience of his English subjects, and though they had not yet resorted to arms, many of them welcomed the invasion of the Scots as likely to aid in bringing their sovereign to reason. The Long Parliament, which met in November, 1640, quickly swept away the Star Chamber, the Court of High Commission, and the Council of the North, and sent Laud to prison and Strafford to the block.

It may be doubted whether Charles trusted his Scottish subjects more than others, or whether it was merely that he saw, or fancied he saw, an opportunity for producing a cleavage among his opponents, and getting his own way when he had set them to quarrel among themselves ; but in this crisis, as at another dark hour in his fortunes five years later, he turned to the Scots. Repairing to Edinburgh, he attended the Presbyterian worship, scattered titles among the leaders of the Covenanters, and conceded the demands of the General Assembly and the Scottish Parliament. These included the abolition of Episcopacy, and from the revenues of the bishoprics further endowments were bestowed on the Scottish Universities. St. Andrews obtained £1000 a year from its own bishopric and priory ; Aberdeen, the bishopric of Aberdeen ; Edinburgh, the bishopric of Edinburgh and Orkney ; and Glasgow, endowments from the bishopric of Galloway and two abbeys and a priory within the same territory.

Charles arrived in Edinburgh on 14th August, 1641, and the University and College of Glasgow having presented to him a supplication for the helping of their poor estate, on 11th September he remitted to the Marquis of Hamilton, the Earls of Argyle, Eglinton, Glencairn, Wigton, and Lanark, Lord Loudon, Sir James Carmichael, treasurer depute, and Sir John Hamilton, justice clerk, to consider ' how the University and

Colledge, professors and members thereof,' might 'be helped and sup-
plyed,' and to report their advice to His Majesty.

The Commissioners reported that the University revenues amounted
to £470 11s. 10d. sterling annually, and the expenditure to £737 1s. 1d.,
leaving a deficit of £266 9s. 3d. ; and they recommended that the University should also be provided with a further sum of £214 13s. 4d. for
the maintenance of a professor of theology, a professor of oriental languages, and six bursars in theology.

The result was that on 11th November the king granted to the University and College the whole feu duties of all lands and baronies pertaining
to the late bishopric of Galloway, the abbeys of Tongland and Glenluce,
and the priory of Whithorn, with all their teinds, both parsonage and
vicarage. At that time the free rental of the bishopric was valued at
£348 8s. 4d. sterling. On the 17th of November—the last day on which
the Parliament of 1641 sat, and the day on which Charles gave a banquet
in Holyrood to the prominent men of the time before his setting out for
England—the Scottish Parliament ratified the king's grant, and suppressed
and extinguished ' the name and memorie of the said bischoprik of Galloway, abbacies and priorie respectivelie foirsaid in all tyme cumming, to
the effect the foirsaidis few maillis, few fermes, teyndis, teynd deuties, and
utheris foirsaidis that belongit to the said bischoprik, priorie, and abbacies
respectivelie foirsaid, and uthers annext thairto, may remain with the
principall, professouris, regentis, and uther memberis of the said Universitie and Colledge of Glasgow as ane testimonie of His Majestie's
favour perpetuallie in all tyme cumming.' The deanery of the chapel
royal of Stirling, with its fruits and rents, was excepted from the gift, and
the king and Parliament made grants in favour of the minister and schoolmaster of Glenluce, and conferred some further means on the magistrates
of Glasgow, partly for the support of a minister for the Cathedral.

What was reserved and what was given to others seem to have excited
misgivings, and a strange scene was witnessed on the day when Parliament
ratified the king's mortification to the University. Principal Strang
appeared before the King's Majesty and the estates of Parliament, and
entered three separate protests for himself and the University that the
revenues of the latter should not be prejudiced by the king's grant to the
city magistrates of the parsonage and vicarage teinds of Glasgow and of
the other kirks of the archbishopric, for maintaining a minister of the
High Kirk in place of the archbishop, and for other uses ; by the parliamentary ratification of the king's charter of general confirmation, of 1636,
in favour of the magistrates ; or by the parliamentary ratification of the
king's grant of the precinct and ruins of the abbey of Glenluce for a manse

and glebe to the minister, with a stipend of a thousand marks out of the bishop's rents, and two hundred marks yearly out of the bishopric of Galloway as a salary to the schoolmaster of the parish of Glenluce.

Before these further endowments had been obtained in 1641, the University had fully doubled the number of the teaching staff contemplated by the *Nova Erectio*. The addition of a fourth regent about 1581 or 1582 has already been mentioned. The *Nova Erectio* provided for a regent to teach the institutes of Greek and to drill and exercise students in both languages. Students were expected to come to College with a good knowledge of the elements of Latin, and when they had obtained a similar knowledge of Greek, they were to be drilled so as to be equally expert in both languages. In 1618, when James Roberton was admitted as a master, he was styled ' *Philosophiae et Rerum Humaniarum Professor.*' It is probable that as time went on it was found desirable that at least some of the students should be taught the institutes of Latin as well as of Greek within the College.

In the record of a meeting held on 25th October, 1637, David Monro is mentioned as one of the regents who attended, and in a later sentence he is described as master of the humanity class. The meeting that day signalised itself by appointing Mr. Robert Mayne, one of the regents, to be professor of medicine in the College for the future, with a stipend of 400 marks. Patrick Maxwell, another regent, was appointed to the place left vacant by the promotion of Mayne, while David Monro was promoted to Maxwell's former place, and William Hamilton, student of theology, was elected master of the humanity class. From this time a separate teacher of humanity, who is sometimes called a regent but more frequently a professor, may be reckoned part of the normal teaching staff, though in the period subsequent to the Restoration pressure on the academic funds caused this chair to be left vacant for a long time. Doubtless more money and more teachers were required to enable the University to develop satisfactorily, but the establishment of a fourth regent, a professor of humanity, a professor of medicine, and a professor of divinity before the additional endowments were obtained in 1641, makes it seem probable that the academic administrators were not really so hard pressed for funds as they sometimes represented.

At the time we have now reached the country rang from side to side with the discussion of religious and theological questions, and questions of ecclesiastical polity and the relations of Church and State. The ministers had for a long time combined with their preaching the functions of discussion and criticism now discharged by the press, and, whether their turn of mind was thoughtful or vehement, they exercised a great influence

in their particular districts.   But as yet there was only a slender equipment
for the training of young men for the ministry after they had gone through
their course in arts.   At Glasgow the principal was the only teacher in the
faculty of theology, yet Glasgow could claim among its sons so great a
theologian as Cameron, and had sent forth such learned and accomplished
men as Dickson and Baillie, who were about to become its earliest professors of divinity and the instructors of men like Durham and Binning.
Nothing could be more natural or appropriate than that the Church, now
that it was freed from the royal coercion under which it had so long
suffered, should endeavour to improve the training of its ministers by
strengthening the staff of their teachers.

The University applied to the General Assembly in 1639 for aid in
establishing and maintaining chairs of theology, and the Assembly recommended the proposal to next session of Parliament, and appointed Commissioners of Visitation to concur with the academic administrators in
inviting any who should be found fit, and for whom maintenance could be
provided, to act as professors of divinity, and also to arrange for their
transference.   The Commission, which included the Earls of Argyle and
Eglinton, the Provosts of Glasgow, Stirling, and Ayr, and a number of
ministers, among whom were David Dickson and Robert Baillie, met at
Glasgow towards the end of January, 1640, and agreed that David Dickson
should be transferred from his ministry at Irvine and appointed professor
of divinity in the University, with a stipend of £800 Scots per annum.
At a meeting of the College managers about a month afterwards Dickson
promised to remove to the College before the middle of March, ' and to
undergo the office and charge of ane professor and Doctor of Theologie
within the said Colledge, and to teache weiklie publick lectours of Theologie in Latine within the samyne, and to attend diligentlie upone the
students thairof for thair instructione.'   For his residence the managers
assigned to him ' that hous heiche and laiche, lyand at the north end of the
said Colledge, presentlie possesst be Mr. Robert Mayine, Professor of
Physick.'

David Dickson was the son of a merchant in Glasgow, and was born
there about 1583.   Educated at the University of his native city, he
graduated as M.A. in 1609, and is said to have applied himself for a short
time to his father's business, in which he was the reverse of successful.
However, in 1610 he became a regent in the University, a position which
gave him an opportunity of extending his own knowledge, and obtaining
practice and skill in the arts of interpretation, exposition, and persuasion.
After being a regent for eight years, he was called to be minister of Irvine,
where he soon made a great impression as a preacher, and secured the warm

goodwill of his parishioners. For publicly denouncing the articles of Perth, he incurred the wrath of Archbishops Law and Spottiswood, and the Court of High Commission banished him to Turriff in Aberdeenshire, but in about eighteen months he was suffered to return to his ministry at Irvine. In 1637 he induced the Presbytery of Irvine to petition the Privy Council against the introduction of Laud's liturgy. The same year he received Robert Blair and John Livingstone, both graduates of Glasgow, and the former sometime a colleague with Dickson in the regency, the two having been driven by the Irish prelates from their positions as ministers in the north of Ireland. Dickson employed them occasionally to preach for him, and for this he was again called before the High Commission, but the power of the bishops was now on the decline in Scotland, and he soon got rid of this trouble.

At the time when the National Covenant had been warmly adopted in all the important centres of the country except Aberdeen, Dickson was sent, along with Henderson, Cant, and the young Earl of Montrose, to reason with the Aberdonians and win them over to the views embraced by the great body of their fellow-countrymen ; and he held discussions with ' the Aberdeen doctors,' Forbes, Baron, Sibbald, and others, while Montrose, in more than one visit, traversed the country, and procured many signatures to the Covenant, allowing those who signed to add qualifications or limitations if they wished, even Huntly himself signing a modified version. Dickson and Baillie were sent from the Presbytery of Irvine to the memorable General Assembly at Glasgow in 1638, and both were prominent members, Dickson making a seasonable and prudent speech when Hamilton, the Lord High Commissioner representing the king, threatened to leave the Assembly, and another notable one in refutation of Arminianism. He was moderator of the General Assembly of 1639, and the same year he was chaplain of a regiment raised in Ayrshire, of which the Earl of Loudon was colonel, which marched to the border under Leslie in the first ' Bishops' War.'

Dickson was not meant to abide alone as professor of divinity, and in 1642 Robert Baillie was appointed second professor in that faculty. Often taking a prominent part in public affairs, and constantly in communication with those who did so, and being besides an observant man and loquacious with his pen, Baillie has bequeathed to us in his letters and journals much valuable and some curious information regarding the events and the *dramatis personae* of his time. He was about sixteen years younger than Dickson, but in the early life of the two men there was a strong resemblance. Both were natives of Glasgow and graduates of its University, in which they both acted for some time as regents, and afterwards became

ministers in Ayrshire.   Both opposed the introduction of Laud's liturgy,
and were members of the famous General Assembly at Glasgow in 1638,
and both acted as chaplains to the troops raised to oppose the king in the
' Bishops' War.'

Baillie graduated as M.A. in 1620, and continued some time longer at
the University, coming under the influence of Cameron, by whose views
he was considerably impressed.   It was in 1626 that he began his short
tenure of office as a regent.   He attained to excellence as a linguist, wrote
Latin well, and was specially skilled in oriental languages.   The thirteen
languages which he acquired included Hebrew, Chaldee, Syriac, Arabic,
and Ethiopic.   He received episcopal ordination, and was presented to the
parish church of Kilwinning by the Earl of Eglinton, to whose son he had
been tutor ; but the changes forced upon the Scottish Church led him to
reconsider his views, and when the cleavage arose over the introduction of
Laud's liturgy, Baillie allied himself with the Covenanters.   He was chaplain to the Earl of Eglinton's regiment at Dunse Law, and has left a
graphic picture of the scene there—the soldiers' growth in courage,
experience of arms, and belief in Leslie's skill, prudence, and fortune ; the
readiness with which all, even the emulous nobles, submitted to the guidance of ' that old, little, crooked soldier ' ; the good sermons and prayers
morning and evening, to which the soldiers were called by roll of drum,
instead of bells ; and the sound from the tents of some singing psalms,
some praying, and some reading the Scripture.   ' True, there was swearing
and cursing and brawling in some quarters, whereat we were grieved ; but
we hoped, if our camp had been a little settled, to have gotten some way
for these misorders ; for all of any fashion did regret, and all promised to
do their best endeavours for helping all abuses.'

Baillie had made a study of the Service Book and Canons, and in
March, 1640, on the solicitation of Johnston of Warriston,[1] he produced
a treatise against the encroaching designs of prelacy, bearing the title of
The Canterburian's Self Conviction.   Towards the end of the year he was
invited by Rothes, Montrose, Argyle, and others, to attend the committee
at Newcastle, where the Scots army then was, and to bring with him copies
of the treatise, with the warrants and proofs for it.   He reached the camp
on 6th November, and was nominated one of the commissioners to proceed
to London to negotiate with the king, among the others being the ministers
Henderson and Blair, and the Earls of Rothes, Loudon, and Dunfermline.
On their arrival in London, Baillie drafted The Charge of the Scottish
Commissioners against Laud, archbishop of Canterbury, and Henderson

[1] It is probable that Johnston was himself an alumnus of Glasgow, and that he is to be
identified with the 'Archibaldus Jhonstonus' whose name occurs in a list of students
belonging to the higher classes enrolled in 1630.

put the finishing touches to it. Other tracts from Baillie followed—*A Parallel of the Liturgy and the Mass Book* ; *Antidote to Arminianism* ; and *A Large Supplement to the Canterburian's Self Conviction*. He seems to have had nearly simultaneous offers of a professorship from all the four Scottish Universities, and in the summer of 1642, not without some reluctance to give up his ministry at Kilwinning, he agreed to accept the invitation to Glasgow.

The University thus secured as professors of divinity two men of learning and ability who had previously gained some experience in academic teaching, and who were prominent in the counsels and controversies of the Church.

A Commission of Visitation from the General Assembly met at Glasgow in September, 1642 ; found that the profession of divinity lately established was most necessary ; and ordained that Baillie should have £800 Scots of stipend, with a convenient residence or 100 marks additional to provide one ; and that he should have an equal right with the principal and Dickson to an augmentation of stipend if funds were available. In distributing the subjects to be taught in the faculty of theology, the Commission directed that the principal should explain the hard places of Scripture, go through the commonplaces of theology, and preside at disputations ; that Dickson should go through the text of Scripture, handle 'casuall divinity,' as he could overtake it, and regulate the students in their composition of homilies ; and that Baillie should teach the controversies, oriental languages, and chronology. The course was to be completed in four years under the regulation of the faculty.

The principal desired that he might be relieved of the great weight of the affairs of the College—doubtless the collection of subscriptions and superintendence of the work of renovating and enlarging the buildings— by which he was greatly hindered in his teaching, but the visitors, while appointing a committee to consider this and other matters, desired the principal in the meantime to continue his teaching work as well as his other engagements would permit, and entreated him to bear his present burden till he could be relieved without prejudice to the interests of the College. Dickson continued as professor of divinity at Glasgow till 1650, when he was transferred to the corresponding chair at Edinburgh, and in January, 1651, Baillie was promoted to fill the vacancy, and held the first chair of divinity, as it was called, till 1661, when he became principal. Between them Dickson and Baillie trained a very large number of those who became ministers in the south and west of Scotland.

During the first sixty years of the seventeenth century the number of students and graduates continued in a course of nearly constant but not rapid increase. For the first half of the period the record of students enrolled for each year is contained in one list, but afterwards it is broken up into several. Sometimes there is a list for each class from the first to the fifth, sometimes one list for the three higher classes, and one each for the fourth and fifth, sometimes only a list for the fourth class, and sometimes there is no record at all for a year or two. In a few cases a list of students of theology is inserted along with the others, but this is exceptional. 26 students are given for the year 1651, 86 for 1653, 27 for 1654, 125 for 1657, and 8 for 1658. On the other hand, the graduation lists show that there were 28 graduations in arts in 1654, and 25 in 1658. It is not credible that if there were 125 students in 1657, there could have been only 8 next year ; still less is it credible that if there were only 27 students in 1654, 28 could have received degrees that year, or that with only 8 students in 1658, 25 could have obtained degrees. For the years in which it exists, the list of graduations is probably a full one, but the list of students enrolled can be only partial, and the actual number of students must have been greater than the number whose enrolment has been recorded.

The University having invoked the aid of the General Assembly in 1639, received a good deal of attention from that venerable body for some time afterwards, and a number of Commissions of Visitation were appointed, some of which did not meet at all, while others, though they held one or more sittings, failed to complete the business with which they were expected to deal. Such men as the Earl of Loudon, the Lord Chancellor, the Marquis of Argyle, and Johnston of Warriston, were too busy to give much of their time to the organisation and settlement of academic affairs, and probably the others named along with them, though they might have been competent to carry out the work, did not care to act in the absence of those who might be regarded as their chiefs.

The Commissioners were hampered in another respect, for it was not clear that the Assembly had full power to deal with the affairs of the University. When the Visitation met at Glasgow in 1640, the governors and masters of the University, while acknowledging the care of the General Assembly in appointing this ecclesiastical Visitation, feared that some clauses in the act of Assembly might be interpreted so as to prejudice some of the civil privileges and other rights of the University, and humbly entreated the Commissioners to condescend in such a way as might secure the University and its members from such inconveniences. The Commissioners declared that they were to proceed only in ecclesiastical things and in an ecclesiastical manner, that in any civil matters they would proceed only with the advice and consent of the governors and masters, and that a representation would be made to the next General Assembly to secure such an entry in their books as would safeguard the University.

The Visitation of 1640 laid down that the masters should read some portion of Scripture in their several classes, morning and evening, and should take means to ascertain ' what conscience each scholler makes of secret devotion, morning and evening.' They also sanctioned a scheme proposed by the masters which distributed the portions of the teaching work in arts to be done in the several sessions of the curriculum ; and appointed that the master of the humanity class should go through a compendium of history and what further should be prescribed to him by the faculty. It was ordained that students should convene by 1st October, and that the masters, having examined and ' promoved' their students, should begin to teach by the 24th of that month ; and that not only the four lower classes, but also the magistrand class should remain in College till the date of the graduation. It was also laid down that the National Covenant, according to the explanation of the Assembly of 1639 and the warrant of the Privy Council to that effect, should be subscribed by all the students of the University, except such as were not native Scots or whose parents and estates were outside the kingdom, and registers containing the students' signatures were to be kept. Masters and regents were also to sign at the time of their entry to office. The provost and bailies of Glasgow and Patrick Bell were requested to ascertain the contributions and expenditure for the fabric of the College, and also the sums promised and still unpaid, in order that means might be taken to collect them.

The Visitation of 1642 from the General Assembly directed the dean of faculty to see ' that the regents be short in their nots,' that students be examined on the former lesson before the next be taught, and that every student have Aristotle's text in Greek. It was enjoined that disputations should continue among the students in their classes and in the public schools, and that means should be taken to stir up emulation between the classes by theses, themes, disputations, declamations, and otherwise. The regent of the magistrand class was to continue to teach till 1st June, and no student of his class was to leave the College before the graduation day, except by special leave of his master, and subject to a fine of eight shillings for each day he was absent in excess of the time allowed—the fines to be used to procure books for the library. Students who did not enter by 1st October were to be subject to a fine of two shillings for each day's absence in the first week, four shillings for each day's absence in the second, six shillings for each day's absence in the third, and so on for the rest—the fines in this case also going to the benefit of the library.

Every student in the College was required to have a Bible and to wear a gown, and in all places students must speak Latin among themselves. Further, students were freed from going to church on week days, except when their professors preached, and were to be exercised in lawful games, such as ' gouffe, archarie, and the lyk,' but were to abstain from ' carding, dicing,' and other forbidden games.

The Visitors declared that the profession of medicine was ' not necessar for the Colledge in all tyme comming,' but allowed Mayne, the existing professor, to hold the chair during his life.   Having regard to the custom that had hitherto prevailed, under which every regent had continued for years in the same profession, and the students had to change their masters yearly, the Visitors thought it profitable and expedient that this should be altered, and that every master should take his own students through all the four classes.   Upon this, the regents gave in an overture claiming that, as every regent was to take his students through all the classes, their stipends should be brought nearer to an equality, and stating that they had agreed among themselves that the augmentations already designed to them by His Majesty's favour should be disposed of by assigning fifty marks each to the first and second regents, a hundred marks to the third, two hundred to the fourth, and one hundred to the master of humanity. The 1640 Visitation had ordained that there should be a meeting of the faculty on the first Tuesday of every quarter, and that a record of their transactions should be kept ; but the 1642 Visitation found ' it necessar for the good of the Universitie that the facultie conveine the first Tuysday of everie month, and lykwyse at what other tymes they find convenient.' They also recommended that the principal and masters should make an effort to collect the sums of money owing to the College building fund, and especially that the Lords of the Treasury should be petitioned for what was promised by the king.

Some years after this, delegates from the various Scottish Universities held meetings and arranged a detailed order and plan of studies in the several classes of the faculty of arts, as well as a scheme of disputations and public examinations.   On 10th November, 1648, the dean reported to a meeting of the regents at Glasgow what had been done by the delegates till the beginning of September, and all their acts were approved and ordered to be recorded in the academic register.   A portion of the course in philosophy had been left to be adjusted by Glasgow College, and John Young was appointed to draft this.   He seems to have done the work promptly, for on 27th December, 1648, the whole scheme was read over in the hearing of the regents at Glasgow and approved by them.

In the fifth or Latin class the teacher was to begin by reading selections of verse and prose suited to the capacity of his students, and daily to give out portions of grammar to be repeated next day. At least on alternate days the students were to be exercised in versions from English into Latin and Latin into English, and those who had the ability might express themselves in verse. In the last months of the session members of the class were to be taught some of the works of Joannes Sleidanus. On the Saturdays they were in the morning to be examined on the prelections of the week, in the forenoon to carry on disputations, and in the evening to have readings from Buchanan's version of the Psalms, to be repeated from memory on Monday. On Sunday they were to read the Catechism, and in the evening give an account of their reading, as well as of the sermons they had heard.

The fourth or Greek class (*novitii*) commenced with Latin versions, and towards the end of October the principal or the dean of faculty prescribed themes, which were to be rendered by the fourth class in Latin and by the third class in Greek. This seems to mean that students from the Latin class of the preceding session who were now joining the Greek class were to be tested in Latin ; and students who had taken the Greek class in the preceding session and were now entering the logic class were to be tested in Greek. Theses were at the same time prescribed to members of the first and second class. About the beginning of November students of Greek addressed themselves to the Greek grammar of Clenardus, and by and by added reading of the New Testament, the orations of Isocrates, and the poetry of Homer, Hesiod, and Phocylides, committing to memory considerable passages from Isocrates and Homer. Thrice a week they were exercised in translating from English into Latin and Greek, those who had the faculty being invited to compose verses, and near the close of the session they learned the rudiments of Hebrew from Buxtorf's *Epitome.*

During the greater part of October the students of the three upper classes repeated carefully the dictates taught in their classes of the preceding year, after which came the public examinations for promotion to higher classes. When these were over, members of the semibaccalour or logic class entered upon the study of the logic of Burgerdicius, followed by the divisions of oratory from Vossius, with demonstrations of the precepts of rhetoric from the speeches of Cicero and Demosthenes. From the beginning of February they studied Porphyry, and proceeded to Aristotle's *Categories, De Interpretatione, Prior Analytics, Topics,* and *Refutations.* They were drilled in logic and rhetoric by analysis of Latin and Greek authors, and by handling simple and compound themes. After 1st February theses were composed twice a week by the students and publicly corrected by the regents. On the Saturday mornings students revised the work of the week, and from half-past ten held disputations, while they also exercised themselves in declamation.

The second or baccalour class, roughly corresponding to the modern ethics or moral philosophy class, after the examinations for promotion, entered on the study of the *Later Analytics*, followed by the *Ethics*, *Politics*, and *Economics*, with arithmetic and geometry, a compendium of metaphysics, and two books of physics. Theses and declamations continued all through the session in this class.

The first class, being the physics or magistrand one, began with the remaining books of physics, and proceeded to the books *De Coelo*, along with astronomy and Kekermann's geography, followed by *De Ortu et Interitu*, portions of the *Meteorologics* and the *Compendium of Anatomy*.

It was appointed that all the classes should meet in their auditoriums from one to two in the afternoon for disputations on such subjects occurring in the prelections as the masters prescribed, and on Saturday the two upper classes, with their masters, met in the public auditorium to dispute from ten to twelve—the baccalours disputing among themselves for the first half hour, and the magistrands among themselves for the second, while after eleven o'clock one or more magistrands disputed with the baccalours. From the beginning of May the semibaccalours were also admitted to these public disputations.

The masters were instructed to look to the improvement of the young men in divine as well as in human knowledge. Prelections on the Catechism were to receive special attention, and the students of the fourth class were to learn half the Palatine Catechism and those of the third class the whole of it, while the baccalours and magistrands were to be exercised in the general principles and the controversies against Papists, Lutherans, Arminians, Socinians, Anabaptists, and other enemies of the truth, of which David Parens treats in his *Commentaries on the Palatine Catechism*.

Two stated yearly periods of examination were prescribed—the first at the end of the session, including the examination of students of the magistrand class for the degree of master, and of students of the other classes before they separated for the vacation ; and the second at the beginning of the session before students were promoted to higher classes.

Students of the magistrand class before being admitted to the degree of master underwent a complex examination consisting of two parts. In the initial part they were examined by the first regent in the *Isagoge* of Porphyry and Aristotle's *Categories* and *De Interpretatione* ; by the second in the *Prior* and *Later Analytics* ; by the third in the *Topics* and *Sophistical Refutations* ; by the fourth in the *Nicomachean Ethics* ; and by their own teacher in the *Compendium of Metaphysics*. In the final part of the examination they were examined by the first regent in physics ; by the second in *De Coelo,* and astronomy and cosmography ; by the third in *Generation and Destruction* and the *Meteorics* ; by the fourth in *De Anima* ; and by their own teacher in the *Tractate on Anatomy.*

Members of the second class were examined by the principal in the *Prolegomena to Logic,* the *Isagoge* of Porphyry, and Aristotle's *Categories* ; by the first regent in *De Interpretatione* and the *Prior Analytics* ; by the second in the *Later Analytics* ; by the third in the *Sophistical Refutations* and the *Topics* ; by the fourth in what they had learned from the *Physica Auscultatio* ; and by their own teacher in arithmetic, geometry, and the *Compendium of Metaphysics.*

Students of the third class were examined by the first regent in the *Prolegomena to Logic,* the *Isagoge* of Porphyry, and Aristotle's *Categories* ; by the second in *De Interpretatione* ; by the third in the *Prior Analytics* ; by the fourth in the rest of what they had learned of logic, whether from Aristotle's or some other system ; and by their own teacher in rhetoric and the orations of Cicero on which he had prelected.

All the regents took part in testing the proficiency of students of the fourth class in Greek grammar and the application of it to the authors read in the class.

The examinations at the beginning of the session for promotion to higher classes followed the same order, but greater exactness was expected, and students from the Greek class of the preceding session had to give a specimen of their skill in reading authors they had privately studied, apart from those on whose works they had heard prelections.

Probably this scheme of study and examination is not very different from what had been previously in use at Glasgow, but as representing the outcome of deliberations of representatives of all the Scottish Universities, it is remarkable how much the curriculum was still dominated by Aristotle, and not less so the scheme of examinations. The second and third classes were examined at the end of the session, mostly on his works, and again at the beginning of next session when they came up for promotion to higher classes, and yet again at the end of their session in the magistrand class students had to face a final and formidable ordeal to test their knowledge of the Stagyrite. The disputations and some of the other exercises in which students engaged should, if well managed, have been of great value ; for education consists, or should consist, not merely in receiving knowledge into the mind, but also in training the mind to make the best use of the knowledge it possesses. Some parts of the discipline might perhaps be revived with advantage even in these modern times, when mute listening and the taking of notes have been carried rather too far.

In 1643 it was determined that no student from the Grammar School should be admitted to the University unless he had finished the five years' course of study there, instituted with the sanction of the moderators of the College, unless in any exceptional case where the faculty might give leave.   It was mostly a course in Latin—grammar, translation of Latin authors, and discipline in Latin prose, verse, and conversation—but in the latter part of the time scholars learned rhetoric and Greek grammar.   They also received religious instruction, first in the vernacular and afterwards in Latin.   They had further to learn dialogues, orations, and especially comedies where different parts were presented dramatically.   These they declaimed surrounded by a ring of spectators, that they might acquire good expression and action.   It was ordained that the school should be inspected twice a year by visitors appointed by the Town Council and the College, and after these examinations an order of merit was made out, and prizes and distinctions awarded.

On the request of the dean in 1642, a senate [1] of the faculty declared that those entitled to elect the dean were the rector, the principal, the vice-chancellor, the divinity professors, the ministers of the Church of Glasgow —city and landward—along with the regents and the preceptor of the Grammar School.   From these, four assessors were to be chosen by the dean, with consent of the Senate, to assist him in dealing with the affairs of his province, but in the weightier matters reference was to be made to the Senate itself.   The Senate also declared that the examiners of students were the dean, the principal, and the regents, with the preceptor of the Grammar School ;   and that it belonged to the dean, the rector, and the principal to call to order any preceptors who did not perform their duty faithfully.   It is doubtful whether these deliverances were sound in all their details.

In 1644 Principal Strang applied to the Committee of Estates, claiming that, in virtue of the privileges of the College, it should enjoy immunity from excise, and the claim was strongly pressed by James Dalrymple, one of the regents, who had been the bearer of a letter on the subject to the Earl of Loudon, the lord chancellor.   A somewhat guarded and niggardly assent was given, and Lord Loudon wrote to the principal that the committee ' have condescendit that quhat is spent within the Colledge for thair enterteinment sall pay no excise ; but leist it suld be ane preparative to utheris to sute the lyk immunitie, the committee wald not condescend to give out any extract or writ heirupon.'

---

[1] This is one of the earliest instances in which we encounter the word senate as applied to the University administrators, and it is curious to find the senate and faculty, afterwards so sharply opposed to each other, conjoined as they are here.

A few years after Strang had been appointed principal, efforts were made to provide new buildings for the University, and a public subscription list was opened. According to the heading given in the book containing the list of subscriptions, the movement was begun for the purpose of building a new library, furnishing it with books, and otherwise enlarging the fabric ; but renovating the buildings soon came to be the main object. Little was done for the library, and it would not have required a large part of the buildings to accommodate all the books it then contained. Michael Wilsone had in 1607 mortified £500 sterling for rebuilding the decayed part of the fabric and founding a bursary, though the money was not immediately received, and in 1619 Alexander Boyd, one of the regents, bequeathed a thousand marks for rebuilding the College ; but these sums did not go far, and in 1630 an appeal was made to the public. The list of contributions given or promised is a long one, but there is evidence that many of them were not promptly paid.

It is to the credit of the University authorities that they were among the first to subscribe, the principal giving 500 marks (with a subsequent contribution of £100, diverted from Blackfriars Church with consent of the Town Council) ; while of the regents John Rae gave £100, Robert Baillie 100 marks, George Young 40 marks, and William Wilkie 50 marks ; and Zachary Boyd, minister of the Barony, who held office at one time or another as rector, dean of faculty, and vice-chancellor, gave liberally to the University during his life and bequeathed a large sum to it at his death. He began with a contribution of 500 marks. This was in 1630 when the subscription list opened, and during the next six or seven years there was a response which for the times may be called liberal, though it was hardly adequate to the magnitude of the work.

In 1633 Charles I. promised £200 sterling, but it was left to Cromwell to make payment twenty-one years afterwards. The Marquis (afterwards the Duke) of Hamilton—a prominent but ill-starred actor in the affairs of Scotland, who had served under Gustavus Adolphus, and was destined to defeat at Preston and execution afterwards—promised 1000 marks in 1631, but a quarter of century elapsed before the money was paid by the trustees of the sequestrated Hamilton estates in 1656. The Earl of Abercorn gave 600 marks, the Earl of Angus 500 marks, the Earl of Dunfermline 400 marks, the Earl of Morton 500 marks, the Earl of Strathearn 500 marks, Viscount Lauderdale 300 marks, the Earl of Montrose (afterwards the warrior Marquis) 400 marks, the Earl of Rothes 14 dollars, Lord Napier 200 marks, Elizabeth Douglas, Lady Nithsdale, 100 marks, and Rachel Johnston, Lady Stenhouse, £20. It is gratifying to find that the movement obtained considerable support from the Highlands.

H

The Earl of Seaforth contributed 400 marks, Sir Donald Macdonald of Sleat £100, Hector Maclean, younger of Douart, £100, John Macleod of Dunvegan 100 marks, and Archibald Lord Lorne (then practically in possession of the Argyle estates, his father having turned Catholic and gone abroad) 500 marks. At the outset the Town Council of Glasgow gave 2,000 marks, and a further sum of £50 afterwards; the towns of Stirling and Ayr each contributed 300 marks, and the burgh of Irvine £100. James Hamilton, provost of Glasgow, gave 100 marks, and there were contributions from other merchants and citizens.

In 1641 Thomas Hutcheson of Lambhill bequeathed £1,000 for rebuilding the south part of the College, and by his direction it was invested at interest, so that when it came to be used in 1654 it had increased to £1,851 5s. 6d. Other members of the nobility and many country lairds also contributed, but, apart from a multitude of ministers, there are few names of professional men in the list, except some notaries and one or two doctors of medicine. The ministers of Glasgow and the south and west of Scotland supported the movement well, and as far north as Perthshire there were many clerical contributors. The names of half a dozen prelates also occur, Spottiswood, archbishop of St. Andrews, giving 1,000 marks, two successive archbishops of Glasgow 1,000 marks each, an earlier bishop of the Isles 600 marks, a later bishop of the Isles 200 marks, the Bishop of Galloway 200 marks, and the Bishop of Dunblane 200 marks. In 1632 eighteen Scottish gentlemen holding positions ' at the court of Ingland' gave subscriptions ranging from 100 to 300 marks; and David Muirhead and William Muirhead, both resident in London, gave £100 sterling and 100 marks respectively.

Viscount Stirling, a poet and politician of the time (some lines in whose tragedy of *Darius* are believed to have suggested to Shakespeare the passage in the *Tempest* beginning, ' The cloud-capp'd towers '), gave a sum of £500, stipulating that one or two chambers bearing his name and arms should be provided in the College for the use of his children and members of his house while being educated there. There is a further entry setting forth that there was ' given be Richard and Thomas Couts, sons to Sir Richard Couts, knicht barronet, for adorning their chamber, fyftie four pounds Scotts money.'

Directions were given in 1646 that John Grahame, the provisor, should levy certain specified rents from the students who occupied the College chambers. Forty-one apartments were enumerated, and the rent varied from ten to thirty shillings for each, but some apartments marked as studies were let for six shillings each. Seventeen of the chambers were supplied with iron chimneys, for which a separate charge, varying from ten to twenty-four shillings, was made—nearly as much as was charged for the chambers. The rents were exacted before entry, ' so that they quho first entre shall pay the quhol duetie for the chalmber and chimney, and if any one afterward be placed in the chalmber, the first payer or payers shall have the relief of the rest *pro rata*.' Two or three of the chambers were marked as ' in the Arthurlie,' a portion of the building still bearing the name of that early benefactor.

Preparations costing £1,022 10s. were made in 1631, and from 1632 to 1635 the work of building was in active progress, the outlays in that period amounting to £10,473 2s. 2d. Between 1635 and 1640 progress was slower, the outlays amounting to £7,823 4s. 6d. Afterwards, in Gillespie's time, the renovation and extension of the buildings were pressed forward, and money spent perhaps rather hastily. Now and again there is evidence of contracts being made for joiner and slater work, but most of the building was reared by workmen employed and paid directly by the University—quarriers, sawyers, carters, barrowmen, masons, wrights, slaters, blacksmiths, and others. It appears from the accounts that in 1632 the daily wages of masons ranged from tenpence to one shilling and threepence, while a mason's apprentice received one shilling and eightpence a week, and a barrowman four shillings a week. A blacksmith received fifty marks for sharpening twenty thousand irons for masons. The principle of compensation for injury to workmen seems to have been recognised, for there is an entry—' Mor to J. Quantanes man that had a sor finger hurt in our work, xxs.' The workmen were frequently treated to drink, sometimes drink-money was given them instead, and occasionally the rulers of the University regaled themselves with a glass of wine. Bread was sometimes given to the workmen, but it seems to have borne about the same proportion to drink as in Falstaff's tavern bill. Gloves for masons, wrights, and slaters are also charged in the accounts, and there is an entry for a sandglass to keep the masons' hours.

In connection with the new building arrangements Blackfriars' Church, often called the College Church, was made over to the Town Council. This old structure, representing the Church of the Blackfriars or Dominicans who had been the friendly neighbours of the College in the days before the Reformation, stood within the University grounds some distance to the rear of High Street, with a narrow churchyard in front reaching forward towards the street. The church had been in a more or less dilapidated condition for many years, and the College had incurred considerable outlays for repairs which were not of a thorough character, so that in 1635, when the transaction took place, the structure was nearly ruinous, and urgently needed repairs which must have proved costly to the University.

The Town Council having undertaken to make the repairs if the church were placed in their hands, and having shown their interest in the University building scheme by subscribing two thousand marks, the academic managers made over the church and churchyard to the Council, with a space of ground eleven ells wide along both the south and the north walls of the church, which the Council were allowed to use for building enlargements at their discretion. The most commodious place and sittings in the church after the Council's seat were reserved for the rector, dean of faculty, regents, and students, as well as the use of the church at the yearly graduation in arts, and other public occasions not interfering with the holding of divine service ; and the Town Council undertook to relieve the College from the burden of repairing and maintaining the church. At the same time four of the low chambers lately built in the north part of the University were assigned to the use of burgesses' sons who were students.

The year 1645 witnessed the beginning of a lamentable episode in the history of the city, which caused a temporary removal of the classes beyond its borders. A severe outbreak of the plague occurred, and the disease continued, with some fluctuations of intensity, for fully three years. Efforts were made to arrest its spread, and when these proved unavailing the sufferers were removed to wooden buildings with straw beds, which had been hastily erected on the Muir to the north of the town. The councillors in turn visited the plague-stricken patients, and healthy people in the town were forbidden, without leave of the magistrates, to hold any communication with the sufferers who had been removed to the Muir, while the best medical skill then available was procured, the services of a certain Dr. M'Cluir and of John Hall, then the chief surgeon in Glasgow, being retained. Ordinary trade and industry were nearly suspended, and most of those who could afford to leave the sadly changed city did so.

Under the advice of David Dickson, the professor of divinity, who had long been minister at Irvine, the teaching work of the University was transferred to that old seaside town, and there the classes met in sessions 1645-1646 and 1646-1647. In the first of these years the board of the bursars at Irvine is charged from the opening (which normally would be 1st October, 1645) to 1st May, 1646, while the board of the principal and five regents there is charged for a half-year. Next year the session at Irvine was a longer one, as is shown by the following account: ' Item to Johne Grahame, maltmane, for furnisching of the hous and for the in- tertenement of the Principall, Maisters, and Bursoris at Irving frome 1 October, 1646, to 1 August, 1647, j^{m}ix^{c}lxl. viijs. 8d.' There is a record of a further expenditure of £372 for the house rents of the principal,

Dickson, Baillie, and the four regents, and the expenses of their removal to Irvine, Paisley, and Glasgow.

Both arts and divinity classes were transferred to Irvine, and the statistics of attendance and graduation in arts do not show any noticeable falling-off as compared with other years. Among the students in 1646 was Lord Niel Campbell, son of the Marquis of Argyle, at that time the most powerful of Scottish subjects ;[1] while among the graduates in 1647 was James Durham, afterwards a notable and accomplished minister, who held for some months the rather incongruous position of Presbyterian chaplain to Charles II. Durham was a man of good education and exceptional piety, and while still very young served as a captain in the civil wars. Having on one occasion called together his company for prayer, David Dickson, happening to ride past, was surprised and delighted with the young captain's powers in that branch of devotion, and, regretting to see such talents wasted on civil or military affairs, persuaded him to become a minister. The influx of so many students, and of teachers like Dickson, who had long been minister of Irvine, Baillie, who had formerly been minister of Kilwinning, Dalrymple of Stair, an estate not many miles away, and occasional visits from Zachary Boyd, the vice-chancellor of the University, and probably other officers and administrators, must have quickened the life and activity of the old town. There is evidence too that it did not extinguish the hopefulness and enterprise of the visitors, for it was during the sojourn at Irvine in April, 1647, that David Monro and John Dickson, two of the regents, resigned office so as to emancipate themselves from the promise they had given not to marry, a step they now contemplated. They were immediately re-elected to office without restriction to the single state of bachelor.

The early part of session 1647-1648 was held at Paisley, the teaching staff, with their pupils, having by that time ventured so far on the way back to Glasgow. From the ratio of the amount paid for the board of masters at Paisley to the amount for six months' board at Irvine, the classes seem to have been conducted at the former place for only a little more than two months, and probably teaching had been resumed in Glasgow about the new year of 1648. At the beginning of next session in the autumn of 1648 students seem to have been slow to come forward, and the public examinations and the promotions to higher classes were postponed till the beginning of February. It would appear that not only students but teachers also had been slow to present themselves at the beginning of this session, and a fine was denounced against any teacher who

[1] The eldest son, Lord Archibald, who became Earl of Argyle, and was executed after the insurrection of 1685, was enrolled as a student of Greek in 1643.

did not come forward to begin the work of the session in good time.   It seems likely that the plague was still claiming its victims in the autumn of 1648.[1]

It is probable that Baillie, who had been minister at Kilwinning, and James Dalrymple of Stair, who was one of the regents in the first year of the exile at Irvine, had been instrumental, along with Dickson, in choosing that place of refuge for the University in the time of the plague.   Born in 1619, Dalrymple was educated at the University of Glasgow, and became captain in Glencairn's regiment, which formed part of the force raised to bring Charles I. to reason in his management of Scottish affairs. Early in 1641 the young captain came forward, attired in his military uniform of buff and scarlet, to dispute for the office of regent then vacant in the University, and carried the appointment against several competitors. He continued as a regent for about six years only, and it was not till after his withdrawal from that position that his abilities came to be fully known. Having applied himself during his regency to the study of law, he was prompted to try his fortune as a practitioner in that faculty, and some time after resigning his academic position he was admitted an advocate in 1648. Under Cromwell he was appointed a judge of the Court of Session, on the recommendation of Monk, who described him as 'a very honest man, a good lawyer, and one of a considerable estate'; while under Charles II. he became Lord President.   He was not in haste to place himself in opposition to the government of the day, but there were limits he did not care to exceed, and by and by the stringent and oppressive measures of the government induced him to retire from public life, when he completed his great work on *The Institutes of the Law of Scotland.*

He withdrew to Holland for some years, but under William of Orange he was restored to office as Lord President of the Court of Session, and took a leading part in the public measures of that eventful time.   Knighted at the Restoration, he was made a baronet of Nova Scotia in 1664, and in 1690 Viscount Stair.   The Massacre of Glencoe left a blemish on the name of Dalrymple, though it was the Viscount's son rather than himself who was implicated; and Sir Walter Scott has given to the family a weird and sombre fame in the treatment accorded to them among the *dramatis personae* of *The Bride of Lammermoor.*   Dalrymple may fairly be reckoned the ablest man among the lay teachers at Glasgow in the seven-

---

[1] It is curious to note that about the same date, on account of the plague, the teaching of the University of Aberdeen had to be removed from that city and conducted for a time in the buildings of the derelict University of Fraserburgh, a seminary which had been sanctioned by James VI., but soon fell into decay when its principal offended that monarch.

teenth century, and it appears from the testimony of John Snell and others
that he was also an able teacher.

It is said to have been Dalrymple's retirement from the office of regent
that opened the way to the appointment in October, 1646, of Hugh
Binning, a young man who had shown extraordinary and precocious powers
as a student. He was not quite nineteen when he gained by competition
the post of regent over other candidates of maturer years and respectable
acquirements. He taught with ability and success for a short time, till,
having qualified as a clergyman, he was appointed minister of Govan, and
in that position continued to preach with great fervour and eloquence till
he was cut off by consumption at the age of twenty-five. In the division
of ecclesiastical parties prevailing in his later years he took the side of the
Protesters; but he was a temperate partisan and would fain have healed
the divisions between Protesters and Resolutioners, and wrote a treatise
on *Christian Love* to help towards that end. Selections from his works
were published in 1732 and again in 1829.

Baillie's large share in the memorable events of his time often called
him away from his duties as professor of divinity, yet his prominence in
public affairs must have reflected credit on the University. He possessed
great information and considerable experience, was widely known and
generally esteemed, and, with greater firmness and insight, might himself
have been a leader of men. But he was better fitted to sketch and record
the personages and events of his day, to grumble, criticise, and wonder
what the outcome would be, than to read the characters of men and the
signs of the times, or to seize the right moment for action and decide
swiftly on the action that would be effective. It was the misfortune of
the Covenanters that, after the death of Henderson, they had no chief
really able and worthy to lead them, for though Argyle and Warriston
were men of capacity and astuteness, they fell short of the needful standard.

In 1642 Lord Maitland, afterwards the Earl and Duke of Lauderdale,
brought an invitation from the parliament of England, and the Commission of the Scottish General Assembly appointed Alexander Henderson,
George Douglas, Samuel Rutherford, George Gillespie, and Robert Baillie
as commissioners to the proposed General Assembly of Divines at Westminster. All of these were ministers, but on Baillie's proposal three ruling
elders—the Earl of Cassilis, Lord Maitland, and Johnston of Warriston—
were added. It does not appear that Cassilis or Douglas ever took part
in the Assembly, and the other commissioners were at first rather disinclined to the employment. But in 1642 the great Civil War broke out
in England, in its early stages the armies of the parliament fared ill, and
it became very important to secure the assistance of Scotland. With a

view to this end, Sir Henry Vane (the younger) and other commissioners from the English parliament, with two ministers, Marshall and Nye, came to Edinburgh in August, 1643.

Subsequent history has shown the possibility of two countries living together in peace and friendship, though they may not have the same ecclesiastical polity or the same confession or profession of faith. But at that time an overstrained desire for uniformity of ecclesiastical doctrine and organisation manifested itself, and the Scots, who had previously suffered by the attempts to impose the Anglican polity and forms upon them, now vainly thought they could extend their system to England. The English Commissioners proposed a civil league between the two countries, and this would have been the wiser course, but the Scots generally favoured a religious bond, and Henderson drafted the Solemn League and Covenant, which was swiftly adopted by the Scottish General Assembly and Convention of Estates. Its subscribers bound themselves to labour for the preservation of the Reformed religion in Scotland, and for the reformation of religion in England and Ireland in doctrine, worship, discipline, and government, according to the Word of God and the example of the best Reformed Churches; to endeavour the extirpation of popery, prelacy, heresy, and schism; and to defend the privileges of parliament and the person and authority of the king. The league was so worded that, after all, England was not bound to the establishment of Presbytery.

Commissioners were ordered to proceed to London to support the ratification of the Covenant, and Lord Maitland, Henderson, and Gillespie, as well as Robert Meldrum, having arrived there, were admitted to the Assembly of Divines to be present and debate upon occasion. The Covenant passed both houses, and was solemnly sworn in St. Margaret's Church, Westminster, towards the end of September. The Westminster divines having called for Baillie and Rutherford, the two reached London on 18th November, and on an order from the house, 'without which no mortal man may enter to see or to hear,' they were admitted to the Assembly, and welcomed in a long speech by Dr. Twisse. Early in 1645 Baillie and George Gillespie were deputed to return to Scotland to give an account of the proceedings to the General Assembly at Edinburgh, bringing with them the *Directory for Public Worship*, which superseded Knox's *Book of Common Order*. Baillie reported the progress made with the abolition of ceremonies and of Episcopacy in all the king's dominions, and said they now had a fair prospect of the establishment of Presbytery.

After he had been only a short time with his family at Glasgow, he was ordered back to London; and the vessel in which he sailed being driven by stormy weather to the coast of Holland, he spent some days at Middleburg and Rotterdam before making his way back to Westminster. Baillie had preached before the English House of Commons in 1644, and in July, 1645, he preached before the House of Lords in the Abbey Church at Westminster, and was thanked for his sermon, which was printed by order of the house. In December, 1646, he obtained leave to return home, and next month he reached Edinburgh, bearing the *Confession of Faith* and the new metrical version of the psalms. The Assembly adopted the first of these, with some limitations, as 'in nothing contrary to the received doctrine'; and remitted the second work (of which Francis Rous, a member of the Long Parliament, was partly author and partly editor, and which reproduced much of an earlier version by Sir William Alexander of Menstrie, afterwards Earl of Stirling) to the revision of a committee, instructing them to make what use they could of the versions of the Laird of Rowallan and of Zachary Boyd. The latter had cherished a vain hope, encouraged by some flattering friends, that his version of the psalms might be adopted, and the Assembly showed their consideration for him by making this recommendation, but even the men of that unpoetical age who accepted Rous's metrical translation of the psalms could not bring themselves to accept Boyd's. As a result that version of the psalms which has so long held its place in the musical part of Scottish worship was adopted, though organs and hymnaries are now pushing it somewhat into the background.

The tide of the Civil War turned against the king, but the rise of the Independents prevented the hopes of the Covenanters from being realised. In July, 1647, Charles rejected proposals made to him by Cromwell on behalf of the army, and ominous hints were heard about bringing the king himself to justice for the bloodshed of the war. The Scots were attached to monarchy, though they had opposed the measures of Charles, but now they were alarmed by the ascendancy of the Independents and the danger which seemed to threaten the king. In December, 1647, the Lord Chancellor Loudon, the Earl of Lauderdale, and the Earl of Lanark, acting for his brother the Duke of Hamilton, made a secret treaty with Charles, known as the Engagement, under which he was to be restored to power by a Scottish army, the king agreeing that Presbyterianism should be established in England for three years, the Covenant ratified by act of parliament, and the Independents and other sectaries suppressed.

The proposal to raise a Scottish army to aid Charles was carried by a small majority in the Scottish parliament in 1648, Argyle and others opposing the measure as inconsistent with the treaty with England, and tending to make Scotsmen companions in arms with those who had been enemies of the Covenant. A cleavage began in the ranks of the Covenanters, and difficulties were found in raising an army.   The Town Council of Glasgow reported a general unwillingness to engage in the war from want of satisfaction as to its lawfulness, and the members of the Council and the Town Clerk were sent to prison, while soldiers were billeted on the citizens. An army was at length raised, but inadequate in numbers, and consisting mostly of raw levies, indifferently equipped, and unable to meet on equal terms the veteran soldiers of Cromwell.   Leslie and other experienced officers refused to act unless the Church was satisfied, and the Duke of Hamilton was himself left to command.   In 1642 the duke had been chosen chancellor of the University of Glasgow—the first time a layman was called to that office—and in the troubles and vicissitudes of the period he had been repeatedly thrust into prominence, but he was not the man to win a victory from Cromwell, and in a three days' fight at Preston, Wigan, and Warrington, his forces were cut to pieces.   Hamilton's unfortunate expedition hastened the fate of Charles.   The Presbyterians were still strong in the English parliament, and would have come to terms with the king, but the army was stronger than the parliament.   'Pride's Purge' excluded the Presbyterian members, Charles was put on trial, condemned, and executed in spite of a vehement protest from the Scottish Commissioners in London.

After the defeat of Hamilton the direction of Scottish affairs fell to the party opposed to the Engagement, and in January, 1649, the Estates hastily passed an Act of Classes, distinguishing four grades of delinquency among the opponents of the Covenant, and excluding them from civil and military office till they had proved their faithful repentance.   Yet next month, having proclaimed Charles II. as king, they resolved to send a deputation to Holland to invite him to accept the Covenant and the crown.   The Commissioners included the Earl of Cassilis and Robert Baillie, and their secretary was James Dalrymple, who had been a regent at Glasgow only two or three years before.   Having reached the Hague and been admitted to an audience on 27th March, Cassilis made a speech in name of the parliament, and Baillie another in name of the Church. Charles did not give the satisfaction required, and the Commissioners returned, commending his sweet and courteous disposition, but lamenting that he was surrounded by a very evil generation of English and Scots.

The proceedings of the Commissioners were approved by the parliament and the General Assembly and thanks voted to them, but Baillie was drawn into a pamphleteering warfare with some of the 'evil generation.' He declined to join the next deputation sent to negotiate with Charles at Breda in 1650, but among the Commissioners was John Livingstone, minister of Ancrum, a graduate of Glasgow, who has left a curious account of the proceedings, while Dalrymple was again secretary. Livingstone was averse to going, as he distrusted his own aptitude and capacity for such an undertaking, and had little confidence in the intentions of some of the other Commissioners; but by the persuasions of David Dickson, James Guthrie, and Patrick Gillespie he was prevailed upon to go. During all the time of the negotiations at Breda Charles 'continued the use of the service book and of his chaiplans, and many nights he was balling and danceing till near day.' Yet Livingstone thought the king so tractable and courteous that, if the Commissioners had been in earnest, he would have granted all their desires at the outset.

When Charles landed at Speymouth in June, 1650, he came to a distracted country, which was not rendered more united or tranquil by his presence. He had accepted the Covenant, and further promises were exacted from him. Yet few believed in his sincerity or his likelihood to abide by his promises if circumstances should alter in his favour. An increasing party among the Covenanters looked with distrust on the measures which were followed, and though rooting out heresy was one of the objects of the Covenant, they began to think they might more easily endure a sectary like Cromwell than a prodigal and voluptuous cynic without religion or conscience, such as Charles was. As a concession to them, the policy of the Act of Classes was pursued, and thousands of men were weeded out from the army of Leslie. After the defeat at Dunbar the party opposed to the acceptance of a malignant king grew bolder and more defiant. Their leaders, Johnston of Warriston, and two obstreperous ministers, James Guthrie of Stirling and Patrick Gillespie of Glasgow, drew up a manifesto—*Causes of a Solemn Public Humiliation upon the Defeat of the Army*. At the end of October a remonstrance was presented to the Committee of Estates denouncing the policy of the government and objecting to Charles being accepted as king till he gave evidence of the reality of his profession. The remonstrants or protesters, as they were now called, also gathered a considerable force in the south-western shires, which, however, was soon crushed at Hamilton by Major-General Lambert.

The fortunes of the war suggested the need for filling up the ranks of the army, and for this purpose relaxing the Act of Classes. The Commission of the General Assembly, having been asked for their advice on the matter, passed successive resolutions that all might be admitted to the army except such as were excommunicated, forfeited, notoriously profane, or professed enemies of the Covenant; and that under certain safeguards those who had been shut out from the Committee of Estates might now be admitted. The Act of Classes was repealed, but a heated controversy continued among the clergy.   A General Assembly at St. Andrews in July, 1651, confirmed the resolutions of the Commission, and those who adhered to them were henceforth called resolutioners.   The Assembly likewise intimated that all who were not satisfied with the public resolutions should be cited as liable to censure.   Upon this, twenty-two ministers gave in a protest against the lawfulness of the Assembly on the ground that both the king and the Commission had interfered with its constitution.   The Assembly replied by deposing three of the leading protesters, including James Guthrie and Patrick Gillespie.

Cromwell's victory at Worcester ended the war, but the strife of resolutioners and protesters was still heard in the land, and Baillie, who had been one of the leading resolutioners, had to yield precedence for a time to Patrick Gillespie, who had been a fiery and vehement protagonist on the other side.   Gillespie was on good terms with Cromwell, who, when in Glasgow, sent for him to talk over affairs, and in the course of a year or two he was made principal of the University, notwithstanding Baillie's opposition.   About the time when Strang became principal, Zachary Boyd was appointed minister of the Barony Church, and the two, having been companions in early youth, renewed their acquaintance and friendship. Both were strong royalists and not very favourably inclined to the National Covenant of 1638.   Indeed both Boyd and the moderators of the College at first refused to sign, and Baillie, then minister of Kilwinning, paid them a visit with a view to induce them to subscribe, but was not successful.

The University granted a commission to four representatives in the eventful Assembly which met in the Cathedral of Glasgow in 1638, but the Assembly would not recognise their right to appoint more than one, and the commission was annulled, though it seems to have been understood that the principal would remain a member.   But probably he had not much heart for the work, and when Hamilton, who represented the king, withdrew from the Assembly, Strang also ceased to attend, excusing himself on the ground of the annulling of the commission issued to four representatives.   He had subscribed a protestation against elders, which was held to be inimical to the Assembly itself, and done other things which gave offence, and a Commission of Visitation to the University was appointed and caused some apprehension, though it does not seem ever to have met.   Subsequent visitations from the Assembly have already been mentioned.   They gave little trouble to the principal, but he seems to have resorted to some diplomacy in order to secure his own predominance in the College, and to have been opposed to the public measures then generally in favour.   In 1646 a letter and a treatise addressed by Strang to Dr. Walter Balcanquhal, found among the king's papers which fell into the hands of the victors after the battle of Naseby, were sent down to Scotland, and did not tend to improve the principal's standing with the government.

The General Assembly of 1646 appointed Commissioners to examine Strang's dictates—short notes of the instruction he gave to his students— and they reported to the Assembly of next year that some expressions in them occasioned scruples in the minds of grave and learned men, but that after conferring with Dr. Strang and hearing his explanations, they were satisfied of his orthodoxy, and that Dr. Strang had volunteered to add some words to render his meaning more explicit, and the Commissioners thought this acceptable. Strang suffered from want of circumspection and tact, and some who bore him no goodwill took occasion to make the later years of his tenure as principal unpleasant. Baillie, who previously thought the principal was following an ill-judged and inadvisable course, says, 'by great studie and violence Dr. Strang was made to dimitt his place.' In April, 1650, Strang gave in his resignation, which was accepted by the Visitors, and the faculties of arts and theology reluctantly acquiesced. The Visitors gave him a testimonial of orthodoxy, and he was allowed an annuity of a thousand marks from the University. He died in June, 1654, having spent his latter days in revising his treatise, *De Voluntate et Actionibus Dei circa Peccatum*, which was published by the Elzevirs at Amsterdam after his death. Another of his works, *De Interpretatione et Perfectione Scripturae*, was published at Rotterdam in 1663.

Nearly a year elapsed from the time of Dickson's removal to Edinburgh in February, 1650, before Robert Baillie was appointed to succeed him in January, 1651. The Commissioners of the General Assembly wished James Durham, whose graduation at Irvine has already been mentioned, and who afterwards became minister of Blackfriars Church, Glasgow, to be appointed to the chair, but this design was laid aside when the General Assembly in July, 1650, nominated him to be domestic chaplain to the king. The position was no doubt a trying one, but Durham was a man of prudence as well as piety, and for about eight months ministered as Presbyterian chaplain to Charles II. and his court, probably as well as man could do. After Durham became chaplain the academic administrators took steps to make it clear that the place to which he was called in the College was vacant, and they caused surprise and annoyance to the Town Council by also declaring his place as one of the ministers of the town vacant. After Baillie had himself been promoted to be first professor of divinity in succession to Dickson, Robert Ramsay, another of the city ministers, was chosen as his colleague, but the Town Council, disapproving of what had been done regarding Durham, seem to have used their influence to prevent Ramsay from accepting. About March, 1651, Durham returned to Glasgow and unsuccessfully laid claim to the professorship to which he had been appointed in the preceding year.

There was a considerable interval between Baillie's promotion in January, 1651, and October, 1652, when John Young, who had been a regent in arts since 1645, was appointed to succeed him. By reason of 'the junctors and incidents of the Colledge affaires,' there was a further interval before Young was released from the teaching of his class in arts and began to teach in divinity. On 13th January, 1653, the moderators resolved that on the 21st of that month 'he should have ane publict prelectione upone the last verse of the 17 Psalme, *pro more sueto* and emitt theologicall theses, that so thairupone with the ordinare solemnities he might be installed in the said professione of Theologie.' At the time of Young's formal appointment to the divinity chair, the moderators directed that, 'according to the ordour formallie observed in sicke cases, programes to be given out for inveiting all able students in philosophie to dispute for that plaice, that the samen may be conferred upone such of the competitors as sall appeare most qualified for the discharge of the samen.' The election of a new master to fill the vacancy caused by Young's promotion did not take place for some time, Mr. Robert M'Cward being admitted to office on 4th August, 1653.

Among 'the junctors and incidents of the Colledge affaires' helping to explain the want of promptitude in filling up vacancies in the teaching staff, it is probable that the long vacancy in the office of principal counted for a good deal. After Strang's resignation there was some talk of appointing Patrick Gillespie, a proposal which Baillie characterised as 'exceedingly absurd.' Baillie had considerable faith in his own qualifications for the post, but his time was not yet, and he and some others were sent as a deputation to St. Andrews to invite Robert Blair—who had been a regent at Glasgow in his early days, and was now minister of St. Andrews and a man of good standing and influence—to become principal. Blair seems to have been not unwilling, but some obstacles prevented his acceptance ; and Robert Ramsay, who a little before this had received an ineffective call to be professor of divinity, was now made principal. Baillie states that in June, 1651, he was 'sent to Perth for Mr. Ramsay's call,' and this is understood to mean that he was sent to procure a presentation to the office of principal in favour of Ramsay from Charles II., who was then in Perth or its neighbourhood. Ramsay was admitted to office, and took part in at least one meeting held on 27th July, 1651.

At this meeting the moderators put on record their conviction that the offices of principal and professors of divinity were so exacting that the most diligent services of the ablest men hardly sufficed for them ; that the College had been moved to liberate the principal from the ministry of Govan to which he had formerly been bound ; and that, if the principal and professors accepted full charges as ministers, it might give the town and their parishes a share in electing them and controlling their work, which would be inconsistent with the welfare and privileges of the University. They therefore adopted a resolution against the principal or the professors of divinity holding office as ministers, though they were allowed to preach and administer the sacraments, so far as the moderators judged consistent with their academic duties.　They further declared that the College should be free to choose any qualified person to be principal or professor of divinity though he was not a minister at all.　A few weeks after this Ramsay died, and the office of principal was again left vacant.

It has been pointed out that Patrick Gillespie, one of the ministers of Glasgow, was on good terms with Cromwell, and that, as one of the leading remonstrants or protesters, he was in sharp antagonism to Baillie, who was conspicuous as a resolutioner.　But Cromwell was now in the ascendant, and the Commissioners whom he appointed for the government of Scotland resolved to nominate Gillespie to the office of principal, and sent an order to that effect to the moderators of the University.　When the rector, George Lockhart, commissary of Glasgow, communicated this order to a meeting of the moderators, Baillie says that John Young, James Veitch, and Richard Robertson were willing to accept Gillespie as principal, but the majority, consisting of George Young, dean of faculty, Zachary Boyd, vice-chancellor, Robert Baillie, and Patrick Young, protested against his admission.

In this state of matters the rector professed he had no vote, and acknowledged the faculty had declined to elect Gillespie, but said that as a private man he would support him.　Cromwell's Commissioners then wrote stating that they had been informed the moderators were not unanimous in desiring Gillespie's appointment, and that some were directly or indirectly opposing it, which might discourage him from accepting the office.　The Commissioners asked who were for and who against the appointment, and desired those who opposed it to give their reasons.　Baillie gave several reasons, alleging that the University had the privilege of electing a principal as well as other masters, that Gillespie was disqualified on account of his having been deposed from the ministry by the General Assembly, and that he did not possess the measure of learning necessary.　However, at a meeting of the faculty on 14th February, 1653, from which four members were absent, including the dean and Zachary Boyd, the latter being then on his deathbed, Baillie says that Gillespie explained that, though as yet he could not fully and finally accept the office of principal, he would offer till next meeting of the General Assembly to accept so much of the charge as was consistent with his ministry in the town, and to supervise the discipline of the College and do what else he was able. Gillespie then withdrew, and Baillie advised an adjournment till next day, pointing out that four members were absent, two of whom he alleged were not summoned, and urging that it was a new thing to have a principal in part and not fully, for a time and not finally—a principal with a full ministry in the town, and with no invitation from the College, but only invited by some private men, whose invitation a meeting of the faculty had declined to sustain. Baillie does not seem to have secured any support this time, and the rector having put the matter to the vote, it was decided to accept Gillespie, who was then called in to the meeting and inducted.

Baillie's objections were not frivolous, but they were hardly so strong as they looked at first sight. Gillespie's learning in the oriental languages with which the principal had to deal was probably not very great, and certainly far inferior to Baillie's. The deposition of Gillespie from the ministry by the General Assembly was a sinister fact, but no attempt seems to have been made to enforce it, and Gillespie having actually continued a minister for nearly two years, the sentence might be looked upon as having lost its force. According to a decision of the Court of Session afterwards given, the vice-chancellor had no right to sit and vote as an ordinary administrator, and if his vote were withdrawn from the so-called faculty meeting, the other votes recorded would have been equal, and the rector's vote, which was favourable to Gillespie, would have turned the scale. Baillie declared that it was a new thing to have a principal accepting office temporarily and under conditions, but if he had directed his attention to the case of Boyd of Trochrig in 1615, he would have found that it was not unprecedented, though it might not be very constitutional. The resolution of 1651 that no principal should have a full ministerial charge may have been partly intended to hinder Gillespie's appointment.

As for Baillie's contention that the moderators had a right to elect the principal, it would be hard to justify it either from the constitution or practice of the University; and after the Restoration, when his own turn came to be a candidate for the office, he entirely discarded this doctrine, and actively solicited a presentation from the crown in his own favour. It will be noted that Gillespie undertook, with some reservations, to carry on the work of principal till next General Assembly. However, the Assembly never had an opportunity of considering or deciding the case, for it had no sooner met in July, 1653, than it was summarily dismissed by

ZACHARY BOYD

Minister of Barony Parish, Glasgow

A liberal benefactor of the University, and sometime Rector and Vice-Chancellor

BORN circa 1585. DIED 1653

From oil painting in the Senate Room, University of Glasgow

Colonel Cotterel, supported by a troop of horse and a company of musketeers, and did not meet again till after the Revolution.

Gillespie signalised himself as a builder. Strang had done something considerable in this way, but Gillespie far excelled him in the boldness and magnitude of his undertakings. Shortly after his appointment he entered on a great scheme of renovation and extension of the University buildings, and he pressed it forward, as Baillie thought, with energetic prodigality. In the three years from January, 1654, till December, 1656, a sum of £28,034 Scots had been expended, the outlay at that time exceeding the income by £334. Two years later the total expenditure had risen to £35,857, being this time about £4 within the income. Gillespie had subscribed £600 to the building fund, Baillie and John Young £200 each, James Veitch, regent, £80, and the other regents, Patrick Young, Andrew Burnett, and George Sinclair, £66 13s. 4d. each. In January, 1656, the moderators, with a view to prevent the interruption of the work which was sometimes likely to occur, owing to the sums destined to the purpose not being punctually paid, resolved that money might be borrowed from time to time as the necessity of the work required, but not to a greater amount than 5,000 marks; and that the principal and interest of the borrowed money should be repaid, either from the first and readiest portion of the rents due to the University, or from the sums mortified for building. They also put on record that 1,000 marks had already been borrowed from George Murdoch and 600 marks from Mrs. Binney, which sums were to be reckoned as part of the 5,000 marks authorised to be borrowed, and were to be paid in the manner laid down.

The death of Cromwell and the unsettled condition of the country which followed hindered the work, of which a considerable portion still awaited completion. In December, 1659, the moderators, considering that several sums were owing to workmen and for furniture, and that from want of the execution of the law they could not then recover the moneys which should be available, passed resolutions to safeguard sums already lent by certain of the masters. At the preceding Martinmas, Gillespie had lent 5,000 marks, Baillie 500, John Young 500, and Andrew Burnett and George Sinclair 250 marks each, all to aid in defraying the expenses of the buildings. It was now resolved that these loans should be repaid with interest when funds were available; and that, should any one of the lenders leave his charge in the College or be removed from it before repayment, he should have a right to payment before the others. Up to Martinmas, 1660, a further sum of nearly £5,000 had been spent.

It is not known who was the architect either in Strang's or Gillespie's

I

time ; but, as the work was in progress about thirty years, there may have been several successive architects, though the structure showed uniformity of design   The completed buildings had extensive grounds adjoining, and were of a quaint, old-fashioned style of architecture, with windows and gables everywhere prominent, and consisted of three ranges parallel to High Street, enclosing a larger inner court or quadrangle and a smaller outer one, the middle range between the two courts having a tall steeple, bearing a clock made by a Glasgow blacksmith.   The steeple and some parts of the buildings about the inner and outer courts were reared in Gillespie's time, and towards the end of it the buildings fronting High Street, in particular the fore hall, the principal's house, and the gateway and arch leading from High Street into the outer quadrangle.   Houses for Baillie and John Young, the two professors of divinity, were also included.   Towards the end of 1658 Baillie wrote that his house had been cast down by Gillespie, to make room for a new and more showy one with worse accommodation.   He complained that for a year he would be very badly accommodated, and added that he bore these things because he could not help it.   An entry in the accounts for 1657 shows that Baillie had a stable which was thatched with straw.

Principal Strang and Zachary Boyd had been close friends, and probably Boyd's friendship for the principal first enlisted his interest in the University, while afterwards the high offices he held as rector, dean of faculty, and vice-chancellor, confirmed that interest, and, as he remained childless notwithstanding two marriages, determined him to leave the great bulk of his property to the University.   The death of Boyd about the time Gillespie became principal opened the prospect of coming into possession of his bequests, while a sum of £1,000 left by Thomas Hutcheson of Lambhill for building purposes had accumulated at interest till it had nearly doubled, and 2,000 marks bequeathed by John and Robert Fleming were to be available when a certain amount of progress had been made with the work of erection.

These circumstances and the favour in which he stood with Cromwell encouraged Gillespie to give rein to his ambition and proceed with a building scheme on a large scale.   Further sums of considerable amount were received within the next six or seven years.   The £200 sterling promised by Charles I. in 1633 was paid by order of Cromwell in 1654, and the 1,000 marks promised by the Marquis of Hamilton in 1631 was paid in 1656. The Commissioners for the Government of Scotland for some time contributed £20 sterling a month, while in 1659 a further contribution of £500 sterling from them was being paid in instalments, and next year the Town Council subscribed £1,000.   Considerable grants were also made from the stipends of vacant parishes—among them the Barony, Sorbie, Galston, and Whithorn.

Of all the donors to the building fund, Zachary Boyd was the most munificent. He was educated at the Universities of Glasgow and St. Andrews, and was some time a regent in the protestant College at Saumur in France, where his cousin, Boyd of Trochrig, afterwards principal at Glasgow, then held a chair. Having returned to Scotland, he was in 1623 appointed minister of the large suburban district of Glasgow known as the Barony parish, and soon began to take an active interest in University affairs. He was several times elected rector and dean of faculty, and for a long time held office as vice-chancellor, sitting and voting as an ordinary administrator without any further qualification, though this was probably not constitutional. At first he refused to take the Covenant in 1638, but afterwards he consented and signed. When Cromwell came to Glasgow a few weeks after his victory at Dunbar, the magistrates fled before him, as did also most of the ministers, but Boyd remained and preached in the High Church. Baillie escaped to the Island of Cumbrae, leaving, how-ever, his family and goods to the courtesy of Cromwell, which he acknow-ledges to have been great, for he kept his soldiers so well under control 'that they did less displeasure at Glasgow than if they had been at London, though Mr. Zachary Boyd railed on them all to their very face in the High Church.' Cromwell listened with patience to the preacher's invective, and having afterwards sought an interview, is said to have overwhelmed Boyd, not by physical force, but by a prayer of two or three hours' duration.

Boyd tried what Fielding calls the trade of 'authoring,' his chief prose work, bearing the rather funereal title of *The Last Battel of the Soule in Death*, being of an allegorical and dramatic nature, giving a kind of fore-taste of Bunyan; while his metrical effusions—mostly very uninspired versions of Scripture—were named *Zion's Flowers*. But such as they were, Boyd was unwilling that his works should be allowed to die, and he left triple instructions with his legatees for their being printed. For this purpose, which was to be faithfully carried out at the sight of the faculty, he assigned in January, 1648, in favour of the College 4,000 marks, being part of a bond for 6,000 marks granted to him by Lord Loudon. Having perhaps become distrustful of Loudon, in December of the same year he assigned to the College, to be employed for printing his works at the sight of Lord Boyd, the ministers of Glasgow and the Barony, and the laird of Glanderston, 5,000 marks due to him under a bond by the Earl of Glencairn.

In December, 1652, a few months before his death, Boyd executed a

more lengthened and detailed settlement, under which, 'for my guid affec-
tioune to the advancement of pietie and learning, and my singular respect
to the florisching of the Universitie and Colledge of Glasgow,' he mortified
and disponed to it the sums due to him under a number of bonds, namely,
6,000 marks by Lord Loudon, 5,000 marks by the Earl of Glencairn, 8,000
marks by Sir William Muir, elder of Rowallan, 3,000 marks by Sir George
Maxwell of Nether Pollok, £500 due by George Ross of Broomhill, and
900 marks by the Estates of Scotland, with all the other debts and sums
of money, 'bookis, guids and geir quhatsumewer' pertaining to him.
He reserved his own life-interest, as well as the life-interest of his second
wife (Margaret Muir, third daughter of the laird of Glanderston), in the
sums of money secured to her by her marriage contract or by bonds in
which her name was mentioned, and directed that payment should be made
to her of 3,000 marks owing under a bond by Sir William Muir, younger
of Rowallan, in satisfaction 'to hir of the lyk sowme of hir tocher obleeist
to be refoundit to hir be our contract of marriage'; and some small
bequests were made to acquaintances and servants.

Boyd specially provided that out of the readiest of the sums made over
to them, the principal, professors, and masters should expend a sufficient
amount to print an edition of a thousand copies of his works in a folio
volume ; and that all the rest of the money should be employed for the
new buildings of the College, 'quhairof he that is cheiff of the name of
Boyd sall hawe his choyce of the best two chalmers it sall pleiss him to
choyce, and that he hawe power of the keyes to bestow them upone any he
pleaseth, they being studentis in the said Colledge.' The testator desired
that Dr. John Strang and Mr. Robert Baillie should revise his manuscripts, giving them a certain discretion what to print, and for their
encouragement offered them the whole edition ; but in case Strang and
Baillie declined the work of revision, he empowered the University
to appoint one or more able, godly, and learned men to act in their
stead.

After Boyd's death in March or April, 1653, the University thought
it advisable to come to an understanding with his next of kin, who probably
would not much like the settlement ; and in consideration of a payment of
a thousand marks, they agreed not to raise objections, and to take any steps
deemed requisite to corroborate the rights of the College. The question
remained of making a settlement with Boyd's widow, who did not long
remain in the single state. It is said that she endeavoured to persuade her
first husband to remember in his will Mr. James Durham. She failed in
this benevolent effort, but when Zachary Boyd was no more, after a swift
courtship she became the wife of Durham. In February, 1655, the

College resolved to pay her seven years' purchase of the life-rent to which she was entitled, amounting to fully 7,000 marks, so that the remainder might be available for building purposes.

In February, 1655, the moderators ordained that a marble statue of Boyd should be placed in a suitable part of the new buildings, and by and by the statue was erected over the gateway within the College court, with an inscription commemorating Boyd's munificence to the University in founding three bursaries for students of theology and contributing so liberally to the funds for new buildings. Still nothing was done, and there is no evidence that anything was attempted, to carry out Boyd's desire to have his works printed.

The building scheme was foremost in the thoughts of the University administrators, and to it they postponed the printing scheme which had been foremost in the thoughts of Boyd. There is reason to believe that they contemplated publication when the bond of 6,000 marks due by the Earl of Loudon could be realised; but Loudon, from having been the Chancellor of Scotland, had fallen into poverty and disrepute. An ineffectual attempt was made to enforce payment in 1657, and in a decreet of poynding issued fully twenty years later, it was stated that no interest had been paid from 1657 to 1676. The second Earl, against whom the decreet of poynding was obtained, went abroad and died at Leyden in 1684, and no part of the 6,000 marks was ever recovered. This failure to secure payment of Loudon's bond may perhaps be held to free the University administrators from the imputation of intentional breach of trust in regard to the publication of Boyd's works, but it is not a complete defence, especially as Boyd provided that the printing should be done with the readiest of the sums he bequeathed. But, except as a miscarriage of justice between a munificent donor and his beneficiaries, the failure to publish need not be much regretted.

Cromwell was-friendly to the University, and called Gillespie to London shortly after his appointment as principal, to discuss the affairs of the University and probably other affairs bearing on the state of the country. Gillespie remained eleven months in London, and seems to have lived in a good style, for the College paid one pound sterling a day for his personal expenses, with £50 sterling for other expenses, and he received £150 sterling from his own party, the Protesters, and a further sum from the town of Glasgow, for representing their interests or negotiating for them with the government of the Commonwealth, besides £200 sterling from Cromwell himself. The thrifty and frugal nature of his rival, Baillie, was irritated and scandalised at the principal's sumptuous manner of living, and he declared that never bishop in Scotland lived at so high a rate.   However, Cromwell's benefactions flowed in upon the institution as well as the individual.

On 4th August, 1654, he issued an ordinance providing that the sums of money mortified to the University, as well as the portion of the University revenues payable from the estates of persons under sentence of fine or forfeiture, should still be paid to the University in as ample a manner as formerly.   On the 8th of the same month the Lord Protector, considering 'the great advantage which may redound to the people of this commonwealth inhabiting in Scotland that the Universities there should receive both countenance and encouragement and be provided for with competent mainteynance for the members of the said Universities, for the better training up of youth in pietie and good literature,' granted to the University of Glasgow the superiorities of the lands belonging to the late bishopric of Galloway, the abbeys of Tungland and Glenluce, and the priory of Whithorn, with the feu-duties, customs, and casualties pertaining to them, as well as the superiorities of their parsonage and vicarage teinds, excepting the superiority of the deanery of the Chapel of Stirling ; and further granted 200 marks sterling yearly from the customs of Glasgow for the education of pious and hopeful young men who were students of theology and philosophy in the University.   On 17th November, 1654, a charter under the great seal, expressed at somewhat greater length, confirmed the grants made by the ordinance of 8th August preceding, and set forth that the principal, professors, and regents should pay yearly at Whitsunday 'ane Scots pennie in name of blench dewtie,' 'if it be asked allanerlie.'   There was another ordinance of the Protector respecting the bishopric of Galloway, with its abbeys and priory, which, besides recording the grant, ordained that the Commissioners for visiting Universities and Schools should take special care that none but godly and able men were authorised to enjoy the livings of the ministry, respect being had to the choice of the more sober and godly part of the people, though they might not be the majority.   The ordinance did not explain how the more sober and godly part were to be discriminated from the rest.

With the exception of the allowance from the customs of Glasgow, these grants were mainly reiterations of earlier ones made by Charles I. ; but on 8th July, 1657, the Protector by a charter under the great seal confirmed all previous grants in favour of the University, especially his own gift of the bishopric of Galloway, with its abbeys and priory ; and further granted the revenue up to a limit of £200 sterling a year of the deanery and subdeanery of Glasgow, with the churches and benefices of Hamilton, Monkland, Campsie, Killearn, Luss, Cardross, Erskine, Glasgow, Ayr, Tarbolton, Cumnock, Cambuslang, Douglas, Carstairs,

Eaglesham, Durisdeer, Morebattle, Stobo, Ettleston, Sanquhar, Roxburgh, Eskirk, Ancrum, and Kirkmahoe—all of them churches lately
belonging to the former dean and chapter of Glasgow—and the churches
of Peebles and Maybole, and the abbacy of Corseraguel in Carrick. He
also granted to the University the vacant stipends of the churches of which
the academic administrators were titulars, for the first year of vacancy, if it
should last so long, or for the whole of any shorter period ; confirmed the
immunities and exemptions granted by any Kings or Queens of Scotland ;
and declared that the University in all time coming should be free from all
tributes, collections, and taxations, ordinary and extraordinary, imposed
or to be imposed.

The Protector likewise conferred the right of printing bibles in any
language, ' with all sortes of buikes relating to the faculties of theologie,
jurisprudence, medicin, philosophie, philologie, and all other buikes what-
sumever, the same being ordoured and priviledged to the presse be our
said Universitie, or any persone to be named be the said Universitie.' If
the commonwealth had stood, the liberty of printing might have been
valuable, and the conditions do not seem to have made it imperative that
the University should directly maintain a printing press, but rather appear
to have allowed any book to be printed under privilege if ordered by the
University, though an outside printer might do the work. On 9th
September, 1658, only six days after the death of his father, Richard
Cromwell granted out of the College revenues an addition of a hundred
pounds sterling a year to Principal Gillespie's salary ; and, conditionally on
the revenue formerly belonging to the dean and chapter of Glasgow yielding a sufficient amount, ordained that it should contribute a further sum
of £100 to the University, besides the £200 already provided for. On
29th November following, the moderators approved of this augmentation
of the principal's salary, having heard his own free offer renouncing the
benefit of the gratuity to be allowed him under a resolution passed in
June, 1656, for settling the affairs of the bishopric of Galloway.

These affairs required a good deal of settlement. Early in 1656 the
moderators, Baillie himself included, put on record an acknowledgment
that they owed Cromwell's gift of the bishopric to Gillespie's diligence
and mediation, and desired that he would bestir himself to make the gift
effectual. They also requested and authorised him to endeavour to put
the College in orderly and legal possession of the superiority of the lands
included in the gift, and, in return for the expenses he had lately incurred
in the service of the College and those to be occasioned in the prospective
settlements, granted him half of the profits that might accrue from the
entry of vassals to the bishopric. The negotiations extended over a con-

siderable time, for in April, 1658, the moderators commissioned Gillespie to treat in their name and conclude with all parties interested, and in view of the work involved exempted him from his other duties, especially from prelections on theology.   Two or three years before, they allowed Gillespie on account of the pressure of business to choose an amanuensis from among the students of divinity.   In 1656 the augmentations of the bishopric appear to have yielded about £358 sterling, and the compositions received from the entries of vassals from 1654 to 1660 amounted to £2,461 sterling.

Some other transactions concerning teinds and kindred matters may be mentioned here.   Following on a decree that had been pronounced in the case, John Stewart of Balshagray granted in 1655 a charter to the College for an annual payment of thirty-six bolls of oatmeal and forty-four shillings and twopence in money from his lands of Whiteinch Meadow, Hyndland, Balgray, and Balshagray.   The same year the College excambed the lands of Ballagan, of which the Buchanans had long been tenants, to Sir John Colquhoun of Luss for a payment of meal along with a feu-duty of £12.   In 1659 the University purchased from Anna, Duchess of Hamilton, her right to the teinds of Calder and Monkland. The Duchess' right seems to have hindered the University from reaping the full benefit of the subdeanery of Glasgow bestowed by Cromwell in 1657, and hence it was considered advisable to purchase the teinds, and to invest in them the funds belonging to the Wilsone, Boyd, and Struthers bursaries.   Next year the gentlemen freeholders of Lanarkshire ordered their collector to suspend exacting from the College the cess of the tithes of Calder and Monkland.   A new claimant appeared, however, in the person of Lord Kilmarnock, who after some time agreed to withdraw his claim on receiving a sum of money to be determined by the Provost of Glasgow and the Bishop of the Isles.   These arbiters awarded him 10,000 marks Scots, and Kilmarnock made over his rights to the University.   Finally, in 1664, by a charter under the great seal, Charles II. granted to the University the patronage of the churches of Calder and Monkland, with their teinds and emoluments, constituting the subdeanery of Glasgow, which had been resigned into his hands by the Duke and Duchess of Hamilton.

In June, 1651, the moderators declared it expedient that the stipends of the principal, professors, and regents should be fixed and certain, and ordained that in future they should be in accordance with a report made by the Visitors of the General Assembly and Parliament which had been ratified by the Assembly in 1650, and that none of them should have any further claim founded on bygone right or custom.   They also laid down

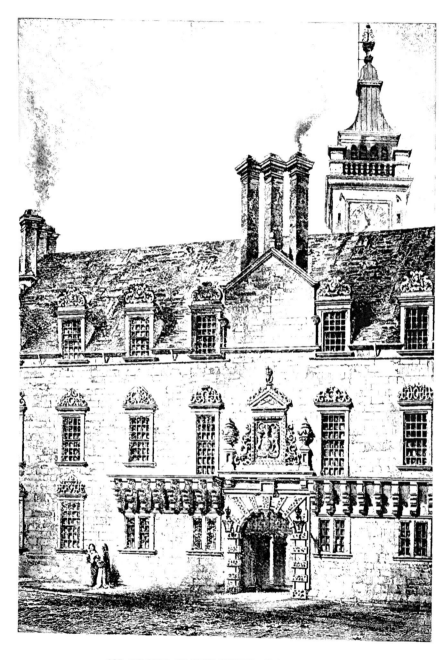

OLD COLLEGE IN HIGH STREET—MAIN ENTRANCE

From Drawing by R. W. Billings

that the board of the regents should be defrayed for the whole year from the College funds; and that, for the breeding of the youth who dined at the College table and the keeping of good order there, it was necessary that the principal should in all time coming diet at the College table, having his board defrayed at the public expense, like the regents, and having, also like the regents, an allowance for the two months of the vacation at the same rate as for the rest of the year.

The cost of the College table increased very considerably during the first fifty or sixty years of the seventeenth century. In 1608 a sum of £30 Scots per quarter was allowed for the board of each master, and £16 13s. 4d. for that of each bursar, the purveyor being further allowed £30 for fuel and ten marks for the cook's fee. In 1658 an agreement was made for the maintenance of three tables—one for the principal and four regents, at £54 Scots each per quarter; a second for bursars in theology, at fifty marks each per quarter; and a third for bursars in philosophy, at £24 each per quarter; and a further payment of £90 for servants' fees, linen, and fuel. Baillie grumbled against these lavish arrangements, as he considered them, declaring that the masters used to have the best table in the country without paying more than fifty marks a quarter.

There was a rule in those days that each bursar should give a silver spoon or its equivalent in money 'for upholding the plenishing of the house.' Previously the value of the spoon amounted to £5 5s. Scots, but by 1649 it had risen to £5 10s., and by 1653 to ten marks. In 1655 it was ordained that students of philosophy maintained from the endowment derived from the customs of Glasgow should also give a silver spoon, seeing they had fully as good an allowance as other bursars.

Cromwell's bursaries from the customs of the Tron proved to be only of a temporary character, but Zachary Boyd founded three bursaries in theology, and the foundation made by Thomas Hutcheson in 1641 for a librarian was ultimately converted to a bursary, while the foundation made about the same time by Margaret Graham for the encouragement and reward of a student of theology who recorded special providences, soon failed from loss of the capital fund. For Boyd's bursaries £2,000 Scots was made over to the Town Council for maintaining two bursars, and £1,000 to the dean of guild and Council of the Merchant rank for maintaining the third. Though founded in 1635, the bursaries did not come into operation till after Boyd's death in 1653.

In 1655 it was enacted that bursars in theology, as well as those in philosophy, should at their entry pay ten marks Scots for increasing the stock of books in the public library; in return for which they were to have access to the library, but not to be allowed to carry books out of it. In

1659 a regulation was laid down for a levy for behoof of the library to be exacted from students generally, excepting only such as were poor and lived upon charity. For this purpose students were divided into three ranks, the first rank being ordered to pay six shillings sterling at matriculation and five shillings at examination; the second rank three shillings at matriculation and the same sum at examination; and the third rank two shillings at matriculation and two at examination; while every graduand was to pay at least ten marks at the time of laureation, and for extraordinary or private laureation £36 at least.

Each person who presented himself for examination or laureation when he came to the Black Stone was required to bring the quaestor's certificate that he had paid at the rate appropriate to him. So far as I know, this is the earliest mention now extant of the Black Stone which was associated with examinations for the next two hundred years, and may probably have been in use long before 1659. Latterly this stone, a piece of black marble, formed the seat of a chair on which the candidate sat whilst under examination, but there is no evidence that in the earlier times it formed part of a chair. Candidates undergoing examination may have stood upon this stone, so mysterious in its origin, and, to many generations of students, so fateful in its associations.

Early in 1655 the moderators remarked on the ingratitude of many of the students towards the regents and the loss sustained by the latter on account of students neglecting to pay their 'schollages.' It was said that no little 'deboshing' had arisen from some students keeping back the money received from their parents to make these payments, and applying it 'to their own particular and oftymes profane uses.' A strict regulation was enacted for payment of 'schollages' in future, at the rate of twelve shillings Scots per quarter for students of the first rank, six shillings for students of the second rank, and four shillings for students of the third rank; but the regents were forbidden to exact payment from poor students who could not maintain themselves or did so with difficulty. Further, out of regard to the Town Council and the kindly feelings which should subsist between the city and the University, the moderators determined that sons of citizens and burgesses should not be liable to pay at the rate laid down for others, but should pay only at such a rate as the Town Council and the moderators agreed upon after conference. Payment of fees by students was no new thing, for long before the Reformation, though other names might be used, the regulations provided for the payment of matriculation fees, class fees, and degree examination fees.

The bodies that transacted the business of the University during this period were not very clearly defined, and some individuals took part in the administration without being very fully warranted by the constitution, while indeed the name of the institution itself was very inconstant.   In the *Nova Erectio* the word University occurs only once, and that in a reference to the chancellor, and for the most part the word used is *Academia* or *Collegium*.   In documents of the period the principal and regents are often spoken of as belonging to the College, but perhaps almost as frequently as belonging to the College and University.   Sometimes we even come on such a designation as chancellor of the College.   The rector and dean are usually described as pertaining to the University, and yet both of them may be found in meetings of the faculty.   The word pedagogy is still occasionally applied to the institution.

A letter of Charles I. to members of the Privy Council recalls the slender estate of the Universities and Colleges of Scotland, and asks them to enquire and report on the subject.   A financial statement drawn up in 1637 in reference to this enquiry is headed 'Ane Information concerning the University and Colledge of Glasgow,' and there is no distinction between the property and revenue of the one and the other.   Charters and documents of the era of the Commonwealth use the word University rather than the word College ; and in 1661 Charles II. recommended the Privy Council to pay what sums they should find convenient for defraying the debts of the University of Glasgow for new buildings.

The records of meetings during this period are rather scanty, yet they disclose a medley of bodies, without system or clearly defined constitution, taking part in the business.   Ministers were inclined to claim rather a wide range for their activity, and as clergymen were frequently chosen to be rector and dean of faculty, and these high officers were wont to nominate assessors, more and more ministers were brought into the number of academic administrators.   The *Nova Erectio* also gave a footing to the minister of Glasgow as a visitor.   Now and again the chancellor took part in the business meetings, and for a long time the vice-chancellor did so. The Senate and the faculty, the two bodies which afterwards managed University and College affairs respectively, both come into view, but without the sharp distinction which was afterwards drawn between them.

Early in 1623 the whole senate of the academy (*senatus academiae universus*) laid down a regulation that no one should attain to office or dignity unless he took the oaths of supremacy and allegiance.   In 1642 at a meeting of the senate of the faculty (*senatu facultatis habito*) it was declared that those entitled to take part in the election of the dean and to be members of his court were the rector, the principal, the vice-chancellor, the professors of divinity, the ministers of the churches of Glasgow, urban and rural, the masters and regents, and the preceptor of the Grammar

School, and that out of these the dean, with the approval of the senate, should choose four assessors, of whose advice and assistance he should make use, referring to the senate itself in the more weighty affairs.

Under date 1st March, 1626, there is a record: '*Quo die in publica gymnasii aula habitis academiae comitiis*' at which there were present the chancellor, the rector, the dean of faculty, the principal '*reliquique magistri academiae et assessores rectoris, ab his adeoque senatu academiae universo . . . decretum est ut potestas concedendi ludendi veniam in gymnasio sit penes solum gymnasiarcham aut ejus vicarium.*' In this record there is a blending of the senate with the comitia, entirely out of keeping with later usage. In 1643 at a meeting of the council of the faculty of Arts ('*concilio facultatis artium habito*') a rule was laid down against receiving pupils from the Grammar School unless they had completed the full course there.

The Visitation of 1640 ordained that there should be a meeting of the faculty on the first Tuesday of every quarter. A body known as the faculty was gradually evolved which did not correspond to the faculty of Arts or any other faculty as the term is now understood, but which took part in general academic business. It would be hard to say whether some meetings that transacted important business should be regarded as comitia, congregation, council, senate or faculty—for instance, the meeting which in 1621 freed the principal from the ministry of Govan, and the meeting which in 1637 established a chair of medicine. It would have been well if the managing body of the University had been definitely constituted and duly authorised, rather than that it should be a body of fluctuating membership, frequently including individuals who had no clear right to take part in the proceedings.

Some writers have bewailed the departed grandeur of the University after the Reformation, and the pope's bull was certainly conceived in a more generous spirit than the *Nova Erectio*. On paper the bull authorised a large and noble organisation of the University and of its separate faculties; and conferred on the institution and its graduates the full franchises and privileges of the great academic brotherhood of Europe. In the period before the Reformation there were two or three regents in arts, and during part of it there were intermittent teachers in canon law, civil law, and theology. The *Nova Erectio* provided for three teachers in arts and one in divinity, but they rose to five in arts and three in divinity, and a chair of medicine was added in 1637. The number of students greatly increased, the University came to possess property and revenues which, though still inadequate, compared favourably with those of the period before the Reformation, and its buildings were vastly improved and extended. The earlier scheme was a grand one, but it was only very partially realised ; the later scheme was a modest one, but it was much more than realised. Judged by the standard of life and work, there was no need for wailing over departed grandeur in the second century of the institution as compared with the first.

III. 1660–1688.

The twenty-eight years from the Restoration to the Revolution were not years of plenty or of progress in the University. The number of students did not fall short of the average for the preceding generation, and during the earlier part of the time the number of graduates was also fully maintained. But the re-establishment of episcopacy withdrew a large part of the revenues which the University had enjoyed for the last twenty years, Gillespie's lavish expenditure on building left a heavy burden of debts behind, while near the end of his tenure he demolished a portion of the old buildings without rearing new ones to replace them, and this work had to be done by his successors.

The lessened income occasioned a reduction in the number of the teaching staff, and the distracted state of civil and ecclesiastical affairs in Scotland would probably have caused a reduction in the number of students also, but the strict tests in the English Universities attracted not a few English students to Glasgow, and there were also some Irish and a few foreign students. After the death of Baillie the most notable men connected with the University during this period were Gilbert Burnet, the historian, who was professor of divinity from 1669 till 1674, and Archbishop Leighton, who held the office of chancellor for a few years about the same time. George Sinclair, one of the regents, also deserves mention as an early and by no means a barren worker in the field of engineering and applied science.

Patrick Gillespie had been in high favour with Cromwell, had received considerable grants from him, had preached in his presence in London and the neighbourhood sermons which after the Restoration were deemed seditious, and had prayed for him as supreme magistrate. When Charles II. regained his throne these things counted against Gillespie, as well as his share in the Western Remonstrance and *The Causes of God's Wrath*, and worst of all his arrogant and offensive bearing towards Charles himself when the latter was in Scotland in 1650 and 1651, of which the king retained a lively and somewhat vengeful recollection. He had also come to be on ill terms with the civic as well as the national authorities, for his ostentatious and meddlesome disposition led him to interfere with the Town Council election in 1658, and to stir up trouble with the town over the appointment of a successor to the Reverend James Durham, who died that year. Yet for a time there was some expectation that Gillespie might be allowed to continue as principal, and in some measure he began to suit his demeanour to the new circumstances. Conscious that he himself was not in favour, he sent his wife to London in June, 1660, to offer his humble duty to the king, and to solicit from him for her husband a pardon and continuance in the office of principal. Mrs. Gillespie was related to John, sixth Lord Sinclair, a Covenanter who had afterwards turned Engager and Royalist, and seems to have had considerable influence ; and Gillespie had some trust in Lauderdale, for whom when a prisoner he had done some good offices with Lambert.

Baillie, who now aspired to be principal, wrote to Lauderdale warning him against the persuasions of Mrs. Gillespie, adding—'You are too wise to be enchanted by the siren's song.' Mrs. Gillespie received no countenance in London, and had to return with her mission unaccomplished. In August, 1660, Lauderdale replied that, so far from pleading for Gillespie, he had obtained a grant for another to be principal, and waited only for a formal presentation from the king. However, the matter was not settled immediately, and at the beginning of 1661 Baillie wrote to Sharp, afterwards the apostate Archbishop of St. Andrews, claiming that after Dr. Strang's death the first place in the College was due to himself, and referring to efforts made by John Young, his colleague as professor of divinity, to procure the place. Baillie disliked Gillespie much, but he disliked Young more, and declared—'I could ever have lived rather with Mr. Gillespie than with him, and if he should be the man, I think I would leave the house and go to a country church.' However, Baillie's ambition was gratified, and on 23rd January, 1661, the king granted a warrant appointing him principal.

Baillie states that Gillespie was removed to prison on 1st October, 1660, for his crimes against the State, and Wodrow that he was imprisoned in Stirling Castle. But if he was in a regular prison, it can only have been for a short time. He had so many powerful friends that he was mildly treated, and, though perhaps nominally a prisoner, was allowed to live for a year in the principal's house. Indeed so far was he from being alarmed or overawed, that he kept closely in his possession a charter chest with the College writs and a number of books and documents, and positively refused to surrender them till a settlement was made. On 25th September, 1660, Gillespie's stipend was arrested by order of the Committee of Estates, on the ground that he had refused to sign a bond for keeping the peace and disowning the Remonstrance, and was otherwise guilty of seditious and dangerous practices.

On 6th March, 1661, he appeared before the parliament in Edinburgh to answer the charges made against him. He made a fair speech by way of vindication; gave the sense in which he interpreted the *Western Remonstrance* and *The Causes of God's Wrath*; admitted that he had received money from Cromwell, but declared that it was all for University uses, and that he had not put a farthing into his own pocket, and pleaded that draining the usurper's coffers for so good an end could be no disservice to the king. The *Caledonian Mercury* of that time gives a friendly and apologetic account of Gillespie's appearance before parliament, declaring it was a pity such a man should be ensnared in mistakes, for he was generous and public-spirited, as was shown by his improvement of the University of Glasgow by enlarging the fabric and increasing the bursaries. If there was merit in fanatics of either kind, the *Mercury* judged this man had the larger share.

He appeared again before the parliament towards the end of May; renounced the *Protestation* and some expressions in *The Causes of God's Wrath* and *Lex Rex*; acknowledged that he had given offence to His Majesty by the *Remonstrance* and otherwise, which he now regretted and disclaimed; and therefore cast himself on the king's mercy, humbly desiring the Commissioner and the parliament to proffer his petition to His Majesty.

The length to which he had gone in the way of confession and supplication was a great grief to the more steadfast Protesters with whom he had previously been associated. Rutherford on his deathbed bewailed Gillespie's falling off from his former testimony, and James Guthrie, who had now come within the shadow of the scaffold, exclaimed—'And hath he suffered so much in vain, if it be yet in vain!' But he had done penance to such an extent as to enable Lord Sinclair and other powerful friends to induce parliament to deal tenderly with him as compared with others whose offence was not greater. He seems to have come to an understanding with the College authorities that his emolument should be paid till Candlemas, 1661; but on 12th July, the last day of the session, parliament ordered that he should receive the arrears of his office and service up to Whitsunday of that year.

The moderators of the College were surprised and indignant, and in September they presented a petition to the Privy Council, setting forth that parliament had appointed a Commission of Visitation, but they could not be prepared to receive the Commission without their charter chest and documents; that the king had declared Gillespie never had a right to be principal, but was an intruder by the power of the late usurpers, and had conferred the office and emoluments on another, who could not obtain them without deliverance of the College writs and principal's lodging, which Gillespie refused to deliver, though often importuned to do so. The petition also complained that, in virtue of the clauses he had obtained from parliament, Gillespie laid claim to more than nine thousand marks, though he had left the College overwhelmed with debt, so that they had been unable that year to keep a table, and none of the masters had received two-pence of his stipend. The petitioners desired that Gillespie should be ordered to deliver the College writs and the house he occupied, and, till the claims had been further investigated, that the Privy Council would suspend the execution of the order he had obtained.

There can be little doubt that the wrath of Baillie speaks through this petition. The Privy Council granted warrant to Gillespie to proceed to Edinburgh to answer the petition, notwithstanding his confinement or being under restraint, and appointed the Lord President of the Court of Session and the Lord Register as impartial auditors, with the Lord Chancellor as oversman, to hear the differences of the parties and if possible to settle them. After this Gillespie appears to have surrendered his house and the charter chest, and the parties to have moderated their hostilities and gradually found their way to some arrangement. A form of discharge by Gillespie, dated 1664, with blanks for the day and month of signature and for some other particulars, has been preserved, and probably indicates the terms on which a settlement was reached. It bore to be a discharge by Gillespie to the moderators of the University for the arrears due to him, granted in consequence of their having made him their assignee to the sum of 4,000 marks, the equal half of a sum of 8,000 marks, due to them by the deceased Earl of Loudon, and certain annual rents specified in the assignation. The 4,000 marks were doubtless part of the money due by Loudon under the bond to Zachary Boyd, which was accumulating in amount owing to the interest not being paid, and, as neither principal nor interest of this loan ever was paid, it must have been a barren bargain for Gillespie.

Baillie had now attained his ambition to be principal of the University, but his tenure of office was short and troubled. Though a Covenanter, he had ever been a warm Royalist, and he rejoiced at the king's restoration, but the overthrow of the Presbyterian Church and the re-establishment of Episcopacy wounded his spirit, broke his health, and hastened his death. His vexation was all the greater because these changes were in a great measure brought about by men like Sharp and Lauderdale, with whom he had long been in friendly alliance, and in whose integrity and steadfast-less he vainly trusted. On general public grounds he lamented the alterations made in the Church, but as the head of an institution sorely burdened with debt, he had further reason to regret the revival of prelacy, inasmuch as it withdrew from the University the revenues of the bishopric of Galloway with its abbeys and priory, which had been of great service during the preceding twenty years.

Presbytery was not immediately overturned, indeed in August, 1660, the king declared his intention to protect and preserve the government of the Church as settled by law, and to call a General Assembly as soon as practicable; but in the earlier months of the year 1661, the 'drunken parliament,' as it was called, made the king absolute, and by a sweeping rescissory act cancelled all the legislation of the preceding twenty-eight years. The result was that the laws on which the Presbyterian polity rested were abolished; and at a meeting of the Privy Council held in Edinburgh on 5th September, 1661, a letter from Charles was read intimating his firm resolution to restore the 'Church to its right government by bishops, as it was by law before the late troubles, during the reigns of our royal father and grandfather of blessed memory.' In December following Fairfowl, Hamilton, Sharp, and Leighton, four Presbyterian ministers, met in London to be created bishops, and bring back with them to Scotland the apostolic succession. The two first had been ordained during the time Scotland was under Episcopacy, and passed for clergymen in the view of English churchmen; but Sharp and Leighton had been ordained by the laying on of the hands of the Presbytery, which was considered unapostolic and ineffective, and so they had to submit to be made clergymen *de novo*. Hamilton was appointed to the see of Galloway, Fairfowl to Glasgow, Sharp to St. Andrews, and Leighton—who on the return journey wearied of the company of his brother bishops and left them at Morpeth—to Dunblane and afterwards to Glasgow.

On 19th April, 1662, Fairfowl as Bishop of Glasgow made his public entry into the city, accompanied by the Earl of Glencairn—who then enjoyed the double distinction of being chancellor of the kingdom and chancellor of the University—and a number of nobility and gentry, and was received by the citizens and magistrates. Though a man of boisterous mirth and careless life, he preached on the first Sunday 'soberly and well,' according to Baillie. It was proposed that the chancellor and the bishop should have a collation in the College on the Monday, and though Baillie reasoned much against the needless outlay which this would involve, he was outvoted. The collation took place, and it is said that £200 did not pay the expense. John Young, the professor of divinity, made a speech of welcome to the distinguished visitors, without the knowledge of Baillie,

K

who was confined to his room by an illness which proved fatal in the month of August following. Glencairn brought the bishop and others of the company to see the principal, and Baillie regaled them with the best sac and ale in the town, but excused himself from addressing Fairfowl as ' my lord.' About a year before this Baillie had written to Lauderdale declaring that, if the latter had advised the king to the measures then being pursued in regard to the Church, Baillie counted him 'a prime transgressor and liable among the first to answer to God for that great sin ; and the opening of a door, which in haste will not be closed, for the persecution of a multitude of the best persons and most loyal subjects that are in all the three kingdoms.'

Baillie had been pleading with Lauderdale and others for aid to the funds of the University, which was now loaded with debts and deprived of a great part of its previous endowments, but he did not live to see any substantial relief afforded. It is curious to find, however, that while the change in the ecclesiastical establishment alienated a large portion of the revenue of the University, it also led to a great number of parishes being left without ministers for a longer or shorter time, and it was from the vacant stipends thus occasioned that the first crumbs of financial relief were procured. The University having petitioned the king for aid in paying off the debts incurred for buildings newly erected, and providing the funds required to defray the cost of buildings still awaiting completion, Charles on 17th August, 1661, recommended the Privy Council to order payment for these purposes of such a portion of the vacant stipends as they should find convenient. It was in the south-western shires, where the doctrines of the Protesters prevailed, that the vacancies fell thickest.

In 1649 parliament abolished patronage in the Church, and the Assembly conferred the right of election on the kirk session, and from 1649 to 1660 ministers had been elected under this arrangement. An act was now passed declaring that these ministers had no right to their livings, and must before 20th September, 1662, receive presentation from their patrons and collation from the bishops, or else demit their appointments. The ministers in the diocese of Glasgow did not comply, and Middleton, the lord high commissioner, the Earls of Glencairn, Morton, Linlithgow, and other Privy Councillors, came to the west to concert further measures. In the forehall of the College of Glasgow the Privy Council met on 1st October, 1662, declared the churches vacant, prohibited the ministers from exercising any part of their ministry, and required them to remove from their parishes by 1st November following. The time was afterwards extended to 1st February, 1663, but nearly three hundred ministers, mostly in the south and west of Scotland, relinquished their livings rather than submit.   A hue and cry was sent over the country and men of indifferent character and training were accepted to fill the vacant offices, but many of the charges remained unfilled, and for a number of years after this we hear of grants from vacant stipends.

In dealing with the king's recommendation for aid to the University, the Privy Council consulted Burnet, who had succeeded Fairfowl as Archbishop of Glasgow, and Burnet reported that the College was specially interested in the churches of Renfrew, Govan, Kilbride, Calder, Easter and Wester Monkland, and Dalziel, and earnestly desired that the vacant stipends of these parishes should be assigned to it.   The Council then granted a warrant for the application of the bygone vacant stipends of these parishes to the payment of the building debts and completion of the University buildings.   In October of the same year, parliament passed an act making a further contribution of £600 sterling out of the vacant stipends of the diocese of Glasgow to be applied to the same purposes, and it was then stated that the debts amounted to about £1,100 sterling.

The lessened funds from which the University suffered after the Restoration led to a reduction in the teaching staff, which did not regain its full strength till after the Revolution.   The chair of medicine was discontinued (though it would be unfair to blame the Restoration for this, seeing that the Visitors from the General Assembly in 1642 declared for its discontinuance); the chair of humanity remained dormant till after the Revolution, except for a fitful interval of revival for some years after 1682; and after Baillie was made principal there was no attempt to appoint a second professor of divinity.   The principal, a single professor of divinity, and four regents in arts made up the teaching staff.

An act of parliament was passed in June, 1662, declaring it was necessary that principals, professors, and regents in Universities should be well affected to the king and the established government in Church and State, and that for the future none should be admitted to these offices or allowed to continue in them but such as were of pious, loyal, and peaceable conversation, submitting to and owning the government of the Church by archbishops and bishops.   The principal, professors, and regents at Glasgow were to have the sanction of the archbishop, and to take the oath of allegiance in his presence.   The act also provided that none should afterwards be permitted to preach in public or in families, or to teach in public schools or act as tutors to children of persons of quality, without license from the ordinary of the diocese.

We have no record of immediate compliance being required from professors at Glasgow, but in July, 1663, Robert Erskine demitted his office as regent, probably from dislike to the new order of things.   The subject was revived early in January, 1666, when the archbishop produced an order of the king's Commission for Visitation of Universities that principals and professors should take the oath of allegiance in presence of the archbishop, with attestation that they submitted to and owned the episcopal form of church government, on pain of being deprived of office. As a consequence George Sinclair, who had been a regent for about twelve years, demitted office in March, 1666. He seems to have been on good terms with his colleagues and even with the archbishop, for in the preceding year the faculty, with the archbishop's consent, allowed him the use of one of the houses of the professors of divinity. Sinclair was recalled to office in the University after the Revolution. The oath of allegiance does not seem to have been warmly welcomed, but three months after Sinclair's demission the masters, in presence of Archbishop Burnet, appointed that all students of philosophy should swear and sign it before graduation, and that office-bearers in the College should also sign, on pain of forfeiting their offices.

In 1661 a resolution of parliament provided for the visitation of the Universities, but some time elapsed before it was carried out. The Commissioners of Visitation met at Glasgow on several occasions from July to October, 1664, and among them were the Archbishop of Glasgow, the Provosts of Glasgow and Ayr, the Duke of Hamilton, the Marquis of Montrose, the Earl of Argyle, Lord Cochrane, Sir James Turner, and John Hay, parson of Renfrew. The Commissioners seem to have been invested with ample powers to do everything except the one thing needful—to improve the endowments. After enquiry they drew up what appears to have been for the times a moderate and judicious scheme of extension. In their report the Commissioners recalled with regret the wider ramification of faculties and range of studies and graduation before the Reformation ; but declared that the University had still the power to create, not only masters of arts, but doctors and bachelors in theology and other faculties ; and recommended that such degrees should be more frequently conferred. The state of the finances of the University disclosed in their report was very bad—so bad that we can hardly believe it applicable to a normal year.

In sterling money the yearly revenue amounted to £555, but after deducting £179, mostly for ministers' stipends payable by the University, the net revenue was £376. The salaries of the principal and professors amounted to £289, and other necessary charges and disbursements (mainly made up, we may suppose, of interest on debt, maintenance of the College table, salary of the œconomus, and wages of College servants) to £416, making a total yearly expenditure of £705, and leaving a deficit of £329.

It was found that the extraordinary debts—mostly for buildings, no doubt—amounted to fully £2,833, or about seven and a half times the free annual revenue. The Commissioners must have expected that relief would somehow be obtained, for they recommended the masters to carry out and complete the new buildings as soon as possible; and they also recommended that a number of professors should be added to the teaching staff—at least one additional professor in theology, besides a professor of humanity, a professor of mathematics,[1] a professor of medicine, and a professor of civil and canon law. They gave some compassionate advice regarding the library, which was declared to be very small for a University, enjoining the masters to take the greatest care of it, and punctually to pay over for its benefit the small matriculation and examination fees, as well as the contributions from bursars of theology and philosophy.

Masters and students were enjoined to wear their gowns in the College, and students to do so in the streets as well. The common table was to be maintained as hitherto, and it was recommended that as many of the students as possible should sleep and diet in the College. Students were directed to speak Latin, and a fine was denounced against those who spoke Scots. Students in arts were recommended to practise the good and useful exercise of oratory and rhetoric, and were to be taught as formerly logic, metaphysics, physics, and ethics, the text of Aristotle being diligently and succinctly gone through. They were also to be instructed in some good abridgment of the various parts of mathematics, at least arithmetic, geometry, geography, and astronomy. The principal and the professors of theology—there was only one such professor at the time, but the Commissioners recommended the addition of another—were to see that their students went through the whole body of theology and the Holy Scriptures, and to exercise them in homilies; as well as to see that they had some knowledge of antiquity, the fathers, councils, ecclesiastical history, and chronology; and that they were proficient in Hebrew and Greek, and had some touch of Chaldee and Syriac.

The session was to last from the beginning of October till the end of July, and regulations were laid down against students leaving before the

---

[1] Among the additional professors required the Commissioners include 'Ane professor of mathematickes whiche this Universitie formerlie had, and by the erectione and fundatioune aucht to have.' It is possible that there may have been further evidence available in 1664 than now, but certainly neither the foundation by the town nor the *nova erectio* provided for a professor or regent in Mathematics. The *nova erectio* did indeed include Arithmetic and Geometry as adjuncts to the other subjects taught by the second regent. Some regents may have given greater prominence than others to Mathematics, but I should think it extremely doubtful whether there ever was before this time a teacher appointed for the specific department of Mathematics and confining himself to that department.

proper time.   The session closed with graduation in arts, and besides the degree examination leading up to that ceremony, there were examinations at the beginning of the session before students were promoted to higher classes than those already attended, and before the vacation further examinations on the work of the session.   Strictness in personal religion is generally believed to have been relaxed after the Restoration, but the regulations now laid down might have come from a puritan commission. The students, with the principal and masters, were to attend church on Sunday in their gowns.   The masters were to meet with the students on Sunday morning and evening and exercise them in sacred lessons.   The masters were also enjoined to see that each student, whatever his rank, should have a Bible and read portions of it at fit times, and should be careful to seek God, chiefly in secret prayer.

The Visitors to Glasgow recommended several matters for consideration by the general Visitors of all the Universities, among which were the institution of a sort of inter-university congress, to meet annually and to have power to hold special meetings; the establishment of a common course of order and discipline, so far as consistent with the foundations and 'approvable customs' of the several Universities; the taking of the oath of allegiance by the governors, masters, and students, at least by such students as were graduates; and the requiring of testimonials from any student of one University who wished to be admitted to another.

In 1667 the Privy Council forbade the collectors of cess to exact payment from the College of the proportion of taxation then granted to the king at which the teinds of the lands of Calder and Monkland had been rated, and instructed the collector to pay back what had been exacted.   In 1682 it appears that a party of military had been quartered upon the College to extort payment of an assessment laid on their lands and heritable property as their proportion of a supply of £150,000 sterling, spread over five years, granted to the king by the Convention of Estates held at Edinburgh in July, 1678, and continued in 1681 for other five years.   But the College and the managers of the city hospitals having presented a petition to the Commissioners of the Treasury, pointing out that Colleges and hospitals were expressly exempted from contributing, the Commissioners, acting on the advice of the Lord Advocate, freed the lands mortified to the College.

In 1670 Charles II. by a charter under the great seal, granted to the University the subdeanery of Glasgow, with its annexed kirks of Calder and Monkland, the teinds great and small, and the parsonage and vicarage, and confirmed all former mortifications of the subdeanery to be united to the patrimony of the University; and appointed that the professor of divinity should enjoy the honours and privileges of subdean of the chapter of Glasgow, with a chalder of victual and a hundred marks annually from the revenues, provision being also made for the ministers of Calder and Monkland. Probably it may have been out of consideration for Gilbert Burnet, who was then professor of divinity and on good terms with Lauderdale, that this arrangement was made, an arrangement afterwards ratified by parliament.

In 1672 an act of parliament was passed authorising the masters to sell their feu-duties and ground annuals in the city and its neighbourhood, which were said to be so small as scarcely to pay the cost of collection, on condition that the proceeds were applied to the uses of the College. Another more fruitful act of parliament passed in 1672 granted for the next seven years the vacant stipends in the dioceses of Glasgow, Galloway, and the Isles to the University, except that for the first year half of the sum from the diocese of Glasgow was bestowed on the University of St. Andrews. In May, 1685, an act of parliament provided that in future the vacant stipends of all churches should be employed by the patron for pious uses within the respective parishes, particularly in building or repairing bridges—a very useful but not a very pious purpose, as the word is now understood—repairing churches, and maintaining the poor ; but that for the next five years vacant stipends in the dioceses of Glasgow and Galloway should be assigned to the University.

With a view to encourage professors and masters of Universities and Colleges, the Privy Council in 1672 prohibited all persons not publicly authorised according to act of parliament from gathering scholars and teaching them philosophy or the Greek language. They also laid down a regulation that students changing from one University to another should be required to produce certificates from their former masters before admission to the second University ; and that degrees should not be conferred on students coming from other Universities unless, as the meaning appears to be, they gave a certain amount of attendance in the University where they desired to graduate. The Privy Council in the same year issued an order prohibiting the rector and masters from allowing any person to teach a class till he had taken the oath of allegiance, from which it seems likely that the thing prohibited had been done.

John Young continued as professor of divinity till 1665. He had never been a clergyman, and was known as 'the maiden midwife,' yet by a peculiar turn of fortune he died a bishop-elect. After the death of David Fletcher, bishop of Argyle, Sharp wrote to Lauderdale in May, 1665, that after consulting with the Archbishop of Glasgow and the Earl of Argyle, he had conferred the bishopric on John Young as the fittest person on many accounts to succeed to the office. The promotion seems to have come upon Young as an ominous thing, for, if it did not set him to make his will, at all events it induced him to execute an assignation of three bonds for a total sum of ten thousand marks, which probably represented most of his wealth. His wife, Marion Campbell, a daughter of the laird of Blythswood, had a life interest in nearly the whole of this amount, and he provided that after her death the money should pass to his brother Patrick Young, one of the regents, or his brother's heirs, or to the elder or younger of two married sisters or their heirs ; and failing all these, to the principal and masters of the University for the maintenance of three bursaries in theology. It appears that the conditions for this bequest passing to the University were never realised, and strangely enough Young died a few days after signing the assignation.

The chair remained vacant for four years, during which time probably there was little teaching in theology save what Edward Wright, who succeeded Baillie as principal in 1662, found opportunity to give. The next professor, Gilbert Burnet, afterwards chaplain to the Prince of Orange and Bishop of Salisbury, was one of the most notable men of his generation, an adviser and to some extent an actor in the great events which happened in that period, and author of numerous historical works, of which the *History of His own Time* is the most important and interesting. His father was a successful lawyer in Edinburgh, rather averse to the Covenant and inclined to prelacy ; while his mother was a sister of Johnston of Warriston, an astute leader on the other side.

Young Burnet was educated at Aberdeen, in 1662 was introduced to Bishop Leighton, and next year, at the age of nineteen or twenty, paid a visit to England, and made the acquaintance of Cudworth, Boyle, Tillotson, Stillingfleet, and other men of mark and influence. Then he spent some time on the continent, pursuing further studies in Holland, and made a stay of some length in Paris. On his return to Scotland, he became minister of Salton, and though still a very young man, was soon brought into communication with members of the government and with Leighton, who had now become Archbishop of Glasgow, regarding the policy to be followed in the distracted state of civil and ecclesiastical affairs in the country. Some of the moderators of the University met him at the Duchess of Hamilton's, and were so favourably impressed that they invited him to undertake the duties of the vacant chair of divinity. Burnet is said to have been rather disinclined to leave his quiet ministry at Salton and the parishioners to whom he was greatly attached, but Leighton interposed his influence, and at the close of 1669 Burnet was admitted as professor of divinity.

Burnet and a number of other clergymen went on circuit through the western shires preaching in favour of Leighton's scheme of ecclesiastical compromise, under which bishops were to be perpetual moderators of presbyteries, while ministers were to be ordained by the bishop with the concurrence of his presbyters, not in the Cathedral but in the churches in which they were to serve; and church affairs were to be managed in presbyteries and synods by the free votes of presbyters or the majority of them, and every third year synods were to be held in which bishops might be censured if found guilty of any fault. Like Patrick Gillespie, Leighton had been some time a minister under what we may call the Covenanting dispensation and afterwards principal of a University, and he further resembled Gillespie in having procured endowments from Cromwell for the University of Edinburgh, as Gillespie did for Glasgow. Yet after the Restoration Leighton was comforted and Gillespie tormented.

But any external comfort that might be supposed to attend Leighton's promotion was marred by his inability to change in any substantial measure a policy and a course of events which he was far from approving. He was cultured and contemplative, tolerant and peace-loving, but he lacked robustness, and had in his composition almost as much of the courtier as of the saint. As for his scheme of accommodation, the bishops, except Leighton himself, did not wish it, indeed Archbishop Burnet of Glasgow had been dismissed by the king from his see for a remonstrance against allowing ejected ministers who had lived peaceably to re-occupy their pulpits if still vacant, or to be appointed to other vacancies; and Lauderdale declared it would be rash to make such a change in the constitution of the Church unless it were to be followed by some practical result. The Presbyterians knew how at the beginning of the century bishops had been introduced as perpetual moderators, how unavailing the restriction had proved, and how soon a modified Episcopacy was likely to develop into an unmodified one. Leighton, who looked upon the controversies of the religious parties around him as 'a drunken scuffle in the dark,' had a conference with some of the leading Presbyterians at Holyrood chapel, but they declined to enter the pitfall prepared for them, and he afterwards resigned his archbishopric, tired of wearing a mitre and being helpless to do any real good.

The bustling activity of Burnet, his fondness for mingling with the world, and the alertness with which, while attending to the affairs of his own province, he became acquainted with persons noted for their rank or learning or influence, must have made him a valuable acquisition to the staff of University teachers and managers. It is said that, in his course of forenoon instruction, on Mondays he made his students explain a head of divinity and exercised them in propounding and defending theses; on Tuesdays he delivered prelections on divinity in Latin; on Wednesdays he lectured on the Gospel of Matthew; on Thursdays he expounded a Hebrew psalm or explained some portion of the ritual and constitution of the primitive church; and on Fridays he made each of his pupils preach a short sermon on an allotted text, the professor adding his comments and criticisms.   In the evenings he read and discoursed on a portion of Scripture, and enquired into the progress of his pupils in the several branches of their studies, encouraging and directing them as he found occasion.

Burnet was a frequent visitor at Hamilton Palace, and the Duchess having employed him to put in order the papers of her father and uncle, he was led to compile the *Memoirs of the Dukes of Hamilton*, a work in which Lauderdale offered to assist him by supplying such information as he could furnish regarding the transactions of the time to which it referred. In 1673 Burnet went to London to obtain a license for publishing these *Memoirs*, and had interviews with the Duke of York and with the king, who named him to be one of the royal chaplains.   He had previously helped to prevent variance from arising between the Dukes of Hamilton and Lauderdale; but in the session of parliament held towards the close of 1673, when Lauderdale asked for the usual grant to the crown, Hamilton proposed that before any grant was made the grievances of the country should be made known to the king.   In consequence of this, certain monopolies on salt, tobacco, and brandy were removed, and Lauderdale cut short any further opposition by summarily dissolving the parliament. Burnet was on friendly terms with Hamilton, and Lauderdale blamed him as the underhand instrument of the opposition offered in parliament to the measures promoted by the court.   Burnet went to London in 1674 with a view to defend himself.   He was coldly received by the king, who ordered his name to be removed from the list of chaplains, and upon this Burnet made up his mind to resign his chair at Glasgow and try his fortunes in London.

David Liddell, who had been dean of faculty since 1665, was appointed to succeed Burnet in the chair of divinity, and continued to hold it till his death in 1682, when Alexander Rosse, parson of Perth, was elected his successor.   After holding the professorship for five years Rosse was made Bishop of Moray, and Dr. James Wemyss, parson of Kirkliston, was chosen professor of divinity under circumstances which must have been rather tantalising to John Tran, who had been a regent since 1669.   The masters put on record a resolution that Tran, who had been at extraordinary pains to fit himself for the employment, should be appointed professor of theology when the next vacancy occurred, without further election if a vacancy occurred during their administration. If a vacancy did not occur in their time, they earnestly recommended their successors to appoint him, since they had previously been about to elect him to the office, but with Tran's own consent had elected Dr. Wemyss. This was an unavailing measure, for Wemyss was deprived of office after the Revolution and Tran was not his successor.

In the summer of 1686 Thomas Gordon, who had been elected a regent four years previously, went to London and, without acquainting the principal or professors of his design, obtained a presentation from James VII. to be professor of oriental languages. This was setting up a new professorship, and the king in his presentation to Gordon ordered ten thousand marks from the vacant stipends then vested in the University by act of parliament to be set aside as an endowment fund, from which an annual salary of six hundred marks should be paid to the new professor. The masters considered the project unreasonable and impracticable, but in order to enforce his claims under the king's presentation, Gordon summoned them before the Privy Council. After examining the whole matter, and particularly the intromissions of the College with the vacant stipends, the Privy Council found that no such endowment could be provided, but ordered the masters to admit Gordon as professor in virtue of the king's presentation, but without a salary, and this was done in January, 1687.

A few years before this the moderators of the University made an effort to re-establish the professorship of humanity, and the scheme they adopted may have suggested to Gordon the plan of endowment embodied in the presentation which he obtained from the King. In March, 1683, James Young was admitted as professor of humanity, and three months later the moderators resolved that six thousand marks should be collected from the vicarage teinds of Old and New Monkland and invested, the interest being assigned as a salary to Young as long as he continued in office. It does not seem that this investment was ever carried out, and the scheme did not succeed. Young had also been appointed by the Town Council as College librarian, but in 1687 he obtained some employment outside the College, and demitted his office as professor; and the faculty having represented that he could not conveniently continue to act as librarian, he made his brother his deputy in that office. The faculty then suppressed the humanity class for a time till the College revenues should improve, and ordered payment for the past five years at the annual rate of twenty pounds sterling to be made to Young as soon as practicable from the teinds of Monkland. Four-fifths of this sum remained unpaid in 1696, the moderators declining to make payment, on the allegation that while Young had charge of the library it was damaged by his negligence.

The University still claimed and exercised jurisdiction in affairs that should naturally have belonged to the law courts of the realm. On 18th August, 1670, a student named Robert Bartoun was tried before the rector, Sir William Fleming of Ferme, and four assessors, namely, David Liddell, dean of faculty, and Walter Forsyth, William Blair, and Thomas Nicolson, three of the regents, on the very grave charge of having shot and killed Jonnet Wright, servant to Patrick Wilson, or at least of having been art and part in the crime. The indictment was given in by John Cumming, writer in Glasgow, acting as procurator-fiscal for the University, and by Andrew Wright, cordiner, nearest of kin to the deceased woman. A jury of fifteen was empanelled, and Bartoun, who pleaded not guilty, was defended by Thomas Sheirer, his procurator. They demanded proof, and upon this Andrew Wright withdrew from the prosecution, as he could produce no witnesses to substantiate the charge. Cumming, on the other hand, adhered to the indictment, and called four witnesses, but the nature of their evidence has not been recorded.

Before giving in their verdict the jury requested that they might be secured from detriment in case they should afterwards be challenged for taking part in the trial, as they were not clear regarding the University having the right to hold criminal courts for the trial of such cases, and no warrant had been produced to them. The rector and his assessors answered that the objection came too late, but *ex abundanti gratia* guaranteed them from all detriment. The jury gave a verdict of not guilty, and it has been surmised that they may have been influenced by a sense of the responsibility a verdict of guilty would have brought upon them. For the University, too, it would have been a very serious thing to hang a man, and altogether foreign to its proper functions.

Josiah Chorley, a piously inclined Englishman, has left an interesting account of the arrangements at Glasgow when he studied there in 1671 and 1672. Chorley began his University course at Trinity College, Cambridge, but withdrew from it on account of the strict terms of conformity which prevailed, and came to Glasgow in February, 1671. In consideration of his previous studies he was allowed to join the baccalour class under Mr. John Tran, 'whose excellent qualities would fill a large volume.' 'Keen as was my appetite for learning, here was rich provision enough to satisfy it in daily dictates, disputations, etc.' The College bell rang at five in the morning, and the roll being called, every student had to answer his name. The day was spent in private study and public exercises, and at nine in the evening the chambers were visited by the regents. On Sunday students met twice in their classes for religious exercises, and they accompanied the principal and regents to church both in the forenoon and afternoon, ' so that there is no room for vain ramblings and prophanation of the day.'   Chorley declared that the public worship in the churches, even when the archbishop preached, followed the same manner in all respects as in the Presbyterian congregations in England, so that he wondered why there should be any dissenters, till he was informed of the renunciation of the Covenant, the imposition of the hierarchy, and other measures that had been adopted.   He also noted a comely appearance of religion throughout the whole city, the reading of Scripture and singing of Psalms being heard in most houses, while sauntering and playing were prohibited both in and out of church time.

In the beginning of April, 1672, lecturing ceased in the magistrand class to give time for the examinations and preparations leading up to graduation, or laureation, as it was called ; and all the students going forward to that ceremony contributed to an assessment for defraying the expenses.   Chorley declined to be public orator, but was sent to Edinburgh ' to invite the grandees there to our laureation,' and set out ' furnished with gloves and theses, which I first presented to the patron, the laird of Colchun, upon white satin.'   He then waited on Archbishop Leighton, who accepted the theses, but ' with all demonstrations of humility' excused himself as unworthy to receive a present of ' fine fringed gloves.'   Chorley pressed him to accept, and the archbishop continued to protest and retire till he reached the far end of the chamber, and then consented.   'But it was amazing to see with what humble gratitude, bowing to the very ground, this great man accepted them.'   After waiting on Sir James Turner, whom he describes as ' steward of our University,' he called for Professor Gilbert Burnet, but found that he was out of town, attending the Earl of Tweeddale in his last illness.   On a second visit to Burnet's lodging next morning, the professor being in bed, ' sent for me up, made me sit down on his bedside, after I had delivered my message to him.   Then he told me he was come home this morning as soon as the Earl was dead.   After much more discourse about the affairs of our Colledge, and his compliments to my tutor, I took my leave of him, and soon after of the city, and returned to Glasgow with all expedition ; was kindly received by my good tutor, to whom I related all the transactions, and delivered all the compliments, etc.   Blessed be God for good success in this journey!'

The laureation was held in the Tron Church on the 18th of July, 1672, in presence of a crowded audience, including many clergy and gentry. The presiding regent offered a prayer in Latin, introduced the business of the day in an eloquent speech, and propounded the theses.   Disputations followed, ' wherein every clergyman and gentleman present, or as many as would, called out what scholar he pleased for his respondent, and opposed upon any thesis that he read, the regent all the while moderating in the pulpit.' After this long exercise Jonathan Low, an Englishman who had shared the same chamber with Chorley, and who had been appointed to act as public orator at the ceremony, 'pronounced his declamation very well.' The graduands were then sent out into the churchyard, and, being called in the order of merit assigned to them, re-entered the church and stood there in the same order, when the principal read his injunctions to them out of the College statute book, and pronounced the title of master of arts over them, the regent closing the proceedings with a solemn prayer and thanksgiving.

The money required to defray the expenses of graduation was raised by an assessment levied from the graduands, and from among these graduands certain individuals whom Chorley calls officers were chosen to collect the assessments, and to provide gloves and arrange for the printing of theses. Chorley, who was one of the collectors, tells us that after the laureation the officers met to adjust accounts and pay the expenses of the ceremony, which they did to the satisfaction of the students by whom they had been elected. It was proposed that every officer should have a dollar for his pains, though Chorley objected to this, and that the surplus should be handed over to the regent. Finally it was carried that each officer should receive half a dollar, and after this had been deducted, a large purse was presented as a valedictory offering to the regent. Chorley was many years troubled about the half dollar, and eventually sent a letter with a guinea to Tran, 'begging his pardon and prayers to God.' The number who received the degree of master of arts at the ceremony described by Chorley was twenty-six, and some points mentioned by him regarding the order of merit do not quite agree with the lists preserved in the University. It will be seen that in those days students were allowed a considerable share in making the arrangements for graduation, but students of the present day will probably not regret being freed from the assessment for expenses to which their predecessors had to submit.

In 1667 the masters laid down a stringent regulation that every student who rented a chamber in the College should give a written acknowledgment of his responsibility for keeping the fabric in the same condition as at the time of his entry; and that everyone guilty of breaking glass windows or doing other injury to the buildings should forthwith be whipped and expelled. Various occurrences among the students showed that they shared the feeling of aversion, then so widely prevalent in the country, to the policy of the government. When Lauderdale and the bishops brought the Highland Host, chiefly consisting of men from Athole and Breadalbane, to Ayrshire to coerce landowners into giving a bond for keeping, not only themselves and their families, but also their tenants and cottars away from conventicles, and from dealings with forfeited persons, intercommuned ministers, and vagrant preachers; and when the terrible ordeal had failed, and the mountaineers were returning homeward by way of Glasgow, laden with booty, it is said that a band of students, assisted by other youths from the town, stopped the bridge of Glasgow in the face of nearly two thousand Highlanders, and would not suffer them to pass till they had delivered up their spoils, consisting of pots, pans, bed clothes, wearing apparel, and the like. If two thousand armed Highlanders submitted to be dealt with in this way, they must have been in an unusually docile mood. An order by the Privy Council that none should be admitted to graduation unless they took the oath of allegiance was followed by a complete cessation of public graduations from 1676 till after the Revolution.

Within a year or two after the battle of Bothwell Bridge the students at Glasgow ostentatiously wore the blue ribbon of the Covenant and other emblems distasteful to the rulers then in power. For this several of the leaders, William Johnston, Earl of Annandale, among them, were summoned before the masters and the archbishop, Arthur Ross. Annandale made a spirited defence of himself and the others, and was called to order by his regent for styling the archbishop sir, instead of my lord, and asked to remember that he was addressing a greater person than himself. Annandale haughtily retorted: 'I know the king has been pleased to make him a spiritual lord; but I know likewise that the piper of Arbroath's son and my father's son are not to be compared.' Nothing further could be made of the matter.

Some further bursaries were founded during this time. Captain Ross of Rosseyle designed to leave lands capable of maintaining six bursaries in philosophy, with 200 marks a year each, and six in divinity, with 300 marks, a third of whom were to be at Glasgow, and the rest at King's and Marischal College, Aberdeen; but the conditions of the bequest were complex and unfortunate contingencies occurred, so that the project proved like a magnificent prospectus followed by a very slender dividend. After long delay a single bursary of £4 3s. 4d. sterling was established at Glasgow. In 1672 a more fruitful foundation was instituted when the Earl of Dundonald mortified the lands of Milton and Arratshole in Kilbride, Lanarkshire, to maintain four bursars in philosophy and three in divinity, retaining the patronage to himself and his heirs. David Adamson, minister of Fintry, in 1674 left 800 marks Scots for a bursary in arts, to be held by the son of a tradesman within the seven incorporate trades of

Stirling, the patronage being assigned to John Campbell of Dowan, who conveyed it to the convener court of Stirling. In the same year Leighton, who had been chancellor, placed £150 sterling in the hands of the Town Council to maintain a bursary, and after his death his sister, acting on a recommendation he had left, paid a further sum of £150 for a second bursary.

James Fall, who, on a presentation by the king, was admitted as principal in 1684, relates that a general Commission of Visitation of the Universities of Scotland sat at Edinburgh in June, 1687, to which returns were given in from Glasgow regarding the foundations, finance, and regulations. A special Visitation was appointed to meet at Glasgow on 29th August following, but a quorum did not appear. Visitations had previously been held in 1681 and 1683, but their transactions were not very important. In 1681 it was prescribed that students should meet for public prayers at six in the morning and six in the evening—a regulation favourable to early rising—and should also have private prayers in their chambers morning and evening. The masters were to recommend students to read the Scriptures, and to take account of so many chapters as they found convenient every Saturday or Sunday.

The Visitation found that graduations ought to be public in all the Universities, but that for several years this practice had not been followed at Glasgow, and asked the principal and masters to give reasons. They answered that about four years previously they received intimation of an order by the Privy Council that none should be admitted to graduation without taking the oath of allegiance, and that so few would comply with this requirement that they could not incur the expense of a public graduation. They added that students who had been admitted to private graduation had taken the oath; and that several who were refused admission to the degree without the oath went to Edinburgh and were allowed to graduate there without it. The Visitors considered that all the Colleges should give full obedience to acts of Council, and renewed their regulation against students changing from one University to another without certificates.

The Visitation from the General Assembly in 1642 declared in favour of 'regenting.' But in 1681 the Visitors, considering that by the *Nova Erectio* each master and regent should be fixed to a certain class, and that this had been the practice till the late troubles, ordered that this method should be followed in future. Almost the only important act of the Visitors of 1683 was to rescind this order and restore the practice of 'regenting.' Having previously declared that 'regenting' was inconsistent with the foundation, they had now to provide excuses; so they

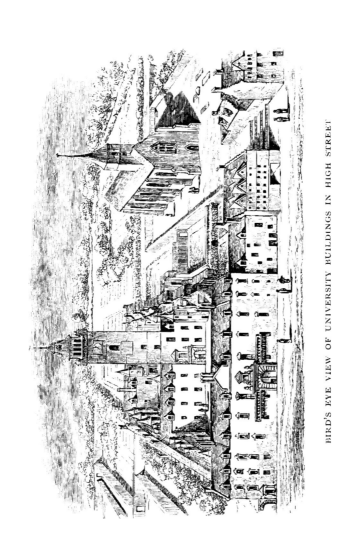

BIRD'S EYE VIEW OF UNIVERSITY BUILDINGS IN HIGH STREET

At the close of the Seventeenth Century

By Captain John Slezer, R. A., 1693

declared that it was the more profitable way, and more in harmony with the uniformity among the Universities recommended by the King in his commission.

The frequent breakdown of meetings for want of a quorum in these three Visitations from 1681 to 1687, as well as the limited amount of their work, is suggestive. Perhaps the Visitors were conscious that the measures of the government and the state of the country did not tell in favour of the higher learning, and that, without further endowments, of which there could be little prospect till the country was better governed, effective reforms in the University could hardly be carried out. And they may have suspected that, though the King simulated an interest in the Universities, there was no earnest purpose of affording them real help. Upon the failure of the meeting at Glasgow in August, 1687, nothing further seems to have been done, so far as the Western University was concerned, till after the flight of James and the advent of William and Mary. And when the news of William's landing came, the students burned the effigy of the pope in fellowship with those of the archbishops of Glasgow and St. Andrews.

CHAPTER III

FROM THE REVOLUTION TO THE END OF THE EIGHTEENTH CENTURY

I. 1688-1727

THE Revolution did not bring about an immediate and decided expansion of the University, but it introduced a new and more settled era which soon told in its favour. With the exception of two or three short-lived insurrections, the country returned to a state of order and tranquillity, the sounds of warfare were hushed, and ecclesiastical strife, though not extinguished, was less acute and less absorbing to the general body of the people. The University endeavoured to realise the plan of extension sketched by the Commission of 1664, and before the date of the Union of England and Scotland, it had added professorships of mathematics, Greek, and Latin, and lectureships on history and botany. A physic garden was instituted in 1704 in connection with the last subject, and this was the beginning of a school of medicine which soon became an active and ever-expanding department of the University. A chair of medicine was instituted in 1713, to which was almost immediately added a lectureship in anatomy, and a chair of anatomy was founded in 1720 or earlier. A chair of law was founded in 1713, while to the single chair in the faculty of divinity which had been maintained since the Restoration, a second chair was added in 1709 to deal with Oriental languages, and a third in 1716 to deal with Church history, though in this last case an acting professor was not appointed till 1721. An allowance of £300 a year had been obtained from King William some years before, and in 1697 or 1698 he granted a tack of the Archbishopric of Glasgow for the better payment of the gift ; and Queen Anne and George I. made some further grants.

With the establishment of a permanently separate chair of Greek in 1704, that subject was withdrawn from the province of the regents. After this it was only in the three subjects of physics, ethics, and logic that the system of 'regenting' continued, and the Commission of 1727 ordered it to be discontinued in these three subjects also, every professor appointed after that date being fixed to a definite subject.   The number of students, which before the Revolution may have been 120 or 150, quickly increased, there being 250 in 1696, and 400 in 1702.   The change from Episcopacy to Presbyterianism created a great demand for ministers, and for some years brought to the University a large number of students both in arts and divinity who were destined for the Church, but when this temporary pressure ceased and the ranks of the ministry were filled, the students continued about as numerous as before.   During the time of Principal Stirling there was much wrangling and strife among the managers, and several earlier Commissions having proved insufficient to restore peace and order, an abler and more keen-sighted Commission appointed in 1726 issued next year a code of regulations which were of greater importance than any which had appeared since the *Nova Erectio*, and which exercised a considerable influence on the organisation and management of the institution for more than a hundred years.

The news of the flight of James and the coming of William caused uncertainty and suspense in the University, but no very violent disturbance.   All recognised that important changes in Church and State were impending, and as the policy of William on many public questions had not been declared, many hastened from Scotland to London, not so much to learn William's views as to influence them, if possible, to their own advantage.   Principal Fall set out for the southern metropolis on 26th January, 1689, and did not return till the end of April.   Glasgow had by this time declared for the Prince of Orange.

Towards the end of the preceding year an attempt was made to raise troops in the city for the army of King James, but it was not very successful, and the magistrates, not finding the recruits who had enlisted amenable to control, disbanded them on 23rd January, 1689, at the same time resolving to maintain a night guard of sixty men for prevention of robbery and outbreaks of fire.   The next day the majority of the magistrates and Council signed an address to the Prince of Orange.   At the end of session 1688-89 Fall, at the request of his colleagues, again betook himself to London, but neither of his visits seems to have had any important result.   Some repairs and improvements about the College were interrupted early in the session of 1688-89, and the maintenance of the common table was discontinued, but tolerable order and discipline were preserved throughout the session.   But some young men set up as private teachers of philosophy in the city, and withdrew a number of students from the University.   Against this breach of privilege, as it was considered,

Fall made a representation to the Earl of Melville, Secretary of State, who wrote to the Provost of Glasgow requesting him to hinder such encroachments on the privileges of the University, but still the private teaching continued all that year.

Changes or reforms in the Universities depended largely on the new settlement of the Church, and there was some delay in completing this settlement. The Prince of Orange was not at first very zealous to restore the Presbyterian polity in Scotland. He never took very kindly to Scottish affairs, and was rather impatient when they assumed such magnitude as to divert his attention from subjects in which he cherished a greater interest. Nor was he very studious to conciliate public opinion, but so far as he did regard it, the opinion of his English rather than his Scottish subjects impressed him. He found, however, that Scottish Episcopalians were by no means favourable to himself or his government, and under the advice of Carstares he assented to the re-establishment of Presbyterianism.

William Carstares, who soon came into special relation with the University of Glasgow owing to the appointment of his brother-in-law as Principal, was a Scottish Presbyterian minister who had been an agent and a messenger in the projects and negotiations of Argyle, Baillie of Jerviswoode, Monmouth, Russell, and others with a view to some kind of intervention to secure better government. On the discovery of the Rye House plot, in which he was not concerned, Carstares was arrested and sent to Scotland, where the law allowed harsher usage of prisoners, and where he endured the torture of the thumbkins, and would have had to endure the torture of the boot but for an accidental change of hangman which brought in a new man incompetent as yet for the work of torture. Carstares afterwards made a declaration regarding the negotiations in which he had been engaged, having previously stipulated that it should not be used as evidence against any one ; and was subsequently allowed to go abroad. He returned to Holland, and was appointed chaplain to the Prince of Orange, who valued his personal character and abilities, and came to place great reliance on his knowledge of men and parties in Scotland and England. At the Revolution he crossed to England in the same vessel with William, was soon appointed Scottish chaplain to the King and Queen, had apartments assigned to him in Kensington Palace, and was ordered to be in constant attendance on the King's person. He came to be known as ' Cardinal Carstares,' and through the King he wielded a greater influence over Scottish affairs than the official ministers of State.

The Convention which met at Edinburgh in the spring of 1689 offered the crown to William and Mary, accompanying the offer by a claim of right which declared that Prelacy was an intolerable burden, contrary to the inclinations of the people, and that it ought to be abolished. Various circumstances, including the successful obstruction offered for some time to the measures of the government by Montgomerie and other malcontents of 'The Club,' delayed legislation on ecclesiastical affairs, but in the summer of 1690 Presbyterianism was re-established. On 25th April an act was passed restoring ministers who had held charges before 1661 and had afterwards been ejected for refusal to own Episcopal authority. Only about sixty of these ministers now remained, and by a later act of 7th June they were empowered to admit others, whether ministers or elders, to share in their authority, to visit parishes throughout the country, and to depose ministers deficient in ability, in moral character, or in soundness of faith. Parishes from which the ministers were withdrawn were declared vacant. On 26th May the Confession of Faith was read in Parliament, approved, and ordered to be recorded in the statute book. On 19th July a further act was passed abolishing patronage, and conferring the right of presentation on the heritors and elders in country parishes and on the municipal corporations and elders in burghs—the congregations having a right to object to presentees, and the Presbyteries to judge of the efficacy of the objections. It was also enacted that each patron should receive 600 marks Scots by way of compensation, and as the University held the patronage of several parishes, it was interested in this provision.

Parliament now turned its attention to the state of Universities and schools, and on 4th July passed an act declaring that no principals, professors, or office-bearers should be admitted to the Universities or allowed to continue in them without taking the oath of allegiance, subscribing the Confession of Faith, submitting to the Presbyterian form of Church government which had been established, and being found of a pure, loyal, and peaceable 'conversation,' and of sufficient scholarship and ability for their employments. The act also appointed Commissioners or Visitors to the Universities to try the professors and others then in office, and to remove the inefficient or disaffected, and those who would not conform to the prescribed conditions.

The Commissioners were also empowered to regulate the foundations, revenues, and manner of teaching in the Universities, and to appoint committees of their number to visit the several Universities and report to the general Visitors, who might determine matters as they thought fit. The special Visitors to Glasgow were also instructed to report on all the schools in which Latin was taught within the shires of Lanark, Renfrew, Bute, Argyle, Dumbarton, Dumfries, Wigtown, and Ayr, and the Stewartries of Annandale and Kirkcudbright. The committee were to enquire into the qualifications and efficiency of the schoolmasters, and whether they owned the new government in Church and State. Before long a number of schoolmasters from widely separated districts, including Inveraray, Dumbarton, Greenock, Lanark, Ayr, Moffat, Dumfries, and Penpont, appeared before the Commissioners at Glasgow; but the Commissioners soon came to think they had enough to do with the University, and recommended that the enquiry regarding the schools should be delegated to Presbyteries. This was done, but progress was slow, and years later reports from many Presbyteries were wanting. It was well, however, that the attention of the government was directed to the condition of the schools throughout the country, and the enquiry and discussion that took place doubtless helped to promote the legislation of 1696 providing further means for the establishment and maintenance of parochial schools.

At the end of August, 1690, the Commissioners to Glasgow met in the high common hall of the College. They included Lord Carmichael, Sir John Maxwell of Pollok, John Anderson, Provost of Glasgow, the laird of Craigends, and several ministers. All of them were described by Principal Fall as men of great honour and justice, as well as moderation and temper. The principal, Dr. James Wemyss, professor of divinity, and the four regents, William Blair, John Tran, John Boyd, and George Sinclair, were called before them and asked to take the oath of allegiance and the assurance—an acknowledgment of William as rightful as well as actual King—to sign the Confession of Faith, and to submit to the established form of Church government.

The principal declared that as the conditions were complexly composed he could not take them with a good conscience. Wemyss, Blair, and Boyd also declined. George Sinclair, who had recently been reappointed to the office of regent which he had held from 1654 to 1666, accepted the conditions and explained that he had not yet been installed. The committee agreed to recommend him to the general Visitors. John Tran also accepted the conditions and declared his readiness to purge himself from any accusation of scandal, if required. Further procedure in his case was reserved for the general Commission, before which, on 6th September, Tran was allowed to take the oaths. At Edinburgh on 26th September, 1690, Fall, still declining to accept the conditions on the ground that they were 'a complex engagement,' was deposed by the general Commission. He was dismissed with compliments, however, and received the public thanks of the Commission for his fidelity and good administration of the revenues. At the same time James Wemyss and William Blair, who still persisted in declining the conditions, were deposed. Though John Boyd had at first refused, on further reflection he agreed to comply, and craved the Commission to make enquiry into certain charges and aspersions brought against him.   Intimation was made at the Cross of Glasgow that objectors might appear before the committee, but none appeared, and on 15th October the committee recommended the general Commission to continue Boyd as a regent, and this was done.

The Archbishop of Glasgow fell with the fall of Episcopacy and the office of Chancellor became vacant, but for some little time the other chief officers of the University appointed before the Revolution were not displaced.   Archibald Inglis, rector of the church of Glasgow, had been elected rector of the University in 1686, and he was reappointed in the three succeeding years.   In March, 1690, however, David Boyle of Kelburne was elected by the votes of three 'nations,' and he immediately took oath and entered upon office.   James Creighton, rector of Kilbride, was chosen dean of faculty in 1685, and reappointed from time to time till in December, 1690, Patrick Simpson, minister of Renfrew, 'a reverend prudent man of age and experience,' was chosen to succeed him.   The office of chancellor remained vacant till 30th September, 1692, when the rector (Sir John Maxwell of Pollok), the principal, the professor of Divinity, the four regents, and the professor of Mathematics met and appointed John, Lord Carmichael, to that high office, recording his election and his merits in a sounding Latin minute.

The appointment of principal belonged to the Crown, and soon after Fall had been deposed the office was bestowed on William Dunlop, cousin and brother-in-law of Carstares, the King's chief adviser in Scottish affairs. Dunlop was a son of the minister of Paisley, and had himself been trained for the ministry, but was too much of a Presbyterian to obtain promotion in the Church in the era of the Restoration.   For some time he acted as tutor or chaplain in the family of Lord Dundonald—a family from which Claverhouse chose his wife—and a few days before the battle of Bothwell Bridge he brought to the insurgents the draft of a manifesto setting forth in what was conceived to be temperate and politic language the stern necessity which made them take up arms.   He continued some years longer in his native country, and married his cousin, Sarah Carstares, but feeling that the times were adverse, he emigrated to Carolina about 1682 or 1683, and was for some years not only an active colonist but also a preacher and major of militia.   Mrs. Dunlop remained in the old country, not forgotten by her brother William, who declared she was very dear to him and would find it so, 'if Providence shall capacitate me to testify it.'

After the news of the Revolution, Dunlop returned to Scotland, and was presented first to the parish of Ochiltree and shortly afterwards to the church of Paisley. In the course of the year 1690 Dunlop rendered notable service to William by aiding in the disclosure of a conspiracy in favour of James, in which Montgomerie, the Earl of Annandale, Lord Ross, and other chiefs of 'The Club' were concerned. The leaders hastened to betray each other, and the power of 'The Club,' which had long hampered the action of the government and the progress of business in Parliament, was at an end. Becoming alarmed for his own safety, and perhaps thinking that Dunlop's influence with Carstares might be helpful in procuring the clemency of William, Ross had sent for Dunlop, and, professing to be in great trouble of conscience, desired his prayers to enable the penitent to open his heart. Prayer and confession followed. Ross told Dunlop all he knew, and Dunlop, with consent of the penitent informer, conveyed news of the plot to Melville, the Secretary of State. Fresh from this service, Dunlop, instead of becoming minister of Ochiltree or Paisley, was appointed by the King to be principal in succession to the deposed Dr. Fall. On 24th November, 1690, Dunlop appeared before the Privy Council, and took the oath of allegiance, the assurance, and the oath of faithful administration; and on 11th December, after delivering an inaugural discourse before a very full meeting of members of the University and others, he was inducted to office.

The faculty parted on good terms with Fall, the deposed principal, giving him an exoneration for his management, and salary for the half year to ensue, amounting to £73 8s. They also allowed payment of half a year's salary to William Blair, the deposed regent, and James Wemyss, the deposed professor of Divinity. The case of Thomas Gordon, regent and regius professor of Oriental Languages, gave more trouble. In 1689 the faculty entered on a process against him for a scandal, but he carried his case to the Court of Session and was absolved. He found it prudent, however, to give in a demission of his office as regent, and the faculty showed their discernment of the signs of the times by electing as his successor George Sinclair, who had been regent from 1654 to 1666, when he demitted office rather than comply with the ecclesiastical arrangements of the time.

The Visitors had regarded Gordon as no longer a member of the University after he had demitted his place as regent; but on 20th December, 1690, when a settlement was made with the other deposed members, Gordon came forward with a claim for a salary of 600 marks for three and a half years, in virtue of the commission granted to him by James VII. to be professor of Oriental Languages. According to Principal Dunlop, Gordon 'was very unfitt for our society yet was litigious.' At an earlier stage the faculty had promised a certain amount, and they agreed that, on his giving in a demission of his second academic office, they would pay him a thousand marks out of the vacant stipends.

In September, 1690, the Commissioners of Visitation laid down strict rules that no one, even though he had a presentation, should be received as a master or regent in any University without 'ane previous tryall, and program' to be affixed to the University or College in which he sought appointment, inviting candidates to dispute for the place. It was ordained that the presentee should be obliged to dispute on any 'problematicall subject' if candidates offered, and that he should undergo trial by examination or otherwise if the judges of the University thought fit. The judges were to consider not only the ability and learning of the candidate, but 'other good qualifications complexidlie,' such as good life, prudence, fitness for the place, and affection to the government in Church and State. For the future the admission of any regent was to be null and void if he had not complied with these rules, but they were not to apply to the principal, the professor of Divinity, or any other professor ; and in 1695 it was further enacted that they should not apply to a regent transported from one College to another. As the era of regents was drawing towards an end, these regulations by and by ceased to be operative. Towards the close of 1690 there was an unprecedented competition for a vacant regency, nine candidates (one of whom, William Jameson, was blind from birth) appearing and disputing for a fortnight. They acquitted themselves so well that it was considered there was not one who had not given sufficient proofs of learning to deserve the place. The faculty had difficulty in coming to a decision, but having made a short leet, they resolved to determine the appointment from it by lot, and on 2nd January, 1691, the lot fell on John Law, who forthwith became regent. The faculty considerately ordered five pounds sterling to be paid to each of the remaining candidates.

Apart from the honorarium of five pounds, the eight candidates besides Law were not all unsuccessful, for three other competitors—James Knibloe, William Jameson, and John Loudon—obtained academic appointments in no long time. About five weeks after the close of the competition, the faculty, considering that funds would probably be available from vacant stipends to which the College had right of sufficient amount to enable them to afford a salary of 600 marks yearly, resolved immediately to appoint a fit person to be professor of Humanity and History, and to be counted one of the masters of the University, as the professors of Humanity used to be—the appointment at the outset to be made for two years only, in case the funds from vacant stipends might prove inadequate.

James Knibloe, who had competed with Law for the vacant regency, was shortly afterwards appointed to this profession. He soon quitted Humanity, however, for on 4th December, 1691, it is stated that, as William Leggat had not accepted the profession of Philosophy, and as Knibloe was in charge of the Greek class, the faculty appointed him to be regent or professor of Philosophy, and declared his former profession of Humanity vacant. He continued as regent for three sessions only, and in October, 1694, as the faculty deemed it for the good of the University, he demitted his charge. A parting allowance of 1,300 marks was made to him, 500 of which represented a sum given by him to his predecessor, and 800 being considered due to him as his 'ann.' He was succeeded by Gerschom Carmichael, who had previously held office at St. Andrews, and was elected a regent at Glasgow on 22nd November, 1694. Carmichael held office for thirty-five years, and had a notable reputation in his day.

In providing for the teaching of History along with Humanity the faculty laid stress on the former subject as tending to improve the instruction of youth, especially those of the best quality who might be called to serve their country in civil employments. After the transfer of Knibloe it was still desired to do something for the teaching of History, and in May, 1692, the faculty taking into account that William Jameson, though born blind, had been educated in the University till he had attained great learning, especially in Civil and Ecclesiastical History, and considering that he had no means to support himself and might be useful in these branches of knowledge, appointed that he should employ himself according to his capacity at the direction of the faculty. Some months later it was agreed that he should give a prelection once a week in Latin on Civil History. Jameson is sometimes called professor of History even in University documents, but as his tenure was precarious and he was not admitted to a share in academic administration, he may more properly be regarded as the earliest of University lecturers in the modern sense. He continued to teach for twenty-five years more. The Commission recommended him to the King for an annual allowance, but a number of years passed before it was obtained, and the University made him an allowance beginning with 200 marks yearly, but soon increased to £400 Scots. Jameson was the author of a number of works on ecclesiastical history and polemics, some of which continued to find readers for a century or more. In *My Schools and Schoolmasters* Hugh Miller mentions among the works perused in his youth 'blind Jameson's volume on the Hierarchy.'

George Sinclair, who was reappointed a regent in 1689, soon retired from that office to be made professor of Mathematics early in 1691, with a salary of 600 marks yearly, and the promise of an augmentation if the state of the funds would allow.   Since his time there has always been a distinct chair of Mathematics in the University.   Sinclair was a man of notable industry and perseverance, and one of the earliest Glasgow professors who showed a decided turn for physical and applied science, as is shown both by his professional work and his writings.   He was the author of a number of treatises on Mathematics, Hydrostatics, Coal, Astronomy and Navigation, and other subjects, and of *Satan's Invisible Works Discovered*, a book on witchcraft and ghosts.   Even his books on science sometimes contain a mixture of superstition, but he was not the only author of that age liable to this charge.   Professor James Gregory of St. Andrews made a derisive attack, on Sinclair's Hydrostatics in a pamphlet entitled *The Art of weighing Vanity*, but carefully abstained from questioning an account of the witches of Glenluce which Sinclair had very incongruously brought into his work.   After some time Sinclair retaliated in a manuscript entitled *Cacus pulled out of his Den by the Heels*, now preserved in the University library.

It was less to Sinclair's credit that in 1684 he published under the title of *Truth's Victory over Error*, a translation of David Dickson's *Praelectiones in Confessionem Fidei*, apparently with a design that it should pass for his own.   On ceasing to be a regent in 1666, he set up as an engineer and surveyor, and in this capacity he was extensively employed in connection with mines in the south-west of Scotland, and is said to have first suggested effective means of draining them.   About 1670 he was employed by the magistrates of Edinburgh to superintend the execution of the works for the first water supply brought into the city ; and if not the first, he was among the first who endeavoured to measure the height of mountains by means of variations of atmospheric pressure as indicated by mercury.   In this way he measured in 1668 and 1670 the heights of Arthur's Seat, Leadhills, and Tinto.

The faculty of Arts might now be regarded as having reached its normal equipment as measured by past times ; but on the deposition of Wemyss, the single professor of Divinity disappeared, and though before the Revolution it was reckoned part of the duty of the principal to take a share in the teaching of Divinity, a different course was afterwards followed.   Yet the need of teaching in Theology was perhaps the most urgent academic requirement of the time.   Over a great part of the country, and especially in the south-west, churches came to be vacant by the hundred after the Revolution.   Some of the Episcopal clergy retired voluntarily, some under demonstrations of displeasure from their parishioners, and some were deposed.   To fill the vacancies thus caused, few Presbyterian ministers were left, for those admitted before 1661 were mostly dispersed or dead or enfeebled by age, and since 1661 few had been admitted.

In February, 1691, the faculty resolved that there should again be two professors of Divinity, though there were not funds to allow them such stipends as formerly; indeed it was arranged that the seven chalders of victual and one thousand marks of money which had been the salary of the single professor of Divinity for the last twenty years should be divided equally between them. Better stipends were promised as soon as the King restored the bishopric of Galloway or provided some other grant. George Meldrum, minister of Kilwinning, and James Wodrow, minister at Glasgow, were chosen to be the two professors, but considerable delay occurred in the procedure required in the Church Courts to obtain liberation from their pastoral charges, and ultimately, through the intervention of the General Assembly, Meldrum was transferred to Edinburgh. When, on 22nd February, 1692, the principal reported this to the faculty, they ordered a new call to be given to Wodrow as sole professor of Divinity.

Though outside the University, Wodrow had been teaching in the interval. The training and experiences of this worthy man had been of a strangely chequered character. He graduated as M.A. at Glasgow in 1659, and then studied Divinity for three years, but disliking the turn ecclesiastical affairs took after the Restoration, he did not enter the Church, but continued to act as tutor to pupils of the Grammar School and students of the University till 1673. In that year he was licensed to preach by a number of Presbyterian ministers, among whom was Donald Cargill. For several years Wodrow preached in houses and in fields at the call of the people, and under the direction of ministers indulged and not indulged. In the severe times after Bothwell Bridge he retired to his native Eaglesham, and having among his other studies given some attention to medicine, especially botany and anatomy, he had thoughts of repairing to a foreign University to qualify for a medical degree. Soon after the Indulgence of 1687 he was urged to remove to Glasgow to teach the young men in training for the Presbyterian ministry, and in January, 1688, he settled there. Besides teaching Divinity, he was soon called to be minister of a congregation in the city, and he continued to act in both capacities till settled as professor of Divinity in the University early in 1692, when he brought his students with him. It was natural that the Wodrows should be interested in the sufferings of the Presbyterian Church in the days of its adversity, and Robert Wodrow, a son of the professor, has done more to preserve the memories of that time than even 'Old Mortality' himself.

For a dozen years from 1692 the teaching staff remained without further expansion and with little change in the individual teachers, except that Knibloe having resigned in 1694, Carmichael succeeded, and John Boyd having died early in 1699, John Loudon was chosen his successor, while in the same year Dr. Robert Sinclair became professor of Mathematics, the veteran George Sinclair having died a little before. Meantime the number of students was rapidly increasing. Before the Revolution they may probably have numbered from 120 to 150. In 1696 there were about 250, as is proved by the signatures attached to a bond of association occasioned by the discovery of a plot for the assassination of the King, the signatories to which bound themselves to defend his person and government and to avenge it upon his enemies if he came by a violent or untimely end. The next half dozen years witnessed an extraordinary expansion, for in 1702 Principal Stirling recorded that there were fully 400 students—106 in the first class, 69 in the second, 102 in the third, and 46 in the fourth, the remaining 80 being students of Divinity. The students at this time included a large number from Ireland and a sprinkling from England, while, besides the democracy, there were still many sons of the landed and titled aristocracy of Scotland.

Chambers were still let in the College for the accommodation of students, and a single chamber sometimes lodged more than one, but when the total number reached four hundred, the majority must have lodged outside. Teaching was to a large extent carried on by means of slow lecturing—notes dictated by the regents to the students ('dictates')—and by disputations among the students themselves, supplemented by oral examinations, comments, criticisms, and explanations by their teachers. Latin was the ordinary language used in communicating instruction, and probably it too often caused students to see things through a glass darkly, instead of face to face. It is hard to believe, however, that the teacher would never deviate into English, if he found it difficult to get his students to follow him. Certainly Wodrow, the professor of Divinity, made free use of English, and so did Andrew Ross, the first of the unbroken line of professors of Latin.

In June, 1691, in view of the necessity of conferring degrees on students whose course was finished, the faculty empowered Principal Dunlop to confer degrees on qualified candidates, pending the appointment of a chancellor. Till a chancellor was elected, they also empowered the principal to do all other things which the vice-chancellor might or could lawfully do. On 26th December, 1693, the faculty made regulations for the stenting or assessment of students about to graduate, who had to defray the expenses of the ceremony and provide an honorarium for the regent of the magistrand class ; and they enjoined strict economy in the ceremony, perhaps as much out of consideration for the magistrand regent as for the students.   The graduands were to meet and choose stentmasters acquainted with the taxable capacity of their constituents, and the stent-masters having fixed the assessment for others, were to propose an assess-ment for themselves, which might be confirmed or modified by a general meeting of the other assessed students.

While the number of students was rapidly increasing, the University felt itself straitened for lack of funds.   Dunlop and Carstares had already been in correspondence on this subject, and the latter had represented to the King the needy condition of the Scottish Universities and the urgent expediency of improving their endowments.   William treated the appli-cation with Dutch caution, and in April, 1691, Carstares could only write that he had spoken to the King about allowing the Universities some part of the Bishops' rents, and that he seemed more inclined to do so than to grant them to individuals.   On 28th August, 1691, the faculty resolved that Principal Dunlop should proceed to London as soon as the King returned from abroad, and should urge him to aid the revenues of the University.   On the 17th of the following month they made provision for the expenses of the principal's journey, instructed him to produce the report of the Visitation of 1664 as evidence of the needs of the University, and to represent that the revenues, derived as they were from tithes, in ordinary years, when the price of victual was £5 Scots per boll, fell short of the necessary expenses by £606 Scots.

The University formerly had right to the vacant stipends in the bishoprics of Glasgow and Galloway, and on the appearance of a consider-able number of vacancies in 1689, the masters, in anticipation of a great sum accruing to them, made necessary repairs on the fabric ; but though compositions amounting to £2,475 sterling were actually arranged for the vacancies, the Privy Council had gifted them away, and the University, which was burdened with a debt of nearly £1,000 sterling, was dis-appointed of this relief.   Formerly there had been two professors of Divinity, and both were urgently required, but the University now had enough to do to support one, and for want of funds had been obliged to suppress a chair of Medicine and a chair of Humanity and Civil History which formerly existed.   The necessity for a chair of Mathematics and Experimental Philosophy had obliged the masters to appoint a professor to teach these subjects, but there were no endowments for the chair. Instruments and apparatus were also required for Experimental Philo-sophy, and the scanty and impecunious library urgently called for support. The College buildings needed repair, and Blackfriars' Church, which formerly belonged to the University, and where its members used to attend worship, was completely ruinous, and neither the University nor the city could spare funds to restore it.

Several expedients for relieving the University were persuasively submitted for consideration by His Majesty. He was reminded that in 1641 Charles I. had granted the bishopric of Galloway as a perpetual mortification, but this had been taken away, greatly to the detriment of the University, on the restoration of Episcopacy in 1661. Now that Episcopacy was abolished, it was hoped that the King would make effectual the pious intentions of his royal grandfather. Charles I. had also intended to bestow on the University a good part of the revenue of the arch-bishopric of Glasgow, and the grant was ready for the King's signature when the Duke of Lennox prevailed to obtain it for himself ; but as that family was now extinct and the King had the bishopric at his disposal, the whole or a part of it might be granted to the University, and would suit even better than the bishopric of Galloway, being more conveniently situated and adjacent to the places where the University had tithes. It was also suggested that a sum resulting from the abolition of patronage in the Church might be assigned to the University for repair of buildings.

Early in 1692 the principal gave an account of his mission, and reported that the King showed a ready inclination to support the University of Glasgow, but was extremely busy with other affairs and not prepared to say what method would be followed. The faculty then requested Carstares to accept of a commission that he might 'agent the same affair at court,' and Carstares having agreed to do so, they gave him instructions similar to those furnished to the principal. In March, 1693, Dunlop informed the faculty that the King had granted a signature for £1,200 sterling to the Scottish Universities. This was followed in 1695 by the King granting a charter appointing that the £300 apportioned to the University of Glasgow should be paid from the revenues of the bishoprics of Glasgow and Galloway. Payments did not begin till after the charter of 1695 was issued, and in November, 1694, the principal informed the faculty that he had carefully made up the accounts, and found 'that the debts of the Colledge do dayly so grow that the revenue will run to ruin if not supported by some royal grant.' The faculty again requested the principal to proceed to London and wait on their Majesties to represent the needs of the University.

The grant of 1693 had been destined to the maintenance of a foreign professor of Theology—a measure favoured by Carstares, who believed in Dutch professors and perhaps intended to pay a compliment to William— and ten bursars in Divinity. This destination was not very acceptable to the moderators of the University of Glasgow, who wished to see their debts paid, and who, as there were already not a few bursaries in Divinity, were content with the addition of a smaller number than ten.   For the £300 in the charter of 1695 the Commissioners of the Treasury were required to allocate a portion of the dioceses of Glasgow and Galloway sufficient to yield the amount ; and the destination was altered so that £230 a year was to be applied towards the extinction of the debts of the University, and the remaining £70 to the support of four bursars in Theology, each receiving £10 annually during three years' study at Glasgow, and £40 in the fourth year, during which he was required to study at some foreign Protestant University.   After the debts were extinguished the Sovereign was to determine to what purpose the £230 should be applied.

Payment under this grant began to be made in 1696, but, whether from trouble in allocating a portion of the dioceses sufficient to yield the amount, or from unreasonableness on the part of the government officials, there were difficulties in settling with them.   Through the influence of Principal Dunlop a better arrangement was made, and the University obtained a nineteen years' tack of the archbishopric of Glasgow commencing in 1698, at five pounds Scots per boll of victual.   A considerable allowance was made for factorage, and in virtue of a letter from the King the University was allowed to retain £300 at settlement.   The University at the outset paid a grassum of £1,000 sterling—granted by the King to Carstares—and for the time this increased its debt, but it was agreed that a tenth part of the grassum should be allowed yearly to the masters when settling with the Treasury.   This tack of the archbishopric, with the payments considerably enlarged by George I., was continued from time to time by successive sovereigns till 1825, and was one of the main financial resources of the University.

A detailed financial statement for the five years from 1690 to 1694, with some figures for later dates, was submitted to the Commission of Visitation in 1696.   The yearly revenue was set down at £12,374 17s. 2d. Scots, and the yearly expenditure at £14,211 2s. 2d., leaving an annual deficit of £1,836 5s.   The masters submitted that, apart from the £70 for bursaries, the King's grant of £230 sterling (£2,760 Scots) would just suffice to pay the yearly deficit of £1,836 5s., and the interest at six per cent. on debt, leaving the University in possession of tenpence Scots yearly from the grant.

Dunlop takes credit to himself for his part in obtaining from Parliament in 1693 an enactment that teinds should not be bought from any College at nine years' purchase, and an exception of the Colleges from the

Parliament's Commission for plantation of kirks. In 1696 Dunlop was again using his influence with the Parliament at Edinburgh, and he obtained an act for the more speedy and easy collection of the College revenues, and a gift of the vacant stipends which had been in the patronage of the College.   In the same year 1696 the University received the sum of 1,200 marks (£66 13s. 4d. sterling) allowed by the act of Parliament of 1690 as compensation for loss of the ecclesiastical patronage of the two parishes of Old Monkland and Cadder.   Dunlop was for some time much engaged in negotiating and bargaining on behalf of the University with heritors in regard to teinds and vacant stipends, and the faculty in November, 1693, considering that the state of the funds did not permit them to reward him liberally, ordered that he should receive ten per cent. on sums outside of the ordinary revenue of the College which had been secured or might afterwards be secured through his exertions.

The Parliamentary Commission appointed in 1690 moved slowly. This may have been partly due to uncertainty regarding the financial aid to be provided for the Universities, but in proportion to the length of time the Commission existed and the bustle occasionally displayed, the results were slender.   Early in 1695 the Commissioners sent out a number of proposals and recommendations on which the several Universities were invited to report their opinions.   These proposals were briefer and less formal than the draft ordinances of recent University Commissions, but in principle they were much alike.   After the Universities had reported their opinions, some of the proposals were passed into enactments, either in the original form or in a modified one, while others were allowed to drop.

It was proposed that the regents, each in turn, should act as 'hebdomadars' in supervising the students who had chambers within the College ; and rules were suggested for the wearing of gowns, but in the case of students the object was, not to give them a costume which by conventional association of ideas might come to be regarded as the proper garb for youths engaged in academic pursuits, but to discourage wandering and mischief by making it more easy to detect red-gowned offenders. The masters were decidedly altruistic in their views on the subject, and did not relish a proposal to lay down regulations for the costume to be worn by themselves.

The Universities were also invited to give their opinions regarding the length of the session and the order of classes in the curriculum.   The Commission recommended that the professor of Greek should be fixed to the subject, as there were fewer eminent scholars in Greek than in philosophy, and that students should confine themselves to Greek during the

M

year of their attendance on that class.   Another recommendation, not by any means suitable to the case of Glasgow, where a chair of Mathematics had been established, was issued, that every year the regents should teach some rudiments of Mathematics to their students.   The Commissioners also recommended that a uniform course in philosophy should be prepared, which, after adjustment and approval, should more or less supersede the practice hitherto followed by the regents of dictating short notes ('dictates') to their students on the several branches which they taught.   The preparation, revision, and discussion to which this abortive proposal gave rise lasted half a dozen years or more.

In other subjects discussion was kept within endurable limits, and regulations were issued.   The session in all the Universities was to begin on 1st November and extend to 30th June, the regent of the magistrand class ceasing his teaching on 1st May, to give time for holding the degree examinations; but Colleges which had been wont to begin before 1st November were allowed to continue to do so, provided the regular work of the session was not commenced before 1st November.[1]   This exception seems to have been granted at the instance of Glasgow, where the custom was to open on 10th October.   A general rule for the preliminary examination of arts students in the Scottish Universities was laid down on 1st August, 1695.   None were to be admitted to the first or Bajan class of any College but upon strict trial of their proficiency in Latin, or to the Semi or second class without similar trial of their proficiency in Greek. This regulation shows that the idea of a compulsory preliminary examination is not a novelty first conceived in the latter part of the nineteenth century.   It was also enacted that students should be examined in their classes at the beginning of the session, the general enrolment of students being completed in time for this examination, and in case any student received special permission to enrol later, he was to be subjected to examination as well as others.   Students were also to be publicly examined in their classes at the end of the session, and were not at liberty to cease from attendance till this examination was over.

At the end of their course students were to be strictly examined in presence of the masters and regents, and none admitted to the degree of master of arts unless the faculty of the College found them sufficiently qualified.   The vicious or immoral were not to receive the degree till they satisfied the masters of their amendment.   Strangely enough, the faculty of Glasgow argued against a strict degree examination as an indispensable condition of graduation.   They approved of all students being examined, and of the degree being withheld from the stupidly ignorant and incapable; but thought it hard that those who had intelligence and had not

---

[1] The early days were occupied with revision of previous work.

very diligently improved it should be excluded from graduation, alleging that it would discourage them from study. The faculty also pleaded that many who had neglected their time in College had afterwards proved able and useful men. They further argued against a proposal of the Commissioners to give precedence according to order of merit, alleging that it would discourage many from taking degrees, and would impose on the masters a difficult and invidious task. The latter point was not insisted on, but the Commissioners wisely enacted that there should be a strict degree examination.

The Commissioners also laid down a rule that no one should be admitted as a regent under the age of twenty-one years ; and ordered that, pending the preparation of a uniform printed course of philosophy, the regents should submit beforehand to the principal or the dean of faculty the 'dictates' to be taught to their students in the session then ensuing, these being liable to correction by the principal or the faculty. This fore-shadowed one of the functions of the Boards of Studies constituted by the Commissioners under the Universities Act of 1889. In August, 1696, when the Commissioners of Visitation met at Glasgow, the principal informed them that the masters were very diligent, and that the ordinary hours of meeting of professors and masters with their students were from seven to nine in the morning, and from eleven to twelve in the forenoon, with an additional hour from three to four in the afternoon of Monday, Wednesday, and Friday. The professor of Divinity at the same time gave an account of his method of teaching.

Bursars before being admitted were required to produce certificates from the presbytery to which they belonged or from the minister or kirk session of their parish, and after admission, unless their attendance was good and their progress in study satisfactory, they might be deprived. Students were required to wear red gowns constantly during the session, and the masters were to wear black gowns. It had not hitherto been the custom at Edinburgh for students to wear gowns, and the masters there were recommended to introduce it, but Edinburgh showed its good sense in adhering to previous usage. Students were not to be received from one University into another without certificates from their former masters, and masters were required to grant such certificates unless they could give very pregnant reasons for withholding them. Students who were refused certificates without just cause might, however, be received into another College without them—a regulation which might admit of considerable laxity of interpretation. No student was allowed to graduate in any other College than that in which he completed his course, unless he obtained the consent of the masters of the College in which he completed it, which those who conferred the degree were to preserve for their warrant.   The regents in turn held the office of 'hebdomadar' or inspector for a week, and were enjoined to reside within the College during their week of office, and visit the students in their chambers before six in the morning and nine in the evening.   Masters and students were to attend public worship together on Sunday, and students were afterwards to give an account of the sermon.   The regents were to give a religious lesson once a week, and to teach and explain the Confession of Faith, while the students were to repeat the Catechism.

The scheme of providing a uniform text book in Logic, Ethics, and Physics for all the Scottish Universities, if it had been well carried out, might in one respect have proved useful.   In those days it must have been a formidable task for students, with no reasonably adequate text books, to take down from the regents' 'dictates' a proper account of the several subjects ; and, though some of the more clever students may have benefited by the exercise, many students would only accumulate a body of chaotic and inaccurate notes.   On the other hand, a uniform course might have had a stagnating effect if it remained unrevised for any length of time, and the teachers contented themselves with training students to repeat what was contained in the text book, but as the proposal was under-stood at Glasgow, regents were to be at liberty to differ from the text book, and to impart other teaching when they saw fit.

Different parts were assigned to the different Universities to compose, and each University was to commit the task to one or more of the regents in philosophy.   The work which each University produced was to be criticised by the other three, and this did not expedite matters.   Logic and General Metaphysics were assigned to the two Colleges of St. Andrews, general and special Ethics to Glasgow, general and special Physics to King's and Marischal College, Aberdeen, and Pneumatics or special Metaphysics to Edinburgh.   The moderators at Glasgow resolved that John Tran should compose the course on Ethics, Economics, and Politics, and Tran agreed to do so.

Long drawn out endeavours and elaboration followed, and finally the papers on the proposed uniform course were put into the hands of Gilbert Rule, principal of Edinburgh University, and after his death in 1701 could not be found.   After all the years of preparing, discussing, and revising, it is pitiful to see how the laborious trifling ended.

The common table for regents and foundation bursars established by the *Nova Erectio*, and afterwards so managed as to admit other bursars and students who paid for their entertainment, was maintained, with some intermissions, till the Revolution, but little is heard of its existence afterwards. The marked increase in the number of teachers, bursars, and students which soon took place may probably help to account for this. But a considerable number of students continued to live in rooms within the College which they hired as lodgings ; and about 1695 the Commissioners wished to see this arrangement more widely carried out in all the Universities, though it was pointed out that at Glasgow there were not enough chambers to accommodate half the students, and that for the most part parents preferred to have their sons board and lodge with some outside person on whose supervision the parents relied. Two or three years before this, in May, 1692, there is a record that the faculty ordered intimation to be made to students of philosophy to take up their lodgings in the College chambers next session, when the principal would see them conveniently bestowed.

In 1693 James Dunlop was appointed chamberkeeper, with a salary of 100 marks yearly out of the chamber rents, the remainder of which was to be applied to repair of buildings. For each of the upper chambers a charge of six shillings sterling was to be made ; for the middle chambers on the second story, four shillings ; and for the lower chambers, two shillings and sixpence. In 1712 the rents were considerably advanced, ten shillings being charged for the highest rooms on the south side, eight shillings for the highest on the north-east and some others, six shillings for the rooms on the middle story, and four shillings for those on the lower. The masters were to see the students subscribe at entry an inventory of the furniture in their rooms, and at the end of the session the furniture was to be redelivered in good condition along with the keys.

In 1711 Principal Stirling entered into an agreement with Alexander Eagle, the cook, to supply three diets daily ' with meat and drink ' for all the English students who might desire to board within the College, these students paying £3 sterling for each three months' board and proportionally for other periods. To enable him to provide for these boarders, Eagle was to have the use of the kitchen, brew-house, ovens, and utensils, as well as of a room to be used as a dining hall. But some of the students concerned liked better to dine than to pay. Eagle seems to have looked on his agreement with the principal as a guarantee that the latter would see him paid, but Stirling repudiated this interpretation, and in January, 1712, barely two months after the working of the scheme began, Eagle had to make a declaration that, though the principal had bound himself to do everything that was proper to secure payment from English students dieting within the College, yet he was not obliged to pay what these students or their guardians ought to do, but only to secure such effects as defaulters might have within the College.

For some time after the Revolution disturbances and offences among students in the Scottish Universities were more frequent than usual. In view of this the Privy Council on 9th March, 1693, authorised the principals, regents, and masters to fine students guilty of tumults and disorders, the fines being allocated to the use of the library, and the magistrates of the several University towns being required to interpose their authority to the sentence of the masters, and assist in carrying it out by imprisonment if necessary. Fines were to vary with the rank of the offenders, the maximum for a nobleman or his eldest son being £150 Scots ; for younger sons of noblemen, for barons or their eldest sons, £100 ; for the younger sons of barons or gentlemen, and for sons of burgesses, £50 ; and for sons of craftsmen or yeomen, fifty marks—in addition to the cost of repairing the damage in all cases. Sometimes the offence might be of the nature of an ill-timed frolic, or dealing in a light-hearted manner with an affair which should be taken seriously. Thus in 1702 Patrick Brown, a magistrand student, was expelled for giving in the name of Francis Montgomery to be prayed for by the congregation at the Sunday service— Montgomery being so far from ill or afflicted that he was sitting in the College pew at the time.

Sometimes disputes between the students and townspeople gave rise to serious disorders. About the New-year 1704 the townspeople resented some misconduct by the students, and appear to have carried off one or more of the latter to prison. Some students then seized the keys of the prison, and made an attack on the house of William Wilson (probably the jailor). The citizens retaliated by entering the College, drawing their swords, and shooting among the unarmed students even in the inner court —pronounced to be a high violation of the privileges of the University which in the memory of man was never known to be equalled. The magistrates and the College masters afterwards met and endeavoured to come to a settlement.

An effort was to be made to frame regulations by which, without prejudice on either side, disorderly students might be regularly secured till they were delivered to the principal to be duly punished. There seems to have been an acknowledgment of the jurisdiction of the College over its students outside its own precincts. Occasionally students brought discipline upon themselves by carrying arms and challenging each other to duels. The mention of duels in connection with the University naturally recalls the passage in *Rob Roy* where Scott describes the encounter with swords between Rashleigh and Francis Osbaldistone in the College gardens, ended by the opportune intervention of the redoubtable Macgregor. Scott did not err in regard to the character of the place and time, or the hot temper of the young irascibles who preferred sword play to reasoning.

Principal Dunlop's influence helped to lead the University into a financial enterprise but too well known in Scottish history—the Company in Scotland trading to Africa and the Indies, usually called the Darien Scheme, although it had much wider aims than merely the formation of a settlement at Darien. Of the four hundred thousand pounds sterling subscribed for this great but ill-starred undertaking, fifty-six thousand came from Glasgow. Dunlop himself invested a thousand pounds in the venture, and under his advice the University resolved to contribute a thousand pounds. The three regents, Boyd, Tran, and Law, each invested £100, and Dunlop was instrumental in procuring contributions from some gentlemen in the West of Scotland. As already mentioned, Dunlop had spent some years in the Colony of Carolina, and his experiences there may have led him to take an interest in a Company which had for one of its aims the settlement of Scots Colonies ; and the Company showed their appreciation of Dunlop's support by making him a director, but he does not seem to have been a very active one.

The Scots have been blamed for credulity in entering on this enterprise. But even if the charge be made out, they were not more credulous than other men, for when a portion of the capital was offered for subscription in London, it was taken up with eagerness and alacrity till the interference of the English Parliament, stirred up by the clamour of monopolists who alleged that the commerce of England would be ruined by the success of the new Company, obliged the London shareholders to withdraw. The merchants of Hamburg were also ready to support the Company, had they not been hindered by the strenuous hostility of King William's English Resident there and of his Envoy to the Court of Lunenberg. The Isthmus of Panama was selected for the site of the new colony as a place fitted to command the trade of both the Atlantic and Pacific coasts of America, and to be a stage in the long sea passage between Europe and India, China, and other countries of the far east ; and the unhealthy summer climate of Darien was the direful spring of disaster to the enterprise. The Act of Parliament incorporating the Company empowered them to make settlements, and to build cities, harbours, and fortifications in any place in Asia, Africa, or America which was uninhabited, or where they had the permission of the natives, and where they did not encounter the previous claims of any European sovereign. They were also empowered to make treaties and to defend themselves from attack.

In July, 1698, three vessels with twelve hundred men on board sailed from Leith, and in the early days of November their passengers landed at the projecting point of the Gulf of Darien. Some huts were erected as the beginning of a town, called New Edinburgh, fortifications were thrown up, and the natives proved not unfriendly, but after the lapse of some months and the approach of summer, the pestilential climate, aggravated by the want of provisions, and of clothing and equipment suitable to the country, made havoc with the health and lives of the settlers. From May to September, 1699, additional ships, with reinforcements of men and new supplies, were sent out, but the remnants of the first settlers had fled before the reinforcements arrived. The later emigrants found desolation where they expected prosperity, dissension and disease aggravated their situation, and the Spaniards—-emboldened by the ill success of the expedition, and the freezing attitude towards it of King William, who wished to have the support of Spain in his European policy—laid claim to the territory which the Scots had occupied.

The views of some writers on the question of territory are remarkable. There are no bounds to their righteousness when righteousness can be made to tell against a rival company. One might fancy that in forming their numerous foreign settlements the English had never deviated a hairbreadth from the principles laid down in the Sermon on the Mount. When the Spanish forces were mustering, two hundred Scots whose health had not been shaken, with Campbell of Finab, a dauntless and experienced old soldier, at their head, rapidly crossing the Isthmus, attacked and routed a greatly superior force under Don Balthasar at Tubacantee. When the victors returned to the Colony they found it blockaded by a number of Spanish men of war. Campbell and other daring spirits would have resisted against all odds, but finding they could not carry the majority with them, they contrived to make their escape in a small vessel, and left the majority, who were broken by reverses, starvation, and disease, to capitulate to the Spaniards and evacuate the settlement. Two more ships with additional emigrants from Scotland arriving after the evacuation, narrowly escaped being seized by the Spanish garrison.

The settlement of a colony at Darien was not the sole object contemplated, but the Company never recovered from the great disaster which befell the colony, though its other business lingered on in an enfeebled condition for a number of years. Scotland had put forth an unwonted effort in order to provide the capital, and severely felt the loss. Suffering begot discontent, and there were complaints both loud and deep regarding the King's attitude. As a director, Dunlop no doubt had his share of anxiety, while Carstares, his brother-in-law, often helpful in Scottish affairs, seems to have made up his mind not to offend William however things might go. Probably the disaster which befell the Company helped to shorten Dunlop's days, for he died in the prime of life on 8th March, 1700, within five months of the time when news of the first great reverse at Darien reached Edinburgh. The money invested by the College was repaid in 1708 (out of the Equivalent Grant, as we may assume) through the principal's son—Professor Alexander Dunlop. The amount returned was £3,624 Scots, and the faculty determined to invest £3,081 of this amount, and to pay the yearly produce, estimated at £160, as an augmentation to the salary of the professor of Humanity, who also received £240 from grassums of the vicarage of the Subdeanery and £300 from Queen Anne's grant. Within a month of the death of her husband, Carstares obtained from King William a pension of £60 a year for Mrs. Dunlop.

It was more than a year after Principal Dunlop's death before his successor was appointed, but on 8th May, 1701, the King presented John Stirling, then minister at Greenock and previously at Inchinnan, who had been recommended by Sir John Maxwell, the rector. Stirling was an intimate friend of Robert Wodrow, the Church historian, and took part with him eighteen or nineteen times in conducting the communion services at Eastwood; while for seventeen years the two rode together between Glasgow and Edinburgh to and from the meetings of the General Assembly and Commissions of Assembly three times a year. Wodrow says 'the principal was an excellent gospel preacher and preached much'; that 'he was a person of public spirit, and singularly sweet in prayer, and very much taken up in ejaculatory prayer, even to his being mocked for it by his enemies'; that 'he was a person of great weight in our Synods, Commissions, and Assemblies'; that he was 'once Moderator of the Assembly, and when he was Moderator our Form of Process was passed by the Assembly, in which he had a good share'; and that as principal he 'contributed much to promote the prosperity of the College.' Without disputing Wodrow's estimate of Stirling the clergyman, one may doubt whether he has not been rather partial to Stirling the principal. There was much strife and unrest in the University during his time, he seems to have been too peremptory in his relations with many of his colleagues and partial in his relations with others, and the part he took in the financial affairs of the institution was by no means helpful. The University did not gain by exchanging Dunlop for Stirling. But though Stirling's tenure was a troubled one, especially in the latter part, it is fair to add that notwithstanding this, the development of the institution went on apace, the teaching staff being doubled in his time.

A portion of the College garden having been set apart for botanical purposes, the faculty in 1704 appointed John Marshall, surgeon in

Glasgow, to be keeper of the Physic garden, as it was called, and to instruct students in Botany. The faint beginnings of a Medical School had now appeared, and the University had begun to examine candidates for the degree of M.D. The chair of Medicine was refounded in 1713, and a chair of Anatomy was established in 1720 or earlier, the chair of Botany being for a long time combined with it. The country had reached a stage at which a Medical School might have prospered, but its development was hindered by the aversion to teaching displayed by Johnstoun, the professor of Medicine, and Brisbane, the professor of Anatomy and Botany. Surgeons from the city were called in to teach Anatomy while Brisbane neglected that duty, and students seem to have been attracted in appreciable numbers; but it was not till Cullen and others had succeeded to the places of the early and indolent professors, and other needful subjects began to be taught, that the Medical School had a fair opportunity to develop.

The ancient and honourable subjects of Greek and Latin were the next to obtain separate chairs. Greek had been taught from the time of Melville, but it belonged to the province of the regents, and was liable to be taught by any of them in rotation with other subjects, while the regent who taught Greek was directed by the *Nova Erectio* to teach Latin as well.[1] In 1695 the Commission proposed that the professor of Greek should be fixed to the Greek class, but the answer from Glasgow was that there was no reason to fix the Bajan regent more than the rest, every regent being qualified to teach Greek. Afterwards it was pleaded that the Bajan regent should not be fixed to Greek, but that when a vacancy occurred a professor eminent in Greek might be appointed. For a number of years the faculty evaded the wishes of the Commission, but early in 1702 the Commissioners minuted that St. Andrews and Glasgow had not yet fixed constant masters for teaching Greek on pretence of some difficulties and scruples, and ordered that they should do so by October next. Upon this, the masters at Glasgow petitioned that they might not be required to carry out the order till a vacancy occurred, as the present regents had been chosen more especially for proficiency in philosophy. A short respite was obtained, but in 1704 the death of John Tran created a vacancy which was filled up by the appointment of a professor of Greek. The faculty referred to the statutes and found it was warrantable to settle the appointment without a trial by combat, that is, without following the programme of public disputation which the Commissioners had laid down in 1690 for appointment of masters and regents but not of professors.

[1] About the end of the 16th and beginning of the 17th centuries one regent was sometimes confined to Greek.

Alexander Dunlop, son of the late principal, was the preferred candidate, and as a trial of his ability he was required to give an analysis of eleven lines of Homer. He was also instructed to attend at the principal's house, so that any master desiring satisfaction regarding the candidate's knowledge of Greek might have access to him. On 26th September, 1704, it was minuted that Dunlop's analysis of the eleven lines of Homer had been approved, and that he had attended at the principal's house and satisfied such of the masters as called. Dunlop then took the oath of allegiance and the oath *de fideli*, promised to sign the Confession of Faith, and entered on his tenure of office which lasted forty-two years. As an administrator he was active, and as a teacher one of the foremost men of his time at Glasgow. In 1708 Queen Anne assigned a sum of twenty pounds yearly as an augmentation to the salary of the professor of Greek.

By the *Nova Erectio* the first regent was required to exercise his students in both Greek and Latin, though the former was his leading subject. Separate masters or professors of Latin were sometimes appointed, but the office was rather insecure and liable to temporary extinction when there was pressure on the funds. James Roberton was elected professor of Philosophy and Humanity in 1618, but he probably taught Latin in the same way that some later regents taught Hebrew, as an addition to the ordinary work of a regent. David Monro was master of the Humanity class in 1637, and after this a teacher of Humanity may be reckoned as part of the normal teaching staff. William Hamilton succeeded Monro in 1637, and in 1642 there was a master of Humanity, for he was remonstrating about his inadequate salary. In 1648 John Dickson resigned his place as Humanity master on very short notice, and William Strang, the principal's son, was appointed to succeed him. The Commission of 1664 included a professorship of Humanity as part of the rightful equipment of the University, and, as already stated, James Young was professor from 1682 to 1687, when he obtained an appointment outside the University and the chair was suppressed for the time.

In October, 1705, about a year after Dunlop had become professor of Greek, the faculty impressed with the necessity of reviving the professorship of Humanity, and considering that the grassums of the vicarage of the subdeanery if all invested would yield a yearly salary of £20 sterling, resolved to re-establish the professorship in October, 1706. A few days later Andrew Rosse, a student recommended by the Presbytery and the University of Edinburgh, offered himself as a candidate. As a trial of his skill he was required to submit an English version of the letter of Tiberius to the Senate in the third book of the *Annals* of Tacitus, and a Latin version of Lord Loudon's speech to the King in *Rushworth's*

Collections, and shortly afterwards his versions were 'well approven.' He was admitted to office on 4th June, 1706, the faculty having previously enacted that the professor should not teach grammar, except that he might go over the substance and the fundamental rules with his students in the beginning of the year, and that no students should be admitted to the class unless they had learned the three parts of grammar, their knowledge of these parts being tested by examination before they were admitted.

A long paper by Rosse explaining his method of teaching is extant, and bears evidence of his having taken pains to make his teaching clear, effective, and interesting. Moreover, while other professors still followed the traditional method of lecturing in Latin, the professor of Latin had the good sense to make free use of English in teaching and exercising his students. Rosse also instituted a class for higher instruction, which was attended by some who had completed the course and graduated, and by some who were not otherwise students in the College. In this course the professor did all the speaking, dealt with grammar, criticism, and Roman customs, and prelected on Latin authors. Such was the origin of the private Humanity class, as it was long called, but which under recent regulations has become the honours Humanity class. A similar class has long existed in Greek, but probably its origin was somewhat later. In 1708 Queen Anne assigned £25 a year to the professor of Humanity.

Professor Wodrow had the sole work of teaching the students of Divinity, and devoted himself to it with diligence and care. In his later years, when age and infirmity had crept upon him, the burden grew rather heavy for the old man, and he agreed to quit £400 Scots a year to help to provide a salary for a second professor of Divinity, a like sum being available on account of the salary hitherto paid by the University being now paid by the Treasury, while the University agreed to add a further sum to bring the second professor's salary up to £1,000 Scots. This being arranged, the moderators of the University on 18th October, 1705, appointed Professor James Wodrow's son, Alexander Wodrow, one of the ministers of Glasgow, to be second professor of Divinity, but unfortunately he died almost immediately, and his father, after struggling on a little longer, died on 25th September, 1707.

In a little time John Simson, a graduate in Arts of Edinburgh, who had been a student of Divinity under Wodrow in 1694, and afterwards became minister of Traquair, was appointed, his induction taking place in November, 1708. Simson married Principal Stirling's niece, and in academic controversies usually supported the principal. He was also related by marriage to Robert Dick, one of the regents, and by consanguinity to Robert Simson, who became professor of Mathematics in

1711. Simson seems to have regarded himself as too great a man to be understood and criticised by country ministers. Whether his views on the rather abstruse questions which afterwards brought him into trouble be regarded as dangerous or not, if he had adopted them conscientiously and held them with earnest conviction, caring more for them than for his status and emoluments, his course of thought might have been respected. But when his status and emoluments came to be in danger, he sheltered himself behind the most orthodox declarations.

In the Act of Security which accompanied the Treaty of Union in 1707, it was declared that the Universities of St. Andrews, Glasgow, Aberdeen, and Edinburgh should continue forever. It was also enacted that every professor, principal, regent, or master should before his admission subscribe the Confession of Faith as the confession of his faith, and bind himself in presence of the Presbytery to conform to the discipline and worship of the Established Church ; and this test was not repealed or modified till 1853. In 1709 the Scottish Universities acquired Stationers' Hall privileges (of little value at first), but as regards their general organisation and endowments the Parliament of the United Kingdom left them for a hundred and fifty years to continue, if so they might, with little assistance from it. The Scots Parliament, almost with its dying breath, ratified and confirmed King William's grant of £300 sterling yearly to the University of Glasgow ; and recommended the Queen to grant some augmentation of the salaries of the professors in the four Universities. Stirling repaired to London in the summer of 1708 to use his influence with a view to procure a royal grant, and was so far successful that Queen Anne, by a charter, dated 22nd September, 1708, granted to the University of Glasgow from the Civil List of Scotland an annual sum of £210, to provide salaries of £40 yearly to the professor of Oriental Languages, £40 to the professor of Mathematics, £25 to the professor of Humanity, and £30 to the professor of Botany ; and augmentations of £22 yearly to the principal, £11 to each of the three professors of Philosophy, and £20 to the professor of Greek. In connection with the procuring of this grant and some expenses incurred by Principal Stirling the faculty voted to him a sum of £3,216 Scots.

Forty pounds a year being now available as a salary for a professor of Oriental Languages, steps were taken for making an appointment. The main business of the professor was to teach Hebrew, a subject taught in some form since the *Nova Erectio*, under which the principal was teacher of Hebrew and Syriac. When the principal did not teach, Hebrew might have been expected to fall to the lot of the professor of Divinity, or one of the professors of Divinity if there were two ; but latterly the teaching

of Hebrew had been assigned to a regent or professor in Arts.   Thomas
Gordon's brief tenure as professor of Oriental Languages under a presentation from James VII. has already been mentioned.   John Tran had
been teaching Hebrew before Gordon was made professor, and he again
taught the subject after Gordon's demission.   In addition to his emoluments as a regent, Tran received 300 marks yearly for this work.   Upon
Tran's death in 1704, the faculty committed the teaching of Hebrew to
Dr. Sinclair, professor of Mathematics.   Shortly after the announcement
of Queen Anne's grant, the faculty on 12th January, 1709, by desire of
the Chancellor, the Earl of Hyndford, and with the consent of the Rector,
Sir John Maxwell of Nether Pollok, elected Charles Morthland to the
office.

Morthland had been an assistant master in a country Grammar School,
and it may be doubted whether his attainments in Hebrew were at all
extraordinary.   It was made a condition that he should stand his trials,
but the faculty considerately allowed him the greater part of a year to
prepare, and during that time he appears to have studied at the University
of Utrecht.   In October, 1709, Morthland produced testimonials from
Reland, professor of Oriental Languages at Utrecht, and successfully
underwent his trials, it being also reported that several members of faculty
had conversed with him to their satisfaction, which probably means that
he went through some sort of friendly oral examination.   The faculty
pronounced him fit for the profession of Oriental Languages, and he was
inducted to office with more than usual display, the Duke of Montrose,
the Lords of Session then on circuit in Glasgow, and the Lord-Advocate
being invited to hear his inaugural address.   From the circumstances of
its foundation and endowment this chair might naturally have been
retained in the patronage of the Crown, like that of Law or Medicine,
but it has been left in the hands of the University.   As the forty pounds
granted by the Queen was considered an insufficient salary, the faculty
resolved to continue to Morthland the £200 Scots formerly paid to the
regent or professor who taught Hebrew.   Morthland established a course
extending over two years, and including some Chaldee and Syriac as well
as Hebrew, and he taught Arabic when students desired it.

The occurrence of Mar's insurrection[1] gave the University an opportunity of ingratiating itself with the Hanoverian King and his government, and immediately afterwards a third chair was added in the faculty
of Theology.   It is recorded that the faculty on 3rd August, 1715, being

[1] On a rumour of a French and Irish invasion on behalf of the Pretender in 1708, the
principal and professors agreed to subscribe for the maintenance of a company of fifty-one
soldiers for forty days.

certainly informed of the popish pretender's design to invade Britain, in order to show their concern for religion and their zeal and affection for the person and government of King George, agreed to maintain a company of not fewer than fifty foot soldiers for forty days after the time of their being called up by public authority, engaging to pay sixpence a day to each soldier.   The principal was asked to inform the Duke of Montrose, then Chancellor of the University and one of the Secretaries of State, of their resolution, and request him to lay the matter before the King, that His Majesty might be pleased to order officers and arms for the company.

On 18th August the principal informed the faculty that he had written to the Duke of Montrose with an account of their offer, and that the Duke having resigned office as Secretary before receiving the letter, had placed it in Lord Townshend's hands.   Townshend wrote in acknowledgment stating that he had communicated their offer to the King, and was directed to return hearty thanks for their zeal.   The principal was particularly desired to acquaint the faculty with His Majesty's sense of their affection to his person and government, by which they had secured a just title to the King's favour when the concerns of the faculty should require it.   Respecting officers and arms they might depend on what was necessary for their security, but the King hoped there would be no occasion to proceed further in the way proposed, as the government had taken the necessary measures for the security of Glasgow and the neighbouring country.   Three regiments were to be transported from Ireland, a regiment of dragoons despatched, and a regiment of foot levied, to be commanded by Brigadier Grant, while further reinforcements would be sent if needful.   By 17th September the faculty were informed of the rising in the north, and that Argyle, the King's general in Scotland, had sent pressing messages to the magistrates of Glasgow to despatch as many of their men as they could to Stirling.

The faculty then resolved to advance as much money as would maintain fifty men for twenty days, at sixpence a day for each man, the principal subscribing for eight, the professor of Divinity for five, Gerschom Carmichael and Alexander Dunlop for four each; and as the majority of the masters were then absent, a precept was ordered to be drawn on any of the factors for contributions which the absentees were afterwards to repay. The faculty ordered that a further advance to maintain the company should be made if needful, and that in the meantime pay for twenty days should be handed to the commissary appointed to receive money for supporting the men, who were presently to march.   On 4th November it was reported that several members had paid to Alexander Dunlop their second moiety for the maintenance of the fifty men, and the faculty in view of the continuance of the insurrection, resolved to make an advance for twenty days more, being sixty days in all, if needful for suppressing the rebellion—all the payments being made out of the several members' own money.

The battle of Sheriffmuir was fought nine days later, and though it was not a positive victory or defeat for either side, the cause of the insurgents afterwards went from bad to worse, and soon ended in ignominious failure. With the resources available in 1715, Montrose or Dundee or even Prince Charlie might have shaken the throne of George, but it was folly to enter on an insurrection under a commander of such pitiful incapacity as Mar.

It seems to have been on the hint conveyed by Lord Townshend of the King's favour when academic affairs should require it, that the University caused a representation to be made to George I. of the need for the endowment of a chair of Ecclesiastical History and for augmentations to the slender salaries attached to certain existing chairs. The representation was successful, and on 4th July, 1716, the King granted an additional sum of £170 yearly from the revenues of the archbishopric of Glasgow, £100 of which was allocated as a salary to the professor of Ecclesiastical History, and £70 to the improvement of the smaller salaries. Ecclesiastical History had previously been taught as well as practicable, and there are notices of its having been dealt with by Melville, Baillie, and others. Several years elapsed after the grant had been procured before a professor was appointed, and it has been suggested that the delay may have occurred out of consideration for William Jameson, the blind scholar appointed to lecture on History in 1692, who died about the time when the first appointment was made.

But the University was in a troubled state, and the principal may have been waiting for an opportunity to introduce a new professor who would be likely to support his policy. In January, 1720, James Dick, minister of Carluke, received a commission from the King to be professor of Ecclesiastical and Civil History or second professor of Divinity. In March following, the Commission was submitted to a University meeting, and it was resolved by a majority to send a deputation to the Presbytery of Lanark with a view to procure the release of Dick from his charge at Carluke.

Forbes, the professor of Law, dissented from this resolution, pointing out that the King's commission merely required them to receive and admit the person presented, on his offering to them his presentation ; and that the prosecution of the matter before the Presbytery appeared to belong to His Majesty's Solicitor, as in the case of the Rev. James Chambers recently

ROBERT SIMSON, M.A., M.D.

Professor of Mathematics, 1711-1761

BORN 1687.   DIED 1768

From oil painting in the Senate Room, University of Glasgow

appointed principal of King's College, Aberdeen. Forbes also dissented because Principal Stirling, being uncle-in-law to the presentee, Robert Dick being his brother, and John Simson married to his sister-in-law, they should not have voted on the question, and then the vote would have been carried in the negative. Gerschom Carmichael, Alexander Dunlop, and Robert Simson joined in the dissent. The question was carried to the General Assembly, and that reverend court declined to sanction the transference of Dick, so that his presentation never took effect. In August, 1721, William Anderson was admitted as professor. He was a son of the minister of Drymen, near the seat of the Duke of Montrose, and probably his promotion had been owing to the Duke's influence. Having now a professor of Divinity, a professor of Ecclesiastical History, and one of Oriental Languages, the faculty of Theology was, for the times, tolerably well equipped.

Towards the end of 1712, having obtained from the rector, Sir John Maxwell, an opinion that an effort should be made to establish a chair of Law and a chair of Medicine, and to procure from Queen Anne for their support an allocation of part of the unappropriated portion of King William's grant, the faculty resolved to petition the Queen accordingly. As most of this grant of King William's had been destined in the first instance to the payment of the College debts, we may infer that by this time these debts were nearly if not quite extinguished.

In December of the following year the Queen assigned from this source a salary of £90 a year for a professor of Civil Law, and £40 a year as a salary for a professor of Medicine. Professor Alexander Dunlop was sent to Edinburgh to consult with the rector, Sir John Maxwell, then Lord Justice Clerk, and others, with a view to the selection of a suitable incumbent for the new Law chair. He brought back a report that William Forbes, advocate, was very strongly recommended, and on 28th January, 1714, the faculty appointed him professor of Civil Law; and next day they passed a number of regulations regarding the new chair and students of Law. It was provided that those entering for the study of Law who had not formerly been students of the University should matriculate and make certain payments to the College servants. Law students were to be 'stented' for the library by their own professor, in order to provide the necessary books on Law.

To prevent encroachments on the provinces of previous professors, it was laid down that the professor of Law should teach nothing but Civil, Feudal, Canon, and Scots Law—surely a sufficiently wide range for one man's energies. It was thought probable that some Law students might need to attend classes in other subjects, and the faculty agreed to consider the conditions under which they might be admitted to such classes ; and recommended Professor Forbes to see that his students were duly prepared for the study of Law by having a competent knowledge of languages and philosophy.   In August, 1714, the faculty having informed themselves of the practice of other Universities at home and abroad, ordained that in point of precedence the professor of Law should rank next to the professor of Divinity, and the professor of Medicine next to the professor of Law. The establishment of a chair in Law was a distinct gain to the University and the legal profession, and the choice of Forbes as professor was a fortunate one, as he proved a capable teacher and administrator.

The allocation of the grant of £210 from the Civil List of Scotland made in 1708 by Queen Anne led to a dispute between Dr. Sinclair, professor of Mathematics, and the principal.   In December, 1709, Sinclair was called to order for having in a recent visit to London blamed the principal for the distribution of the grant.   Sinclair owned that he had done so, and pleaded that he was not then aware that the distribution had been made by the Queen's charter of gift, though he had since learned that this was the case.   He also admitted having used expressions in disparagement of the masters and professors.   He promised to write to London acknowledging his mistakes, but six weeks later he had changed his mind and declined to do so.   Stirling admonished him for contumacy, and on 26th May, 1710, he agreed to demit office from 1st December following.   It is curious to note that in 1729, when a new Sovereign reigned, and a new principal and a new professor of Mathematics were in office, George II. made a fresh allocation of the £210, under which £62 was apportioned to Mathematics in place of £40 assigned in 1708.

Sinclair's demission made way for the most eminent professor of Mathematics that ever occupied the chair—Robert Simson, who late in life graduated as M.D. at St. Andrews, where his brother was professor of Medicine, and thus became a doctor in the same faculty as his predecessor. A native of West Kilbride, Ayrshire, Simson, at the age of fourteen, entered the University in 1701, under the regency of John Tran.   He was intended for the ministry, but found in Mathematics a more congenial study, and taking things leisurely, he graduated as M.A. in 1711.   The faculty seem to have had him in view for the chair when Sinclair's withdrawal was announced, and on 8th March, 1711, they nominated him to the chair, provided he should satisfy them on trial.

Simson had previously gone to London, where he spent about a year in friendly communication and discussion with some of the most eminent mathematicians of the day, but without becoming exactly a pupil to any of them.   Upon his return, the faculty on 9th November, 1711, required him to solve two geometrical problems, and to give a specimen of how he would begin to teach Geometry and Algebra. Next day Simson went through his trials successfully, and a few days later was admitted to the chair, which he held for the long period of fifty years, devoting himself with diligence and success to the restoration of the work of the ancient geometers, especially Euclid and Pappus, and achieving a reputation which enhanced that of the University. It should be mentioned to his credit that—though probably his appointment had been partly owing to the influence of his uncle, John Simson, the professor of Divinity, and of Principal Stirling—he soon became an opponent of their unenlightened policy.

Robert Dick, who had previously been tutor to the Master of Belhaven, having been elected a regent in philosophy, was admitted to office on 22nd October, 1714. When 'regenting' was abolished in 1727, he became professor of Natural Philosophy. Even before his time we can discern the beginning of an interest in science, and of the employment of apparatus and instruments for teaching purposes. In the statement of the needs of the University which Principal Dunlop was commissioned to lay before the King in 1691, apparatus for Experimental Philosophy was included. In 1693 a telescope eight feet long, a prism, and tubes for weather glasses were laid up in the library ; and a number of books presented about this time by George Sinclair, professor of Mathematics, who had decided scientific leanings, relate to Physics, Astronomy, and allied subjects.

In 1704 a Botanic Garden was formed in the College grounds and a teacher of Botany provided. By this time or shortly after some physical instruments and apparatus had been procured. They were placed under the charge of the regent who for the time taught Natural Philosophy, the professor of Mathematics being also allowed the use of those appropriate to his students. In 1712 the faculty enacted that each regent who had the custody of the instruments should receive them according to inventory ; and return them under the same check and in good condition when his triennial turn of Physics was over. He was also to levy a 'stent' or assessment from the students for the maintenance of the instruments, but this assessment was not regularly and probably not often exacted. In 1726 some additional instruments, costing nearly £30, were procured from Hawksby of London.

Next year Dick was fixed to Natural Philosophy, and during the period of about thirty years in which he and his son held the chair accounts amounting to over £300 for instruments can be traced in the minutes, while indications of additional expenditure sometimes occur without the amount being stated. A complete apparatus for electrical experiments is mentioned among additional articles procured in 1749. In 1730 payments began to be made to Henry Drew for assistance in working the instruments and showing experiments in the course which Dick conducted twice a week in Experimental Philosophy. Drew is elsewhere described as a hammerman, and for a long time he received an annual allowance for keeping the steeple clock in order. He was the earliest laboratory assistant or demonstrator of whom we have record.

It is further evidence of the interest in Experimental Philosophy in Glasgow that in 1725 a gentleman from England designed to give a course in that subject, and applied to the Provost for permission. 'But the Provost, douce man,' declined to countenance the venture unless the consent of the University were obtained. Principal Stirling and John Loudon waited on the chief magistrate to return him hearty thanks and strengthen him in this resolution. The academic visitors were kindly received, and the Provost and eldest Bailie declared they looked on the interests of the University as their own.

Dick succeeded John Law, who had been a regent from 1691 till the breakdown of his health compelled him to demit his office in September, 1714. 'Dictates' and disputations made the staple of his teaching, as appears from the following declaration by him : ' My opinion is yt disputs and dictats must be kept up as usually till we see furder about us : reformations cannot be sudden in these cases, but must go on by slow degrees, till we can say yt the remedie is at least better yn the disease, if any be.' The other two who continued as regents along with Dick till the system of 'regenting' was abolished were Gerschom Carmichael, appointed in 1694, and John Loudon, appointed in 1699. Carmichael was for a long time very popular with the students, but in the latter part of his tenure being won over to support the policy of Principal Stirling, he became less of a favourite. He edited the works of Puffendorf, and was the author of a Latin manual of Logic which appeared in 1720, and a *Synopsis Theologiae Naturalis* published in 1729, works which had a considerable repute in their day. As a teacher he stood above most of his colleagues. He is sometimes credited with being the originator of the Scottish school of philosophy, and the impulse and direction which he gave to the mind of Hutcheson told on later generations of students. When 'regenting' was abolished in 1727, Carmichael chose the Ethics class and Loudon the Logic class, in accordance with an option allowed by the Commissioners.

Early in 1704 Carmichael and Loudon impugned the accuracy of the minutes of certain meetings, declaring that several things were minuted as acts of the faculty which were neither written by the clerk nor in presence of the faculty, nor as much as ever read in their presence, but which had been both written and signed privately by the principal acting both as praeses and clerk. The faculty, however, approved the minutes, and Carmichael and Loudon being censured and threatened with further proceedings, retracted.

In giving an account of the troubles and dissensions which arose about this time I have made some use of a small book published in Dublin in 1722 and of which Wodrow and others say that James Arbuckle, a lame student, was the author. Arbuckle graduated as M.D. in 1724, and settled in Dublin, where he had a respectable practice, and enjoyed the friendship of Swift. Arbuckle's narrative though not free from bias, nor from such minor inaccuracies as naturally beset an author who has no access to ófficial documents, is strongly corroborated from other sources, and appears to be trustworthy in the main.

During Dunlop's time the students had been deprived of their rightful share in the election of the rector, and they do not seem to have made any determined effort to resist. But in Stirling's time the majority of the masters, finding their own rights seriously threatened, made common cause with the students, and then came the tug of war. Allegations were made that the University authorities in the unsettled state of affairs after the Revolution were apprehensive that convening the students for the purpose of such an election might lead to tumults and disturbances. There were considerable disorders among the students occasionally, but there is no evidence of their having occurred in connection with the election of rector, and the apprehension of disturbances was probably only a pretext for confining the franchise to the principal and professors, who preferred to make the election themselves. In 1690 David Boyle of Kelburne was elected by the votes of three 'nations.' Next year it is recorded that, the *comitia* having been held in the ancient manner, Sir John Maxwell was elected by the votes of all the 'nations.'

For 1692 there is a double entry—the first stating that the Senate determined to continue Maxwell, and the second that, the academic *comitia* having been held, it was declared that Maxwell was to be rector. This marks a transition stage in which for a few years the principal and professors having made their choice, assembled the students, announced the resolution arrived at, and expressed a hope that the students concurred in the election. This was little more than an empty form, but the apprehension of the rulers of the University that public meetings of the students would give rise to tumults cannot have been very deep-seated, since they actually convened such meetings and no disorder happened. The Senate sometimes made the election, but generally it was the faculty, and always the latter from 1709 to 1716. During all this time, from 1691 onwards, Sir John Maxwell continued rector. This was an unprecedented length of tenure, and most of the members of the body which had usurped to itself the power of election desired a change of rector, but, as things were now managed, the majority could not count on making their wishes effective. It had come to be the practice for the principal to give in a leet of three names from which the rector was to be chosen, and the principal took care that two of the nominees should be practically outside the range of appointment.

Stirling's colleagues complained that, without consulting them, he transacted important business regarding loans, investments, payment of accounts, and orders to tradesmen for executing work ; that considerable sums were expended on the principal's house and that of the professor of Divinity without the knowledge or consent of the other masters ; and that he sometimes travelled on College business without taking previous instructions from the faculty, and drew upon the factors for payment of his expenses, though the payments had not received the previous sanction of the faculty. It was also alleged that important business was transacted during the vacation, in the absence of many of the masters ; that even a deed made by the majority of the society had afterwards been set aside by less than half the number of those who first determined the transaction ; that weighty affairs were decided without a quorum ; and that the principal had several times laid his veto on what had been concluded by the majority, a proceeding which was both unreasonable and without warrant in the constitution or usage of the University.

There was no fixed clerk responsible for writing the minutes, keeping the College books and papers, and allowing the masters reasonable access to them. The minutes of meetings, as well as the charters, writs, bonds, and securities, were retained by the principal in his own custody, without any inventory or effective means of securing their production, if required.[1] The faculty sometimes had occasion to hold meetings in the absence of the principal, and in such cases had no access to their own books. The method of writing the minutes was irregular, the principal dictating extempore to the person acting as clerk for the time, but the minutes might afterwards be scored, interlined, and margined by the principal or by his direction, while the requests of members who desired to have dissents recorded were refused. It will afterwards be seen that a great part of the enactments made by the Commission of Visitation in 1727 was designed to guard against these evils.

---

[1] This complaint is hardly warranted so far as the existence of an inventory is concerned, for Robert Alexander of Blackhouse made out a comprehensive inventory in 1712.

Notwithstanding all this, Stirling had supporters among the masters. He could count on Morthland and John Simson, generally on Rosse, sometimes on Dick, and the deans of faculty were usually among his followers. James Brown, minister of the church of Glasgow, was dean from 1704 till his death ten years later, when he was succeeded in 1714 by John Hamilton, one of the city ministers. Hamilton was continued till 1718, and seems to have been an obsequious supporter of the principal. But the irregularities by which the administration was now affected turned the majority of the professors into an opposition, of which Dunlop, Forbes, Robert Simson, Johnstoun, and for some time Gerschom Carmichael were leading members, though latterly Carmichael's son having been, through the principal's influence, provided with a remunerative appointment, the father's opposition disappeared. The contest came to a crisis over the election of rector. The opposition professors probably chose this question in the consciousness that the method of election then followed was illegal, that to challenge it would procure for them the support of the students, and that if they could restore the constitutional method of election and secure an independent and impartial rector, the principal would be shorn of the extravagant powers he had assumed, and other irregularities would be corrected.

On 1st March, 1717, Professors Forbes, Johnstoun, Carmichael, Loudon, Dick, Dunlop, and Robert Simson joined with the students in electing Mr. Muir to be rector, the election being conducted according to the ancient and unrepealed statutes. But though the opposition professors and the students had on their side the statutes and long-continued usage only recently departed from, the principal and his partisans raised a loud outcry, and laid their version of the case before the Chancellor, the Duke of Montrose. Maxwell, a fast friend of Stirling's, who had been art and part with him in the unwarrantable elections, and who must have felt the recent proceedings as a call to order, probably helped the Duke to procure the appointment of a Royal Commission to enquire into the divisions and disorders in the University. The Commission was invested with ample powers, but does not seem to have been well constituted or well disposed for carrying out in an efficient and impartial manner the work that should have been done.

They met in September, 1717, and their president intimated to the masters concerned in the 'irregular election,' as it was called, that the Commissioners looked upon all the steps in that affair as most unwarrantable and tending to create division, to destroy good order, to discourage learning, and to introduce confusion into the College. The professors who had taken part in the election were warned that the Commissioners expected more decent and peaceable behaviour in future, and that they would apply themselves to the discharge of their duties and the propagation of learning and probity, ' with due respect to the superior officers in the College.'   On 5th November the Commission laid down regulations for an election of rector to be held on the eleventh of the month, excluding the students from voting and prohibiting them from meeting on the election day ; and providing that the rector when elected should nominate two assessors, the University meeting also appointing two.

When the election day came eight professors declined to take part in the proceedings, but the minority declared Sir John Maxwell re-elected. Maxwell nominated Mungo Graham of Gorthie to be vice-rector, and Professor John Simson and John Gray, one of the ministers of Glasgow, to be assessors.   The opposition professors were unwilling to take part in the election of assessors under the Commissioners' new arrangement, and absented themselves from a meeting held on 28th January, 1718, for that purpose, though the principal sent message after message by the beadle to require their attendance.   At a meeting held three days later Forbes, the professor of Law, for himself and other seven professors, including Rosse, who for this time joined the opposition, gave in a declaration that as, notwithstanding their respect for the Commission of Visitation, they could not for several weighty reasons vote in the last election of rector under regulations made by the Commission, so now they could not vote in electing assessors to him ; and that their sitting or voting at any meeting attended by persons who thought themselves entitled to be present in consequence of the Commissioners' regulations should not infer that the subscribers of the declaration acquiesced in anything inconsistent with the just rights and privileges of the University or any of its members.   The minority then elected George Campbell, minister of Glasgow, and Professor Morthland to be assessors—partisans of the principal, as the two assessors nominated by Maxwell were.

The students were now roused to action.   Carmichael delivered an oration to them in praise of liberty, and the opposition professors aided them with money and advice.   Mr. Edmonston and Mr. Butler, two students of Divinity, went to Edinburgh and raised proceedings in the Court of Session in the name of the whole body of the students.   The Court was disposed to give the students a fair opportunity to establish their rights if they could produce evidence in support of them.   But when Edmonston and Butler returned to Glasgow Professor Simson gravely dismissed them from his class, and pronounced sentence of expulsion against them, telling them that what he did was purely for their good.   The two expelled students having applied to the Court of Session, obtained an order for restoration, and Simson reluctantly and with an ill grace obeyed the order of the Court and readmitted them.

Successive Royal Commissions made rules for the election of rector from year to year, and while the Court of Session might have declared what was the law prior to 1717, it would have been of little avail if a later Commission had power to alter the law and lay down new regulations. This consideration may have induced the Court and perhaps the pursuers in the case to wait the final outcome of the Commissions, and fortunately the ultimate regulations laid down by the Commission in 1727 obviated the need for the Court's intervention. The students also succeeded in interesting a number of members of parliament in their cause, and several members, including Lord Molesworth, a correspondent of Shaftesbury and friend of Hutcheson, undertook to support a petition which the students were preparing for presentation to the House of Commons, when the dissolution of 1722 prevented them from carrying out the plan, at least for the time. It is curious to note that on 25th April, 1722, when the news of Lord Molesworth's re-election reached Glasgow, a number of students, along with William Hamilton, master of the Grammar School, lit a bonfire in front of the College gate, and drank some healths, after which some of the townspeople became rather unruly. Gerschom Carmichael appeared, and ordered the College servants to put out the fire, but some students, among them John Smith, the son of a Dublin publisher, opposed its extinction. For this Smith was on 1st May expelled from the University; but in October, 1726, in deference to a recommendation from the Royal Commission, the faculty rescinded and annulled this sentence.

A Royal Commission of Visitation appointed in 1718 went further wrong than its predecessor of the previous year. They considered the previous Commissioners had been too lenient in not inflicting adequate censure on the 'offending masters'; that the distractions and divisions were injuring the reputation of the University, and discouraging parents from sending their sons to study under masters who could not be at peace among themselves; that students were encouraged to take sides and parties after the example of the masters, to the detriment of order and discipline; and that the head of the College was discouraged in the exercise of his duty, and suffering abroad in character and reputation. The extraordinary thing is that while the Commissioners saw all these evils, they did not earnestly and resolutely address themselves to the task of finding out where the responsibility really lay.

Without bringing home any actual misdemeanour to the 'offending masters,' as they were pleased to assume them to be, without showing that they had violated any statute or failed in any obligation founded on reason or sound policy, the Commissioners on 22nd October, 1718, suspended 'Mr. William Forbes, professor of Civil Law, Dr. John Johnstoun, professor of Medicine, Mr. Gershom Carmichael, Mr. John Lowdoun, Mr. Robert Dick, professors of Philosophy, Mr. Alexander Dunlop, professor of Greek, and Mr. Robert Simson, professor of Mathematics, from exerceing any part of their office and profession within the College of Glasgow, other than their teaching and exerceing as usuall their ordinary discipline in their classes, and receiving their ordinary sallary and emoluments . . . and that untill the first day of October next in the year 1719, reserving to the Commissioners power to continue or shorten the said interim prohibition as they shall see cause.'

The principal had a further success in regard to the election of the dean of faculty. On 26th June, 1718, the ordinary day for the election, the Rev. John Hamilton, who had been dean for some years, was not re-elected, the majority making choice of the Rev. John Miller, minister of Neilston. Against this election the principal protested on the rather inconclusive grounds that the books and records respecting the election of dean were in the hands of the Commission of Visitation, and that without the books a new dean could not be admitted ; and further that a considerable number of members of faculty had privately resolved to discontinue Hamilton as dean and to elect another, though no proposal to that effect was brought up for discussion in the faculty till the day of the election. The members who wished a new dean had given the principal to understand that they would find a man who would not be deterred from entering on office by any discouragement the principal might give him, but they did not realise their aspirations, for Mr. Miller, though elected, made no sign of accepting. The principal invited the Commission to observe that there was no dean, and the circumstances having been considered, the Commission on 1st October, 1718, declared the office vacant. The other professors being suspended, this gave the principal and the minority who adhered to him an opportunity to choose one of their own partisans, and on 23rd October, 1718, John Scott, one of the ministers of Glasgow, was chosen. He was continued till 1721, when George Campbell, another city minister, was chosen. In 1723 and 1724 Scott was again appointed, and for the next two years John Hamilton was recalled to his old office, to be succeeded in 1727 by John Gray, another city minister. In the controversy that was going on, the influence of the deans appears to have been generally on the wrong side.

When the day for the election of rector in 1718 was reached, Graham of Gorthie, as vice-rector, presided, and made an explanation which threw grave doubts on the validity of Maxwell's election in the preceding year.

The warrant under the great seal creating the Commission required the Commissioners to deliver to the University a copy of the regulations which they enacted, bearing the signatures of a quorum of the Commissioners, but the regulations actually delivered and under which the election was held were signed only by the Clerk. It was then determined to delay the election, and to apply to the Commission of 1718 for fresh regulations, and when these were obtained, Mungo Graham of Gorthie was unanimously elected rector in a very full meeting of the masters.

The Commissioners though excluding the students from the election of that year, undertook to consider their claims maturely and determine according to what should seem to them just. This plausible arrangement seems for the time to have disarmed the opposition professors who, being under suspension, were powerless to affect the result, but on their agreeing to concur in the election of Graham for that year they had their suspension taken off. Carmichael and some others, however, protested that this interim arrangement should not prejudice the rights of the students; and the students themselves, having in vain demanded admittance to protest against the proceedings, 'took instruments' at the door, and in a public and orderly manner marked their dissent. Only two further elections from which the students were excluded have been recorded. These were held on 22nd November, 1720, and 24th November, 1721, under regulations specially framed for each occasion, and Robert Dundas of Arniston, Lord Advocate, was elected both times. He was no great friend to the students, and blamed the masters for receiving petitions from them, alleging that petitions were instruments of riot and sedition. No further election is recorded till 15th November, 1726, when the ancient procedure was followed, and George, Master of Rosse, was elected by the votes of all the 'nations.'

There must, however, have been at least one election in the interval probably in November, 1724, for in March, 1725, the principal informed the faculty that the students had 'riotously insulted' the house of Hugh Montgomerie of Hartfield, then rector, and had rung the great bell of the College to convene their comrades. A number of students were summoned to answer for the disorder, but their answers have not been preserved. The principal, Carmichael, and Dunlop were appointed to wait on Mrs. Montgomerie and express their concern for the disorders committed. Montgomerie had been a member of the Commission of Visitation in 1718, and was probably distasteful to the students, but this was an unfortunate lapse from the good order which the students generally maintained throughout the proceedings.

There was a double return in 1727, under circumstances which are not now well known, the Master of Rosse being re-elected, and James Hamilton of Aikenhead being also returned. The faculty decided in favour of Hamilton, but next year the Master of Rosse was again elected. By this time stable regulations had been laid down regarding the election of rector and a number of other important subjects by a Royal Commission specially appointed on 26th August, 1726 ; and, as already remarked, it will be seen that most of their legislation was directed to redress the grievances and irregularities of which the opposition professors and the students complained.

The Commissions of Visitation in 1717 and 1718 had been to a considerable extent composed of ministers and others in Glasgow and the neighbourhood, more or less amenable to the principal's influence, and their one sided character may be inferred from the fact that in 1718 Sir John Maxwell was himself a member, though one of the most important questions to be dealt with was whether the mode of election by which he had been kept in office for more than a quarter of a century was sound. A better selection was made for the Commission of 1726, which included Erskine of Grange and Fletcher of Milton, two judges of the Court of Session, Charles Arskine, the Solicitor General, Patrick Grant of Elches, Advocate, John Campbell, formerly Provost of Edinburgh, Principal Wishart of Edinburgh University, William Miller, minister at Edinburgh, James Alston, minister at Dirletoun, and the Earls of Findlater and Ilay.

As the questions to be discussed were largely of a constitutional and legal nature, there was a strong leaven of lawyers ; and as the former Commissions, mainly composed of local men, had been nibbling and bungling for years without any approach to a satisfactory and abiding settlement, the new Commission was composed of new men selected from outside the local area. The Commission had power to regulate as well as to enquire, and they held a number of meetings at Glasgow and Edinburgh, enquired into the policy, government, and discipline of the University, inspected the records so far as they threw light on the questions under consideration, and made themselves acquainted with ancient usage and recent practice. They also called the principal and professors before them and heard their evidence. Some previous indications were given of the resolutions to which the Commissioners were tending, and on 19th September, 1727, they laid down a body of statutes by which in a great measure the University continued to be regulated till the passing of the Universities (Scotland) Act of 1858.

They ordained that the rector should be annually elected on the 15th of November (or on the 16th when the 15th fell on Sunday), and that the right of election 'is in all and every the matriculate members, moderators or masters, and students in the said University,' the electors voting by nations in the ancient manner, each nation choosing a procurator and an intrant to collect the votes and declare the result, while, in the case of an equality of votes, the former rector, or failing him, the penultimate rector, should have the casting vote.   The general matriculation of gowned students was appointed to be on the lawful day immediately preceding the election, matriculation being allowed at other times when required; while ungowned students, in order to take part in the election, were required when matriculating to promise to attend their classes for three months at least, and to repeat the promise every subsequent year of attendance.   Due notice of the election was to be given by posting up 'programs' in the ancient manner, and it was declared 'that the "nations" in electing their rector shall not be under restraint of limitation by any leet to be given in to them.'   With slight modifications from the original statutes, the boundaries of the 'nations' were reaffirmed, but the name Glottiana was preferred to Clydesdalia and Loudoniana to Thevidalia, while Transforthana was suggested for Albania.

As regards meetings, the Commissioners statuted and ordained that the minutes of each meeting should be adjusted and settled at the next, and should then be fairly entered in the faculty book and signed by the principal and the clerk; the faculty being allowed, however, if members could conveniently stay, to adjust and subscribe the minutes at the original meeting.   What was concluded by the majority at any meeting was to take effect, liberty being granted to have dissents and protests recorded. In case of the principal's absence, the eldest of the four regents[1] was empowered to call and preside at meetings, and to do everything competent to the principal.   In the meetings of masters of the University the majority of the constituent members was to be a quorum, and meetings of faculty were to be summoned the day before by the beadle.   Any three members might requisition the principal or eldest regent to call a meeting, and, in case of refusal, might themselves call it; and in the absence of the principal and the eldest regent, any meeting of faculty might choose a chairman for the time, the chairman, whether official or occasional, having only a single casting vote, never a double vote.   In case of the absence of the principal and eldest regent, any three members might likewise call a meeting.

Four ordinary meetings of the faculty, consisting of the principal and all the professors of the University, were appointed to be held every

---

[1] For this purpose the professors of Physics, Ethics, Logic, and Greek counted as regents.

session, namely on the first Friday of November, the second Friday of January, the last Friday of March, and the last Friday of April, and further meetings might be called as occasion required.   No orders for payment of money were to be made except at a meeting of faculty ; where a sum of £10 or upwards was involved, the order was not to be issued till eight days after it had been proposed ; and no new burden on the revenue was to be ' passed or done in the time of vacance.'   It was laid down that no member of the faculty should journey on the affairs of the College unless by appointment of the faculty, and any person so appointed was to take the instructions of the faculty, and upon his return to report his diligence and give an account of his expenses to be revised and approven.

The clerk was obliged to mark all dissents and protests, with the reasons of them, to give extracts, and to make patent to the masters the books and accounts of the faculty for inspection when required ; a room in the College being appropriated to him, in which were to be kept the current faculty books and such other books and accounts as were frequently needed ; while all the College papers, deeds, writs and charters were to be inventoried and placed in a chest in the clerk's room.   This charter chest was to have three keys, to be kept by the principal, the professor of Law, and the eldest regent, respectively.   Collated and attested copies of old books, statutes, and proceedings of the faculty and of Visitations were to be made, and to be kept by the clerk for the use of the masters.

The Commission ordered that accounts of the bursary foundations should be kept, that the College should maintain the full number of bursars, though the patrons neglected to present, and that bursaries should not be divided, but that patrons should be at liberty to conjoin two or more into one.

A full inventory was to be made of all the University's estates and debts, and the lodgings and chambers were to be rentalled.   The silver plate and furniture were also to be inventoried, and the persons who had the custody of such articles were to be obliged to give a receipt and an undertaking to produce them when required.

The state of the University accounts seems to have called imperatively for attention from the Commission.   'Forasmuch as the accompts of the College since Principal Dunlop's death are in such disorder that the state of the University's revenue cannot be known without making from their books a journal and ledger, appoints and ordains the faculty to cause journalise the accompts for the time bygone above mentioned, and to bring the same into a ledger book, so as the balances thereof may be known.'   A committee of the Commission had met at Glasgow and looked into the accounts, with the assistance of Thomas Harvey, a Glasgow merchant, 'who went through the same with much labour,' and the Commissioners judged Harvey to be the fittest person to bring the accounts to order, and recommended the faculty to pay him for the trouble he had already taken and for his further services.

To secure accuracy and efficiency for the future in accounting and in the collection of revenue and making of payments, the Commissioners laid down special regulations in regard to the factor. Hitherto one of the influences tending to confusion had been the existence of more than one factor. It was now ordained that for the future there should be only one factor for uplifting and receiving of the rents and revenue belonging in any manner of way to the University; and no principal or professor was to be eligible for the office, nor any person bearing a nearer relation than cousin-german by consanguinity or affinity to any principal or professor. The factor was to keep an exact cash book, journal, and ledger open at all times to the inspection of the masters. He was to submit his accounts annually to be passed and approved by the faculty, and to make oath that he had fully accounted for his transactions, and had not received more than he charged himself with, nor obtained any abatement or consideration in settling precepts or payments. The vouchers were to be laid up among the faculty papers. The accounts were to be given in for inspection by the masters three weeks before being passed, and were not to be passed nor tacks set in the vacation. The factor was not to receive more than £60 a year for the whole work committed to him, and no allowance was to be made to him for the Candlemas advance of money to bursars, which was to be continued as formerly. He was also forbidden to detain, as factors had hitherto done, fifty marks yearly from the stipends of the ministers of Kilbride and Renfrew. The factor was to find sufficient caution for his management, 'and to do exact diligence for the subject committed to his care.'

The Commissioners forbade the granting of tacks of teinds or other subjects below their just value, and required that tacks should be granted only at a meeting of faculty and not till eight days after the proposal had been made.

Some regulations were laid down about teaching, the most important of which was the final abolition of the system of 'regenting' and the fixing of the three professors of philosophy each to a definite subject. The master of the 'Semi' class (Logic) was to teach Logic and Metaphysics and that part of Pneumatics *De Mente Humana*; the master of the 'Baccalour' class (Ethics), the remaining parts of Pneumatics *De Deo*, and Moral Philosophy; and the master of the 'Magistrand' class (Natural Philosophy) was to 'teach and go through a course of Physics and Experimental

Philosophy.' The Commissioners allowed the masters of the three philosophy classes then in office, Carmichael, Loudon, and Dick to make their
election which classes they were severally to take.   Carmichael chose
Moral Philosophy, Loudon Logic, and Natural Philosophy fell to Dick.
The Commissioners fixed them and their successors to these particular
classes, subject to a reservation in favour of the survivors of the three
existing professors, that when a vacancy should happen in any of the three
chairs, the survivors should have access according to their seniority 'to
take the vacant business, if they preferred it to their own.'   The masters
were to begin teaching annually on the 20th October, after which date
during the session the professors of philosophy and Greek were not 'to
teach any other thing than their own proper business,' and the Natural
Philosophy and Moral Philosophy classes were not to close earlier than the
Logic class.

The professors of Divinity, Law, Medicine, Oriental Languages, and
History were required to teach their respective subjects annually whenever
five students applied to them and to 'give not under four lessons every
week.'   They were to continue their 'Colleges' (the teaching of their
subjects) from the first day of November to the last day of May, or, if the
general course were completed sooner, they were afterwards to give weekly
prelections till the end of May.   The professor of Botany and Anatomy
was required to teach Botany from 15th May to 1st July every year if five
students offered ; and it was declared that Dr. Brisbane, who then held
the double chair, was obliged to teach Anatomy as well as Botany, beginning his teaching of Anatomy as soon as ten students offered, and if ten
students did not offer by 1st November, he was afterwards to give a weekly
prelection on Anatomy till 15th May.

As regards precedence, it was ordained that the professor of Divinity
should come next after the principal, and that the other masters should
follow in the order of seniority from the time of their admission to office.
All subordination between the students of Moral Philosophy and Natural
Philosophy was removed, and students who were Scotsmen were not to
have access to either of these classes unless they had been in the Logic
class either in Glasgow or some other Scottish University.   Scottish
students who had taken the Logic class might afterwards enrol in either
Moral Philosophy or Natural Philosophy, from either of which they might
have access to degrees in arts, provided they had 'studied the business in
both these classes under the professors of these respective classes, and that
they gave proof of a competent knowledge in all parts of philosophy and
in languages' ; and Scotsmen who had studied no part of philosophy out
of Scotland might have access to degrees if they had actually studied all

the parts of philosophy in some of the Universities of Scotland. This regulation might have been clearer, but it involved that Scottish students desiring to graduate should go through the classes of Logic, Moral Philosophy, and Natural Philosophy, and should afterwards be examined in these three subjects and in languages (Latin and Greek), but attendance on classes in languages was not made compulsory. Inferences were drawn about the requirements in the case of students who were not Scotsmen, in dealing with whom the University afterwards fell into discreditable laxity, but the regulation enacted nothing positive concerning them.

Within ten days after the passing of these important statutes, Principal Stirling died on the 28th or 29th September, 1727, in his sixty-first year. After providing for relatives, he made several bequests for benevolent purposes, and left his collection of books and a sum of £166 13s. 4d. to the University library.

At that time England and Ireland scarcely afforded a University education to citizens unless they came within the fold of the established church, and this brought to the Scottish Universities numbers of students belonging to the dissenting churches of these countries, especially such as were destined for the ministry. Glasgow had probably a larger share of these English and Irish students than any other Scottish University. During the time Carstares was principal, the University of Edinburgh seems to have looked with longing interest on students who came from the south side of the border, and would fain have attracted as many of them as possible to the modern Athens.

Among the English dissenting clergy of that time Daniel Williams favoured Glasgow, and Edmund Calamy was more friendly to Edinburgh. In 1709 Calamy made a tour of Scotland, and Edinburgh created him a Doctor of Divinity. He proceeded to Aberdeen and there the degree was repeated. Next he came to Glasgow, and on 17th May received a third degree of Doctor of Divinity, the University having the day before conferred that degree *in absentia* on Daniel Williams. Carstares, calm and courteous though he usually was, wrote an angry letter to Stirling. He was offended at the way Glasgow doctorates were given generally, and specially offended because in the diploma issued to Calamy, while reference was made to the degree of D.D. conferred by Aberdeen, the degree granted by Edinburgh was passed over in silence, which he seemed to take as an implication that Edinburgh had no right to confer a Doctor's degree. Stirling replied that he would not answer the charge then, though he could do so, but would leave Carstares' angry expressions to his own review when the heat was over. Dr. Williams bequeathed some property and funds to the University to establish bursaries for the education of English

o

students. Such of the bursars as were Masters of Arts were to receive higher stipends and to give tuition to undergraduate English students. The scheme has since been modified by the Court of Chancery, and has been in operation for about 200 years. Some of the bursars have risen to distinction in other departments of learning and activity than those which relate specially to the clergy.

About the time when the Royal Commission laid to rest the long and acute controversy respecting academic management, the teaching of Professor Simson in the faculty of Divinity originated another controversy which roused a widespread and fiery interest in the country generally. Twelve or fifteen years before this Simson had caused disquiet by teaching doctrines savouring of Arminianism. Webster, one of the ministers of Edinburgh, brought the reports against him before the Synod of Lothian and Tweeddale, and afterwards before the General Assembly of 1714. As instructed by the Assembly, he laid his complaint before the Presbytery of Glasgow, and Simson gave in answers. The case came before the Assembly of 1715, and they appointed a committee of thirty ministers and six elders to continue the investigation. The rebellion delayed the work of the committee, but their report was presented to the Assembly of 1717. Simson declared his adherence to the doctrines of the Confession of Faith, and protested that, instead of believing the errors of which he was accused, he had often refuted them. But the Assembly found that some of his expressions might bear a heterodox meaning, and prohibited him from using such expressions in future.

After an interval of some years during which he was influenced by Dr. Samuel Clarke's work on *The Scripture Doctrine of the Trinity*, Simson passed from Arminianism to Arianism. Several Presbyteries urged the General Assembly of 1726 to enquire into his teaching. The representatives of the Presbytery of Glasgow explained to the Assembly that the Presbytery had sent two or three of their number to confer with the professor, who sent them a letter admitting that reports were in circulation against him, but denying their accuracy and giving a statement of his teaching regarding the Trinity. The Assembly then instructed the Presbytery to proceed with the investigation, and appointed a committee to correspond with and assist them. Simson objected to be questioned about his views, and his letter to the Presbytery might bear different senses, which Lord Grange [1]—by no means a faultless man himself—char-

---

[1] James Erskine of Grange, brother of the Earl of Mar who raised the insurrection, was an elder in the Church, a member of many General Assemblies, a correspondent of Wodrow's, and a concealed Jacobite. He was a judge of the Court of Session, and outwitted Walpole, who passed an Act excluding judges of that Court from the House

acterised as ' the art of teaching heresy orthodoxly.' Simson's students were examined, but, as his lectures were delivered in Latin, it was difficult to get an exact statement of the very words in which his views on somewhat abstruse questions had been expressed.

But from the evidence given it appeared that the professor had said that Christ, though He is eternal, does not exist of necessity ; had declared that the independence and necessary existence of the Son were things we knew not—philosophical niceties, impertinent terms, not to be used in speaking of the Trinity ; had affirmed that the Father was before the Son not in time but in causality, unless we were to suppose that God was not able to create from eternity ; and had said that the unity of essence in the Trinity could not be numerical essence, for, if they were numerically one, they could not be three distinct persons. Professor Simson at this stage gave in a paper with a long account of the Arian and Sabellian heresies, and a statement that he had been led to quit all hypotheses for explaining the doctrine of the Trinity, and confine himself to phrases used in the Scriptures and the standards of the Church ; and had taught that the Son had all life in Himself and was infinite and eternal in His being and other attributes.

This did not satisfy the Presbytery, who proceeded to libel the professor. This brought the lawyers into the case, and they contested everything, and cross-examined the witnesses at great length. Simson was frequently too ill to attend, but the Presbytery completed their work in time for the Assembly of 1727. After long and stirring debates it was found proven that Simson had denied the necessary existence of the Son. The next article as to the independent existence of the Son disclosed greater difference of opinion in the Assembly, and some explanatory words were added in the course of the debate, thus altering the libel after the evidence was taken. It was unanimously decided that this article was not proven, and many believed that the Assembly did not wish to be committed to a positive assertion of the independent existence of the Son. After a further long debate it was found proven that Simson had denied the numerical oneness of the Trinity. Simson appeared at the bar expressing the most orthodox opinions on the questions involved in the articles proven against him. The trial could not be finished during that year's sitting of the Assembly, and it was remitted to the Presbytery and the committee to ripen matters for next Assembly, the professor being meantime suspended.

of Commons, by resigning his position as a judge, after which he was elected M.P. for the Stirling burghs in 1741. But his most remarkable action was to arrange for his own wife being kidnapped and secluded in St. Kilda, probably to prevent the disclosure of any indiscreet babbling on her part about her husband's share in Jacobite plots.

The Presbytery found further articles of the libel proven, and began a fresh libel, charging Simson with disregarding the Sentence of 1717, and uttering expressions that might bear an Arminian meaning. The Assembly of 1728 held further debates on the case, and received from Simson a retraction of the errors charged against him. The reverend Court was much perplexed what to do with the offender, for the case had thrown the country into a ferment of discussion and unrest. It was resolved to continue Simson's suspension, to print the process and circulate it to the Presbyteries, so that they might send Commissioners to the next General Assembly fully instructed to give a final decision. The Presbyteries were informed that Simson had given in papers asserting the necessity of the existence of Christ, and that the title of supreme and only God was equally applicable to Father and Son, also affirming that the three persons in the Trinity were one substance or essence in number, and therefore his sentiments were sound ; but it had been proved that he had taught things inconsistent with these truths, and moreover he had neglected opportunities of giving earlier satisfaction to the Church regarding his opinions. The Assembly of 1729 suspended Simson from preaching, teaching, and all exercise of any ecclesiastical power or function till another Assembly thought fit to remove the sentence ; and also recorded their judgment that it was not fit or safe that he should be employed in teaching Divinity or instructing young men designed for the ministry.

The University used its influence on behalf of Simson, and in 1727 Principal Stirling protested before the Presbytery that, though he owned the Presbytery had the right to try Simson for alleged errors, yet the proceedings of the Presbytery should not derogate from the power of the University to try and to judge its members. A similar plea was tendered to the Assembly in 1729, with a recommendation that Simson's suspension should be taken off ; and complaint was made that, though the process had been sent to the Presbyteries, it had not been sent to the Universities, notwithstanding that the University of Glasgow had a very direct interest. Mr. Forbes, the professor of Civil Law, cautiously abstained from joining in the representation to the Assembly, explaining that he could not pass judgment on the process not having sufficiently considered it. The results of this celebrated trial were more formidable to Neil Campbell, who succeeded Stirling as principal, than to Simson himself. The latter during the remaining ten or eleven years of his life retained his emoluments and was released from teaching ; and, though no other principal since the Revolution has been required to conduct a class, Campbell had to teach Divinity to the students of that subject.

II. 1727–1761.

THE chair of Practical Astronomy, founded in 1760, was the only new professorship belonging to the period of thirty-four years from 1727 to 1761, but the institution of a lectureship in Chemistry in 1747, on which its early holders Cullen and Black shed a lustre, was an event of no less importance. Cullen was professor of Medicine, and lectured on Botany and Materia Medica as well as on Chemistry, and his work as a teacher put new life and vigour into the Medical School, while Black's researches on latent heat made his career at Glasgow memorable. Within the University in this period James Watt was sheltered and encouraged, and the brothers Foulis set up their printing press and established their academy of art, while Wilson, the professor of Practical Astronomy, who had previously been a typefounder and still continued that business, transferred his foundry to a site within the University grounds.

The great teachers in the faculty of arts included Moor in Greek, Hutcheson and Smith in Moral Philosophy, and Simson in Mathematics. Leechman and Anderson both appeared on the scene, and while as teachers they did not achieve such distinction as some of their colleagues, they out-stripped all of them as fighting men, though the dust and din of their contests belong to the next section. Leechman during the later years of his tenure as professor of Divinity was vice-rector, and presided in what were called University meetings, while faculty meetings, in which the principal was the normal chairman, were extinguished; yet Leechman's great work on becoming principal was to restore faculty meetings and extend their powers and functions. The prosperity of the faculty of law was in some danger from the appointment of Cross as professor, Cross being as little inclined to teach law as Brisbane and Johnstoun had been to teach Anatomy and Medicine; but he had a shorter tenure than they, and consequently did less mischief. Both Lindesay and Millar who came after him were men of diligence and ability.

The teaching of modern languages received some countenance and encouragement, and for a number of years from 1730 onwards the University made a small annual grant to a French gentleman residing in Glasgow and teaching his native language. Afterwards Professors Anderson and Cumin taught French and Italian, and a number of books were procured for the use of students of these languages. Among the more distinguished students belonging to this time were Smollett, Boswell, William Hunter, 'Jupiter' Carlyle, Black, Robison, and the elder William Hazlitt. The last having come over from Ireland in expectation of a bursary which he did not obtain, was more than once helped by small grants of money voted to him by the administrators of the College. In 1740 the administrators showed their fellow feeling for Marischal College, Aberdeen, which was then making an effort to improve its buildings, by voting a sum of £20 for this purpose.

A few years before 1727 a scheme of building houses for professors had been discussed and adopted, but its execution fell mostly within the dates of the present section. It involved the borrowing of money and in other respects was an injudicious undertaking. The Duke of Chandos had made a gift to the University of £500 through the chancellor, the Duke of Montrose, who was empowered to name the use to which it should be put. Montrose destined it for the erection of a new building for the library, and allowed it to be lent at interest for some years, so as to increase the amount available. The building, which cost about £1,500, having proceeded very slowly, was ready for occupation in 1744, and a few years after this catalogues of the collection of books were prepared by Professors Rosse and Hamilton.

Neil Campbell, minister of Renfrew, having been appointed by the king to be principal in December, 1727, was admitted to office on 8th February following. He was not a man of exceptional learning or administrative ability, but he entered on office at a time when the landmarks of the constitution had been laid down afresh, and when the condition of the University might be regarded as prosperous and hopeful, and during his tenure much valuable work was done and great names were associated with the University. Campbell's chief employment for the first dozen years was to conduct the class of Divinity from Simson's suspension till his death in 1740. In 1748 Campbell claimed some remuneration for this work, pointing out that he had not made the claim earlier on account of the College debts ; that, upon Simson's suspension, it was feared that Divinity students would betake themselves to other Universities, which would have been adverse to the interest and credit of Glasgow ; that the faculty had given him hearty thanks in November, 1731, for teaching the class during the three preceding sessions ; and that the work was burdensome to him on account of other duties. There were recent instances of grants of £25 and £30 for carrying on classes by deputy or during a vacancy in a chair, and he hoped to receive at least £25 a year for what he had done.

But for a time his pleading was in vain, the University meeting declaring that the principal was and always had been obliged to teach Divinity, and that the University had a right to insist on his doing so. Some years later the meeting took a more generous view of matters, and appear to have been at a loss to find an excuse for making a grant to Campbell. In 1751, although it was several years before the lease of the archbishopric expired, Campbell was authorised to negotiate regarding a new lease, and it was agreed that he should have £100 as an acknowledgment 'of the pains and application he will use in obtaining it,' and that an additional £100 should be paid when a new lease was obtained on the same favourable terms as the current one.

About 1753 Campbell was smitten with palsy and rendered unable to attend to business, and probably his colleagues would have viewed with satisfaction his removal to a residence outside the College. In 1754 his house having become dilapidated, the University meeting offered him £20 a year to provide for a house so long as his own was not repaired or rebuilt, and £10 for the expense of removal. He did not remove, and in 1756 he was asked whether he would prefer to have repairs made on the part of his house still standing or to remove. He replied that he could not live in the house as it was, and intended to go to a house in the city. This intention was not carried out, however, and rather more than a year later, it was resolved to make a proper addition to what remained standing of the principal's house, rather than to build a new one. Campbell died on 22nd June, 1761, and was succeeded by William Leechman, who had been professor of Divinity since 1743.

A few years after his appointment Andrew Rosse, professor of Humanity from 1705 to 1735, came to an understanding with Dunlop regarding the arrangements for students attending the Latin and Greek classes in the same year. In December, 1734, it was reported that Rosse was hindering the students of Humanity who had likewise enrolled in Greek from attending the latter class. A committee was appointed to intimate to the students concerned that they should attend the Greek class at the same hour as formerly, and to admonish the students of Humanity to proper behaviour. It was stated that Rosse did not give satisfactory answers to some questions put to him, and probably his temper as well as his health had become infirm by this time.[1] In November, 1735, he gave in a demission of his office in favour of his son, George Rosse, M.A., which, after a week's delay, was accepted. For his trials young Rosse was appointed to translate into English a speech of Portius Cato from Livy, and to translate into Latin the Duke of Argyll's speech for a standing army ; and his work having been approved, he became professor of Humanity on 11th December. The elder Rosse at first proposed to reserve his salary during his life, but as this was not accepted, he agreed to

[1] In 1726 and 1727 Frederick Carmichael (a son of Gerschom's) taught the Latin class for some time, the health of Rosse having given way.

demit both office and salary. Not succeeding in his purpose with the meeting, the elder Rosse turned to the younger and procured from him an obligation to pay over to his father, as long as the latter lived, the whole salary of the chair.

The University was not a party to the arrangement, but, as the years passed, the younger Rosse wearied of doing the work under the conditions to which he had agreed, and applied for some allowance, representing to the University meeting in June, 1746, that he had taught Latin for more than ten years without any remuneration but the fees paid by the students. Early next year it was carried by a majority to give him some encouragement, the allowance during his father's life being fixed at 400 marks Scots, conditionally on the University having a surplus of 200 marks at balancing the year's accounts. The claims of the Rosses did not stop here, for on the death of the elder Rosse, his widow in 1751 claimed an 'ann.'[1] The meeting declared there was no foundation for the claim, but agreed to pay her £50 ex gratia.

George Rosse died on 26th August, 1754, and Moor agreed to teach the private Latin class and Leechman the public one from the opening of the session till a successor should be appointed. With a view to the appointment, the vacancy was ordered to be advertised in the Edinburgh and Glasgow newspapers. On 2nd December, 1754, George Muirhead, professor of Oriental Languages, was transferred to the Humanity chair, it being provided that he should receive no salary till the death allowance to the heirs of his predecessor was paid. In the policy of litigation and other measures pursued by Leechman after he became principal, Muirhead was one of his steadfast supporters. He was an early member of the Literary Society of Glasgow, and was associated with Moor in editing the edition of the *Iliad* published by the Foulises and much admired in its day. The professor was a near kinsman of Agnes Muirhead, the mother of James Watt, and introduced Watt, then a lad of eighteen on a visit to Glasgow, to the notice and acquaintance of a number of other professors who afterwards became his friends and patrons. Muirhead was professor of Humanity for about nineteen years, dying in 1773, and two or three years later his brothers presented £100 to the University as a permanent fund, the interest of which should be used to provide book prizes to students in the Latin class.

[1] The allowance called an 'ann' was authorised in 1655 when the moderators made a regulation that when the office of a principal, professor, or regent became vacant by death or otherwise, except by reason of censure, the retiring office-bearer, or in case of death, his heirs, should receive the whole emoluments due at the time the vacancy occurred and for six months afterwards, the successor, if appointed within six months, being liable to a proportionable deduction to prevent the burden of a double stipend falling on the College.

FRANCIS HUTCHESON, M.A.

Professor of Moral Philosophy, 1730-1746

BORN 1694.   DIED 1746

From oil painting by John Foulis in the Senate Room, University of Glasgow

Owing to advancing age and failing eyesight, Alexander Dunlop retired from the professorship of Greek in 1746. In the contests which took place he was frequently on the same side as Hutcheson, and Hutcheson was so much concerned about the election of Dunlop's successor that he declared the soul of the College depended on it. After some delay (which may have been arranged for the purpose of bringing on the election at the time most suitable to those who were laying their plans with a view to it) the demission was accepted on 27th June, 1746, Dunlop being allowed to retain during life his salary and his house in the College. The meeting recorded their regret at parting with a colleague whose ability and diligence had brought the knowledge of Greek to a flourishing condition in the University. Dunlop did not long enjoy his retirement, dying towards the end of April, 1747.

James Moor, who now became professor of Greek, was the son of a schoolmaster in Glasgow, but early lost his father. While a child measles deprived him of the sight of one eye, yet he was a voracious reader, and Andrew Stalker, a bookseller, admitted him to free perusal of the contents of his shop. Moor entered the University in 1725, and though afterwards 'much renowned for Greek,' he seems while an undergraduate to have applied himself with special ardour to Mathematics and Natural Philosophy. He graduated as M.A. in 1732, presenting on that occasion a thesis *De Systemate Mundi*, which he defended *sine praesidio*, as the phrase went. He was some time tutor to the Earl of Errol and the Earl of Selkirk, with whom he travelled abroad, and subsequently he was tutor to the son and heir of the Earl of Kilmarnock. During this time Moor applied himself closely to study and drank strong tea to keep off drowsiness. From this excess of study and tea his health and temper suffered permanently. He was for some time librarian to the University, holding the post at a time when the books were transferred to new buildings, and quitting it only when he became professor of Greek. Moor's son stated that his father paid £600 to Dunlop, the retiring professor, for the appointment, and that the money was advanced by the Earl of Selkirk.

Shortly before Moor was made a professor, the cause of the Stewarts was finally defeated at Culloden, and the Earl of Kilmarnock, Moor's former pupil, was among the captured chiefs of the insurgents. Kilmarnock was soon afterwards condemned to death, and at the request of his relatives, Moor, who was a firm adherent of the reigning family, repaired to London to plead with the Government for a pardon, but his efforts were unavailing. Moor was appointed vice-rector in 1759 and again in 1761 (on the latter occasion by his old pupil the Earl of Errol), and in the early stages of the controversy regarding the powers of the rector and the principal he upheld the rights of the former, but soon went over to the side of Leechman.   He continued as professor till 1774, but in the last third of his tenure his work was much interrupted by illness, and there were some interruptions before this.

Within a period of eighteen years three famous men, Hutcheson, Smith, and Reid, held the chair of Moral Philosophy.   On the death of the veteran Gerschom Carmichael in 1729, Hutcheson was elected to the vacant profession.   His grandfather, an Ayrshire man, settled as a Presbyterian minister in Ireland, where his father followed the same profession. As a student Francis Hutcheson is said to have entered Glasgow University in 1710, and his name appears in the Logic class list for 1711.   Afterwards he passed through the course both in Arts and Divinity.   Of the professors under whom he studied, Alexander Dunlop, Gerschom Carmichael, and John Simson, the heretic, seem to have impressed him most.   Some years after leaving the University he set up an academy in Dublin, and carried it on for eight or nine years, gaining experience which must have helped to develop his exceptional capacity as a teacher.   He imbibed the teaching of Shaftesbury and to some extent of Butler, Berkeley, and Locke, made the acquaintance of Lord Molesworth, and soon became an active member of the little society gathered round him.   Through the influence of James Arbuckle, an M.D. of Glasgow, who practised in Dublin, and being lame and sprightly, was nicknamed by Swift 'Wit upon Crutches,' he began to write articles for the *Dublin Journal*.   In 1725 he published an *Inquiry into the Original of our Ideas of Beauty and Virtue*, and three years later an *Essay on the Nature and Conduct of the Passions and Affections, with Illustrations upon the Moral Sense*.   In the year of the publication of the *Inquiry* he was introduced to the vice-regal court of the Lord Lieutenant, the scholarly and accomplished Lord Carteret, afterwards Earl of Granville, who dispensed a liberal hospitality and played the part of Maecenas to all and sundry.   Offers of a place in the Episcopal Church were conveyed to Hutcheson.   His father was alarmed and wrote to remonstrate with his son, who replied in a long and somewhat wavering epistle, to which he added the following postscript: 'Pray write me further on this subject, and assure yourself that there is no ground for uneasiness.   Were I disposed in that way, there is nothing to be got worth acceptance, without some evil compliance to which I would not submit.'

On 19th December, 1729, Hutcheson was elected by a majority to the profession of philosophy left vacant by the death of Carmichael, and on 20th February following the faculty appointed that he should make discourses to be delivered before them in the following subjects, namely, in Logic—*De Scientia Fide et Opinione inter se Collatis* ; in Ethics—*An sit una tantum Morum Lex Fundamentalis, vel si sint plures, quaenam sint?* and in Physics—*De Gravitatione Corporum versus se mutua.*

The preparation of three theses or discourses in different departments of philosophy was a circumstance quite unique, but at the outset it was not clear whether Logic, Ethics, or Physics would fall to the province of Hutcheson; for the regulations made by the Commissioners in 1727 empowered John Loudon, the senior of the two surviving regents, who then taught Logic, to make choice of Ethics or Physics if he thought fit, and after him Dick, the other surviving regent, who then taught Physics, might have chosen another subject. But Loudon and Dick both elected to continue teaching their former subjects, and happily Moral Philosophy fell to Hutcheson.[1] It was then the custom for the academic company to welcome a new professor over a glass of wine. Hutcheson was admitted on 3rd November, 1730, and on this occasion the good cheer seems to have been more than usually abundant, an account of nearly £5 for wine being paid next month, and a further account for wine, fruit, and 'biskets' shortly afterwards.

After beginning work as a professor Hutcheson for some time taught Puffendorf and the 'Compend' of Gerschom Carmichael, but by and by he developed a set of written lectures, published after his death as his *System of Moral Philosophy.* He was by no means tied to his manuscript, however, and as he expounded morals, jurisprudence, and government, ancient ethics, and natural religion, new matter and new illustrations streamed from his mind, and gave freshness and variety to his discourse. A man of cheerful and buoyant disposition, of good natural ability, well informed in the topics of Moral Philosophy and well trained to discuss them, speaking with eloquence and enthusiasm to students whose awakened interest and youthful ardour responded to the power and the charm of his teaching, endeavouring, not only to discipline the intelligence of students, but also to inspire them with worthy aims and noble views of life and its duties and opportunities, and ready to counsel and befriend students as occasion arose—Hutcheson soon became the most distinguished and the most popular professor of his time. Adam Smith, who was one of his pupils, characterised him as 'the never to be forgotten Hutcheson';

---

[1] Mr. Scott, a recent biographer of Hutcheson, asserts that Loudon was coerced into choosing the Logic class by a threat from some English students that they would go to Edinburgh unless Hutcheson taught Moral Philosophy. He further accuses the College meeting of overriding the statutes in allowing Loudon a choice of subjects; but he cannot have read the regulations applicable to the case, else he would have found that it was the statutes and not the College meeting that allowed Loudon this choice. See *Munimenta*, vol. II. p. 578.

and though the lectures varied little from session to session, many students attended them four or five years together.

He retained a strong interest in Ireland, visiting it frequently, reckoning Belfast superior to Edinburgh or Glasgow, keeping up a ceaseless correspondence with acquaintances in the Emerald Isle, sometimes helping to procure honorary degrees for them, and taking a warm interest in Irish students. Hutcheson's friendship with Hugh Boulter, Archbishop of Armagh, procured from him in 1733 a gift of £250 to found three bursaries for students of Medicine, Law, or Divinity from England or Ireland. One of the witnesses of the deed of foundation was Ambrose Philips, a disciple of Addison's and author of some minor works written in a style called namby-pamby from a play on the author's name.

Hutcheson took a fair share in the business of the University, the library being one of the departments to which he devoted attention, and occasionally he acted as clerk in the absence of Robert Simson. He is said to have drawn up a scheme adopted in 1739 regarding the professors' houses, which could not be equally distributed, some professors having new houses, some old ones, and some none at all. The plan then temporarily adopted was to exact a yearly rent from those who had new houses, and to make a small allowance to those having old ones, and a larger allowance to such as had no College house. When elections to chairs in the patronage of the University were being made Hutcheson worked with a will for his favourite candidates. He aimed at securing a majority of College administrators of like mind with himself, and while he doubtless worked for ends which he considered good, he had no keener sense of fairness than other men, so far as means and methods were concerned. Hutcheson befriended the Foulises when setting up their printing business in Glasgow. Shortly after the publication of the *Treatise on Human Nature* he came into communication with Hume, and they corresponded for some years, Hutcheson criticising Hume's views and advising him with regard to dealings with publishers. Though differing widely on points of philosophy, they corresponded in a friendly manner, but in 1744, when Hume was a candidate for the Moral Philosophy chair at Edinburgh, Hutcheson's influence was used against him. Hutcheson died at Dublin on 8th August, 1746, at the comparatively early age of fifty-two.

On 1st October following, Thomas Craigie, professor of Hebrew in the University of St. Andrews, was appointed to succeed him. In December, 1749, the University meeting allowed Craigie to build a new house, with its front in line with that of the forehall, and to expend a sum of £400 upon it—to be repaid on his death or on the College providing him with another house. The work was afterwards begun, but Craigie did not live to see it finished. In April, 1751, he was allowed to cease teaching and go to the country for the benefit of his health, Leechman conducting the class for the remainder of the session. His health did not return, and in September, 1751, he obtained leave of absence for the following session, that he might betake himself to a warmer climate. Four of his colleagues agreed among them to carry on the work of the class— Leechman taking natural theology and the first book of Hutcheson's Ethics, Smith taking the other two books on jurisprudence and politics, and Rosse and Moor the remaining part of the work. Craigie died at Lisbon on 27th November, 1751, and on 22nd April of next year Adam Smith was unanimously elected to succeed him.

Smith had come to Glasgow as a lad of fourteen in 1737, and studied under the 'never to be forgotten Hutcheson,' giving close attention also to Mathematics then taught by Simson, and to Natural Philosophy by Dick. In 1740 he went to Oxford as a Snell exhibitioner, and having returned in 1746 to his native Kirkcaldy, he by and by repaired to Edinburgh and began to lecture on rhetoric and literature under the patronage of Lord Kames. In January, 1751, he was elected professor of Logic at Glasgow, and having delivered a dissertation *De Origine Idearum* was admitted to office. He did not immediately settle in Glasgow, and Hercules Lindesay taught the class till the end of the session. Smith is said to have improved on Loudon's methods of teaching, but as he taught Logic for one session only, our estimate of him as a teacher must be formed from his work in Moral Philosophy.

Smith's course in Moral Philosophy embraced four divisions—natural theology, ethics, general jurisprudence, and the nature of political institutions. It will be seen that this division differed little from Craigie's, and indeed it was partly derived from Hutcheson. The section on ethics was published in 1759 as the *Theory of the Moral Sentiments*, and proved a success at the time, though it would not have ensured a permanent reputation for its author. The last of the four sections, after much further study and elaboration, was given to the world in 1776 as *The Wealth of Nations*.

Smith prepared his matter and committed it to paper, but did not content himself with merely reading to his students a set of lectures fashioned in his study. He rather chose to think out the subject afresh in their presence, setting out with a number of leading statements or ideas, which he explained, illustrated, and exhibited in relation to each other. He was sometimes rather slow and hesitating at first, but became more fluent and animated as he went on, defending his tenets, combating objections to them, and pouring forth illustrations—somewhat diffuse, but with the main doctrines still discernible through all the mazes of his oratory.

Both on his students and on the academic and literary circles of Glasgow he made a great impression, and his opinions formed an outstanding theme of talk and discussion among intelligent townspeople of all classes. Without any powerful external impulse his mind might have betaken itself to the study of commercial and economic problems, but twelve or thirteen of the most vigorous years of his life spent in the industrial and mercantile community of Glasgow gave him further occasion and opportunity for such pursuits—pursuits which came within the scope of his teaching as he interpreted it.   Provost Cochrane was the founder and the leading spirit of the Merchants' Club of that time, which collected information and sharpened the wits of its members by discussions on the nature and principles of trade in all its branches.   Cochrane led the next generation of Merchants to wider views and ventures than had formerly prevailed, and Smith, who was one of the members, doubtless owed something to the Club and its founder.   William Paterson and John Law had already shown the strength of the Scottish mind in practical finance, and it was now reserved for Adam Smith to show what the Scottish mind could accomplish in dealing with financial and economic theory.

Apart from his professorial lectures, Smith was not successful as a public speaker, but his conversation sometimes merged into lecturing.   In the company of strangers he was rather shy and embarrassed, but among friends he was full of matter, and could be both easy and exhilarating in his manner.   He fell into some of the failings of philosophers, and was apt to be too introspective, too busy with the train of internal ideas, too often wanting in presence of mind and in attention to what was happening around him.   Not only was he absent-minded, but he was also inclined (if one may use an expression so paradoxical) to soliloquise in company, and in his more or less unconscious habit of thinking aloud sometimes uttered unfavourable opinions on those who were present.   Probably he has suffered something from story-tellers, and while he was a professor he cannot have been so absent-minded and blundering as they would make him out, for he was not only an active administrator but one to whom his colleagues usually had recourse when difficulties arose or questions requiring to be warily dealt with.

As quaestor he rendered considerable service to the library, and in 1762 he was appointed, along with Trail and Williamson, to examine the state of the College manuscripts and consider as to a proper method for their preservation.   As dean of faculty he presided for several years at meetings which, whether constitutionally or not, transacted a great part of the academic business.   He assisted in drafting a bill which passed through Parliament in 1757 for improving the regulations of the Hamilton

Bursaries, and he was sometimes employed to clear the accounts of the Archbishopric with the Barons of the Exchequer in Edinburgh, and to submit the accounts of the ordinary revenue and of the Subdeanery for a sort of audit which they had to undergo at the Treasury in London.

A large part of the revenue was derived from teinds, and the management of this rather intricate department gave rise to much discussion and negotiation, a full share of which fell to Smith. He was intimately concerned in the proceedings against Professor Rouet when the latter withdrew from the University and went to Utrecht as tutor to Lord Hopetoun's son. He was one, and probably one of the most active, of a committee that in 1762 drew up a long report on the provinces and powers of the rector, the principal, and the dean, and of the meetings over which they presided, a report involving considerable research and reflection, and foreshadowing to some extent the decisions of the Court of Session nine or ten years later. Sometimes he negotiated with the city authorities, as in the case of the exaction in 1757 of a tax on the meal brought into the town for the use of students.

Near the end of his professorship Smith was engaged in two projects of a rather incongruous character—one having in view the establishment of an academy, under the direction of the University, for dancing, fencing, and riding ; and the other being the taking of measures to prevent the establishment of a theatre in the city. The first of these projects was considered on 22nd December, 1761, Smith being appointed to write to the rector, the Earl of Errol, to procure his patronage and assistance, while Anderson was to communicate with such neighbouring gentlemen as were thought likely to favour the plan. In concerting measures against the intended theatre, Leechman, Smith, Clow, and Trail were, on 25th November, 1762, appointed a committee to confer with the Magistrates. The University and the City sent a memorial to the Lord Advocate, and other means of preventing the setting up of a theatre were discussed, but the opposition failed. There is no suggestion in the records that the company which then came to Glasgow was more objectionable than other theatrical companies, or that Smith was behind his colleagues in offering opposition. This is all the more curious because afterwards in *The Wealth of Nations* he taught that it was the duty of governments to encourage public amusements and diversions, especially dramatic representations.

Charles Townshend, a brilliant and fickle statesman of that time, had become the second husband of the Duke of Buccleuch's mother, the Duke being then a minor, and Townshend half in jest and half in earnest took a notion to employ Smith, who, besides his reputation as a professor, had come to be favourably known by his *Theory of the Moral Sentiments*, as tutor and travelling companion to the young Duke.   Shortly after the publication of that work, Hume hinted at Townshend's intention, and also hinted that Townshend was by no means reliable.   At the same time Hume made two vain attempts to see Townshend in order to persuade him to send the young Duke to Glasgow, not thinking that terms would be offered sufficiently tempting to induce Smith to quit his professorship. However, after the lapse of some time the offer was made in 1763.   On 8th November of that year Smith applied to the dean of faculty's meeting for leave of absence, as some interesting business would probably require him to leave the College for some part of that winter.   The meeting allowed him leave of absence for three months if his affairs should require it.   Having attended his last meeting on 10th January, 1764, he quitted the University immediately afterwards, not for three months but alto- gether.   He repaid his students the fees collected for that session, for the remainder of which Thomas Young, student of Divinity, was, on his recommendation, appointed to teach the Moral Philosophy class, Smith paying his salary.   Having arrived at Paris with his pupil on 13th February, next day Smith wrote a letter finally resigning his chair, and declaring his warm interest in the welfare of the College.   The University meeting in turn recorded their sincere regret at the removal of Dr. Smith, whose *Theory of the Moral Sentiments* recommended him to men of taste throughout Europe, and whose talents in illustrating abstract subjects and assiduity in communicating useful knowledge distinguished him as a professor, and at once afforded the greatest pleasure and the most solid instruction to the youth under his care.

Robert Simson held the chair of Mathematics for fifty years ending in 1761.   His fame rests on his own researches and excogitations, chiefly in ancient Geometry, rather than on his teaching, though a number of good mathematicians were taught at Glasgow in his time, including Colin Maclaurin and Matthew Stewart, who became professors of Mathematics in Edinburgh University, William Trail, professor of the same subject in Marischal College, Aberdeen, John Robison, professor of Natural Philosophy at Edinburgh, Moor and Williamson, who held chairs in his own University, and others.   Of Simson's methods of teaching not much is to be learned from the College records, but from other sources it appears that he taught two classes in Mathematics, separately organised to suit the capacity of his students.   About 1728 he became clerk to the University meeting, and held that post till he resigned his chair.   He rendered con- siderable services, not merely in performing the ordinary duties of clerk, but also in deciphering and transcribing some of the old records of the

ADAM SMITH, LL.D.

Professor of Logic, 1751-1752, and of Moral Philosophy, 1752-1764

BORN 1723. DIED 1790

From Tassie Medallion in the Hunterian Library, University of Glasgow

University. His long services must have made him familiar with many details of the constitution and working of the University, yet his opinions on such matters were not always reliable, for in 1755 he declared that neither the Statutes of Visitation nor the *Nova Erectio* appointed the calling of meetings by the principal except for discipline, and that the calling of meetings by him for other purposes was an innovation—a statement entirely at variance with the regulations of the Commission of 1727, within his own time if not within his memory. In 1750 the University meeting voted a sum of fifty guineas to him for transcribing the Rector's Book ; and about two years afterwards he applied to the meeting for some recognition of his services as clerk. The meeting declared that the office had always been performed without reward, but acknowledged that a great and unusual burden of business had been laid upon Simson which he had faithfully and cheerfully executed, and voted a grant of £250 to him, of which £100 was to be paid immediately, and the rest when a new tack of the archbishopric should be obtained, or when Simson, who was considered the only member of the society capable of executing the task, should prepare an inventory of the College papers, an index of the minutes, and an abridged account of the University from its foundation. Simson was largely instrumental in procuring a good part of the collection of Roman stones in possession of the University.

In June, 1760, there was nearly £100 still unpaid of the sum voted to Simson, and he applied to the faculty for payment, stating that he needed money for an octavo edition of Euclid's *Elements and Data* which he had prepared for the press. The request was granted, and Simson agreed to assist the College law agent in making an inventory of the writs and titles to property which had not yet been inventoried. Simson was now seventy-three, and probably age was beginning to impair his memory and other powers, for Professors Buchanan and Wilson were desired to remind him of his undertaking and assist him in carrying it out. In May of the preceding year he had presented a memorial, recalling that he had been professor of Mathematics since 1711, and stating his wish to retire that he might have opportunity to finish some works on Geometry before he was disabled by age. He also stated that the professor of Oriental Languages, Mr. Buchanan, who was fully capable of teaching the Mathematics classes, had agreed to do so on condition of his succeeding to the chair, and desired the meeting to give Mr. Buchanan an assurance to that effect. Ten days later, at Simson's request, the meeting postponed consideration of the memorial till October, and from one cause or another the retirement was delayed. Buchanan died on 21st June, 1761, and from a protest by Leechman, who was made principal about that time, it appears

P

that some members contemplated that the next professor of Oriental Languages should be appointed to teach Mathematics also, and to succeed to the chair when it became vacant. It is not clear whether this was Simson's plan.

On 19th October, 1761, Simson demitted office and gave up all right to his house in the New Court of the College, but retained possession of chambers in the Outer Court, and stipulated that James Williamson, minister at Closeburn, should be elected as his successor. The meeting accepted the proposals, and entered a panegyric on Simson in their minutes: 'Whereas Dr. Simson, from a happy union of elegant taste and force of genius in the science of his profession, was the first to discover and understood in its full extent the Analytical Geometry of the ancients after it had been lost for so many ages, and after it had been entirely mistaken or despaired of by the best modern mathematicians, as is evident from the writings of some of the greatest among them (Dr. Wallis, Dr. Barron, and Sir Isaac Newton)—the University meeting do on this occasion declare that they consider it as one of the highest and most lasting honours which this or any University can hope or wish to boast of that so sublime a discovery in so very noble a science was first made by a professor in this University, first taught by him to the students here, and first published to the world in his writings, in which he has already most ingeniously restored some of the lost books of the Analytical Institutions of the ancients, and proposes to employ the remaining leisure of his life in restoring and publishing the rest of them, for the accomplishment of which valuable design, of so much importance to the advancement of true science, the University meeting do wish and pray that he may long enjoy the blessing of a fresh and vigorous old age, and they entreat Dr. Simson to be entirely assured that they will at all times heartily embrace every opportunity of testifying to him their affection, esteem, and veneration.'

Simson was not very prompt in delivering the keys which he held as clerk, and on 29th April, 1762, the University meeting required him to deliver his keys and the University papers still in his hands, and sent a committee to explain that the appointment of a clerk was under consideration. Simson declared he was well pleased to hear another clerk was about to be elected, and on 11th May, 1762, Dr. Joseph Black was appointed to that office, and Simson delivered up the keys of the clerk's rooms and the charter chests. He continued to reside in the College chambers till his death on 1st October, 1768. His books and papers were made over to the University and placed in the library, and the University purchased two telescopes which had belonged to him. In December, 1769, William Cochrane, an artist trained in the Foulis Academy, was employed to make a copy of Dr. Simson's portrait, for which he was afterwards paid £6. Moor reckoned himself inconveniently lodged, and within a little more than three weeks from the death of Simson applied for the rooms he had possessed, and was authorised to occupy them immediately. Simson's executors agreed to vacate the rooms speedily, but gently hinted they considered the action precipitate, upon which the meeting declared they intended no disrespect to the memory of Simson or to his executors.

In his younger days Simson had been jilted by a lady who preferred a satyr to Hyperion, and afterwards, as 'Jupiter' Carlyle relates, he eschewed female society, save when once a year he drank tea at the principal's, and his mood brightened in the presence of the gracious and beneficent Miss Mally Campbell, who was always his first toast. He was a member of the Literary Society in which all the talents of Glasgow were brought to a focus, and he founded a club which held weekly meetings. On the Saturday afternoons he walked to a tavern in Anderston, then a village some distance outside the town, where he gathered a number of friends round him at dinner. Professors Cullen, Smith, and Moor were among the members of his club, as well as the brothers Foulis, and amid free-hearted hospitality and varied and sprightly talk 'the minutes winged their way with pleasure.' Simson was chief of the meetings and sometimes enlivened the company with songs—Greek odes set to modern music being among the number—but, like a worthy man, he kept within the bounds of moderation and closed the meetings in time for members to reach home in 'elders' hours.' He continued to enjoy these social gatherings till a few months before his death, and when he died the club died with him.

The efforts of the two Dicks to procure apparatus and make some progress with experimental and laboratory teaching in Natural Philosophy have already been mentioned. Robert Dick, M.D., succeeded his father as professor in 1751, and died on 22nd May, 1757. Joseph Black described him as one of the most sensible and manly fellows he ever knew; John Robison declared he 'had infinitely more knowledge than his successor' (John Anderson), though the latter was 'much more popular'; and James Watt cherished a grateful recollection of Dick's kindly interest and help in preparing him to enter on life.

After the second Dick came John Anderson, who, though neither a great man nor a great scientist, was a capable and energetic teacher, and for many years the most notable member of the academic society. His career was stormy and combative, and there was keen controversy over some of the steps leading to his appointment. He had previously been for a short time professor of Oriental Languages, and was a member of

the electing body.   On 6th September, 1757, it was proposed to name a
day for the election, but by the casting vote of the rector (the Hon. Patrick
Boyle) it was carried to delay.   It was afterwards carried to resume consideration of the subject on 30th September.   Moor, Lindsay, Smith, and
Black protested against both resolutions, because they were carried by the
casting vote of the rector, including the vote of Anderson, one of the
candidates.   The 30th September passed without anything being done,
but on 20th October it was minuted that the session was ten days begun,
and that a number of students were waiting to join Natural Philosophy ;
and a resolution was passed to hold the election next day.   Smith protested against an election next day and against Anderson voting on a
question concerning an election in which he himself was a candidate.
Moor, Black, and Muirhead joined in objecting ; but the election was held
and Anderson was appointed.   Smith, who did not vote, explained that he
would have concurred in Anderson's election, but regarded the procedure
as irregular, and protested against its forming a precedent.   Black adhered
to this protest.   Next day Moor and Black were appointed to inspect
the instruments and deliver them to Anderson, who was to give a receipt
for them ; and, as the room in which they were stored was too small,
Smith and Clow were to look out for a proper room to accommodate them.

Just before this, Anderson had persuaded his colleagues to vote a sum
of money to procure books with a view to his teaching Italian, but his
transference to the Natural Philosophy chair interfered with the plan,
which was afterwards taken up by Cumin.   Anderson very soon attracted
an exceptionally large following of students, including a strong infusion
of tradesmen and townspeople, who found it useful to attend his instruction, though not taking a full University course.   He had an unusually
strong hold on the good will and support of the townspeople ; and though
he sometimes dealt harshly with individual students, he was still very
popular with the general body of them.   He was fearless and often far-
seeing as an administrator, but he had violent disputes with his colleagues,
and indulged in heated and abusive language.   Some of his chief quarrels
were with Professors Moor, Hamilton, Trail, and Macleod, but his
greatest and bitterest difference was with Principal Leechman, with whom
he had begun in concert.   Anderson was a better administrator than the
principal, but his violent vituperation of the latter went beyond the bounds
of fairness and decency, and gradually alienated Anderson's colleagues
from him, till at length he stood alone.   Anderson was instrumental in
procuring the restoration of three volumes of Zachary Boyd's manuscripts
which were lost before the Revolution and afterwards came into the hands
of Bernard Baine, a London apothecary ; and in redeeming the manuscript

book of subscriptions to the building fund beginning about 1631, which had fallen into the hands of Mr. Bell, a Linlithgow lawyer, and was returned by him for a guinea. He was also concerned in procuring many of the Roman stones in the University collection.

The professorship of Practical Astronomy was the only one added to the equipment of the University in the long period from 1721 to 1807. In 1754 it appears that a number of astronomical instruments had been acquired, probably in connection with the Natural Philosophy class, in which Physical Astronomy was taught, for on 24th June of that year the University meeting approved of a plan for raising public subscriptions to build an Observatory in which they should be placed for use. The proposal was not promptly acted on, but the subject was revived when on 20th January, 1756, it was announced that Alexander Macfarlane, a merchant in Jamaica, whose taste for Astronomy led him to establish an observatory there fitted with the best instruments the times could afford, had bequeathed to the University, in which he had formerly been educated, the whole of these instruments. The meeting resolved to confer the degree of LL.D. on the donor's brother, the laird of Macfarlane, whose knowledge of Scottish antiquities was declared worthy of academic recognition, and a silver box with the University and the Macfarlane arms was ordered for the diploma. By the end of October, 1756, Macfarlane's instruments had arrived, and £8 was ordered to be paid to Captain Wylie of the *Caesar* for their freight, besides £2 of a gratuity for taking care of them on the voyage; but as several of them had 'suffered by the sea air,' James Watt, who happened to be then in Glasgow, was asked to clean the instruments and put them in order, for which work £5 was paid to him. In May, 1757, it was resolved to build an observatory at a cost of £400, the site being in the upper eastern part of the College Green; and on its completion the instruments were ordered to be placed in it in June, 1760. It proved rather damp, and efforts were made to overcome this by digging ditches round the basement, painting the walls with linseed oil, and other means. To preserve the amenity of the place and keep the view from being obstructed, two neighbouring plots of ground at Dovehill and the Butts were purchased for about £500, and the Town Council having been asked to aid an institution so useful in promoting navigation and commerce, made a gift of a third plot.

When the University came to possess an Observatory equipped with instruments, an observer became necessary. A separate professorship was not contemplated, but it was proposed that an assistant attached to the chair of Natural Philosophy, from which certain parts of Astronomy were then taught, should also act as observer. The interest of some of the

Scottish nobility seems to have been invoked, communications being made through the plausible and officious Rouet, whose own projects soon came to be mixed in the discussions.   In May, 1759, a proposal was made on behalf of the Earl of Hopetoun to give £400, the interest of which should be applied towards making up the salary of an astronomical observer, on condition that the College granted leave of absence for four years to Professor Rouet to enable him to go abroad as tutor to the Earl's son. It is to the credit of the majority that they declined to accept this offer. Through the influence of the Duke of Argyle, George II. intervened, and, by a royal warrant dated 11th January, 1760, founded the chair of Practical Astronomy, with which was combined the office of observer, the crown granting a yearly allowance of £50, and appointing Alexander Wilson to be the first professor and observer.   Wilson graduated as M.A. at St. Andrews in 1733, passed some time as assistant to a surgeon in London, entered on business as a typefounder at St. Andrews, and having improved the method of casting type, set up a foundry for the purpose at Camlachie, near Glasgow, probably between 1740 and 1745.   Business connections associated him with the Foulises, and about 1748 he was nominated typefounder to the University.   After giving an inaugural dissertation on Comets, Wilson was inducted on 17th February, 1760.

The University had proposed the appointment of an assistant to the chair of Natural Philosophy who should act as astronomical observer, and though what was done went beyond their application, the title of Practical Astronomy given to the new chair seemed to emphasise the work of observing.   It was not considered that the professor was obliged to lecture to students, as that was not done at Greenwich or elsewhere in Great Britain ; but Wilson, being willing to do so, was authorised to give instruction in the three following branches to students who applied to him—the application of spherical trigonometry to the solution of astronomical problems, the construction of astronomical tables and making calculations by them, and the construction of astronomical instruments and methods of using them in making observations.   The physical parts of Astronomy were stated to belong to the professor of Physics.   Wilson continued his typefounding business, and in a little more than two years the University erected a building for his foundry in a small garden adjoining the Botanic Garden.

Even in this period modern languages were not altogether neglected in the University.   In December, 1730, the faculty reckoning that 'it is of considerable advantage to have residing and teaching in this place a native of France who understands and can pronounce his own language accurately, and Mr. Francis Buord who has these qualifications having shown his ability in teaching these several years byepast in this place,' though he had few scholars and would be obliged to go elsewhere unless further encouraged—ordered £5 to be allowed to him, half of the sum being paid then and the other half at the end of the session. Buord continued to teach and to receive this modest allowance for nine or ten years. He must have fallen into ill health, for in October, 1738, instructions were given to pay him the second moiety of the usual grant 'in case he lives to Whitsunday next.' He struggled on, living and teaching a little longer, the annual grant for the following session being voted to him in October, 1739, and 'he having died very poor,' the second moiety of it was paid to his widow in March, 1740. In February, 1744, £5 was voted to Mr. Barenger for teaching French in the preceding session, and a similar grant was authorised for next session. John Anderson contemplated teaching French along with Italian just before being transferred from Oriental Languages to Natural Philosophy, and it seems probable that he actually taught French for a time. Shortly afterwards Professor Cumin took up the teaching of French. In March, 1766, he represented that he had been teaching the French language and proposed to teach Italian, and asked for a grant to procure a small library for students of these languages. A later minute narrates that Cumin had received from Anderson a small library of French classics which cost £28 4s. 6d., of which £14 4s. 6d. had been refunded to Anderson in contributions from students, and Cumin paid the remaining £14 on receiving the books. The meeting agreed to grant £25, on the understanding that the whole of the French books should belong to the University, and that £11 should be used to procure Italian books.

In January, 1731, the faculty enacted that the fees payable by students to professors for attendance on any of the classes in philosophy, Mathematics, Greek, or Latin should not be less than £1 10s., and this fee was not to include the private classes taught by any of these professors. Up to 1727 certain small sums were payable by students at the time of their graduation in arts to the three regents in philosophy, but in that year the Commission of Visitation enacted that after the death of the regent to whom the Logic class should fall these graduation fees should be equally divided between the professors of Moral Philosophy and Natural Philosophy. There were no further fees for examination or graduation in arts except small sums to College servants. In 1732 it was resolved that of the five shillings paid for fees to servants by students who graduated as M.A., 2s. 4d. should be given to the bedellus, 1s. 6d. to the porter, 8d. to the furnisher of coal and candle, 4d. to the scavenger, and 2d to the porter's servant; while of the 21s. 6d. similarly paid for the degree of Doctor in any faculty, 1s. 6d. was assigned to the seal, and from the remaining 20s. each of the servants was to receive four times as much as in the case of M.A.   There is a statement in 1748 that half of a fee of £15 for the degree of LL.D. should go to the professor of Law and the other half to the library.   Ten years earlier there is a statement that half of a fee of £20 for the degree of D.D. should be expended on furnishing the new library.   Probably the other half should have gone to the professor of Divinity, but as John Simson was then under suspension, there is no record of the payment having been made to him.   In 1732 it was laid down that the professor of Medicine should receive £8 of the fees for M.D., and that £2 should be assigned to the library for procuring books, the remainder being given to the servants and for diploma and seal. The whole charge must have been £11 1s. 6d. at least.

In 1748 it was laid down that for the future no higher degree, that is, no doctorate, should be conferred on any one who had not previously obtained the degree of M.A.; and shortly afterwards it was ordered that every person receiving the M.A. degree with a view to become eligible for a higher degree should pay a fee of £3 for the former.   This arbitrary and ill-considered regulation was sometimes enforced and sometimes ignored.

William Forbes had been a capable professor of Law, but in the last two or three years of his tenure he was too infirm to conduct the Law class and it was carried on by Hercules Lindesay.   When Forbes died on 23rd October, 1745, there was an inclination to claim that the University had a right to appoint to the chair, as it had appointed Forbes, but counsel having been consulted seem to have given an unfavourable answer, and the meeting resolved to request the Duke of Argyle to use his influence to procure the appointment of Lindesay.   This recommendation was not followed, and on 26th March, 1746, the king appointed William Cross, Advocate, to succeed Forbes.   The appointment turned out worse than indifferent.

Cross had gone to London to present to the Duke of Cumberland the diploma for the degree of LL.D. conferred on him by the University,[1]

---

[1] Prince Charlie spent the closing days of December, 1745, in Glasgow, held a review on the Green, and exacted considerable supplies for his men.   The townspeople were strong Hanoverians, and had recently raised a regiment of 1,200 in support of the established Government.   The University professors were Hanoverians too, and on 28th Nov., 1745, resolved to subscribe funds to maintain a company of 50 men in the service of the Government for 30 days, or longer if needful, at eightpence a day, as against sixpence at the time of Mar's rebellion.   On 3rd February, 1746, the University resolved to send the principal and the rector to wait upon the Duke of Cumberland at Stirling, congratulate

and also to deliver another diploma for the same degree to Sir Everard Faulkner, the Duke's secretary. Having been introduced by Faulkner to the Duke, Cross presented the diploma with the compliments of the University, and was very graciously received. Thinking perhaps that his great acquaintances would impress the University meeting, he represented that the troubles in the country had prevented him from preparing for his prelections on Law, and desired to be excused from teaching next session, but his colleagues considering the importance of having Law taught and that it would be detrimental to leave it untaught that year, insisted on its being taught and requested an immediate answer. However, on 19th November Lindesay was allowed to teach the class, at the professor's request. The session passed, and when the next one came Cross was as unwilling and unready as before. On 14th October, 1747, the meeting declined to allow the Law class to be taught by deputy, and insisted that the professor should remove to Glasgow and teach himself, beginning at the stated time. Cross agreed to come as soon as he could settle some affairs at Edinburgh, then he found that these affairs took longer than he had anticipated, and in a third letter he stated that it was extremely inconvenient to move his family at that time of year, and hoped the University would allow Dr. Lindesay to teach for that session. Next session he would reside in Glasgow or resign his office. The meeting agreed to the proposal, on the understanding that Cross sent a plain and final declaration of his intentions before the beginning of May, and they resolved not to allow the Law class to be taught by deputy afterwards.

Even next session Cross was slow to begin. It is minuted on 21st November that, on application, he had agreed to teach the Pandects as well as the Institutes for that session. But he soon found or invented difficulties, and in a letter to the rector, submitted to a meeting on 1st December, 1748, contended that he was not obliged to teach unless five students offered for one branch; but said that if the meeting thought otherwise he would try to teach the Institutes and the Pandects that winter as well as the low state of his health permitted. The meeting decided that the statutes required him to teach both the Institutes and the Pandects to the five students who had applied, and he was ordered to begin teaching

him on his safe arrival to command the king's forces, assure him of the inviolable attachment of the University to His Majesty and the royal family, and express their hearty desire for the defeat of the rebels and the extinction of the rebellion. On 27th June, the faculty considering the obligation of the whole kingdom to the Duke, who had ' put an end to the unnatural and wicked rebellion,' ' unanimously and with the greatest cheerfulness agreed to confer the degree of Doctor of Laws upon His Royal Highness.' Some readers may think the record would have been more romantic if they had conferred the degree of Doctor of Laws on Prince Charlie.

in the Divinity Hall on the following Monday. A difference then arose between the professor and his students regarding the fees to be paid, and it was under discussion at a meeting on 27th December, but, as he left the meeting through indisposition, it remained unsettled. Some weeks later it was intimated that, on the advice of his two physicians (Cullen and Hamilton), Cross had gone to the country for two or three weeks. On 1st February, 1749, the clerk was instructed to ask whether Cross expected to return and resume duty, or whether it would be necessary to provide a substitute, but at the end of the month there was no positive answer, and Cross was requested immediately to name a substitute with the sanction of the University, if he could not resume duty himself. By the 20th March no answer had been received, and the University meeting intimated they considered he had not treated them as he should have done. They required him to return forthwith or name a substitute approved by the University; and if he failed to do one or the other, the meeting resolved to take what methods they thought proper to do the University justice. By 31st March Cross had agreed to Lindesay teaching for the rest of the session, and Lindesay was again appointed. The indolent valetudinarian never returned to teach, and in January, 1750, it was announced that Hercules Lindesay had been appointed professor of Civil Law, in succession to Cross, who had demitted office.

Lindesay was an efficient professor and accomplished in other subjects besides Law, having taught the Logic class for session 1750-51. He is said to have been the first professor of Law who discarded Latin and lectured in English, though the credit of this change is often assigned to his successor. In June, 1746, the faculty considering that Lindesay had taught the Civil Law class with great success and approbation for several years, and had thus been of considerable use to the University, conferred the degree of LL.D. upon him. Lindesay held the chair only a little over eleven years, and died on 2nd June, 1761. Next day the University meeting considering it of the highest importance to have the vacancy properly filled, resolved to send a letter by that night's post to Lord Bute, recommending John Millar, Advocate, as a proper person for appointment. Leechman, then vice-rector, having signed and forwarded the communication, Bute replied from London on 10th June in the following terms: —' I received the letter you sent me in name of the University of Glasgow. I have ever held that honourable seminary of learning in the highest estimation, and shall be happy to contribute anything in my power towards its greater perfection. The present opportunity of supporting the applications of so many respectable personages I embrace with real pleasure, and I hope in a few days to transmit the royal nomination, which, from the character I have seen drawn of Mr. Millar, cannot fail to do honour to our young sovereign, from whose parental eye the University of Glasgow is not concealed.' Millar's commission as professor was sent down shortly afterwards.

In the 18th century LL.D. was the only degree conferred in the faculty of Law, with the exception of a single case of D.C.L. in 1745, and of LL.B. in 1771. Though generally conferred *honoris causa*, the degree might be obtained by passing an examination and producing and defending a thesis. Civil Law and Canon Law were usually included in the examination, and sometimes authorship of a book on legal subjects, supplemented by a thesis on a subject prescribed to the candidate, was accepted as a qualification. The degree of LL.D. was less frequently conferred in the 18th century than in more recent times, and this was the case also with the degree of D.D. Of honorary degrees the Earl of Selkirk had the distinction to receive in 1745 the solitary D.C.L. conferred by the University. The degree of LL.D. conferred on the Duke of Cumberland in 1746 has already been mentioned. In 1752 the same degree was conferred on the Hon. Colonel York, ambassador to the States General, who had done considerable good offices on account of the University to Mr. Robert Foulis when he went to France and Holland in quest of foreign assistance and patronage for his printing establishment and for the academy he was about to set up. Next year the degree was conferred on James West, Secretary of the Treasury, described as a person of great worth and merit who had shown a particular regard to the interests of the University. It was declared that it would be for the honour and advantage of the University to give him some particular mark of their regard. Early in 1754 the faculty, considering that the Hon. William Murray, Solicitor General, had long been employed as counsel for the University, and had always shown a great regard and friendship for it, conferred the degree upon him. The future Lord Mansfield did honour to the roll of Doctors of Law. The same year the faculty unanimously resolved to confer the degree on Robert Dinwiddie, Governor of Virginia, a native of the city and alumnus of the University, who by his high office did honour to both, and might have occasion to promote their interest. In 1762 Adam Smith was made a Doctor of Laws in recognition of his universally acknowledged reputation in letters, and his having taught jurisprudence for many years with great applause and advantage to the University. Six months later Moor offered himself for the degree, in consideration of his literary merit, his long standing as a master of arts and professor, and his having studied Law under Hercules Lindesay ; and he too was made a Doctor of Laws.

After his suspension in 1729 John Simson, professor of Divinity, continued to reside in his house at the College and to attend meetings and take a fair share in the general business, though his days of teaching were over.   He kept or wished to keep a cow or cows in the College, for it is stated that in 1732 a committee was appointed to inspect the 'closses' of the professor of Divinity and Mr. Rosse to see whether a byre might be conveniently built for the use of the professor of Divinity, without prejudice to Mr. Rosse.   In June, 1736, Simson protested, not without good reason, against the election of John Loudon, the professor of Logic, to be dean of faculty, because the *Nova Erectio*, by appointing the dean one of the visitors, had constituted him a check on the administration of the principal and regents, and had made him, along with the rector and principal, a judge of the behaviour of the regents.   Professor Dick had been chosen to the office in 1734, and Simson declared he would have protested then, but Dick took some time to consider whether he would accept, and Simson was absent from the meeting at which Dick actually accepted.   Professors were frequently elected as dean for some time after this, Adam Smith repeatedly holding the office.   Simson ventured on more dangerous ground when he asserted there was no instance of such an appointment since the *Nova Erectio*.   There were several precedents, for Professors Dickson, Baillie, and John Young had all held the office of dean, but the appointment of an ordinary administrator to be a visitor was mischievous and objectionable.   Simson died suddenly on 2nd February, 1740.   His widow, Jean Stirling, a niece of Principal Stirling's, received payment of the salary of his chair till 10th October following, and shortly afterwards the University borrowed money from her to help to complete the new building for the library.   Simson's daughter married Dr. John Moore, author of *Zeluco* and the *View of Society*, and became the mother of the hero of Corunna.

On 20th March, 1740, Michael Potter, minister of Kippen, was elected professor of Divinity, the other candidate being John Maclaurin, one of the ministers of Glasgow, and brother of Colin Maclaurin, the mathematician.   The majority for Potter must have been rather narrow, the principal, and Forbes, Johnstoun, Dick, and Rosse, being opposed to his election.   Some criticisms by the minority have been recorded, the principal declaring that he could not find any two or three masters who could from their own acquaintance give any satisfying account of Potter's sufficiency ; while Forbes declared he was aware Mr. Maclaurin was competent to fill the chair, but regarding Mr. Potter who had been elected he knew no more than 'that he is minister of Kippen, and is said to be some years above sixty,' so that he could not concur in applying for his release from his pastoral charge.   Potter delivered his inaugural address before the *comitia* on 27th November, 1740, and was admitted to office on 4th December.   As was then the custom in the case of the professor of Divinity, an allowance of 500 marks Scots was made to defray the expenses of his removal.   Though not elected under very auspicious circumstances, Potter soon gained the confidence of his colleagues, and was unanimously chosen dean of faculty in 1742 and again in 1743, but he died on 29th November of the latter year.

He was succeeded by William Leechman, born in 1706, and educated at Edinburgh University, who became tutor to Mure of Caldwell, afterwards one of the Barons of Exchequer in Scotland and a man of considerable influence.   Through the friendly interest of the Caldwell family Leechman was made minister of Beith at the age of thirty.   An acquaintance, soon ripening into a close friendship, sprang up between Leechman and Professor Hutcheson, the latter describing Leechman as 'one of my Scotch intimates who sees all as I do.'   In Hutcheson's slighting estimate Beith was 'an obscure hole' where Leechman 'preaching to a pack of horse-copers and smugglers of the rudest sort' was 'so much lost.' Hutcheson, who preferred Belfast to Edinburgh or Glasgow, wished Leechman settled as minister of a congregation there, in succession to James Kirkpatrick, for whom the professor of Moral Philosophy had kindly helped to procure simultaneously the degrees of M.D. and D.D., but the project was not effected.   For some little time before Potter's death Hutcheson and some of his colleagues were looking forward to it, and with indecorous haste had begun to scheme and plan for Leechman becoming his successor, Hutcheson declaring that the appointment would 'put a new face on Theology in Scotland.'   On the very day of Potter's death Hutcheson wrote to Mure of Caldwell, urging him to stir the Duke of Montrose, Chancellor of the University, and the Marquis of Tweeddale, Secretary of State for Scotland, to use their influence with the patrons of the chair in favour of Leechman.   The appointment was made at the University meeting on 13th December, 1743, when Simson, Dunlop, Morthland, Hutcheson, Rosse, and Hamilton voted for Leechman ; and the principal, Loudon, Forbes, Johnstoun, Dick, and Anderson for John Maclaurin, the same worthy candidate to whom Potter had been preferred. The rector, George Bogle, gave his casting vote for Leechman, and his election was declared carried.

Professor William Anderson protested against the 'pretended election,' on the rather slender ground that the salary of the professor of Divinity was mostly derived from the Subdeanery, which by royal charter was conveyed to the principal and professors, and that therefore the rector had no right to interfere. Dunlop counter-protested that Anderson's version of the institution of the profession of Divinity appeared to be inaccurate, that if there was anything in his objection it should have been stated before the election took place, and that no such views were put forward at the time of the election of Potter. The rector protested that he had an undoubted right to call and preside at any meeting for the election of a professor of Divinity. The judges of the Court of Session determined otherwise about thirty years later when the question was submitted to them, and decided that the patronage of chairs in the gift of the University should be exercised by the faculty or principal's meeting, not by the rector's. Though in accordance with the practice followed then and for some time afterwards, Leechman had been elected by the wrong meeting.

A committee was appointed to draw up reasons for loosing Leechman from his ministry at Beith, and Hutcheson and Hamilton having waited on the Presbytery of Irvine, he was loosed. On 5th January, 1744, a letter was produced from Leechman, accepting office and desiring his acceptance to be recorded. Prior to his admission he had to appear before the Presbytery of Glasgow to sign the Confession of Faith, and the Presbytery, probably somewhat perplexed by the disputes about his election, and perhaps influenced more or less by consideration for Maclaurin, a member of their own body, unwisely refused to allow Leechman to sign when he appeared on 4th January. Leechman, who was afterwards accompanied by a Notary, protested that the refusal of the Presbytery was contrary to law, that he was not responsible for not signing but ought to be reputed as having signed, and that he would sign before any other Presbytery if lawfully called upon. The rector, and Dunlop, Simson, Rosse, and Hamilton joined in the protest. Leechman reported to the University meeting on 11th January what had happened at the Presbytery, and stated that he had signed the Confession on being licensed to preach and again on being ordained minister of Beith. In the circumstances the majority of the meeting determined to admit Leechman—the minority protesting—and on 12th January he was admitted. He appealed to the Synod against the action of the Presbytery, and the Synod seem to have reversed the decision, though there were some ineffectual appeals to the Assembly, and a process against him for alleged heresy in a sermon on prayer which he had published ended in failure, and was not very creditable to those who instituted it. On 26th June, 1744, Leechman was elected dean by a majority, and probably the division between his supporters and opponents was still pretty keen, but next year he was elected unanimously.

After the death of Professor Hamilton, Leechman was appointed vice-rector in June, 1756, and, except for a short interval in which he was allowed leave of absence on account of ill health in the summer of 1759, he continued to hold that office till he became principal in July, 1761, after the death of Campbell. During this time the meetings of faculty (or principal's meetings) were suppressed, and the bulk of the College business, which, by the decisions of the Court of Session in 1771 and 1772, rightly belonged to the faculty, was transacted by the University meeting presided over by the vice-rector. It is true that the University meeting had previously drawn much of the faculty business to itself, but never so entirely as during the time Leechman was vice-rector. Yet Leechman's great work in the University was the share he took in procuring these decisions, and altering a practice for which he was especially responsible at a time when it reached its climax.

Charles Morthland held the chair of Oriental Languages from 1709 till his death on 4th September, 1744. Along with Dunlop of the Greek chair, he advanced money for building a number of new College houses and supervised the work of their erection. There were seven professors of Oriental Languages in the sixteen years from 1745 to 1761, four of whom were transferred to other chairs, while two died. Upon Morthland's death, the Lord Advocate claimed that the appointment belonged to the Crown, and asked for a copy of the deed of foundation and for information regarding the footing on which the chair stood. His view was not maintained, and on 22nd October, 1744, the University meeting appointed Alexander Dunlop, son of the professor of Greek and grandson of Principal Dunlop. The new professor was acting as tutor at Geneva to the son of Sir James Campbell, and in December he was allowed to delay commencing his professorial duties till spring. A further extension of leave must have been given, for he was not inducted till 23rd October, 1745. The salary of the chair which had accrued during his leave of absence helped to provide the equipment required to begin the teaching of Chemistry, and Dunlop formally moved the institution of teaching in that subject.

He died on 4th September, 1750, and on 31st October William Rouet, son of the minister of Jedburgh, was appointed to succeed him. In April, 1752, Rouet petitioned for an augmentation of salary, and Professors Hamilton and Dick followed his example. Relief came to Rouet in another way, for William Anderson having died shortly afterwards, he was appointed by the King to be professor of Ecclesiastical History. George Muirhead, the next professor of Oriental Languages, was transferred to the chair of Humanity in December, 1754, and about a fortnight later John Anderson, son of the minister of Rosneath, was appointed to the former chair. Anderson, who was then in France, was instructed to begin duty at the opening of next session ; but, at the request of the Archbishop of Armagh, the University meeting in February, 1755, allowed him to continue another year with his pupil, Mr. Campbell, in France. However, Anderson returned sooner than was expected, and was inducted on 25th June, 1755. About two years later a vacancy having occurred in the chair of Natural Philosophy by the death of Robert Dick, junior, Anderson was appointed to succeed him. On 31st October, 1757, James Buchanan was appointed professor of Oriental Languages, but he died on 21st June, 1761, and on 15th July Robert Trail was appointed to succeed him. Trail had the shortest tenure of all, being transferred to the chair of Divinity in about six weeks, on Leechman's being made principal. Short tenures and frequent changes then came to an end, the next professor, Patrick Cumin, elected on 26th October, 1761, having a tenure of fifty-nine years, the longest on record at Glasgow. He was the son of Patrick Cumin, a minister in Edinburgh, and also professor of Ecclesiastical History in the University there. Besides teaching his own subject, he deserves honourable mention for having taught French and Italian within the University for thirty years.

Rouet, who became professor of Ecclesiastical History as already mentioned, seems to have been a man of respectable talents, who took care to cultivate the acquaintance and goodwill of those whose patronage and influence might be useful to him, and he could put forward very specious professions of acting from regard for the University when pursuing his own designs and interests. Though less than the statutes of 1727 prescribed, two lectures a week seem to have been all the teaching that was expected from the professor of Ecclesiastical History, and as he was twice commissioned to repair to London on University business which detained him a long time, Rouet appears to have come to think lightly of his teaching duties. During the greater part of his tenure he did not teach at all, and the ending of his tenure gave rise to one of the longest and keenest controversies in an age when long and keen controversies were far too common. On being transferred from the chair of Oriental Languages to that of Ecclesiastical History, he stipulated for reserving precedency as reckoned from the date of his election to the former chair, and though such reservations were made in some other cases, it is doubtful whether they were consistent with the regulation on precedence laid down by the Commission of 1727.

Rouet soon took a considerable part in academic business, one of his early successes being the ending of a lawsuit about teinds with the laird of Garnkirk. In 1753, probably after Principal Campbell had been laid aside by palsy, Rouet was commissioned to go to London to endeavour to bring to a settlement a long pending lawsuit with Balliol College regarding the Snell exhibitions, to arrange questions regarding the Williams foundation, and to negotiate regarding the renewal of the lease of the Archbishopric. He was recommended to the countenance of the Dukes of Argyle and Montrose and the Earl of Hyndford. He returned from his long mission on 27th April, 1756. A decree had been passed by the Master of the Rolls by which the Williams estates in Hertford and Essex, which by a deed of lease and release executed about thirty years before were conveyed only to the professors then named, were now conveyed to the existing professors and their successors. The Snell affairs were not settled, but new regulations had been drafted and sent down by the Court for consideration by the University of Glasgow, as well as by the Chancellor of the University of Oxford, the Master of Balliol, the Provost of St. John's, and others. A committee appointed to consider regarding the payment of Rouet's expenses investigated previous cases in which Principal Stirling and Principal Gillespie had been in London negotiating with the Government, and found that Gillespie had been allowed £1 1s. a day for eleven months, and Stirling sixteen shillings and eightpence on one occasion and twenty-five shillings on another, which the committee deemed exorbitant. They recommended that Rouet, who had been fully two years and three months in London, besides the time occupied on the journey, should be allowed six shillings and eightpence a day, besides travelling expenses and some other allowances, amounting altogether to £330 15s. 11d. In addition, his outlays on behalf of the University had to be refunded, amounting to £356, but about £200 had already been paid.

In December, 1756, on the advice of their London solicitor, the meeting resolved to send Rouet back to London to help in managing the litigation and arrangements with Balliol. He was also employed in negotiating and communicating with respect to a bill passed through Parliament that session for improving the regulations of the Hamilton bursaries and making some changes on King William's bursaries. Rouet was in no haste to return, and on 6th February, 1759, the meeting resolved to request him, as soon as possible after entrusting the management of the Balliol suit to some proper person at London, to return to Glasgow—at furthest within four weeks. Rouet was back by 28th April, accounts for his outlays and expenses were passed on 3rd May, and he was thanked for his diligence and activity in managing the Chancery suit with Balliol College and their lessee, and bringing it to a successful issue after it had been twenty-one years in the court.

Rouet had been so much absent on University business that he seems

Q

to have come to think the University would not seriously object to his being absent some years on his own.   In May, 1759, the Earl of Hopetoun offered £400 as the nucleus of a fund to provide an astronomical observer, if leave of absence were granted for four years to Rouet that he might go abroad as tutor to the Earl's son.   The majority of the meeting were against acceding to the proposal, but before the end of the year Rouet went abroad notwithstanding.   On 23rd January, 1760, Moor brought Rouet's absence under the notice of the meeting, and on 2nd February the meeting proceeded to consider and deal with the matter, the facts alleged being unanimously acknowledged as incontestable.   It was resolved to proceed to determine finally on the case that day rather than to allow a month's delay, and, on a further vote being taken, it was resolved to declare Rouet's place vacant.   Leechman, Simson, Clow, and Anderson protested against both these resolutions.   The meeting found that Rouet, who had gone abroad as tutor to a young nobleman, not only without leave, but after leave was refused, was guilty of wilful desertion of office, breach of duty to the Society, and acting contrary to his engagement promising fidelity and diligence in the discharge of his office ; and considering the pernicious tendency of a precedent subversive of discipline and authority, they declared that he had forfeited office as professor of Ecclesiastical and lecturer on Civil History, that his office was vacant, and that Rouet was no longer a member of the Society, but deprived of all rights, privileges, and emoluments enjoyed by him as a professor and member of the University.

The minority gave in a long protest at a subsequent meeting.   They referred to the leave of absence granted to Anderson on the solicitation of the Archbishop of Armagh, declared it monstrous to deprive a man of office without citing him or sending him one requisition to attend his duty, and that no professor could be secure if on any alleged fault, his colleagues were to deprive him without intimation, admonition, or summons ; alleged that leave of absence was not refused to Rouet, because the request was not put forward by him ; and asserted that they knew no gross breach of duty on Rouet's part, nor of his acting contrary to his engagement.   They pointed out that they did not propose that under no circumstances should Rouet's office be vacated, but they had asked for a month's delay and would have accepted a shorter period if it had been offered.   Lindesay, Moor, and Smith were appointed to draw up answers, and they declared the University had no power to execute a legal summons in a foreign country, argued that if a letter had been sent by post its receipt could not have been proved, and that in the case of the principal whose constant attendance could best be spared, the *Nova Erectio* provided that his office should be rendered vacant if he were absent three nights without leave, and that in his case no summons was necessary. Rouet was present when the request in the Earl of Hopetoun's name for leave of absence was presented. He supported it as well as he could, and it was refused in his presence. On his admission he took oath—'*Sancte polliceor me in munere meo obeundo studiose fideliterque versaturum.*' Could a private tutor at Utrecht do this? or could a person retaining office and deserting duty act agreeably to his engagement?

Probably some of Rouet's powerful friends had used their influence with the Government to prevent a new appointment being made—at all events, time passed and there was no sign of a fresh appointment. In September, 1761, the University meeting resolved to petition the King to fill up the vacancy. The minutes of 2nd February, 1760, recording the deprivation, and also the protests and answers, were sent to the rector, the Earl of Errol—no doubt for communication to the Government. On 27th October following Errol wrote from London to Adam Smith : ' I am this moment come from Lord Bute, and he desires me to inform the University that the King's orders are that you immediately vacate Rouet's place *de novo*, and that everything may be done in a legal way. As soon as this is done His Majesty will appoint a successor. There is a necessity to comply with this, else it may be of the worst consequence to the University. I could do no more : I said all that was possible, but to no effect. One thing Lord Bute told me is that he is engaged to nobody, but that the man who is recommended as the fittest for filling the place properly will be his man. I beg to hear from you soon on this subject, and I likewise hope our address will be sent up immediately.' [1]

When this letter was communicated to the University meeting on 11th November, they resolved to send Smith and Millar to Edinburgh to consult James Ferguson of Pitfour and James Burnet of ' Mountbodie,' advocates, regarding the legality of the deprivation, more particularly whether in the circumstances the want of a formal summons invalidated the sentence, whether desertion of office after leave of absence was refused was sufficient to justify deprivation, whether the sentence if otherwise legal should have been intimated to Rouet, and what was the proper and legal method of proceeding to vacate the office *de novo*, supposing the sentence to have been informal. Smith and Millar gave in the signed opinion of the two advocates on 26th November. They considered the want of a citation to Rouet was a material defect in the proceedings against him which might properly be taken notice of before another presentation

---

[1] This allusion is to a congratulatory address on the King's marriage.

was granted ; and that Rouet's desertion of office after leave of absence was refused was sufficient to warrant deprivation, though they would have advised that no further censure or reflection on his conduct should have been expressed in the sentence. If Rouet had been cited beforehand, they did not think the sentence need have been intimated to him afterwards, as it would have been incumbent on him to appoint some person to appear in his behalf, and to inform him of the proceedings. The Court of Session was the only authority that could cite persons who were abroad, but the Court could not delegate its powers. A letter to Rouet might be sent to some gentleman residing in the place where he was and might be delivered before witnesses, after which it was not probable he would deny receiving it. This was not strictly legal, however, and if there was reason to apprehend an after challenge, the proper way to secure against it was to execute a summons against Rouet before the Court of Session, referring to his oath the fact of his being refused leave of absence and of his going abroad and continuing there. If he appeared in answer to the summons, the case would be tried, and if he did not, counsel considered a decree might be passed against him in his absence, and would be effective. Though this form of summoning was sufficient for legal purposes, they advised that Rouet should also be informed by letter of the proceedings contemplated.

Thus cautioned, the meeting, in respect to His Majesty's command, took into consideration and reversed the minute of 2nd February, 1760, declaring the profession of Church History vacant and Rouet no longer a member of the Society, being informed by counsel there were some informalities in the procedure. Moor and Muirhead protested against reversing the sentence, Hamilton explained that he voted for reversing it, not from a belief in its illegality, but for the sake of the University and in compliance with His Majesty's order, while Clow desired it marked that he protested against the sentence *ab initio*. The principal, apparently solicitous for his own safety, sent a letter desiring the advice of the University meeting regarding the procedure to be followed. The meeting recommended him to send a letter to Rouet, pointing out to him by their advice that it was known he had been absent more than two years without leave and had been employed as a private tutor in foreign parts, that the University had suffered by the total interruption during all that time of the lectures on Ecclesiastical History, that he had given no reasons for his departure nor sent any apology for deserting his office ; and ordering him to appear before a meeting to be held in the faculty room at noon on the third Tuesday of January, 1762, with certification that, if he failed to do so, the meeting would proceed to deprive him of his office and declare him no longer a member of the Society. The principal was also recommended to summon Rouet at his house, where Mrs. Rouet was living as if nothing had happened. Both parts of the recommendation were carried out.

On 19th January, 1762, Rouet did not appear, but the principal produced a long and smooth-tongued letter from him. His conduct in the whole matter had been fair and honest, and he thought far above the censure of any candid and ingenuous man. He did wish to return after three years' absence a member of the Society, but only if it could be done on terms equally honourable and advantageous to the University. The arrangement with the Earl of Hopetoun rather injured than improved Rouet's pecuniary interests. Five members, including the rector, supported the proposal to grant leave of absence, and if Rouet himself had voted the meeting would have been equally divided, so that any censure passed on him would apply equally to many of his colleagues. Everyone had a right to desert office when he pleased, leaving it to the proper judges to proceed in accordance with the known laws of decency and good manners to declare the office vacant. A noble lord had informed him that a duke had undertaken to obtain the consent of the masters to his absence on a promise being given by a great person then still in power to obtain His Majesty's warrant for £50 as a yearly salary to an astronomical observer in the University. He would not say how far this condition, faithfully executed by one of the parties, had been complied with by the other; but if he had resigned when he left Glasgow he might have injured the University and the gentleman who was to be the first holder of the new office. In this state of affairs he had taken public leave of all his colleagues in September, 1759, and left them to declare his place vacant when they saw no proper alternative to prevent it. His private engagements rendered it impossible for him to attend the meeting on the third Tuesday of January, and his colleagues might take what steps they thought proper, but it would be a favour if they would not proceed to declare his office vacant that day, till he received an answer to some letters he was then posting. A delay of two months could neither strengthen nor prolong the legal claim he had to his salary and house till Whitsunday next. If he were asking too great a favour, then he must bid adieu to the University, but it would be his duty and pleasure to support its public character and interests in any future condition of life in which he might be placed. He demanded that the letter should be recorded in the books of the University as the only justification of his conduct with which he would ever trouble his colleagues.

The members of the meeting were astonished at Rouet's claiming salary, and unanimously declared that he should have no salary after Martinmas, 1759. At a later meeting on the same day a further letter from

Rouet, dated Utrecht, 22nd December, 1761, was produced in which he declared that he was desirous to prevent the University from losing time or spending money in further prosecuting the affair, and therefore he resigned his professorship. The meeting accepted the resignation, declared the office vacant, and ordered intimation to be sent to the Earl of Errol. Rouet persisted in his claim to salary till the date of his resignation, and the University was very slow to comply. But Rouet had powerful friends, among them Mure of Caldwell, one of the Barons of the Exchequer. Rouet petitioned the Barons of the Exchequer; and they referred his petition to the University. The University gave in answers, Rouet replies to the answers, and the Barons of the Exchequer gave it as their opinion that he was entitled to salary till the date of his resignation. At length on 6th January, 1767, the University meeting ordered payment, four members dissenting.

Before this, Rouet wrote from Caldwell offering his services to bring another Chancery suit about the Snell foundation to a settlement, and the University meeting requested him to assist in the affair, and to see their agent frequently while Rouet remained in London. Millar and Wight dissented from this arrangement, thinking it indelicate to give Rouet trouble seeing he was engaged in litigation with the University, and fearing that arguments might be founded upon it in the process. In March, 1767, the meeting went so far as to appoint Rouet, then in London, their attorney in reference to the Chancery suit about Snell's foundation, with power to adjust accounts, settle the balance of costs, let the charity estate, and settle the points in dependence. By the end of April Rouet reported that the Snell estate had been let to the highest bidder at a clear rent of £580, that he proposed to settle the accounts with the former lessee, and that the sum in the lessee's hands, with the profit and rents for the last two years and the money paid into court and forfeited by Balliol, would pay the costs of the suit and the £300 demanded by the new tenants. The meeting recorded their unanimous and hearty thanks to Rouet for his care and activity. However, they found, as on some previous occasions, that a good deal remained to be done after Rouet had given a plausible account of the progress he had made. Matters were not completed expeditiously, nor did Rouet find the Master in Chancery so favourable to his pecuniary claims as the Barons of Exchequer had been, the Master being unwilling to allow the whole of Rouet's charges. On 7th March, 1770, instructions were given to Mr. Sharp, solicitor in London, to try to get the case finished as soon as possible before the Master, and to accept £200 or a smaller sum, if he could do no better, as a full payment for Rouet's charges for attendance on the suit.

During this period the degree of D.D. was not frequently conferred. It was almost invariably an honorary degree, but on 2nd June, 1732, James Kirkpatrick, minister in Belfast, a friend of Hutcheson's, applied for the degrees of M.D. and D.D., and offered to submit to examination. He was at once admitted to trial for M.D., and on 5th June the degree was conferred. On the same day it was resolved to admit Kirkpatrick to trial for D.D., Forbes and two others dissenting. They argued that the degree was normally an honorary one, and that the University had never determined what kind of trial should be held if it were to be given by that method; that Simson, the professor of Divinity, who otherwise should have been one of the chief examiners, was under suspension and therefore not qualified to act; that there was no dean of faculty, nor could one be elected till the statutory day (26th June), yet it was the dean's province to appoint the subject of thesis on such occasions; and that Kirkpatrick held and avowed opinions contrary to the Confession of Faith. The majority, however, summarily carried through the proceedings, and Kirkpatrick was created both an M.D. and a D.D. in the space of six days from the date of his application. In 1745 Samuel Clark, dissenting minister at St. Albans, was created a D.D., on the recommendation of Dr. Isaac Watts of Stoke Newington, Dr. John Guise of London, and Dr. Philip Doddridge of Northampton. On the last day of 1754 William Leechman, professor of Divinity, was created a D.D., in recognition, as the faculty declared, of his universally acknowledged merit, learning, and ability. The degree was conferred in 1756 on John Taylor, dissenting minister at Norwich, who was described as eminent both in Divinity and Oriental Languages, as appeared from his published books, especially his Hebrew Dictionary. At the same time a similar honour was conferred on Matthew Stewart, formerly minister at Rosneath and then professor of Mathematics at Edinburgh, father of the more famous Dugald Stewart. In October, 1758, Adam Smith recommended William Robertson, one of the ministers of Edinburgh, for an honorary degree, declaring that he was a person of great worth and learning and of uncommon ability both in speaking and writing. The faculty acted on the suggestion, and Robertson became a D.D. Robertson's historic works had not yet appeared, but Smith did not judge amiss in making the recommendation. Thomas Vance, minister in Dublin, who taught an academy in that city, was created D.D. in 1768, it being laid down that he should pay ten guineas to the public library and two guineas to the College servants. This seems to have been an act of clemency both to Vance and to the College servants, for the former paid a smaller fee than the normal, and the latter had a larger sum divided among them. Occasionally the degree was conferred on American colonists. Thomas Clap, president of Yale College, Connecticut, and pastor of a Presbyterian church in Windham, was created a D.D. in 1748, a sermon by the president with another specimen of his good learning having been transmitted, and he having been recommended by the Duke of Hamilton. In 1756 the faculty conferred the degree on Francis Alison, one of the professors in the Academy of Philadelphia, being assured it would much conduce to the promoting of solid piety and useful learning in that part of the world. The Rev. Samuel Finley, President of the College of Princeton in New Jersey, was made a D.D. in 1763, an application having been made on his behalf accompanied by very strong recommendations.

In 1722 the faculty resolved to build eight new houses for professors, and, as under this arrangement two professors would be left without houses, they were to receive such payments from their colleagues who possessed houses as would compensate for the inequality. As appears from a minute of 1726, rents were to be charged for the houses, which were to be assigned to masters by direction of the faculty. The later custom by which a professor's right to choose a house depended on his seniority was not recognised as yet. A beginning was made, and by 1726 four houses were partly built, but as the University had not funds to carry on the project, Professors Dunlop and Morthland agreed to advance money on the security of the houses built and to be built. Six new houses were erected instead of eight, and were completed in 1744 or earlier. In that year Morthland conveyed to the University certain lands which he had purchased from Archibald Roberton of Bedlay and others, and which adjoined those of the College. The houses were built partly on the newly acquired ground and partly on ground previously owned by the University, in an angle between High Street and the New Vennel, and had an open area in front forming the College New Court, as it was called. Afterwards Professor Craigie, during his brief tenure of the Moral Philosophy chair, built another house in line with the Forehall, leaving an entry fourteen feet wide into the New Court ; and in 1768 the University erected an additional one, raising the total number of houses to eleven. Occasionally a number of College chambers were grouped together and made to serve as a house for a time.

In May, 1743, the professors who occupied new houses informed the University meeting that the 'stent-master' of the Town had 'stented' their houses for the town's proportion of the land tax, and that on their refusing to pay, soldiers had been quartered upon them. This being considered contrary to the privileges conferred on the University by several bishops and by sundry Kings of Scotland, and ratified by Parliament, the meeting ordered their agent to raise a process of declarator of the rights of the University; and further that, as the University had a right to the customs of the Tron for which the Town paid only a hundred marks Scots and refused to show by what title they held them, the right to these customs should be insisted upon in the process. An action in the Court of Session followed, but it was not pursued to the end, the University and the Town having agreed to refer the question as to 'stenting' the College houses and lands to arbitration—George Sinclair, advocate, being the arbiter named by the University, and Thomas Miller, advocate, the one named by the Town. On 5th January, 1747, the decision of the arbiters was laid before the meeting, and in the main it was favourable to the University, but in some points fell short of expectation, for objections were urged and Robert Simson proposed that it should not be accepted. For a time, however, the professors seem to have escaped the house tax, but other taxes were impending, and in 1756 Simson, Rouet, and Dick were appointed to consult a lawyer about the immunity of the University from the window tax. In February an opinion was submitted from James Ferguson and Thomas Miller, advocates, and a petition was drawn up to be laid before the Commissioners of Supply. The petition was unavailing, and in 1758 the College law agent was instructed to enter an appeal against the College houses being subject to window tax, every time the houses were surveyed; while in 1759 Leechman was appointed to correspond with ministers and Lindesay and Buchanan with other Universities with a view to proper measures for freeing the University from the window tax. In 1768 Professor Stevenson, whose house was in Virginia Street, some distance outside the University, reported that he was being assessed for it, and the University meeting ordered him not to pay the assessment, and undertook to defend him in case legal proceedings were raised. The minute bears that the Rev. John Corse, dean of faculty, being in the same position as Stevenson, the meeting made a similar order in his case. When the Town Council in the same year were promoting an Improvements Bill in Parliament, the University entreated the Hon. Thomas Fitzmaurice, M.P., and Robert Wood, M.P., to give their close attention to a bill conferring the power of levying taxes, in order that the University and its members might be exempted according to their ancient and unquestionable privileges. Eventually when the members of faculty were unable to maintain the immunity of the University from the house and window tax, they procured immunity for themselves by paying these taxes from the College funds, which they ordered to be done in April, 1783. It is to the credit of Leechman that he dissented from this measure.

The building and maintaining of professors' houses proved a heavy burden on the academic funds.   Much expense and also much wrangling would have been avoided if this impolitic scheme had not been carried out.   For the professors were not on an equal footing as regards these College houses, some having new ones, some old ones, and some none at all.   A plan devised in 1739 of levying a larger contribution from those in the first class, and a smaller contribution from those in the second, in order to make a payment to those in the third, did not answer the purpose and was not long followed.   Professors who retired generally retained their houses and often their salaries too, and for many years the acting professor in the most vigorous period of his life might have to carry on the work of the chair without either.   Leechman, who was sometimes as mindful of the law as of the Gospel, had an old house allotted to him at the outset, but in March, 1752, he claimed a right to choose one of the new houses according to his precedency,[1] or at least according to seniority as a professor.   The meeting unanimously declined to admit this, but offered to make the house he then occupied as convenient as practicable, and to lay down a rule that in future the professor of Divinity might on his appointment either enter immediately into possession of the house held by his predecessor, or wait without a house till a vacancy occurred to which he might succeed by seniority.   Leechman raised an action at law, but in June, 1753, it was resolved to submit the question to arbitration, and Leechman's old friend Mure of Caldwell, then rector, was appointed arbiter.   In November following, the meeting allowed Leechman to make choice of the first vacant house, and he had not long to wait, for Professor Rosse having died in August, 1754, Leechman made choice of his house. Repairs, alterations and additions were almost constantly being made to the houses, and inordinate expenses were incurred.   Indeed there can be little doubt that during a great part of the time from 1722, when this housebuilding project was resolved upon, down to the passing of the Universities Act of 1858, more money was spent on professors' houses than on the public buildings of the University.

A proposal for insuring the buildings was under consideration in 1760, but was suffered to drop for some years.   In December, 1769, however, the buildings, books and instruments were insured for £9,200, at an annual charge of £10 1s.   The allocation of the sum insured is not mentioned, but, when a new insurance for £13,950 was taken out in 1793, the professors' houses were much more heavily insured than the public buildings.

During the first fifty or sixty years of the eighteenth century the library

[1] By the statutes of 1727 the professor of Divinity took precedence next after the principal.

underwent considerable expansion, and in 1744 was provided with new buildings, about half the cost of which was defrayed from funds presented by the Duke of Chandos. Before the Reformation there was little money to spare for books, but gifts of books, consisting mostly of the works of Aristotle, Porphyry, and Peter Hispanus, and commentaries upon them, were made by Bishop John Laing in 1475, by Duncan Bunch, the venerable principal regent, and in 1483 by John Brown, a former regent. For a considerable time after the Reformation more books were obtained by gift than by purchase. They consisted largely of Aristotelian literature, along with editions of the Classics, biblical and theological works, and books on philosophy and history, with some on medicine, geography and miscellaneous subjects. George Buchanan presented twenty volumes chiefly in Greek, among them being the works of Plato, Plutarch, Demosthenes, and Strabo. A considerable number of additional books were acquired by gifts or bequests made by Archbishop Boyd, John Howison, minister of Cambuslang, William Struthers, one of the ministers of Edinburgh, Alexander Boyd, one of the regents (who also left a thousand marks for renovating the buildings), Archbishop James Law, and Zachary Boyd. The scheme of subscriptions for renovating and extending the University begun in 1630 included the building of a new library and furnishing of it with books; but as the design was actually carried out little was done for the library, and the Commission of 1664 described it as very small for a University. Subsequent donors down to about the time of the Union included John Snell, the founder of the Snell exhibitions, Sir George Mackenzie, Lord Advocate and founder of the Advocates' Library, Principals Fall, Dunlop, and Stirling, William Carstares, and Queen Anne.

About 1615 some of the young men who had just graduated in Arts presented a number of valuable books as a token of gratitude and respect to their *alma mater*, but the custom was soon discontinued. Students had been previously assessed for contributions to the library, and in 1637 and again in 1659 fresh regulations were laid down. The scheme of 1659 provided for the triple taxation of students, from whom contributions, graded according to the positions of their parents in the social scale, were to be levied at matriculation, at degree examinations, and at graduation, with an exception in favour of very poor students. In connection with matriculation the Bajan regent was forbidden to admit any student to his class unless he produced the quaestor's certificate for his contribution to the library; and at the time of examination and laureation every person who came to the fateful Blackstone, which then guarded the pathway to graduation, was obliged to show the quaestor's certificate for payment of his library dues.   Probably there was a good deal of evasion and irregularity in the payment of these dues, notwithstanding all the regulations, and the want of any clear and compulsory system of yearly matriculation made evasion easier.   Previously students had greater freedom in the use of books outside the library, but the regulations of 1659 forbade the librarian to give students books to be removed from the premises, except by special warrant.   In 1715 the librarian was authorised to lend to students, upon a note from the principal or their respective professors, such books as were proper for them, the students being obliged to return them within a fortnight.   Contributions had been levied from bursars of Philosophy before 1655, and in that year the moderators resolved that bursars in Theology should also contribute, and ordained that the latter at their entry should pay ten marks Scots for augmenting the public library.

Provision was made for a librarian in 1641, when Thomas Hutcheson of Lambhill, one of two brothers whose wealth has ministered to the cause of education and benevolence in Glasgow for two centuries and a half, mortified 2,000 marks Scots to provide a stipend.   The appointment after Hutcheson's death was vested in the Town Council of Glasgow, and the librarian was to be a master of arts and the son of a burgess of Glasgow. The books were to be delivered to each successive librarian by a signed catalogue, and on his retiring at the end of his four years of tenure, he was to be exonerated in the same way.   It seems to have been felt that the annual interest of the 2,000 marks hardly afforded sufficient remuneration, and probably the moderators thought they would have better control over the librarian if they paid some part of his stipend and had some share in making the appointment.   In 1651 they resolved to augment the stipend by adding a hundred marks yearly out of the College revenues, but on condition that the College should have a right to make the appointment alternately with the Town Council, and this arrangement, though by no means free from objection, continued for more than a hundred years. Nearly coeval with Hutcheson's foundation a sum of 2,500 marks provided by Margaret Graham, widow of John Boyd of Coatdyke, Kilmarnock, was mortified, and the annual proceeds of three-fifths of it destined to purchase new books for the library, while the proceeds of the other two-fifths were assigned to a student of Theology for collecting and recording the rarest passages of God's providence happening in Scotland and witnessed by famous living persons.   The modest provision thus made for increasing the number of books in the library would in time have come to be very serviceable, but unfortunately before the scheme had been long in operation the capital funds were lost.

James Brydges, eighth Baron Chandos, had held the very lucrative post of Paymaster of the Forces abroad from 1707 to 1712 and amassed a large amount of wealth. Montrose, then Chancellor of the University, had been a cabinet minister, and Chandos, who sat in the House of Commons till 1714, may have become acquainted with him in that capacity. At anyrate in 1720, the year after he had been made a duke, Chandos announced his intention to make a gift of £500 to the University, it being afterwards left to Montrose to prescribe the manner in which the gift should be applied. In 1726 he decided that it should be used to provide a new building for the library, but allowed the faculty to postpone the execution of the work for three years, if the money, which had been lent at interest since 1721, was not sufficient for a suitable building. Five years passed and the work was not yet begun.

Meantime an attempt had been made to bring the Vice-Chancellor, who was nominated by Montrose, into the faculty meetings as a member qualified to sit and vote in the transaction of business. In November, 1727, when this attempt was made, Dunlop, Johnstoun, and Robert Simson requested some delay till members who had doubts on the matter might consult the records and statutes to see whether there was any warrant for such a step. At first the majority supported the claim, but the minority having raised a summons of reduction and declarator in the Court of Session against the Chancellor's sitting and voting in meetings himself or by his deputy, the majority in November, 1728, agreed to join in the summons. In 1731 the Court decided that the Vice-Chancellor could not sit or vote in the meetings of the faculty unless he were a member of that body independently of his office as Vice-Chancellor; that the faculty had power to name any member of the University to be interim Vice-Chancellor till the Chancellor gave a deputation to another; and that the Vice-Chancellor as such had no further power than to confer academic degrees. Probably neither the Duke of Montrose nor Mr. Hamilton whom he had made Vice-Chancellor was well pleased with the decision. Hamilton withdrew from office, and in April, 1732, the faculty appointed Principal Campbell to be Vice-Chancellor till the Duke of Montrose nominated another or the University made a change.

Montrose now began to chide the faculty for delay in erecting the building for the library, and intimated that, unless the matter were settled and an assurance given before Martinmas, 1731, he would call for the money out of their hands and employ it for the purposes proposed by the donor. The faculty resolved to begin building in spring, requested Deacon Dreghorn and John Craig to furnish plans and estimates, appointed a committee to supervise the work, and sent a respectful and conciliatory

letter to the Duke, intimating what had been resolved upon, stating that
they would have complied with any intimation of his views about the
time for beginning to build, and pointing out that they had inferred from
his allowing a delay of three years that the Duke himself regarded the
sum as insufficient, and that the object of the further delay was to obtain
a larger sum to provide a worthier monument of the donor, and a more
commodious building sufficient for the reception of all the books the
University should acquire for many years to come.   The foundation stone
was laid some time before 27th June, 1732, and Dreghorn and Craig
drew plans and supplied estimates, but the work was not carried out by
contract, the University paying the workmen and sometimes allowing
them bread and ale in addition.   The faculty were wiser in this affair
than the Duke of Montrose, and, as they were not suffered to wait a
sufficient time before beginning, they had to wait a considerable time
before ending the work, which extended over twelve years, and involved
the borrowing of a good deal of money, including £100 from the widow
of a Glasgow minister, £100 from Professor Johnstoun, £60 from Professor Brisbane, £100 from Professor Dunlop, and £160 from the widow
of Professor John Simson.   Altogether the building cost about £1,500,
about £800 of which was derived from the Chandos fund with interest
upon it.   For three years from 1736 the work seems to have come almost
to a stand, but at the end of that time the committee recommended that
the University should borrow money to complete the building, and when
this had been done the work again went slowly forward and was completed
in 1744.
     The old library had been filled to overflowing, and the accessions had
been left in the keeping of the several professors.   In May, 1743, a committee was appointed to have the books placed in the new library, and an
alphabetic catalogue, as well as a catalogue of the different treatises in each
volume, prepared.   The buildings do not seem to have been ready for
this order to be fully carried out, and in June, 1744, Dunlop, Simson,
and any other professor who might be in town were appointed a committee
to see the books placed in the new library—both those from the old library
and those which Loudon or any other master might have—and at the
same time Rosse and Hamilton were appointed to make the catalogues
ordered in the preceding year.   The work of transference must have been
done this time, for in May, 1745, special payments were made to John
Bryce, the bedellus, and the other servants for carrying the books into
the new library buildings.   Some were still left in the old repositories,
however, for in 1755 Adam Smith and some others were commissioned
to inspect the books in the old library, to consider which of them should

be placed in the new, and how the remainder should be arranged.   Rosse and Hamilton required some years to make up the catalogues, and in June, 1750, they were allowed £80 for compiling them.   James Moor, afterwards professor of Greek, was librarian at the time the new library came into use, and no doubt took a leading part in arranging its contents.

In 1730 John Orr of Barrowfield presented £500 to the University that the interest might be used in purchasing books.   He directed that in the first place the writings of the ancient Greek and Latin authors before the year 350 A.D., not already in the library, should be procured, and that afterwards the University meeting might purchase whatever books they deemed proper.   When the gift was announced on 27th June, 1730, the faculty instructed Professors Dunlop, Robert Simson, Loudon, and Johnstoun to wait upon Mr. Orr that night and convey to him the cordial thanks of the University ; and further determined to ask him to sit for his portrait to be executed by Mr. John Williamson.   Orr had been a student in Arts and afterwards in Divinity, but, having married a lady of some means, betook himself to trade.   A vessel of which he was one of the chief owners was lost, and Orr was reduced to great straits. His wife had a wealthy uncle who did little to befriend him, but Professors Dunlop, Johnstoun, Robert Simson, and some others lent him money to set up anew in business.   After a time he began to prosper, and gradually paid off what he had borrowed.   By the death of the uncle at the beginning of 1730, he suddenly came into possession of £42,000.   He had preserved his literary tastes and his attachment to the University, and one of his first acts after coming into possession of great wealth was to bestow this substantial benefaction on the library.   Mr. Orr was elected rector in 1731 and again in 1735 and 1741.

Principal Stirling, who died in September, 1727, left 3,000 marks Scots (£166 13s. 4d. sterling) for the use of the library, to be paid after the death of his widow.   Mrs. Stirling died in December, 1738, and, there being several legatees, the faculty joined with them in measures to make the legacy effective, and interest on the mortification was first paid to the University at Martinmas, 1740.

In 1770 £100 was bequeathed to the library by Robert Dinwiddie, who had been created an LL.D. thirteen years before.   He was a member of a Glasgow family that had extensive trading relations with the American colonies, and was himself appointed Lieutenant Governor of the colony of Virginia, a position in which he afforded the earliest opportunity to George Washington to display his talents for public affairs.

In 1732 the University meeting made an agreement with the Town Council that the tenure of the librarian should for the future be *ad vitam aut culpam*, instead of changing every four years with the expiry of the period prescribed by Hutcheson when he provided the librarian's stipend ; but the principal and some others opposed the arrangement.   The majority of the members of the University meeting and of the Town Council seem to have been steadfastly favourable to the proposal, but Principal Campbell, Professors John Simson and Johnstoun, and Provost Ramsay, with the Dean of Guild and the Deacon Convener, obtained from the Court of Session in 1735 a suspension of the contract on the subject, and so the old arrangement had to be continued till more sensible views prevailed.

In 1752 and for some years afterwards repeated orders were given for 'stenting' or assessing students for the benefit of the library.   In 1754 the process was said to have been intermitted on account of the change from the old library to the new and the making up of catalogues, but it is doubtful whether previous 'stenting' regulations had been firmly and uniformly enforced for any considerable time.   In this year, however, it was enacted that all students, except those of the Humanity class and such as were quite unable to pay (of which their professors were to judge), should contribute—those of the lowest condition paying two shillings, and others, two shillings and sixpence, three shillings, four shillings, or five shillings, as their condition would allow.   These 'stents' were to be collected annually in January before any 'stent' was imposed for class libraries, and after paying for four years students, if they attended longer, were to be free from further exactions.   When some new regulations were adopted in 1768, Anderson protested against professors being allowed twenty volumes at a time, as they could change their books every day and might have any number in the vacation.   He objected to trustees making privileges in favour of themselves, and proposed that each member of faculty should contribute two shillings a year at least, and when this was not seconded, declared he could not remember any instance in Britain where those who imposed a tax had exempted themselves.

An act of parliament passed in 1709 first conferred Stationers' Hall privileges on the Universities of Scotland.   It provided that nine copies of every book published should be delivered to the warehouse keeper of the Company of Stationers, one copy being destined to the library of each of the four Scottish Universities.   In case of failure, a penalty might be recovered by an action before the Court of Session.   For many years the University did not receive the full number of books to which it was entitled, but from about 1756 more careful attention was paid to securing the fruits of Stationers' Hall privileges.   In November, 1768, Professor Hamilton, as quaestor for the library, represented that the books from

Stationers' Hall were not sent regularly, the University not having a London agent.   He was authorised to get a power of attorney for some proper person in London to be agent, suitable remuneration being allowed, in order that the books might be sent down at least once a year.   Some earlier arrangement may have been made, but in 1774 John Murray, the founder of the well known establishment bearing his name, was appointed to get the books for the University from Stationers' Hall, 'for which trouble he is to receive a guinea *per annum* during the pleasure of the meeting.'

In November, 1730, the University paid accounts for the *London Gazette* for two and a half years preceding, for *Votes of Parliament* for the three preceding sessions, and for the *Speeches and Addresses* for last session.   These were procured through James Wemyss of the Post-office at Edinburgh, while Daniel Montgomery, postmaster at Glasgow, supplied the *Edinburgh Gazette*.   The *Caledonian Mercury* was also ordered to be procured for the future.   Subsequent minutes show that the newspapers mentioned continued to be procured for a long time.   In 1736 the clerk was ordered to write to the Edinburgh postmaster whenever he omitted to send at the normal time the newspapers supplied by him, and ask him in such cases to send them by the next post.   In 1742 the *London Evening Post* was taken in addition to the *Gazette*, while next year it was the *St. James's Evening Post*, and in 1760 the *London Chronicle*. In 1765 the meeting agreed that the newspapers should lie on the table of the Charter room from twelve to two o'clock each post day ; and that they should afterwards be sent round to the masters in the order of seniority, each being recommended to keep them for only one hour before sending them to the next in order.   For some years from 1766 the *London Daily Gazetteer* is mentioned along with the *London Chronicle*, but by 1772 or earlier it seems to have been discontinued.   In 1730 the lectures on Anatomy to be delivered next session by Mr. Paisley were ordered to be advertised in the Edinburgh newspapers and 'here in town,' and this was the earliest advertisement of University classes, so far as I have noticed.   In June, 1752, the University adopted the new style, and ordered that for the future the session should open on 10th October by that reckoning.   Next year Rosse and Cullen were appointed to advertise the opening in such newspapers as they thought proper.   In 1768 the order for advertising the opening of the session was again minuted, and next year the advertisement was ordered to be inserted in the *London Chronicle* and Edinburgh newspapers in the beginning of September. Advertising was now firmly established, and other papers, including some in Ireland, were afterwards added.

R

Printing had for some time been intermittently carried on within the University itself. Early in 1715 Donald Govan, junior, was appointed University printer for seven years, two chambers, a cellar, and a garret being allotted to him. He was to maintain two printing presses, with skilled workmen and sufficient founts of type, including Greek characters, and enough Hebrew and Chaldee to print a small grammar. Very few works are known to have issued from his press in the College, and it is doubtful whether he completed the time stated in the agreement ; but towards the close of 1715 a newspaper published three times a week began to be issued. It was sold at the printing office within the College and at the Post-office, advertisements being received at both places, but it had only a short existence. It appears from the minutes of 26th June, 1738, that Alexander Miller, printer, had obtained accommodation within the College before that date, for on that day the principal and five professors were appointed to find a room for storage of his papers, which were then in a garret above the library. Miller's position within the College seems to have been rather precarious, but he continued till 1741 at least, and shortly afterwards came the brothers Foulis, who, under the patronage of the University, gained an honourable name as printers, and made a notable effort for the advancement of Art.

Robert and Andrew Foulis were the sons of a Glasgow maltman. Robert, the more resolute and energetic, was born in 1707, and Andrew in 1712. Robert was bred as a barber, and while following that occupation, attracted the notice of Professor Hutcheson, whose class he attended for several sessions. Andrew was educated at the University, and for some time taught Greek, Latin, French, and other subjects. Their course of life for some time is not well known, but Robert seems to have given up the barber trade, and the two brothers, having a keen thirst for knowledge, read widely. In 1738 they went abroad and spent some time in Paris, receiving advice and encouragement from the venerable Thomas Innes of the Scots College, who was favourably impressed by their talents, but said—'their damning principle is their latitudinarianism . . . with an aversion to persecuting any for their different sentiments in religious matters.'

A letter had been written that summer conveying a request from the University that Innes would forward by the hands of Robert and Andrew Foulis a copy of a charter by Robert II. concerning the founding of a chaplainry in the Cathedral, and a request seems also to have been made for copies of a number of documents carried away by Archbishop Beaton at the time of the Reformation. They were transcribed at the expense of the gentlemen of the Scots College, who would not allow the University to pay, and the Foulises carried back not only a copy of the charter mentioned, but notarial copies of the Bull of Pope Nicholas V. founding the University, the Charter of Protection by James II., the Grant of Privileges by Bishop Turnbull and his Chapter, a document *De Collegio Fundando in Glasgu*, 1537, and copies of several old charters by William the Lyon and others.[1] The brothers again went abroad in 1739. On both occasions they used their opportunities to confer with such literary and scientific men as they could meet, and having access to the best public libraries, they paid particular attention to books, especially valuable editions of Greek and Latin Classics, of which there was then rather a scanty supply in the United Kingdom, most of such works having to be imported. They collected a considerable number of books of this description, and sold them in London at a profit.

Robert now attended a printing establishment in Glasgow, to gain a practical knowledge of that art. In 1741 he set up as a bookseller in the city, and having resolved to add printing to his business, he made a careful inspection and comparison of the characters used by various printers, and ordered founts of type from Wilson and Baine on the models he judged best. On 31st March, 1743, he presented a petition to the University meeting, exhibiting specimens of his printing which were considered well deserving of encouragement, and was appointed University printer, with all the privileges belonging to the office, but with a restriction against using the designation on any works except those of ancient authors, unless permitted. Andrew Foulis was associated with his brother in carrying on the business, but Robert was the mainspring of the firm. The University minutes sometimes mention the firm of R. & A. Foulis, but perhaps quite as often it is Robert Foulis the individual who is mentioned. As printers the Foulises paid great attention to accuracy, clearness, and elegance of type, qualities for which the productions of their press gained a high reputation. Besides works of their own time on general and miscellaneous subjects, they published numerous books by French and Italian authors in the original languages, as well as translations of them, and many editions of Greek and Latin classic authors. Professors Rosse, Moor, and Muirhead supervised the publication of some of these, and they were thought to be almost perfect at the time, though no editions

---

[1] In 1767 Principal Gordon of the Scots College presented to the University two handsome volumes, being a transcript of the Chartulary of the Cathedral of Glasgow, containing papers from 1116 till the Reformation. He had supervised the work of transcription, compared the copies with the documents copied, and attested the whole. Gordon, who acted on the suggestion of Professor Cumin, received a cordial vote of thanks, and a present of books from the Foulis press.

printed nearly a century and a half ago could satisfy the keen and disciplined criticism of the present day, fortified by the results of all the research and discussion that have since taken place. A famous edition of Homer was issued in four folio volumes—the *Iliad* in 1756, and the *Odyssey* in 1758—copies of which the University presented to the Kings of Spain and Sicily, and to a number of eminent statesmen and other prominent men, including William Pitt, Mr. Pratt, Attorney General, the Earl of Granville, the Duke of Argyle, and others. The firm also reproduced the works of many standard English authors, and published books and treatises by a number of professors, among whom were Hutcheson, Moor, Leechman, and Richardson. In 1756 they issued an edition in Latin and one in English of *Euclid's Elements*, edited by Professor Robert Simson.

Robert Foulis by and by conceived the idea of setting up an Academy of the Fine Arts in Glasgow. It was a bold venture, for there was then no such institution in the United Kingdom. The Academy of St. Luke, set up in Edinburgh in 1729, perished before it could well be organised; and the Royal Academy of Arts in London was not instituted till 1768. With this project in his mind, Foulis went abroad in 1751, spending some months in Holland, where he received the countenance of Colonel York, the British ambassador, in his enquiries and negotiations. He was nearly two years abroad on this occasion, and shortly after his return he set up the Academy about the beginning of 1754. The University allowed him the use of several rooms for his students, and the occasional use of the faculty hall for exhibitions of pictures and works of art. Probably it was partly from insight into the relations of things and partly from a desire to enlist the support of the commercial community of Glasgow, that Foulis gave the following account of his views. He had, mainly in his foreign tours and experiences, observed 'the connection and mutual influence of the arts and sciences upon one another and upon society,' and 'the influence of invention in drawing and modelling on many manufactures. And 'tis obvious that whatever nation has the lead in fashion must previously have invention in drawing diffused, otherwise they can never rise above copying their neighbours.' He represented that by supporting the Academy the merchants and manufacturers of the city would be encouraging a finer kind of manufactures, which, though it might not yield an immediate return, would in the long run repay the outlay incurred. The scheme, however, was generally considered as bordering on the quixotic, and Foulis himself said 'there seemed to be a pretty general emulation who should most run it down.' It was not only the plebeians of commercial Glasgow who shook their heads over the venture, for members of high society were ready to do likewise. Charles Townshend (who took a kindly, if not strong, interest in the Foulises) and the Earl of Northumberland dissuaded them from the attempt, and the Duke of Argyle thought they should keep to their printing. Andrew Foulis would have given way, but Robert was determined to proceed.

Notwithstanding the cold scepticism of the many, he was not without respectable support. The patronage of the University and the free use of their rooms lessened the cost of the undertaking and gave it credit and distinction; and Mr. Campbell of Clathic, Mr. Glassford of Dugalston, and, at a later time, Mr. Archibald Ingram—three Glasgow merchants—opened their purses to support the new Academy. In 1757 Sir John Dalrymple endeavoured to enlist the support of the citizens of Edinburgh —Adam Ferguson and Dr. Cullen assisting—and they appear to have raised upwards of £150 in subscriptions. The Academy attracted a considerable number of students, who were stimulated by the prospect that those who gave proof of superior talent would be sent to continue their study in foreign parts at the expense of the institution. Payen, a painter, Aveline, an engraver, and Torrie, a 'statuary,' as he was called, were the teachers, and under them students were taught painting, engraving, moulding, modelling, and drawing. The productions of the students were exhibited within the University, and, with a view to attract wider attention, some of them were shown in the shop of Robert Fleming in Edinburgh. A special exhibition was held in the University in 1761, at the time of the coronation of George III., and David Allan, one of the pupils, has left a sketch of it, with a copy of Rubens' Daniel in the Den of Lions in a prominent place, and the smoke of a coronation bonfire in the background. The Duke of Hamilton gave some countenance to the Academy, and students were allowed to copy pictures at Hamilton Palace. Lord Cardross, afterwards Earl of Buchan, while a student of the University, also attended the Foulis Academy, and, among other things, produced an etching of the Abbey of Icolmkill.

David Allan, James Tassie, and other notable artists were trained in the Academy, which probably did as good work as the times and circumstances would permit. The institution was carried on for more than twenty years, but towards the end of the time it fell into difficulties, and the care and thought required for its management could ill be spared from the printing business, and that also declined. The Foulises in their old age were beset with difficulties when least able to cope with them. Andrew died suddenly in 1775, and in the spring of next year Robert removed a great part of the pictures and other works of art to London, where, contrary to the advice of the auctioneer, they were sold at an unseasonable time and brought very low prices. Robert never saw Glasgow again, dying at Edinburgh on the homeward journey, on 2nd June, 1776. When the University wished to recover possession by the following Martinmas of all the rooms the Foulises had occupied, Andrew Foulis (Robert's son) acknowledged that he had no claim on the rooms and could only hold them by favour, but asked for indulgence, pointing out that more time would be needed, as, owing to the great number of pictures, the Academy could not be at once cleared without great inconvenience and loss. He agreed to clear the forehall and one of the Academy rooms by Martinmas, but begged the University, after having so long encouraged and protected the Academy, to allow him the use of two rooms till the pictures could be properly disposed of. He stated that he had neither the power nor the intention to carry on the Academy, but would confine himself to printing, and hoped the faculty would grant him their favour and protection. He was allowed to retain the use of some rooms, and for a number of years was employed as University printer. When the remainder of the pictures were afterwards sold in London in the early part of 1779 the University purchased two for £50—the Martyrdom of St. Catherine, by Jean Cossiers, and the Carrying to the Tomb, attributed to Raphael, but more probably the work of some pupil of that great master.

The granting of so many rooms to the Foulises sometimes involved the University in inconvenience if not in sacrifice. Soon after Williamson became professor of Mathematics he complained of inadequate accommodation for his class, and the meeting agreed to assign to him one of the rooms occupied by the Foulises. Upon this, Robert Foulis presented a memorial which probably contained a respectful remonstrance. The meeting declared that Foulis possessed the room at the pleasure of the University, but from regard for his services and the position of his Academy for painting, they allowed him to continue in possession for the time, as Williamson did not insist on getting the room if he could be provided with reasonable accommodation elsewhere. Again in 1769, when measures were being taken for improving and enlarging some of the classrooms and providing new accommodation for the clerk, the Foulises were required to give up some rooms, but afterwards a committee was appointed to survey all the rooms which they possessed, with a view to determine whether less space might not suffice for them, and in the end they seem to have been very leniently treated.

In 1755 the University lent the firm £150 on the security of a piece of vacant ground opposite the College and of their printing house in Shuttle Street. This ground was afterwards purchased by the University in 1766 for £300. The loan was allowed to continue, the security of some houses in Bridgegate being taken instead. The bond over the Bridgegate houses and the printing house in Shuttle Street remained after the death of the brothers, and the University having purchased the printing house at £50, can have had little if any loss by the loan. The Foulises were booksellers as well as printers, and in the former capacity supplied a large number of books to the library. For a number of years it was usual to appoint a committee to examine the lists given in by the Foulises, and select from them the books to be ordered. In 1755 the University purchased from the brothers the Clementine manuscript of the Octateuch of the Septuagint, described as one of the most ancient and valuable manuscripts in Europe. Next year the meeting presented for the use of students in the Academy two volumes of the *Musaeum Florentinum*, and in 1768 allowed the Foulises to borrow the manuscript of Calderwood's *History of the Church of Scotland* to collate it, with a view to their publishing a new edition, a bond of £200 against loss or damage being taken.

The accessory art of type founding was also carried on in connection with the University for a very long time. In April, 1762, Professor Wilson represented that, though he had been appointed type founder to the University more than twelve years before, he had not hitherto applied for such accommodation as was granted to those employed in arts subservient to learning; but now that he had to reside within the College, he found it impracticable to carry on the business conveniently without a founding house near at hand. On the motion of Adam Smith, it was agreed that the University should build the foundry in a convenient place, at a cost of not more than £40, Wilson paying a reasonable rent, and agreeing that, should the building become useless before the University was compensated for the outlay, he should pay such compensation as might be awarded by arbiters. The building was erected in the little garden adjoining the Physic Garden, not far from the Chemistry Laboratory, and cost about £59. The yearly rent was fixed at £3 15s.—a proposal by Moor that Wilson and his son should occupy the building rent-free, but should pay seven and a half per cent. on the outlay, and hand over the foundry in good condition for carrying on the business if they ceased to use it for type founding, being rejected. In 1769 Wilson having applied for an addition to the building, and the University having erected it at a cost of £57 14s., an additional rent of £3 9s. 3d. was imposed.

The most memorable instance of the University giving recognition and assistance to struggling merit occurred in the case of James Watt. As a youth of eighteen he had come to Glasgow in 1754 to spend some time with his maternal relatives, and he remained till May, 1755. His father had met with reverses, and it was necessary that young Watt should be early settled in some business in which he could support himself. His own earnest desire was to become a mathematical instrument maker. His relative, Professor Muirhead, introduced him to the notice of some of the other professors, among the rest to Dr. Dick, professor of Natural Philosophy, under whose advice he determined to spend a year in London, in some workshop where he could improve his skill in the practice of the business he intended to follow.

It was no easy thing to find a master to admit him to a short irregular apprenticeship such as he wished, but at length, by the exertions of a friend to whom Dick had recommended him, this was accomplished. Having completed the engagement, he left London at the end of August, 1756, and two months later he was in Glasgow. On 25th October Dick asked him to stay and help to unpack the astronomical instruments presented to the University by Alexander Macfarlane, which were expected to arrive next day from Jamaica. Four days later the minutes bear that the instruments had arrived and were found to have suffered by the sea air, in consequence of which the University meeting appointed Moor and Dick to request Watt to clean them and put them in order. For this work Watt was paid £5 about a month later.

Watt now desired to set up business in Glasgow, but though he was abundantly possessed of the real qualification—ability to do good work—he lacked the conventional qualification, for he had not served a regular apprenticeship, nor was he the son of a burgess, nor married to the daughter of a burgess ; and he was prohibited from opening a shop for the exercise of his craft within the burgh. In these circumstances it was by the friendly interposition of the University that Watt was enabled to establish himself in business. In the summer of 1757 he was allowed to occupy an apartment and to open a shop in the College itself, and to style himself mathematical instrument maker to the University. His means were slender, his health feeble and uncertain, ' and melancholy marked him for her own.' He talked of failure and of abandoning his projects and endeavours, but worked and persevered notwithstanding. He was very keen in the pursuit of knowledge, and so willing to enlighten those who applied to him that he brightened when invited to solve a problem. His shop was a resort for students with a turn for science, and both students and professors had much to learn from the mathematical instrument maker to the University.

Dr. Robert Dick died on 22nd May, 1757, but besides his kinsman

JAMES WATT, LL.D.

Whose great work on steam was done within the Old College

BORN 1736.   DIED 1819

From oil painting by John Graham Gilbert in the Senate Room, University of Glasgow

Muirhead, Simson, Millar, Black, and Anderson were among Watt's friends, as well as John Robison, who, while still a student, made Watt's acquaintance when the latter had newly come to the University. Robison had an aptitude for Physics, and at first was rather mortified to find himself excelled by a workman. After some years' absence, Robison returned to the University, and was lecturer on Chemistry for a few years, renewing his acquaintance with Watt. Dr. Black, then engaged in the researches on latent heat which made him famous, was a close friend, and for him Watt made a small organ and afterwards an ingeniously contrived machine for drawing in perspective. He had been asked to construct an organ for a Masonic Lodge, and though he did not know one musical note from another, he accomplished his task through his insight into the mathematical theory of music and his wonderful skill in designing and executing mechanical contrivances. In the College workshop he made not only mathematical and nautical instruments, but also flutes, guitars, harps, violins, organs and other musical instruments, before he had accomplished anything notable with steam.

Not long after becoming professor of Natural Philosophy, Anderson employed Watt to make repairs on the instruments of the department, for which work a sum of £5 5s. was ordered to be paid on 26th June, 1760. The day before, Anderson had been authorised to spend £2 to recover the model of the steam engine from Mr. Sisson, a highly skilled maker of astronomical instruments in London. Somehow the model engine did not answer the purpose.

Watt's attention had been directed to steam engines in 1759 by John Robison, who threw out an idea of applying steam to propel wheeled carriages, but when, soon after this, Robison left the University, the prosecution of the idea was abandoned. Watt made further experiments with steam in 1761 and 1762, and next year Anderson asked him to repair the model of the Newcomen engine, for which he was afterwards paid £5 11s. in June, 1766. On this Newcomen engine he worked and experimented for a long time, receiving occasional hints from Dr. Black, and while thus engaged he discovered the great defect of previous engines and how to remedy it. Condensation had been effected in the cylinder by injecting cold water, which not only cooled the steam but the whole metallic substance of the cylinder, involving great waste of power and enormous consumption of fuel. To remedy this he contrived a separate vessel for condensing the steam, between which and the cylinder an opening was made every time the steam was to be condensed, and thus the cylinder was always kept in condition for working hot and dry. For years after this Watt continued to experiment and contrive further improvements on the steam engine, but the separate condenser was his most vital achievement.

In 1769 Watt made a survey, and submitted estimates for a canal, nine miles long, from Glasgow to Monkland. The promoters of the canal wished to procure a cheap supply of coals for the city, and at Monkland the price was hardly eighteenpence a ton. The University meeting, considering it becoming to support public-spirited designs, and that they were interested in measures for procuring the necessaries of life at as reasonable rates as possible, agreed to subscribe £200 to the undertaking. Anderson, while wishing success to the canal, and stating that he might himself subscribe, protested against this resolution, declaring that, if it was for the advantage of the College to have cheap coals, so would it be to have cheap shoes and cheap shirts, and thus the College money might be risked in a tan-work or linen manufactory.

Watt was engaged in supervising the construction of the canal from June, 1770, till the end of the year 1772. For a long time after opening his workshop in the College he had doubtless looked on himself as permanently settled in Glasgow, and in 1761 he made an offer by letter to take a lease from the University of a garden for nineteen years, but the only minute on the subject ends with the tantalising statement that the proposal was to be considered at next meeting.

In 1763, in anticipation of marriage, he quitted the apartments in the College which had been his home for six years, but his workshop continued there till the time of his finally leaving Glasgow, about the end of 1773. Watt was further associated with the University as an honorary graduate, as the founder of a prize, and as an adviser regarding the heating arrangements of the building erected for the Hunterian Museum.

' Jupiter' Carlyle, who became minister of Inveresk, after a course in Arts at Edinburgh, held a bursary and studied Divinity and some subjects in Arts at Glasgow in 1743-4 and 1744-5. In his *Autobiography* he gives a comparison of the two Universities, partly borrowed from Dr. Johnson, and many interesting particulars of student life in his time. He asked Mr. Edgar, a former student, for introductions, and Edgar gave him one to Miss Mally Campbell, the Principal's daughter, assuring him that he would find her ' more sensible and friendly than all the professors put together and much more useful to me. This I found to be literally true.'

At the opening of the session in 1744 Carlyle set out to walk from his father's manse at Prestonpans to Glasgow. The first day he reached Foxhall, near Kirkliston, and next day was storm-stayed at Whitburn by a deluge of rain. Having ingratiated himself with the landlady of the inn there by presenting her little girl with some ribbons, bought from a pedlar who was also sheltering from the storm, he was charged only 3s. 6d. for board and lodgings for four days, at the end of which he was lucky enough to find a chaise returning from Edinburgh which conveyed him to his destination.

In his second year he lodged in an apartment in the College, 20 feet by 17. He counted it better than lodgings he had in the town in the previous session, and, though it had only bare walls, he never had a cold or cough the whole winter. A College servant lit his fire, and 'a maid from the landlady who furnished the room came once a fortnight with clean linen.' He was a member of a students' literary society which met in the porter's lodge of the College to criticise books and write abridgments of them, and to hear discourses which students had to prepare as part of their work in the Divinity Hall. He also joined a club which met in a tavern, and besides regaling itself with literary conversation, drank a little punch and partook of beef steak and pancakes, the charge to each member seldom exceeding a shilling a night. Some young merchants and several clergymen were attracted to the meetings.

Carlyle was also admitted to Professor Robert Simson's Friday Club, and, as was his custom, made himself acquainted with good families and notable people. In Stirling's time the students had shown an inclination to act plays, and though discouraged, the inclination survived. Arrangements were now made for presenting the tragedy of *Cato*, Carlyle taking the title-rôle, Mr. Robert Bogle that of Sempronius, and Miss Campbell that of Marcia. The play was well rehearsed, though never acted before an audience, and the promoters succeeded in one of their chief purposes, which was to become better acquainted with the ladies. Hutcheson gave Sunday evening lectures on Grotius' work, *De Veritate Religionis Christianae*, which were well attended by townspeople as well as students. Carlyle says that Alexander Dunlop, besides being eminent for Greek, had strong good sense and capacity for business, and was believed, with the aid of Hutcheson, to direct and manage all the affairs of the University.

III.   1761–1800.

THIS was a period of controversy and quarrelling, and the great controversy concerned the provinces and powers of the senate and the faculty, though questions regarding factorage and finance and the expediency of a Royal Visitation were keenly disputed. The Senate, or

University meeting, as it was also called, consisted of the principal and professors, along with the rector and the dean of faculty; and the faculty consisted of the principal and professors only. The principal was the normal chairman of the faculty, and the rector was chairman of the Senate, but was empowered to nominate some other member of Senate to be vice-rector. The vice-rector presided in the rector's absence, and sometimes unconstitutionally exercised the rector's powers as a visitor.

The faculty consisted of fourteen members, and the Senate of sixteen, namely the fourteen included in the faculty, and the rector and dean. It is plain that if two distinct administrative bodies were required for the management of academic business, they should have been more distinct than this. As things went the rector's meeting had drawn most of the business to itself, but decisions by the Court of Session in 1771 and 1772 placed the administrative powers mainly in the hands of the faculty. A few years later a further action was raised in the Court of Session to settle the manner in which the factor should keep his account books and perform his duties, and the questions at issue having been remitted to the decision of the Visitors, certain rules were laid down in 1775, which Mr. Morthland, the factor, with the countenance of Principal Leechman and some others, year after year disregarded, and he finally became bankrupt, owing several thousand pounds to the University, great part of which was never recovered. Mr. James Hill, writer in Glasgow, was then appointed factor, greatly to the advantage of the University, and his descendants or the firms to which they belonged have ever since been factors. Under Mr. Hill's advice the faculty gave closer attention to the management of teinds, and in a short time obtained a considerable improvement of revenue from this source. With the consent of the Visitors, repeated augmentations to the salaries of the principal and professors were voted.

Moor taught Greek for part of this period, and was succeeded by John Young, while Richardson held the Humanity chair from 1773. Jardine taught Logic from 1774, either as professor in his own right or as assistant to Clow, and disciplined the faculties of his students for active and decided usefulness, though he did not lead them far into the debatable land on which the Hegelians think they have since shed light. Reid conducted the Moral Philosophy class for sixteen years from 1764 to 1780, and in his old age continued as nominal holder of the chair for other sixteen, while Archibald Arthur taught the subject. John Anderson, who continued as professor of Natural Philosophy till 1796, came into sharp antagonism with the principal, and endeavoured by rather strained means to procure a Royal Visitation to regulate the affairs of the University. Some years before this a number of the leading medical practitioners in

Edinburgh had contemplated making an effort for a similar end ; and in those days, when the regulation of Universities was regarded rather as a prerogative of the crown than a function of parliament, such a visitation might have done much good. There were numbers of questions calling for settlement which would have been more fitly dealt with by a body possessing legislative powers than by the law courts. But by this time Anderson was estranged from all his colleagues, and though he had strong support from the townspeople and considerable support from the graduates, his endeavour failed. In his later years Anderson was isolated, and indeed he suffered a minor form of excommunication, being suspended from taking part in the *jurisdictio ordinaria.* Dr. James Brown who was appointed to succeed him in 1796 proved to be a professor of the same type as Cross, the professor of Law, had been.

The number of students in Arts and Medicine increased considerably towards the end of the eighteenth century, and the Medical School gained by the appointment of a lecturer on Materia Medica in 1765 and one on Midwifery in 1790, while the opening a few years later of the Royal Infirmary, to which the University subscribed a considerable sum, gave opportunity for regular instruction in Clinical Medicine and Clinical Surgery. Millar enjoyed a good reputation as professor of Law, and the faculty of Divinity, serving as it still did to train the ministers of a practically undivided church, had a large following of students. By the death of Dr. William Hunter in 1783 the University became heir to the treasures contained in his Museum and Library.

Leechman as vice-rector had summoned and presided over University meetings at the time when the principal's meetings were for some years extinguished, but no sooner had he been appointed principal on 6th July, 1761, than he adopted a new attitude. According to previous appointment a University meeting was held on 15th July to admit Mr. Millar, who had just been appointed professor of Law, and to appoint a professor of Oriental Languages, in succession to Buchanan, who died on 21st June. Leechman informed the meeting that he had been appointed principal and had resigned office as vice-rector, and that unless the rector were present to preside there could be no meeting. All the members present took a different view, considering themselves legally summoned and entitled to transact the business for which they were called together, and they entreated Leechman to attend. Adam Smith brought a message that, if the meeting would not proceed to the election of a professor of Oriental Languages, Leechman would consider about coming to preside as vice-rector. The meeting declined to agree to the proposal, and Smith having communicated this to Leechman, the latter finally refused to attend.

Smith, being dean of faculty, was then appointed to preside, and the meeting having admitted Millar to the chair of Law, afterwards elected Robert Trail, minister of Banff, to be professor of Oriental Languages. The rector, the Earl of Errol, attended a meeting on 26th August, at which the proceedings of 15th July were approved; and at a later meeting on the same day in the new principal's house, Leechman resigned office as professor of Divinity, produced the King's commission for his new appointment, took oath, and was admitted as principal. The rector thinking it improper and unconstitutional that the principal should be vice-rector, appointed Professor Moor to that office. As usual in other cases, Leechman was appointed vice-chancellor.

A University meeting was held on 26th November, 1761. The Earl of Errol had been re-elected rector but not installed, and the tenure of Moor as vice-rector was deemed to have expired. The principal presided, but desired it to be recorded that he considered the meeting illegal and unconstitutional, and only consented to it for the sake of peace and to prevent the University business from being retarded. Moor then protested against a meeting called by the principal in reference to the admission of Williamson to the chair of Mathematics as being illegal and contrary to the practice of the University. Upon this, Leechman, Trail, Smith, Moor, Anderson, Clow, and Muirhead were appointed a committee to examine the statutes and practice of the University with regard to the jurisdiction and powers of the rector, the principal, and the dean of faculty, and to present a report on the subject. On 19th April, 1762, Moor was appointed to give in a statement on the side of the rector, supported by proper vouchers from the charters, statutes, and usage of the University, and the principal to do the like on his side, while Trail, Clow, Muirhead, and Millar were appointed to receive and report upon the claims they put forward. The Earl of Errol having been installed as rector on 28th May, 1762, appointed Moor vice-rector, and confirmed the minutes of the meetings held since the rector's re-election in the preceding November. Leechman then protested that, as the committee on the rights of the rector and the principal had not yet reported, this confirmation should not prejudice any rights of the principal. On 13th August, 1762, a long report, signed by Adam Smith, Joseph Black, John Millar, and Alexander Wilson, was submitted regarding the powers of the rector, the principal, and the dean, and the meetings held by them. It reviewed the evidence from the statutes, records, and practice of the University, and summed up in favour of the principal's meeting having the main share of the ordinary business. In view of the statutes of 1727, the committee could hardly have come to any other conclusion. It had been alleged that the

Royal Commissioners of 1727 were not well acquainted with the ancient statutes and practice of the University, and had made regulations inconsistent with them. The committee did not admit this, but pointed out that, even if such were the case, the University meeting was undoubtedly subordinate to the Commissioners of Visitation, and could not set aside the statutes of the latter. The report, which gave evidence of industry and reflection, did not assign quite so much power to the faculty as the Court of Session afterwards did, and it asserted a power of appeal from the faculty meeting to the rector's to which the Court of Session gave no countenance, while it failed to take sufficient account of the powers which the rector, the dean of faculty, and the minister of Glasgow possessed in their capacity of visitors under the provisions of the *Nova Erectio*.

Moor, who described himself as appointed by the University meeting to maintain the rights of the rector, and pathetically remarked that he had had only one day to formulate objections, gave in a feeble paper on the other side. He went back to the early period of the University, and some of his arguments, though not presented with that design, show the difficulty of applying the *Nova Erectio* to the altered circumstances which the lapse of time and the development of the institution had brought about, and suggest that fresh legislation would have solved academic problems in a better way than legal decisions could have done. Skirmishes between the parties continued to occur from time to time. In June, 1763, Moor took exception to the passing of accounts on the report of a committee appointed by the principal, and in October following, the principal dissented from a resolution of the University meeting to build a new Chemistry laboratory, urging that the matter should have been dealt with in the principal's meeting, and questioning (as he well might do) the right of the vice-rector to be a visitor of the College. In the preceding May the principal, Clow, Trail, Moor, Smith, and Millar were appointed a committee to collect and put together all facts relating to the powers of the meetings held by the rector and the principal; and they drew up memorials which were submitted to a meeting held in the end of October.

It was resolved to ask the principal and Adam Smith to lay the memorials before the rector. The rector at that time was Thomas Miller, then Lord Advocate, afterwards Lord Justice Clerk, and finally President of the Court of Session. He had been educated in the University of Glasgow, and his services were more than once invoked as adviser or arbiter on one side or the other in disputes between the Town Council and the College. The University meeting was held a few days afterwards, with the rector present, but a number of members were now beginning to think that to settle the questions which had been raised would need more wisdom and authority than they could muster within their own ranks. It was agreed to lay the memorials which had been prepared before Mr. Miller, the Lord Advocate, and Mr. Ferguson, Dean of the Faculty of Advocates, for their opinion. A formal opinion from these gentlemen was never submitted, but after some time Miller advised that, to put an end to disputes and uncertainties, members of the University should agree among themselves to raise an amicable process of declarator in the Court of Session to determine the points at issue.

On 25th January, 1766, a proposal was made to institute the process in the Court of Session, but, when it came to be considered at next meeting, an amendment was carried to appoint a committee to enquire fully into the statutes and records regarding the offices and powers of the magistrates of the University—to begin their enquiry at the end of that session, and to present a report to the first meeting in the ensuing session. On 15th February Trail, Millar, and Black were appointed to conduct the enquiry. The minority thought they had had enough of this, and on 10th April it was announced that they had raised a lawsuit in the Court of Session. On 22nd April it was proposed to appoint a committee to watch over the litigation during the vacation, to employ and instruct agents, and to authorise the factor to make the necessary payments. The principal then read a paper, which was also signed by Moor, Anderson, Wilson, and Reid, stating that it was with concern and reluctance they had applied to the Court of Session, but they wished to prevent endless disputes about the forms of doing business, and to stop what they considered violations of the constitution. They were willing to submit to the colleagues who differed from them their reasons for thinking the main lines of the constitution were as marked in the summons of declarator, if these colleagues would within three weeks lay before them the facts and reasonings on which they based a different opinion ; and to withdraw the whole declarator or any part of it as soon as it was shown not to be founded in the charters and statutes of the College and in immemorial practice. A full presentation of the merits of the case might produce complete or partial agreement ; or, if litigation must go on, the case would be more fully and clearly put before the judges, and the duration and expense of the process lessened. They proposed that the expenses should be paid from the public money if the rector and dean consented, or that the question of costs should be left to the Court when the case was decided ; but that in the meantime the needful money should be advanced by individuals, and that no person or committee should be authorised to draw on the factor. Any accounts incurred should afterwards be laid before the meeting for inspection and approval in the usual way before being ordered for payment.

Muirhead declared that as dean of faculty the statutes gave him power to check improper applications of the funds, and he therefore declined to vote. The vice-rector, Clow, before putting the question to the vote, protested that the *Nova Erectio* gave the rector a personal power to check the misapplication of funds. The appointment of the proposed committee was then carried by a majority, and Trail, Black, Hamilton, Millar, Cumin, Williamson, and Wight were appointed. Leechman made a strong protest, to which Anderson, Wilson, and Reid adhered. The vice-rector, Clow, then gave in a protest for himself and Muirhead, the dean of faculty, setting forth that they, agreeably to the powers committed to them by the constitution, disallowed the employment of public money to carry on or defend the process of declarator, till the expenses were awarded by the Court, and that they prohibited drafts on the factor for that purpose. They further desired the principal to intimate this prohibition to the factor, and to admonish Trail, Black, Hamilton, Millar, Cumin, Williamson, and Wight to desist from attempting to employ public money in such a manner, on pain of prosecution according to the statutes. The principal then admonished the majority of the meeting, and Millar protested against the admonition.

On 24th April Williamson required the meeting to order the vice-rector and the dean to lay before the meeting their authority for desiring, without consent of their assessors, the principal to admonish the gentlemen so treated at last meeting. Trail, Black, Millar, and Wight supported Williamson's requisition. The vice-rector and the dean, while not holding themselves bound to answer, declared they thought the admonition altogether necessary, from regard to the interests of the public and of the gentlemen named, both because they considered the voting away of the public money without their consent as highly criminal, and because this was the second occasion on which the same gentlemen pretended to dispose of the public money in opposition to half the society, and against the vice-rector and the dean. The gentlemen sat in the University meeting only as assessors to assist with their advice, but not possessed of the funds, far less entitled to dispose of them in opposition to the rector and the dean. For evidence and authority they referred to the *Nova Erectio*.

The principal offered to give in his reasons to a subsequent meeting. After this the meeting recorded their opinion that the conduct of the vice-rector and the dean in desiring the principal to admonish the University meeting was unprecedented and unwarrantable. The vice-rector and the dean protested against this sentence, as they called it, as unjust, illegal, and tending to debar them from the exercise of their rights, and reserved to themselves power to call to account those who had passed it. The principal also dissented, and Anderson and Wilson adhered to his dissent. Wight protested against Muirhead's claim of a personal power as dean of faculty to check the application of public funds, and Trail, Black, Millar, Cumin, and Williamson adhered. An action of suspension was intimated to the meeting against their ordering the College seats in Blackfriars' Church to be let for the ensuing session ; and Trail, Millar, and Williamson were appointed to draw up defences and to instruct the College agent. Anderson protested against College money being used in this cause, and the principal, Clow, Muirhead, and Wilson adhered. There were many animated and contentious meetings in this period, but few of them could excel the two which have just been described.

Arrangements had recently been made for holding chapel services in the Common Hall during the session, and these were now swept within the vortex of party strife and strategy. By an arrangement between the University and the Town Council, Blackfriars' Church, which had been struck by lightning and destroyed twenty or thirty years before, was re-built, and opened for worship early in 1702. The University contributed nearly a sixth of the cost, and a considerable amount of the accommodation was allocated for the use of students and of the masters and their families. Burial places were also assigned to the University on the east and north sides of the churchyard, and there the dust of many worthy and respected teachers and members of the institution were laid to rest till the railway came to dispossess them. There appear to have been separate services at an earlier time, for in 1736 and 1737 there is a record of payment of a small fee to James Stewart, a senior student, for precenting in the Common Hall during the preceding session ; but early in 1764 the students gave in a petition for the institution of separate chapel services in the College. The consent of the Presbytery of Glasgow was obtained, and it was deter-mined to hold the services in the Common Hall, which would not only accommodate professors and students but also allow some of the sittings to be let. It was further resolved that the sittings in Blackfriars' Church long held by the College should be let, and the chapel expenses defrayed from the resulting seat rents. On 29th November, 1764, a committee was appointed to manage the affairs of the chapel, the preachers receiving a guinea for each service, but no costs being incurred beyond what could be paid from the seat rents. For the first session the income amounted to about £140, and the expenditure to about half that sum. The committee were authorised to arrange for thirty services, and to allow fifteen guineas for each of two preachers, or ten guineas for each of three.

Shortly after this a proposal was made to appeal to the public for subscriptions to build a chapel and a Museum for Natural History ; but it was opposed by Trail, Black, Hamilton, and Millar on the ground that the present accommodation for the chapel was sufficient, that only urgent necessity could justify an appeal to the public, and, that as there was little prospect of getting a sufficient sum by subscriptions, a burden might be laid on the University funds.   On 10th June, 1765, it was determined that when subsisting arrangements made by the committee had expired some one possessing the full ministerial character should be appointed as chaplain.   On 5th November the principal desired that no further steps should be taken to supply paid clergymen to officiate in the chapel till it was ascertained who had the right to the seats in Blackfriars' Church, and could dispose of the money obtained by letting them.   After some wrangling and protesting, Leechman offered to officiate next session without payment, and with no further assistance than such of his colleagues as were ministers chose to give, adding that he considered the principal, without any desire or appointment by any meeting, was entitled to preach in the chapel whenever he pleased, and always if he pleased.   A vote was taken and the meeting decided not to accept the principal's offer.   Amid further wrangling and protesting, it was carried that Wight, who had succeeded Rouet as professor of Church History, should be appointed to officiate in the chapel, with power to him to employ any minister or preacher of the Church of Scotland to supply his place when he thought proper, and that he should receive an allowance of £50 for the session—the appointment of chaplain to be made annually.   Clow, the vice-rector, who presided at the meeting, dissented from the measures resolved upon, and signed the minutes under protest.

Muirhead, Moor, Anderson, and Wilson now procured a suspension from the Court of Session against letting the seats in Blackfriars' Church, thus cutting off the revenue from which the chaplain and other expenses were to be paid.   The resignation of Professor Black, which was accepted on 27th May, 1766, altered the balance of parties.   The King issued a commission on 30th June to Dr. Stevenson to be his successor, but it was not presented till 16th September, and in the meantime those who had formerly been the minority now finding themselves sufficiently strong, went promptly to work and reversed many of the measures which had recently been adopted.

On 9th June, 1766, a resolution was carried that Wight should have no salary as chaplain, in respect that the Court of Session had meantime prohibited the letting of seats in Blackfriars'.   Wight and other four members dissented, but the carrying of the motion showed that the former minority had become the majority, and they were emboldened to proceed further.   Leechman referred to the action of the University meeting in empowering Wight to exclude everyone from preaching but such as he should invite.   The principal considered this an injury to himself, and asserted his right to preach to the students and masters in the Common Hall without any appointment by the meeting or invitation from Dr. Wight ; and declared that he was in lawful possession of the keys of the Common Hall, as well as other parts of the College, and would yield his right of possession to no person whatever.   If the chapel services were continued next session, he would preach on the opening Sunday and after-wards when he thought proper ; and if the society returned to worship in Blackfriars' Church, he would renew the Sunday afternoon lectures on moral and religious subjects which he gave to students for three sessions from the time of his appointment as principal till the College chapel was opened.

The new majority then set to work, and the appointment of Wight as chaplain was reversed, as were also the appointment of the committee on defences in the process of declarator, and the committee to conduct the defence in the action of suspension against letting the College seats in Blackfriars' Church, five members protesting against the first of these resolutions.   The minute of 24th April, 1766, censuring the conduct of the vice-rector and the dean in the exercise of what they claimed to be their right—advising the principal to admonish the majority that carried one of the resolutions now reversed—was renounced and abrogated.   A further resolution creditable to the new majority was carried that, in prosecuting the actions of declarator and suspension, the requisite funds should be advanced by the members concerned till the Court of Session decided regarding expenses.

It was afterwards resolved that the principal should carry on the ser-vices in the chapel during the ensuing session, under a vague reservation that, if ill health or other circumstances prevented him, the chapel com-mittee should employ preachers at a guinea per sermon as often as the principal or his colleagues or stranger ministers did not officiate gratis. But though determined to assert his right to preach in the chapel, and though he may have borne a great part of the work in session 1766-67, his zeal to officiate soon waned, and in March, 1767, he proposed that the services should be conducted by hiring preachers with the chapel funds, and this was carried against a counter proposal by Trail to return to Blackfriars' Church.   It was also resolved again to let the College seats in that church, the suspension having been removed.   After this paid chaplains · usually officiated, and in no very long time the office was again conferred on professors who received special remuneration for their services.

The action of declarator in the Court of Session continued, and from time to time books, charters, deeds, and papers were sent in, many of them old, but some new or recent. Their total number and volume were formidable, and there was little wonder though the Court required some time to digest them. Early in 1771 the Court decided (firstly) that the whole revenue and property of the College of Glasgow, excepting the mortifications for bursaries or other purposes which were otherwise conveyed, were by the *Nova Erectio* and subsequent charters and statutes of the College vested in the principal and masters, who had the sole right of administration, and that the rector and his assessors had no legal power to meddle with or dispose of the College money ; (secondly) that by the *Nova Erectio* the rector, the dean of faculty of the University, and the minister of Glasgow were appointed Visitors of the College, and any surplus revenue, after paying the masters' salaries and other standing burdens, was to be applied to pious and necessary uses of the College by their advice and consent, or by the advice and consent of a majority of them, without which the acts and deeds of the administrators in disposing of surplus revenue should not be valid ; and (thirdly) that by the *Nova Erectio* the principal and masters as administrators were bound to lay the accounts of their administration of the revenue before the Visitors, otherwise the accounts should not be valid or authentic.

A further decision of the Court obtained in 1772 at the instance of Anderson established (firstly) that the Visitors had power to see that all things in the College were rightly administered according to the *Nova Erectio* and the statutes of Royal Visitation of 1727, and might by their own authority reduce all things to order, so far as conformable to that charter and those statutes ; (secondly) that professors were subject to the daily ordinary jurisdiction of the principal, and that the principal and all the professors, with the advice of the rector and the dean of faculty, had the sole right to try any professor for negligence or misconduct, and to inflict censure, suspension, or deprivation ; (thirdly) that the right of election to professorships in the gift of the College belonged solely to the faculty meeting as described in the statutes of 1727, together with the rector and dean of faculty, presided over, not by the rector or dean, but by the principal or other person who might take his place according to the regulations of 1727, and that when a vacancy occurred in a professorship of this description, it belonged to the faculty to deliberate about filling it up, and to fix and intimate the day for the election, the faculty being empowered to make the appointment though

either or both of the rector or dean did not attend ; and (fourthly) that
when a vacancy arose in the office of principal or in any professorship in
the gift of the King, it belonged to the faculty meeting of the College,
not to the rector and his assessors, nor to the *comitia*, nor to the Senate of
the University, to intimate the vacancy, and in case the King omitted to
fill it up, it belonged to the faculty to make the appointment as law and
equity should direct.[1]

These decisions controlled the general administration till the Universities Act of 1858, but a further decision by the Court of Session on the
Muirhead case in 1809 introduced what was in practice a most unfair
distinction between College professors, who were members of faculty,
and University professors who were not, and this notwithstanding that
the statutes of 1727 had declared that the faculty should consist of 'the
principal and all the professors of the University.' By the decisions of
1771 and 1772 the powers of the faculty meeting were fortified, and little
was left to be done by the Senate, at which, if present, the rector presided,
except that some shreds of business were assigned to the dean. The
apparent strengthening of the powers of the Visitors was of little avail.
The rector, often an absentee, was seldom active in the general business,
and could not delegate his power as a Visitor, while, till about the time of
the Muirhead decision, both vice-rector and dean were usually professors,
and from 1803 to 1857 Taylor and Macfarlan held concurrently the offices
of principal and minister of Glasgow and did not act as Visitors. The
decisions of 1771 and 1772 were undoubtedly beneficial in putting an
end to uncertainty and disputes regarding the powers and functions of the
various officers and meetings, but they did not put the administration of
the University on a satisfactory basis.

Anderson had previously called attention to the loose and irregular
manner in which Matthew Morthland, the factor, kept the accounts of
the capital, revenue, and expenditure. Morthland, who was now an old
man, seems never to have been specially zealous or capable, though in
selfishness he was not deficient. In April, 1773, Anderson declared that
soon after he became a professor he objected to the manner of keeping
accounts as irregular and illegal, and that during the last twelve years
many complaints had been made and many orders to the factor recorded,
with no other effect than to swell the minutes, for neither the faculty nor
the factor had attended to them. Anderson now invoked the intervention
of the Visitors, but they were slow to take action. The factor had been

---

[1] So far as the office of principal was concerned, this was distinctly contrary to the
Nova Erectio, which provided for a different method of election in case the King omitted to
appoint.

repeatedly ordered to give in a proper bill of arrears with his annual accounts, and those previously furnished having been indistinct and unsatisfactory, an emphatic call was made upon him early in 1775 to furnish separate lists of arrears for each branch of the revenue. Morthland sent in an account of arrears, and claimed £840 for expenses in collecting the revenue for the last 28 years. Being required to state the grounds for this claim, he gave in a memorial in which he stated items of expense amounting not to £30 but to £50 a year, including charges for rent of rooms, clerks, messengers, stationery, hiring, etc. Clow, Anderson, Cumin, and Reid having been appointed a committee to investigate the claim, reported that all necessary and proper expenses had already been allowed to him ; and declared their opinion that he had no shadow of a reasonable claim. Upon this, the faculty declared Morthland had no right to £30 a year or any other annual sum for extraordinary expenses, and allowed him some days to relinquish the claim, warning him that unless it was withdrawn they would consider it as equivalent to the resignation of his office. Morthland sent a letter stating that he had told them the truth about his expenses, but must submit to the judgment of the faculty, and that he would never ask redress except from themselves. The majority, among whom Leechman, Trail, Clow, and Millar were most active, voted Morthland's letter satisfactory, while Anderson, Hamilton, Wilson, Reid, Richardson, and Young dissented.

Anderson then raised an action in the Court of Session, and after some time it was, agreeably to the desire of the parties, remitted to the ordinary Visitors of the College—the rector, Lord Cathcart, the dean of faculty, John Corse, and the minister of Glasgow, the Rev. John Hamilton. After hearing parties and considering the case, the Visitors gave their decision on 12th October, 1775, at Shaw Park, near Alloa, from which the decision itself came to be called the Shaw Park decree. They found that the statutes of 1727 were the rule in all points to which they extended ; that the accounts should be kept in the regular way of bookkeeping, the factor keeping an exact cashbook, journal, and ledger, open at all times to the inspection of the masters. These rules had not been observed for some time, but for the future they must be rigidly observed and enforced. The factor should charge himself in his accounts with the whole revenue of the College, and discharge himself by disbursements, deductions, and arrears. In his next account he should also charge himself with the outstanding arrears, that whatever could be recovered might be placed to the credit of the College. The faculty were warned to be careful to get from the factor an exact bill of arrears ; and that, if indulgence were granted in any case, it must be with due regard to the interests of the College and in such a way as not to open a door to further claims. The factor's statement of accounts should show the exact financial condition of the University, and for the future he was appointed to give in his annual statement on 15th or 16th March, so that there might be time to examine and pass the accounts before the vacation. It was found that the factor's claims for extraordinary expenses were inconsistent with the statutes and inadmissible, and that he should give a full discharge to the faculty at every clearance of accounts. The faculty were further directed to discontinue the practice of allowing the factor to uplift unpaid arrears and apply the interest to his own uses. The Visitors allowed the expenses of the process to be paid from the common funds.

Morthland's friends grumbled at the decision, and Leechman, Clow, Millar, Williamson, Wight, and Stevenson presented a reclaiming petition to the Visitors, craving that the decree might not be enforced till the Visitors had reviewed it. On 28th March, 1776, the Visitors after hearing Leechman, Clow, and Millar in support of the reclaiming petition, and Anderson and Reid in support of the decree, refused the petition. Leechman, though vanquished, argued still, and Morthland was little moved. He continued to be factor for eight or nine years more, persisted in his habits of evasion and delay, and paid little attention to peremptory messages and even occasional threats of dismissal. Many serious blunders were found in his bookkeeping, he gave in the annual accounts long after the date when they were due, and there were large sums of outstanding arrears without any sign that he had used reasonable diligence to recover them.

Accountants and lawyers were brought in at considerable cost to assist Morthland, and to make up the books from materials to be supplied by him, but it was very difficult to get him to supply materials. Anderson, Wilson, and Reid had been appointed a committee to see the Shaw Park decree carried out, and for some time they exerted themselves to bring the factor to reason. At first they had the support of the majority of the faculty, though a considerable minority, among whom the principal was most prominent, opposed their efforts and sheltered and excused Morthland.

In April, 1778, the faculty dissolved the committee, and instituted a new one, consisting of the same members but without power to employ lawyers or do anything to incur expenses. Anderson, Wilson, and Reid thought this would prevent them from doing anything effective, and they declined to act. By and by the principal, Clow, and Millar were appointed to assist Mr. Hill, another gentleman called in from the outside, to put Morthland's accounts in order. Afterwards Hill wished his instructions to be modified, upon which Wilson and Reid remarked that he had never had any difficulty till the new committee came into existence, but for some time he had done nothing but state objections. The former committee found that Morthland owed considerable sums to the College in the accounts for the Armagh bursary, the Hastie bursary, and the grassums of the Subdeanery, while in the accounts for the year 1773 a mistake of an opposite nature was found, the factor having charged £388 against himself, instead of crediting it to himself. Even the second committee, though consisting of members partial to Morthland, reported great confusion and irregularity in his accounts. In June, 1779, the committee reported on some differences between the new rental made up by Mr. Hill and the charge contained in the factor's annual accounts, and mentioned that arrears, evidently amounting to a large sum, though the exact amount was not stated, were jotted on a number of separate papers, and there was no appearance of diligence having been done for any part of it. By this time the new committee seems to have grown tired of its work, for a day or two later Anderson and Reid were appointed to correct the errors observed and such others as might be observed in the new rental, and during the vacation to get the books posted in accordance with the Shaw Park decree.

Notwithstanding the remissness of the factor, there was a prospect of some surplus revenue, and Clow, Anderson, and others made suggestions for its application. In October, 1776, the faculty agreed upon a scheme, which to a great extent followed the suggestions Anderson had made, and included a considerable outlay for extending the building of the library, rearranging the books, and providing new catalogues, £850 for building a new chapel, £500 to rebuild part of the front of the College which was not in good condition and had hitherto been let to tenants, £300 for fitting up a house intended to be built in the front of the College, and £500 for improving and ornamenting the buildings and grounds. A few weeks later these proposals were submitted to the Visitors for their sanction. The Rev. Robert Findlay, dean of faculty, and the Rev. John Hamilton, minister of Glasgow, who acted on the occasion, refused their consent for the time, until the debts of the College should be ascertained and a distinct statement of the surplus produced. Afterwards in April, 1780, the visitors approved of extending the library buildings and erecting two new houses for professors.

In June of the same year two Visitors, the Earl of Lauderdale, rector, and Alexander Dunlop, dean of faculty, whose views had somehow approximated to Leechman's, minuted that the revenue of the society had greatly increased within the preceding twenty years, and imputed this to the care of the principal and professors and of the factor. They were of opinion that the method of keeping accounts followed by Morthland was in harmony with that of factors for gentlemen in Scotland, and with some modifications might have been well adapted to the circumstances of the College ; but as the faculty, in consequence of their interpretation of the Shaw Park decree, had resolved to introduce a somewhat different method, the Visitors agreed that it should be carried out, in order that the faculty might judge of its expediency. The principal added a note to the Visitors' docquet, stating that he agreed in the greater part of their judgment, but could not submit to the whole, since it did not prevent further expenditure of public money contrary to the statutes, as represented in one of his protests. This note by Leechman gave Anderson an opportunity to remark at a subsequent meeting that the principal had constituted himself a visitor to the visitors. Leechman had often given his judgment on the visitors before, but this time he had adopted a new method, putting on record his opinion in a sederunt by himself.

Four or five more years passed without Morthland greatly changing his ways, and in January, 1785, he resigned, and the principal was appointed to write conveying to him an expression of the faculty's approbation of his conduct as factor. On 10th June of the preceding year the faculty resolved to present to him a piece of plate with a suitable inscription as a mark of their appreciation of his services. The account for the plate, amounting, with interest, to £31 9s., was somehow left unpaid for four or five years, and by that time the faculty had doubtless altered their estimate of Morthland. After his resignation a committee reported that many important alterations on his accounts were absolutely necessary. It was very difficult to induce him to hand over part of the balance in his hands to enable the new factor to make necessary payments, and it was found that he owed £3,300 to the College, and considerably over a thousand pounds to five of the foundations. An action was raised against Morthland and his cautioners, and the old man died in 1788 or 1789 leaving his affairs in a bankrupt state. Two of the foundations, being safeguarded by the bond of the cautioners, were repaid in full, but the other three and the College itself only ranked for dividends on the bankrupt estate along with other creditors. The loss fell all the more heavily on the College in consequence of the Court of Session deciding that Morthland's cautioners were not liable for his intromissions with the revenues of the Archbishopric after the expiration of the tack subsisting when the bond of cautionery was granted. For a large part, probably the larger part, of the sum actually recovered the College had to wait eighteen years, when Morthland's widow died, and some property or funds of which she had the liferent became available.

The strife with Morthland gave rise to other strife. Anderson, who had been instrumental in procuring the Shaw Park decree and exerted himself to make it effective, in July, 1778, printed in a quarto volume the Process of Declarator of 1775 concerning the management of the revenue of Glasgow College, and took means to make the work accessible to the public. In November following Leechman desired to have the original papers of the Shaw Park decree put into his hands. Anderson pointed out that by an order of the faculty of 10th May, 1777, these papers had been put into the hands of Reid, who was then clerk, it being laid down that extracts should be given to those who required them and paid for them, and that Anderson and Leechman should be allowed to consult the papers together. After declaring that Leechman had made serious allegations against the visitors and some of his colleagues, Anderson went so far as to say that to trust him with the papers would be like trusting a person accused of forgery with the proofs. Anderson offered to supply the principal's notary with copies of any papers in his hands if the principal would pay for them. If this did not satisfy Leechman, he might apply to the Court of Session to have the papers put in a court of record.

Early in 1779 it was carried that the papers put into Reid's custody in May, 1777, should be put into the hands of the clerk then in office,[1] but Reid declined to part with them, unless he had an order from the visitors and a receipt which he had given for the papers was returned. On 9th March of next year the principal demanded that Reid should be peremptorily required to obey the former order. Reid desired to be furnished with the request in writing, that he might answer it at next meeting, and on 16th March he declared that he needed no peremptory order to induce him to give obedience to the faculty when their orders were within the line of their authority and his duty. He knew only two ways in which, consistently with fidelity and safety, he could give up the papers—either by the consent of the parties who deposited the papers with him, and the return of the receipt he gave for them, or by the sentence of a judge who had authority to compel him. He never desired the trust, and accepted it in the hope that the animosity and jealousy of the parties would subside, and in the belief that they would be satisfied with the access to the papers to which they had both agreed when the documents were deposited with him. If these answers did not satisfy the faculty, Reid relied for protection on the laws of his country.

Anderson had a number of disputes with students and with professors, as well as with the principal, which helped to bring him into the position of estrangement and isolation in which he latterly stood. In April, 1773,

[1] Richardson was clerk at this time.

James Prossor, a student of Natural Philosophy, described as the son of an Irish gentleman of ample means, brought a complaint against Anderson, first before the rectorial court, and afterwards, as there were doubts regarding the powers of that court, before the faculty. The students were moving out of the lecture room into an adjoining room to witness some experiments, and Prossor stepped over a rail to shorten his journey. Anderson came behind, pulled him by the coat, and, as Prossor alleged, pushed him down among the seats at a place where there was danger of his being hurt by projecting iron spikes. When the class had dispersed Prossor waited on the professor, and offered to apologise if he had done wrong in stepping over the rail, but insisted that Anderson should apologise to him for the rough usage he had undergone. Anderson refused, but, by his own account, offered to refer the matter to arbitration. On reaching his lodgings, Prossor sent a note stating that he was leaving the College next day and would be no longer under its jurisdiction, and that he looked for a proper apology to be made in the morning class, otherwise Anderson might expect shortly to hear from him as a gentleman. Prossor attended the class in the morning, when Anderson having gathered a body of eight men in a side room, called them forth and ordered them to seize Prossor. They did so, and professing they were to carry him to be examined before the Sheriff-Substitute, dragged him from the College through the streets, and lodged him in the common room of the prison among miscellaneous prisoners, where he remained for five or six hours till he was let out on bail tendered by Professors Millar and Hamilton. Anderson had intended to make the occasion still more dramatic, and endeavoured to procure a party of soldiers to make the arrest, but in this he did not succeed. He also wrote to Sheriff-Substitute Weir warning him against readily accepting bail, alleging that the prisoner would break it and beat his professor. The faculty would have proceeded to take evidence and consider the case, but Anderson procured its advocation to the Court of Session, and so cut short the academic trial. Prossor, who afterwards went to study at Edinburgh, took no part in the action at law, and Anderson was absolved by the Court, though his procedure had been harsh and indefensible.

In the spring of 1783 Arthur and Jardine observed James Wilson, a student of Natural Philosophy who boarded with Anderson, leaping in the College garden, against which there was a rule on which Anderson was said to have laid stress. They reported this frivolous occurrence to Richardson, who sent the bedellus with a message to Anderson about Wilson's conduct. Anderson sent a message to Arthur and Jardine that Wilson did not know there was a rule against leaping in the College garden, and desisted as soon as he was informed about it ; but Richardson said they would not take Wilson's ignorance as an excuse. So much had been made of this trifle that Anderson convened a meeting of the *jurisdictio ordinaria*, which could find nothing to condemn, and grumbled at being summoned. Wilson afterwards spoke rather hotly to Richardson, which in the circumstances was not unnatural, and as there were no witnesses to the interview, Richardson might have excused him. But Wilson was called before the meeting and asked to sign an apology in writing, which he declined to do ; and his father, who came up from Newcastle, approved of his declining. Wilson had declared himself no longer a student nor subject to College discipline, but sentence of expulsion was pronounced against him. Anderson, who had communicated with Wilson's father and probably advised the son as to the course he should follow, was censured for his part in the affair.

In 1784 Andrew Crawford, a student whose means were slender, procured towards the end of the session a teaching appointment for part of the day, and requested Anderson to excuse him from attendance at the hour for examination, and allow him to attend at the morning hour and the meeting for experiments. Anderson refused the request, and with ill-judged severity dismissed Crawford from the class in presence of his fellow students. Crawford having petitioned the faculty, they ordered Anderson to re-admit him. The professor gave an angry representation of the affair to his class, and said the faculty were overthrowing academic discipline. He was summoned before the faculty, but instead of appearing, sent a letter inviting them to take their precognitions and give him a libel. When he received a libel he would wait upon the faculty and stand upon his defence as law directed, and particularly with the aid of counsel, open doors, extracts, and some other meeting place than a private house. He was again summoned next day, and appeared, but declined to say anything unless the reports were put in writing and given to him. The meeting desired some further answer, and stated their unwillingness to proceed with the formality of a regular trial, and their readiness to admit any proper explanation.

Anderson declined to give any account of the affair, though warned that refusal would be considered inconsistent with his duty and would subject him to consequences. He was then ordered to withdraw, which he did, protesting against the faculty's procedure, but offering to give answers to questions put to him in writing or recorded in the minutes. The meeting unanimously found that the disrespect and contempt shown in refusing to give any satisfaction concerning his conduct was inconsistent with the duty of a professor, subversive of order and discipline, and deserving of academic censure, and they therefore suspended Anderson from all exercise of academic discipline in the Common Hall and other meetings of the *jurisdictio ordinaria*, and declared that he should remain under this censure till the faculty received satisfaction concerning his behaviour.

Anderson was almost always at variance with some of his colleagues. One of his earliest disputes was with Moor, who seems to have been the aggressor. The strife began in a tavern, there was talk of a challenge, and the two professors were fined, and for a time during the vacation suspended from office. About fourteen years later a complaint by Anderson was one of the chief circumstances leading up to the resignation of Moor. In 1762 Anderson accused Hamilton of falsifying the minutes, but afterwards apologised. At the time when the chapel services were being established Trail took needless offence at a statement by Anderson that he knew cases in which students of Divinity neglected to attend public worship and misspent the time when they should have been in church. Trail repeatedly and warmly insisted that Anderson should name the offenders or suffer censure, but he failed to persuade his colleagues. On 11th January, 1783, there was a furious quarrel between Anderson and Macleod, the professor of Church History. The former had been enquiring into the conduct of the Hon. Mr. Fitzroy, a student who boarded in Macleod's house, and upon whose integrity there seem to have been some reflections. When brought before the College meeting he did not maintain his defence, but intimated that he was no longer a student, on which proceedings were stayed. Macleod believing the reflections on Fitzroy to be unfounded, read a paper and made a speech full of invective against Anderson, and the latter gave his antagonist the lie direct and shook his cane at him across the table. Though affirming that he had been greatly provoked and that his behaviour was directed to Macleod only, Anderson asked pardon of the principal and the faculty for what had occurred, but by the principal's casting vote it was determined to proceed with the consideration of Macleod's complaint. Anderson presented a bill of advocation and tried ineffectually to have the case removed to the Court of Session. He then insisted on a libel, and when the faculty reluctantly gave way to this request, he gave in a list of witnesses, some of whom were in India, America, and on board ships of the Navy. But Macleod's complaint seems to have lost force from its being found that Anderson's suspicions against Fitzroy were not groundless.

Leechman and Anderson were further divided, if that were possible, by an article contributed by Mr. Disney, a dissenting minister in London, to the *Gentleman's Magazine* for September, 1783, reflecting on the conduct and administration of Principal Stirling, and accusing him of embezzling some thousands of College money, which it was said the Commission of 1727 had obliged him to refund.   The records of the Commission give no countenance to these allegations that money was embezzled and refunded.   What they do state is that the accounts of the College since the time of Stirling's predecessor were in such disorder that the financial state of the University could not be ascertained without making out *de novo* a journal and ledger ; and that the Commissioners gave instructions for this being done.   Disney's article was founded on memoirs left by William Robertson, who graduated at Glasgow in 1724 as M.A. and in 1768 as D.D., who was expelled from the University in 1725, but whose sentence of expulsion was rescinded next year in deference to a recommendation by the Commission of Visitation, and who, after acting as a curate, rector, and vicar in the Church of Ireland at various places, became chaplain to Lord Cathcart, the British Ambassador to Russia, and finally was appointed master of Wolverhampton Grammar School.

Leechman brought the article before the faculty, and they desired him to write to Disney furnishing a vindication of Stirling.   Anderson, who went to London about this time, laid before Disney evidence or arguments in support of the charges against Stirling, but failed to convince him, and Disney published in a subsequent issue of the *Gentleman's Magazine* the vindication which Leechman had sent.   Leechman now began to be concerned about the Process of Declarator leading up to the Shaw Park decree, which Anderson had printed in 1778, apprehending that in after years unfavourable judgments might be formed regarding himself, as had happened in the case of Stirling ; and he asked the faculty to take into their consideration the Process of Declarator of 1775 concerning the management of the revenue, and to record their judgment upon it for his exculpation.   Upon this, the faculty on 3rd May, 1784, declared they regarded the insinuations and aspersions against Leechman as totally unfounded, and characterised them as scandalous and unwarrantable. They expressed their sense of the prudent economy of the principal in the administration of the public funds, which had been commended by the ordinary visitors after they had recently enquired into the whole period of Leechman's administration.   The faculty thought it necessary to furnish means of opposing the public and authentic approbation of his colleagues to the misrepresentations of an individual, so that Leechman's character might escape the violence offered after so great a distance of time to that of his predecessor.

Leechman had renewed his demand for the Shaw Park papers, and on

7th May, 1783, Reid was ordered to deliver them to the clerk (Jardine). At next meeting, two days later, Reid declared that his giving up the papers would depend on whether Anderson, who gave them to him and took his receipt, had put them into the hands of Reid personally or into his hands officially as clerk, and whether Anderson would return Reid's receipt and consent to his delivering the papers. Anderson was not present, nor had he given Reid an answer to these questions, but he sent a communication to the clerk which, after some altercation, was put into Reid's hands. Anderson signified that he would consent to Reid giving up the papers and would return his receipt, but only under protestation that no after challenge should be competent for any alleged alteration of the papers while in Reid's custody, and requiring this to be inserted in the minutes. In consequence of this, Reid gave up the papers, calling attention to Anderson's protestation. The meeting received them, declaring they paid no regard to the protestation.

A meeting was fixed soon afterwards to examine the papers and Anderson was ordered to attend. He disregarded the order, and the meeting expressed their high disapprobation of his behaviour. Patrick Wilson having been appointed clerk, the meeting proceeded on 10th June to consider the papers, and much against their will consented to allow a memorial by Anderson to be recorded. After giving a history of the papers and of the principal's efforts to get them out of Reid's hands, he pointed out that Leechman had said injurious things of the visitors and of Anderson, and was publicly called upon to prove them, and it was therefore proper to take care of the authentic papers presented to the visitors. The three visitors concerned in the Shaw Park decree were all dead, and it was desirable to get a judicial examination before the death of the other parties interested or concerned—Leechman, Reid, Anderson, the clerks to the visitors, and the notaries. As Anderson had not succeeded in his efforts to get this done, he now by the advice of his lawyer, protested against any after challenge. The meeting expressed their renewed disapprobation of the protest and the time and manner of its being introduced, and admonished Anderson to be more circumspect for the future in his conduct in such matters.

The *jurisdictio ordinaria* having resolved that prizes should be given for the two best orations delivered in the Common Hall on the Saturdays, Anderson gave in a memorial to the faculty against it, but the faculty highly approved of the resolution and recommended that it should be carried out. They also highly disapproved of Anderson's conduct in the affair, especially of a letter sent to the principal in which he threatened that, unless certain views of his were followed, he would tell his students

JOHN ANDERSON, M.A.

Professor of Oriental Languages, 1755-1757, and of Natural Philosophy, 1757-1796

BORN 1726.   DIED 1796

From oil painting in the Glasgow and West of Scotland Technical College

that he looked upon the innovation as a piece of folly and oppression. They prohibited him at his peril from executing his threat or giving any representation to his students unless directed.   In 1770 Anderson had given a sum of £20 for the encouragement of Natural Philosophy and good elocution among the Masters of Arts of the University, to be regulated by a deed of donation which he was to draw up.   Shortly afterwards Archibald Arthur, who became assistant and successor to Reid, added five guineas to the fund.   No deed was executed, but essays or treatises were invited, and meetings of Masters of Arts, usually attended by professors as well, were held to adjudicate on the work submitted.

When sharp differences arose between Anderson and his colleagues, some of them professed to discover great dangers in the working of this scheme, and thought it monstrous that in the course of discussing and awarding the prize Masters of Arts should hold meetings and be at liberty to speak and vote against professors.   They were jealous of Anderson's influence with the graduates, and as no deed had yet been executed, they feared that even after his death he might vex them still.   The new prizes now proposed seem to have been devised as a set-off against Anderson's, and shortly afterwards the faculty withdrew their consent to the holding of meetings in connection with the latter, and returned the fund, which had increased to about £53.   When the proposal had been fully discussed the new prizes took the form of three silver medals awarded annually, one for a discourse in Theology, one for a discourse in Philosophy, and the third for the best specimen of elocution.   The earliest awards were made on 1st May, 1785, one medal being assigned to Stevenson M'Gill, M.A., for an essay on the Authenticity of St. Matthew's Gospel, a second to John Sommers, M.A., for an essay on the Ebbing and Flowing of the Tides, Mr. Sommers also carrying off the medal for elocution.

Anderson had hitherto made free use of the power of dissenting and protesting, and getting his reasons, which were sometimes expressed at great length and in very forcible terms, entered in the minutes; but the faculty had begun to think of checking this also.   Henry Dundas, a man who wielded greater powers than some of the kings of Scotland, was rector from 1781 to 1783.   His functions as visitor seem to have led him to peruse the minutes, and the faculty or some of its members requested his advice how far they were obliged to insert inordinate protests.   Dundas gave his opinion that the faculty had a discretionary power to prevent the insertion of extraneous or indecent matter, whether presented in the form of dissent, protest, or otherwise.   A meeting was held on 17th May, 1784, to consider a number of protests tendered by Anderson.   The faculty expressed the opinion that the papers contained many misrepresen-

T

tations and falsehoods, and refused to record them, but offered to do so if they were put into a decent and regular form.   They also resolved, in view of long and improper papers being sometimes given in as protests and reasons of protests, burdening the records and causing expense, that if such papers were inserted in future, the members who gave them in should pay for their being engrossed.

Anderson's valour remained, but his discretion had departed.   For a long time he had generally been in a majority, and though he afterwards fell into a minority, he had respectable allies, Reid and Wilson frequently sharing and supporting his views, and the former suffering no little vexation in consequence of his reluctance to give up the Shaw Park papers which Anderson had committed to him.   But ill-considered and vituperative methods had estranged the last allies among his colleagues, and, so far as they were concerned, he now stood alone—alone but not subdued. His next effort was to procure a Royal Commission to investigate and regulate the affairs of the University.   Such a Commission might have found enough work to carry out, for the University had outgrown the *Nova Erectio*, supplemented as it was by the statutes of 1727, the administrative bodies stood in need of reform, and the Medical School was a comparatively new department steadily rising into greater importance, yet there had never been a systematic code of regulations for it, and the want of provision in the faculty of Medicine for a specific curriculum and a certain standard of efficiency in all the Scottish Universities had already induced the leading physicians of Edinburgh to draw up a memorial for a Royal Visitation.   Anderson might have known that his attempt, unsupported by any of his colleagues or of the higher officers of the University, was not likely to succeed; but probably he now felt towards the managers of the University as the witch in *Macbeth* towards the sailor:

> ' Though his bark cannot be lost,
> Yet it shall be tempest-tost.'

In the summer of 1784 he applied unsuccessfully to the Marquis of Graham, then Chancellor of the University, and to the Lord Advocate to aid him in procuring a royal warrant.   Later in the year he set about procuring petitions to the King from the students and the citizens of Glasgow, with both of whom he had great influence.   His opponents asserted that he was by no means scrupulous in his methods, that he intrigued with the students, and caused handbills and strongly-worded papers to be distributed.   Petitions were laid out for signature in shops and elsewhere, porters were stationed in the street to ask passers-by to sign, adherents of Anderson canvassed from house to house, and notaries public were employed to give the proceedings an air of regularity and legal form. Anderson seems to have regarded a petition from the Masters of Arts as of special importance, and to them he addressed a circular letter, carried about to many by his own servant, soliciting their support. In this letter he sketched the course he intended to pursue, and gave an estimate of the support accorded to his petition. ' In a short time I shall set out for London and carry fifteen petitions to the King for a Royal Visitation, viz., a petition from the Masters of Arts, which, with one from the Masters of Arts in Ireland, will be subscribed, it is believed, by more than fifty; a petition from most of the Irish students; a petition from more than one hundred and fifty students of every denomination; a petition from the Trades House and fourteen incorporations; a petition from the merchants, traders, manufacturers, and other inhabitants of Glasgow, amounting, it is said, to four thousand; and ten petitions from individuals who have received injustice from the University: that is, there are petitions from a number equal to three-fourths of the students that were at the University last year, and from more than two-thirds of the inhabitants of the city. Whether a Royal Visitation will be granted in consequence of these petitions may be thought by some to be doubtful, but there are two things of which there can be no doubt—a Royal Visitation was never asked by so many and such a variety of persons; and if it is not granted, the University must for many years fall into such contempt that it will not answer the end of its institution.'

At a meeting on 24th February, 1785, the Trades House of Glasgow passed a resolution which was published in the newspapers two days afterwards, setting forth that for a considerable time there had been great animosities and divisions among the professors and students, in consequence of which the latter were decreasing in numbers and suffering in their education. The House agreed to present a petition to the King for a Royal Visitation to enquire into the past conduct of professors and students and to order such remedies as might be judged proper. The Deacon Convener was appointed to sign the petition for the Trades House, after which it was to be laid before the fourteen Incorporated Trades, that they might, if so inclined, authorise their Deacons to sign. At the next meeting of the Trades House, Leechman, now bending beneath the weight of years, appeared, and in his own name and that of the professors and lecturers protested that the averments of the resolution and the petition were untrue, calumnious, and injurious to the University; that they had been made, not only without proof, but without previous communication with the University, and without proper measures to ascertain the facts; and that the Deacon Convener and other members of the Trades

House should be liable for all damage arising to the University or to individual members of it from the publication of these averments.

Anderson laid his petitions before Lord Sydney, Secretary of State for the Northern Department, to whom also the faculty sent a memorial setting forth their views. Sydney consulted the Lord Advocate, the Chancellor of the University (the Marquis of Graham), and the Rector (Edmund Burke), and on 17th June, 1785, intimated to Anderson that the petitions had received the fullest consideration, but that, though there was every disposition to redress grievances, it was not judged to be either necessary or expedient to appoint a Royal Visitation in the present case. The complaint might be remedied by the ordinary visitors or by a law court, and the extraordinary intervention of the Crown seemed more likely to injure the discipline of the University than to promote the peace and good order of that respectable seat of learning. Sydney at the same time wrote to Leechman, forwarding a copy of the reply to Anderson, and stating that he hoped the decision would tend to suppress discontent and discourage the making of applications of this nature to the Crown, which should not be made while the ordinary means of redress remained open ; and concluded by saying—'I have not failed to mention to His Majesty all the steps which have been pursued by me in consequence of Mr. Anderson's representations, and I have His Majesty's commands to acquaint you that he sees no reason to be dissatisfied with your conduct, or in any degree inclined to entertain an opinion to your disadvantage or to the discredit of the University.'

The sands of life were running rather low with Leechman, who was now seventy-nine years of age, and doubtless it had been very consoling to the old man to receive an assurance of the King's approbation, following on the panegyric which his colleagues had recently bestowed on him. The protest he made in March against the action of the Trades House must have strained his physical powers, early in May he became unable to attend to University business, in November he was entirely prostrated, and he died on 5th December, 1785. He bequeathed a considerable number of books for the use of Divinity students.

Lord Sydney in replying to Anderson had suggested application to the law courts, and the latter, who was no novice as a suitor before them, promptly turned to the Court of Session, in which before the close of the year 1785 he raised an action against the Chancellor, the Marquis of Graham, the Rector, Edmund Burke, the other two visitors, and the professors of the University, containing seven conclusions of reduction and as many of declarator, and claiming £5,700 as solatium and damages, besides £500 for expenses of the process. The first article had reference to a new rule passed in February, 1782, in regard to the attendance of students who were not Scotsmen before they became eligible for graduation in Arts, it being contended that the new rule affected the graduation fees due to the professors of Physics and Ethics.   The second concerned the dismissal of Andrew Crawford from the Natural Philosophy class and the order of the faculty that he should be re-admitted.   The third asked reduction of the sentence of the faculty of 6th April, 1784, suspending Anderson from the *jurisdictio ordinaria*.   The fourth related to a resolution of faculty of 10th June, 1784, abolishing the institution by Anderson of annual prizes for Natural Philosophy and elocution.   The fifth related to the faculty's narrative and comments intended to exculpate Principal Stirling from reflections made upon him in an article in the *Gentleman's Magazine* in 1783, in which the faculty gave a severe account of Anderson's relation to Leechman and a eulogistic account of the latter.   The sixth concerned the refusal to enter Anderson's protests in the minutes. The seventh complained of the refusal to give Anderson extracts of the proceedings in the process with Macleod, in regard to which the defenders stated that Anderson had circulated in the town a narrative from his own point of view of the matters to be proved in evidence, and that they thought it their duty not to allow any part of the evidence to get abroad till the whole was finished.   The decision was given in November, 1787, and the Court assoilzied the defenders on the first, second, third, and fifth articles, and also the fourth article, but on this point the Court gave no decision concerning the return of Anderson's fund for prizes, as the article contained no conclusion on that subject.   The Court sustained the defences regarding the sixth and seventh articles, reserving right of redress to Anderson in case of unjust refusal to insert proper protests or to give extracts when duly demanded at the conclusion of a case.

A number of students were brought into trouble by joining in the petition for a Royal Visitation or inducing others to join.   David M'Indoe, a student of Divinity, was one of the chief offenders. Thomas Kennedy, another student of Divinity, and John Hamilton, a student of Natural Philosophy, complained that having been influenced by M'Indoe to sign the petition, and having afterwards desired their names to be removed, M'Indoe refused this.   Richardson informed the faculty that a number of very young students in his class, from eleven to fourteen years of age, had been improperly enticed by M'Indoe to add their signatures; and these students, to the number of fifteen, now appeared and expressed their regret for having signed, and their desire to have their signatures cancelled.   M'Indoe wished to be allowed counsel, and, upon this being refused, insisted on having the charge against him put in writing before answering. The faculty then expelled him, and M'Indoe transferred the controversy to the church courts. After his case had been before the Presbytery and the Synod, the former body was proceeding to take him on trial for admission to the ministry, when the General Assembly reversed the decision of the Synod, and ordered the Presbytery not to proceed further until the sentence of expulsion from the University should be removed. M'Indoe then applied to the faculty, and after a tardy submission and apology, the sentence of expulsion was withdrawn on 21st November, 1785.

Alexander Humphreys, M.A., an Irish student of Anatomy attached to Anderson's views, was summoned to answer for a defamatory publication addressed to Dr. Taylor, minister of Glasgow. Dr. Taylor and Dr. Meek, dean of faculty, as ordinary visitors, had published a letter in the newspapers contradicting the allegations to which the Trades House had given countenance, and bearing witness to the prudent management and prosperity of the College; and Humphreys' paper seems to have been an abusive rejoinder. When summoned, Humphreys declined to appear unless accompanied by such persons as he chose, and the faculty not only expelled him but deprived him of his degree of M.A. This is the latest instance, so far as I am aware, of the withdrawal of a degree granted by the University. William Clydesdale, a student of Divinity, was also expelled for having signed along with Humphreys a paper called *The State of the Facts*, which was printed and circulated after the protest made by Leechman before the Trades House, and contained a disparaging account of the proceedings of the faculty and railing invective against the visitors and professors. A resolution was passed not to admit a number of students who had been present at a meeting which authorised the publication of *The State of the Facts*, till they should petition the faculty and either clear themselves or make a proper submission, and on complying with the condition a number of them were admitted. It is noted that several of the students who brought discipline upon themselves were paupers who had been received to their classes without payment of fees, and this circumstance was considered an aggravation of the offence. Dr. Taylor having raised an action in the Court of Session against Anderson as the real author of the defamatory paper issued in name of Humphreys, recovered £250 by way of damages and expenses. The faculty also recovered damages from Peter Tait, proprietor of the *Glasgow Journal*, in respect of a paragraph which appeared in that paper, and of which Tait refused to disclose the author's name. The paragraph accused the faculty of giving fabricated extracts to the Synod in the M'Indoe affair.

Down to this time, and indeed down to the time of the passing of the

Universities Act of 1858, though professors benefited by an increase in the number of students and the consequent increase in the class fees accruing to their teachers, the University itself gained little in this way. Students were charged a few shillings for behoof of the library, and there were petty charges for bell ringing, heating and lighting, and small fees of various kinds to servants; but there was no regular matriculation fee destined to the general funds of the University. A large number of students attended without matriculating, and students who matriculated did not enrol in this way every session of their attendance. The examination fees for graduation in arts were, by a regulation of the Commission of 1727, divided between the two privileged professors of Ethics and Physics; the examination or graduation fees in Medicine and Law went mostly to the professors who examined, but a certain part was apportioned to the library; and the greater part, if not the whole, of the fees for the degree of D.D. also went to the library. Under the system introduced by the Act of 1858, though the class fees still went to the teacher, the University had a considerable revenue from matriculation and examination fees, especially from the examination fees of medical students. In earlier times when the University had no revenue from such fees, it was all the more important that there should be careful and efficient management of the other sources of income. For the forty years ending with 1784 during which Morthland was factor, it is tolerably clear that the financial management might have been improved. But with the gradual progress of the country, the Archbishopric became more valuable and the share accruing to the University improved, while some of the teinds yielded a better return. Even in Morthland's time it is probable that the amount of money lent on heritable security had increased, and besides this a number of separate investments were made which helped to increase the yearly income. Among these were the purchase in 1776 of feus at Stobcross for £3,375, and next year of feus at Balgray for £1,500, and at Broomielaw for an immediate payment of £470 and a yearly payment of £15.

When the faculty set about appointing a successor to Morthland they encountered a difficulty in consequence of the regulations made by the Commissioners of 1727 having limited the factor's salary to £60 a year. On this point the faculty desired to have the opinion of Henry Dundas as counsel, but, as it could not conveniently be got, they procured the opinion of Mr. Cullen and Mr. Blair, Advocates. Counsel considered that the Commissioners could only have intended to enjoin a proper economy, and not that the revenues of the University should go to ruin for want of a proper factor. The College funds as well as the work of the factor had increased since 1727, and the emoluments of different professions and employments had also increased.   It could not be doubted that if the Commissioners had foreseen these changes, they would have allowed for an increase in the factor's salary.   Upon this, the faculty resolved to give the new factor the £60 stated in the statutes of 1727, the emoluments according to former usage for managing the College mortifications, and a further sum of £40 to be continued as long as deemed expedient.   On 13th January, 1785, James Hill, writer in Glasgow, who had done a large part of the work in the later years of Morthland's tenure, was unanimously appointed factor.   Six years afterwards his son, James Hill, junior, was associated with him in the office, and ever since members of the Hill family or the firms to which they belonged have been factors to the University, and have discharged the duties with great efficiency and credit.

In 1789 Mr. Hill pointed out that the granting of tacks of the teinds of the parishes of Govan, Renfrew, and Kilbride on moderate grassums would greatly improve the College revenue, and advised the faculty to examine their rights to the teinds and give him proper instructions.   A memorial was then submitted to Mr. Robertson and Mr. Cullen, Advocates, and they gave a clear opinion that the College had full right to the teinds of the three parishes.   The faculty considering their rights indubitable, and that the rental according to which the teinds had been paid for some time was not that 'good and sufficient rental' which they were directed by the Act of Parliament confirming them in possession of these teinds to make up, resolved in February, 1790, that heritors who had not valued their teinds should be asked to take leases at moderate grassums or to pay the legal teind, the factor being authorised to show the College titles and the opinion of counsel to the law agents of the parties concerned.   To the natural man a call to make further contributions in the form of teinds is unwelcome, and the heritors of Govan by one strategy or another put off the evil day as long as they could.   They desired to inspect documents, and many charters and papers concerning teinds, as well as College records bearing on the subject, were produced to them ; and after taking the opinion of counsel they answered that the proposals of the College were unjust and oppressive, and altogether unnecessary in the existing circumstances of the College revenue.   In March, 1792, the College having been advised that the proper procedure was to execute an inhibition of teinds before the separation of the crop and then bring an action for payment of the true value of the tithe, resolved to instruct their agent at Edinburgh to execute the appropriate summons against James Ritchie of Craigton, president of the committee of heritors negotiating with the

College, Thomas Lithan of Kelvinside, and Robert Houston Rae of Little Govan, it being considered best to summon only a few heritors at first.

Subsequently the heritors proposed to give a certain percentage more of teind, and being asked how much, after some delay they answered in the summer of 1793 that, if the College had a legal right to augment the charge for teinds, the *quantum* was no doubt a fifth of the rent. There were proposals to appoint a practical farmer on each side to determine the rent, one fifth of which was to be fixed as the permanent teind, and some further time was spent in considering and discussing the plan, but it was not carried out. In December, 1795, the heritors enquired whether the College would grant leases to them at the old teind and a grassum of one year's duty, the terms usually allowed to the heritors of Cadder and Monkland. They were told they had been misinformed regarding Cadder and Monkland, and that the proposal they had made was inadequate, but that the faculty would be prepared to grant leases on moderate grassums. They next enquired on what general principle the grassums would be fixed, and were informed that the faculty would be willing to receive proposals from any heritor of Govan either for a lease of his teinds or for valuation by arbitration, regard being had to the recent augmentation of the minister's stipend, the expenses of the process the College had been obliged to raise, and the proportion of the existing teind to the real rent. The heritors were still slow to commit themselves, and were warned that unless they put forward, before 14th November, 1796, some proposal for a settlement, the faculty would proceed against them in the process of spuilzie of teinds which was begun some years before. A week or two later Mr. Rae offered to proceed with a valuation of his teinds, or to give a grassum of £70 or £80, the yearly payment continuing as before; and was informed that his offer of grassum was inadequate, but that the faculty were willing to proceed with a process of valuation.

At the close of 1796 intimation was ordered to be sent to the heritors that the faculty were prepared to fix the grassum by ascertaining a fifth part of the rental of each heritor, deducting from that fifth the tithe then paid, and quadrupling the remainder for a grassum. It was afterwards stated that the heritors preferred valuation to leases; and the factor was instructed to say that proposals would be received from each heritor either for a tack or for valuation; and to suggest that each heritor should supply a note of the rent and area of his lands, with an estimate of what rent they would bring in a nineteen years' lease, and a statement of deductions claimed on account of improvements made within the last seven years of which he had not reaped the benefit. If the faculty and the heritor agreed, a decree of the Court might be obtained on facts admitted ; or if a difference arose, it might be settled by calling in a neutral person. . Probably the heritors, having stood out for eight or nine years, now felt that the resources of procrastination were exhausted, and that, if the process for spuilzie of teinds were pressed to a conclusion, they could not make a good defence.   They seem now to have submitted to the inevitable, and the tedious controversy was brought to a close greatly to the advantage of the University.   At the end of 1798 Mr. Hill submitted a rental of the parish of Govan after the valuation of teinds and the granting of leases to heritors who had not valued them ; and on 15th January of next year the faculty ordered a special payment of a hundred and twenty guineas to be made to him for his trouble and attention in carrying through the arrangements regarding these teinds.

Having come within sight of a settlement with the heritors of Govan, the faculty instructed Mr. Hill to intimate to the heritors of Renfrew and Kilbride who had not valued their teinds or taken leases, that they would be expected to take leases for nineteen years and pay grassums, or to pay an additional sum as teind from 1798 onwards.   These heritors were more easily dealt with, probably because they knew what had happened to their brethren in Govan.   Within a month it was announced that an agreement had been made with Day Hort M'Dowal, fixing his teinds for Walkinshaw in Renfrew at 24½ bolls of meal and a sum of £40 ; and some months later the teinds of Mr. Speirs of Elderslie were fixed at £110 yearly.   A new agreement made with the burgh of Renfrew in March, 1801, fixed the teinds of the lands belonging to the community of Renfrew and the proprietors of lands within the burgh, excepting Lord Glasgow, Mr. Speirs of Elderslie, and Mr. Campbell of Blythswood.   By appointment of both parties the College factor had reported on the extent and value of the lands, and his report was taken as the basis of agreement. It was stipulated that the payments should be—for lands belonging to the burgesses lying within the burgh, 36 bolls meal, 16 bolls bear, and a sum of £20 8s. 8d., the provost and magistrates collecting and paying over the money for which a small sum was to be allowed to them ; for the Mosslands and Muir and Newmains and Millands, belonging to the burgh, £40 ; for the lands of Porterfield three bolls meal, two bolls bear, and a sum of £10 4s.   Prices were to be regulated by the fiars prices annually struck by the principal and professors, and the agreement was to hold until the College insisted on the delivery of the *ipsa corpora* of the victual. No great changes were immediately made on the teinds of Kilbride, but in 1813 the heritors agreed to an augmentation of fifteen per cent. on the sums at which their lands were valued by a decreet arbitral, and a few years later the teinds of this parish were estimated to bring in £300 of additional yearly revenue.

During this period the College acquired a good deal of property in the city itself, probably quite as much from a desire to improve its own surroundings as to secure investments. In 1788 a house called Wyllie's Land, between the principal's house and Blackfriars Church, was purchased for £690, and in 1790 some other subjects on the east side of High Street below the principal's house ; while four years later two contiguous areas of ground near the Molendinar and bounded on the north by Duke Street were acquired. But the most important purchases were on the west side of High Street, opposite the College, where in 1766 a vacant area of ground belonging to Robert and Andrew Foulis, over which the College had given them a loan about ten years before, was bought for £300. Six or seven years afterwards a house and yards in the same neighbourhood were bought from Walter Somerville for £350. In 1774 a committee was appointed to inspect the Mealmarket, which it was said the town authorities were willing to sell.

Nothing came of the project at the time, but it was afterwards revived, and the College acquired the Mealmarket by excambion nearly twenty years later. A meal market had long been held in a portion of Blackfriars' Churchyard, but the church was enlarged when it was taken over by the Town Council from the College in 1635, and the displaced market was accommodated in a building on the west side of High Street facing the College. There the Mealmarket long remained, but latterly portions of it were devoted to other uses than dealing in meal. A similar establishment having been tried successfully at Edinburgh, a Correction House in which idle and unruly persons were set to work was opened in Drygate about 1636. A few years later a successful factory was established side by side with the Correction House, and the latter seems to have fallen into disuse. But with the growth of the city, it was again found necessary to take measures for the correction of indolent and unruly persons, and about 1778 the granaries of the Mealmarket were transformed into a Correction House, or, as it was now called, a Bridewell.

The Faculty again turned their attention to the condition of the west side of High Street opposite the College, and formed a design to buy a number of the old properties there, with a view to their being cleared away, and replaced by a new street of proper width and lined by handsome buildings. In 1787 a committee was appointed to examine the boundaries of the College property on the west side of High Street, and consider about buying more ground in that quarter. Early next year it was resolved to enquire on what terms the Town Council would sell the buildings and grounds of the Mealmarket, and, though more than five years were spent in communication and negotiation, the transaction was completed this time. Towards the end of 1791 the faculty purchased for £1,050 two houses and a garden belonging to the heirs of James Barr, rector of the Grammar School, adjoining houses on the south side of Broad Close. It was suggested that the College might exchange this property for the existing Mealmarket, and that Barr's ground would afford a suitable site for a new one. This suggestion proved fruitless, but in 1792 further purchases were made, including two tenements in Broad Close belonging to William Lindsay, writer, estimated to be worth £750, a property adjoining the Bridewell, costing £500, and a house in Shuttle Street under the College printer's premises, with a small yard behind, costing £105. At length in December, 1793, the principal delivered a registered submission and decree arbitral between the magistrates and the faculty for exchanging the Mealmarket and Bridewell for certain property at the Butts belonging to the College. Part of the ground at the Butts was used as the site of Barracks to accommodate about a thousand infantry, built by the Government in 1795. It was found that the ground at the Butts which the town acquired under the excambion was hardly sufficient for the purposes intended, and an additional area was purchased from the College.

Matters were now ripe for proceeding to form the new street extending from the west side of High Street and having its open end facing the entrance to the College. The faculty seem to have wished to provide a model of the kind of buildings desired, and early in 1793 they procured from Mr. James Adam, architect, London, plans for the first building erected in College Street, as it was called ; and it was built for the College by Andrew Macfarlane at a cost of about £3,500, including some alterations on the contract. The tenement seems to have been occupied in 1795, among the tenants being Mr. Mundell who succeeded the younger Andrew Foulis as printer to the University. A bad vent in one of the houses gave trouble, for though it was treated by John Robb, 'Smoke Doctor,' it shortly afterwards occasioned an outbreak of fire. The town's fire engine was summoned, for the attendance and services of which the town, as was then the custom, exacted a fee of £2 11s. 2d. Fortunately the fire was soon extinguished and the loss was covered by insurance. In 1803 the faculty put the tenement up to auction at an aggregate price about equal to the cost of erection, the various flats being offered separately. Professors Young and Davidson and Mr. Graham, the College law agent, having bought a portion of the property, in order to avert any suspicion of partiality on account of their direct connection with the College, offered to give back their purchases to the faculty at the price they had agreed to pay, but the faculty declined to accept the offer.

No large or striking addition was made to the University buildings during this time, but some departments obtained an appreciable increase of accommodation, generally by means of patching and remodelling. In 1763, in Black's time, it was resolved to build a new Chemistry laboratory at a cost of £350. Soon after he became professor of Natural Philosophy, Anderson drew a crowded attendance of students. Some of the students were tradesmen and townspeople who did not take a full course in any faculty, but there are many students who have not time to do so and yet acquit themselves creditably in life; and it would be for the advantage of the University if professors in general stood as well with the towns-people as Anderson did. In May, 1768, he presented a memorial pointing out that his classroom had been twice enlarged within the last few years, and provided accommodation for only about 70 students, and that last session he had to divide his class into two and deliver the same lecture twice in the same day; that the two College rooms allowed for keeping the instruments of the department were quite insufficient, and the space for experiments altogether inadequate. Anderson suggested that a new classroom should be provided by heightening the walls of the Common Hall, but in February, 1769, another plan was adopted by which four rooms above the premises occupied by the Foulises for binding were converted into a classroom for Physics, while the previous experiment room was turned into an apparatus room. This plan was carried out at a cost of about £240. The lectures in Divinity had previously been delivered in the old library, but it was not well adapted to the purposes of a class-room, and in 1778 it was resolved to divide it by partitions and convert it into a suitable lecture room for Divinity, a library for the Divinity Hall, and a large room available for such purposes as might afterwards be determined. In 1782 nearly £200 was spent in rebuilding the back wall of the Logic classroom and otherwise improving that room. The number of students in Anatomy seems to have been rapidly increasing, and considerable improvements in the Anatomy rooms were made in 1770, 1783, and 1791, the former Materia Medica room being annexed to Anatomy in the year last mentioned, and a new dissecting room provided, while Materia Medica was accommodated in remodelled chambers previously occupied by the Clerk, the Clerk in turn finding accommodation in the steeple. In 1800 the Anatomy classroom was extended so as to provide sittings for about 200 students, about double the number it could previously accommodate. In 1780 it was resolved to build two new houses for professors, raising the total number to thirteen, and to make a considerable addition to the library, and the work, which appears to have been finished early in 1782, cost about £2,000.

In 1784, 1794, and 1799 the faculty on reviewing the state of their finances found themselves in the happy position of having a considerable surplus, and on each of these occasions they voted additions to the salaries of the principal and professors. Hitherto the fixed salaries had been rather modest, but the professors in Arts and Medicine had a considerable income from the fees of their students, and the official residences provided for the principal and professors aided their emoluments. Still, though the addition of 1799 followed rather quickly on its predecessor, the augmented incomes did not go beyond due bounds. Early in 1784 a committee reported that there had been considerable savings during the last twenty-one years, chiefly from the tack of the Archbishopric, and the faculty—considering that the salaries of the principal and professors had not been augmented from College funds for more than a century, except a small and partial augmentation in 1729, that the expenses of living had greatly increased and taxes and other burdens had been imposed, while large augmentations had been made to the stipends of ministers and to the salaries of professors in other Colleges—deemed it for the interest of the University that the principal and professors should be enabled to support their character in a manner suitable to the increased expense of living; and resolved that an augmentation of £30 a year should be made to the salary of the principal and each of the thirteen professors; that £3 yearly should be added to the stipend of each of the four foundation bursars; and 200 marks to the salary of the librarian, to compensate him for the withdrawal of that sum as an allowance to the keeper of the old library under the arrangement made with the Town Council. At the end of March Alexander Hutchison, dean of faculty, and William Taylor, minister of Glasgow, two of the visitors of the College, put on record that they had examined the state of the funds from 1761 to 1781, considered they had been managed with attention and care, and being assured of their sufficiency, sanctioned the augmentations. On the page where this has been recorded an autograph note has been added: 'April 10th, 1784. Edm. Burke, Rector, approves.' Two months later it was determined to make an addition of £20 to the allowance of £30 formerly given to Dr. Irvine as lecturer on Chemistry and Materia Medica.

In May, 1794, a resolution was passed to make a further addition of £40 to the salaries of the principal and professors, of £2 to each of the foundation bursars, and of £20 to each of the three lecturers on Chemistry, Materia Medica, and Midwifery. In August, 1799, a committee on the

College revenue reported that there was a surplus of £867 6s. 4½d. Parliament had enacted that corporations should be taxed to the extent of at least a tenth of their surplus revenue, and the faculty ordered that £86 15s. should be entered in the income tax return, and authorised the factor to pay that sum. It was believed that the yearly surplus of fully £800 would not only be maintained but increased. The faculty considered there had been an unexampled rise in the price of every article of consumption, and a diminution of their salaries by the late taxes, doing away entirely with the advantages arising from the former augmentations. It was deemed a duty to preserve their condition and rank as public instructors of youth, and they accordingly resolved that there should be a fresh augmentation of £50 a year to the salary of each of the fourteen members of the faculty. As Parliament had enacted that surplus revenue should bear a tax of one-tenth, it was thought better that there should be little or no surplus to be thus taxed. This time, notwithstanding the unexampled rise in the price of every article of consumption, no augmentation was provided for the lecturers or foundation bursars.

It is curious to see what a demand there may be among mankind for things of hardly any real benefit or helpfulness, what a stir in procuring and distributing such merchandise, and how individuals and communities may be enriched by the traffic. It would hardly be too much to say that tobacco made Glasgow great. The city had some trade in tobacco in the seventeenth century, and during the greater part of the eighteenth it continued to expand. From 1760 to 1775 Glasgow was the great European emporium for tobacco. In 1772 the whole import into Great Britain was 90,000 hogsheads, and of this amount Glasgow imported 49,000; while in the same year Glasgow exported to France 20,744,943 lbs., to Holland 14,932,543 lbs., and to Germany 3,868,027 lbs. The city was therefore much interested in the trade with Virginia, Maryland, and other American colonies, and aggrieved and alarmed at the prospect of American independence. After the news of the disastrous surrender of Burgoyne and his army at Saratoga, special efforts were made to raise additional forces. The city authorities lent their aid, and an effort was made to involve the University in its corporate capacity.

In January, 1778, it was moved that the faculty, from concern for the honour and interests of the Government and zeal for the best of kings, should give a thousand pounds of their unappropriated College funds, besides whatever sums individual members might subscribe, to be applied for expeding the necessary levies for the war. This motion was rejected, Dr. Reid recording his dissent. It was carried, however, that the principal should send round a subscription paper among members of faculty recommending them to contribute, and that the sum thus raised should be handed to the Treasurer of the City of Glasgow to aid in raising a battalion. In 1782 when peace had come in sight, an address was presented to the King in name of the chancellor, rector, principal, and professors. They allowed the reverses of the war and the loss of America to fall out of view, and referred with gratification to the victories of Rodney, and the advent of a new order of things in Ireland which now got rid of Poyning's Law. They approached the throne with congratulations on the late glorious success of His Majesty's arms, and the prospect of such a peace as might secure the rights of mankind and the interests of the British empire. While exulting in the protection and security derived from their happy system of government, they rejoiced in its extension to the sister kingdom, and looked forward with satisfaction to the stability and power which must arise from the union of hearts and interests throughout His Majesty's dominions.

There was some apprehension of an invasion by Napoleon in 1798, and on 12th January an Act of Parliament was passed authorising corporations to subscribe to the national defence. On 17th March, 1798, the faculty resolved to subscribe £300 for the defence of Great Britain in the critical juncture then existing, to be charged on the revenues of the Archbishopric. Millar, the professor of Law, protested against this, holding that the academic funds were intended for the particular uses of the University, that any occasional surplus was not meant for the use of the nation at large or for fleets or armies, and that the administrators had no power to divert funds from their normal uses. He also alleged that the money was solicited, not from any sudden alarm or great and unexpected danger, but as an expedient for substituting the contributors in place of others who had already been taxed. A committee appointed to answer the protest declared that the faculty had from time to time applied surpluses in building houses, augmenting incomes, making contributions to the building of churches, hospitals, schools, and bridges, opening streets and roads, purchasing pictures, and even in purposes of common charity. The propriety of the particular use and its relation to their own body were always matter of discretion with the administrators, and none of these applications were more clearly within the faculty's discretion than the vote for the defence of the country against an enemy who had denounced an implacable hatred against its independence, property, laws, and government.

In June, 1798, there was received a list of nineteen students lately expelled from the University of Dublin for being leading and active members of treasonable societies in Trinity College ; and it was resolved

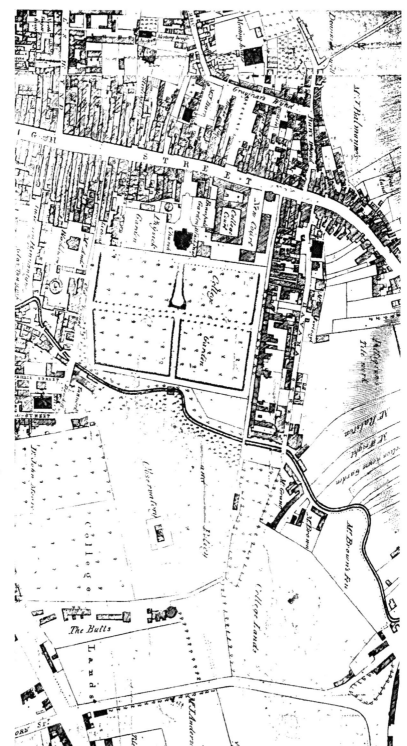

PART OF PLAN OF HIGH STREET, 1778

Showing Site and Surroundings of Old College

From an actual Survey by John McArthur, for a plan of the City of Glasgow, Gorbells and Calton

ot to admit any of them at Glasgow while they continued under sentence of expulsion at Dublin.

James Boswell, himself an alumnus of the University, acted as a sort of guide to some distinguished visitors who came to see the ancient seat of learning in High Street. He was not very fond of study or of the legal profession which his father wished him to enter, and in early manhood he made a tour of the continent, and met Voltaire and Rousseau, from the latter of whom he obtained a letter of introduction to Paoli, the warrior patriot of Corsica. Boswell repaired to Corsica, and obtained an introduction to Paoli at his palace by means of Rousseau's letter. He was received with distinction and kindness, spent some weeks in the island, and after his return home published through the Messrs. Foulis of Glasgow a lively and amusing account of Corsica, with memoirs of Paoli, of whose conversation he had made copious notes which he now reproduced. The work had a great but ephemeral popularity, and was translated into German, Dutch, French, and Italian. Paoli would have freed Corsica from the Genoese, but the Genoese sold it to France when they could no longer hold it themselves; and though Paoli for some time maintained a gallant struggle against a great French army, he was at length overpowered and took refuge in Britain. Boswell renewed his acquaintance, and when Paoli, accompanied by Count Burzyuski, paid a visit to Scotland in September, 1771, he escorted them to Glasgow, where on 6th September they paid a visit to the University. The report of the great Corsican leader's presence in the city quickly spread, and a crowd gathered at the University to see him. It was vacation time, but a goodly company of professors, including Reid, Anderson, Moor, Muirhead, Trail, Wilson, and Stevenson, received the distinguished visitors, and conducted them through the buildings, which were seen to great advantage. They also inspected the printing establishment and academy of Art of the brothers Foulis, and a contemporary account states that the Foulises were 'transported with enthusiasm' to see such visitors. Before leaving, the company were served with wine and refection in the library.

About two years afterwards Boswell came to Glasgow in company with a yet greater acquaintance than Paoli. On 28th October, 1773, Dr. Johnson and Boswell, after their famous tour in the Hebrides, arrived in Glasgow, and took up their quarters at the Saracen's Head in the Gallowgate, then the great inn of the town. Next day Professors Stevenson, Reid, and Anderson breakfasted with Johnson and Boswell, and afterwards the two latter were received within the College by the principal and professors. Johnson also paid a visit to the principal at his house, and the conversation turned on the translation of the New Testament into Gaelic.

Professors Reid and Anderson and the brothers Foulis dined and drank tea with Johnson and Boswell at their hotel, after which the professors left, and Boswell withdrawing to write a letter, Johnson soon tired of the conversation of the Foulises, and entreated Boswell to rejoin the company. 'You have come to me for refuge,' said Boswell. 'It is of two evils choosing the least,' was the reply. In the evening Johnson supped at Anderson's house. The distinguished visitor was better pleased with the appearance of the town than of the old College, the latter seeming to be 'without a sufficient share in the magnificence of the place'; yet learning was an 'object of wide importance, and the habit of application much more general than in the neighbouring University of Edinburgh.' But it is doubtful whether Johnson had made a sufficiently thorough survey of academic affairs in the two places to justify the comparison. Johnson's exaggerated reputation and robust dogmatism of deportment seem to have scared the Glasgow professors, and they had little to say, but this did not propitiate Nemesis. 'I was not much pleased with any of them,' Johnson wrote to Mrs. Thrale.

In June, 1792, Professor Wilson informed the faculty that William Herschel of Slough, the celebrated astronomer, was to visit Glasgow early next month, and out of respect to him the faculty recommended the vacation committee to invite him and his friend John Komarzewski to a dinner in the forehall of the College, to which such other gentlemen as the committee thought proper might also be invited. At the same time the Senate resolved to mark their sense of his eminence as a practical astronomer and of the sublime discoveries made in the heavens by means of his highly improved telescopes, by conferring upon him the degree of LL.D., and ordered a diploma to be prepared, and presented to him when he came to Glasgow.

Some marks of hospitality were shown to other visitors of less note than those just mentioned. In May, 1787, the faculty, considering that the late custom of entertaining strangers visiting the College had led to considerable inconvenience and unnecessary expense, resolved that no more wine should be put in the hands of the porter for this purpose. They added that when persons of eminent rank and character visited the College it could not be improper to treat them at the public expense, and directed that wine and other things should be procured from a tavern for the immediate occasion, on an order from the principal or from two or more professors to John Maclachlan, the bedellus, who was to keep an exact account of these disbursements, with the names of the professors ordering the collation and of the strangers entertained. The janitor still sold wine within the College without paying a license, and though the revenue authorities sometimes threatened and objected, they do not seem to have made any very determined effort to stop the practice, while the faculty regarded it as part of the privileges of the College and gave it their countenance and support. Dinners were given at the rector's installation, and after William Hunter had left his splendid benefaction to the University an annual dinner in commemoration of him was instituted. A dinner to the clergy who officiated at the sacrament held in connection with the College chapel seems to have recurred as regularly as the seasons, and sometimes a dinner was given at the induction of a new minister to Govan, of which church the faculty were patrons. The records show that for some years dinners were usually provided by May Forrest, the College porter's daughter, who seems to have been an expert at cookery and purveying. Another custom that prevailed from generation to generation while successive Dukes of Montrose held the office of chancellor, was to send a deputation, consisting of the principal and a number of professors, to wait upon the Duke at Buchanan Castle and offer him the compliments of the University.

It became necessary to correct a practice concerning graduation in Arts which was introduced to oblige Irish students but gave rise to undue laxity. Before his appointment as a professor, Francis Hutcheson had been at the head of a private teaching academy in Dublin, and there were several other similar institutions about that time and afterwards connected with the Presbyterian part of the community, who had then no access to University education in Ireland. Now and again when a capable and energetic teacher presided, these academies might do good work, but there was no security for this. Under the influence of Hutcheson, however, the University unwisely determined to allow students from such academies to be admitted to a degree in Arts after two years' attendance at Glasgow. These Irish academies may have deteriorated as time went on, but they were never on a footing to justify the resolution. The students from them were often poorly prepared at their entrance to the University, and many of them endeavoured to curtail the length of their attendance to the very minimum that would be accepted. By and by there were loud complaints of the ill consequences of granting degrees in such circumstances, and in May, 1764, the University meeting enacted that no foreign student, as the phrase was, who had not attended part of his course in some other University should be admitted to trial for a degree in Arts till he had regularly studied two sessions in the University of Glasgow, and attended at least Natural Philosophy and Moral Philosophy in separate sessions, besides being qualified to undergo examination in the other parts of philosophy and in languages ; that any foreign student from another University must produce certificates of his standing and behaviour in the former University, and must study six months at Glasgow before being admitted to trial; that every candidate for a degree in Arts, whether he was Scottish or foreign, must undergo an examination in Virgil and the first 'decad' of Livy, and in Zenophon's *Memorabilia* and the first books of Homer's *Iliad*; and that any candidate might if he chose be examined in Mathematics or any other branch of academical knowledge and have his proficiency in that branch certified in the diploma, as well as his being taught it at Glasgow when that was the case.   The fourth rule, if it had been allowed to continue, might have proved a step towards options in the choice of subjects for the degree, but it was rescinded in 1771, mainly at the instance of Reid, and instead of extra subjects being recorded in the diploma, separate certificates were allowed to be given for them.

It is curious that so great a mathematician as Simson did not use his influence to secure the inclusion of Mathematics as one of the subjects in which candidates for graduation in Arts should necessarily be examined, but it was not so treated in his time.   His successor Williamson having represented that some students without any proper knowledge of Mathematics entered the Natural Philosophy class and afterwards became candidates for graduation, a regulation was laid down on 31st December, 1765, that after 10th June following the professor of Mathematics should examine all candidates for degrees in Arts on the same footing as other professors.   Leechman protested against this regulation.   Mathematics was not yet made a regular subject of the curriculum.

After the death in 1750 of John Loudon, professor of Logic, the graduation fees in Arts were, in conformity with a regulation of the Commissioners of 1727, divided equally between the professors of Natural Philosophy and Moral Philosophy, and the existence of these fees formed a vested interest which did not tend to facilitate reforms in the regulations for graduation in Arts.   In 1771 Anderson put forward a proposal on behalf of himself and Reid to surrender these graduation fees during their tenure of office, on compensation being made to them by the faculty, the amount being determined by arbitration.   The arrangement did not profess to bind their successors or finally to put an end to the fees, and no change was effected.

Meantime the Irish difficulty continued, and about 1772 Dr. Trail, Bishop of Down and Connor, though friendly to the University, sent strong remonstrances, pointing out that he had incurred much disapprobation for admitting into orders persons who had obtained degrees after two years' attendance at Glasgow, and that, if degrees continued to be granted on such terms, he would be obliged to reject applicants founding upon them. The Irish Presbyteries and Synods now joined in the outcry, and a motion was made in the Irish House of Commons to prevent bishops from accepting as a qualification for admission to holy orders Scottish degrees obtained upon two years' attendance, and it would have been carried but for a promise made by the bishops that they would not for the future admit such degrees. The University had been slow to take effective action, but the scandal had now become so great that in February, 1782, the Senate resolved that foreign students who had not studied at another University should not be admitted to degrees on a shorter standing than Scotsmen. Anderson protested, and at a meeting a few days later Reid dissented. On 5th March a further resolution was passed that students from other Universities wishing to complete their course at Glasgow should before their admission be tested by a committee of faculty, who should also enquire as to their previous good behaviour. Reid was still a member of Senate and of faculty, but Arthur was now teacher of Ethics. Anderson renewed the proposal for fixing by arbitration the amount to be paid to himself and Arthur on their surrendering their claim to graduation fees. It was not accepted, and a motion was carried that the professors of Ethics and Physics should not be entitled to compensation from the faculty for any loss they might sustain in consequence of the regulations lately passed for graduation in Arts.

The degree of B.A. seems to have remained dormant from the Reformation till in 1774 it was conferred on one candidate, and again on a single candidate in 1775. On 26th March, 1776, when the list of students in the Physics class and of magistrands was adjusted, it was resolved that any students whose names appeared in it might apply for B.A. if they had studied philosophy for two sessions, and from this time, though not usually in great request, the degree continued to be given till it was abolished in 1861.

William Richardson, who held the Humanity chair from 1773 to 1814, might almost be said to form a connecting link between Rob Roy and the Empress Catherine of Russia. Born at Aberfoyle in 1743, as a boy of seven he witnessed some of the proceedings in the abduction of a wealthy widow by the sons of Rob Roy, for which one of them was afterwards hanged ; and having completed a distinguished course in Arts at Glasgow and attended two or three sessions in Divinity, he abandoned the idea of entering the Church, and in early manhood resided four years in the Russian capital as secretary to Lord Cathcart, the British ambassador, and tutor to his sons. Through the influence of Cathcart, who was rector at the time, Richardson was appointed to succeed Muirhead. Besides being an efficient and successful professor, he was a prolific author, his works including—*Poems chiefly Rural; Analyses of Shakespeare's Characters;* a tragedy; a lyrical drama; *Anecdotes of the Russian Empire;* contributions to *The Lounger, The Mirror,* and *The Edinburgh Magazine and Review;* and an *Essay on Celtic Superstition,* written in connection with the controversy concerning Ossian. He had readers and admirers in his day, and his works are still readable, though not read. He was long a familiar figure in the General Assembly, to which he was returned as representative elder by the Presbytery of Dunblane.

Moor, the professor of Greek, was appointed clerk to the University meeting in 1766, but was soon incapacitated by ill health, which troubled him considerably during the remainder of his tenure. In October, 1766, Thomas Young, who conducted the Moral Philosophy class for the latter part of the session when Smith retired, was appointed to teach the public and private Greek classes when the professor's health hindered him from acting. Next year Moor was authorised to employ John Gillies, when needful, to conduct the Greek classes. Gillies, whose merit, learning, and assiduity Moor declared would make him acceptable, afterwards proved an author of note, whose Histories of Ancient Greece, of Frederick the Second, and of the World from Alexander to Augustus are not yet entirely forgotten, while his translations of Isocrates and Lysias further attest his interest in Greek studies.

Towards the end of 1767 in Moor's absence, as it seems, his household goods at the College were poinded. A bill accepted by Moor had been protested, in consequence of which he had been charged by the Magistrate to pay the debt contained in it, and afterwards a warrant of warding and poinding had been executed against him. His colleagues maintained that Moor as a member of the University was not subject to the jurisdiction of the City Magistrates, but the Magistrates declined to recognise this doctrine. Moor with all his talents and acquirements was somewhat heedless in his manner of living, and has been described as taking 'little thought of College convention or Church discipline.' One result was that in his later years he was straitened for means, and in 1769 sold his collection of medals to the University for £32.

In November, 1772, a student named James Mathie, with the concurrence of his father, complained that for no other fault than that of repeating the present and future of a Greek verb after the professor, which witnesses did not think was done in ridicule, Moor lifted a heavy wooden candlestick from the floor and struck Mathie several blows with it, not desisting even when the latter fell among the seats. While thus belabouring his victim, Moor was vociferating wretch! scoundrel! puppy! and Mathie when leaving the room turned round to the infuriated one-eyed professor and said : 'You old blinker, you shall pay for this.' Mathie afterwards withdrew his complaint, but the meeting could not condone such a violent outburst, and served a libel on Moor, who tried to maintain that he had done only what he considered necessary for the discipline of his class. Temporising measures failed to end the case, and Moor having at length appeared, denied the charge and called for a proof. Evidence was then taken, the libel was found proven, and in March, 1773, a deliverance was adopted declaring that Moor's behaviour was unbecoming a professor, hurtful to discipline, injurious to those on whom such outrageous discipline was exercised, and highly censurable. His former offences were recalled, and he was warned that any further offence would be visited with the highest censure.

A few days later Anderson brought a fresh complaint against Moor, the nature of which does not appear. Moor represented that, as he was too ill to teach, John Young was teaching for him, and he was ordered to appear and answer the complaint before resuming teaching, otherwise the meeting would proceed against him as contumacious. Other affairs retarded the progress of the case, but when, on 25th March, 1774, a meeting was held for the trial of Moor, the principal announced a proposal from him to resign if allowed to retain his house and salary, on condition that John Young should be immediately elected as successor. He pointed out that he was now the senior professor, advanced in years and broken in health, and that he was asking no unusual concession, but one which during his tenure of office had been granted to three or four of his colleagues. The meeting, while willing to make a suitable allowance for a colleague who had spent so much of his life in the service of the University, declared it was too much for any professor to be permitted to name his successor, and that if there were precedents for such things, an immediate stop should be put to them. After this Moor resigned office, reserving for life his salary and his house in the inner court. Though the faculty had declined to enter into a bargain with Moor regarding the appointment of John Young as his successor, the latter was elected professor immediately after Moor's resignation.

Moor was the author of a useful, though incomplete, Greek Grammar, long a standard work for Glasgow students ; and wrote several odes, one of which, *The Linnet* or *Happiness at Home*, gives some indication of his domestic circumstances. Finally he composed his own epitaph, prefaced by some lines to Professor Richardson. In this piece, which would hardly make a poetical reputation, though it reads tolerably, he claimed to be a good deal of a scholar and something of a poet, and tried to preserve an appearance of gaiety even at taking leave of life and quitting the world—

' sad supine step upon the dorsum,' as he called it.   He died on 17th September, 1779.

From a letter of Hume to Cullen it appears that the former would have liked to become professor of Logic at Glasgow when Smith was transferred to Moral Philosophy, but the appointment was given to James Clow, an M.A. of 1731, who had been tutor to the Earl of Galloway's children.   Clow acted for some time as clerk, and also held office as dean of faculty, and several times as vice-rector.   In 1761 he received the thanks of the University meeting for investigating and putting in order the accounts of a number of bursary foundations, as well as of the arch-bishopric for crop 1758, and of the grassums of the Subdeanery.   He retired from teaching Logic in 1774, George Jardine being appointed to conduct the class as his assistant and successor, while Clow retained his house and salary and continued an administrator.   Towards the end of 1774 a committee was appointed to continue Blackhouse's inventory of College papers, and the execution of the work devolved on Clow, who in May, 1775, gave in an inventory of writs in the charter chest and papers in the clerk's chamber.   A vote of thanks was passed, and he was asked to furnish notes on any further measures which should be taken regarding College papers, upon which he made a number of suggestions for improving the arrangement and cataloguing of these documents.   When Leechman in his last illness was disabled from attending meetings, granting precepts, or conducting correspondence, Clow was appointed to transact the business usually falling to the principal, with power to do whatever was competent to the principal in such matters.   In 1785 he was offered the degree of LL.D., but while declaring his affection and respect for the University, on account of his great age and other circumstances, he declined to accept it.   In February, 1787, Clow resigned his office and emoluments, except his College house, in favour of Jardine, and he died on 9th July, 1788.

George Jardine, the next professor of Logic, had been a student of diligence and promise, and graduated as M.A. in 1765.   He was some time employed as tutor to the sons of Mure of Caldwell, superintending their education at an academy in Paris.   Mure had been an acquaintance and friend of David Hume, and in consequence of this association Jardine procured introductions to some notable literary men of the day in Paris— Helvetius and D'Alembert among the rest.   Jardine was a candidate for the Humanity chair in 1773, when Richardson carried it by only one vote.   Next year he became assistant and successor to Clow, and though not an administrator as yet, sometimes took an important part in academic business.   In May, 1775, on its being announced that he was going to

Oxford on his own account that summer, he was empowered to negotiate with Balliol College and Snell's Trustees concerning the Snell foundation on which some surplus funds had accrued, while Balliol College desired the exhibitioners to be removed from it.   He was appointed clerk to the faculty in 1781, and from about this time two rooms in the College were assigned to him, while other two for which he paid rent, were on the death of Leechman added to his accommodation.

After the death of Clow, in order that there might be a College house for every professor, the rooms possessed by Jardine were declared a College house to be called No. 14.   He was one of the warmest and most helpful supporters of the scheme for the establishment of an Infirmary in Glasgow, and in January, 1793, the faculty appointed him a manager of the Royal Infirmary, for which a charter had now been obtained from the crown. The appointment was renewed for many years, and for a long time Jardine acted as secretary of the new institution.   He taught the Logic class for fifty years, and taught it well, giving first an account of the powers of the mind and the means of training them, with a short exposition of Aristotle's Logic, and afterwards dealing with composition and rhetoric, including the principles of taste and criticism.   Students were required to meet at a separate hour to give an account of the morning lecture, and exercises and essays were prescribed to discipline them in the application of the rules and principles enunciated in the lectures.   At the outset the professor read and criticised the exercises, but in the latter part of the session students were required to give in written criticisms on each other's work. A keen interest was maintained, and the students, stimulated by the competition of their fellows, and aided and encouraged by an able and sympathetic teacher, worked with a will and to good purpose.

On 22nd May, 1764, Thomas Reid, professor of Philosophy in King's College, Aberdeen, was elected to succeed Smith at Glasgow, and on 11th June it is recorded that Reid 'whose ability and qualifications for the professorship of Moral Philosophy are well known to the masters,' took the oath of office and was admitted.   He belonged to a family which had long been settled in the lower part of Deeside, holding in early times the lands of Pitfodels, while one of his ancestors was the first minister of Banchory after the Reformation.   One of this minister's sons was physician to Charles I., and author of some forgotten treatises on Medicine ; another was Latin and Greek secretary to James VI., wrote Latin poems, some of which found a place in the *Deliciae Poetarum Scotorum*, and bequeathed a fund to support a librarian at Marischal College, Aberdeen ; while a third translated Buchanan's *History of Scotland*.   Reid's mother belonged to a Lowland offshoot of the wild Highland clan Macgregor that had adopted the name of Gregory, and hardly any family could vie with the Gregories in the number of distinguished professors they continued for some generations to produce.

Reid was born at the Manse of Strachan, Kincardineshire, in 1710, and it is notable that his contemporary Immanuel Kant, the great German philosopher, was also descended from a family named Cant long settled in Strachan, one of whom was a Covenanting worthy. Reid graduated as M.A. at Marischal College at the age of sixteen, and for three years held the office of College librarian which his kinsman had founded. In 1737 King's College, as patrons of New Machar, forced him on the unwilling parishioners as their minister, and he preached to them the sermons of Tillotson and Evans, instead of composing sermons of his own. Hume's *Treatise on Human Nature*, published in 1739, roused him to read, observe, and reflect, but he did not rush hastily into print. 'The first heir of his invention' seems to have been an *Essay on Quantity*, published in 1748, combating the view contained in Hutcheson's *Inquiry* that mathematical measures could be applied to the subjects of moral science, such as merit or virtue. In 1752 he was appointed professor of philosophy in King's College, Aberdeen, where he was required to teach in rotation Natural History, Physics, and Mental Philosophy. For half a dozen years before leaving Aberdeen Reid's mind was disciplined and his opinions developed by his connection with the Aberdeen Philosophical Society, a 'wise club' in which he and other studious northern spirits worked diligently at intellectual problems. The discussions in this society helped Reid, Gerard, Beattie, and Campbell to 'rough hew' a number of valuable works, including Reid's *Inquiry into the Human Mind on the Principles of Common Sense*, published just before he entered on the work of the chair of Moral Philosophy.

In Reid's opening lecture at Glasgow he expressed his regret at not having had the good fortune to be personally acquainted with Smith, and was evidently conscious of difficulty in taking up the work of so famous and so popular a man. Of Smith's system he knew only what had been published, and said he would count it a favour if any among his audience would furnish him with notes of Smith's prelections, whether in Morals, Jurisprudence, Politics, or Rhetoric. He would always be desirous to borrow light from every quarter, and to adopt what appeared sound and solid in every system ; and desired to live no longer than this openness to education and information lived with him. In those days students frequently attended the Moral Philosophy class for several sessions, and there were some in the class before whom Reid confessed that he feared to speak without more time for preparation. There seem to have been between four and five hundred students attending the University when Reid began to teach, and he declared that about a third were Irish—'stupid Irish teagues,' he called them. In his class-room Reid was not a brilliant teacher or one to excite enthusiasm. He did not trust himself to speak extempore, and he was not a good reader. But his reputation as an author, the calm and meditative dignity of his age, and the stamp of an earnest, patient, laborious seeker after truth which characterised his clearly stated doctrines, procured for him an attentive hearing.

Reid was much interested in Watt's improvements on the steam engine and in Black's scientific researches and discoveries, and in his second winter at Glasgow he attended Black's lectures on Chemistry. He kept up an active correspondence with old friends in Aberdeen, and made some interesting comparisons between it and Glasgow. Shortly after coming south he declared : 'There is certainly more of religion among the common people in this town than in Aberdeen ; and, although it has a gloomy enthusiastical cast, yet I think it makes them tame and sober. I have not heard either of a house or of a head broke, or of a pocket picked, or of any flagrant crime since I came here. I have not heard any swearing in the streets, nor seen a man drunk (excepting, *inter nos*, one professor) since I came here.' About a year afterwards, writing to a friend at Aberdeen, he said : 'I think the common people here and in the neighbourhood greatly inferior to the common people with you. They are Boeotian in their understandings, fanatical in their religion, and clownish in their dress and manners. The clergy encourage this fanaticism too much, and find it the only way to popularity. I often hear a gospel here which you know nothing about, for you neither hear it from the pulpit nor will you find it in the Bible.' This severe description is hardly consistent with the claims often made that Hutcheson, Leechman, and, as some would fain say, John Simson had done much to improve and enlighten the West of Scotland.

Reid soon came to have many friends in Edinburgh—Dugald Stewart, Dr. Gregory, and Lord Kames among the number—and occasional visits to Edinburgh were notable events in his life. 'One goes,' he said in 1766, 'in the stage coach to Edinburgh before dinner,[1] has all the afternoon there, and returns to dinner at Glasgow next day.' The acquaintance with Kames was perhaps the most notable. Reid was slow and reserved, Kames alert and keen to discuss ; but though their temperaments and many of their views were in strong contrast, they continued fast friends from 1767 till the death of Kames in 1782, Reid usually spending a good part of the College vacation at Blair Drummond with Lord Kames. In 1774 Reid contributed a brief account of Aristotle's Logic to Kames'

[1] By dinner Reid evidently meant the midday meal.

Sketches of the History of Man, and this was his sole publication during the sixteen years he taught at Glasgow.

Shortly after coming to Glasgow, Reid, as appears from his correspondence, saw with regret the divisions and bickerings among his colleagues, but he took his full share in University administration notwithstanding, and followed what he believed to be the line of duty in circumstances which must sometimes have been very disagreeable, as in the case of his custody of the Shaw Park papers about which Leechman and Anderson quarrelled.   Though they were at last estranged, for a very long time Reid was an administrative ally of Anderson.   With the advance of age Reid was troubled with deafness, and in May, 1780, he retired from teaching, and Archibald Arthur was appointed assistant and successor with sole charge of conducting the classes, and receiving for his remuneration the fees paid by students, while Reid kept the salary of the chair, his College house, and his position as one of the University administrators. Released from teaching, Reid set himself to put the matter of his lectures into a form suitable for publication.   His *Essays on the Intellectual Powers* appeared in 1785, and *Essays on the Active Powers* in 1788.

Reid was a member of the Literary Society which long flourished in connection with the University, and took his share in its work.   The Society was established in January, 1752, and then or subsequently included among its members, Cullen, Black, Adam Smith, Moor, Robert Simson, Anderson, Reid, Mure of Caldwell, Oswald of Scotstoun, Graham of Dugalston, Lord Cardross afterwards Earl of Buchan, David Hume, Robert and Andrew Foulis, and many others.   Till discourses in regular form should be prepared, accounts of new books were given at the three weekly meetings held on 16th, 23rd, and 30th January, Dr. Cullen dealing with the *Cosmology* of Maupertuis, Mr. Smith with David Hume's *Essays on Commerce*, and Mr. Clow with Harris's *Hermes*.

On 7th February the first regular discourse was given by Professor Moor, *On Historical Composition*.   After papers had been read individuals gave their views in the course of a friendly discussion, and the varied talents and accomplishments of the members, as well as the wide range of subjects brought under review, gave weight and interest to the proceedings.   Dugald Stewart declared that 'by watching his gradual decline with the courage of an indifferent observer, and employing his ingenuity to retard its progress,' Reid had 'converted even the infirmities of old age into a source of philosophical amusement.'   His last contribution to the proceedings of the Society, submitted the winter before his death, was a dissertation on *Muscular Motion*, describing in his own way the changes which occur in human muscles with the advance of age, and endeavouring to account for them. In 1794 he contributed another interesting paper, *Observations on the Danger of Political Innovation*, suggested by the French Revolution, from which Reid, like many others, at first hoped much, but afterwards hope gave place to apprehension. On the authority of a statement by Richardson, Reid is usually credited with having written the account of the University in Sinclair's *Statistical Account of Scotland*, though the records would rather suggest that the work might have been a composite one. During the summer of 1796, though he was eighty-six years of age, he was punctual in attending meetings of faculty, and was appointed a member of the committee for attending to business emerging in the vacation. He still entertained views of the future, and his old colleague Anderson having died early in the year, Reid made choice of his house ; but there were some questions to adjust with Anderson's executors about improvements, and Reid did not live long enough to enter into possession. He spent part of the summer in Edinburgh with Dr. Gregory, and till within three or four weeks of his death found recreation in solving mathematical problems and working in his garden. In September, 1796, he fell ill, and died on 7th October.

Reid's remains were buried in Blackfriars' Churchyard beside the College, and a tombstone was placed to his memory, and that of his wife and three daughters, who rested in the same spot, by his only surviving daughter Martha, who had married Dr. Patrick Carmichael, son of Professor Gerschom Carmichael, but was now a widow. The dust of Reid, as well as of many other notable University men buried in the same churchyard, was removed to the Necropolis when the ancient buildings and grounds of the University were taken over by the Railway Company, and a recent biographer of Reid tells us that his tombstone was then removed to Gilmorehill. A proposal was long ago made to erect some memorial over the dust of the College worthies dislodged from what was thought to be their last resting place, and it would surely be to the credit of the University that the work should be done without indefinite postponement. And would not Reid's tombstone, with an appropriate addition to the inscription, be better placed over his dust in the Necropolis than hidden away at Gilmorehill?

Archibald Arthur, who now succeeded to the full status of professor of Moral Philosophy, was the son of a farmer in Abbot's Inch, Renfrewshire. He had a distinguished course in arts at Glasgow, and afterwards went through the course in theology. He was licensed by the Presbytery of Paisley, though some members of the Presbytery were rather suspicious about his orthodoxy, including the Rev. Dr. Witherspoon, a voluble preacher and prolific writer, then minister of one of the churches of Paisley, who had previously been Leechman's successor as minister at Beith, and afterwards became president of the College of Princeton, New Jersey, one of the delegates to the convention which set up the republic of the United States, and for some years a member of Congress.   Natural shyness and a slight hesitation in his speech prevented Arthur from making the full impression he might have done, but he was soon appointed chaplain to the University, and in 1774 librarian.   He held the latter post for twenty years, and compiled with great pains and accuracy a catalogue of the 20,000 books then in the library.   Arthur had at various times shown his versatility by lecturing on Logic, Botany, and Humanity, and he conducted the Church History class for a session during the absence of the professor. He survived for only one session after Reid, dying of dropsy on 14th June, 1797.

In August, 1797, James Mylne, who had been chaplain of the 83rd Regiment of Foot, and afterwards minister of the Abbey Church, Paisley, was elected professor of Moral Philosophy, on condition that his admission should not take place until he had resigned his parochial charge and the resignation had been accepted.   The College house No. 14, which had been constituted by grouping together a number of rooms for Jardine in 1788, was assigned to him, and he proposed considerable alterations and repairs, which he was permitted to carry out, the faculty contributing only £30 which they had been willing to spend on repairs.   Mylne is described by Professor Campbell Fraser as 'a strong man unknown in philosophical literature, whose professorial career of forty years made him a familiar figure to generations of Glasgow students.'   He was elected clerk in 1799, he was for a long time chaplain, and in other respects was an active and prominent member of the society, but his *res gestae* fall mostly within the nineteenth century.

In January, 1789, Williamson intimated that he had begun to feel the strain of teaching the Mathematics class, and on his proposal James Millar, son of the professor of Law, was appointed to be his assistant and successor, with full charge of the Mathematics class and right to the fees paid by the students, while Williamson retained his house and salary and continued a member of faculty.   After six years of retirement Williamson died on 3rd June, 1795, and Millar attained to the full status of professor. He had Thomas Campbell,[1] the poet as one of his students, but young Campbell did not take kindly to Mathematics.   He even questioned some of Euclid's definitions, declared that a line must have some breadth, be

---

[1] In 1791 Campbell was appointed to the Leighton bursary.   In 1802 Robert Burns— 'Robert the second,' as his father, the national bard, used to call him—was admitted a bursar on the Hamilton foundation.

it ever so thin, and wrote waggish rhymes on the professor and his class :

> ' As Millar's hussars marched up to the wars
> With their Captain in person before them,
> It happened one day that they met on the way
> With the dangerous *pons asinorum.*'

After twenty-one years of service as professor of Practical Astronomy, Alexander Wilson asked the faculty to send a memorial to the government with a view to procure the appointment of his son Patrick as assistant and successor. The memorial was sent accordingly, but the government regarded the proposed appointment as a bad precedent and did not comply. Early in 1782 the faculty allowed Professor Wilson to employ his son Patrick to assist in the care of the Observatory and instruments, in making observations, and in teaching. In 1784 the faculty renewed their application to the government, and this time they succeeded, but though Patrick Wilson's commission as assistant and successor was dated 28th July, 1784, it was not laid before the faculty till 23rd February, 1786. He was appointed Clerk in 1783 and continued in that office about fifteen years. In October, 1798, 'with sentiments of the highest and most unalterable veneration' for the University, he informed the faculty that symptoms of failing health obliged him to think of retiring ; and that he intended to strengthen the equipment of the Observatory, to the value of several hundred pounds, through improvements made on its former instruments and the presentation of further instruments belonging to himself ; and also to bestow a sum of £1,000 as a permanent fund, the interest of which should be used for augmenting the equipment of apparatus and procuring new books in Astronomy. Though asked to reconsider, Wilson adhered to his purpose, but delayed his resignation for some months, and at his suggestion, the faculty sent a memorial to the Chancellor to be by him presented to the Duke of Portland, Home Secretary, recommending for appointment Thomas Jackson, who taught the Natural Philosophy class during the earlier part of Brown's absence.

The Chancellor declared he could not recommend Jackson, and expressed a hope that the faculty would not expect him to present to the Home Secretary a memorial in which he did not concur. The faculty then asked Henry Dundas to transmit the memorial to Portland, and Dundas did so, at the same time informing the faculty that he considered it impossible for Portland to recommend any one who had not the support of the Chancellor, more especially as the faculty were not themselves unanimous. All this time there was no actual vacancy, for Wilson had never placed his resignation in the hands of the faculty, though he sent it to the Chancellor, and the Chancellor returned it.   Jackson, a worthy and promising young man, rather suffered by the unskilful handling of the affair, but ten years later he was appointed professor of Natural Philosophy in St. Andrews University, an office he filled with credit and success till 1837.   In August, 1799, the King issued a commission to William Meikleham to be professor of Practical Astronomy and Observer, and on 29th October he was admitted to office.

Doubtless Anderson had been keenly disappointed by the failure of his scheme for a Royal Visitation and of his action in the Court of Session. He seems to have discontinued attendance at meetings of faculty, but sometimes sent letters, one of the last being submitted in May, 1795, accompanied by a memorial for the better preservation of the Roman stones which he had helped to collect.   In 1790 Anderson invented a gun the recoil of which was deadened by air stored in its carriage, and this invention not being appreciated by the British Government, he went to Paris next year and presented it to the French Assembly, who ordered it to be hung in their hall with the inscription, 'The Gift of Science to Liberty.'   A six-pounder was formed from his model, and experiments made with it in the neighbourhood of Paris, the notorious Paul Jones being one of those who witnessed and praised the gun's execution. Anderson also suggested the use of small balloons of paper, varnished with boiled oil, for conveying newspapers and manifestoes into Germany, the frontier line of which was guarded by a cordon of troops to keep out inflammatory French literature, and they seem to have served their purpose and been extensively used.   In November, 1792, his colleagues agreed to remove the sentence of suspension from the *jurisdictio ordinaria* passed on Anderson in 1784.

In November, 1794, Anderson informed the faculty that the state of his health, joined to his age, prevented or might soon prevent him from being able to discharge the duties of his chair, and asked the faculty to determine whether the appointment of an assistant and successor or the resignation of his office would be most expedient.   The faculty sent a sympathetic message that they were disposed to contribute everything in their power to his ease and accommodation, and a week or two later he was allowed to employ William M'Ilquham as occasional assistant when the state of the professor's health made it needful.   The arrangement was renewed in December, 1795, by which time the assistant's name had been changed from M'Ilquham to Meikleham.   Anderson died on 13th January, 1796, bequeathing nearly the whole of his property to establish an educational institution intended to supply courses and means of instruction in general and scientific branches of study, and avowedly designed to be a rival to the University. The endowments were not adequate for the realisation of his plan, but Anderson's College has had a number of able teachers and many capable and enterprising students, among them David Livingstone, the missionary, traveller, and philanthropist; and it is said that the Royal Institution in London was partly organised on the model which it supplied. The Medical School of Anderson's College is still conducted separately, but the other departments have, since the foundation of the Glasgow and West of Scotland Technical College in 1886, been merged in that institution.

On 13th April, 1796, James Brown, minister of Denino, and assistant to Nicholas Vilant, professor of Mathematics in the University of St. Andrews, was appointed professor of Natural Philosophy in succession to Anderson. The appointment was one of the most unfortunate ever made. Having taught for one session, Brown conceived himself to be in ill health, and recommended John Leslie, Largo, to conduct the class for next session, but Leslie excused himself in respect that lately a large annuity had been settled upon him; and Thomas Jackson, a young M.A., who had gained the Gartmore prize at the end of the previous session, was appointed. He taught for two sessions, receiving the thanks of the faculty for the ability and diligence with which he had acquitted himself. He was then recommended for appointment to the chair of Astronomy, but the Chancellor did not support the recommendation, and the appointment was conferred on Meikleham. Efforts were made to induce Brown to reside in Glasgow and take at least some part in the teaching of Natural Philosophy, but he evaded doing so, and Meikleham was appointed to teach for him. In May, 1800, Brown proposed that Lockhart Muirhead, then acting as librarian, should be appointed as his assistant and successor, Brown retaining £150 of the annual emoluments of the chair during his life. The faculty did not approve of this, and on 9th June Meikleham was appointed to teach for another session. This arrangement was continued for some time, and in November, 1801, the faculty allowed Brown to be absent till the end of March, 1803, in the hope that his health might be restored, announcing that if not, they must endeavour to come to a permanent arrangement.

In April, 1803, the faculty resolved to procure reports from eminent medical men appointed by themselves on the state of Brown's health, seeing that he had not attempted to teach since 1797, nor even resided in Glasgow. He now began to make proposals, but those first made were considered inadmissible, and reports were procured from Drs. Munro and Wardrop on the state of his health, but, as he agreed to resign on an annuity, they were not opened. Though Brown did wofully little service as a professor, he made a very good bargain for himself, obtaining an annual allowance of £165 for life, £100 being taken from the emoluments of the Natural Philosophy chair and the rest being paid by the faculty. On these terms he resigned in August, 1803, and Meikleham was transferred from the Astronomy chair to that of Natural Philosophy. Brown taught the Natural Philosophy class for a single session, but held the professorship for seven years, and the annuity for thirty-three.

John Millar, whose induction as professor of Law has already been narrated, was the son of the minister of Shotts, and was educated at Glasgow, where he came under the influence of Adam Smith, and abandoned an early intention of entering the church. He was some time tutor in the family of Lord Kames, and made the acquaintance of David Hume. He was called to the bar as an advocate in 1760. From Kames and Smith he received an impulse to trace the progress of Society from early and simple forms to later and more complex ones, and in the course of his lectures sketched the process of development through the stages of savage, pastoral, agricultural, and commercial life. In 1787 he published a *Historical View of the English Government from the Saxon Settlement to the Accession of the House of Stewart*, afterwards continued to the Revolution, consisting largely of material from his lectures. He is said to have been skilled in putting aside irrelevant and perplexing details, and presenting in a clear light the main essence of a subject or the true significance of a question, but in the academic controversies of his time he was often on the losing side.

In 1792 James Millar while still assistant and successor to Williamson, the professor of Mathematics, and while his father was professor of Law, was authorised to give a course of lectures on the law of England. In November, 1805, the faculty again permitted him to lecture on that subject; but Davidson was now professor of Law, and shortly afterwards Millar gave a written acknowledgment that his lectures on the law of England should not prejudice Davidson's right to lecture on the same subject if he chose. The degree of LL.D. was conferred by examination in 1767 on John Tretjakoff and Simeon Desnitzkoy, two Russian students, who had studied in the University for a number of years and obtained the degree of M.A. Towards the end of 1766 Desnitzkoy had a quarrel with Professor Anderson, who excluded him from the seats for the choir, or band, as it was then called, at the chapel service. Desnitzkoy conceiving himself ill used by Anderson, took counsel with Alexander Fergusson,[1] a law student, but without disclosing to the latter the real

---

[1] Son of the laird of Craigdarroch. He afterwards became a friend of Burns, who celebrates him in *The Whistle* as 'Craigdarroch, so famous for wit, worth and law,'

nature of the case. Fergusson advised Desnitzkoy to insult Anderson, and both students fell into trouble. The case was referred to the decision of the Earl of Selkirk, then rector, and Desnitzkoy was obliged to make a public apology before the *comitia*, and promise good behaviour for the future; while the sentence on the other offender was, that 'Alexander Fergusson be taken immediately to prison by the beadle for a little time.' In 1752 the degree of LL.D. was conferred on the Hon. Lockhart Gordon, son of the Earl of Aboyne, who had studied philosophy and law at Glasgow for six years with great applause, and afterwards passed his trials in civil law for admission as an advocate. He followed the military profession for a time and was a Lieutenant Colonel in the army, but latterly was Judge Advocate General of Bengal. In 1766 the degree was bestowed on David Stewart Erskine, Lord Cardross, afterwards Earl of Buchan, who had been a student of the University and given special attention to law. Buchan was a man of no mean ability, but wayward and inflated, and less known to fame than his brother Thomas, who became Lord Chancellor, and Henry, who became Lord Advocate. The latter was also a student at Glasgow.

In April, 1791, the Senate resolved to mark their esteem for the character and abilities of William Wilberforce, M.P. for Yorkshire, and their approbation of his exertions for the abolition of the African slave trade, by conferring on him the degree of LL.D. Wilberforce warmly acknowledged the compliment, declaring that his gratification was not merely personal, as the honour done to him could not fail to reflect credit on a cause in the success of which he was most deeply interested. On receiving the intimation he was doubtful whether he should not send an address to the Senate along with his letter, and waited till he could consult the Duke of Montrose on the point. Next year the Senate forwarded to Wilberforce a petition in favour of the abolition of the slave trade to be presented by him to the House of Commons.

In 1775 the Senate enacted that candidates for degrees in Law must have two years' standing in the University beyond what was required for M.A., and must have attended two years in Civil Law. If they had not the degree of M.A., they must be examined in arts on the M.A. standard, and after an examination in Law by a committee of Senate, must undergo an examination before the Senate, or such other trial as might be prescribed. Three years after obtaining the degree of bachelor or becoming eligible for it, students might proceed to the degree of LL.D., and if they had not the degree of LL.B. must undergo the examination for it; but if they had the degree of LL.B. the Senate was to consider whether further examination was necessary, and might prescribe other trials when deemed proper.   Candidates were to pay £5 to the library, £10 to the professor of Law, and £2 to the University servants and for diploma, two-thirds being paid at the time of taking LL.B., and the remainder when taking LL.D., an additional payment being made when an examination in arts was required.   The regulations were not to apply to honorary degrees, for which there was to be no fee, nor to degrees conferred after particular application on persons advanced in life and of known abilities or eminent knowledge of Law.   These regulations did not attract candidates, and it may be doubted whether they were actually enforced.   In May, 1800, the Senate declared that in all cases fees should be exacted for the degrees of Doctor in Divinity, Law, or Medicine; and that if the graduate was not to be charged, the dues should be paid from the College funds.

Cumin continued as professor of Oriental Languages during the whole of this period, and he further showed an interest in modern languages by voluntarily holding classes in French and Italian for thirty years.   With the advance of age, he found the work of these additional classes too laborious, and in 1797 intimated that he did not intend to continue them. He received the thanks of the faculty; and with their sanction it was arranged that Lockhart Muirhead, librarian, should conduct the classes in French and Italian.   Cumin's health suffered and in March, 1798, he proposed the appointment of an assistant and successor.   At the instance of Jardine, the faculty had in 1790 adopted a regulation declaring that, while a professor disabled by age or infirmity had a right to a provision for life from the emoluments of his chair, professors in such circumstances should submit the whole case to the faculty, that the latter might judge whether a temporary assistant or an assistant and successor should be appointed; and that when a professor proposed the appointment of an assistant or an assistant and successor, the terms and conditions arranged should be stated without reservation in a letter subscribed by both and laid before the faculty.   In consequence of this regulation the faculty, while willing to grant such relief as the circumstances of Cumin's health might require, declined for the time to agree to his proposal.

The Earl of Bute had declared himself unpledged regarding the appointment of a successor to Rouet and willing to support the fittest candidate, and the University meeting recommended James Oswald, minister of Methven.   Oswald and James Beattie, though of less weight than Reid, were sometimes regarded as forming along with him a triumvirate of Scottish philosophers.   But the Earl was not so amenable to guidance this time as in the case of the Law chair, and in May, 1762, William Wight, dissenting minister in Dublin, received a commission from the Crown to be professor of Ecclesiastical and teacher of Civil History, in succession to Rouet, 'late professor and teacher of these Histories.' The wrangle over the appointment of Wight as College chaplain, an episode in the greater controversy about the management and administration of the University, has already been narrated. In June, 1778, Wight was elected professor of Divinity by seven votes to five recorded for Dr. Findlay.

In August Hugh Macleod was appointed to the vacant chair. He applied for leave of absence for session 1779-1780, but was informed that this would be inconsistent with the laws and interests of the University, and was peremptorily required to be in his place on 1st November, 1779. Macleod, who was then at Eton College, intimated that he would comply. There was a good deal of wrangling on the question, but Macleod was allowed to choose a College house before Young, the professor of Greek, though the latter had been longer in office. The hot dispute between Anderson and Macleod has been narrated previously. In December, 1796, Macleod called attention to the broken state of his health, of which there was little prospect of improvement, and suggested that the faculty should represent to the government the expediency of appointing William M'Turk, preacher, whom he described as well known and highly esteemed by all members of the Society, to be assistant and successor. He stated that M'Turk was ready to begin immediately a course of lectures on Civil History, and that he himself would continue to lecture on Ecclesiastical History as long as he was able. The faculty gave the proposal their hearty support, and in February following M'Turk was appointed assistant and successor.

Trail, who became professor of Divinity in 1761, had a dispute with Moor. The latter conceiving that Trail had used him ill in a meeting of committee, rose to complain in the dean of faculty's meeting, and used very forcible language. As Moor was not inclined to make a proper acknowledgment, Trail summoned him to answer in the Court of Session, but the former having withdrawn the offensive epithets and made an apology before the University meeting on 25th January, 1766, was admonished and forgiven. Trail died on 19th October, 1775. Ten years after his appointment he received a payment of £11 because at the outset he was kept some time out of the house belonging to his charge, owing to indulgence shown to the widow of a previous professor; and after his death his heirs were the last to whom an 'ann' was paid under the regulation made in 1655. Having received a report from a committee which investigated the subject, the faculty on 17th April, 1776, abolished the regulation under which 'anns' were granted, declaring that it was prejudicial to the College funds, detrimental to the professors in some cases, and impracticable in others.

On 13th November, 1775, Dr. James Baillie, one of the ministers of Hamilton, was appointed to succeed Trail. He is said to have been of the same family with Baillie of Jerviswood, and he married Dorothy, the only surviving sister of John and William Hunter. Their daughter Joanna had some note in her own time as a songstress and writer of dramas in verse ; while their son, Dr. Matthew Baillie, was a distinguished physician and pathologist, and one of the trustees of the property left by his uncle, Dr. William Hunter, of which so large a share fell to the University. Professor Baillie had only a brief tenure of the chair, dying on 28th April, 1778, after which Wight was transferred from the chair of Church History to that of Divinity. He also had a short tenure, dying on 29th July, 1782.

On 5th September, 1782, Dr. Robert Findlay, then minister of the Ramshorn Church, Glasgow, who had previously been dean of faculty, and had been a candidate for the Divinity chair at the time when Wight was appointed, was elected to succeed the latter. Findlay took special interest in a fund left about 1641 by Margaret Graham for the benefit of the library and of a student of Divinity, but which had been only a short time in operation when it ceased to be traceable. He worked at this subject for a number of years with a persistence which might have done credit to John Anderson. In 1792 the faculty, after considering memorials from him, declared their opinion that if a claim ever existed it must have been cut off by prescription. Findlay dissented and brought the case before the Visitors, but they deemed it incompetent for them to enter upon the merits of a question concerning, not the present administration, but the existence and application of a mortification of which there was no authentic record during the eighteenth century. After this Findlay seems to have approached the Town Council, and letters were received from the Town Clerk, and finally from the Provost, who suggested that the affair should be referred to arbitration. To this the faculty would not agree, and Findlay entered another dissent, Richardson and Jeffray adhering. At the time when the second of the series of augmentations of salaries of professors which marked the end of the eighteenth and the beginning of the nineteenth century was proposed, Findlay dissented. In April, 1800, the faculty resolved on a general increase of class fees, and determined that for each of the curriculum classes in Arts and for Mathematics the fee should be two guineas, for each of the private classes taught by arts professors £1 11s. 6d., for Anatomy, Botany, and Medicine three guineas each, and for Church History and Hebrew one guinea each.

Findlay desired his opinion to be recorded that the professors of Church History and Oriental Languages should admit students to their classes without fee as formerly. The Divinity class still continued to be open without fee.

The degrees of D.D. and LL.D. were not so often conferred in the eighteenth century as in more recent times. Among the more notable recipients of the degree of D.D. during the period with which the present chapter deals were William M'Gill of Ayr, the 'Dr. Mac' of Burns' *Kirk's Alarm*; Sir Henry Moncrieff Wellwood, a man of great sagacity and mental force, to whom the overthrow of the 'Moderates' who had long dominated Scotland was largely owing; William Burn of Minto, whose degree was conferred on the recommendation of Edmund Burke, just after the latter had ceased to be rector; William Ritchie, minister of Tarbolton, and afterwards of St. Andrew's Church, Glasgow, who introduced an organ into that church, and should therefore wear the laurels usually bestowed on Dr. Robert Lee, who, like himself, was a professor in his later years in the faculty of Divinity of the University of Edinburgh; and Roderick Macleod, upon whom the degree was conferred at the request of the University of Aberdeen, where he had previously been sub-principal in King's College, and immediately afterwards became principal.

A considerable addition to the library buildings was made in 1782, but it was two or three years later before the internal parts were finished and fitted for the reception of books. In May, 1776, Mr. Arthur, the librarian, was directed to arrange the books in one of the presses by way of specimen, after which the rest of the books were to be arranged in the manner approved, in order that a proper catalogue might be compiled. The preparation of a new catalogue was begun soon after this, and from time to time notices appear in the minutes sanctioning payments to defray the expenses of the work, which extended over twelve or fifteen years, and was hindered by the limited printing equipment of Andrew Foulis, the younger, and the difficulties in which he was sometimes involved about money. Though it was not in conformity with the regulations laid down by Hutcheson of Lambhill, who provided an endowment for the librarian, Arthur, who had been appointed by the Town Council for four years in 1775, was re-appointed by the University for other four in 1779. An important further step was taken in 1781, when negotiations were opened with the Magistrates and Council, with a view to alter arrangements so that the appointment of librarian should for the future rest entirely with the University. A suspension from the Court of Session had previously cut short a plan of this kind, and this time a strategy was adopted so as to gain the object and yet preserve at least a seeming compliance with the stipulations laid down by Hutcheson.

In February, 1782, the Town Council agreed to an arrangement by which they retained the right to appoint a librarian once in four years, with an annual stipend of 200 marks Scots, but with no further charge than that of keeping the books in the old library, apparently a very small collection ; while the University was left free to appoint a librarian for the general library with such a salary and such a length of tenure as they deemed expedient.   Under the new arrangement the librarian's salary was at first only a little over £22 a year, with some allowance for entering additional books in the catalogue, but in 1800 the salary was raised to £40, including remuneration for entering additions.

Arthur's catalogue was very carefully compiled, and comprised about 20,000 volumes.   It was drawn up after the manner of the catalogue of the Advocates' Library, and contained two lists, one of which was alphabetical, while the other followed the order in which the books were placed on the shelves.   In May, 1787, the faculty ordered a special payment of £210 to be made to Arthur for this work, at the same time stipulating that the catalogue should be completed by June, 1788, but it was not actually issued till 1791.   Arthur resigned office as librarian in October, 1794, and next month William M'Turk was appointed to succeed him. M'Turk resigned in a year, and the faculty then appointed Lockhart Muirhead, who continued librarian till 1827.   It is curious that these three consecutive librarians all became professors in the University.

Robert Dinwiddie, a native of Glasgow, for some time Governor of the colony of Virginia, and frequently mentioned in Thackeray's novel, *The Virginians*, received from the University the degree of LL.D. in 1754 and died in 1770, leaving a bequest of £100 to be laid out in procuring books.   In 1774 Thomas Hollis of Corsecombe, Dorset, bequeathed a further sum of £100.   It does not appear that Mr. Hollis had any direct connection with the University of Glasgow, but he had a special regard for an alumnus, Mr. Thomas Brand of Hide, Essex, to whom he bequeathed his real estate and the residue of his personal property, upon which Mr. Brand assumed the additional name of Hollis.   At his death in 1804 Mr. Brand Hollis bequeathed a third sum of £100, to be laid out on the purchase of books on Government or Civil History or Mathematics for the use of the library.   These three sums have been treated as capital funds the interest of which is applied to the purchase of books.

Professor Robert Simson bequeathed to the University library a valuable and interesting collection of books, and in 1776 the Earl of Stanhope, who had borne the expense of printing Simson's posthumous works, presented a copy to the University. At the same time the Senate accepted an offer by Professor Clow, one of Simson's executors, to present to the University the original manuscripts from which the posthumous works were printed, as well as sixteen or seventeen small quarto volumes containing a variety of Geometrical propositions, entitled *Adversaria*, the works of Pappus with Dr. Simson's notes, and the whole of Simson's papers. As regards the works of Pappus, Clow stipulated that the University should bear the expense of taking a copy of Simson's notes, many of which were written on loose pieces of paper. Principal Leechman bequeathed a considerable number of books, not to the general library, however, but to a separate one attached to the Divinity Hall.

Early in 1797 Mrs. Carmichael, daughter of Professor Thomas Reid, intimated that her father before his death had expressed a desire that such of his books as the College might choose should be given to the public library, and upon this about seventy volumes were chosen, the faculty recording their respect and gratitude for this mark of attention from their late most venerable colleague. Four years before, Mrs. Carmichael presented 386 volumes of medical and other books from the library of her deceased husband, Dr. Patrick Carmichael. In 1786 another Mrs. Carmichael, daughter of Professor William Forbes, made a gift to the library of a manuscript body of Scots Law by her father, extending to seven volumes. The Rev. Dr. James Wodrow of Stevenston in 1795 presented four volumes of original manuscript letters on College affairs addressed by various persons of his time to Principal Stirling. Mr. John Orr of Barrowfield in 1787 gave the works of Virgil printed at Venice in 1488, and the works of Lucretius printed at Paris in 1514 ; and a copy of *Piers Plowman* printed in 1550 was presented in 1788 by the Rev. Robert Boag of Paisley. A work in four volumes, *The Antiquities of Herculaneum*, was received in 1764 as a gift from the King of the two Sicilies. In February, 1772, the Earl of Suffolk, one of the Secretaries of State, informed the principal that George III. had been pleased to present a copy of the *Journals of Parliament* to the University of Glasgow, adding—'It is with particular pleasure that I communicate to you this mark of royal favour.' The principal was instructed to return dutiful acknowledgments for the honour done to the University. In 1799 a copy of the *Proceedings in the House of Lords and in the East India Company on the Evidence given in the Impeachment of Warren Hastings, Esquire,* was presented by the great accused.

John Murray, bookseller, London, was appointed in 1774 to receive books for the University from Stationers' Hall, with an honorarium of a guinea a year for his trouble. Doubtless it was for the advantage of the

University to have an agent in the great centre of publication. Notices appear from time to time of parcels of books forwarded by the Murrays (in 1794 it was Mrs. Murray, and in 1796 and for two or three years afterwards Murray & Highley), and their remuneration, though moderate, soon went beyond the guinea at which it began.

In 1785 Reid submitted to the faculty a letter from Edmund Burke, who had been re-elected as rector in the preceding November, enclosing an application from Dr. Geddes, of Maddox Street, London, for the use of a manuscript in the library containing the Octateuch of the Septuagint. Geddes, whose application was supported by Burke, desired that the manuscript might be sent to the house of the rector in London for collation. The faculty, while willing to allow Geddes, or any one he might appoint, to collate it in Glasgow, thought the document too precious to be sent so far as London ; and in October, 1785, Geddes was allowed to carry it to his lodgings in Glasgow for collation, on his giving a bond for £500 to return it uninjured. Though his light was meteoric rather than abiding, Geddes had a remarkable career.

Sprung from the Banffshire peasantry, he was educated at the Scots College, Paris, and after becoming a priest, was some time in the family of the Earl of Traquair. A young kinswoman of the Earl openly displayed an affection for him, and, though he felt the germs of a responsive passion, his vow of perpetual celibacy made him check it, and he returned to Paris. Afterwards he became priest to a congregation of Catholics at Auchinhalrig, in Banffshire, and carried on a small farm, and having been brought to the brink of ruin by church building and farming, he extricated himself by publishing a translation in English verse of *Select Satires of Horace*. He advised his people to read the Scriptures and think for themselves, and being on good terms with the minister of Cullen, occasionally attended the services of the parish church. These things roused the ire of his bishop, who suspended him from the priesthood. Leaving amid the general regret of Protestants and Catholics, the University of Aberdeen conferred upon him the degree of LL.D., and he repaired to London and set himself to execute a translation of the Bible for Catholics. As a linguist and otherwise he had considerable qualifications for the work, but he made too many digressions into polemical and satirical literature, and, though his productions in that kind were sometimes highly amusing, they retarded his progress with the translation, which in 1797 was published down to the end of the book of Ruth, and never went any further. In 1786 Reid laid before the faculty a short account of the Greek manuscript of the Octateuch, which had been drawn up by Dr. Geddes after collating it. Two or three years later the faculty resolved to subscribe for Dr. Geddes' translation of the Old and New Testaments, and this resolution went hand in hand with another to subscribe for Cowper's translation of Homer into blank verse.

The Caledonian Mercury, one or other of the Glasgow newspapers, and a London newspaper made the professors acquainted with current topics and passing events. At the era of the French Revolution, when there had doubtless been a keen desire for news, the papers were placed in the forehall from the time of their arrival till three in the afternoon, after which they were carried by a College servant from house to house among the principal and professors in the order of their seniority, not being allowed to remain more than two hours in any house, while papers were not delivered or called for earlier than eight in the morning or later than ten in the evening. In 1791 the *Glasgow Mercury* was stopped and the *Courier* taken instead. The *London Chronicle* was taken for many years, and in 1790 the clerk was instructed to ask William Woodfall to send by post his daily paper *The Diary* during the sittings of Parliament. Periodicals seem to have gradually gained in prominence, and in 1777 the quaestor of the library was authorised to expend £25 received for Doctors' degrees on periodicals which were at that time wanting. In 1780 orders were given that the *Monthly Review* should be forwarded by post, and that the issue for each month should lie in the forehall till the succeeding one arrived. A yet quicker delivery was desired, and in 1794 it was resolved that the *Monthly Review* should be brought from London at the beginning of each month by mail coach.

Andrew Foulis, the younger, continued for about nineteen years as printer to the University after the death of his father and uncle, and occupied a number of apartments within the College, of which he was allowed the use during the pleasure of the faculty. He seems to have been generally in difficulties, once at least sums due to him by the University were arrested, he made slow progress in printing Arthur's catalogue of the library, and probably other parts of the University work were not promptly executed. The date for making annual appointments was 10th June, and when that date arrived in 1795, Foulis, who had previously been warned by the Senate, was not re-elected. He was required to vacate the College rooms, and as he showed no alacrity in complying, an action was raised in the Sheriff Court to enforce his removal. A process had also been raised against Foulis for the rent of the printing house from Whitsunday, 1776, and the College law agent was instructed to raise a further action for his removal from premises in Shuttle Street belonging to the College.

Notwithstanding this parade of actions, Foulis was not harshly dealt with, and in April, 1796, the faculty, considering that he had suffered some inconvenience from the taking down of the back wall of the College many years ago, and from having on hand at the expiration of his term of office as printer a number of books for the use of the classes, agreed to allow him £70, on his removing from the printing house and other premises belonging to the College. Under this arrangement Foulis quitted the premises, gave up the keys, and received the £70. Poverty seems to have been his companion to the end, and when he died in 1829 the faculty made an allowance of £5 to defray the expenses of his funeral. For more than a quarter of a century the faculty made an annual allowance for the support of his sister Elizabeth, who had married Robert Dewar, foreman in the printing establishment of R. & A. Foulis, but was soon left a widow. On 18th November, 1795, James Mundell, of whose good character and eminence as a printer the Senate had satisfactory evidence, was appointed printer to the University for three years; and, after the expiration of his first term, he was re-appointed for other three. Mr. Mundell took a shop with rooms below it, in the new tenement built by the faculty in College Street opposite the University.

In 1769 the University agreed to erect an addition to the type foundry carried on by the firm of which Wilson, the professor of Astronomy, was chief partner; and in 1785, 1789, and 1792 Wilson & Sons were allowed to make further additions; while in 1793 the faculty granted them a lease for nineteen years of the yard in which their foundries stood, recommending to their successors the advisability of renewing the lease at the end of that time. The faculty also granted to the firm the use of some rooms in the library which were not otherwise occupied.

In 1738 Robert Simson reported that the Hon. Mr. Drummond had sent from Drummond Castle an inscribed Roman stone found several years before in the pretorium of the Roman camp at Ardoch. A small sum was paid to Simson in 1744 for his outlays in purchasing and bringing from Kirkintilloch a large stone from the Roman wall with an inscription. Orders were given in 1767 that engravings should be made on copperplate of the Roman stones, and as Foulis charged £40 for the work, it is probable the University already possessed a good many more of these stones than the two from Ardoch and Kirkintilloch. The works for the Forth and Clyde Canal were begun in July, 1768, and by and by Roman stones were unearthed in the course of the excavations, and mainly through the activity of Anderson were added to the University collection. In May, 1771, Anderson was appointed to visit the excavations and endeavour to procure some relics which had been brought to light. Shortly after this four Roman stones found at Auchendavy were presented by the proprietors of the canal. In 1774 Anderson intimated that Sir Lawrence Dundas[1] was to make over his Roman antiquities to the College. These included an inscribed stone, and several other stones believed to have formed the sides of a niche for a figure of the Goddess Fortune, to whom there was an inscription.

About 1789 or 1790 engravings from copper plates were issued giving a view of the Roman stones with their inscriptions and figures or ornaments. The faculty in 1810 presented the Roman stones to the Hunterian Museum. In 1779 Provost Clarke and the Magistrates of Linlithgow presented to the University a collection of Roman coins which had been discovered some time before in improving a common belonging to the burgh. In 1782 about a dozen Roman medals were presented by Mr. Fullarton of Carstairs.

After the Revolution not much is heard of the College table which had previously formed part of the normal equipment, and at which professors, regents, bursars, and, so far as accommodation served, other students who chose to pay, had their meals together. All through the eighteenth century, however, it was customary for students to lodge within the College, though the total number was such that only the minority could be accommodated in this way. Chambers in the College were let to students at a small rent, and sometimes two or three shared a room among them, but it was not always poor students who lived in these chambers. Alexander Carlyle, afterwards minister of Inveresk, whose handsome figure and noble bearing caused him to be popularly known as ' Jupiter' Carlyle, lived in a College chamber while attending the University in 1744-5. Among others who lived in College rooms were Simeon Desnitzkoy, a student of good means who graduated in arts and law, and who, along with a fellow Russian, came to the University on the recommendation of Lord Mansfield, both being accommodated with advances of £20 from the College funds when their remittances from Russia were slow to arrive ; and David Woodburn, who for some flippant remarks —such as that more benefit was to be got by attending the theatre than by attending the drowsy shops of Logic and Metaphysics—underwent a trial of nine days, not very fairly conducted before what was called the rector's court, though on this occasion the vice-rector presided, and before the case was concluded, the rector himself appeared and entered an energetic protest against the proceedings. Woodburn afterwards had an honourable career in the service of the East India Company, in which he rose to the rank of Colonel.

It had been the custom to appoint two professors as curators of the

[1] Dundas had cut the first sod of the canal.

College chambers, and in 1760 the curators were asked to prepare as many rooms as practicable for lodging students. In 1768 the rooms do not seem to have been much in demand; and Reid having pointed out that there were many apartments unoccupied by students or others, was allowed with his family to occupy some of them. Gentlemen holding the position of assistant and successor to professors were usually provided with College rooms, and other officials sometimes had similar accommodation. In 1770 the rents of the chambers did not meet the cost of repairs, and it was resolved to have only one curator for the future, to whom those taking rooms were to pay the rent in advance. In 1781 Young became curator, and he continued till the end of the system. Under his management the funds derived from chambers improved, and being invested from time to time, they finally reached in 1817 the sum of £850. Of this amount £100 was allocated to pay the debts of the library and £25 to procure books on Law, while the remainder was transferred to the general funds of the College. A resolution was passed in 1803 that medical students should not be admitted to reside in the College, and by 1817 when the funds were transferred, the letting of rooms to students was discontinued.

Among the students of this time who afterwards reached distinction and whose connection with the University has not already been noticed were, Dugald Stewart, the eloquent professor of Moral Philosophy at Edinburgh; Dr. John Jamieson, whose *Etymological Dictionary of the Scottish Language* is still valuable, though the progress of Philology has not confirmed all the author's views and estimates; Dr. Claudius Buchanan, chaplain to the East India Company, Vice-Provost of the College which Lord Wellesley founded at Fort William, and translator of the Gospels into Persian and Hindustani; Major-General Sir Thomas Munro, eminent in the Indian civil and military service, and finally governor of Madras; Sir John Sinclair of Ulbster, known for his interest in agriculture and as a writer on various subjects, but specially known as the projector and compiler of the old *Statistical Account* of Scotland; Thomas Thomson, advocate, a great antiquarian, of whom Scott said 'he understands more of old books, old laws, and old history than any man in Scotland'; Francis Jeffrey, editor of the *Edinburgh Review* in the days of its power and fame; John Wilson, the breezy freshness of whose *Noctes Ambrosianae* long enlivened the pages of *Blackwood's Magazine*; and William Windham, a politician and orator of the days of Pitt, Fox, and Burke.

Unless the retiring rector was present, a case which seldom happened, the vice-rector presided at rectorial elections, and when the 'nations' were equally divided, the result was determined by his casting vote. A case of this kind happened in 1776, when two 'nations' voted for James Montgomerie, Lord Chief Baron of the Exchequer, and two for Daniel Campbell of Shawfield ; and Professor Alexander Wilson, then vice-rector, gave his casting vote for the former. In 1768 Sir Adam Fergusson of Kilkerran was elected by the votes of all the 'nations' in opposition to Adam Smith, who had only a very slender following. Probably Smith was little obliged to his supporters on this occasion, who appear to have been a handful of discontented students ; and it is not unlikely that Smith may not have been nominated till the very eve of the poll. Henry Dundas was elected in 1781 by the votes of three 'nations,' Rothseiana voting for Edmund Burke. After Dundas had, according to custom, been re-elected and held office for a second year, Burke was chosen as his successor on 15th November, 1783. He accepted office, and signified his impatience to attend the University in person for his admission, but his installation did not take place till 10th April, 1784. He was re-elected at the end of his first year, and installed a second time on 1st September, 1785. On both occasions he nominated Thomas Reid as vice-rector. The next rector, Robert Graham of Gartmore, showed greater impatience to be admitted to office than Burke, for he was elected on 15th and installed on 19th November, 1785. Adam Smith was chosen rector in 1787 and again in 1788. In the former year Francis Jeffrey, then a diminutive but spirited lad of fourteen who had just begun his attendance at Glasgow, harangued the students against giving their votes for Smith, not from any dislike to the *Wealth of Nations* or its author, but because he thought the election was being too exclusively managed by the professors. However, the opposition was withdrawn, and on both occasions Smith was returned by the votes of all the 'nations.' It is usually stated that Smith made no speech at his installation, and that Burke broke down when addressing the academic audience ; but at that time it was not the custom to deliver a full length address such as is now expected, though there may have been a few words of thanks to the electors and good wishes to the University.

During all the time from 1714 onwards successive Dukes of Montrose held office as chancellor, excepting that in December, 1780, the Marquis of Graham was appointed to succeed his aged father, who had resigned two or three weeks before. At his installation in January, 1781, the chancellor, accompanied by the members of Senate entered the public hall, where the students, the lord provost and magistrates of the city, and many other gentlemen had assembled. The oath *de fideli* was administered, and Principal Leechman in name of the Senate addressed the chancellor in a Latin speech. Half a dozen gowned students then gave specimens of their taste and proficiency by pronouncing orations or verses in Latin. The chancellor followed with a Latin speech addressed to the University, and Leechman closed the proceedings by a speech in English followed by a prayer.

CHAPTER IV

THE NINETEENTH CENTURY AND AFTER, 1801–1909

I. 1801–1830

A DECISION given by the Court of Session early in the nineteenth century introduced a new grade of professors who were little better than tolerated aliens. In 1807, without previous communication with the University, the King founded a chair of Natural History and appointed Lockhart Muirhead to be professor. The principal and the professors holding chairs previously founded had accustomed themselves to make augmentations to their salaries, and now saw with apprehension the prospect of additional professors being admitted to share what they considered their exclusive patrimony. They raised an action in the Court of Session to prevent this result. By a strange neglect on the part of the Crown officers, no appearance was made for the Crown, and the court decided that Muirhead was a professor in the University but not in the College of Glasgow. For a decade or two before the end of the 18th century the number of students had been steadily rising, and in the first decade of the 19th century the increase became so great as to necessitate a large extension of the buildings. For this purpose a grant of £2,500 was obtained from the Government, and the faculty were doubtless encouraged to use other funds in consequence of a bequest of more than £10,000 left by Mr. Robert Hamilton, a merchant in Canton, China, though this legacy was not actually received till some time afterwards. A further considerable extension was made in 1831, when new buildings for Chemistry were erected in Shuttle Street.

In 1817 the degree of Master of Surgery was introduced, and, without retarding the steadily increasing demand for Doctor of Medicine, was itself in considerable demand till the unfortunate issue of a lawsuit interfered with its value as a qualification to practise in Glasgow and an area in the West of Scotland, where a charter by James VI. gave the faculty of

Y

Physicians and Surgeons a right to examine practitioners in Surgery. The development in the faculty of Medicine as regards students and graduates, teaching staff and equipment, has been marked all through the 19th century, though the point of interest has changed from time to time. The faculty of Arts, on the other hand, gained no addition to its teaching staff till after the passing of the Act of 1858, unless, for want of a faculty of Science, we count as a professorship in Arts the chair of Engineering founded by the Crown in 1840.

But the faculty made some advance in 1826 when new regulations for graduation were laid down, including provision for graduation with honours. Notwithstanding the laxity of the rules of the Church respecting admission to the ministry, the University of Glasgow in the early part of the 19th century had a longer session in its Divinity Hall and probably a larger number of students than any other Scottish University. Jardine and some others took exception to several instances of pluralities, including the case of Principal Taylor, appointed in 1803, and Principal Macfarlan, appointed twenty years later, both of whom were ministers of Glasgow as well, which left the College for more than fifty years with only two acting visitors, instead of the three contemplated by the *Nova Erectio* ; while Gibb, the professor of Oriental Languages, was minister of St. Andrew's, Glasgow. The University had for more than a hundred and twenty years been aided by the profits derived from repeated leases of the Archbishopric of Glasgow, but the Government declined to renew the lease which expired at Whitsunday, 1825, though the King gave an annual grant of £800 for fourteen years longer. Another most important event which marked the close of the period with which this chapter deals, was the appointment in 1826 of a Royal Commission to enquire into the condition of the Scottish Universities and propose measures for their improvement. After four busy years the Commissioners presented a valuable report, though somewhat wanting in precision as regards the reforms proposed.

Upon the death of Leechman in 1785 the faculty recommended the Rev. Dr. Taylor, minister of the High Church of Glasgow, for the vacant office of principal, but the recommendation passed unheeded, and the Rev. Archibald Davidson, minister of Inchinnan, was appointed. As compared with that of Leechman, Davidson's tenure was peaceful ; and when he died in 1803 Dr. Taylor, without any recommendation from the faculty, was this time successful, the King's commission in his favour being issued only eight days after the death of Davidson. As Taylor made no sign of giving up his ministry, but rather indicated his intention to hold both offices, Findlay and Jardine entered a strong dissent, pointing out that the *Nova Erectio* constituted the minister of Glasgow a visitor of the College, and contending that the principal could not resign office as visitor without resigning his charge as minister, and that, the visitors being now reduced to two, there could be no means of obtaining a decision if a difference arose between them; further pointing out that the principal in 1621 had been released from the ministry of Govan because the pastoral charge had been found hurtful to the academic one; that in previous instances when a minister of Glasgow had been appointed principal, his pastoral charge had been assigned to another; and that, as the stipend of the minister of Glasgow was about £400 and the emoluments of the principal about £500, there could be no plea of necessity.

At his admission Taylor declared that his presentation as a minister did not require him to act as a visitor, and that he would never more do so. Afterwards he gave in a long reply to Findlay and Jardine, containing a good deal of ingenious argument. Ministers of Glasgow, he said, had often held the office of rector or dean, and as such had been visitors. The new foundation by the Town in 1573, which was ratified by Act of Parliament, made the magistrates, along with the rector and dean, visitors of the College, at least so far as funds were concerned. The *Nova Erectio* was not confirmed by Act of Parliament except in regard to the granting of certain teinds, and therefore it could not repeal the new foundation of 1573, for no royal charter could repeal an Act of Parliament. If the dissenters feared the College would suffer from too few visitors, let them take in all the ministers of Glasgow, of whom there were now six, instead of one at the time of the *Nova Erectio*. The business of the College had long gone smoothly with only two visitors; but if it proved inconvenient to have only the rector and dean, the way to the crown was open, and the King might appoint visitors either ordinary or extraordinary. Taylor ended with a devout peroration in which he professed to find the fulfilment of the designs of Providence in what had happened. Now that he had nothing further to wish for in this world, he could say that whatever he had attained had come to him, so far as he knew, without the solicitation of friends, and though the lot seemed cast by chance, its disposal was 'of the Lord.'

Taylor died on 29th March, 1823, and very swiftly afterwards the King's commission was issued to the Rev. Duncan Macfarlan, minister of Drymen, to be principal. When it was given in Macgill, the professor of Divinity, dissented from appointing a day for the admission of the new principal, the *Gazette* having announced that the King had presented Macfarlan to be minister of the High Church of Glasgow, so that it was evidently contemplated that Macfarlan should hold the two offices as

Taylor had done.   Macgill repeated the arguments against their union, and urged the faculty to ascertain whether Macfarlan intended to accept the office of minister of the High Church, and if it were found that he did, to present a respectful memorial to the Government against a union so pregnant with evil.   Millar, Mylne, and Jardine also objected.   The majority did not share these views, and on the 29th of April Macfarlan was admitted as principal.   In the Presbytery of Glasgow Macgill opposed Macfarlan's induction as minister of the High Church, on the ground that the offices of principal of the College and minister of the High Church were incompatible, the duties of each being sufficiently onerous for one man's abilities.   The Presbytery by a large majority set aside the presentation, and declared the presentee 'unqualified'; and the Synod confirmed the sentence.   The General Assembly of 1824, however, reversed the decision, and ordered that Principal Macfarlan should be settled as minister of the High Church.

The chair of Natural History, though afterwards assigned to the faculty of Medicine, was for a long time outside the curriculum in any faculty, and its institution led to such important results that it deserves to be narrated separately.   Lockhart Muirhead, who was appointed librarian in 1795, seems to have been a man of considerable energy and varied accomplishments.   In 1797 he volunteered to continue the teaching of French and Italian when Cumin gave it up.   A motion was carried in the faculty in December, 1803, that it was expedient to appoint a lecturer in Natural History, and Muirhead was immediately appointed.   From 1804 to 1807 a building was in course of preparation beside the College for the reception of William Hunter's Museum, and in the spring of 1807 measures for its removal to Glasgow were being considered.   On 21st April it was resolved to ask Muirhead to proceed to London to superintend the packing and despatch of Hunter's great collections.   A day before, Cumin submitted to the faculty a royal warrant, dated 23rd March, 1807, erecting and endowing a professorship of Natural History in the University, and appointing Lockhart Muirhead to be professor for life, and also keeper of the museum or repository of natural curiosities, granting to him all the rights and privileges which belonged to any other professor in the University, and requiring the rector, dean, and other professional masters to admit him to office in the usual form.   The King also granted the new professor a salary of £100 a year from the bishops' rents or other crown rents or casualties in Scotland.

The clause appointing Muirhead to be keeper of the museum was open to exception, especially as Hunter's great collections were about to be removed from London to Glasgow, and the clause might be construed as an implied claim on the part of the crown to appoint a keeper; but the right of the sovereign to institute a new professorship must be judged on grounds apart from this incidental question. The royal warrant was issued without the knowledge of any of the College or University administrators, but as the faculty had appointed Muirhead to lecture on Natural History in 1803, they could hardly maintain that the subject was unnecessary or the teacher unfit. A change of Government had taken place a short time before, and it is said that the opposition to Muirhead's admission arose partly from political considerations. Nothing was done at the meeting at which Cumin presented Muirhead's commission, but at a meeting on 23rd April, at which the rector, Glassford of Dugalston, and the dean, the Rev. Dr. Duncan Macfarlan, attended, the rector proposed a motion, which was carried by eight votes to six, that the opinion of counsel should be taken regarding the extent of Muirhead's rights in consequence of his presentation. Cumin, Young, Macleod, Jardine, Millar, and Mylne dissented, and at next meeting a protest was taken by a notary public on behalf of Muirhead.

On 10th June the opinion of Lord Advocate Colquhoun, Adam Rolland, and Matthew Ross was laid before the faculty. Counsel considered that it was competent to the crown to establish a new professorship, and to bestow a salary from funds at the royal disposal, and that the professor would have the same rights as other professors in the University to sit and vote as a member of Senate, to be a member of faculty, and to act and vote in the patronage of the faculty and the general management of the funds, to claim a share of future augmentations of salary, and also, in order of seniority, to claim a house. They further considered that matters relating to Hunter's museum must be regulated by his will, and that the King had no right to appoint a keeper of that museum; but though that part of the deed were ineffectual, it would not necessarily invalidate the rest. The presentation was not given under the privy seal of Scotland, and this was considered a defect. They considered the memorialists were not bound to take any steps in consequence of the presentation in its existing form or until some regular deed passed the seals, and under all the circumstances they apprehended that the memorialists might refuse to admit Muirhead till his right to be admitted was duly ascertained.

It was thus only on the point respecting the seal that counsel found any serious difficulty—a point which was afterwards lightly dismissed by the Court of Session, and on which the faculty had previously laid little stress, the commissions of the principal and the professor of Law being sealed in the same way as Muirhead's. Not satisfied with this opinion, the majority resolved to draw up a fresh memorial and procure a further opinion from

Mr. Blair, dean of the faculty of Advocates, and Mr. David Hume. On 17th August the opinion of Blair and Hume was submitted. They considered the King had a right to erect a chair of Natural History in the University and to endow it with funds at his disposal, and that Muirhead when admitted on a commission under the proper seal would be a member of the University entitled to sit and vote in the *Comitia* and in the Senate, and to take part in the election of the dean of faculty. They thought the members of the College were vested with a peculiar and profitable interest which could not be taken away from them or their successors, or impaired by communicating it to others, without their consent express or implied; and on the whole, though with diffidence, concluded that Muirhead when admitted would be a member of the University only, and not of the College.

Soon after this the faculty, notwithstanding strong protests from nearly half their number, raised an action of declarator in the Court of Session. On 15th November, 1807, Lord Advocate Colquhoun was elected rector, which might have induced him to uphold by all legitimate means the credit and good order of the body over which he presided, and to avoid any action or inaction tending to exalt the faculty at the expense of the University. The opinion given by the three counsel originally consulted in favour of the crown's right to establish chairs, and of Muirhead's rights as a professor both of the University and the College, shows what his own better judgment was. Further, his position as chief law officer of the crown required that he should defend the royal prerogative, not as a personal right of the King, but as representing public control in the affairs of the University. Yet when the case came on for hearing, no appearance was made for the crown. On 17th November, 1808, the Second Division of the Court of Session repelled the objections regarding the seal, and found Muirhead entitled to be admitted professor of Natural History in the University, reserving the question of his right to be admitted a professor in the College as alleged to be distinct from the University.

On 12th December, 1808, Muirhead was at length admitted as regius professor of Natural History in the University. On 16th May, 1809, the Court further decided that Muirhead was entitled to sit and vote in meetings of the *comitia* and the Senate, but not to the patronage and patrimonial and other rights of the professors of the College then existing or their successors; or to sit or vote in meetings of the faculty, or to claim a house allotted to the existing professors; but that he was not debarred from claiming an increase of salary from the surplus funds of the University arising from the tack of the Archbishopric or otherwise. The Court pronounced no decision on the question of the custody of the museum, as Muirhead had abandoned all claim to be keeper, ordered that the expenses of the pursuers should be defrayed from the common funds of the College, and recommended that, with the sanction of the visitors, Muirhead's expenses should be defrayed from the same source. On the understanding that matters would be settled in this way, Muirhead agreed not to appeal. In 1812 Muirhead urged his claims on the faculty, and obtained an annuity of £40 from the College funds, the amount being increased to £75 three years later, Muirhead renouncing all claims competent to him against the College, and the faculty declaring that no successor should have any claim to this annuity. It will subsequently be seen that some of the ablest Scottish lawyers questioned the soundness of the decision, believing that it never could have been pronounced if a proper appearance had been made for the crown. The chairs afterwards founded, including Surgery, Midwifery, Chemistry, Botany, Materia Medica, Physiology, Forensic Medicine, and Engineering, were subject to the same disabilities as Natural History till a clause embodied in the Universities Act of 1858 on the motion of Mr. Dunlop, M.P. for Greenock, removed the unjust and invidious distinction.

At the opening of the 19th century the number of students in Arts was probably as great as the total number of students in the University had been a generation before. In 1826 the students in Arts numbered 631, and for the eleven years from 1826 to 1836 the average was 556. At the commencement of the century the session in Arts opened on 10th October and closed on 10th June. It was not, however, compulsory to be in attendance at the outset. The majority came in time to matriculate on 14th November, the day before the election of the rector, but students might delay entering till the public or Blackstone examinations, which began probably a full week or ten days later, and determined whether students were to be promoted to higher classes than those of the previous session. Students were examined in Latin before admission to the Greek class; in Greek before admission to the Logic class; and in Logic before admission to the class of the final year; and each student was deemed to belong officially to a particular class for each session of his course, though he might unofficially attend another. Towards the end of the session a list of magistrands entitled to be taken on trial for M.A. was made up, usually from the Natural Philosophy class, though the regulations left access to graduation open from either the Moral Philosophy or the Natural Philosophy class. The Blackstone examination was an oral one, conducted by the professor of the previous year, who was the more active examiner, and the professor whose class the student wished to enter. One by one students were called upon to seat themselves on the fateful Blackstone chair and undergo the ordeal, while the bedellus, who received a small fee for his attendance, stood behind and turned the sandglass measuring the time of the trial for each candidate.

Moderate as the standard of this examination probably was, it deterred numbers of students from entering certain classes or forced them to enter as private students, for the professors concerned were resolute in enforcing this test on all public students. In Young's time it was proposed that students destined for commercial pursuits should be excused from examination in Greek before admission to Logic, but Young objected to this as an interference with his rights as professor of Greek. It was felt to be a disadvantage to have so long an interval between the opening of the session and the time when the public examinations were held and the classes assumed their full and regular form ; and a remedy was applied, not by fixing the public examinations earlier, but by delaying the opening of the session till the first week in November. Before this change was made the session had been curtailed at the other end. Down to 1810 the other classes continued in session till 15th May, and the Humanity class for some time longer, while the distribution of University prizes and the appointment of lecturers and officials which marked the nominal close of the session took place on 10th June ; but in the spring of 1811 it was resolved to close the session on 1st May, and for about eighty years this arrangement lasted without material change.[1]

It had not been the practice to require attendance in Mathematics for the purpose of graduation, but in March, 1818, Meikleham, Mylne, and Millar, who had been appointed to consider the advisability of requiring it, submitted two alternative plans—either that all students should attend the Mathematics class for one session before entering the class of Natural Philosophy ; or that the rule should apply only to those who wished to graduate, and that other students should be admitted to the Natural Philosophy class on passing an examination in the elements of Plane Geometry, Trigonometry, and Algebra. The proposals seem to have been favourably received, but it is not clear that they were enacted into standing regulations. In November, 1821, Millar proposed that one session of Mathematics should be required for the degree of B.A., but in April following consideration was delayed till information was procured regarding the practice of other Universities. In 1818 Jardine proposed that the class

---

[1] A deed of the year 1733 regulating the Armagh bursaries required bursars to attend from 10th Oct. to 10th June, under penalty of a deduction being made from their stipends, and probably the session then lasted a little beyond the 10th of June. In 1763 it being found inconvenient to have the annual election of Dean on 26th June, which was stated to be some time after the rising of the College, the date of the election was changed to 10th June.

fees paid by students should be raised, and after consideration the faculty resolved that the fee for the gown classes in Arts and for Mathematics should be £3 3s., and for the Roman Law class £7 7s.

In November, 1826, a committee on improving the degree examinations gave in a scheme which, with some modifications, was ordered to be entered in the records, printed, and generally acted on. It set forth that students in the Ethics class who had passed through the junior classes might obtain the degree of B.A. on being examined in Languages, Logic, and Moral Philosophy; and students in the Physics class, or who had previously finished a course of Philosophy, should have access to the degree of M.A. on being examined in the same subjects, with the addition of Mathematics and Natural Philosophy. Provision was made for students graduating with honours in the three departments of Classics, Mental Philosophy, and Mathematics and Natural Philosophy, if they showed a distinguished degree of scholarship and talent in an examination on a more extended range of study in one or more of these departments, the other subjects being passed on the ordinary standard.

Two grades of honours were awarded—honourable distinction and highest distinction—according to the degree of excellence exhibited. The plan thus introduced at Glasgow in 1826 was adopted for all the Scottish Universities by the Commissioners under the Universities Act of 1858, but they explicitly required attendance on classes in all the subjects, added English Literature as a seventh subject in the curriculum, and introduced Natural Science as a fourth department in which honours might be taken. It would seem that before 1826 the practice of conducting the examinations for graduation in Arts in public had ceased, and the new regulations provided for the resumption of the ancient usage of examining publicly all candidates for the degrees of M.A. and B.A. The standard of examination, even for the ordinary degree, seems to have been more strict after this, fewer degrees were conferred, and the number of B.A.s bore a higher ratio to the number of M.A.s than formerly. In the ten years ending with 1826 the degree of B.A. was conferred on 22 students and the degree of M.A. on 278; while in the ten years ending with 1836 the degree of B.A. was conferred on 43 students and the degree of M.A. on 157.

Richardson died on 3rd November, 1814, and for the ensuing session the Humanity class was conducted by Andrew Alexander, M.A., afterwards professor of Greek in the University of St. Andrews. At the meeting in April, 1815, for election of a new professor of Humanity six voted for James Pillans, rector of the High School of Edinburgh, and six for Josiah Walker, collector of customs, Perth, and the principal gave his casting vote for the latter. Both candidates have a sort of connection with great names in literature, for Byron in the headlong wrath of the *English Bards and Scotch Reviewers* spoke of the first as 'paltry Pillans'; and the second, who was some time tutor in the family of the Duke of Athole, met Burns at Blair Castle, and afterwards produced a biography of the bard, in which, as Carlyle points out, he fails to understand his own and the world's relation to Burns, dealing with him in a patronising and apologetic way, as if the public might think it strange and scarcely warrantable that a gentleman and a scholar should take such notice of a rustic. Pillans was afterwards elected professor of Humanity at Edinburgh, and taught with ability and success from 1820 to 1863. Walker, who was fifty-four when transferred to the chair, had a numerous following of students and was soon obliged to divide his ordinary class into two sections, and for several of the later years of his tenure much of the teaching was done by assistants, including Mr. Milligan, afterwards minister of Elie, his own son Josiah, and Mr. Ramsay, who was elected professor after the death of Walker in 1831.

Young, though latterly enfeebled by age, continued as professor of Greek till his death on 18th November, 1820.[1] In April preceding he proposed for appointment as assistant and successor his son Charles, a young man of good promise as a scholar but of weak constitution, who had resigned the Snell Exhibition and sought health by a sojourn in the warm climate of France and Italy. Consideration of the proposal was delayed, and when the father died it was abandoned. During the vacancy in the chair the faculty, in May, 1821—taking into account that the number of students in Greek was very great and that most of them entered the class without previous acquaintance with the language, that more time should be given to their instruction, and that the professor should not be employed in teaching the grammar or rudiments, but should be free to devote his time to instruction in Greek classics and the higher branches—resolved to appoint a separate teacher of Elementary Greek to be remunerated by a fee of three guineas from each of his students. For the time and in the circumstances the plan seems to have been commendable, but it was disliked by Meikleham, Walker, Jeffray, and Freer, as well as by the principal, and three days before the election of the next professor the resolution to appoint a teacher of Elementary Greek was rescinded. On 25th September, 1821, Mr. Daniel Keyte Sandford, B.A., of Christ's Church, Oxford, was elected to the chair of Greek, three votes being given for Dr. Jackson, apparently the professor of Natural Philosophy at St. Andrews, who had previously taught that subject at Glasgow for Professor Brown.

[1] He died while taking a bath in the George Inn, Glasgow.

There was a sharp conflict between the faculty and the Commissioners of Visitation appointed in 1826 regarding extensive alterations which were being made on the house formerly occupied by Mylne of which Sandford had made choice. The Commissioners did not look very favourably on the faculty as an administrative body, and considered the latter had alienated much valuable property on very disadvantageous terms ; and in view of the feus recently granted of parts of the College garden and other College property, concluded that no further feuing should be allowed till arrangements had been made by some competent authority in regard to the administration and management of the College property. They accordingly issued an order prohibiting further feus, sales, or alienations. A committee of the Commissioners appointed to visit Glasgow observed the addition to Sandford's house in course of erection in the outer quadrangle, and disapproved of it as an encroachment on the quadrangle and inconsistent with the style of the rest of the building, and in October, 1827, they issued a prohibition against proceeding further with it till it should be inspected by Mr. Reid, the King's Architect for Scotland, and a report regarding its effect on the safety and amenity of the fabric obtained and considered. They further prohibited all additions to the College buildings or extra alterations upon them without the previous sanction of the ordinary visitors, the rector and dean, till regulations on the subject should be made.

On 12th October the faculty out of respect to the Commission resolved that work on the additions to Sandford's house should be suspended for three weeks, but declared they did not recognise any right or power on the part of the Commissioners to issue such orders and directions as they had sent. Upon this the Commissioners entirely approved of the course taken by their committee, and intimated that the alteration of the building must be stopped and not recommenced without authority from the Commission. The faculty then agreed not to proceed with the building to which exception had been taken till they should hear from the Commission.

Yet by 18th December, when they had obtained two plans from the King's Architect, and one from Mr. Hamilton, a Glasgow Architect, they came to a resolution. Considering that Sandford and others were put to expense and inconvenience, and that the interior of the unfinished building was exposed to injury from the weather, that one of the visitors was in London and the Commissioners not sitting, the faculty determined to proceed with Hamilton's plan, in the hope that, having shown their deference and respect for the Commissioners by complying with their wishes so far as circumstances rendered practicable, the Commissioners would not construe into any mark of disrespect their proceeding with a measure which the urgent necessities of the case would not allow them to defer. This called down a stern reproof from the Commissioners. In every particular the faculty had attempted to evade the resolution of the Commissioners.

The plan adopted did not profess to take down and reconstruct the building, though the order of the Commissioners plainly marked the necessity for these things being done, and was deliberately adopted so as to finish the building formerly commenced, with trifling and partial alterations. The directions given to Hamilton did not appear in the minutes, but the Commissioners believed that if he had been directed to prepare a plan for taking down and reconstructing the building he would not have prepared one for permanently finishing it. The Commissioners were therefore called upon to censure the faculty for their proceedings on 18th December and consequent measures, and did accordingly censure them. They again directly prohibited the faculty from proceeding further with the building, under warning that if the faculty did not comply the Commissioners would proceed to use the high visitatorial powers committed to them. The condition previously laid down regarding the intervention of the King's Architect, the character of the plan, and its approval by the rector and dean were reaffirmed. The faculty then resolved to stop all proceedings with regard to the buildings, to request the King's Architect to favour them with his presence and suggestions for carrying the wishes of the Commissioners into effect, and to send copies of that day's minutes to the Commissioners, the rector, and the dean. When the communications reached him the rector, Thomas Campbell, was so exhausted by care and watching on account of the dangerous illness of his wife, that he declared himself incapacitated from judging of the plan of the building; but the dean, Archibald Campbell of Blythswood, having given his approval, this was communicated to the Commissioners, who answered that the faculty had now fully complied with their wishes and were authorised to proceed with the buildings according to Reid's plan. The buildings were then finished but not the trouble, for, as will afterwards appear, the ordinary visitors disallowed part of the rather inflated expenditure incurred for the work.

Jardine was more than eighty years of age before he relinquished his chair. Near the end of his tenure he received a special compliment from Francis Jeffrey, who when delivering his rectorial address thus alluded to Jardine: 'I cannot resist congratulating myself and all this assembly that I still see beside me one surviving instructor of my early youth—the most revered, the most justly valued of all my instructors—the individual of whom I must be allowed to say here, what I have never omitted to say in every other place, that it is to him and his most judicious instructions that I owe my taste for letters and any little literary distinction I may since have been enabled to attain.' In 1822 Jardine was authorised to avail himself of the assistance of Mr. Robert Young in conducting the Logic class, probably the same person who conducted the Greek class for a session before the appointment of Sandford. In April, 1824, Jardine represented to the faculty that, having taught the Logic class for fifty years, he now found the work too great for him to discharge with comfort and utility. On 10th June following Robert Buchanan, minister of Peebles, was appointed assistant and successor, with a salary of £210 from the fees of students during the lifetime of Jardine, who retained the salary attached to the chair, as well as his house and seat in the faculty and Senate. Jardine died on 28th January, 1827, and Buchanan attained his full status as professor. On rare occasions the degree of M.A. was still conferred as an honorary distinction, and in April, 1828, it was so conferred on Buchanan, as well as on Mylne, the professor of Moral Philosophy.

Mylne had married a daughter of Millar, the professor of Law, and was therefore brother-in-law to Millar, the professor of Mathematics. In their views of public affairs they were friends of progress and rational liberty, and though in that respect they were by no means alone in the University, yet they were in the minority. In Scotland the end of the eighteenth century and the early years of the nineteenth were not favourable to men who held such views, and they were liable to fall under very unjust suspicions. Mylne, who acted as College chaplain for ten years from 1809, suffered in this way. He conducted services in the College chapel on Sunday, 26th March, 1815, immediately after news had reached Glasgow that Napoleon, after escaping from Elba, had arrived in Paris, and that the Bourbon king had fled. The minds of the townspeople had doubtless been fluttered by the news, and some of them put a strange and unwarrantable construction on portions of Mylne's services. The devotions began with reading four or five verses of the 107th Psalm, which were afterwards sung by the congregation, and this passage was so far from being specially selected for the occasion that it had been reached in the course of a regular progress through the Psalms. The verses express satisfaction at the fate of those who had been in a desert place, and had come from north, south, east and west, 'that they might to a city go wherein they might abide.' The sermon was founded on a text in the eleventh chapter of Acts, where Peter is represented as giving the other apostles an account of the first instance of a heathen admitted into the Christian Church, a prelude to the extension of the blessings and privileges of the Gospel to all heathen nations. In the closing part of the service

Mylne read the 5th to 8th verses of the 26th Paraphrase, directing the congregation to sing from the 6th to the 8th verses.   The 5th and 6th verses run : —

> ' Behold he comes ! your leader comes,
> With might and honour crown'd ;
> A witness who shall spread my name
> To earth's remotest bound.
> See ! nations hasten to his call
> From every distant shore ;
> Isles yet unknown shall bow to him,
> And Israel's God adore.'

It was stupid and perverse to think the preacher intended to apply such passages to Napoleon, and would have been ludicrous but for the serious consequences which followed to Mylne.   But some of the hearers perverted Mylne's meaning, and regarded him as exulting in the escape of Napoleon and his arrival as a leader in the capital of France.   Hints or charges of sedition were conveyed to Mr. Barclay, the Procurator-Fiscal. Barclay presented a petition to Sheriff-Substitute Hamilton, stating that he had received information that Mylne in the course of the chapel services introduced allusions to the recent overthrow of the legitimate Government of France with which the Government of this country was in a state of amity ; and that the opinions and allusions alleged to have been uttered tended to create impressions prejudicial to the prosperity and interests of the Government and inhabitants of this country ; in consequence of which the petitioner thought it his duty to apply for an enquiry into the circumstances, and particularly for a warrant to cite and precognosce witnesses.   The Sheriff and the Procurator-Fiscal conducted the enquiry on 30th and 31st March, making their first appearance in the College courts and questioning the servants, after which they examined Professors Young, Jardine, and Muirhead, and Mr. Alexander, then temporarily conducting the Humanity class, as well as some ladies belonging to the families of professors, while Mylne was examined in his own house and permitted to dictate his declaration.   Mylne asked by whose order or upon what information he had been subjected to precognition, but the Sheriff declined to answer, or to give a copy of Mylne's declaration in answer to the queries put to him.

The faculty agreed to transmit a copy of the substance of Mylne's declaration, reproduced as well as he could from memory, to Lord Advocate Colquhoun,[1] along with a letter expressing a hope that the matter would

---

[1] He became Lord Advocate in 1807 as Archibald Campbell of Clathic, but soon afterwards took the name of Colquhoun on succeeding to the estate of Killermont.   He

be thoroughly investigated, and that Colquhoun's friendship for the University and zeal for official duty would afford them facilities for bringing to light the authors of such foul and dangerous aspersions. The faculty also complained of the manner in which the enquiry had been carried out, which they regarded as inconsiderate and accompanied with needless publicity and scandal, leading to the affair becoming matter of talk in the city and unpleasantness from which a different mode of procedure might have relieved them. On 19th April at a meeting held by request of Mylne, the faculty examined Professors Young, Jardine, and Muirhead, and Mr. Alexander, who were present at the service complained of, and having heard their evidence, the faculty recorded their fullest conviction of the propriety of Mylne's conduct and the utter groundlessness of the charge that seemed to have been made against him. Colquhoun at first sent a letter conceived in an official frame of mind, pointing out that till the contrary was established, he must presume that the magistrate acted properly. But the law was open for protection and redress to those who were injured by any magistrate, as well as to any magistrate who was calumniated.

Some time later the Lord Advocate sent a further reply from London. After considering the precognitions and whole proceedings, he was of opinion that no crime had been committed by Mylne, and that no criminal intention could be justly imputed to him ; but he did not acquiesce in the censures on the Sheriff, who seemed to have done his duty to the public in a proper manner, and with every attention to the feelings and convenience of those examined. He regretted that circumstances proceeding from accident merely rendered a precognition necessary. Had there been a violation of law within the walls of the College, in a place of public worship where the young and inexperienced formed part of the audience, that would have been an additional reason with him for making it the subject of public prosecution. The Duke of Montrose, to whom as Chancellor papers regarding the case were sent, regretted the circumstances that had arisen out of a misunderstanding of Mylne's intentions and object as declared by himself, which could not be doubted by any ingenuous mind having regard to the honour and feelings of a person of Mylne's consideration and station in life. The majority of the faculty thought the opinion of counsel should be taken as to further measures, but as some members were averse to further proceedings, Mylne declined the offer.

James Millar, professor of Mathematics, besides teaching his own

---

was an alumnus of the University, and rector from 1807 to 1809, when his supineness in regard to the Muirhead case was remarkable. He did better for the University by helping to procure a building grant of £2,500 in 1810.

subject and endeavouring to secure its inclusion as a necessary part of the curriculum in Arts, was more than once authorised to lecture on English Law, and from 1815 to 1820 he acted as Clerk of faculty. In 1819 Millar obtained a loan of £2,000 from the faculty on the security of seven shares of the Great Canal Stock and his own personal security and that of several friends. In October, 1829, Millar, who had fallen into ill health, recommended Mr. William Ramsay as his assistant, and in December, 1830, proposed that Ramsay, who had conducted the classes with ability and success in the preceding session, should be appointed as his assistant and successor. But the faculty were less inclined than formerly to appoint assistants and successors, and from one cause or another there was more than the usual amount of higgling over the arrangements for Millar's retirement. On 10th December, 1830, Millar sent a further letter withdrawing his proposal for an assistant and successor, and offering to resign his chair on being allowed to retain his salary and house, but on 23rd December it was carried by the casting vote of the principal to accept the resignation on Millar's engaging to quit his College house at Martinmas following. Arrangements for resignation were not completed at this time, and as Mr. Ramsay became professor of Humanity on 2nd November, 1831, upon Millar's recommendation, Dr. William Brown of Edinburgh, was appointed to teach the Mathematics classes for the ensuing session. By 25th November, 1831, it was agreed that Millar should resign, retaining his salary but not his house, and on 16th December the faculty elected Dr. James Thomson, professor of Mathematics in the Belfast Institution, to the chair of Mathematics at Glasgow.

Meikleham, who became professor of Natural Philosophy in 1803, by and by grew tired of the arrangement under which £100 was withdrawn from his emoluments to make up part of the annuity allowed to the inert Dr. Brown, and in June, 1812, proposed that after 1st November, 1813, he should be relieved from this burden, and that the whole annuity of £165 should be taken from the College funds. This proposal was carried by a majority. Meikleham was elected clerk of faculty in 1829 and 1830.

After Meikleham's transfer to Natural Philosophy, the King in August, 1803, appointed the Rev. James Couper, minister of Baldernock, to be professor of Practical Astronomy and Observer in the University. Findlay recalled the resolution adopted in 1797, when Mylne was elected professor of Moral Philosophy on condition that he was not to be admitted till he had resigned his charge as one of the ministers of Paisley and the resignation had been accepted. Findlay therefore, with the concurrence of Jardine and Mylne, dissented from appointing a day for the admission of Couper till he had resigned his pastoral charge at Baldernock, but the majority judged otherwise, and he was admitted on 24th October, 1803. In a very short time Couper retired from the ministry at Baldernock, but he taught no class in Astronomy except for a few years at the beginning, and by and by he gave up observing too. It was alleged that the smoke of the town rendered observing impracticable, and St. John's Church, built about 1819, obstructed the view.

A new Observatory was erected at Garnethill by the Glasgow Society for Promoting Astronomical Science, a body founded in 1808. This Observatory had a good equipment but inadequate funds, and towards the end of 1812 the Directors offered to sell it to the faculty. The proposal had the support of Couper, Meikleham, Mylne, and Jardine, and at first seemed likely to command general approval, but after enquiry and consideration the faculty, in view of the large expenditure recently incurred for new buildings, decided not to purchase. Further efforts were made in 1819 and 1821 to induce the faculty to purchase, but they were unavailing, and the Garnethill Observatory seems to have come to an end. In 1809, Couper's son James was appointed keeper of the Hunterian Museum, and the father was requested to take charge till the son's admission, and to assist him in making himself acquainted with the collection. There is little trace of the son's official doings, and probably the father continued as keeper from this time. In 1820 Couper suggested that his son William, an M.A. of Glasgow of 1811, and M.D. of 1816, should be appointed joint keeper along with him. The suggestion was adopted by and by, if not at once, and in 1830 a salary of £70 was assigned to Dr. William Couper as joint keeper.

After the death of John Millar, the King issued a presentation to Robert Davidson, Advocate, son of Principal Davidson, appointing him to the sole profession of Civil Law in the University, and he was admitted in August, 1801. Davidson began with teaching the Institutes, but in 1802 he stated to the faculty that a number of lawyers in Glasgow had represented to him the importance of a course in Scots Law for young men preparing for the legal profession. He suggested that a daily course of Scots Law should be given in 1803-04, in which session he would also read and explain the Pandects to such students as might apply, and that a course of lectures on the Pandects should be postponed till session 1804-05. It seems to have been two or three years later before the Scots Law class was begun, but at once it became the leading subject, as it afterwards continued to be till towards the end of his tenure, when the attendance fell off somewhat. Davidson had an average following of about thirty-five students each session. There is evidence of a demand

z

in the legal profession for teaching in Conveyancing, which Davidson did not expound at length, for in 1817 Mr. James Galloway, Writer in Glasgow, began to lecture on that subject under the patronage of the Faculty of Procurators.

For a number of years in the earlier part of his time Davidson was much engaged in conducting College business relating to teinds and other legal matters.   He was an officer in the volunteer forces raised early in the century when the country was under apprehension of an invasion by Napoleon ; and in November, 1802, the faculty desired the principal to give a note to Captain Davidson's servant, who was about to procure some articles of provisions, stating that they were being brought to his house within the College, and were therefore not liable to town dues, from which the faculty were resolved to assert their exemption.   As no more is said on the subject, probably the note had the desired effect.   On 22nd April, 1828, the Senate in an unusually beneficent mood towards professors conferred the degree of LL.B. on Davidson, the degree of M.D. on Burns, the professor of Surgery, and the honorary degree of M.A. on Professors Mylne and Buchanan.

Findlay, the venerable professor of Divinity, had evolved a course of prelections of portentous range and elaborate execution, embodying great stores of learning, but less interesting and useful to his students than if it had been prepared with judicious selection and condensation.   He died on 15th June, 1814, at the age of ninety-three.   Cumin, the professor of Oriental Languages, was appointed in 1761, and had shown signs of failing health before the Rev. Gavin Gibb was appointed his assistant and successor on 21st September, 1814, while Hugh Macleod, professor of Ecclesiastical History, who died in 1809, had M'Turk for assistant and successor from 1797.   It is tolerably evident that for some years in the early part of the 19th century the faculty of Divinity must have been influenced by the age and infirmity of its professors.   On 8th September, the Rev. Stevenson Macgill was elected by a large majority to succeed Findlay as professor of Divinity.   The son of a shipbuilder of Port-Glasgow, young Macgill came early to the University, and in 1781 became an M.A. of Glasgow at the age of sixteen.   He then took a leisurely course in Divinity, acting from time to time as tutor in several families, one of which was that of the Hon. Henry Erskine.   Licensed by the Presbytery of Paisley in 1790, he was next year appointed minister of Eastwood, and in 1797 was translated to the Tron Church, Glasgow. He was an active and kindly minister, giving close attention to the affairs of his own congregation and of the city, and taking an interest in the improvement of prisons, the extension of education, and other measures

for social amelioration.   In 1800 he instituted a Clerical Literary Society
among the ministers of Glasgow and the neighbourhood, which was carried
on for a considerable time with beneficial results.   He published *Thoughts
on Prisons*, and in 1809 *Considerations Addressed to a Young Clergyman*,
a work much commended by Zachary Macaulay, father of the historian.

Macgill took an energetic part in the church courts against pluralities,
and advocated a change of the law of patronage by which the appointment
of ministers would have been committed to a body of delegates chosen
by the heritors, the elders, and the heads of families who were communi-
cants and had resided four or five years in the parish.   Though hardly one
of the ecclesiastical leaders, he was heard with attention and respect in the
church courts, and was Moderator of the General Assembly in 1828.   He
was not pleased with the arrangements made regarding the College chapel,
which had come to be very poorly attended, and in 1824 declined to preside
at the dispensation of the sacrament.

The faculty agreed that its members should dine together on 9th
November, 1810, as a testimony of respect to their worthy colleague
Dr. Cumin, who then entered on the 50th year of his professorship of
Oriental Languages.   But Cumin's age brought ills as well as honours.
More than a dozen years before this time he applied unsuccessfully for the
appointment of an assistant and successor.   In November, 1813, having
become very frail, he represented that he needed an assistant to teach the
Hebrew class for the session, and the faculty allowed him to employ Dr.
Couper for that purpose, on condition that Couper should receive no
remuneration from them.   Efforts were being made to secure the appointment of Gavin Gibb, minister of St. Andrew's Church, Glasgow, an M.A.
of 1783, and D.D. of 1804, who had several times been dean of faculty,
as assistant and successor to Cumin, Gibb retaining for the present at least
his ministerial charge.   The opposition of Jardine was feared, and he was
unwilling to compromise even for a limited time the objection he had long
maintained to pluralities.   Richardson pleaded with Jardine and urged
that it would be inconvenient for Gibb to resign his ministerial charge
while Cumin lived, and that some provision might have to be made for
Cumin's family at his death.   Gibb agreed that as soon as he was reim-
bursed for this arrangement, he would resign his ministry, and upon this
Jardine acquiesced in the proposal, and Gibb was appointed assistant and
successor to Cumin on 21st September, 1814.   Cumin died on 27th
October, 1820, and Gibb attained the full status of a professor.

Some months afterwards Jardine asked him to name a time within
which he would resign his ministry in accordance with the undertaking
formerly given, but Gibb refused and had recourse to somewhat disin-

genuous arguments. Jardine moved that Gibb should be called upon by the faculty to say whether he intended to resign his ministry and, if so, at what time ; but it was carried not to take up the motion, as it related to transactions with which the faculty were not acquainted at the time and were therefore not concerned. Gibb was appointed vice-rector by Thomas Campbell in 1827, and in the rectorial election of next year the votes of the 'nations' being equally divided between Scott and Campbell, Gibb gave his casting vote for the former ; but Scott had a keener sense of honour than most candidates in like circumstances, and declined to accept an office which came to him by the casting vote of Gavin Gibb. By 1828 Gibb had fallen into indifferent health, and in November of that year he was allowed to employ Josiah Walker, son of the professor of the same name, as assistant for the coming session. Professor Gibb died on 9th June, 1831.

M'Turk taught Ecclesiastical History for the whole period included in this chapter, though he did not reach the full status of a professor till the death of Hugh Macleod on 22nd May, 1809. His course in Ecclesiastical History extended over three sessions, but as he delivered only two lectures a week,[1] his pace was leisurely. From 1797 to 1802 he also taught a class in Civil History, which seems to have been discontinued for lack of students. For ten years from the opening of the century he was College chaplain, for some time he was clerk of faculty, and in 1814 he was appointed vice-rector by Thomas Graham, Lord Lynedoch.

Among those on whom the degree of D.D. was conferred were Francis Hutcheson, rector of Donaghadee, grandson of the distinguished professor of Moral Philosophy ; Claudius Buchanan, Vice-President of the College of Fort-William, Calcutta ; Thomas Chalmers, then one of the ministers of Glasgow ; and Samuel Hanna, Presbyterian minister at Belfast, and some time Professor of Divinity to the Synod of Ulster. The two last came to be closely related by family ties, for Hanna's son William, who, like his father, was a graduate in Arts of Glasgow, married the daughter of Chalmers, and became his biographer. Chalmers succeeded Stevenson Macgill as minister of the Tron Church, and in 1819 was transferred to the new parish of St. John's, formed to enable him to make a great philanthropic experiment as to what could be accomplished for the improvement and elevation of the poor and neglected part of the population. The Church stood on ground feued from the College. The building and equipment of schools was one of the means on which Chalmers relied in his efforts for the social, moral, and religious amelioration of the masses,

---

[1] This appears from the Report of the Commission of 1830, but in his later years he seems to have given three lectures a week.

and the site for the first school connected with St. John's was procured from the faculty of the College. It is recorded that on 17th February, 1820, the faculty considered a letter from Mr. Montgomerie regarding a steading of ground, sixty-four feet square, on the east side of Macfarlane Street, for building schools for St. John's parish, approved of the benevolent design, and to encourage such good work agreed to accept three hundred guineas as the price, though much below what the steading might be sold for, but on the understanding that if the building on that site ceased to be used as a school and was applied to any other purpose an annual ground-rent of £7 should be charged.

In 1804 Claudius Buchanan wrote from Calcutta, recalling in friendly terms the days when he studied under Richardson, Young, and Jardine, and conveying an offer of prizes designed to quicken public interest in the extension of civilisation and Christianity in the East. Of these, a prize of £100 for a dissertation *On the best Means of Civilising the Subjects of the British Empire in India and Diffusing Christianity* was gained next year by John Mitchell, M.A., minister of the Relief Church, Anderston, afterwards professor of Biblical Literature to the Associate Synod; and a prize of £25 for a Latin ode or poem on *Collegium Bengalense*, by Alexander Macarthur, a student whose name frequently appears in the prize lists of his time. A year or two later the faculty gave their warm approval to Buchanan's design for translating the Scriptures into the eastern languages, and agreed to contribute thirty guineas in aid of the expense.

The fee for the degree of Doctor of Divinity was raised to £20 in 1806, and it was resolved that it should not be conferred without payment, except on clergymen of eminence and in peculiar circumstances, of which the Senate were to judge. In 1807 the Senate appointed that one half of the fee should be divided equally among the professors in the faculty of Theology.

A building for the reception of William Hunter's Museum was in course of erection from 1804 to 1807, but by this time there was great pressure on the accommodation in most departments, and a proposal made in 1806 for the enlargement of the Common Hall and some other parts of the buildings soon developed into a scheme for erecting a new Common Hall and a number of new classrooms, and for improving several of the old classrooms. Plans and specifications were obtained from Mr. Nicholson, but some years later when the building was actually executed, the work was superintended by John Brash, architect, who supplied further plans. In January, 1809, the faculty adopted a memorial to the Government, setting forth that during the past thirty years students had been becoming more and more numerous, owing chiefly to the increase of wealth and population in the West of Scotland consequent on the extension of commerce and manufactures, but partly to the establishment of the Royal Infirmary and the Hunterian Museum. The classrooms had been enlarged as far as practicable, but were still too small, and classes which were too numerous for the rooms normally assigned to them had to be taught elsewhere. Humanity had been taught in the Common Hall for four years, Materia Medica was taught in the Latin Classroom, Logic in the Divinity Hall, while one section of the Greek class was taught in the Divinity Hall, and the other had to be divided into two portions meeting at separate hours. These expedients could hardly be carried on longer, and other classes, especially Chemistry and Anatomy, were crowded and could not be transferred. The Common Hall, in which the gowned students met at stated times, was becoming inadequate, and if the increase of students continued, the meetings would have to be suspended. The faculty thought there was no other way but to pull down most of the existing classrooms, which were old and small, and to rebuild them on a more commodious scale. Though the funds of the College were managed with thrift, the income had of late been somewhat less than the expenditure, but it was expected that there would soon be an annual surplus owing to a rise in the produce of teinds. The faculty concluded by requesting the Government to grant a loan of £8,000 or £10,000 without interest, the memorialists giving security and undertaking to repay.

The memorial was forwarded to the chancellor (the Duke of Montrose), and the rector (Lord Advocate Colquhoun), and shortly afterwards the latter suggested that application should be made to the Lords of the Treasury for a grant in aid of erecting the buildings, and hinted that, on a proper application by the chancellor and rector a grant of £2,000 might probably be obtained. Upon this hint the faculty sent a memorial to the Treasury through Montrose and Colquhoun, and a grant of £2,500 was procured. It was also resolved to appropriate a sum of £1,300 from the funds of the Forfar bursaries to help in defraying the cost, as the deed regulating the foundation empowered the administrators to determine the application of surplus funds, and the invested capital was then more than double the amount required to produce an income sufficient for bursary purposes. The new buildings, completed early in 1813, were placed on the site of the previous Common Hall and its neighbourhood, and included a handsome new Common Hall, and seven large new classrooms, appropriated to Latin, Greek, Mathematics, Logic, Chemistry, Medicine and Anatomy, including dissecting rooms; extensive improvements being also made on the classrooms of Ethics, Materia Medica, and Law. The total outlay amounted to £10,054. A great improvement on the buildings was thus effected, but it was not long before some of the departments began to outgrow the new accommodation provided for them. In 1824 additional buildings, in large part intended to accommodate Surgery, were ordered at a cost of £1,436. In 1830 and 1831 new buildings for Chemistry were erected in Shuttle Street at a cost of more than £3,500. The College Botanic Garden was feued in 1813 and 1814, having apparently been disused for teaching purposes some years earlier, and in 1817 the faculty agreed to subscribe £2,000 to the Royal Botanic Institution, whose Gardens were opened a year or two later at Sauchiehall Road. The abortive negotiations for taking over the Garnethill Observatory have already been mentioned.

The faculty sometimes gave considerable donations and subscriptions for civic, national, or benevolent purposes. In 1803 they contributed £365 in aid of local forces levied to withstand invasion, in 1805 gave £400 to a scheme for supplying the city and its environs with water, and in 1817 subscribed £200 to the Gas Light Company, gas lighting being then newly introduced. Two years later a sum of £100 was advanced to aid in making a road from Duke Street to join the Shettleston Road, and in 1826 £50 for improvements in Duke Street. In 1800 and 1801 a soup kitchen was maintained within the College for the benefit of the neighbouring poor, and in 1820 and again in 1826 the faculty subscribed £100 for the relief of the unemployed in Glasgow. A subscription of £105 was given in 1824 towards the erection of a monument to James Watt ; and next year the faculty granted an annuity of £50 to the widow of Dr. Irvine who began to lecture on Materia Medica sixty years before.

Early in 1802 the faculty consulted Mr. Foss, an attorney in London who sometimes did business for them, regarding the estate of Robert Hamilton, a merchant, described as of Canton, China, though he must have traded in India also. Hamilton died nearly three years before, leaving to the College the reversion to a considerable part of his property, but as yet there had been no direct communication from his trustees. In June a copy of Hamilton's will was received, and in August the faculty considered a letter from his trustees. Mr. Hamilton had conferred a liferent interest in his estate, after payment of certain legacies, on his sister Mary, wife of Thomas Cochrane, M.D. ; and as Mr. Reid, Hamilton's partner, relinquished claims amounting to £2,263 which he might have put forward, and recommended that a sum of £1,414 should be handed to Mrs. Cochrane, the faculty, in testimony of their gratitude and of their kind remembrance of the connection of Mrs. Cochrane's family with the College, authorised the executors to make this payment. There was trouble in dealing with one of the executors who owed £1,400 or £1,500 to Hamilton's estate, but, with the concurrence of Dr. and Mrs. Cochrane, it was agreed that Mr. Foss should take the opinion of eminent counsel and be guided by it, and accordingly the opinion of Sir Samuel Romilly was obtained.   On 11th February, 1823, it was announced that Mrs. Cochrane was dead, and towards the end of next year payment of the residue of Hamilton's estate was made, the College receiving a sum of £11,000 from the bequest.   In 1803 Freer was authorised to purchase a painting of Hamilton at a price not exceeding thirty guineas, and in 1810 Dr. Cochrane proposed that some memorial of him should be placed on the new buildings about to be erected.   The uncertainty of the amount and time of payment of the bequest probably hindered the placing of a memorial at that time, and it is to be regretted that so little is now remembered of a notable benefactor.

The faculty, having previously had before them a proposal for the sale of the patronage of Govan, on 11th April, 1820, in view of the increasing expenses of the College, the straitened state of the funds, and their diminution by the recent augmentation of ministers' stipends, especially the great augmentation of nearly £200 a year granted to the minister of Govan, agreed to accept an offer of £2,100 made for it by Thomas Leishman, grain dealer, Paisley.   The principal, Macgill, Meikleham, and Walker being strongly opposed to the measure, insisted that it should be submitted to the rector and dean as visitors of the College.   They gave in reasons of protest, setting forth that they considered the patronage a sacred trust for the benefit of the community, not as a subject to be bought and sold to the highest bidder without considering the interests of the parish. They regarded such a mode of sale as contrary to the spirit of our ecclesiastical constitution during a vacancy of the parish or the indisposition of the incumbent, when a price far beyond the natural value was offered, and when the purchaser's motive was to secure the living for his son.   The patronage proposed to be sold was acquired as a gift from the Crown, and was bestowed for public purposes and for the good of the parish, from the lands of which the College had long derived benefit.   It was agreed that papers should be drawn up setting forth the views of the majority and of the minority, and that the opinion of Mr. Cranstoun as counsel should be taken whether it was competent to proceed with the sale.   Meantime Leishman was pressing for the completion of the conveyance, but the faculty, in view of the appeal to the visitors, delayed further action, and early in May Mr. Pollock, the minister of Govan, died. On 29th August the faculty called on the visitors to name a time for hearing and deciding the case, and on 10th October it was intimated that

FRANCIS JEFFREY

Literary Critic.   Rector of the University, 1820-1822

BORN 1773.   DIED 1850

By Sir Henry Raeburn, R.A.

In the collection of the Rt. Hon. the Earl of Rosebery, K.G., K.T.

the rector, Kirkman Finlay, and the dean, Archibald Campbell, had declared against proceeding with the sale.

At a later meeting Jardine gave in a paper explaining and defending the views of the majority regarding the sale. The teinds of Govan, with the exception of three chalders assigned to the principal for officiating as minister, were by the charter of James VI. in 1577 appropriated to the increase of the College revenue, and the proposed sale of the patronage was directed to the same object. After the principal ceased to be minister, the patronage was granted to the College by Charles I., not as a sacred trust, as the minority alleged, but apparently as a means of occasionally rewarding young men who had discharged the laborious duties of regent, of whom Hugh Binning was mentioned as an example. The faculty did not regard it as a sacred trust, for about 1771 they sold the patronage of Gorbals which was a pendicle of Govan. King's College, Aberdeen, about twenty years before sold the patronage of at least seven churches bestowed on them by the crown, and the faculty never heard that any disastrous consequences such as were now predicted to religion followed. The faculty were advised by counsel of the first respectability to proceed, in conjunction with the rector and dean, to complete the sale, but for the peace of the society they agreed to refer the matter to the visitors. They regretted the stoppage of a measure which would have prevented dissensions among themselves in making appointments, and which the state of the funds rendered necessary.

The filling up of the vacancy in the parish of Govan led to a keen debate in the faculty, whose members deliberated at great length on the subject on 20th October, 1820. Four days later, the roll being called and the votes marked, Matthew Leishman, Preacher of the Gospel, Paisley, was by a considerable majority chosen as presentee. The case ended well for the Leishmans, as the son secured the parish and the father retained the £2,100 which he had offered for the patronage.

In 1803 the faculty resumed the process of augmentations, and resolved to add £50 a year to the salary of the principal and each professor, and £25 to the salary of the lecturer on Materia Medica, and the visitors gave their approval, declaring, however, that an augmentation of salaries must not be considered a matter of course every time the College funds could afford it. Again in 1814 it was resolved to make a further augmentation of £50, this time as a temporary expedient, on which footing it was continued for a year or two. In 1817 this augmentation was, with the consent of the visitors, made permanent, after the faculty had received a report from a committee of investigation, showing that there was a surplus revenue of between £200 and £300 a year, that an addition of

£200 a year would in future be received from ground recently feued, that in a year or two £300 more would be obtained from the tithes of Kilbride, that by the founding of a professorship of Midwifery £50 a year from the Waltonian funds, hitherto given as salary to a lecturer, would revert to the faculty, that a capital sum of £1,200 would be received from the sale of Craigrossie in Perthshire, and that about £725 of chamber funds might be merged in the general College funds, as the object for which a separate chamber fund was established had ceased. It was only the faculty or College professors who received these augmentations, and in 1817 there were several University professors outside the faculty who received no benefit. In the thirty years from 1784 to 1814 the principal and thirteen faculty professors voted additions to the salaries of themselves amounting to a yearly sum of £3,080, while they also differed from University professors in each possessing a College house.

In 1825 the annual income of the College, managed by the principal and thirteen faculty professors, after deducting public and parochial burdens and payments from teinds for ministers stipends, amounted to £7,726 12s. 10d.,[1] in 1835 to £7,388 19s., and in 1848 to fully £8,000. The annual revenue managed by the Senate (i.e. the principal and all the professors in the University, with the rector and dean of faculty) might, after the grant of £707 was obtained from the Treasury as compensation for loss of Stationers' Hall privileges, be estimated at from £2,000 to £2,500. It included a small amount from funds invested for the library, dues for the library exacted from students amounting to fully £200, a fee of £10 10s. from each candidate who graduated as M.D. (£2 of which went to the library and the rest to the professors who examined), and a fee of £10 10s. from each candidate who graduated as C.M. (divided among the professors who examined)—these two sets of graduation fees producing on the average from £900 to £1,050 yearly, though latterly the C.M. fees fell off somewhat. For the eleven years from 1825 to 1835 the expenditure on general repairs and improvements amounted to £5,833 4s. 8½d.; while the expenditure on repairs and improvements on professors' houses amounted to £4,009 1s. 8d., or, if we add an average of fully £209 paid by the faculty for taxes and water rates on the houses occupied by its fourteen members, to £6,308.

For more than a century and a quarter the University had been greatly aided by the lease of the Archbishopric of Glasgow, first granted by King William towards the end of the seventeenth century, and renewed with

---

[1] This is exclusive of the amount annually collected as class fees by the various professors in the University from their students, which would probably amount to between £6000 and £7000.

unfailing regularity by later sovereigns.   But the lease granted in 1805 was destined to be the last of the beneficent series.   When it was nearing its expiry a petition was sent in April, 1824, to the Lords of the Treasury for its renewal, and was by them referred to the Barons of the Exchequer in Edinburgh for report.   The Barons requested a return giving a complete and accurate rental of the Archbishopric certified by the principal and the factor, showing the lands from which the revenues came, the names of the feuars or vassals, and the sums of money and quantities of each kind of corn which they contributed.   Probably the Government already contemplated refusing a renewal of the lease, and called for this information that they might more easily collect the revenue when they took the management into their own hands.   Further returns were asked regarding the surplus revenue of the College, and the salaries, fees, and emoluments from all sources received by the professors.

Early in 1826 the faculty learned that a minute unfavourable to their petition was to be submitted to the Lords of the Treasury, upon which the principal and M'Turk were sent to London and had interviews with Mr. Herries, Secretary to the Treasury, and other official gentlemen, but after ample discussion the Lords of the Treasury persisted in their refusal of a new lease, pleading that it had been resolved to bring the whole hereditary revenues of the crown under a uniform system of management. They agreed, however, to recommend the King to make for fourteen years a grant equivalent to the average annual profits under the lease.   The grant, dated 7th August, 1826, set forth that George IV., not being disposed to renew the lease of the Archbishopric or to withdraw from the College the advantage it had so long enjoyed, made an annual allowance for fourteen years from Whitsunday, 1825, of £800 from the crown revenues in Scotland, which was computed by the Barons of the Exchequer to be an equivalent to the profits derived from the lease.   Orders were also issued for payment to the professors and other beneficiaries of the salaries and allowances outside of the lease granted to them by King William and succeeding sovereigns, excepting that the £100 granted in December, 1713, to supply deficiency in revenue or pay off debt, was in future to be paid to the professor of Botany as part of his salary, and not to the College.

In 1803, when Napoleon threatened to invade the country, the faculty on 10th June agreed to guarantee a sum of £50 to a fund for securing from loss the officers of volunteer forces about to be raised, in case the Government allowance proved inadequate.   In October following the principal informed the faculty of a subscription then in progress in the city for clothing volunteers and other purposes connected with national defence, and the faculty unanimously resolved to contribute £315. On 12th August, a number of students desirous of being drilled in the College Gardens and instructed in the use of arms laid their proposal before the faculty, and were allowed the use of the gardens. A few days later the students proposed that they should be formed into a volunteer corps for service in any part of Great Britain, in case of actual invasion or of the appearance of the enemy upon the coast, and requested the faculty to place the offer before the Government, in order that the corps might be furnished with arms, accoutrements, drill sergeants, drummers, and fifers, unless the faculty would defray these expenses, the applicants furnishing their own uniforms. It was suggested that the faculty should name members of their own body as officers. The faculty, while commending the zeal and spirit of the students, believed it was necessary to have two companies of sixty men each to form a corps such as the Government would accept, and it being then vacation time, agreed to present the offer to the Government as soon as sixty had enrolled, and to keep the list open till the number of a hundred and twenty was made up from students, members of the University, and others who had been students within a period of five years. The faculty promised to defray the expense of arms and accoutrements for a hundred and twenty out of their own funds or by subscription, and to apply to the Government for drill sergeants, drummers, and fifers. They also agreed to recommend officers as soon as the offer was accepted by the Government, and to take the needful steps to have the corps drilled and exercised. All ranks and grades from the student to the chancellor appeared in arms, the Duke of Montrose being then stationed in Glasgow along with his regiment.

On 7th August, 1822, the Senate adopted an address for presentation to George IV. on the occasion of his visit to Edinburgh. No reigning sovereign had appeared in Scotland since the time of Charles II., and George IV., though a monarch of slender merit, was received with tumultuous applause. The principal and Professors Macgill, Walker, Jardine, and Jeffray were appointed a committee to wait upon the Duke of Montrose at Edinburgh, apparently with a view to presenting the address ; but probably all or nearly all the professors went to see the royal pageantry. A number of College servants were required to attend them, and were provided with scarlet uniforms for the occasion. In November, 1822, the faculty ordered payment to Mr. Leith of an account for £188 13s. 10d. 'for furnishing carriages, etc., at Edinburgh on the occasion of the King's visit' ; and to Professor Walker, who was vice-rector at the time, of a sum of £34 9s. for expenses at Edinburgh of himself and others. The charge for carriages appears to show that the University company were very fond of driving, unless we are to attach a good deal of significance to the phrase 'etc.' The faculty also agreed to contribute their share along with the other Universities of the sum required to purchase a piece of plate to be presented to the Rev. Dr. Lee, in recognition of his obliging attention in accommodating their members with a place 'at the procession of His Majesty on the occasion of his late visit to Scotland.'

In May, 1813, Richardson and Young proposed that application should be made to Parliament for an Act conferring upon the senate the power of electing the rector, and as a preliminary step a committee was appointed to draw up a memorial to be laid before the chancellor and rector. It does not appear whether further measures were taken at that time, but in December, 1819, the senate and the faculty adopted a petition to the House of Commons asking among other things for a change in the mode of electing the rector, and probably the new method desired had been similar to that proposed in 1813. Jeffray and Millar dissented, and it seems other circumstances of discouragement had arisen, for in February, 1820, a meeting of senate called to consider the application to Parliament agreed to delay further proceedings.

Kirkman Finlay, who had been Member of Parliament for Glasgow, Dumbarton, Renfrew, and Rutherglen from 1812 to 1818, was chosen rector in November, 1819. It was then the almost invariable practice to re-elect the rector at the end of his first year, but before that time arrived in Finlay's case the students had discovered something of the proposal to deprive them of their right to take part in the election, and rightly or wrongly came to believe that Finlay favoured the proposal. They were indignant against Finlay, brought forward Francis Jeffrey as their candidate, overcame the strenuous and united exertions of the professors, and returned Jeffrey triumphantly. Two days after the election the senate recorded their high respect for Finlay, and requested the principal to assure him of their regard, and return thanks for the great attention which as Member of Parliament he paid to the interests of the University and of education generally. They further recorded that, from disinterested attachment and a sense of what was due to his public character and services, members of Senate had unanimously voted for his re-election.

On the election day the students formed a procession through the streets to the house of the late rector, and there made some kind of hostile demonstration. The precise nature of their offence is not stated, though it is probable that if they had gone much beyond the limits of what was orderly and constitutional something specific would have been recorded. However, the professors having lost the election, were very severe on the students, and required a number of them to read an apology in their own name and as representing the rest. Previous rectors had usually been installed with little oratory, except perhaps a few words of formal acknowledgment and thanks, but Jeffrey introduced the custom of giving a full-length address on some topic of interest to the students, delivered as eloquently as the rector may. In the course of his first installation speech he exerted himself to allay the excitement that had prevailed, to restore good feeling between the students and their instructors, and to persuade the former that their suspicions against his excellent friend Mr. Finlay had proceeded in a great degree if not altogether from misapprehension.

In 1822 the votes of the 'nations' were equally divided between Sir Walter Scott and Sir James Mackintosh, the latter obtaining a great majority of the votes of individual students. Jeffrey gave his casting vote for Mackintosh, who, after holding office for two years was himself called upon to give a casting vote. At the election of 1824 Glottiana and Loudoniana voted for Brougham, and Rothseiana and Transforthana for Scott, a very few votes being recorded for a third candidate—Mackenzie, 'the man of feeling.' The principal was directed to inform Mackintosh that the 'nations' were equally divided between Scott and Brougham, and that in such a case the statutes gave the casting vote to the former rector, or, failing him, to the immediately preceding rector; and to ask when it would be convenient for him to attend the meeting of *comitia* to give his casting vote. Mackintosh pointed out that he did not see why the words of the statute should not be satisfied by an authentic and formal declaration of his vote given in writing.

The senate replied asserting their belief that according to the principles of public law every vote in an election must be given by the voter personally, unless in cases excepted by special statutes or inveterate usage, and that the rule applied equally to the deliberative and casting vote. They did not know any precedent directly in point, as on all former occasions the rector or vice-rector had been present to preside in the election meeting and to give a casting vote if required. During last year Mackintosh had not been admitted to office and consequently did not appoint a vice-rector. The senate thought that after the necessity of his presence had been notified to the former rector, his absence might be regarded as 'failure' in the sense of the statute. Accepting a vote in writing might open the door to progressive and injurious innovations; and if a rector whose election depended on such a vote afterwards took part in any University business carried by a bare majority, there could be little doubt his vote would be questioned and the University exposed to keen and protracted litigation. If they had failed to satisfy Mackintosh they offered to take the opinion of eminent counsel on the question at issue, the names of Mr. Cranstoun and Mr. Hope being suggested. Mackintosh replied that, after the Senate had reconsidered the subject, he would not discuss it further or desire any other opinion. On 4th April, 1825, Mackintosh attended a meeting of the *comitia* and gave his casting vote for Brougham, who two days later delivered an address on the spread of knowledge and the excellence of Greek studies.

In 1826 Thomas Campbell was elected by the votes of three 'nations,' receiving 280 votes, while Sir Thomas Brisbane received 189, and Canning 83. Unanimously re-elected in 1827, Campbell was in 1828 proposed for a third year. In the early period of the University the rector was often re-elected many years in succession, and even after the Revolution the same thing had occurred ; but for a long time the tenure had not been continued beyond two years, though there was no law against it. The other candidate was Scott. Two 'nations' voted for each, and Gavin Gibb, whom Campbell had appointed vice-rector in the preceding year, gave his casting vote for Scott, who was declared to be elected. John Ralston Wood, student of Medicine, and a number of others gave in a written protest against the election, alleging that the vote given by the vice-rector was not in conformity with the statutes, and they afterwards served a formal notarial protest on the principal and the clerk of senate, and sent intimation to the two candidates. Scott declined to accept office, and a meeting of *comitia* was summoned for 2nd December to hold a fresh election. Feeling ran high, both students and professors were in a pugnacious mood, and Campbell hastened from London to Glasgow to animate his followers. A number of students opposed to Campbell, including Norman Macleod and Archibald Campbell Tait, lodged a protest against accepting votes from John Ralston Wood and other seventeen students who had protested against the last election, arguing that if Wood and the others lost the new election, they might urge their law proceedings about the former one, and, if successful, overturn the new election. The same objectors also protested against certain other students on account of alleged lack of qualification. The election then took place, and three 'nations' voted for Campbell, who was declared elected, while Loudoniana voted for Sir Michael Shaw Stewart. Then the principal and Professors Macgill, Meikleham, Couper, Sandford, Walker, and Buchanan protested that by the constitution and practice of the University it was not legal to elect the same individual for a third year, and that they should not be precluded from taking such measures as they might be advised to adopt in order to have the election or pretended election set aside.

On 5th December, 1828, a meeting of *comitia* was held for the installation of Campbell for the third time.　He encountered a shower of protests and objections such as no rector ever had to face, and there were some who feared that a poet little accustomed to the surge and strife of great popular meetings might be disconcerted by the ordeal.　But Campbell maintained a calm and manly bearing throughout, and before finishing his address had won over many students who were previously his opponents.　To the first protest by the principal and others Campbell answered that his election by the majority of the students to be their rector for a third year was legal and valid, inasmuch as it was not contrary to the constitution or practice of the University, and inasmuch as the statutes contained no enactment disqualifying any one from being rector for a third year.　To a protest which he had received from certain students, he answered that he held the arguments contained in it to be themselves invalid, and would proceed to take the oath of office.　To a second protest from the principal, Macgill, Walker, Meikleham, Buchanan, and Sandford, repeating the former objection, and alleging that Campbell had not such a residence in Scotland as would enable him to discharge the duties of the office, he answered that he held a firm opinion that his election was perfectly legal.

A further protest was made by Robert Dunlop Deans, student of Law—for himself and as procurator and attorney for a committee nominated by a general meeting of students opposed to Campbell held in the Greek classroom after the election—against Campbell being elected for a third year, which was said to be contrary to the laws and practice of the University 'and in breach of a statute passed during the civil wars in Scotland,' it being further alleged that many who voted for Campbell were ineligible.　This protest was answered by a paper given in by John Ralston Wood and others, setting forth that they thought it their duty to the University and to the very eminent gentleman whom, for his great and disinterested services to the College and his warm attachment to its honour, a large majority had elected for a third time, to record the reasons why the protests against his election should be held futile and invalid. The ancient laws declared that the election should be annual, but in no statute whatever was it declared that one who had served for two years should be ineligible for a third ; on the contrary the ancient practice was to elect for a great length of time year after year, and the Commission of 1727 enacted that the ancient statutes regarding the election should be observed.　Those who subscribed the document were ready to prove before the proper court that the other objections were invalid.

Campbell was then admitted to office, and gave a short address dealing mostly with the circumstances of his third election.　He had previously

THOMAS CAMPBELL, LL.D.

Rector of the University, 1826-1829

BORN 1777. DIED 1844

promised the students, assembled not at his bidding but by their own spontaneous enthusiasm, that he would never refuse them any proof in his power of his interest in their welfare.   And when invited to a contested election he could not fly without abandoning his friends, his faith, and all pretensions to moral courage.   He could not say he was in ill health; he could not say it was impossible to come; and he disdained to say it was inconvenient, for that would have been weighing the duty of friendship, like a light or suspected coin, in the little scales of his own convenience.   He announced his intention of giving two silver medals for Latin and Greek verse, and two gold medals for essays—one on the evils of intolerance, and the other on the comparative importance of scientific and classical instruction.   'In my own opinion,' he said 'the importance of science is paramount, but that idea, from an unscientific man, and thus hastily thrown out and unargued, will not of course affect you; still less, I hope, will it cause you to suspect that I would depreciate the beautifying and exalting influence of classical learning.'   This may seem a strange preference for a poet, yet it was at least prophetic of the kind of development the University was afterwards to exhibit.

Campbell named assessors and an *apparitor* as usual, but deferred naming a vice-rector, promising to do so, however, before he left Glasgow. The principal seized upon this as an opportunity for a further protest, holding that the rector should appoint a vice-rector at the first meeting after his admission.   On 18th December Campbell attended a meeting of senate at which Professor John Towers was created an M.A., after which the rector, by the advice and with the consent of the senate, named him as vice-rector.   Once more the principal protested, declaring that his attendance at meetings called by the rector or vice-rector was not to be held as an acquiescence in the election of the rector or the nomination of the vice-rector.   Campbell gave more time and personal attention to University affairs than most rectors of the nineteenth century.   He communicated representations from the students to the Universities Commission, and urged on the latter the propriety of the students continuing to elect the rector.   When the Faculty of Physicians and Surgeons challenged the right of graduates holding the degree of C.M. to practise Surgery in Glasgow and the western counties unless examined and licensed by that body, an opinion of counsel favourable to the rights of the University and its graduates was obtained; but the faculty of the College declined to incur further expenses, and the senate, when applied to for support by the three graduates whose qualifications were impugned, wavered and, but for Campbell, would have left the Masters in Surgery to their own resources.   When the question came to an issue eight voted for a motion

2 A

by Burns to support the Masters in Surgery, and eight against it, upon which Campbell gave his casting vote for the motion. He also attended a series of meetings at which the means of carrying on the litigation were discussed. In November, 1831, Mr. J. Thomson of Clithero presented a marble bust of Campbell, and spoke of the poet as one of the most distinguished sons of the University, and himself as one of Campbell's old and early friends and admirers. The senate received the gift with equanimity, though the principal was authorised to convey their thanks to Mr. Thomson.

In 1829 the Marquis of Lansdowne was chosen rector by the votes of three ' nations,' Transforthana voting for the Hon. Charles Hope. Vainly and alone Macgill protested against the election, alleging that the want of a residence in Scotland unfitted Lansdowne for discharging the duties of the office, and that the Articles of Union required the office-bearers in Scottish Universities to be Presbyterians. Lansdowne wrote that, had he known such an honour was intended for him, he would have tried to be better informed about the functions and obligations of office, and pre- sumed that no personal attendance at Glasgow would be required. The principal was authorised to point out that, in order to exercise his func- tions, it would be necessary for Lansdowne to attend at the University at least one day to be admitted to office.

Scotland and its Universities had moved a long way since the Revolu- tion and the Commission of 1727, but legislators had done little or nothing for the University of Glasgow in that long period. The population of the country had greatly increased, the number of students had trebled, there was need for a wider and more varied curriculum in Arts, for improv- ing and extending the general organisation, for increased endowments, for a more efficient administrative body, and for abolishing the invidious and unfair distinction between the professors included in the faculty and those excluded from it, while the wonderful development of the Medical School had altered the balance of affairs, and demanded fresh adjustments. Such adjustments could not be expected from the ordinary administrators, even if they had power to make them, for, in consequence of the decision in the Muirhead case, the great majority of the medical professors were shut out from the general management and from participation in the funds. Whether or not the Government of the day felt any natural interest in the reform of the Scottish Universities, a number of circumstances con- bined to call their attention to the subject at this time. The University of Edinburgh, then under the control of the Town Council, was at variance with the latter, because the Council proposed to make attendance on midwifery a necessary part of the course for graduation in Medicine, a proposal which the senate unwisely met by claiming for themselves an exclusive right to originate and carry out all arrangements bearing on graduation. Some time afterwards the Court of Session decided in favour of the Town Council, but before the question was brought into Court and while the University and the Council were still warmly discussing it, the former in October, 1825, resolved to petition the Government for a Royal Commission to settle the respective rights of the parties. The University of Glasgow was also exercised by a number of questions. In 1819 the senate and the faculty adopted a joint petition to the Government for an alteration in the mode of electing the rector, for amendment of the rules and regulations affecting the College and University, and for increasing the number of Dundonald bursars. In 1824 another petition was sent up for the renewal of the tack of the Archbishopric which the University had enjoyed since 1698. After much discussion this tack was withdrawn in 1826 and replaced by a temporary annual grant. There had also been litigation with the Faculty of Physicians and Surgeons regarding the rights of graduates to practise Surgery. On many of the questions calling for settlement it was desirable that the decision should belong, not to judges limited by the charters and enactments of a remote past, but to legislators who could 'act in the living present,' and make the best available provision for its needs. Such circumstances led ministers of state to think of the Universities of Scotland, and in 1826 Peel advised George IV. to appoint a Commission of Visitation to enquire into their condition and propose measures for their reform

The Commissioners originally nominated in 1826 were Viscount Melville, chancellor of the University of St. Andrews, the Duke of Montrose, chancellor of the University of Glasgow, the Duke of Gordon, chancellor of King's College, Aberdeen, the Marquis of Huntly, chancellor of Marischal College, Aberdeen, the Earl of Aberdeen, rector of King's College, Aberdeen, Lord Advocate Sir William Rae, Solicitor General Hope, Dean of Faculty Cranstoun, Chief Baron Sir S. Shepherd, Chief Commissioner Adam of the Jury Court, Lord President Hope, Lord Justice Clerk Boyle, the Rev. Dr. Taylor, the Rev. Dr. Cook, the Earl of Rosebery, and the Earl of Mansfield ; while Sir Walter Scott, the Rev. Dr. Lee (afterwards principal of Edinburgh University), Henry Home Drummond, James Moncrieff (afterwards Lord Moncrieff), and the Earl of Lauderdale were subsequently added to the number. At the first meeting Lord Aberdeen was elected chairman, but he soon retired, and Lord Rosebery was chosen in his place. The Commissioners were instructed to frame statutes and ordinances which, upon receiving the approval of the King, were to remain in force until altered by His Majesty. The Commissioners sitting in Edinburgh, with committees meeting in the other University towns, made elaborate and painstaking enquiries, and had nearly completed the task of framing their report and regulations when, by the death of the King, their powers came to an end.   They were re-appointed by the next sovereign, however, and finally completed their task on 28th October, 1830.   The results of their enquiry fill a number of bulky volumes, and another bulky volume contains their report and the regulations which they drafted.   These regulations never obtained the King's approval and so never came into force, but on account of their influence on subsequent legislation their outlines are worth recording.

To a chancellor, chosen for life by the Senate as heretofore, the Commissioners assigned the right of presiding at University meetings, and of calling special meetings of the University Court, but without power to nominate a vice-chancellor.   They proposed that there should be a University meeting, consisting of the chancellor, the members of the University Court, and the examiners for degrees, to be assembled for the installation of the chancellor, and the induction to office of the rector, the principal, and the professors, for the conferring of degrees granted by the Senate, and for the distribution of general prizes—the graduates and students having a right to be present in places assigned to them by the University Court.

The chief administrative powers were committed to a new body called the University Court (to be carefully distinguished from the University meeting), consisting of seven members—the principal; the dean of faculties; the minister of Glasgow (if not a principal or professor); an assessor nominated by the chancellor; an assessor elected by the principal, the professors, and the graduates; and the rector chosen by the principal, professors, matriculated students, and graduates.   No principal or professor was to be eligible for the office of assessor or rector, the office of vice-rector was to be abolished, as well as that of the ordinary visitors, who, it was said, for a long time had not exercised their powers or even been made aware of them.   They proposed to empower the University Court to review all regulations and decisions of the Senate, and to be a court of appeal in every case not excepted; to originate and carry out, after communication with the Senate, improvements in the internal system of the University consistent with the statutes of visitation, and issue, with the chancellor's sanction, directions to secure the attention of professors to regulations regarding the mode of teaching and other duties; to fix and regulate the fees in the various classes; to receive and dispose of representations from the senate, professors, or graduates, and complaints from parents, students or others, not inconsistent with the ordinary discipline of the University vested in the Senate ; after due investigation, to censure a professor or suspend him for a year or less, the Senate having power to provide for the teaching of the class during the suspension ; with the sanction of the chancellor, to suspend a professor for a longer period than a year, or to deprive him of office ; after due investigation, to remove the librarian, janitors and other inferior officers ; to rectify any other abuse to which their attention might be called ; and to enquire into and control the revenue and expenditure, including the funds mortified for bursaries or other purposes, and to dispose for University purposes of all surplus revenue and funds not already appropriated to specific objects. From the extent of the property to be managed at Glasgow, the Commissioners proposed a court of seven members there, as compared with six at Edinburgh and five at Aberdeen and St. Andrews. They commented unfavourably on the management at Glasgow, and declared that recently much valuable property had been feued or alienated on most disadvantageous terms ; and they proposed that no alienation of the property of any Scottish University should be lawful in future except by authority of Parliament.

The ordinary discipline of the University was assigned to the Senate, with right of appeal to the University Court in cases relating to the dismissal or expulsion of students, or to students being prevented from proceeding in the usual manner through the curriculum of study. To the principal was committed the constant ordinary inspection of the professors, and the superintendence of classes, each of which he was to visit at least twice in the session.

The regulations for graduation in Arts required candidates to attend classes for four sessions of about seven months each, the classes meeting five days a week. In each of the first and second sessions students were to attend two hours a day both in Latin and Greek, and during the second session an additional hour a day in the first Mathematics class ; in the third year they were to attend the Mathematics class for an hour a day, and the class of elementary Logic and Rhetoric for two hours a day ; and in the fourth year two hours a day in each of the classes of Natural Philosophy and Moral Philosophy. The Commissioners disapproved of the Greek class beginning with the elements of Greek Grammar, and proposed that for the future the class should begin with the reading of Greek authors, and that at the commencement of the session only those who professed themselves qualified for the work of the class on this footing should be enrolled as public students ; but that others who were not thus qualified might be allowed to attend the class, and if in the first week after the Christmas vacation they could pass a public examination showing their fitness, they might then be enrolled as public students. Otherwise they were to be merely private students and to get no certificates. Only those students who at the beginning of the session professed to have a competent knowledge of the first four books of Euclid and of Algebra to Simple Equations were to be allowed to enrol as public students of the first Mathematics class ; but students who professed themselves competent for the work of the second Mathematics class were to be admitted to it.

After completing the curriculum candidates were to be strictly examined on all the six subjects included in it before they obtained the degree of B.A. Besides the ordinary degree, it was provided that candidates who passed an examination on a wider range of study and on a higher standard might obtain honourable distinction or highest honours according to the degree of eminence displayed. Holders of the degree of B.A. might proceed to the degree of M.A. by attending for an additional session the classes of Natural History, Chemistry, and Political Economy (for the last of which a new chair was to be established) and passing an examination in these subjects of the same kind as for B.A., and a further examination in some branch of literature, philosophy, or science selected by the candidate, so conducted as to secure very high attainments. The views of the Commissioners were not in harmony with those of recent reformers, who aim at restricting the number of subjects in the curriculum for honours and securing a more extended and thorough study of some particular group of subjects.

The examinations were to be conducted, not by the professors, but by four examiners specially appointed by the Senate for B.A. and three for M.A. In case the Senate or any professor were dissatisfied with the decision of the examiners, the Senate might re-examine a candidate and review the decision of the examiners. The examinations, evidently intended to be *viva voce*, were to be open to all who chose to attend, and not more than four candidates were to be examined in a day. The Commissioners promptly put aside doubts and objections that had been hinted, and declared their belief that even in the smaller Universities, and certainly in Edinburgh and Glasgow, there would be no difficulty in finding suitable young men fully qualified for the work of examining, a work which could not be regarded as part of the inherent functions of professors. Separate examiners did the work in the English Universities, and even in the Scottish Universities the professors were not always examiners, for at King's College, Aberdeen, degrees were conferred after the form of an examination by one professor only, none of the others having a right to be present.

In dealing with the faculty of Theology, the Commissioners proposed to add a professorship of Biblical Criticism and to lay down a curriculum of four sessions, in each of which three classes should be attended.   The session at Glasgow hitherto extended to six months, at Aberdeen to three, and at St. Andrews and Edinburgh to four.   They proposed that in all the Universities it should be six for the future.   They recognised the authority of the General Assembly to regulate the course of students preparing for the ministry, but animadverted on the laxity of the Church, which till recently allowed students who merely enrolled their names in the books of the professors for six years, without hearing a lecture or receiving any instruction in Theology in any University, to be taken on trial by the Presbytery for license to preach, if they delivered a certain number of discourses specified by the General Assembly.[1]   A recent enactment required attendance at the Divinity Hall for at least one session, but this was all the length the Church had gone, though a proposal to make attendance on Hebrew for one session compulsory was under consideration.

Apart from ecclesiastical regulations, however, the Commissioners thought it their duty to ascertain the best means of teaching Theology as a science, to establish a degree of B.D. for regular students of Theology, and to limit the degree of D.D. to those who had previously taken that of B.D.   The curriculum for the latter degree was to extend over four sessions of six months, the class in Divinity being taken in each of the first three, along with junior Hebrew in the first, senior Hebrew in the second, and junior Ecclesiastical History in the third, while in the fourth session students were to attend Biblical Criticism and senior Ecclesiastical History.   Students had for a long time been allowed to attend the class of the professor of Divinity at Glasgow and the other Scottish Universities without fee, but the Commissioners thought the reason for the exemption ---difficulty in procuring a sufficient number of young men properly educated for the Church---had long ceased, and that instruction for which no pecuniary sacrifice was made would be lightly esteemed and ineffectual.   They approved therefore of charging fees, a measure just introduced at two of the Universities, and stated that Dr. Macgill at Glasgow and Dr. Chalmers at Edinburgh reported that no complaint or unwillingness to pay had emerged, and that there had not been any falling off in the number of students.   The Commissioners were unduly strict in

[1] There was an extraordinary contrast between the numbers enrolled in the Divinity class as compared with Hebrew and Church History.   In 1819-20 there were 233 enrolled in Divinity—presumably separate individuals—and only 80 in Hebrew and 74 in Church History—the same individuals being probably often reckoned in both the latter classes. The increased stringency afterwards introduced into the regulations of the Church told on the attendance, for in 1831 there were only 105 students in the faculty of Theology, and by 1836 the number had fallen to 72.

their ecclesiastical views and had a strong belief in other men being bound by the Confession of Faith. They proposed that the degree of B.D. should be conferred only on those who signed the Confession and the formulas of the Church of Scotland, and that the principal and professors before their induction and all members of the University Court should subscribe the same documents. They also laid down that no principal or professor afterwards appointed should at the same time be minister of any parish or chapel of ease ; and that, if the principal or any professor in the faculty of Divinity were deposed or suspended from the ministry by an ecclesiastical court on account of heretical doctrine, deprivation from the academic office or suspension from it should follow.

There was only one chair of Law at Glasgow, and from it Civil Law and Scots Law were taught or might be taught, the former subject having fallen into the background. The Commissioners proposed that the degree of LL.D. should be open to Bachelors of Arts who had gone through a curriculum in Law extending over three sessions of six months each. The course in Civil Law was to be attended in the first session, while the course in Scots Law was to be divided into two parts so as to extend over the second and third. A course in Conveyancing had recently been begun at Edinburgh, and the Commissioners gave it their approval, and recommended that it should be taken in the third year along with Scots Law. The Commissioners remarked that only at Edinburgh could a full course in the science of Law be established, but their measures did not tend to make it any fuller even there, for they proposed that a chair of Public Law which had long existed at Edinburgh but which had failed to attract students, should be abolished. It does not seem to have occurred to them that they might have given vitality to the class and strengthened the curriculum by prescribing Public Law as one of the subjects required for graduation.

The Commissioners declared against the appointment in time to come of assistants and successors, but allowed the appointment of a joint professor in case the incumbent of a chair became insane, some provision being made for the latter. They also allowed professors disabled by age or infirmity to resign, retaining a portion of their emoluments at the expense of their successors, but the expediency of the resignation and the terms arranged were subject to the approval of the University Court. The Commissioners declared they had abundant evidence of the mischief arising from the different powers and privileges of the professors included in the faculty and those excluded from it, and that it was essential the distinction should be abolished. They recorded their belief that the decision of the Court of Session in the Muirhead case on which the distinction rested was not well founded in principle, and could not be a precedent against the crown, for which no appearance was made when the case come on for hearing.

The pressure of inadequate funds led the Senate in 1818 to approve a scheme under which students were required to contribute six shillings each year to the library, to the books in which they were to have access. But next year the Senate wavered, and agreed to return the money to students who had paid under the impression that it was compulsory. It was agreed that the registration of medical students at the library, begun in 1803, for which each paid a shilling, should continue ; but after long deliberation the Senate decided against making the payment of six shillings compulsory. The question was afterwards raised whether the library should be open to students by voluntary subscription or should be shut as formerly, and it was carried that it should be shut for that session.[1] Though not very uniformly or rigorously enforced, regulations were adopted in 1820 requiring that each student should pay seven shillings to the library for the winter session and three shillings and sixpence for the summer one, having in consequence a right to borrow books on depositing a reasonable sum as security before taking them out. Professors were not to enrol students in their classes till they had entered and paid the fee at the library. Afterwards it was agreed that the sums paid by the students in the different faculties were as far as possible to be applied in procuring books connected with their respective departments, and that irregular students of Divinity should not be required to pay the seven shillings, but should enrol at the library and pay a fee of one shilling, the other six shillings being required, however, if they were to read from the library. In 1824 it was resolved that part of the sums contributed by students should be applied to the improvement of class libraries.

About the time measures were being prepared for exacting contributions from students, the librarian was allowed an assistant, William Fleming, afterwards professor of Moral Philosophy, being appointed to this post in 1818. Fleming having been appointed to a church, was succeeded by William Park, and when Muirhead resigned in 1827, Park became chief librarian. In 1825 Mr. Elliot of London was appointed to act for the University in rendering effectual the law respecting delivery of books at Stationers' Hall for the use of the University ; and next year Robert

[1] It is not easy to interpret previous references and regulations so as to determine the position of students in regard to the library. Probably the class libraries sufficed for most students, but it seems that, at least when recommended by their professors, they were allowed to consult books in the library, and probably sometimes to borrow them for home perusal. The new regulations of 1820 authorised them to borrow directly and as a matter of right.

Durham, library agent in London, was appointed to procure, on the same terms as were allowed him by the University of St. Andrews, the books not entered at Stationers' Hall, a recent Act of Parliament having apparently altered the conditions regarding them.

In 1818 the Senate having asked whether there were any unappropriated College funds which might be used to aid the library, the faculty voted a sum of £125, intimating at the same time that there must be no more applications of this nature. Yet in 1820 they agreed to lend £1,000 from the Brisbane fund to be applied by the curators of the library in supplying deficiencies and adding such books as might seem necessary. In 1806 the Rev. Mr. Smith of Galston presented an oriental manuscript written in very small characters on paper made of bark and said to contain the whole of the Koran. Twenty years later Mrs. West of Dublin presented the manuscript from which the *System of Moral Philosophy* of her grandfather, Professor Francis Hutcheson, was printed.

In May, 1802, the Senate appointed James and John Scrymgeour to be printers to the University, in succession to James Mundell, who died in the preceding year. In January, 1811, a letter was read from Andrew Duncan soliciting to be appointed as printer, and the Senate appointed him for such time and on such conditions as they might afterwards think proper. In May, 1827, Duncan sent a letter resigning his position, but, as it was ordered to lie on the table, it may not have taken effect immediately, and no further appointment is recorded till four years later.

Of students during this time who afterwards reached distinction, mention may be made of Thomas Graham, one of the ablest chemists of his day ; Andrew Ure, also a notable chemist ; Robert Pollok, who might have left greater works than *The Course of Time* had not a too early death silenced his young muse ; John Gibson Lockhart, son-in-law and biographer of Scott ; George Gilfillan, a man who could write and lecture well, but whose productions sometimes showed greater fancy than firmness ; Cosmo Innes, deeply versed in the legal and ecclesiastical antiquities of Scotland, and deserving to be remembered in the University of Glasgow for having edited its records and charters ; John Inglis, a distinguished ornament of the Scottish bar, who as Lord Advocate framed and brought into Parliament the bill passed in 1858 for the reform of the Scottish Universities, and was afterwards for more than twenty years Lord President of the Court of Session ; Sir William Hamilton, born in the old College, where his father was professor of Anatomy, as his grandfather and grand-uncle had been, and himself famous as professor of Logic at Edinburgh, and author of a philosophic system adversely reviewed by John Stuart Mill, who, according to the partisans of Hamilton, did not understand the subject ;

Archibald Campbell Tait, Archbishop of Canterbury ; Norman Macleod, successively minister of Loudon, Dalkeith, and the Barony parish, Glasgow, whose name is still a household word in Scotland ; and James Begg, minister of Newington Free Church, Edinburgh, whose best work was done in endeavouring to improve the dwellings of the poor, but who also signalised himself as an opponent of ' human hymns' and of the union of the Free and United Presbyterian Churches, and once sent a letter on ecclesiastical affairs to the prime minister, which was described as the first epistle of Begg to Beaconsfield.

II. 1830–1858.

THE interval between 1830 and 1858 witnessed the foundation of three additional chairs in the faculty of Medicine, as well as the chair of Engineering, but it witnessed also the withdrawal of the annual grant of £800 given for fourteen years after the discontinuance of the tack of the Archbishopric. A lawsuit with the faculty of Physicians and Surgeons of Glasgow regarding the validity of the degree of Master of Surgery as a qualification to practise within the limited area assigned to that Faculty by a charter of James VI., was decided against the University, first by the Court of Session and afterwards by the House of Lords, and involved expenses which pressed heavily on the library funds, then almost the only funds at the disposal of the Senate, and even endangered the existence of the library, the contents of which were pledged in security for the costs of the action. In 1846 a bill was passed authorising the purchase by a Railway Company of the old College buildings and grounds, the Company undertaking to provide new buildings and grounds at Woodlands. Adverse times for railways followed, the undertaking was not carried out, and the Company paid a considerable sum in consequence. The increasing number of students made further accommodation desirable, and the faculty, fain to leave the east end, sent a memorial and deputation to the Government for aid in procuring new buildings in a different locality.

A counter memorial was presented from a respectable minority of the Senate, the transference of the medical classes to a distance from the Royal Infirmary being one hindrance, while the strife between the professors within and without the faculty was another, and the project of securing new buildings had to wait. At the election of Lord Dunfermline as dean of faculty in 1841, and again at his admission next year, there was a sharp wrangle regarding the religious test imposed on officebearers in 1707 by the Act of Security, and the warfare was kept up intermittently till an Act of Parliament passed in 1853 greatly mitigated the test. Soon after this the movement for reform of the Scottish Universities began to gather strength, and a measure passed through Parliament in 1858 may be said to mark a new era in their history.   In 1849 Queen Victoria, the Prince Consort, the Prince of Wales, and several other members of the royal family paid a visit to Glasgow, and were received by the members of Senate within the walls of the old College.

William Ramsay, who was appointed to the chair of Humanity in 1831, was the youngest son of Sir William Ramsay of Bamff.   After two or three sessions at Glasgow, where he was frequently a prizeman, he repaired to Trinity College, Cambridge, graduating there just before he became a professor.   He had already been two years on the teaching staff at Glasgow, being appointed to assist Millar in conducting the Mathematics class in 1829, and being afterwards called upon to assist Walker with the class of Humanity.   At first it seemed likely that Ramsay would succeed to the Mathematics chair, but though he would doubtless have made a capable and efficient teacher of Mathematics, the lot fell more appropriately when he was appointed professor of Humanity.   His works on Latin Prosody and Roman Antiquities, though they may be counted somewhat prolix, still attest the great industry and wide and accurate learning of the man from whom students at Glasgow learned their Latin from 1831 to 1863.

Ramsay was one of the chief men in the University as an administrator as well as a teacher, and was the author of a number of proposals for orderly and economic management.   In 1846 he carried a motion that the Senate should petition Parliament against requiring professors of lay chairs to sign the Confession of Faith and conform to the worship and discipline of the Church of Scotland.   Owing to ill health Mr. Ramsay was compelled to spend the winters of 1851-2 and 1852-3 abroad, and the Latin classes were conducted by Mr. William Young Sellar, an alumnus of Glasgow, afterwards professor of Humanity at Edinburgh, Mr. Sellar being also appointed assistant for the following session.   When the Universities bill of 1858 was before Parliament, the attitude of the faculty towards it was defined in four resolutions drafted by Ramsay, and when the bill passed he was elected as the first assessor returned by the Senate to the University Court, his tenure of office at the outset of the new era while the Commissioners were still at work being a time of special interest.

Sandford's trouble in consequence of the rector and dean as visitors challenging the excessive outlay on the repairs and extension of his house, and his own endeavour to become rector, are narrated elsewhere.   But Sandford cherished the yet higher ambition to become a Member of Parliament, and for a few months he realised it, and had the unique distinction of being the only person holding office as professor in a Scottish University and having also a seat in the House of Commons. He had been knighted in 1830, and at the first election for the city of Glasgow after the passing of the Reform Act of 1832 he was one of six candidates for two seats, and, being third in order at the close of the poll, was not elected. In the spring of 1834, however, he was returned for Paisley, and his colleagues, in consideration of the fidelity and success with which he had discharged the duties of his chair, allowed him to bring his professorial work to an end for that session on 17th April; stating that by September they would expect him either to resign his professorship or to withdraw from engagements inconsistent with the personal discharge of its duties. Early in September a letter was submitted from Sandford, bearing that some reasons would have made him wish to remain in parliamentary life, had that course been really open to him. He had no doubt a series of formidable attacks awaited the principles of the constitution and the establishments which flourished under it, and he would gladly have contributed to their defence.

The interests of the College and of other similar institutions were threatened, and he would have been at least a bold and zealous advocate for them. But the irregular hours, the severe labours, and the anxieties of a parliamentary career had been too much for his health and strength ; and medical advice agreed with his own forebodings that perseverance in the fatigues and cares of a political life must soon terminate fatally. But his health had now been so restored that he had the prospect of being able to discharge his academic duties as efficiently as ever. He had accordingly resolved to resume his chair in the College and resign his seat in Parliament. The faculty recorded their regret at hearing Sandford's health had suffered, and the high satisfaction with which they learned his determination to remain a member of their body. Only a few more years remained to him in the work of professor of Greek for which he was so well fitted, as he was prematurely cut off by typhus fever in February, 1838, at the age of forty. A collection of *Greek Extracts* which he compiled with notes and vocabulary long kept his memory green among students of the junior Greek class, in which it continued to be the text-book till within a few years of the time when the class itself was numbered among the things of the past.

Dr. James Thomson gave notice of motion in the senate that, as the vacancy in the Greek chair made a change practicable without affecting vested interests, the Blackstone examination in Greek or other subjects should not be compulsory except in the case of students who were to graduate or to enter the Divinity Hall. This motion does not seem to have been pressed in the senate, but in the faculty on 1st August, 1838, Nichol referred to Thomson's motion, and himself moved that no rights should be vested in the professor about to be elected to the Greek chair which would hinder the carrying out of the objects Thomson had in view. The motion was ruled incompetent from want of notice, and Edmund Law Lushington, M.A., Fellow of Trinity College, Cambridge, was elected professor of Greek without any special limitation, though Buchanan protested energetically against the Blackstone examination being compulsory on all students entering the Logic class. Lushington's ability and eminence as a Greek scholar were everywhere acknowledged, and he made a strong impression on his own students, but he took little share in the general administration. Owing to the illness of his son, which the physicians expected to terminate fatally in a few weeks, the professor obtained leave of absence for some time at the opening of the session in 1856, the classes being conducted by Mr. John Campbell Shairp, an alumnus of Glasgow, afterwards associated with Oxford and St. Andrews, and an author of considerable merit. Lushington continued as professor of Greek till 1875, and in 1884 the rector, Henry Fawcett, having died on 6th November, within nine days of the statutory date for the rectorial election, and there being little time to organise a contest in the usual way, all parties agreed in electing Lushington to the office of rector.

On the death of Jardine early in 1827 Robert Buchanan attained the full status of professor of Logic, and he held the chair till 1864. He was made an honorary M.A. in 1828, was nominated vice-rector by Henry Cockburn, and late in life was appointed assessor for the senate in the University court. He died in 1873 at the patriarchal age of eighty-eight, leaving £1,000 to establish bursaries in Arts.

In April, 1833, Mylne intimated that on account of advanced age he wished to resign, and desired that a committee should be appointed to receive from him the terms of resignation, but a fortnight later the committee intimated that he 'had withdrawn his intention of resigning.' But enfeebled health and defective hearing made it necessary that he should have assistance, and in 1834 he was authorised to employ William Fleming, the professor of Oriental Languages, to conduct the Moral Philosophy class at the hour of examination, and afterwards the range of Fleming's assistance was extended. In 1836-37 Mylne seems to have dispensed with Fleming, but before the close of the session he was authorised to employ William Brown Galloway to assist. Mylne then proposed that a temporary assistant with £200 a year should be appointed to conduct the class for him, or else an assistant and successor with somewhat better remuneration. The latter alternative was not entertained, and Nichol offered to conduct the class as Mylne's assistant, but in September, 1837, the choice again fell on Fleming. Mylne died on 21st September, 1839, and notwithstanding a protest from Ramsay, who urged that the vacancy should be open to full and fair competition and that more time should be allowed for candidates to come forward, the faculty on 10th October appointed Fleming to the chair of Moral Philosophy.

Fleming had been for some time assistant librarian and College chaplain, and afterwards minister of Westruther and Old Kilpatrick, being called from the latter charge to be professor of Oriental Languages in succession to Gibb in 1831. Fleming had the distinction of being appointed vice-rector by Sir Robert Peel. As an administrator he followed an independent and sometimes an isolated course. In 1843 he dissented from purchasing the Observatory at Horselethill, in 1846 disapproved of the proceedings of the faculty in reference to the sale of the old College, and about ten years later objected to the appropriation of a room by the professor of Natural Philosophy for the purpose of a laboratory, as it disturbed the Moral Philosophy class and their professor. Fleming wrote a *Manual of Moral Philosophy*, but in the main both he and Buchanan seem to have aimed at a tolerable standard of efficiency, as they conceived it, rather than at eminence. By the students the one was familiarly known as 'Moral Will' and the other as 'Logic Bob.'

In January, 1832, James Thomson was installed as professor of Mathematics, but his predecessor Millar retained the salary of the chair during his life. Thomson was not only an able and diligent professor, but one of the most reasonable and tolerant of University administrators. He supported the movement for the abolition of tests in the Universities, objected to the high-handed action of the senate in 1840 in setting aside the assessments made by the regular stint-masters and enforcing others made by the principal and regents, and, in opposition to most of his colleagues, held that the regius professors, as they were called, were entitled to be members of faculty as well as of senate. The University suffered a distinct loss when he died on 12th January, 1849.

On 13th April, 1849, the faculty elected Hugh Blackburn, M.A., fellow of Trinity College, Cambridge, as Thomson's successor. In March, 1852, Blackburn pointed out that a number of candidates for the degree of M.A. never attended the Mathematics class, argued from evidence given before the Commission of 1826 that such attendance was necessary, and gave notice of a motion on the subject. A few days later he withdrew his motion, having found the regulation proposed in 1818, which the senate now resolved to enforce strictly in the case of candidates for B.A. as well as for M.A. Blackburn was for a number of years clerk to the faculty, and he took a leading part in the work of administration. He had a strong belief in the powers and rights of the faculty professors as distinguished from others, and was scarcely disarmed even by a clause in the Universities Act of 1858 which abolished the distinction. Having held the chair for thirty years, he resigned in 1879 at a comparatively early age.

Meikleham held the chair of Natural Philosophy till his death in 1846, but after 1838 he seems to have taught little if at all. He was seized with illness about the new year of 1839, and after the class had been left untaught for a fortnight, the faculty requested Dr. Thomson and Dr. Nichol to divide the work of teaching it between them, to which they agreed. In October following, Meikleham being still an invalid was empowered to employ Nichol to assist him in the session about to commence. A year later David Thomson, B.A., of Trinity College, Cambridge, was, on Meikleham's proposal, appointed to conduct the class, and he continued to do so till four or five years later he was appointed professor of Natural Philosophy in King's College, Aberdeen. After this, in October, 1845, the faculty, at the request of Mr. Edward Meikleham, authorised the Rev. John Cunningham, an M.A. of 1836, who by and by became a missionary to the Jews, to teach the class for the coming session. Meikleham's son William, a lawyer in the city, was some time clerk of senate and of faculty and factor for the Hamilton bursary foundation. Towards the close of 1845 he became bankrupt, owing more than £3,000 to the foundation. Part of the debt was heritably secured, and to restore the remainder the members of faculty contributed £1,200 or £1,300, the Duke of Hamilton making good several hundred pounds more.

While the chair was vacant, Nichol gave notice of his intention to move that, in consequence of the advance of science and discovery, it was doubtful whether the arrangements formerly adequate were now sufficient for a full exposition of the various branches of Natural Philosophy during the ordinary University course; and that the faculty should not be hindered by any claim of vested rights on the part of the professor about to be appointed from deliberating on the efficacy of the present or the eligibility of any. proposed arrangements. On 11th September, the day of the election, Nichol brought forward his motion, but the meeting adopted a shorter one proposed by the professor of Medicine that, notwithstanding the appointment of a professor of Natural Philosophy, power was reserved during his incumbency to originate or support any changes in the arrangements for conducting instruction in Physical Science which on due consideration might appear expedient. The new professor on his election and before his admission agreed to this resolution. At the election meeting on 11th September, 1846, the rector (Lord Advocate Rutherfurd) and the dean (Lord Meadowbank) were present along with the ordinary members of the faculty, and after deliberation on the qualifications of the candidates, William Thomson, B.A., Fellow of St. Peter's College, Cambridge, was unanimously elected. The new professor was the son of Dr. James Thomson, professor of Mathematics, and after tuition by his father, he entered the University of Glasgow in 1834 when only a little over ten years of age, and attended for some half-dozen sessions, being apparently most impressed by Nichol, the professor of Astronomy (who taught Natural Philosophy in the year of young Thomson's attendance), and by Thomas Thomson, the professor of Chemistry—both men of marked ability in their respective subjects. After a brilliant career at Cambridge, he now returned at the age of twenty-two, destined to become the most famous professor at Glasgow in the nineteenth century. He reaped the reward promised of old to the man who findeth wisdom and getteth understanding: 'Length of days is in her right hand; and in her left riches and honour.' Having undergone his trial by reading an essay *De Caloris Distributione per Terrae Corpus*, he was admitted to office on 13th October.

As might be expected in the case of a professor who combined great theoretical ability and learning with extraordinary inventiveness and practical skill in mechanical contrivances and the adaptation of means to ends, Thomson at once turned his attention to apparatus. A few days after his admission he was allowed to introduce a gas light into the apparatus room, and part of the instruments being found to be old and of little service, and others of more recent date in a condition needing thorough repair, the faculty in the next five years sanctioned an expenditure of £550 on apparatus. It appears that the first articles desired by Thomson were for experimental research in Electro-Magnetism. Even in domestic affairs he was a pioneer, and in 1852 he erected a gas cooking apparatus in the kitchen of his house. Towards the end of 1855 Thomson procured the fitting up of a room in the neighbourhood of the physical department as a laboratory, which, small and unpretentious as it was, formed the earliest physical laboratory for students within a University. In fairness to earlier teachers it should, however, be remembered that a separate class in Experimental Philosophy, distinct from the general course in Physics, had been conducted so long before as 1730 in the time of the first Dick, in which demonstrations with instruments or apparatus formed part of the instruction; and that Anderson had large classes in Experimental Philosophy, and arranged experiments in separate rooms, bringing

2 B

in his students in successive detachments to witness them.   It was reserved for Thomson to organise separate courses of practical instruction, apart from the lectures course, and in which students worked by themselves; and the results of his own experimenting and research made his laboratory famous all over the world.   Fleming, the professor of Moral Philosophy, whose class met on the floor below, objected to the noise incident to the fitting up and working of the laboratory, and though it would have been extremely unfortunate if Thomson had been prevented from securing accommodation, yet it appears that some generalship was required on his part in order to secure it.   After a time Fleming withdrew his opposition, and the laboratory was enlarged by the annexation of a deserted examination room to the deserted wine cellar of an old professorial house of which it at first consisted.

In 1848 the new professor of Natural Philosophy sent a letter in which he referred to the statutes of 1727, and argued that no degree in Arts could be conferred unless the student had attended the Natural Philosophy class.   Last session, when he was new to the chair, some students were admitted without this attendance, but now he was resolved to maintain the statutes of the University and the efficiency of his office as advised by counsel.   Maconochie moved and James Thomson seconded a motion giving effect to this view, but consideration was adjourned, and at next meeting the professor of Natural Philosophy was asked to prepare a statement of the evidence on which he based his contention.   When this statement had been circulated the senate, still undecided, adopted a motion by Lushington for the appointment of two committees to prepare a statement on each side for submission to counsel.   The result seems to have been unfavourable to the views of the professor of Natural Philosophy, but in March, 1852, he gave notice of motion that no one should be qualified for a degree in Arts unless he had attended a complete curriculum of the Philosophy classes.   This motion was more than once amended, and as finally brought forward in January, 1853, it proposed that after the lapse of another session all candidates should be examined in some branch of Physical Science, namely, in Chemistry or Botany or Natural History, in addition to the subjects required by the existing regulations. The motion was seconded by Nichol, and though not passed, a committee was appointed to consider whether some advance should not be made in the qualifications required for graduation in Arts.

Few students had enough Mathematics fully to follow the teaching given by this great man of science to his class of Natural Philosophy, but it was always interesting to see how much he himself was interested in the subjects with which he dealt.   He had a generous admiration for the great thinkers and workers in science, and would pour forth his tribute to men like Newton, Laplace, Lagrange, Fresnel, and Fourier, or an estimate of their mental equipment and the results they achieved, forgetful of the winged speed of time, till in the last five or ten minutes of the hour he had to compress the scientific principles and maxims which should have formed the subject of his lecture. But sometimes there were short-comings even among his heroes of science. He gave a eulogistic account of Thomas Graham, declaring he had done great things and made im-portant discoveries in Chemistry, but that he would have done greater things and made discoveries yet more important if he had only been a mathematician. He had come within sight of other great discoveries, and nothing could have stopped him except lack of higher Mathematics. Occasionally the professor's indifference to conditions of time and space which would extinguish another man's interest in a question, was remark-able. Shortly after entering his new premises at Gilmorehill he placed some tall glass tubes reaching from the laboratory on the floor below up through the classroom. These tubes were intended to show the rate at which certain liquids diffused through other liquids, and after being filled with clear water some strongly coloured chemical liquid was introduced at the bottom, and was slowly making its way upward, the rate of advance being marked by the colour imparted to the water. The professor gave a formula for calculating the rate of advance, and gravely told his students —'Now if you work that out, you will find that in ten thousand years or a hundred thousand years the colour would be very nearly uniform from top to bottom.'

Even scientific experiments, however carefully planned, may deviate a little from the course they are expected and desired to follow. The professor was once illustrating the distensibility of certain kinds of matter by turning the mouth of a water pipe into a bag formed of india-rubber or some elastic substance. To begin with, the bag might have the area of a sheet of foolscap, and it was placed over a large tub, so that when it burst the contents might fall harmlessly into the tub. But somehow the bag showed no signs of bursting, but swelled and swelled till it reached something like the area of a mattress, with a formidable thickness too. The professor's patience was at length exhausted, he stirred the bag with a pointer, and it burst, resulting in a waterfall of unmanageable dimen-sions and altogether too much for the tub. The floor was flooded, the water showered over the professor's robes and over the students in the nearest bench or two, but even the students who had suffered this rather uncanny bath could hardly abstain from joining in the general laughter which greeted the escapade. Some other experiments were great annual events in the class, and such was the firing of the shot. A log of wood was slung up over the platform in such a way as to swing backward with the impulse imparted to it by a bullet discharged from a gun, and there was a contrivance to fix the log at the limit of its swing, so as to show the distance it had moved, the movement being a rough equivalent to the explosive force of the gunpowder. The professor had been a volunteer and could fire a shot as well as another man, but it was a sight to be remembered to see the amused curiosity with which the students watched him seizing his muzzle-loading rifle, cocking the doghead, seating himself on a front bench, placing the butt-end of the weapon to his shoulder, taking cool and resolute aim through his spectacles, and lastly firing the shot and sending the bullet into the log. This demonstration was wisely reserved for the end of the hour, for it would have required a good while to restore the students to gravity and order.

James Couper, the professor of Astronomy, died on 7th January, 1836, and on 6th February the King appointed John Pringle Nichol, an alumnus of King's College, Aberdeen, who had shown great aptitude and versatility as a lecturer on science, to succeed. Nichol was 'the bright particular star' of his time at Glasgow. He greatly enlarged the stock of instruments, began afresh the making of observations, revived the class for students, and guided the faculty in the purchase of the new Observatory at Horselethill. He wrote and edited numerous works on science, and crowds gathered to his popular lectures, an audience of more than a thousand flocking to hear him discourse on Astronomy. While he made science popular, it was not at the expense of making it worthless, for he threw out ideas that guided and stimulated men who afterwards rose to distinction, and inspired others with an enthusiasm akin to his own. His varied and solid accomplishments enabled him to carry on the work of the Natural Philosophy and Natural History classes when the professors of these subjects were for a time incapacitated, and he also offered to conduct the Moral Philosophy class when Mylne's energies were failing. The students had no reason to regret when an exchange of this kind was made. Nichol was withal a man of marked characteristics, and sometimes exercised his own initiative in a way that was not encouraged by his colleagues.

Within about a year from the date of his induction a sum of £204 was spent in repairs and improvements about the Observatory, and by January, 1843, more than £700 additional had been spent on procuring instruments, a large portion of the amount being paid to Ertel & Sons of Munich for instruments made to order. In 1843 the faculty laid down a rule that no single member should for the future order instruments on his own responsibility; and in December, 1846, a committee after visiting the Observatory reported that the instruments were in good order, but some of those marked in the catalogue were not found, and several were said to be in Ireland in the hands of Lord Rosse. Maconochie, the professor of Law, strongly disapproved of what had happened, and shortly afterwards the faculty issued imperative orders that no officer of the College having the care of its property should remove or lend any instruments from the place appointed for their custody.

The view from the Macfarlane Observatory had come to be obstructed by neighbouring buildings, and the smoke and dust in the atmosphere told against the making of observations. In the year of the new professor's induction a number of gentlemen in Glasgow and the neighbourhood formed themselves into an Astronomical Institution, intending to provide a new Observatory, for which £2,000 was deemed adequate; but when subscriptions to the amount of £1,500 had been intimated the commercial distress of the winter of 1837-8 put an end to the hope of further contributions. In the following winter Nichol, with the consent of the faculty and the countenance of the subscribers, went to London to invoke the aid of the Government, and a grant of £1,500 was obtained, the Lords of the Treasury stipulating that there should be extra-meridional and magnetic, as well as meridional, observations; that the results of these observations should be annually transmitted to the Admiralty and the Royal Observatory at Greenwich; and that facilities should be afforded for giving time to ships.

The promoters then felt themselves able to proceed, and the buildings seem to have been finished in 1841. It was arranged that the subscribers should grant the full use and occupancy of their habitable buildings to the College, that the College should place and maintain the requisite instruments, and that the professor of Practical Astronomy should be observer. But there were still pecuniary difficulties, and these induced the directors to offer to sell the buildings and grounds to the College, and on 5th May, 1843, the faculty, notwithstanding a dissent by Fleming, resolved to offer £1,859, provided the buildings and grounds were handed over free of incumbrances excepting the feu duty. About this time a number of valuable instruments from the old Macfarlane Observatory were transferred to the new Observatory, and Professor Nichol took up his residence in the house attached to it. Early in 1844 the Faculty of the College and the subscribers to the Astronomical Institution forwarded a joint memorial and petition to the Lords of the Treasury, narrating the history and misfortunes of the Institution, and asking the Treasury to agree to the buildings and grounds being conveyed to the College. After some correspondence and explanations the Treasury in March, 1845, gave their consent, on the understanding that the College should fulfil the conditions laid down when the grant of £1,500 was given, and that the Astronomical Institution should be relieved from responsibility. It was found that there had been some miscalculations in regard to the property, there being a second feu duty of £17 10s. in addition to one for £30, which alone had hitherto been taken into account, and that the revenue of the Institution, instead of being £12, was only £2 12s., and was likely to be reduced to £1 16s. On the other hand the creditors of the Institution agreed to accept fifteen shillings in the pound, and after a further protest from Fleming, the visitors on 11th November, 1845, gave their consent to the transaction, and at length the purchase was completed. The Wilson fund for the benefit of the Observatory and Astronomical department had been subjected to some strain in providing the equipment, and in April, 1845, directions were given for the investment of the full capital sum, and for the gradual extinction of debt by applying half the annual proceeds to that purpose so long as necessary.

In August, 1840, Queen Victoria, considering it would be of importance in the education of youth and for the public advantage, erected a chair of Civil Engineering and Mechanics in the University, and appointed Mr. Lewis Dunbar Brodie Gordon as first professor. Mr. Gordon had previously followed the profession of Civil Engineer at Glasgow and elsewhere, as he afterwards continued to do. The question of the accommodation to be assigned for the carrying on of his work in the University gave rise to more than the usual amount of discussion. In September, 1855, Mr. Gordon resigned, and before the close of the year William John Macquorn Rankine was appointed to the chair, on which he conferred no slight distinction, and left a reputation as the father of modern Engineering and the best methods of expounding it. He dealt more persuasively with the faculty than Gordon had done, and for some time carried on his lectures in the examination hall.

In the latter part of his tenure, Davidson did not teach Civil Law, and the attendance at Scots Law fell off to some extent. For some years before his death on 24th July, 1842, the professor had fallen into ill health and the lectures were read by his son, Mr. William Davidson, writer. The next professor was Douglas Cheape, advocate, who held the chair of Civil Law at Edinburgh from 1827 to 1842, when he resigned on account of domestic circumstances. He was never admitted and never even presented his commission at Glasgow, and must have given in his resignation to the Home Secretary immediately after appointment. On 22nd December, 1842, a commission was presented to the faculty appointing

Allan Maconochie to the professorship of Civil Law ' vacant by the resignation of Douglas Cheape, Esquire, late professor.' Maconochie was
admitted on 4th January, 1843, and prepared a series of prelections on
Roman Law, but soon afterwards the Lord Advocate, on behalf of the
Government, made known to him that a course on Scots Law would be
preferred by members of the legal profession in the West of Scotland.
On 13th May the Queen issued a royal warrant setting forth that it was
the will and pleasure of the sovereign that Maconochie should teach not
only the Roman or Imperial Law to such as desired instruction in that
subject, but also the Law of Scotland, and that to him under the designation of Civil Law should belong the exclusive right to lecture in the
University on Law in its various branches and subdivisions.

While still regarding Civil Law as his proper subject, Maconochie
henceforward delivered a course on Scots Law to a class which soon reached
double the average of any previous time. But he was grievously disappointed by the want of a proper library of law books, and the absence
of an appropriate room in which to begin the formation of one by bringing
together the small number of law books scattered throughout the general
library. The great alteration in the law and its practice in Scotland, the
accumulation of reported decisions, the increase of Scottish manufactures
and commerce giving additional importance to commercial and international law, and the continual reference to English authorities and reports,
had completely changed the mode of conveying legal instruction and the
nature and extent of the means requisite for doing so efficiently. He
had been greatly indebted to the Faculty of Procurators, who had shown
an active interest in his chair and admitted law students to their valuable
library ; while the professor, being himself engaged in private practice, had
been enabled at considerable expense to keep up a law library for his own
use. But increasing weakness of sight induced Maconochie to decline
private practice, and in 1853 he intimated that, until adequate accommodation and a suitable law library were provided, he would cease teaching
the class of Scots Law. He recommended the University authorities to
solicit aid from the Government, who could not expect the professor of
Roman Law to teach Scots Law without adequate means for the purpose
and at loss and inconvenience to himself, while he preferred and was ready
to perform the proper duties of his office as set forth in his commission.

Shortly afterwards a motion by Professor Weir was carried that the
committee on the compensation grant to the library should be authorised
to spend a sum of not more than £200 in the purchase of law books,
provided space was found in the library for their arrangement along with
the existing stock of law books. A room being found, a separate library

of law books was formed, and Maconochie seems to have continued his teaching as usual; but he soon succeeded to the estate of Garvock, and at the end of session 1854-5 he resigned the chair of Civil Law and the lectureship of Scots Law.[1] The senate by way of parting recognition bestowed on him the honorary degree of LL.D. He had been a diligent and successful teacher, and was very active as an administrator, much work falling to his share in connection with the abortive proposal for the removal of the College to new buildings at Woodlands.

The appointment of George Skene, Advocate, as successor to Maconochie, followed very quickly. His presentation stated that the profession of Law in the University being vacant, the Queen nominated and presented Skene 'to the sole profession of Law.' This led the faculty to declare that in admitting Skene as professor of Civil Law they did so without assenting to the Queen's right to change the form of a commission, but solely because the profession of Law in general included that of Civil Law. The new professor was a son of Scott's friend James Skene, to whom the introduction to the fourth Canto of *Marmion* is addressed, and from 1837 to 1841 he held the chair of Civil History at Edinburgh, which at that time had a little frequented and unremunerative class. Towards the end of 1841 he was appointed Sheriff-Substitute of Lanarkshire. As an administrator he was less prominent than most professors of Law have been, but he continued to hold the chair till in 1867 he was appointed curator of the historical department of the Register House, Edinburgh.

In a few instances the degree of LL.B. was conferred as an honorary distinction, as in 1840 in the case of Alan Stevenson, Civil Engineer, Edinburgh, the designer of a number of lighthouses; and in 1843 in the case of Archibald Campbell Swinton, professor of Civil Law in the University of Edinburgh. In 1840 the degree of LL.D. was bestowed on James Walker, an alumnus of the University, who became a distinguished engineer, and at a later date founded a number of prizes in the University for the encouragement of engineering students; in 1841 on John Smith, younger of Crutherland, secretary of the Maitland Club; in 1846 on Francis Adams, Surgeon, Banchory, the translator of Paulus Ægineta, a celebrated Greek physician of the seventh century; in 1854 on David Livingstone, the missionary, traveller, and philanthropist; and in 1859 on Francis Richard Sandford, a son of Professor Sandford's, born and educated in the old College, who afterwards continued his studies as a Snell exhibitioner at Oxford, and entering the civil service, held among other posts that of Assistant Secretary for the Colonies, Under Secretary

---

[1] Both the professor and the faculty held this view of his office or offices.

for Scotland, and Secretary for the Science and Art Department.   It was agreed that the charges for the degree given to Livingstone should be paid from the University funds.   Some years after receiving the degree the great missionary, then at the height of his fame, delivered an address to the students in the Common Hall on 25th February, 1858.   It was peculiarly fitting that the University should bestow such recognition as it could on a native of Blantyre, who had been trained in Medicine in Glasgow, though not within its own walls, and who, *ex humili potens*, had proved himself one of the noblest heroes of the nineteenth century.

In consequence of his too generous dealings with relatives and friends, Macgill, the professor of Divinity, in his later years fell into somewhat straitened circumstances ; and this probably explains his putting forward a claim in 1838 for reimbursement of house rent and house and window taxes incurred by him at the opening of his professorship, owing to the house assigned to him in October, 1814, being in such bad repair that he was unable to enter till November of next year.   The principal and Dr. Thomson, who were appointed to examine the claim, reported that it seemed to be well founded, and if made at the time would have been entitled to attention, but that it might be dangerous to reopen the question after so many years.   The advice of Sir James Graham and Mr. Kirkman Finlay as visitors was then asked, and, while desirous that the case should not be made a precedent, they recommended that Macgill should receive £25 as a matter of grace and favour, and the recommendation was carried out.

Macgill died on 18th August, 1840, and in October Dr. Alexander Hill, minister of Dailly, son of Dr. George Hill, a notable leader of the ' Moderate' party and principal of St. Mary's College, St. Andrews, was appointed his successor.   A curious divergence of view arose over his election as commissioner to the General Assembly in 1847.   Ramsay moved and Thomson (the professor of Medicine) seconded that Dr. Norman Macleod of St. Columba's, Glasgow, should be the representative of the senate, but the principal declared that Macleod, not being a master in the University, was not qualified, and his name was withdrawn.   It was then moved and seconded that Hill should be the commissioner, when nine voted for him and nine declined to vote, and the principal declared him duly elected.   On account of Hill favouring the maintenance of tests, James Thomson dissented from his appointment.

William Fleming, who became professor of Oriental Languages in 1831, had only a short tenure, being transferred to the chair of Moral Philosophy in 1839.   George Gray, minister of Maybole, was then appointed professor, and he too had a comparatively short tenure, dying on 23rd June, 1850.   In September following, Duncan Harkness Weir, an M.A. of 1840, then minister of the Scots Church, Manchester, was elected to the chair.   In the later months of his first session, besides his own class, he conducted that of Church History during the illness and after the death of Professor Reid.   In March, 1854, Weir expressed a desire to hold a more advanced class for students of Oriental Languages, and the faculty of Theology was authorised to make the necessary arrangements.   In February of next year he raised in the senate the question of reviving the degree of Bachelor of Divinity, the design was supported by a memorial from the students of Theology, and shortly afterwards on his motion the Senate gave a general approval to the proposal, and remitted to the faculty of Theology to consider the necessary details, and ascertain how far the other Universities would co-operate in the contemplated measure.

After this, representatives of the theological faculties of the various Universities met at Edinburgh at the time of the General Assembly, approved of the revival of the degree, and were of opinion that it should be open to Masters of Arts who had gone through the course of theological study prescribed by the Church of Scotland, and that while each University should regulate its own examinations, there should be as much uniformity between the different Universities as was compatible with the different courses of theological study pursued in them.   A report from the faculty of Theology had previously been submitted, and in January, 1856, Nichol moved that the senate recognised the importance of promoting studious habits and encouraging theological research, but did not think it desirable to create a distinction between young men equally admitted to education and honours in Arts, but who, through differences widely prevalent and with which the senate was not concerned, attended separate theological halls.   The motion also deprecated the want of uniformity in the examinations of the several Universities, and recommended that further time should be allowed to secure a scheme free from the objections stated. The senate declined to adopt the recommendations submitted, but expressed a hope that the efforts that were being made would lead to a scheme free from objections and effective in promoting the study of sacred literature.   Weir, who had thus raised a discussion which bore fruit after many days, was one of the most active and trusted academic administrators, and from 1855 to 1876 he rendered important services as clerk of senate.

William M'Turk who died in March, 1841, had spent most of his life in the service of the University as librarian, chaplain, and professor of Ecclesiastical History, and by his will he left the sum of £1,000 to the faculty, to be accumulated for twenty years and the annual interest afterwards applied to augment the salary of the professor of Church History. He died so soon after the will as to render his death-bed disposal of heritable property invalid, and the legacy was reduced to £300, an unfortunate accident in the case of a chair by no means too affluent. In April, 1841, the Queen appointed James Seaton Reid, who had studied at Glasgow and graduated as M.A. in 1816 and D.D. in 1833, to succeed M'Turk. He had been a Presbyterian minister in his native Ulster, and for a few years professor of Ecclesiastical History in the Royal Academical Institution, Belfast; and took a kindly interest in students from Ireland, procuring the sanction of the faculty to their holding weekly meetings in his classroom. In 1842 he intimated his intention to open a class in Civil History, and procured a grant of £20 to provide maps and chronological tables. For several years he was clerk of senate, and when separate chapel services in the College were given up he negotiated for the accommodation of students in St. Paul's Church. He died on 26th March, 1851, at Belmont, near Edinburgh.

The next professor of Church History was Thomas Thomson Jackson, and his commission was dated 16th April, 1851. He studied for the church, but never held a ministerial charge, was for some time amanuensis to Dugald Stewart, and in 1836 became professor of Divinity and Biblical Criticism in St. Mary's College, St. Andrews, where he remained till transferred to Glasgow. Having held the chair of Ecclesiastical History for twenty-three years, he resigned in 1874, and died at St. Andrews on 24th December, 1878.

In response to a memorial from members of the Kirk Session of St. David's Church, Glasgow, the senate in October, 1831, conferred the degree of D.D. on the Rev. David Welsh, minister of that church, who had just been appointed professor of Ecclesiastical History in the University of Edinburgh. While a student at Edinburgh he had been much impressed by the teaching of Dr. Thomas Brown, of whom he wrote a memoir. In at least one famous scene of church history Welsh was afterward a prominent actor, for having been chosen Moderator of the General Assembly of 1842, it fell to him to preside at the opening of the memorable Assembly of 1843. Having preached the customary sermon in St. Giles on the very appropriate text, 'Let every man be fully persuaded in his own mind,' he delivered the opening prayer in St. Andrew's Church, Edinburgh, read the protest of the founders of the Free Church, and headed their march to Tanfield Hall where the first Assembly of the new church was constituted. After this exodus Principal Macfarlan of Glasgow University was elected Moderator of the General Assembly of the Church of Scotland whose ranks were now sadly diminished. Among other recipients of the degree of D.D., probably the most notable was Norman Macleod, on whom the distinction was conferred in 1858.

In 1846 Nichol gave notice of motion for a return of the degrees conferred in Divinity, with the names and offices of the recipients and the titles of any works they had published before receiving the distinction. Honorary degrees had hitherto been conferred on a motion made and seconded in the senate, of which notice was usually given at the meeting preceding the one at which it was determined; but early in 1856, when the revival of the degree of B.D. was under discussion, Fleming proposed and Nichol seconded the appointment of a committee to report on the best mode of conferring honorary degrees in Divinity and Law. A few weeks later the committee presented a report which was adopted for regulating the procedure in such cases. It was resolved that a committee of senate should be appointed at the commencement of each session by whom all proposals for the conferring of honorary degrees should be considered in the first instance. They were to take into account whether the proposed recipient had been educated at a University or held a degree, whether he was the author of any work of acknowledged merit, whether his occupation and pursuits were such as tended to advance the progress of learning and science, and whether his character and position in society warranted the conferring of the degree. Afterwards the committee were to report to the senate the names of such candidates as appeared to them fit recipients of the distinction. At a later time a separate committee was appointed for each degree, but in essentials the scheme has ever since been in operation at Glasgow, and the Commissioners under the Act of 1889 made it the rule at other Scottish Universities as well.

The Magistrates of Glasgow having recommended that an illumination should take place on 28th March, 1831, in celebration of the second reading of the Reform Bill, the faculty resolved that the front of the College should be illuminated at the expense of the Corporation and a couple of flambeaux placed in front of the Chemistry classroom, but declared that they adopted this course for the preservation of the College property from outrage, and that their action was not to be taken as an admission of the propriety of the Magistrates' recommendation or an approval of the measure of Reform then before Parliament. The students seem to have been less lukewarm, and in January, 1833, the faculty authorised the College servants to prevent them from meeting in the College property for political purposes. In March of next year placards having been displayed calling a meeting of students in the Chemistry classroom for the purpose of petitioning Parliament to consider the Report of the Royal Commission concerning the affairs of the College, the clerk was directed to intimate to the professor of Chemistry that the faculty disapproved of the meeting being held in their property, and hoped he would concur in thinking it should not take place. By this time the Chemistry buildings stood in Shuttle Street, apart from the other academic buildings, and perhaps the students vainly expected they might there enjoy a sort of extra-mural freedom.

Students' clubs representing the two great political parties originated nearly at the same time. In December, 1836, a few weeks after the election of Peel as rector, the Peel Club was founded to commemorate the election, promote Conservative principles, and unite Conservative students, and from it the Conservative Club traces its descent. On 29th November, 1839, the faculty received an application from the Glasgow University Liberal Association for the use of a room in which to hold their meetings with a view to counteract the influence of the Peel Club. The request was not granted. It may further be said that, as the Liberal students founded a Campbell Club to commemorate the third election in 1828 of Thomas Campbell as rector, and as this Club lasted down to 1839 when the other Association came into existence, it is not clear that the Conservatives have the priority.

Mention is made from time to time of Debating and Literary Societies, which appear to have been active in their day but did not prove permanent ; and the faculty in 1844 gave their sanction to the formation of a University Juridical Society, the rules and regulations of which were submitted by Maconochie. The University Missionary Society is mentioned in 1839, but was founded nearly twenty years earlier, and is the oldest subsisting students' society excepting the Medico-Chirurgical, which dates from 1802. In 1855 a room was granted for meetings of an Abstainers' Society, and, though I do not remember any mention of the Ossianic Society in the minutes, it dates from 1828. In November, 1832, the faculty laid down a prohibition against games in which the use of clubs or sticks was necessary. A few days before they had granted to Mons. Foucart, teacher of gymnastics and fencing, the use of a room for teaching the latter subject, which was very prominent and persistent in the 18th century but less so in the 19th. The societies mentioned, as well as some others, supplied opportunities for training the literary and oratorical powers of students, and for social intercourse ; now and again collections of verses, sketches, and miscellaneous articles were published under the name of the *Glasgow University Album;* and in 1836 some students of Medicine brought out a periodical named *The Scalpel,* which the faculty considered too offensive to be suffered to live.

The University gave less countenance to Modern Languages than it had done in the 18th century.   Six or seven years earlier Mr. Russell had been allowed to give some lectures in French in a College classroom, but when he requested accommodation in 1831, the faculty found they had a rule against granting such applications.   Two years later Mr. Black applied for a classroom in which he might teach French, but the faculty, while willing to allow him accommodation for two lectures, would not grant it for the session.   Again in 1834 Mr. Meadows was refused accommodation for the teaching of French and Italian.   In January, 1842, Isaac Pitman, of whom countless students have since been the disciples, applied for the use of a classroom to lecture on Phonography.   He was permitted to give one lecture in the Common Hall on the following Monday, but further the faculty would not go ; and two or three years later they refused accommodation to two teachers of his system.

From a statement in 1854, shortly after the appointment of Lauchlan M'Pherson as janitor, it appears that every student when matriculating had to pay the janitor three shillings, that he received seven shillings and ten pence for every diploma of Doctor that was issued, and two shillings and ten pence for each diploma of B.A., M.A., C.M., or LL.B.   For attendance at the classrooms and providing fuel, the janitor also received two shillings and sixpence from each student in the class of Divinity, and one shilling and sixpence from each student in the two classes of Hebrew and Ecclesiastical History, and he usually received ten shillings from each student nominated to a Snell exhibition.   The bedellus received a shilling from each student at matriculation, and another shilling from students who underwent the Blackstone examination.   In 1813 he was entitled to five shillings for each Doctor's diploma, and this seems to have been raised to ten shillings in 1818 for the degree of M.D., a similar payment being fixed for the new degree of C.M.   A third official, the bellman, had also his fee, and frequently there was much difficulty in collecting it.   The faculty in 1820 desired professors to give their assistance in procuring payment of the dues from students to Daniel Walker, bellringer ; and in 1833 they ordered payment of £10 to Thomas Yuille, another bellringer, to whom the medical students had not paid their dues.   In 1835 medical students were threatened with the loss of all privileges and advantages consequent on attendance unless they paid the bellman, but Yuille continued to have his grievance, till in 1847 he ceased to be a servant of the University. After this the bellman's complaint is heard no more, and by and by the faculty arranged for the collection of coal and bell money on their own account.   Blackburn superintended the collection for some years, and after providing the cost of subordinate doorkeepers, paid a good balance to the College factors.   In December, 1858, the faculty showed their appreciation of Blackburn's diligence and capacity by asking him to draw up a scheme for the future management of coal and bell money, but the opportunity came rather late, for these vexatious exactions were swept away by the Universities Commissioners, who substituted a single payment of a pound at matriculation.

In 1840 there was an exciting controversy over another set of fees which disappeared in the new era under the Act of 1858—the laureation or graduation fees exacted from students, which, under the statutes of 1727, formed a perquisite of the professors of Ethics and Physics, and to which Fleming and Meikleham were as strongly attached as Reid and Anderson had been. The minimum assessment or stint was thirty shillings, and usually about the end of January the students of the Physics or Magistrand class were called upon to elect a stintmaster for each of the four 'nations.' The regulations provided that if anyone so elected did not at once accept office, another should immediately be chosen ; and if no one in a particular 'nation' consented to act, the stintmasters of the other 'nations' should have all the powers that would naturally have belonged to the fourth official. The stintmasters assessed all the students of the year whose attendance qualified them to become candidates for graduation in Arts, but the assessment was not levied unless the student went forward to examination ; and it is said that they sometimes by way of frolic laid a very heavy assessment on students of indifferent scholarship who might be relied upon not to face the examination.

In 1840 the stintmasters were regularly elected, accepted office, and made up a stint roll in which all the fifty-six magistrands were assessed at the uniform rate of thirty shillings. The *Jurisdictio Ordinaria* tried to induce the stintmasters to draw out a new stint roll rating the students at sums varying according to their ability. When afterwards called before the Senate one of them would have given way, but the other three remained steadfast to their first resolution ; and the Natural Philosophy class declined to proceed to a fresh election of stintmasters, declaring that the election already held had been declared legal, that the refusal of the stintmasters to amend the roll could not be held as declining to act, and that by statute the power of stinting resided in the stintmasters, and did not devolve on the principal and regents unless when no student in any 'nation' would accept office. The principal moved, and it was carried by six votes to five, that it should be remitted to himself and the regents to prepare a fresh stint roll. James Thomson dissented, holding the action of the Senate to be illegal and liable to be reversed by a court of law. He considered the stintmasters acted improperly in imposing a uniform stint, but it might have been allowed to pass for the session, and the

Senate might have enacted such regulations as would have prevented the recurrence of a similar incident.   On 12th March, 1840, a revised stint roll attested by the principal and Robert Buchanan was given in, and seventeen of the fifty-six magistrands were raised above the original rate of thirty shillings.   Sixteen students who wished to graduate acquiesced in the new stint roll, and were admitted to examination.   Among those whose names appeared on the list were three who afterwards became professors—James and William Thomson and Duncan Harkness Weir.

Early in 1836 when reports began to circulate regarding the intended foundation of an examining University in London, the Universities of Edinburgh and Glasgow presented memorials to the Government by no means welcoming the project.   Their apprehensions seem to have referred mostly to Medicine and to have disappeared in the light of further knowledge.   The Williams Trustees several times nominated Bachelors of Arts of London to their bursaries in Arts, and questions arose regarding their eligibility for the Blackstone gold medals and their admission to the degree of M.A. after a shorter curriculum than ordinary students. In 1854 the Trustees remonstrated, alleging that if their bursars were not allowed to compete for the medals given in connection with the Blackstone examination, they should be exempted from that examination altogether.   On the other hand the faculty argued that Dr. Williams intended his bursars to enter at Glasgow as undergraduates, and that it was anomalous to send graduates of one University to go through the undergraduate course at another.   The senate further approved of an answer by the principal that the B.A. of London conferred no privilege through which attendance for M.A. at Glasgow could be shortened.

Down to 1848 Sunday services continued to be held in the Common Hall, and near the beginning of the session and again towards its close the sacrament was dispensed.   For a long time there seems to have been a good attendance, but from about 1820 or earlier it fell off, and for most of the remaining time, notwithstanding admonitions and threats, only a handful of students attended.   M'Turk, who was chaplain at the beginning of the century, was succeeded by Mylne in 1809.   He resigned in 1819, and the professors of Theology agreed to take charge of the services, but in 1821 it was arranged that half the services should be conducted by Macgill and M'Turk and the other half by William Fleming, afterwards well known as a professor.   Next year Fleming and John Fairie were appointed chaplains, and the former being called to the regular ministry in 1826, was replaced by Mr. Johnston, while next year Johnston was in turn replaced by Ebenezer Russell.   Fairie continued till 1828, though Macgill twice objected to him as unsuitable, and in 1827 threatened to bring the chapel arrangements under the consideration of the faculty's civil or ecclesiastical superiors, and for reasons stated to the principal claimed leave to absent himself when Fairie officiated.   In 1826 it was resolved that the names of students who had not given their professors valid reasons for absence should be called in the chapel every Sunday, and offenders were to be fined sixpence for each absence without excuse.   To have enforced the regulation against the general indifference or opposition of the students would have put the professors, who were not themselves very exemplary in attendance, to some trouble, and it does not seem to have been enforced.   In 1832 Fleming, now a professor, was again appointed chaplain, and he continued to officiate till 1839, with a salary of £50 and an allowance of £20 for communion elements.   It was then agreed that, till a chaplain should be appointed, the professors in the faculty of Theology should officiate or find others properly qualified to do so. For some years from 1840 professor Grey acted as chaplain, then Dr. James Aitken for session 1845-6, afterwards Robert Graham, and finally Robert Reid Rae appointed in 1847.

Attempts had been made from time to time to secure better attendance, and further regulations were adopted in 1838, but they proved unavailing. In November, 1844, a committee gave in a long report on the subject, resting the case for continuing the services rather on regard to use and wont and the opinion of authorities in bygone times than on good results achieved in the present.   Most of the professors, except members of the faculty of Theology and others, like Fleming and Buchanan, who were clergymen, had now become tired of the state of affairs, and Maconochie moved that the religious services in the Common Hall should be discontinued, and a committee appointed to secure accommodation in the High Church, where students might have the benefit of attending the ministrations of a high official of the University ; or in some other city church if an arrangement for the High Church were impracticable.   The principal does not seem to have wished the students to form part of his congregation, and gave his casting vote for an amendment that the chapel services should be continued.   Maconochie, Ramsay, Nichol, Lushington, and William Thomson (professor of Medicine) dissented, and declined to take part in carrying on chapel services, experience having shown that the system was not in keeping with the existing state of the University.

When at the close of the session a precept was authorised for payment of the chapel expenses, Maconochie dissented, and at a later meeting in August, 1845, he entered a protest in which he did not spare the reverend gentlemen concerned.   He and others had opposed the maintenance of unprofitable services, and recommended a return to the ancient usage of the University, but this was negatived by the votes of the clerical members.   The services were placed in the hands of the faculty of Theology upon religious principle, and as there had been no mention of salary, he did not think they were to claim remuneration for the assertion of their religious principles.   Reading a few of their manuscript sermons for the benefit of the institution to which they belonged and in support of their declaration of religious principle, might have been done gratuitously.   About £85 had been voted by the reverend gentlemen to be paid to themselves, and they refused rendering any account or giving any explanation, except that the professor of Ecclesiastical History, having on certain occasions employed strangers to preach, stated his claim at £4 4s., leaving the other three reverend gentlemen to account for £80 16s., which they declined to do.   It was a rule in the administration of public money that specific accounts or vouchers should be produced, and the statutes of 1727 provided that no order for payment should be granted till eight days from its proposal.   He was not opposed to proper remuneration to the faculty of Divinity when properly authorised, nor did he wish to be obstructive regarding continuance of public worship in the Hall; but he intended to appeal to the Visitors and take legal means to prevent this irregular appropriation of College funds.

The faculty agreed to lay the matter before the Visitors, and it was forthwith submitted to them, but no immediate decision was reached.   In April, 1846, the principal and Hill gave in answers to Maconochie's protest, in which they claimed that in the Church of Scotland and in most Christian Churches no such thing was known as a precise rate of payment for a given amount of clerical labour.   When payment was ordered for services performance of which was directed by the faculty and the amount of which was the same from year to year, the rule as to the proposal lying ten days on the table did not apply.   Any alterations which it might be thought advisable to introduce should not be retrospective, so as to affect the reasonable remuneration of services performed at the request of the faculty.   Maconochie, believing that he had attained his purpose—the right of insisting on specific and detailed accounts before any payments from the College funds—withdrew from further procedure, and placed a letter in the clerk's hands releasing the Factor from the fetters imposed by the judicial measures Maconochie had taken; the faculty consented to the rendering of specific accounts; and the matter was declared ended. The chapel services were continued for two sessions more, but in November, 1848, Maconochie carried a motion that the attempt to carry on worship in the Common Hall should be abandoned, and accommodation provided for the students in one of the city churches.   After this Reid, who had a more open mind that the other clerical professors, had an interview with the City Chamberlain, and reported that there were several of the city churches in which accommodation might be had. The faculty chose St. Paul's, in which about a hundred sittings were reserved for the College, the professors being assigned cushioned seats behind the students so as to have them in view during the service. Seats were retained in St. Paul's till the University moved to new buildings in 1870.

There seems to have been no inclination to return to Blackfriars, the church with which the College was of old associated, though it stood within the University grounds, and its churchyard held the dust of many deceased professors and their kindred. A railing costing £73 was erected round the College burying ground in 1827 and an additional lair purchased for £15, and in the same year a sum of £10 was contributed for repairs on the church. In 1840 the principal was authorised to negotiate with the Magistrates and Council for the sale of the College seats in the church, which, since the establishment of a College chapel in 1764, had been let and the proceeds paid to the College funds. After some time the sale of seats was effected, and in 1847 arrangements were made for the investment of the £600 which had been realised, it being laid down that the sum should be available at any future time for the purpose of building a College chapel.

One of the most important events affecting the library was the abolition of Stationers' Hall privileges, and another was the pledging of its contents and the application of part of its revenue to meet the costs incurred by the senate in an unsuccessful action regarding the degree of Bachelor of Surgery. Subsequent measures regarding copyright altered the provisions of the Act of 1709 under which the Scottish Universities first acquired the right to obtain free copies of all books published in the United Kingdom, and latterly the privilege was regulated by an Act passed in the 54th year of the reign of George III. But in 1836 an Act was passed which rescinded the provision for the delivery of a copy of every published book to each of the Scottish Universities through the Stationers' Hall, and authorised the Lords of the Treasury to fix the amount of the annual compensation grant to be paid to each University in consequence of the change.

A committee was appointed to assist the librarian in making up a report to the Treasury of the value of the books received from Stationers' Hall for the three years preceding the passing of the Act of 1836. The committee seems to have made a good case for the University, bringing out an annual value of £809 10s. 4d., and in January, 1838, a communication was received from the Lords of the Treasury fixing the annual compensation grant at £707, with which the senate expressed satisfaction. After the House of Lords in 1840 pronounced a decision adverse to the University in their lawsuit with the Faculty of Physicians and Surgeons regarding the degree of Bachelor of Surgery, the senate had to face costs amounting to £1,684, and the library suffered for misfortunes not its own.   Most of the academic funds were in the hands of the faculty of the College, who were not parties to the lawsuit, and the senate, who carried it on, possessed little except the library with its funds, and the fees paid for certain degrees.   The senate indeed had no money to make an immediate payment, and had to raise the far larger part of the sum by means of a bond over their estates, funds, and revenues.   The contents of the library were pledged in security, and for a number of years a considerable portion of the library funds were diverted from their natural purpose, in order to pay interest on the debt and gradually to reduce the principal.   In April, 1851, arrangements were made for extinguishing the liabilities then existing, but this involved an advance which had to be met by appropriating for some time longer part of the contributions paid to the library by students.   The admission of graduates to the use of the library in 1857 begets surprise that it did not happen earlier

After the resignation of Lockhart Muirhead in 1827 William Park, who had been sub-librarian for 18 months, was chosen as librarian, having to find security for £2,000 for faithful discharge of duty.   Park having become minister of Airth, Nathaniel Jones, previously assistant librarian to the Faculty of Physicians and Surgeons, was appointed in 1845 to be University librarian, at an annual salary of £84, half of which was paid by the faculty and half by the senate, the security in his case being reduced to £1,000, and it being provided that in future the librarian should be annually appointed on 1st May.

In 1833 Mr. C. W. White presented a copy of the works of Zenophon in folio, printed by Henricus Stephanus in 1561, which appears to have belonged to James VI., and afterwards to various others.   As the University library possessed a copy of this edition formerly belonging to Zachary Boyd, the Senate directed this copy to be placed in the Hunterian Library.   In March, 1852, Miss Marjory Ettles, Stirling, announced a presentation of rare and valuable old books by her sister, the widow of Dr. Ebenezer Brown, Inspector General of Hospitals, who had been educated in the University.   The collection included about thirty volumes, mostly in Italian but some in Latin, forming beautiful specimens of early printing from about 1470 to 1500 and a little later.   There was also an old illuminated manuscript Bible, for the modern binding of which Dr.

Brown accounted by supposing it was a device to conceal its value at the time when the French under Buonaparte were in Italy, where Dr. Brown procured the books. This collection was also sent to the Hunterian Library. Another donation of some considerable local importance was announced in 1847 by Dr. Smith of Crutherland, secretary of the Maitland Club, who intimated his intention of bequeathing to the University, to be kept in the library in a place apart, copies of the publications of the several literary and archæological societies of which he had been a member ; and also to make over a collection, bound in 42 volumes, of tracts relating to the civil, ecclesiastical, commercial, and political affairs of Glasgow, the bringing together of which had occupied a great share of his attention for many years.

In August, 1846, a letter was submitted to the faculty from Dr. Smith as secretary of the Maitland Club, stating that the Club at their last annual meeting had expressed a desire to print a collection of documents illustrating the history of the University, and would endeavour to produce a work worthy of the subject. The faculty allowed access to the records, charters, and documents, and appointed the principal, Fleming, William Thomson (professor of Medicine), Maconochie and Reid a committee to act along with the editor, Mr. Joseph Robertson. A few months before this, on the proposal of Thomson, who was then clerk to the faculty, it was resolved that, as a tribute to the memory of benefactors and for convenience in administration, the deeds instituting bursaries, scholarships, and other foundations should be printed, with biographical notices of the founders. Fleming and Reid were associated with Thomson in carrying out this work ; and as Fleming was a member of the Maitland Club and Principal Macfarlan its vice-president, the discussion regarding the printing of the deeds of bursary and other foundations and the research among old documents to which it gave rise, may have suggested the larger undertaking, which was issued towards the end of 1854 as *Munimenta Almae Universitatis Glasguensis*. Mr. Robertson planned the work and edited rather more than a fourth of the first volume, and was succeeded by Mr. Cosmo Innes, on whom the work of editing mainly fell. The first volume deals with Privileges and Property, the second with Statutes and Annals, and the third with Members and Economy, while the fourth contains an index and lists of University officers, including administrators, regents, and professors. Under this system the contents of a particular volume in the original records may be disintegrated and the fragments scattered through several of the printed volumes, while many of the documents are of such a kind that it is not easy to say under which heading they might most naturally appear. Valuable as the work is for the long period from 1451 to 1727 which it covers, probably it would have been improved by reproducing the original volumes as they stood, and by supplying a fuller index containing other things besides names of persons and places.

The type foundry built in 1762, in the small garden near the Physic Garden, for Alexander Wilson, who was also professor of Astronomy, had been carried on ever since by himself or his descendants, and had undergone extension from time to time. The Wilsons had also an establishment in London. In September, 1834, application was made to have the lease changed to a feu, and to this the faculty consented; but almost immediately afterwards Mr. Alexander Wilson, resolving to discontinue business at Glasgow, offered the foundry premises to the faculty for £400. The faculty would not give more than £350, and with this sum, and a stipulation that for fifty years to come no other type founder should be allowed to use the building, Wilson had to content himself.

On 2nd May, 1831, Hutchison and Bookman were appointed printers to the University for a year, but in March, 1832, applications were laid before the senate for the office of printer by Mr. Bookman, Mr. Hutchison, and Mr. Khull, and on 25th February, 1833, Mr. Khull was appointed printer till 1st May, 1834. He held the position till 1843 or longer. On 1st May, 1848, George Richardson was chosen printer, and the appointment was continued to Robert MacLehose, who purchased Richardson's business in 1872. In April, 1853, Mr. Charles Griffin of London was, on his own application, appointed publisher to the University, and the office was long held by himself or his firm, Charles Griffin & Co. In 1871 Mr. James MacLehose, who had been bookseller to the University since 1862, was appointed publisher also, and both appointments are still held by the firm which he founded.

In April, 1839, the senate had some apprehensions in consequence of the expiry of the patent of the Queen's printer for Scotland, who had hitherto enjoyed an exclusive right to print Bibles, and the prospect of all printers being allowed to do so in future on their coming under an obligation to produce a pure text. The senate feared this might endanger the purity of the text, and diminish the confidence of the people of Scotland in the sacred volume and their reverence for it. They resolved therefore to offer their services in conjunction with those of the other Universities of Scotland in superintending the printing of the Scriptures, and with this object to send a memorial to the Government and petitions to both Houses of Parliament. The matter was differently arranged, however, and since that time printers in Scotland who are about to bring out an edition of the Bible have to procure a license from the Lord

Advocate and conform to instructions issued by the Queen in Council on 11th July and 28th December, 1839.

In 1831 Henry Cockburn, Advocate, was elected rector, having secured 203 votes and a majority in two 'nations,' while Joseph Hume, M.P., had 170 votes and a majority in one 'nation,' and John Gibson Lockhart, Scott's son-in-law, 159 votes and a majority in one 'nation.' Cockburn was unanimously re-elected in 1832, and in 1833 he was proposed for a third time, the rival candidate being Professor Sir Daniel Sandford. Loudoniana and Transforthana voted for Cockburn, while Glottiana and Rothseiana voted for Sandford, the individual votes for the former being 175 and for the latter 153. The vice-rector Professor Buchanan declined to give a casting vote, and Cockburn, as the preceding rector, was called upon to perform that invidious duty, and voted for himself. He declared that he would have voted for his opponent if that gentleman had been clearly or even probably eligible, but he held it to be certain that Sir Daniel being a professor in the College was ineligible. The principal and six professors protested and twenty-one students followed a similar course.

Some things done or attempted by Cockburn during his tenure were much to his credit, though they seem to have made him anything but a favourite with the faculty. Early in 1832 a committee of faculty reported that accounts for alterations and improvements on Davidson's house amounted to £524, and on Sandford's house to £827, being an excess above what the faculty had sanctioned of £287 in the former case and of £380 in the latter. However, the faculty agreed to pay the charges. Towards the end of the year Cockburn and the dean of faculty, as visitors, gave their opinion that whatever had been expended on the houses without the previous sanction of the faculty should be replaced to the funds. The two professors concerned struggled hard, and their colleagues did what they could to secure at least a mitigation of the sentence. At length in April, 1833, the end of the long controversy was reached, and the visitors in respect that the irregularity they wished to check had been acknowledged, and that the payments to be made would probably prevent its repetition, allowed the matter to be settled by accepting a modified sum of £70 from Davidson and £100 from Sandford.

Cockburn in 1832 transmitted memorials from the students regarding some arrangements concerning the library, in which an improvement seems to have followed, and respecting the mode of awarding the Snell exhibitions, which the faculty delayed to consider. Early in 1834 Cockburn sent a further letter requesting the faculty to consider and dispose of the question, and strongly arguing that, though other circumstances might be admitted to consideration, the exhibitions should be awarded after a public examination of the candidates.   He urged that this would render difficult if not impossible the appointment of persons absolutely unfit in respect of knowledge and ability, and that such appointments were un-questionably believed to have been made ; that it would relieve the patrons from the pest of solicitation and enable them to refer to a test which would deter or extinguish unworthy candidates ; that it would excite greater interest among the students generally regarding these valuable prizes ; and tend to check any actual partiality in the minds of the patrons and probably destroy its imputation.   He might concede that under the exist-ing system partiality existed to as limited an extent as it ever did in human nature, but could the public be got to believe it ?   Adverse imputations were strong and general, and although the College might say the world was in error and to be despised, surely it was politic for the administrators of an institution whose welfare depended on its public reputation to avoid unfavourable appearances.

On 13th March, 1834, the faculty adopted a deliverance in which they cited the long list of exhibitioners, many of whom had risen to distinction, as evidence that the patronage had not been mismanaged.   To make the exhibitions an object of competition by public examination would not remove any material inconvenience actually existing, and would produce serious injury to the exhibitioners, the students, and the College.   If the faculty were to decide by the results of examinations, they must overlook other essential qualifications, and appoint candidates unsuited to the pur-poses of the foundation and unqualified to sustain the honour of their University.   On the other hand, if they allowed greater weight to the general character and merits of a candidate than to the display made in the examination, they would be more loudly and plausibly blamed than at present ; and those who did not attribute partiality to the patrons might suspect some blemish or defect in the unsuccessful candidates, which might be deeply injurious to them.   So far as sound principles, amiable dis-positions, and correct conduct created a preference, the faculty owned they were liable to it ; but hinted that the allegations that they were influenced by selfish or personal motives proceeded from disappointed candidates whose own solicitations had been unsuccessful.   The faculty could not consistently with their duty adopt a measure by which the appointment would be decided in whole or in part by public competition.   M'Turk alone declared in favour of public examinations, though Macgill dissented from some of the views of the faculty.

Stanley and Peel were the next two rectors—the former elected in 1834 by all the 'nations' and a majority of 148 individual votes, and the latter in 1836 by three 'nations' and a majority of 100 individual votes. Both elections made much stir at the time.   Immediately on the declaration of Peel's return, Norman Macleod, still a student and still keen at electioneering, with some others hastened to the Royal Exchange with the news, and a number of merchants at once resolved to invite the new rector to a public dinner.   It is said that in three days 1,250 citizens signed the invitation, and nearly 3,500 persons were present on 15th January, 1837, at the memorable banquet given in his honour, for which a special temporary building had to be erected.   Peel's installation as rector aroused great interest.   The law students petitioned for admission without procuring library tickets—that is, without enrolling and paying a fee of seven shillings—and a number of graduates who were refused admission sent a letter of complaint and remonstrance to the rector.   Peel himself seems to have been not a little elated, for he declared that he had come to be installed as rector with greater satisfaction than he felt on assuming office when called by his sovereign to be Prime Minister, a statement surely begotten of momentary impulse rather than permanent conviction.   After Peel came Sir James Graham, who during his tenure appeared to favour the provision by Government of salaries for unendowed regius professors, and afterwards when Home Secretary brought in bills for Medical Reform with provisions adverse to the Scottish Universities. Next came the Marquis of Breadalbane, Fox Maule, and Andrew Rutherfurd, the last of whom helped to pass the bill for the sale of the old lands and buildings of the University and the provision of new, and endeavoured to procure a reform in the law regarding University tests, and to induce the faculty to provide accommodation for the first professor of Engineering.   On the expiry of Rutherfurd's tenure in November, 1846, Glottiana and Rothseiana voted for William Wordsworth, while Loudoniana and Transforthana voted for Lord John Russell.   Nichol as vice-rector gave his casting vote for the latter, who was declared elected, notwithstanding objections from some few students.   Arrangements were being made for Russell's installation in October or November, 1847, but a time of Chartist unrest, Irish disaffection, and foreign revolutions was impending, and he wrote that he was unable then to visit Glasgow, on account of the anxious state of public affairs.   In November of that year the students deviated from the usual course and instead of re-electing Russell, chose Mure of Caldwell for rector, Loudoniana alone of the "nations' voting for Russell.   Mure, like his predecessor, had only one year's tenure, Macaulay being chosen by a majority in all the 'nations' on 15th November, 1848. The election literature on this occasion seems to have been very bitter, and the faculty admonished the students on the gross impropriety of the imputations against individuals of high character and official position made and repeated in the handbills which had been circulated ; and declared their strong reprehension of the scurrilous language addressed by the students to each other.   Macaulay's term of office happened to be near the fourth centenary of the University, and his rectorial address, delivered on 21st March, 1849, gave a retrospect of the condition of affairs at the opening of each successive century in its history.[1]   The rector was then on the crest of the mounting wave of celebrity which followed the publication of the first two volumes of his *History*, of which three editions were sold in as many months, and his address was very successful.   It was afterwards published at the request of the students and inscribed to them 'by their friend, Thomas Babington Macaulay.'   The day after his installation at the University he received the freedom of the city, an event which in prospect made him very uneasy.   'Having made my way in the world by haranguing, I am now as unwilling to make a speech as any timid stammerer in Great Britain.'   However, he had a great reception from a crowded meeting in the City Hall, what he said was well received, and he was vehemently applauded at the close.

In the summer of 1849, at the request of the principal and all the professors then within reach, Macaulay agreed to sit for his portrait to Sir John Watson Gordon, and it was painted in the spring of next year. Mr. James Keith, printseller and publisher, 60 Princes Street, Edinburgh, had undertaken to defray the cost and to present the portrait to the University, on condition that he should have the sole right to publish an engraving from it.   In November, 1850, Keith made over to the University the property of the picture, reserving only a right to its temporary use for the purpose of taking the engraving which was to be executed in the best style, the process requiring, according to Keith's estimate, a year for its completion.   In February, 1855, a letter was received from Keith, who had now removed to London, stating that he had handed over

[1] Some of Macaulay's kindred and many of his clan have been students at Glasgow.   It seems probable that Aulay Macaulay, matriculated in 1703, was the minister of Tyree and Coll in the first decade of the 18th century, to whom, as the historian's great-grandfather, Trevelyan traces back the ancestral line.   Two of the historian's uncles, Aulay Macaulay and Kenneth Macaulay, were matriculated in 1772 and 1787 respectively.   Aulay Macaulay held the Exchequer bursary, and graduated as M.A. in 1778, after which he directed his course southward, and was some time employed as a private tutor.   He became acquainted with Thomas Babington, owner of Rothley Temple in Leicestershire, and they made a tour in Scotland, paying a visit to the Manse of Cardross, where Aulay's father (the historian's grandfather) was minister.   Babington fell in love with Miss Jean Macaulay, a daughter of the manse, whom he married in 1787.   It was in their house at Rothley Temple that Lord Macaulay first saw the light, and in compliment to its owner he was christened Thomas Babington.

the portrait, and requesting that it should be placed along with other portraits in the Hunterian Museum. There can be little doubt that Keith's chief aim was as much concerned with the engraving as with the portrait. He persuaded the principal and professors to request Macaulay to sit for the portrait, but it may be doubted whether Macaulay, with his proud, independent disposition, would have consented if Keith had approached him and made a frank disclosure of his intentions.

At the end of his tenure Macaulay was called upon to give a casting vote, two 'nations' having voted for Palmerston and two for Sheriff Alison in November, 1850. The principal having transmitted to the former rector an extract of the statute regarding the casting vote, and an intimation that according to usage this vote was given in a meeting of *comitia*, Macaulay replied that he was unable to attend. The senate then called upon Mure, the rector who preceded Macaulay. He was abroad at the time, but, on his return, gave his casting vote in February, 1851, for Alison. In November, 1852, the Earl of Eglinton was elected by the votes of three 'nations,' Glottiana voting for the Duke of Argyll. Eglinton narrowly escaped the one year's tenure which had befallen Russell and Mure, for in November, 1853, Loudoniana and Rothseiana voted for him, while Glottiana and Transforthana voted for Alfred Tennyson, but Harry Rainy, the vice-rector, gave his casting vote for the Earl. In 1854 the Duke of Argyll was chosen by the votes of all the 'nations,' upon which George Palmer, John Marshall Lang, and James Brown gave in a protest against the election '*quia vi atque armis, contra leges Universitatis atque Urbis Glasguensis, transacta est.*' In 1856 Edward Bulwer Lytton was elected, and his tenure fell at the time of passing the Universities (Scotland) Act.

In 1830 and 1837 addresses were presented to King William and Queen Victoria on their accession, and further addresses were presented to the young Queen on her marriage and on the birth of the Princess Royal and the Prince of Wales. When the Queen visited Scotland in 1842 an address of homage and welcome was presented to her, and also an address to Prince Albert. Seven years later the Queen was received and addresses presented within the halls of the University. The royal visit to the city was announced a fortnight beforehand, and on 1st August, 1849, the senate adopted addresses to be presented to the Queen and the Prince Consort. The address to the Queen set forth that the Chancellor, rector, dean of faculties, principal, and professors gladly availed themselves of the opportunity to welcome Her Majesty to their ancient establishment which owed its origin to the zeal for the diffusion of knowledge by which so many of her predecessors had been distinguished. They hoped that a large and increasing number of youths might be trained to high mental culture within the walls of the University, imbued with a love of literature and science, and devotedly attached to those principles of social order and constitutional loyalty of which Her Majesty was the faithful guardian and the exalted object.   It was their earnest wish and prayer that Providence might perpetuate to Her Majesty the large measure of domestic happiness which He had bestowed; and might prolong her reign in prosperity and tranquillity over a people intelligent, contented, free, and worthy of their freedom.   In the address to Prince Albert they offered him the tribute of their respectful homage and affectionate regard.   They contemplated in him the consort of their gracious and beloved sovereign, endeared by his personal character to all classes, and an enlightened patron of the literary and scientific pursuits which it was their object to teach and promote.

It was the vacation time and many professors were absent, but the summer committee pressed forward preparations for the visit.   The forehall, in which the Queen was to be received, was stripped of its furniture and pictures, its walls washed down, its ceiling whitewashed, and the oak panelling revarnished.   The somewhat dingy walls fronting High Street and in the first court were cleaned by setting fire-engines to play upon them with water.   At the main entrance the balconies were repaired and the royal arms regilded.   The floor of the forehall was covered with drugget, except a platform for the royal visitors placed at the upper end and laid with a rich velvet carpet.   On the platform handsome walnut chairs richly covered with crimson satin were placed for the Queen, the Prince Consort, and the younger members of the royal family.   A table on which the mace might be laid was placed in the centre of the room, and covered with rich gold cloth formerly used at the court of Tippoo Sahib, Sultan of Mysore and son of Hyder Ali, lent for the occasion by Lady Leith.   The only other article of furniture was the Blackstone chair, the carving of which had been cleaned and the ornaments repaired.   An alighting platform covered with crimson cloth was provided in front of the entrance, and crimson cloth continued from it to the foot of the staircase and along the stair.   In case the royal visitors should extend their inspection further, the Museum was cleaned, a stair carpet laid down, and the chairs and settees in the cupola room renovated, while the Roman stones, as objects likely to interest Prince Albert, were washed and placed round the Museum court.   The College servants received new uniforms, and to brighten the entrance showy plants from the Botanic Gardens were arranged on the balconies.   The day before the Queen's visit Colonel Gordon, her equerry, inspected and approved the arrangements, but suggested the provision of a boudoir or retiring room, upon which the faculty room was hastily fitted up for that purpose.

The Queen had been spending some days in Ireland, and on Saturday, 11th August, embarked from Dublin for Scotland. Stormy weather arose, and the royal yacht Victoria and Albert with its accompanying fleet anchored in Loch Ryan till Monday. On that day the voyage was resumed, and in the afternoon the Queen visited Loch Lomond, the royal yacht being moored for the night in Rosneath Bay. On Tuesday, 14th August, 1849, the royal passengers were transferred from the Victoria and Albert to the yacht Fairy, which reached Glasgow at midday. At the Broomielaw Lord Provost Anderson and the magistrates went on board with an address, and were severally introduced to the Queen, who knighted the Lord Provost on the spot. Attended by a troop of Glasgow yeomanry and escorts of cavalry and police, the sovereign then drove through decorated streets and cheering crowds to the Cathedral. Soon after one o'clock the Queen, the Prince Consort, and four royal children, including the Prince of Wales, attended by the ladies and gentlemen of the royal suite and the civic authorities of Glasgow, arrived at the College gate.

The high magistrates of the University, the chancellor (the Duke of Montrose), the rector (Macaulay), and the dean of faculties (Colonel Mure) were not present, and Principal Macfarlan and a company of professors received the royal visitors, and conducted them to the forehall, where the Queen and Prince seated themselves on the chairs of state which had been provided. The addresses were then presented and most graciously received, after which the members of senate present—Professors Hill, Burns, Thomas Thomson, Robert Buchanan, William Couper, Fleming, John Couper, Nichol, Andrew Buchanan, Pagan, Reid, William Thomson (professor of Medicine), Rainy, Arnott, and Allen Thomson—were severally introduced to the Queen, by whose gracious courtesy they were much impressed. Her Majesty having, on account of the shortness of the time allowed for her visit, declined to inspect the Museum or any other part of the buildings, the royal party were conducted back to the entrance by the members of the University, of whom they then took leave in the most condescending manner. The senate recorded their deep sense of the honour conferred on the University by a personal visit from the sovereign, and their especial gratitude for the high compliment paid by the Queen and the Prince Consort in receiving the addresses within the College Hall. They anticipated the happiest results from a visit evincing the unabated favour of the crown towards their ancient seminary, confirming the attachment to the sovereign by which they trusted its members had ever been distinguished, and animating all connected with it to redoubled diligence in the discharge of their duties.

In 1838 a memorial was forwarded to the Government asking for the renewal of the annual grant of £800 given for fourteen years from 1825 in place of the lease of the Archbishopric; and the principal repaired to London to invoke the aid of the rector[1] and other persons of influence. In January of next year a memorial was again sent, and the principal was requested to proceed to London and Edinburgh to urge the claims of the College.   On 1st April, 1839, the principal produced a correspondence on the subject, and a memorandum of a conversation with the Chancellor of the Exchequer, who did not admit that the lease of the Archbishopric from 1698 to 1825, followed by a grant of £800 for the last fourteen years, established a right to its continuance.   The claim must be determined by the present state of the College and its funds, and by the report of the Universities Commission appointed in 1837, which he would examine upon its arrival and afterwards take his measures.

The affair did not prove to be a simple one or capable of easy and rapid adjustment.   The Commissioners who reported on the University of Glasgow in 1839 earnestly urged the abolition of the distinction between the regius professors, as they were called, and the faculty professors.   They recommended that the grant of £800 should be continued but placed under the control of the University Court, who in disposing of it could take into account the different circumstances of different chairs.   But the University Court did not exist and did not come into existence till nearly twenty years later, and to have continued the grant of £800 to the faculty would have confirmed their monopoly of privileges which the Commissioners desired to see abolished.   At the time the Commissioners reported in 1839 there were six regius chairs outside the faculty, and by next year three more had been added.   Before many years had passed Government had bestowed some salary on chairs which had no original endowment, and had raised the salaries of some which were originally very small, but the endowment for Midwifery was not raised beyond the original sum.   Before 1858 the nine regius chairs received from royal and parliamentary grants the following annual sums: Natural History, £150, Surgery, Institutes of Medicine, and Forensic Medicine, £75 each, Midwifery, £50, Chemistry and Botany, £200 each, Materia Medica, £100, and Civil Engineering, £275.   It is not clear that the amount granted after 1839 in salaries and additions to salaries in the case of these chairs made up an equivalent for the annual grant of £800.

In consequence of the University or College holding the teinds of

[1] Sir Robert Peel was rector till November, 1838, after that Sir James Graham.

various localities, its administrators were frequently called upon to subscribe to schemes for building churches, and in most cases they consented,
either from love of the Church or from fear of the law, for refusal would
probably have led to litigation.   In 1832 the faculty subscribed £75 for
a chapel of ease in the village of Partick, and in 1833 £50 for a chapel
at Baillieston, next year £50 for a chapel or church in Airdrie, and in
1837 £50 for a church at Strathbungo.   In 1847 the faculty as trustees
for the Dundonald farms in East Kilbride agreed to give £50 to aid in
building a schoolmaster's house there, and at the same time refused to
give any contribution for the erection of a manse at Partick.   Towards
the end of the same year the faculty considered a draft bill forwarded to
them by Dr. Leishman, the minister of Govan, to be submitted to
Parliament for authority to feu the glebe of Govan.

The faculty concluded they were not called upon to oppose the project,
but suggested some amendments for the purpose of safeguarding the
access to the church and churchyard, and preserving the fitness of the
church for accommodating the congregation.   In February, 1848, they
approved of the bill as amended in Parliament, and allowed Dr. Leishman
personally to take to London a charter of 1630 by Charles I., as evidence
that the patronage of Govan was vested in the College.   The faculty in
1837 voted a sum of £20 for repairing and upholding the monument
at Killearn to George Buchanan.   When the ravages of cholera elsewhere
were exciting attention and anxiety, a society was formed in Glasgow for
adopting precautionary measures against the fatal disease, and in December, 1831, the faculty agreed to subscribe £100 for the purpose.   About
two months later the disease appeared in the city.   A subscription was
given to the Cholera Hospital, and on 16th February, 1832, a meeting
of senate, specially convened, authorised the professors to grant to students
who wished to leave town certificates of attendance counting as a complete
session, the professor of Divinity being left to his own discretion, in view
of his special relation to the laws of the church.   Sandford moved and
Badham seconded that the classes should be adjourned for a fortnight, but
the Chamber of Commerce and the Magistrates and Council made representations against this, and it was not carried.   In 1854, at the time of
the Crimean war, the faculty subscribed £105 to the Patriotic Fund.

In 1845 a prospect arose of the University being removed almost
without effort or expenditure on its own part to new buildings on the
high ground at Woodlands, facing the eminence across the Kelvin on
which it actually found a site a quarter of a century later.   It was a time
when projects for the construction of new railways were rife, and in
August, 1845, the Agents of the Glasgow, Airdrie, and Monklands

Junction Railway Company opened negotiations with the faculty of the College for acquiring a strip of ground sufficient to allow the formation of a line with a terminus in High Street; but by November the proposal was altered to one for exchanging the existing lands and buildings of the College for new lands and buildings to be provided elsewhere. An Act of Parliament authorising the scheme was passed on 26th August, 1846, and to it there was annexed a long agreement made by the parties. The Company became bound to provide not less than seventeen acres at Woodlands, with sufficient classrooms and laboratories, as well as accommodation for the museum and library, to be made over to the faculty of the College for the same ends and uses, and with the same rights and privileges, as the lands and buildings they previously possessed. The lands and buildings at Woodlands, and the principal, professors, students, and officers of the University and College were to be exempted from all taxes, burdens, jurisdictions, and imposts in the same manner and to the same extent as they were then exempted by royal grant or charter or Act of Parliament or immemorial usage, except that the lands were to remain liable to the poor rates of the Barony parish. Further lands extending to at least three acres were to be provided at Woodlands, on which the Company were to erect thirteen dwelling-houses for the principal and professors, but the immunity from local and parochial burdens was not to extend to these houses or their occupants.

At an early stage of the negotiations the professors in the faculty of Medicine insisted on the provision of a new hospital, if the College buildings were to be removed to a great distance from the Royal Infirmary, to which there was an acknowledged right of resort for the instruction of medical students. At first the Railway Company, while indicating their willingness to subscribe £1,000, professed to regard the hospital scheme as one for the citizens, but finding they were not likely to obtain their ends without further concession, they gave way. It was agreed that within two years from the passing of the Act the faculty should purchase between the site of the new College and the river Clyde ground for the erection of a new hospital, with not fewer than 120 beds for patients, to be under the charge of the medical and surgical members of the University, and accessible for education in clinical, medical, and surgical practice, under regulations to be framed by the senate, the Company being obliged to pay the cost of one acre of ground, as well as an initial sum of £10,000 towards erecting the hospital, and a yearly sum of £500 to aid in maintaining it.

The plans, prepared by Mr. Baird of Glasgow, were subject to approbation by the Lords of the Treasury, as was also the agreement between

OLD GATEWAY AT GLASGOW UNIVERSITY—A RELIC FROM HIGH STREET

the Company and the College annexed to the Act. The Lords of the Treasury sent the plans to London architects for report and revision—first to Barry and Pugin and next to Mr. Blore—and years passed in communication and discussion. In September, 1848, the principal and the professor of Law reported the purchase within the time allowed by the Act of a site for the new hospital, being a plot of 10,600 square yards at the west side of North Street and south side of Sauchiehall Street, at a price of £10,600, with a feu duty of £10 an acre. The eastern half had already been paid, and the price of the western half remained to be paid at Whitsunday, 1849. Intimation of the purchase was made to the Railway Company, and they were asked to pay £4,840 for the acre to which the agreement bound them. The Directors professed surprise and stated that, from the time that had elapsed since the College Removal Act was passed, they thought all idea of building a new College and hospital had been abandoned, and had long considered themselves freed from any obligation under the Act and relative agreement. If the College had purchased ground, they must not look to the Company for any part of its price or of the cost of erecting the hospital. The College law agent then expressed the unqualified astonishment of the Removal Committee that the Railway Company should resile from the agreement, pointed out that the proposals originated with the Company after the faculty had made known the serious nature and magnitude of the undertaking, and urged that the agreement having been ratified by Act of Parliament had become a public deed in which the Crown, the University, and the public had acquired an interest as well as the faculty, who as administrators were bound to require its fulfilment.

On 12th March, 1849, the Removal Committee reported that they had submitted a memorial and taken the opinion of Lord Advocate Rutherfurd, John Marshall, Charles Neaves, and John A. Wood on the question between the College and the Company. Counsel thought the agreement between the parties was still binding, and that the delay in obtaining the consent of the Treasury to the plans and specifications was not attributable to the faculty, but was incident to the nature of the undertaking and the requirements imposed by the legislature. The College should promptly and strenuously endeavour to procure the sanction of the Treasury to the plans and specifications, and on obtaining approval should tender them to the Company for execution, and it might be reasonable to offer a period of four years from the date of approval for completing the building. If the Company refused, the faculty should institute an action in the Court of Session concluding for implement of the agreement, or, if the defenders would not implement within a specified time, that they should deposit under the authority of the Court the sum they had undertaken to pay for execution of the buildings and other purposes, the faculty being authorised to enter into contracts for execution of the work; or, finally, concluding for damages in case of failure or delay in implement of contract. Counsel thought the faculty would be entitled to be relieved from the cost of the ground which the Act gave authority for acquiring at the expense of the Company, and to be indemnified for other expenses incurred during the subsistence and prosecution of the agreement, even though the agreement should ultimately cease to be binding from delay on the part of the Treasury or other cause not implying delay or negligence on the part of the faculty.

On 1st May, 1849, it was reported that an action had been raised against the Company *ad pactum praestandum*, that arrestment had been made of an unpaid call of £2 10s. in the hands of the shareholders, and that a sum of £15,000 on the property of Woodlands had been secured by an inhibition recorded against the Directors of the Railway Company. On the preceding day the College agents had intimated to the agents of the Company that the plans and specifications for the new College had been approved by the Lords of the Treasury and others concerned, and were accessible for the use of the Company in proceeding to build or enter into contracts. By the beginning of November Peter Blackburn of Killearn, chairman of the Company, intimated that a committee had been appointed to confer with the faculty in order to settle the claims of the latter by a reasonable compromise. Negotiation moved slowly at first and the Company showed some inclination to approach Parliament for a repeal of the College Removal Act, but in May, 1850, terms of settlement were arranged and signed. The Company undertook to pay £12,700 for breach of contract and for expenses which the College had incurred, and as the Company desired to secure a winding up Act, to the passing of which the faculty had procured a promise of opposition on the part of the Treasury, the faculty now prevailed on the Treasury to withdraw their opposition.

It was agreed that in the proposed winding up bill a clause should be introduced providing that the remainder of the £12,700, after paying the expenses incurred and making good any loss in selling or feuing the ground purchased for the site of a hospital, should be held as a separate fund, the proceeds of which should be applied with the approval of the visitors to repairing or renewing the buildings. As a result £10,000 was set apart as a fabric fund. The Glasgow, Airdrie, and Monklands Junction Railway Company did not stand alone in being unable to carry out its undertakings. The great utility of railways had been fully demonstrated, and railway enterprise, still in its early stages, was stimulated to an exaggerated and unhealthy activity, new projects being put forward without sufficient adaptation of means to ends.   Bad harvests, depression in other trades, and social unrest and agitation aggravated the state of affairs, public confidence received a rude shock, and many railway schemes proved ruinous.   The Removal Committee of the College recorded their opinion that, in the state in which railway property then stood, the faculty might consider themselves fortunate in the settlement.

During the time with which this chapter deals two questions concerning the Scottish Universities were after long discussion settled by Acts of Parliament, the one having reference to the abolition or mitigation of tests, and the other to a reform in the constitution and organisation of the Universities.   The Act of Security and the Act of Union of 1707 required professors and officebearers, before or at the time of their admission, to acknowledge and subscribe the Confession of Faith of the Church of Scotland as the confession of their faith, to conform to the worship of that Church, submit to its government and discipline, and never endeavour to prejudice or subvert them.   At the time of the Union the imposition of Episcopacy from the south was feared, but this apprehension had long since passed away, and the events and circumstances of the time forced into prominence the need for reform regarding the test.   At Glasgow there had been controversy before the Disruption, and afterwards others besides members of the Free Church urged amendment of the law.

There was a sharp wrangle over the election of the dean of faculties on 1st May, 1841.   The retiring dean, Kirkman Finlay, attended to take part in the election, a thing most unusual if not unprecedented, and Nichol protested against his attendance.   A shower of other protests followed—one against John Couper and Nichol because they had not produced evidence of having signed the Confession of Faith, another against Burns and Hooker as Episcopalians, who could not have complied with the conditions laid down by law, and a third against Lewis Gordon because he signed the Confession of Faith before the Presbytery of Edinburgh, instead of that of Glasgow.   The principal proposed that Sir Archibald Campbell of Succoth should be dean, and this was seconded by Jeffray; while Thomas Thomson proposed Lord Dunfermline,[1] and this was seconded by James Thomson.   Including Finlay's vote for Campbell, ten voted for each candidate, and the rector, Lord Breadalbane,

[1] James Abercromby, third son of the famous soldier Sir Ralph, was Speaker of the House of Commons from 1835 to 1839, and his elevation to the peerage as Lord Dunfermline in the latter year left a seat vacant at Edinburgh which was filled by the election of Macaulay.

gave his casting vote for Dunfermline.   The supporters of Campbell then protested against the validity of the election.   When Dunfermline came forward on 29th April, 1842, to be admitted to office, the principal and several others renewed their protest against his election, but on a vote being taken the Senate resolved to admit him.   Fleming then read an extract from the Act of Security and asked whether Dunfermline was prepared to comply.   The latter declined to answer unless the Senate thought it a question which ought to be put, and the Senate resolved that, as it had not been the practice to put such a question to former deans and rectors, it should not be put on that occasion.   Dunfermline was then admitted, Fleming entering a further protest.   Some speedy means of composing the strife for a time must have been found, for only three days afterwards Dunfermline was unanimously re-elected dean.

The reformers having resolved to petition Parliament against the test, a notable trial of strength was impending, and at a meeting of Senate on 7th November, 1843, Fox Maule and Sir Thomas Macdougall Brisbane, the rector and dean, were present to give their help.   Resolutions moved by Thomas Thomson and seconded by Brisbane were carried against a counter motion by the principal.   The resolutions, which were intended as the basis of a petition to Parliament, pointed out that no tests were required for matriculation or graduation, that circumstances had altered greatly since 1707, that dissenters had greatly increased in number, and their exclusion would not only restrict the choice of teachers however high their qualifications, but would probably lead to the establishment of other seminaries and the withdrawal from the University of students whose fees formed the main part of the remuneration of professors.   It might be proper that theological professors should belong to the Church of Scotland, but there was no reason for similar exclusiveness in regard to chairs of literature, philosophy, and science.   The subscription of lay professors at Edinburgh had long fallen into disuse without hurt to religion or education, and in all the Universities the law was violated in the case of the chancellor and rector.   The Senate appointed a committee to draw up a petition to Parliament, correspond with other Universities, and take measures for promoting the end contemplated.   About a week later the principal and a number of others who had dissented at the time, gave in reasons, alleging that the petition was contrary to a fundamental and essential condition of the treaty of Union, inconsistent with the constitution of the British Empire and with the oath taken by the Queen at her accession to maintain the Church of Scotland, and injurious to the University.   The dissentients regretted that the majority of the Senate should exhibit themselves in the fantastic and undignified position of asking what they might be assured the British legislature could not, would not, and ought not to grant.

It was not at Glasgow that the worst trouble occurred. At Edinburgh Charles M'Douall was appointed in 1847 joint professor of Hebrew, but on account of his not taking the test the Senate refused to admit him, and afterwards the Court of Session granted an interdict against his induction ; and again in 1850 Patrick Macdougall, another member of the Free Church, was presented by the Town Council as professor of Moral Philosophy, but the academic authorities declined to recognise his induction by the Council, and though he was allowed to teach the class, he was not admitted to the Senate till the law had been altered three years later. At St. Andrews the Presbytery drew up a libel against Sir David Brewster, principal of the University, and proposed that he should be expelled from it for adhering to the Free Church. In 1845 a bill dealing with the question was brought into the House of Commons by Andrew Rutherfurd, a former Lord Advocate, at that time rector of the University of Glasgow, and Macaulay, then M.P. for Edinburgh ; and the reasonableness of the reform was so clear that the Government showed signs of hesitating to oppose it, and well indeed they might, for they were just engaged in passing a measure for establishing Colleges at Belfast, Cork, and Galway, the chairs in which were left open to men of every creed, and Peel had declared it was needless to enquire into the theological opinions of those whose business was merely to teach secular knowledge.

The Government did, however, use their influence against the second reading of Rutherfurd's bill, and it was rejected by the slender majority of eight. In 1852 Mr. Moncrieff, then M.P. for Leith, as Rutherfurd had been, attempted to carry a bill, but was defeated. Next year, however, he succeeded in passing a measure enacting that for the future all professors, excepting those belonging to the faculty of Divinity, should, instead of taking the test formerly prescribed, make a declaration that they would not as professors and in the discharge of their official duties endeavour to teach or inculcate any opinions opposed to the divine authority of the Holy Scriptures, or to the Westminster Confession of Faith as ratified by law in 1690, and would not exercise the functions of their professorial office to the prejudice or subversion of the Church of Scotland or of its doctrines or privileges. The Act of 1853 thus followed in the main the indications for a settlement contained in the petition from the University of Glasgow ten years before.

It had been intended that the regulations drafted by the Commission of 1830 should come into force on receiving the approval of the King, but the changes were so great as to suggest the expediency of procuring the sanction of Parliament, and for some time Parliament was occupied by Reform and other exciting topics. In 1835 a bill for regulating the University of Glasgow was brought in by the members for the city, Mr. Oswald and Mr. Dunlop. It followed in the main the recommendations of the Commission of 1830, and proposed to create a Court—consisting of the rector, the principal, the dean of faculty, an assessor chosen by the Senate and graduates, two assessors appointed by the crown, and one assessor appointed by the Town Council—to hold and administer the property of the University, to exercise a regulating power over the professors and lecturers, and, after consultation with the Senate, to modify the educational system. The faculty denounced this measure as subverting the constitution of the University, establishing a Court with absolute and irresponsible powers, favouring the other professors at the expense of the faculty, and confiscating property. Early in 1836 the Lord Advocate communicated the heads of a draft bill for appointing a board of Royal Visitors to regulate the Universities of Scotland, and in June it was announced that the bill had been brought into the House of Lords by Lord Melbourne, and read a first time. The faculty petitioned against this bill, urging similar considerations to those advanced against the bill of the previous year ; and resolved to ask the Duke of Wellington to present their petition and support its prayer, and also to ask the support of the Duke of Buccleuch, as the infirm health of the chancellor, the Duke of Montrose, prevented him from attending the house. Politicians seem to have been perplexed by the voluminous report and varied recommendations of the Commission of 1830, and the bill of 1836 being strongly opposed by the General Assembly and by the Town Council of Edinburgh, was suffered to drop.

On the advice of the Government, King William in November, 1836, appointed a Commission of Visitation to the University of Glasgow, and the appointment was renewed by Queen Victoria in October, 1837. The Commissioners were Viscount Melville, chancellor of the University of St. Andrews, Sir James Wellwood Moncrieff, a judge of the Court of Session, Lieutenant General Sir Thomas Macdougall Brisbane, Rev. Dr. John Lee, one of the ministers of Edinburgh, John Wilson of Thornley, near Paisley, and Alexander Earle Monteith. They were directed to enquire into the organisation, educational system, finance, and other concerns of the University, and to make such regulations as they deemed most conducive to the improvement of education and the beneficial administration of academic affairs—such regulations being 'consistent with the laws and government of church and state as by law established.' The Senate were allowed six months during which they might submit draft regulations to the Commissioners, and both were directed to have regard to the report of the Commission of 1830, though modifications were permitted. The Senate were far from welcoming the appointment of the Commissioners, and recorded their opinion that in various respects the powers entrusted to them exceeded the constitutional limits of the royal prerogative.

The Government seem to have appointed the Commission in the vain hope that they would settle the question of University reform without requiring Parliament to pass an Act; but the Commissioners found the task too formidable for them, and contented themselves with homologating in the main the recommendations of their predecessors of 1830, and indicating some points of difference. The Commissioners who reported in March, 1839, were of opinion that the Court should have a certain ill-defined power of enquiry and control regarding all the pecuniary concerns of the University, and should be authorised to dispose of surplus or unappropriated revenue in the manner most conducive to the interests of education; but it appeared to them not to be necessary and to some of them not to be desirable that the court should 'supersede the senate in the ordinary administration of the affairs of the University or in the management of its property.'[1] They earnestly recommended the Queen to renew the annual grant of £800 which expired in the following May, but recommended that it should be placed at the disposal of the University Court in the same way as surplus revenue. With a view to give weight and influence to the Court, they proposed that it should be empowered to appoint the principal and all the professors, subject to the crown having a veto on the nomination, which the Commissioners thought would seldom if ever need to be exercised. They confirmed with emphasis the opinion of their predecessors in 1830 that the distinction between faculty professors and regius professors should be abolished, and both classes put on the same footing in regard to rights and privileges, including the right to share in surplus funds not already appropriated, believing that the appropriation of such funds to the faculty professors to the exclusion of others originated in usurpation. By this time the Government of Lord Melbourne had been greatly weakened. Peel returned to office in 1841, but the minister who proposed the appointment of the Commission of 1826 had his hands full of other measures, and the question of University reform was indefinitely postponed.

The miscarriage of the scheme of 1846 for removal did not reconcile the faculty to their accommodation on the ancient site. The grounds

---

[1] The administration and management, with some minor exceptions, had for a long time been in the hands, not of the senate, but of the faculty.

there, extending to twenty-six and a half acres, were valuable in them-selves, associated with the University almost from its earliest days, and, though near the smoke and dust and din of a great working population, there is no proof that the health of the students suffered, and the professors generally lived to a good old age. Besides, the grounds were so ample that new buildings might have been erected a sufficient distance off High Street to be free from its noise and disturbance. Of the existing buildings the houses of the faculty professors were mostly of no great age, the last having been built so recently as 1838, a large part of the public buildings had been erected in the 19th century, and some classrooms insufficient for the larger classes might have served for smaller ones if the larger classes had been accommodated elsewhere. But many of the classrooms were old, inadequate to the uses assigned to them, and expensive to keep in order ; while, owing to the introduction of new subjects and the increase in the number of classes, the total number of classrooms was too small, even if their size and accommodation had been satisfactory. There was therefore real need for the provision of additional buildings, but the case for removal to a new site was by no means so clearly made out.

In January, 1852, the faculty appointed a committee to consider the adequacy or inadequacy of the various parts of the buildings, with a view to prepare the way for measures to remedy insufficiency. On 19th November the committee reported, and Professor Jackson laid on the table a memorial to the Queen which the committee had approved. The faculty ordered it to be printed, and instructed the committee to take steps for bringing it under the notice of Her Majesty and her advisers. At the eleventh hour it was resolved to request the co-operation of the Senate. It was pointed out that the project might involve a change of site, and to allay the apprehensions of the medical professors, Allen Thomson moved that the medical department should not be removed from proximity to the Royal Infirmary unless a hospital satisfactory to the medical professors were established near the new University and College buildings. The Senate then agreed to concur with the faculty in presenting the memorial, and on the last day of November, the rector, the Earl of Eglinton, attended a meeting at which it was approved and signed. The memorial urged that the existing accommodation had long ceased to be adequate, that it was bad in quality and objectionable in point of situation, being sur-rounded by a dense mass of the lowest order of the labouring population, and by many chemical and other manufactories which polluted the air, while the state of the sewerage was unsatisfactory, and altogether the circumstances were most unfavourable to the youth attending the Uni-versity. Since the beginning of the 19th century the buildings of other

Universities and Colleges in Scotland had been renewed in whole or in part, but the University of Glasgow had been left to contend with evils by which it must soon be overpowered unless aided by Her Majesty's gracious intervention. The memorial hinted that the sum advanced for new buildings might be recovered, if the old buildings and grounds were taken over by the Government, who could wait for a favourable opportunity to dispose of them.

The regius professors generally disapproved of the scheme, and a counter memorial was presented to the Lords of the Treasury by John Couper, Andrew Buchanan, Pagan, Rainy, Walker Arnott, and Anderson. They pointed out that removal to a new site was the real object of the other memorial, and that the project was supported chiefly by those professors who had houses within the University, and who, if the proposal were carried out, would acquire more modern houses in a more fashionable locality, though the existing houses were in all respects adequate to the reasonable needs of the professors. None of the other localities proposed would be nearly so convenient for the great body of students as the existing one, which could readily afford sites for additional classrooms and a new library, without materially curtailing the recreation ground. Though the University was surrounded by a dense population, there was no proof that the students had suffered in health or otherwise, and the professors living within it had long been remarkable for longevity. In the event of removal to a distant site, the Royal Infirmary would be lost to the Medical School of the University and left in the hands of rivals, and there was no prospect of a new hospital being provided.

The agitation for removal was one of many evils arising from the present anomalous constitution of the University, by which nine out of the twenty-three professors were debarred from sitting or voting in meetings of the faculty, which was vested with the control of the buildings, lands, and funds, excepting the books and moneys of the library ; and it was urged that no public money ought to be given for improving or extending the buildings or other purposes till a Royal Commission had enquired and reported regarding the question of abolishing the distinction between the faculty and the regius professors. About this time John Couper, Andrew Buchanan, Pagan, Rainy, Gordon, Walker Arnott, and Anderson presented a memorial to the first Lord of the Treasury, the Earl of Aberdeen, urging the abolition of the distinction, and the admission of the regius professors to share in the general administration and management of University property, and to participate in any unappropriated surplus that might arise. The evils arising from the distinction had not lessened, and the memorialists believed they would continue to increase

till effective measures were taken by the crown to carry out the recommendations of the Commissions of 1830 and 1839. The Commission of
1830 had declared that in the circumstances in which it was pronounced,
the decision in the Muirhead case on which the distinction rested could not
form a *res judicata* against the crown. The Government now took action
and in the summer of 1854 a summons of declarator at the instance of the
Crown was served on members of the faculty and others, and for some
years after this we encounter references to the slow progress of the case
in the Court of Session. But it was from Parliament that relief was to
come, and the fulness of time was at hand.

A little before this the faculty professors resorted to a strategy in the
Senate, of which they formed the majority, directed against their less
fortunate colleagues. Maconochie moved that, as the memorialists and
others alleged that the decrees in the former action were incompetently
pronounced, the Senate resolved that an action be again raised to determine the matters in question, and, as members of faculty might be
considered as disqualified, the seven memorialists should be nominated a
committee to raise and conduct the action at the charge of the Senate.
When the motion was discussed in February, 1854, John Couper proposed
a direct negative, and stated that neither he nor any of the other six would
act. The motion was carried by nine votes to six, but Couper and the
others on the same side dissented, and their refusal to serve on the proposed
committee made the carrying of the motion a barren victory. Couper
afterwards gave in reasons of dissent by the minority, alleging that they
had never attempted to obtain a settlement by political influence or any
other means except a fair and open representation of their case. It was
not a mere dispute between two sets of professors, but an important public
question, involving the rights of the crown and possibly requiring the
intervention of the legislature. As the memorialists had appealed to the
crown and their application had been entertained, it would be unbecoming
and inconsistent with the respect due to the advisers of the crown, were
they to raise an action at law to try the question at issue, and such an action
in whatever way it might end would involve a ruinous waste of academic
funds.

In April, 1853, the faculty appointed a committee to proceed to
London to press their memorial on the Government, and on 4th November
the committee reported the result of their visit. They had an interview
with Lord Aberdeen, who expressed himself willing to make enquiries
through the Board of Works into the allegations of the memorial, and
added that the Chancellor of the Exchequer must be consulted. The
deputation then applied through Colonel Mure, dean of faculty, for an

interview with Mr. Gladstone, but Mr. Gladstone was busy, and preferred to dispense with it. The deputation then stated that they had been unwilling to return without being able to say that they had represented to the Government the inadequacy of the present accommodation and the unsuitability of the present position of the College, and so relieve the College from the responsibility of submitting to these evils without having made every effort to remove them. The Chancellor was more oracular than encouraging, and in a note to Colonel Mure replied that he did not agree in what appeared to be the view of the Glasgow deputation that, when they had pointed out to the Government certain evils affecting the University, it rested with the Government to remove them by an expenditure of public money. The University itself, he imagined, would be slow to admit that it was a mere department under Government control, for the state and management of which Government was responsible. When important questions respecting the relation of the Scotch Universities to the nation were at issue, Mr. Gladstone felt that they could not be summarily disposed of, and even were that obstacle out of the way, he felt that before Government could undertake the pecuniary responsibility it would be necessary for him to gather into one view the various wants and demands of the Scottish Universities, which ought to be considered together, in order to the adoption of a rule which might rest on some principle and might have the promise of permanence. He had not entered into the incidental but vital question of the division of opinion in the University with reference to removal, but he did not see how the Government could undertake to settle that matter for the University. The deputation rejoined that former Governments had practically acknowledged their responsibility by erecting buildings for the other Scottish Universities at the public expense in the present century under circumstances less urgent, while in the same time the crown had created nine regius professorships at Glasgow without providing for their accommodation. When the report was presented the faculty requested the principal to remind Lord Aberdeen of his promise to enquire regarding the buildings and site of the College.

Public opinion was slowly ripening in support of reform in the Scottish Universities. The graduates began to show some signs of interest, though their first aspirations were rather timid and indefinite. In May, 1849, a memorial was received from Archibald Watson, minister of St. Matthew's, and James Bryce,[1] one of the masters in the High School, the chairman and secretary of a public meeting of graduates in Arts which had been held recently, which set forth that these graduates cherished a grateful attachment to the University and desired to maintain their con-

[1] Father of the Rt. Hon. James Bryce, the British Ambassador to the United States.

nection with it, an end which they conceived would be best attained by their being admitted to such privileges as it might be in the power of the senate to bestow. Admission to the library seems to have been one of the desired privileges. The senate met the proposal with inert civility, and authorised the faculty of Arts to receive any further communication on the subject. At a much earlier time the question of the representation of the Scottish Universities in the House of Commons had been raised, and in August, 1831, the senate undertook to co-operate with the University of Edinburgh and the other Scottish Universities in endeavouring to obtain due representation, should there be a probability—so they added— of the Reform Bill passing in its present shape. In 1853 the senate of the University of Edinburgh resolved to petition Parliament that, in any measure for altering the representation of the country, the Scottish Universities should be represented, and, though the senate at Glasgow declined to consider the question at that time, in less than a year they came round to a more favourable view. In February, 1854, a meeting of senate was called to receive a deputation from an association of Scottish graduates whose object was to obtain parliamentary representation for the Universities of Scotland through a constituency formed of their graduates and existing members. The interest of the senate seems to have been rather languid, for a quorum did not appear, but the principal stated that he believed the sentiments of his colleagues were generally favourable to the object in view.

An association formed some time before for the improvement and extension of the Scottish Universities sent a deputation in April, 1857, to press their views on Lord Advocate Moncrieff, whose father had been one of the most active members of the Commissions of 1830 and 1839. Moncrieff undertook to bring in a bill, and set himself to prepare one, but public and parliamentary interest being then centred on the Mutiny in India, there was no immediate prospect of passing the measure, and it was not introduced. A change of Government took place in February, 1858, but John Inglis, the new Lord Advocate, who had studied at Glasgow and gone thence as a Snell exhibitioner, obtained Moncrieff's draft bill, which provided for the appointment of an Executive Commission with power to carry out the reforms deemed advisable, and altered it by adding clauses in which Parliament itself defined the future constitution of the Scottish Universities, instead of leaving the Commission to do so.

On 22nd April, 1858, Inglis introduced his bill. He began so low that he was very indistinctly heard, and there were calls of 'Louder' and 'Speak up'; but instead of raising his voice, he turned his back to the Speaker and addressed the members in front of him, and from that time to the end of his speech not a single complete sentence reached the reporters, who prefaced their account of his speech by the saving clause—'He was understood to say.' He submitted that his proposals were not of a novel character, but mostly founded on the recommendations of the Commission of 1830, at the same time acknowledging his obligations to Moncrieff. He expressed the opinion that, so far as the faculty of Arts was concerned, the Scottish Universities had lost sight of their proper objects and descended below the requirements of the age, so that great excellence in any one department of knowledge was no longer a distinguishing characteristic of their students—evils which he attributed to the small value set on degrees. To raise the estimation in which degrees were held and create an intelligent body of graduates would be of great advantage, and with this aim he proposed to allow graduates a certain share in the administration by admitting them to the General Council, a new body to be constituted at each University. He also proposed the constitution of University Courts, with considerable powers of patronage and some powers of regulation and control, the general administration being assigned to the senate; to provide increased endowments from the public funds; to improve, where necessary, the salaries of existing professorships, and to endow some new chairs; and to strengthen the teaching in subjects which required it by the appointment of assistants to the professors. The bill also provided for a temporary Executive Commission, with large powers to regulate the administration of the Universities, the apportionment of endowments, and the conditions of conferring degrees in the several faculties, as well as to carry out other purposes for which the bill itself did not contain detailed provisions. There were murmurs from Edinburgh against transferring the management of the University from the Town Council, and from Aberdeen against the union of King's and Marischal Colleges, but on the whole the bill introduced by Mr. Inglis was well received in the House.

Shortly after its introduction the faculty of the College of Glasgow discussed the bill, and, while concurring in its preamble, adopted resolutions proposed by Ramsay setting forth four objections to its provisions. It was urged that the clause which empowered the University Court, after due investigation, to censure, suspend, or deprive a professor, as well as some other clauses, appeared as if directed against a class of notorious delinquents for the coercion and punishment of whom the expedients adopted against ordinary offenders were insufficient; and that the clause if passed would reduce professors, on whose character, powers, and energy the efficiency of the Universities largely depended, to the position of ushers in a school, and render the office no longer an object of ambition to those best qualified to fill it.   Secondly, the General Council was likely to prove injurious and subversive of discipline.   Though professors were admitted as members, they would be completely overwhelmed by the graduates.   After graduating in Arts, many young men continued to study Medicine, Law, and Divinity, and such students might take part on a footing of equality with their professors in the proceedings of a solemn deliberative court, and might argue with and outvote them.   The existence of the Council would offer inducements to the restless, discontented, and turbulent to dispute and resist the authority of the professors, and to fabricate grievances.   The third objection referred to the taking away of the patronage of the professors, many chairs being in the gift of the faculty, along with the rector and dean.   It was pointed out that the Town Councils of Edinburgh and Aberdeen, as well as a number of individuals and mixed bodies, were patrons of chairs, and the faculty claimed that professors were as able as these to estimate the qualifications of candidates, and not more likely to be swayed by improper influences.   Fourthly, the faculty protested against the vast and, as they believed, completely unconstitutional powers of the Commissioners who for four or five years were to be vested with all the powers of the Crown and the two Houses of Parliament, and were to be absolutely irresponsible.

The senate adopted the same objections, except the one relating to patronage, and appointed the principal and Rainy to proceed to London to urge amendments, but it was by the faculty that the greatest efforts were put forth.   They ordered a petition embodying their objections to be presented to the House of Commons through the dean of faculties, Mr. Stirling, and appointed the principal, Ramsay, Nichol, and Blackburn a deputation to repair to London, and endeavour to procure amendments. The first three met in London on 2nd June, and Blackburn joined them eight days later.   Together or separately they interviewed the Lord Advocate, the Duke of Montrose, the rector (Bulwer Lytton), the dean of faculties (Mr. Stirling), Lord John Russell, Sir Edward Colebrooke, Sir John Ogilvie, Mr. Alexander Finlay, Mr. Monckton Milnes, Mr. Edward Ellice, Mr. Andrew Stewart, M.P. for Cambridge, formerly a Glasgow student, and many others.   Their arguments and those from representatives of the other Universities induced the Lord Advocate to make a number of changes before the second reading, restricting the summary powers originally granted to the Court over the professors, depriving the General Council of the power of adjourning and limiting it to two meetings in the year, and providing that the ordinances made by the Commissioners should be submitted to the Queen in Council for approval before coming into force.   The deputation urged other amendments, at least three of which were ultimately embodied in the bill—that students actually enrolled in University classes should be excluded from the General Council, that the students should continue to elect the rector, and that parties whose interests were affected by the ordinances of the Commissioners might be heard by the Queen in Council before the ordinances were approved.

On 25th June the faculty heard a report of the doings of the deputation and the progress of the bill.   Mr. Alexander Murray Dunlop, M.P. for Greenock, an advocate who had been the chief legal adviser of the founders of the Free Church and the author of their Claim of Right, and whom his friends sometimes called the modern Johnston of Warriston, had given notice of two amendments, the first transferring the administration of the funds to the University Court, and the second abolishing the faculty by enacting that henceforth no distinction should be recognised between the professors in the University of Glasgow.   The deputation could not believe that the House would pass such clauses, but they called the attention of their friends to the necessity of resisting them if proposed.   The deputation expressed their special gratitude to Mr. Stirling, Mr. Peter Blackburn, and Sir William Dunbar.   Professor Blackburn had remained in London, Nichol was soon to rejoin him, and the faculty authorised the whole deputation to repair to London when the bill came before the House of Lords.   On the 16th of July there was much disappointment when it was reported that Mr. Dunlop had carried his amendment abolishing the distinction between the faculty professors and the professors hitherto excluded from the faculty, and it was resolved to make an effort to have the clause embodying this change rescinded or modified.   A letter was sent to Lord Redesdale, the convener of committees in the House of Lords, urging that the clause was unconstitutional, inasmuch as it summarily decided a question of right which was then on trial in the Court of Session. The aid of the chancellor, the Duke of Montrose, was also invoked on behalf of the faculty.   On 21st July Nichol reported that he had found Montrose most anxious to meet the views of the faculty, that Dunlop's clause abolishing the distinction between the faculty professors and the senate professors had been rejected by the Lords, and that he had the promise of the Lord Advocate[1] that it would not be re-introduced in the Commons if the Government could prevent it.   Mr. Dunlop had also carried a clause against the Government, opening the office of principal at Glasgow, Aberdeen, and Edinburgh to laymen without distinction of Church.

[1] This promise was not given by Mr. Inglis, but by Mr. Baillie who succeeded him as Lord Advocate.

Forgetful of the strength of the faculty of Medicine in the Scottish Universities, the framers of the bill proposed that no graduates should be admitted to the General Council excepting Masters of Arts, a proposal to which the medical profession very naturally objected.   The Royal College of Physicians of Edinburgh petitioned for the admission of Doctors of Medicine, urging that medical graduates underwent more rigid examinations and pursued a more varied and extensive course of study than were required for any other profession.   Afterwards a great meeting of medical graduates of Edinburgh University endorsed this view, and protested against the invidious and unfair exclusion of Doctors of Medicine from the Council.   Mr. Adam Black, one of the members for Edinburgh, made a wiser suggestion, and moved that the Council should include graduates in Arts, Medicine, Law, or Divinity ; but as the bill passed it admitted only Masters of Arts and Doctors[1] of Medicine, along with the chancellor, the members of the University Court and senate, and such persons as satisfied the Commissioners before August, 1861, that they had regularly attended University classes for four complete sessions, two of which must have been in the faculty of Arts.   It was thought that, as many students who took a full course in Arts neglected to graduate, if admission to the Council were restricted at the outset to graduates in Arts and Medicine and those whose qualifications depended on their holding office, the number of members would be too limited.   But when the new system was organised, mere attendance was no longer to qualify for membership.   The neglect of graduation was not quite so marked at Glasgow as at Edinburgh.   At the latter the degree of M.A. was conferred on 250 individuals in the twenty years preceding 1863, while at Glasgow it was conferred on 350, and the degree of B.A. was conferred on 256 individuals in the twenty years ending with 1861, when it was abolished.   It was left to the Representation of the People Act of 1868 to widen the Council by admitting, in addition to Masters of Arts and Doctors of Medicine, Bachelors of Divinity, Bachelors of Laws, Bachelors of Medicine, Bachelors of Science, and holders of any other degree that might afterwards be instituted.

Mr. Bouverie, M.P. for the Kilmarnock Burghs, moved that the chancellor, whose appointment the bill left in the hands of the senate, should be elected by the General Council.   The Lord Advocate disliked the proposed change, but it commended itself to the House, and the Home Secretary, Mr. Walpole, said the point was not of great consequence, and if the general feeling were in favour of the amendment, the Government

---

[1] In the case of Doctors of Medicine attendance during a certain number of sessions was required, but under the Act of 1868 possession of the degree sufficed.

15, 16,

9, 13,

7, 8,

6,

5,

24, 25,

26, 19,

14, 27,

21,

22,

20, 18,

12,

11,

4,

5,

3,

2,

THE SENATE LEAVING THE OLD COLLEGE IN 1870

ARRANGED IN ORDER OF PRECEDENCE

1. Rev. Principal Barclay.
2. Rev. Professor John Caird.
3. Professor Lushington.
4. Professor Andrew Buchanan.
5. Professor Harry Rainy.
6. Professor Sir William Thomson.
7. Professor Allen Thomson.
8. Professor Blackburn.
9. Rev. Professor Weir.
10. Rev. Professor Jackson.
11. Professor Thomas Anderson.
12. Professor Macquorn Rankine.
13. Professor Grant.

14. Professor Nichol.
15. Professor Gairdner.
16. Rev. Professor William P. Dickson.
17. Professor George G. Ramsay.
18. Professor Veitch.
19. Professor Cowan.
20. Professor Edward Caird.
21. Professor Young.
22. Professor Roberton.
23. Professor Berry.
24. Professor Leishman.
25. Professor Alexander Dickson.
26. Professor Macleod.

would not object. The amendment was accordingly accepted. Mr. Dunlop proposed that students and none but students should elect the rector; and Inglis, in view of the amendment allowing the General Council to elect the chancellor, assented to the proposal, and it was carried. Dunlop was less successful in an amendment intended to deprive the senate of the general administration of the property and revenues, which, after being opposed by Inglis, was defeated by 85 to 22. By a majority of 82 to 58, however, his proposal to open to laymen the office of principal at Glasgow, Aberdeen, and Edinburgh was carried against the Government. Mr. Baxter, M.P. for the Montrose Burghs, moved, and Mr. Dalglish, one of the members for Glasgow, seconded that no part of the money provided by Parliament should be applied to the endowment of theological chairs. Mr. Inglis opposed this amendment, and it was rejected by the slender majority of 102 to 94.

Dunlop proposed the insertion of an additional clause, one of the most important in the bill so far as Glasgow was concerned, providing that from and after the passing of the Act there should be no distinction among the professors of the University of Glasgow, that they should all be professors of the University and College, and equally exercise the functions formerly exercised by any of the professors, no claim being given, however, to participate in the income or emoluments already appropriated to existing chairs. Mr. Blackburn opposed the amendment, urging that it related to a matter on which a suit had been raised by the crown, and that it was contrary to the practice of Parliament to legislate on a matter which was *sub judice*. Mr. Buchanan, one of the members for Glasgow, said it was true the question was *sub judice*, but it was one which had been in course of preparation for litigation for at least twenty years, and he saw nothing to prevent it from occupying the tribunals of Scotland for twenty years more. He considered the subject one of the most important connected with University reform; the distinction had given rise to an immense deal of heartburning between the different sets of professors; and it was desirable to put an end to the litigation. Lord Palmerston and Sir James Graham supported the amendment, and the Lord Advocate believing its design was to secure that the functions and duties of the professors, whether of the College or of the University, should be the same, saw no reason to object to the clause, and it was added to the bill.

Shortly after this, Mr. Inglis was appointed a judge of the Court of Session, and took his seat on the bench as Lord Glencorse on 14th July, 1858, being succeeded by Mr. Charles Baillie as Lord Advocate. When the bill reached the report stage a clause, not much desired but tolerated on account of its being merely permissive, was added on the proposal of

2 E

Mr. Gladstone. It provided that if the Queen, during the existence of the Commission appointed under the Act, should issue a charter for the foundation of a National University for Scotland, the separate Universities, or any of them, might surrender to the Commissioners their powers of examining for and granting degrees, and might become Colleges of the new University.

The bill now passed to the House of Lords, and the Lords struck out the clause abolishing the distinction between the faculty professors and the other professors of the University, and the amendment opening the office of principal to laymen. The end of the session was at hand, and the Scottish members had mostly left London, believing that the session was virtually over so far as Scottish business was concerned ; but on hearing what had happened, a number of them, including Sir James Anderson, Mr. Baxter, Mr. Buchanan, Mr. Dalglish, Mr. Dunlop, and Mr. Crum Ewing, hastened back. Fortunately many of the supporters of the Government had now left, and though Lord Advocate Baillie had promised to representatives of the faculty that the clause removing the distinction to which they clung should not be restored if the Government could prevent it, no division was challenged when it was proposed that the Commons should disagree with the Lords' amendments on this subject and on the opening of the office of principal to laymen. The chancellor of the University of Glasgow, the Duke of Montrose, was in charge of the bill in the House of Lords, and on 29th July, when the order of the day for considering the Commons' reasons for disagreeing with their Lordships' amendments was reached, he declared his opinion that the views of the other House on the bill were erroneous ; but fearing that if the Lords insisted on their amendments the bill would be lost, and having regard to the importance of the measure and the value of the improvements it would introduce into the Scottish Universities, he moved that their Lordships should not insist on their amendments. After some murmurs and grumbling the House agreed, and the bill received the royal assent on 2nd August.

III. Summary of History since 1858.

The Act of 1858 assigned to the senatus academicus, consisting of the principal and professors, the superintendence and regulation of the teaching and discipline, and the administration of the property and revenues of the University, subject to the control and review of the University Court. It was an immense advantage at Glasgow to get rid of the distinction between the faculty professors and the regius professors, as they were called, and to have all of them vested with the same administrative powers. The majority of the faculty professors were strongly attached to their exclusive rights, and when Principal Barclay was being inducted they left the regius professors out of account and out of the list of invitations. Even after the passing of the Universities Act a number of the faculty professors endeavoured to continue the distinction, professing to be waiting for an intimation from the Commissioners when the Act should come into force; but the Court of Session made short work of their opposition, declaring that the legislature had made it perfectly clear there was equality of rights among the professors from the date when the Act passed.

Two new bodies, the General Council and the University Court, now came into existence. The constitution of the Council has already been described, and it was a decided gain to have the graduates permanently connected with the University through its membership. The Act provided for the Council electing the Chancellor and one Assessor in the University Court, and meeting twice a year to consider questions affecting the welfare of the University, on which they were empowered to make representations to the Court, whose deliverance was to be returned to the Council. The Court, besides being authorised to review all decisions of the senate and to enquire into and control their financial administration, was empowered to fix the fees in the various classes; to effect improvements in the internal arrangements of the University after communicating with the senate, securing the sanction of the Chancellor, and submitting the proposals for the consideration of the General Council; to require professors to observe regulations regarding the mode of teaching or other duties; and, subject to the approval of the Queen in Council, to censure, suspend, or deprive a professor, upon sufficient cause shown and after due enquiry. Except at Edinburgh, the patronage of chairs previously in the gift of Universities or Colleges was transferred to the Court.

At the outset of the new system interest centred, not in the doings of the ordinary administrators, but in those of the Commissioners appointed under the Act who had been entrusted with large powers to regulate the educational, financial, and administrative affairs of the Universities. Among the Commissioners were the Duke of Argyll, three judges of the Court of Session—Lord President M'Neill, Lord Justice Clerk Inglis, and Lord Ardmillan—Mr. James Moncreiff, afterwards a judge of the Court of Session, Mr. William Stirling of Keir, afterwards Sir William Stirling Maxwell, and Mr. Murray Dunlop, M.P. By a fortunate coincidence Lord Justice Clerk Inglis, the author of the Act, was called upon to preside over the Executive Commission which carried its provisions into effect, and his unfailing attendance at meetings and the ability and skill with which he guided the deliberations of the Commission were recognised on all hands ; while Mr. Robert Berry, Advocate, afterwards professor of Law in the University of Glasgow, made a most efficient secretary.

The Universities Act of 1858 was a temperate and cautious measure, and it was temperately and cautiously administered. At Glasgow only three new chairs were founded, namely, those of English Literature, Conveyancing, and Biblical Criticism. Except for the addition in Arts of English Literature and in Medicine of Zoology, hardly any change was made in the number of subjects and the curriculum for graduation in these two leading faculties. The lower degree of Bachelor of Arts was, however, abolished. In other respects perhaps the most important changes made were those which concerned examination. In Arts two professors had been entitled to certain fees from students entering for the degree examination, and in Medicine the larger part of the graduation fees was divided among the professors who examined. As it was for the credit of the institution that fees from candidates for examination should no longer be allocated to professors, the practice was abolished ; and examination fees, whose amount was regulated by ordinance, were henceforth made payable to the general University fund ; while it was laid down that three additional examiners in Arts and three in Medicine should act along with the professors in conducting degree examinations, and should be remunerated from new parliamentary grants. Previously, though the degree examination in Medicine was divided into two sections, it was the custom here as in Arts to take the examination in all the subjects at the end of the course ; but the Commissioners gathered the subjects into groups or departments in which the student was henceforth examined at successive stages in his course. In Arts the old but evergreen subjects of Latin and Greek formed the department of Classics ; Logic, Moral Philosophy, and English Literature, that of Mental Philosophy ; while Mathematics and Natural Philosophy formed the third department. Candidates were left free to take the departmental examinations in any order they pleased. The Commissioners introduced an honours examination in all the Universities on nearly the same system which had been organised at Glasgow in 1826—a system which had borne good fruit, though not on a very extensive scale—but, besides the three departments for the ordinary degree, they added Natural Science, including Botany, Geology, Zoology, and Chemistry, as a fourth department in which honours might be taken.[1]

[1] In 1870 the Queen approved of an alteration of the ordinance allowing students to

After the new regulations came into force there was a marked increase in the number of graduations in Arts, the degree of M.A. being conferred on 1,841 students in the thirty years from 1864 to 1893, no fewer than 1,255 of these degrees belonging to the last thirteen years of the period. The increase was due partly to a rise in the number of students, but also in a great measure to the enhanced estimation in which degrees had come to be held. The number of honours degrees—scarcely exceeding an annual average of three in the earlier part of the time, but rising to more than nine in the later—also showed a notable increase. Mental Philosophy proved the most attractive department for honours students, the number of successful candidates nearly equalling those in Classics and Mathematics put together, while in Natural Science only seven candidates obtained honours during the whole period. About twelve per cent. of the graduates in Arts obtained honours, some few had honours in two departments, and one had first class honours in three departments. The general effect of the regulations framed by the Commission over which Inglis presided was to produce a race of graduates in Arts reaching a tolerable standard of general efficiency in the seven predestinated subjects of the degree, rather than to render great excellence in some department a distinguishing characteristic of Scottish University students, an end which he had indicated as desirable when introducing the Universities Bill. But it must be remembered that large numbers of students entered the University without sufficient preparation, and for them it was better to attain a tolerable standard of general efficiency than to attempt highly specialised and advanced studies. Further, it seems to be now generally recognised that great excellence in any department is to be secured by reducing the number of subjects of study, a method which may be judicious and effective, but yet it involves limitations.

The Commissioners brought the existing chair of Forensic Medicine at Glasgow into the faculty of Law, and established a new chair of Conveyancing there, while at the same time they framed a general ordinance regulating the curriculum and conditions on which the degree of Bachelor of Laws (LL.B.) should be granted in all the Scottish Universities, or such of them as possessed the needful equipment. Glasgow had hitherto stood ahead of the other Universities in granting degrees in Law after a course of study and examination or other trials ; and though the number of degrees thus conferred had not been large, the system was quite normal ; but in the development of a teaching staff for the various subjects the Western University was by no means foremost. Edinburgh had a special

take the honours examination in any department, though they had not previously passed the ordinary examination.

advantage as being the chief seat of the Law Courts in Scotland, and chairs of Civil Law and Scots Law were founded there by taking into the University in 1710 and 1722 teachers who had previously been lecturing in these subjects to supply an actual demand for professional training. In 1816 Macvey Napier, an alumnus of Glasgow who succeeded Jeffrey as editor of the *Edinburgh Review*, was appointed lecturer on Conveyancing by the Society of Writers to the Signet in the Scottish metropolis, and in 1825 he too was taken into the University as professor of his subject. In Marischal College, Aberdeen, a lectureship in Scots Law and Conveyancing was established in 1819, the subjects being taught in alternate years. At Glasgow a lectureship on Conveyancing had been established a little before this, but not within the University. It was with the countenance and support of the Faculty of Procurators that Mr. James Galloway, a member of that body, began a course of lectures on Conveyancing in 1817. The Faculty had expressed their confidence in his qualifications to teach the subject and approved of the prospectus of his lectures, and they showed their substantial interest in the undertaking by voting £127 10s. to defray the initial expenses. Mr. Galloway continued his lectures for a considerable number of years, and they were published in 1838 after his death. Again, it was by the aid of the Faculty of Procurators, who agreed to give an annual salary of £105, that the Commissioners were enabled to provide for the teaching of Conveyancing, and to establish a chair in the University in 1861, the patronage being vested in the Dean and Council of the Faculty. Anderson Kirkwood, the first professor, was appointed in 1861 and began to lecture next year, but after a brief tenure he retired in 1867. He continued, however, to take a lively interest in the affairs of the University, was a member of the Court as Assessor for the General Council from 1867 to 1887, and secretary of the Court from 1874 to 1887. He contested the parliamentary constituency of Glasgow and Aberdeen Universities against Mr. Watson in 1876, and, though unsuccessful, commanded a respectable following.

The Commissioners, after consulting the Faculty of Advocates and other legal bodies, framed an ordinance providing for the degree of LL.B. being conferred on graduates in Arts who had gone through a curriculum of three years in Law, embracing attendance on courses of 80 lectures in Civil Law, Scots Law, and Conveyancing, and courses of 40 lectures in Public Law, Constitutional Law and History, and Medical Jurisprudence. The degree was conceived as an academic distinction rather than as a professional qualification, and included subjects not required by Writers and Solicitors or even by Advocates, while the previous possession of a degree in Arts excluded the great body of Law students from aspiring to its possession.   It was only at Edinburgh that all the subjects were taught, and in order to secure their being taught there the Commissioners were obliged to revive a dormant chair of Public Law, and to divert the teaching of another chair from Universal Civil History and Antiquities to Constitutional Law and History.   Candidates were allowed to take part of their course in another University than that in which they wished to graduate, but for some time progress was rather slow.   At Edinburgh only 24 candidates, including some few who had begun their course at Glasgow, obtained the degree in ten years from its institution, and it was more than ten years before any one at all obtained it at Glasgow.

The Commissioners considered the question of laying down regulations for graduation in Divinity, but found difficulties which appeared to them so formidable that they took no action.   In 1855 delegates from the several Universities had suggested a scheme for the degree of Bachelor of Divinity (B.D.) which would have confined it to members of the Church of Scotland, and on the ground of this exclusiveness it was next year rejected by the senate at Glasgow.   In 1862 the senate approved of reviving the degree under regulations which would have permitted students after graduating in Arts to attend the Theological Hall of any Scottish University, or to attend Theological Halls or Colleges presided over by one or more graduates in Divinity of some Scottish University, and recognised for the purpose by the University Court.   The Universities of Edinburgh and St. Andrews wished to impose at least one year's attendance in the Divinity Hall of the University in which the degree was sought ; and the University of Aberdeen, while leaving the conditions of attendance to be decided by the Commissioners, wished to have security that the degree should be conferred only on members of churches whose doctrines were in substantial agreement with the Westminster Confession of Faith and the Thirty-nine Articles.   The Commissioners evidently desired to leave graduation open to students outside the Church of Scotland, but they objected to the proposal to admit to graduation students who had not received any part of their theological education in the University.   They pointed out that 'the Universities of Scotland, as teaching bodies, have not hitherto been in use to confer degrees in faculties in which they afford instruction, except on persons who have studied within their walls as students in such faculties ; and this usage, depending as it does on an important feature in their constitution, ought not lightly to be infringed upon.'

As the Commissioners did not accept any of the plans suggested to them and had no plan of their own to meet the exigencies of the case, their only course was one of inaction. ' On the whole we concluded'—so their Report runs—' in the absence of any experience to guide us in a matter of acknowledged difficulty and delicacy, that it was better for us to abstain from issuing an ordinance, which would interfere with the free action of the Universities themselves.' Soon after the Commissioners' powers had come to an end the University of Glasgow enacted regulations for conferring the degree of B.D., and in 1866 it was conferred on four candidates. The degree was intended for graduates in Arts, but a relaxation was made in favour of former students in Arts who had not graduated, if they had been admitted as members of the General Council in virtue of a proviso in the statutes which allowed a specified amount of attendance prior to 2nd August, 1861, to qualify for enrolment. At the outset students from Scottish Theological Halls were alone admitted, but in 1869 it was agreed to admit students who had graduated in Arts at Glasgow and afterwards taken a due course of study in a Theological College in England or Wales. The scheme also allowed graduates in Arts of any recognised University to obtain the degree of B.D. on completing a due course of theological study, at least two years of which must be in the University.

Under clauses inserted in the Act at the instance of Mr. Gladstone, the Commissioners were empowered to enquire how far it might be practicable and expedient that a new National University for Scotland should be founded, of which the existing Universities, or such of them as gave their consent, should become Colleges. Towards the end of their tenure the Commissioners requested the Universities to give their opinions on the proposal, and not a single reply in its favour was received, the senates of the four Universities, and the University Courts of St. Andrews, Glasgow, and Aberdeen declaring against it, while the answer from the Edinburgh University Court alone among the replies ' received evidenced the existence of any doubt on the subject, intimating that within that body there was a difference of opinion.' Mr. Gladstone, who had conceived the project, was at that time a member of the Edinburgh University Court, and probably this explains the reason for a difference of opinion in this single instance. The Commissioners declared ' it is impossible for us to report that such a measure would be practicable, and our own deliberations have led us to the conclusion that it would not be expedient.'

An early ordinance passed in July, 1859, fixed a compulsory matriculation fee of ten shillings for the winter session and five shillings for the summer one ; but ordinance No. 22, which regulated the general financial affairs of Glasgow and passed in March, 1862, fixed the matriculation fee at £1 for the whole academic year, or ten shillings for the summer session by itself. The Commissioners did a kindness to the students by adding

THE VERY REV. JOHN CAIRD, D.D., LL.D.

Principal and Vice-Chancellor of the University of Glasgow

BORN 1820.   DIED 1898

that 'no fee shall be chargeable against any student for cleaning, lighting, or heating of classrooms, or for the attendance of College servants,' purposes for which in the past rather vexatious exactions had sometimes been made. Fees of definite amount were also prescribed for the degree examinations in Arts, Law, and Medicine, and these fees were made to form part of the general University fund. In the ordinance and a schedule annexed to it the endowments of the several chairs were set forth, as well as an estimate of the class fees, and, while the class fees might vary, it was laid down regarding other portions of their emoluments that no member of senate should receive in virtue of his office as principal, professor, or examiner any further sum than was specified in the ordinance, except that the senate, with the approval of the University Court, were allowed to pay reasonable remuneration for any special services rendered by a principal or professor. As the ordinary administration rested with the senate, this provision was intended to check the working or imputation of interested motives. The Commissioners revised the regulations of a number of the bursary foundations so as to render them more beneficial, but found less work of this kind to be done at Glasgow than at Aberdeen and St. Andrews.

The Act did not fix the maximum amount to be devoted to the improvement of the Scottish Universities, and there was thus an unrivalled opportunity of giving them effective financial aid. In addition to a temporary charge for compensation to professors deprived of office by the union of the two Universities and Colleges of Aberdeen, and the money necessary to provide pensions to aged and infirm principals and professors, the Act authorised the Lords of the Treasury to pay such sums as the Commissioners should recommend for additional teaching by means of assistants to professors, for remuneration of examiners, for increasing the salaries attached to professorships and other offices, and for the endowment of new professorships. The Commissioners were probably as mindful of the interests of the taxpayers as of the Universities, and they did not show any special consideration for Glasgow. The total of the yearly sums (apart from pensions) allocated to it amounted to £1,805, as compared with £4,043 17s. 10d. to Edinburgh,[1] £1,680 to Aberdeen,[2] and £1,094 1s. to St. Andrews. The grants to Glasgow included £200

[1] This includes not only the sums allocated under ordinance No. 23 and for Examiners, but also a sum of £200 assigned to the chair of Sanskrit. The £3,345 mentioned at page 133 of the second volume of Sir A. Grant's *Story of the University of Edinburgh* falls considerably short of the mark.

[2] There was also a temporary charge of £2,446 12s. 4d. for compensation to seven professors who had been deprived of office by the union of the Universities.

as a salary to the new chair of English Literature, and the following sums as increments to salaries—£250 to the principal, £50 to each of the professors of Natural History and Midwifery, £25 to each of the professors of Surgery and Forensic Medicine, and £75 to the professor of Institutes of Medicine ; salaries of £100 to an assistant in each of the classes of Natural Philosophy, Greek, Humanity, and Mathematics, a like amount to each of two assistants in Chemistry, £50 to a joint assistant in Materia Medica and Forensic Medicine ; and £80 to each of three examiners in Arts and a like number in Medicine.

In adjusting with the Lords of the Treasury the arrangements for pensions to principals and professors the Commissioners proposed more favourable conditions than those conferred by the general regulations of the civil service, but they failed to impress the Treasury with their views, and ordinance No. 26, passed in April, 1862, fixed the rate of pensions to principals and professors retiring from office on the ground of age or infirmity at one-third of their emoluments on completion of ten years of service, with an additional sixtieth of their emoluments for every year of service up to the thirtieth, when the maximum pension was reached, amounting to two-thirds of the emoluments.   The Commissioners recommended that no pension should fall below £150 a year or should exceed £600, but the Lords of the Treasury did not agree to this.   If the limit of £600 had been adopted, there would have been a considerable saving, first to the Treasury, and afterwards to the Universities, which under the Act of 1889 have to bear the burden of pensions.   In one case a professor whose total emoluments the Commissioners estimated in 1862 at £662 has for thirty years drawn a pension of £1,073.

Petitions from the authorities of the University of Glasgow regarding the condition of the buildings were remitted by the Home Secretary to the Commissioners for consideration and report.   At their request Mr. Robert Matheson, Assistant Surveyor for Scotland in the office of H. M. Works, met Mr. Stirling, one of the Commissioners, on the spot, and made an inspection of the buildings.   He described the sixteen classrooms (half of which had been erected within less than fifty years) as affording accommodation altogether insufficient in amount and bad in quality—ill ventilated, ill lighted, and, except in two cases, without any means of heating but a stove or fireplace at the professor's platform.   The joisting of some of the upper classrooms had subsided, the flooring was dilapidated throughout, and the stone staircases leading to classrooms were inconveniently small and ill constructed.   Mr. Matheson considered that any attempt to improve or adapt the building would prove inadequate and unsatisfactory.   The Museum and the Library, though inadequate, could be improved and extended; but if the classrooms were discontinued this would not be desirable. The Commissioners reported that the buildings were utterly unfit for the purposes of the University, and were 'placed in a quarter of the town densely peopled with the lowest of the population, and in an atmosphere darkened with the smoke and polluted by the effluvia of chemical and other manufactories,' so that 'it would be difficult to select an academic seat less eligible or attractive.' The 26½ acres occupied by the College and its grounds, though most ineligible for the purposes of the University, were of greater commercial value than an equal quantity of land in better localities, and the Commissioners urged the expediency of removal to a new site.[1] For this purpose they reckoned as available £50,200, being the value of the College buildings and grounds and of the Chemistry buildings in Shuttle Street, £15,000 derived from the Railway Company for breach of the removal contract of 1846, and £20,000 for the Hunterian coins, which the University had no means of exhibiting and which the Commissioners thought should be sold. They favoured the selection of a site in the west end of the city and to the north of the Clyde, which they reckoned might cost £24,000, while the buildings could be erected for £84,000, giving a total outlay of £108,000, or £22,800 in excess of the value of the College property. On the south side of the Clyde a less eligible site might be obtained for £6,000, and if that locality were chosen the deficit would be only £4,800.

The powers of the Commissioners came to an end on 1st January, 1863, and the removal of the University to new buildings was carried out in a manner that greatly transcended their estimates. Towards the end of 1863 the City of Glasgow Union Railway Company came forward with a proposal to purchase the College buildings and grounds, and on 29th July of next year an Act of Parliament was passed under which they were to obtain possession in five years, at a price of £100,000. It is probable that the Union Railway Company was not the only one that might have been disposed to offer for the 26½ acres of land adjoining High Street, so invaluable for railway purposes, and that with skilful management a better price might in a short time have been obtained. However, in prospect of the £100,000, the University authorities made a fresh appeal to the Government, and in May, 1864, the Treasury agreed to propose to Parliament a grant of £21,400, on condition that £24,000

---

[1] The need for new buildings was completely made out, but the disadvantages of the site in High Street were probably exaggerated. If things were as bad as represented, not the University alone but also the Cathedral and the Royal Infirmary should have been removed, and something ought to have been done for the working population.

required for the erection of a hospital, which, in the interest of the Medical School, was included in the new scheme, should be raised by subscription. The senate about this time appointed a Removal Committee consisting of all its members, with Dr. Allen Thomson as convener ; a Committee on Subscriptions, with Principal Barclay as convener ; a Committee on Financial Arrangements, with Mr. Anderson Kirkwood as convener ; and a Committee on Superintending the Erection of New Buildings, with Dr. Allen Thomson as convener.   In July, 1864, the lands of Gilmorehill, extending to 43 acres, were bought for £65,000, on the understanding that a portion should be made over to the City Corporation, and some months later the adjoining lands of Donaldshill, containing 14 acres, were purchased for £16,000, while five or six acres of land at Clayslaps were acquired at a price of £17,400 as a site for a hospital, but afterwards exchanged for additional ground at Donaldshill.   The value of the site and grounds actually retained by the University was reckoned at about £42,000.   Towards the end of 1864 Mr. George Gilbert Scott, London, was selected as Architect, and sketch plans were in course of preparation and discussion for about a year, the completed working plans being received early in 1866.

It was estimated that for the buildings then contemplated a sum of £266,000 would be required, and as the funds in hand were quite inadequate, a public meeting to organise means of raising subscriptions was held in the Forehall on 2nd May, 1865, with Mr. Archibald Orr Ewing in the chair.   Statements were made by the chairman, the principal, and Dr. Allen Thomson ; and Lord Belhaven, Sir Archibald Alison, Sir Archibald Islay Campbell, Sheriff Glassford Bell, Bailie Raeburn, and Mr. James Mitchell spoke in support of the resolutions proposed.   A numerous committee, with Mr. Orr Ewing as convener, was named by the meeting to co-operate with a Committee of the General Council of which Mr. James Alexander Campbell was convener, and a third Committee of members of the University Court and Senate of which Principal Barclay was convener.   The citizens and others responded generously to the appeal made to them, and their ready and liberal subscriptions greatly encouraged the promoters of the scheme.

The position of the site on Gilmorehill having been determined, the ground was levelled to a depth of nine feet from the highest part of the hill.   This work was commenced on 6th June, 1866, Dr. Allen Thomson cutting the first sod.   By the end of October offers for the various parts of the work were accepted, Mr. John Thompson of Peterborough securing the contract for mason work at £111,042, and for carpenter and ironmonger work at £32,958, while the smaller contracts in the departments of the slater, smith and ironfounder, plasterer, plumber, glazier, and painter were allotted to Glasgow firms, and raised the total to a sum of £191,020. Mr. Thompson brought his men and machinery to Gilmorehill in the end of November, but the preliminary work of measurements, excavations, and the making of sheds and roads occupied some months, and it was not till 4th April, 1867, that the first stone of the building was laid. The great bulk of the building stone required was obtained from quarries within the grounds of Gilmorehill. A strike which broke out among the masons retarded the work for some time, but when this was overcome building operations were energetically pressed forward, upwards of a thousand men being employed.

About this time a further effort was made to secure more substantial aid from the Government, and on 4th May, 1867, the Duke of Montrose, as Chancellor of the University, introduced to the Prime Minister, the Earl of Derby, and the Chancellor of the Exchequer, Mr. Disraeli, a deputation headed by Lord President Inglis, then rector of the University, including Mr. Dalglish and Mr. Graham, Members for the City of Glasgow, and a majority of the Scottish Parliamentary Representatives. Shortly afterwards the Secretary of the Treasury indicated to the Duke of Montrose that a liberal grant would probably be given, and in January, 1868, the principal was informed that the Treasury intended to propose a vote of £120,000 to be paid in several instalments, on condition that an equal amount was raised by subscription. Fortunately the subscriptions by citizens of Glasgow and others were so liberal that there was no difficulty in realising this condition. The enterprise having thus received generous support from the state, was next honoured by the gracious countenance of Royalty. On 8th October, 1868, in presence of a great assemblage for whom a temporary wooden platform to accommodate 20,000 had been erected, the Prince and Princess of Wales laid the memorial stones in the piers of the archway leading from the south corridor into the cloisters. The honorary degree of LL.D. was on this occasion conferred on the Prince of Wales and Prince John of Glücksburg who accompanied him. A subscription of £500 was given by the Queen, and one of £105 by the Prince of Wales.

Notwithstanding the activity with which the work of building was carried on, it was necessary to arrange with the Railway Company to delay their occupation of the old College till 29th July, 1870, a year later than the time stipulated. Even with this extension, there was some difficulty in preparing the new building for the accommodation of the classes at the opening of next session, but on 7th November, 1870, a little more than three and a half years from the date when the first stone of the building was laid, the inaugural meeting was held in the lower hall of the Museum. The Duke of Montrose presided, and Professor Lushington delivered the inaugural address, after which speeches were made by Lord President Inglis, Sir Thomas Edward Colebrooke, Mr. Edward S. Gordon, M.P. for the Universities of Glasgow and Aberdeen, Principal Barclay, Mr. Archibald Orr Ewing, and Professor Allen Thomson.

The Architect had a good opportunity to produce a stately and symmetrical building, being unfettered by previous conditions, such as the existence of neighbouring edifices with which the new building must be brought into relation or harmony. He had also a commanding site, with ample clear space around to give a full view of the structure, which was placed on the crest of an eminence overlooking the Kelvin and the West-end Park and sloping steeply towards the river, which here forms a strong curve on its way through the Park, subtending both the eastern and the southern aspect of Gilmorehill. The buildings form a great rectangle, with the main blocks facing south and north and having a frontage of 540 feet, and the Bute Hall making a cross connection in the middle of their length, and leaving quadrangular courts on each side. Towers of somewhat greater height than the general elevation are placed at the east and west end of the south front, and in the middle of its length there rises, over the main entrance, the great central tower, topped by a spire reaching a height of about 290 feet. Between the towers the height above ground of the buildings in the south front hardly satisfies the eye, and in this respect the north front, where the full height of the walls is in view, has an advantage. The Bute Hall, for the superstructure of which the late Marquis of Bute contributed £45,000, and the Randolph Hall, connected with it, were built fully a dozen years later than the rest, and the spire of the tower was completed in 1888. The Hunterian Museum and the Library occupy a great part of the north block, and in the east quadrangle classrooms for the faculties of Divinity, Law, and Medicine were placed, though some of the last have now been removed to separate buildings, while the west quadrangle affords accommodation to the faculty of Arts. The professor of Astronomy has a house attached to the Observatory, and the other thirteen professors formerly included in the faculty are provided with houses just outside the west quadrangle, so placed as to prevent extension of the public buildings in the direction in which it would most naturally have proceeded. The site and grounds and the buildings contemplated in the original scheme, including a contribution of £30,000 towards the provision of a hospital, cost upwards of half a million, of which more than half was made up by subscriptions and legacies. This is exclusive of large undertakings carried out within the last eight or ten years, which mark a new era in the extension of the University buildings.

The veteran Principal Macfarlan died on 25th November, 1857, and was succeeded by Thomas Barclay, D.D., a native of Unst in the extreme north of Shetland.   He presided over the University at the time it underwent reform and expansion under the Act of 1858, and also witnessed its transfer to new buildings at Gilmorehill.   After his death early in 1873, the office of principal was held for a quarter of a century by John Caird, D.D., who had been professor of Divinity since 1862.   He was at once a philosopher and an orator, a man of great intellectual gifts, of unassuming personal worth, and most lovable character.   Caird was a son of the University, receiving his training in Arts and Divinity within its walls, and after he had shown himself the most eloquent preacher in the country, he returned to its service, to be for thirty-six years one of its brightest ornaments, and though he died at a good old age, the University can hardly yet forbear the *desiderium tam cari capitis*.

In its new home the University continued its course of orderly progress, with capable and diligent teachers in almost all the departments, and men of high academic reputation in not a few.   The addition of English Literature to the faculty of Arts was an important accession, and doubly important when it was taught by so brilliant a professor as John Nichol.   His portrayals of authors and works, of periods and movements, were those of a man possessed of much knowledge gained at first hand, and well acquainted with the estimates of others, but giving forth estimates of his own, expressed with such freshness and spirit, such clearness, force, and elegance, that it was hard to say whether they were more instructive or entertaining.   There were flashes of pleasantry and satire too, but they seldom interfered with the fairness of his judgment, and his views, even when one did not agree with them, were stimulating and suggestive. From 1863 to 1906 Humanity was taught by Mr. George Gilbert Ramsay, who had the longest tenure on record of that chair, and had also to organise and educate probably the largest class that ever came under the control of a single professor in the University, sometimes exceeding 600 in number.   On the retiral of Mr. Lushington in 1875, Mr. Richard Claverhouse Jebb became professor of Greek.   He was a brilliant scholar, a man of fine literary tastes and powers, and a most effective teacher.   Yet some of the elements which contributed to his success in teaching were by no means transcendental in their nature, and might readily and profitably be put in practice by others.   Mr. Jebb exercised a wise discretion in avoiding too great detail, and giving just so much as was good for his students at the particular stage which they had reached.   He also avoided setting too long passages of translation for the daily task, but he was remarkably methodical in accomplishing what was prescribed ; and while ready to accept an honest attempt on the part of a student, though it was not very successful, he had a certain minimum standard of proficiency, and Shylock himself could hardly have been more resolute in exacting it.

Mr. John Veitch, who had previously taught Logic at St. Andrews, became professor of Logic and Rhetoric at Glasgow in 1864, and held the chair for thirty years.   He had studied under Sir William Hamilton at Edinburgh, and been for a short time his assistant, and throughout life continued to be his admirer and defender.   The promise of Veitch's youth was in considerable measure realised, but as time passed and views of philosophy different from those with which he set out came to be more widely accepted, he did not embrace them.   He delivered a number of lectures on Rhetoric—by no means the least interesting part of his course —and sometimes his expositions of philosophy were marked by rhetorical qualities.   His literary leanings and robust Border characteristics appear side by side in a number of works in prose and verse which he has left behind.   Edward Caird, a younger brother of Principal Caird, held the chair of Moral Philosophy for 27 or 28 years from 1866, and retired on being appointed Master of Balliol College, Oxford.   During his long tenure a very large number of students came under his teaching, some of whom have in turn become professors and continue his influence.   After the retirement of Mr. Blackburn, William Jack, LL.D., held the chair of Mathematics for thirty years, resigning in 1909.   Sir William Thomson, who had been knighted in 1866 for his share in the successful laying of the Atlantic cable, was created a peer in 1892 under the title of Lord Kelvin, and continued as professor of Natural Philosophy till 1899. Special celebrations were held in 1896 to commemorate the 50th year of the professorship of this great man of science, and they evoked a lively interest not only in the University of Glasgow, but among Universities and scientific institutions and societies at home and abroad.

Robert Grant, LL.D., became professor of Astronomy in 1859, and the results of a considerable part of his work have been made available to astronomers in a *Catalogue of 6,415 Stars for the Epoch of* 1870, deduced from observations made at the University Observatory from 1860 to 1881, which was printed at the expense of the Government, on the recommendation of the Council of the Royal Society.   After Rankine, whose incessant activity and numerous valuable works in his own subject brought credit to the University, died prematurely in 1872, James Thomson, LL.D., elder brother of Lord Kelvin, was appointed professor of Engineering, having been previously professor of the same subject in

UNIVERSITY BUILDINGS AT GILMOREHILL—SOUTH FRONT

Belfast.   In the theory of Mechanical Science and allied subjects he was a man of great ability, and gave proof of his insight by pronouncing an unfavourable opinion of the system adopted for heating the new University buildings by forcibly introducing heated air into the apartments. The opinion was soon amply confirmed by experience, and the original arrangement was gradually replaced by a system of hot water pipes.

The chairs of Astronomy and Engineering naturally suggest the evolution of the faculty of Science, to which, when it came into existence, they were assigned, though as yet reckoned within the faculty of Arts. After long discussions by the General Council and the Senate on the working of the regulations for graduation in Arts, the question of reviving the degree of B.A., and the advisability of giving greater prominence to scientific subjects, either by modifying the Arts curriculum so as to include them or by instituting new degrees in Science, the Senate submitted to the Court a detailed scheme of examinations for the degree of Bachelor of Science, and stated that they proposed to hold examinations for the various departments as soon as arrangements could be made.   The Court approved of the scheme which had been framed, and authorised the Senate to carry it out as soon as practicable.   Accordingly intimation was made in the University Calendar for 1872-3 that the Senate, with the approval of the Court, had resolved to establish a degree of B.Sc. open to candidates who pursued a course of study and passed examinations in four subjects of the Arts curriculum, and also in four subjects from a specified list in one or other of the departments of Biological, Geological, or Engineering Science, or in the department of Law.   Like most other new ventures, the degree was subjected to somewhat severe criticism, and it would have been better if the rather incongruous department of Law, which was omitted after 1876, had never been included.   The other three departments remained, improvements in the regulations were made from time to time, and the degree of B.Sc., first conferred in 1873, though it did not attract a very large number of candidates, amply justified its existence.

The foundation of a chair of Naval Architecture in 1883, following upon a lectureship on the same subject conducted for two or three years previously by Mr. J. G. Lawrie, extended the range of scientific teaching to one of the greatest industries of the Clyde.   Some time before, Mrs. John Elder, the widow of a famous Glasgow shipbuilder, had given £5,000 as an additional endowment for the chair of Engineering, and towards the end of 1883 she provided an endowment fund of £12,500 for the chair of Naval Architecture, which was forthwith founded by the Senate, and Mr. Francis Elgar, Naval Architect, London, became the first professor.   He resigned in 1886, on being appointed Director of

Dockyards to the Admiralty, and was succeeded by Mr. Philip Jenkins. Mr. Jenkins died prematurely in 1891, when Mr. John Harvard Biles, the present incumbent, was appointed.

The Commissioners under the Act of 1858 provided for the holding of a voluntary preliminary examination in Latin, Greek, and Mathematics, and allowed candidates who passed to omit attendance in the junior classes of the several subjects, those who did so in both Latin and Greek being allowed to graduate in Arts after three sessions of attendance. Though, after some time, a moderate percentage passed this preliminary examination, the great majority entered without doing so, and among them were many whose preparation was very inadequate. After 1870 there was a considerable increase in the number of Arts students, and in March, 1875, the University Court at Glasgow resolved to request a conference with the Court at Edinburgh on the expediency of introducing an entrance examination. After the conference had taken place the Court at Glasgow resolved that it was expedient, in concurrence with the University of Edinburgh, and, if possible, the other Scottish Universities, to institute such an examination for all entrants in the junior classes of Latin, Greek, and Mathematics, commencing with session 1876-77. In 1876 a Royal Commission was appointed to enquire into the state of the Universities, and by and by they presented a Report, not without points of merit and interest, but which did not greatly influence the course of future legislation. The existence of this Commission seems to have been looked upon by some of the Universities as an impediment to their taking action on their own account, and in March, 1876, the Court at Glasgow, after receiving a communication from Principal Sir Alexander Grant of Edinburgh, regretted that no alternative was left but to postpone action. The question was revived early in 1882, and in April the Court approved of the main principles of a scheme framed by the senate applicable to public students in Arts under the age of seventeen. The subjects included were English, Latin, Greek, Elementary Mathematics, a Modern Language, and History, and students were required to pass in English and two other subjects. The other Universities were again invited to join in the movement, but they sent replies auguring more of an inclination to discuss than to act The regulations were therefore brought into operation in November, 1883, at Glasgow only, and remained in force till they were superseded by the higher requirements of the preliminary examination introduced by the Commissioners under the Act of 1889.

Two schemes recommended by the General Council and relating to the province of the faculty of Arts may now be noticed. In 1880 the Court sanctioned the institution of the title of Literate in Arts, open to those attending for at least two sessions, taking five classes in Arts, and passing examinations on the M.A. standard.   The title was not a degree, and conferred no graduate's privileges.   In 1887 the Court dealt with a proposal which had been under discussion several years before, and authorised the senate to constitute a Board for the Extension of University Teaching.   The Board was empowered to select lecturers from graduates of Glasgow or other Universities, to determine the subjects to be taught, and to make other arrangements.   University certificates were not given in connection with this scheme, but the lecturers were authorised to give certificates to those who acquitted themselves satisfactorily in examinations on the work done.   Probably the main reason why no great measure of success attended either of these schemes, is that the Scottish Universities are so accessible and democratic that earnest and resolute aspirants find means to enter as regular students, though many of them have previously spent a number of years in business.

Local Examinations were instituted by the University in 1877, and for some time attracted a considerable number of candidates from Glasgow and various outside centres, of which Dumbarton, Greenock, Hamilton, Kilmarnock, and Rothesay were the most important; but the Examinations were discontinued in 1893, the Leaving Certificates of the Education Department having become accessible to the great majority of the schools concerned.

At their conference in 1875 the University Courts of Glasgow and Edinburgh had under consideration the question of raising the class fees in Arts and Medicine.   After the conference the Court at Glasgow approved generally of raising the class fees, but resolved that it should not be carried out till entrance examinations in Arts were introduced.   In 1878 the senate asked the Court to consider further, in conjunction with the University of Edinburgh, the proposal to raise the class fees, and some further communication and discussion followed, but no action was taken at Glasgow.   The Commissioners had provided for allowances being made for class expenses to the professors of Natural Philosophy, Chemistry, Anatomy, Materia Medica, and Forensic Medicine, and in 1874 a question was raised whether allowances should not also be made in the case of Physiology and some other classes, and the senate requested a deliverance on the subject from the University Court.   Experiments and practical teaching were gradually entering more largely into the work of many classes, but there was no specific provision for payment from the University funds except in the cases laid down in the ordinance, and the burden of acquiring apparatus and articles illustrative of the teaching, and of preparing and demonstrating experiments fell for the most part on the professors. The system was not fitted to encourage the development of experimental and objective teaching. On the other hand, as the number of students increased, the emoluments of the professors from fees also increased, and in several cases separate practical classes were instituted from which additional fees were drawn ; and though some professors were obliged to spend considerable amounts in payment of assistants rendered necessary by the more numerous attendance of students or the institution of practical classes, the advantage in most cases lay with the professors. There was no urgent case for the raising of class fees in the faculties of Arts and Medicine, and such a measure would have entailed great additional burdens for retiring allowances. In all the circumstances the Court acted prudently in not raising them.

In 1867 Mr. Robert Berry, who had been secretary to the Universities Commission, was appointed to the chair of Law in succession to Skene ; and in the same year Mr. (afterwards Sir) James Roberton succeeded Kirkwood as professor of Conveyancing. Berry held his chair till in 1887 he resigned after being appointed Sheriff of Lanarkshire, and Roberton till his death in 1889, the former being succeeded by Mr. Alexander Moody Stuart, and the latter by Mr. James Moir, the present incumbent. Mr. William M. Gloag became professor of Law in 1905, on the retirement of Mr. Moody Stuart. After long dormancy in the teaching of Civil Law, Berry revived it in session 1873-74, and the number of students in the faculty of Law continued steadily to rise, being 84 in 1865, 170 in 1875, and 239 in 1885. But though the number of students was rising, it was fully a dozen years after the ordinance passed before anyone obtained the degree of LL.B. under it. The first to do so was Mr. William Galbraith Miller, and but for his tenacity of purpose further years might have passed before the degree was granted. He attended all the subjects then available at Glasgow, and his exertions seem to have aided the revival of the teaching of Civil Law. Having attended the remaining subjects at Edinburgh, he returned to become a candidate for the degree of LL.B. at Glasgow, but there was still a difficulty, for the ordinance required that there should be a Board of six examiners—either Bachelors of Law under its conditions or professors of Law in a Scottish University. No such Board had as yet been constituted, but, at the request of the faculty of Law, the Court in April, 1874, appointed three additional examiners in Law, and at length in 1875 Mr. Miller was the first to receive the degree of LL.B. under the new regulations.

Before this the academic authorities at Edinburgh, disappointed with the results of the regulations for graduation in Law made by the Commissioners, communicated in 1872 their desire for an alteration of Ordinance

No. 75 so as to introduce a degree in Law which should be easier of attainment and more in demand than the degree of LL.B. A question of some interest arose whether an ordinance originally made applicable to all the four Universities could be altered except by the assent and at the instance of the whole of them. The University of Edinburgh, however, seeing no prospect of securing the concurrence of all the other Universities, resolved to apply to the Queen in Council for approval of an alteration of ordinance sanctioning the introduction of the degree of B.L. at Edinburgh alone, and leaving the ordinance unchanged so far as the other Universities were concerned. There seems to have been no difficulty in obtaining the approval of the Queen in Council to a change on the general ordinance which was to apply to only one University, and further instances of the same kind occurred. After some hesitation the University Court at Glasgow procured a similar, though not identical, alteration sanctioning the degree of B.L. in the Western University, where it was first conferred in 1874—a year earlier than the degree for which the ordinance originally provided. The degree of B.L. might be obtained on a minimum curriculum of two years, including attendance on Civil Law, Scots Law, and Conveyancing, and as a fourth subject either Public Law, Constitutional Law and History, or Medical Jurisprudence—Moral Philosophy or Political Economy being allowed in certain circumstances to count instead of Civil Law or the fourth Law subject. The candidate, if not a graduate in Arts, was required to pass an examination in Latin, as well as in Logic or Mathematics, and a third subject of the Arts course, with the option of French or German instead of Greek. For the next 20 or 25 years the average annual number of LL.B. degrees was almost six, and of B.L. degrees a little over seven.

In the summer of 1877 Professor Lorimer of Edinburgh, by arrangement with the senate at Glasgow, delivered a course on Public Law at the latter place. Later in the year Mr. Scott Dickson (afterwards Lord Advocate) was appointed lecturer on Constitutional Law and History, and next year was succeeded by Mr. Alexander Ure (the present Lord Advocate). In 1878 Mr. Galbraith Miller, who headed the list of Bachelors of Laws under Ordinance No. 75, was appointed lecturer on Public Law, so that from this time there was a full staff of teachers in all the subjects of the legal curriculum.

In 1863 the Rev. William Purdie Dickson, minister of Cameron, Fife, was appointed to the new chair of Biblical Criticism founded by Ordinance No. 22 of the Commissioners under the Act of 1858. In ten years Dr. Dickson was transferred to the chair of Divinity left vacant by the promotion of Dr. Caird to be principal, and he continued as professor of Divinity till 1895, when he retired. He was a man of extensive and exact scholarship, and rendered valuable services to the University, not only as a professor, but also as curator of the library for fully thirty years. He was succeeded in the chair of Biblical Criticism by the present incumbent, the Rev. William Stewart, D.D., who had been minister of St. George's in the Fields, Glasgow. The vacancy in the chair of Divinity in 1895 was filled by the appointment of the Rev. William Hastie, D.D., who at an earlier stage had been principal of the General Assembly's Institution and College, Calcutta, a man distinguished alike by the extent and solidity of his learning, the strength and uprightness of his character, and the urbanity and kindness of his disposition. He died prematurely in 1903, and was succeeded by the present professor, the Rev. Henry Martyn Beckwith Reid, D.D., formerly minister of Balmaghie.

In 1877 the Rev. James Robertson, D.D., who had been for more than a dozen years a missionary at Beyrout, Syria, and had thus been long in direct contact with eastern life and manners, was appointed professor of Oriental Languages. Besides conducting the regular classes in Hebrew for Divinity students, he gave considerable attention to Syriac and Arabic, and since 1902 there has been a separate lectureship on Arabic, the lecturer being Mr. Thomas H. Weir, B.D., a son of Dr. Robertson's predecessor in the chair of Oriental Languages. On Dr. Robertson's retirement in 1907, the Rev. William B. Stevenson, B.D., was appointed to the chair, the title of which was changed by the Commissioners under the Act of 1889 to Hebrew and Semitic Languages.

On the resignation of Dr. Jackson in 1874, the Rev. William Lee, D.D., son of Principal Lee of Edinburgh University, after a ministry of fully thirty years at Roxburgh, was appointed professor of Ecclesiastical History. Upon Dr. Lee's death in 1886, the crown appointed as the next professor the Rev. Robert Herbert Story, D.D., Rosneath, whose robust character, ready and fearless speech, and devotion to the Church of Scotland had made him one of the foremost men within her pale, while as an author and a man of altogether notable personality his name was familiar all over the country. After being twelve years a professor, he was appointed principal on the retirement of Dr. Caird, and the Rev. James Cooper, D.D., Aberdeen, became professor of Church History. Dr. Story signalised his tenure as principal by a movement for the extension and better equipment of the University. In some respects the scheme, which was inaugurated in 1900, fell at an inopportune time. Subscriptions were being asked for the families of the troops engaged in the South African war, and for new buildings for the Technical College and the Royal Infirmary; and, on the other hand, the creation of the Carnegie

Trust in 1901 gave rise to an impression in some quarters that no further aid was needed by the Scottish Universities. In these rather untoward circumstances it was a tribute to the influence of Principal Story that by 1906 a fund of £75,000 had been raised. But the principal was not destined to see the full fruition of this and other plans for the welfare of the University in which he was deeply interested, as he died on 13th January, 1907. The vacancy was filled by the appointment of a layman, Donald MacAlister, M.D., who in 1908 was created K.C.B.

In 1887 under the will of Adam Gifford, a wealthy judge of the Court of Session, there was founded in each of the four Scottish Universities a Gifford lectureship on Natural Theology, a capital fund of £20,000 being assigned to Glasgow for the purpose. This lectureship has no direct or official relation to the faculty of Theology, and the founder desired the lecturer not to rely on revelation, but to treat the subject as a strictly natural science like Astronomy or Chemistry. Some have looked upon the scheme as an endowment of doubt, and in other respects probably the gift might have been made more helpful to the Universities.

In 1863 Mr. Robert Scott succeeded Mr. Jones as librarian, and in 1867 was followed by Mr. Robert B. Spears, who died in 1878. Mr. James Lymburn succeeded in January, 1879, and on his retiral in 1905, the present librarian, Mr. James L. Galbraith, was appointed. A number of gentlemen purchased the library of the late Sir William Hamilton and presented it to the University in 1878. Other gifts include 15,000 volumes bequeathed by Mr. William Ewing, books on Palestine from the library of the late Dr. Alexander B. M'Grigor, selections from the libraries of the late Professors Veitch and Hastie, and Migne's *Patrologie* presented as a memorial of the late Professor Dickson. For a number of years the library, which now contains about 200,000 volumes, has benefited by an annual grant of £100 from the Bellahouston Trustees for scientific periodicals, and a subvention of £1,000 a year from the Carnegie Trustees. Something has of late been done for the Hunterian collections by the publication of Dr. George Macdonald's *Catalogue of Greek Coins*, defrayed by the late Dr. Stevenson of Hailie, Largs; of Dr. John H. Teacher's work on the *Anatomical and Pathological Preparations*; and of Dr. Patrick H. Aitken's *Catalogue of Manuscripts*, issued as a memorial of the late Professor Young.

Among those who have been students of the University since 1830 mention should be made of Sir Henry Campbell-Bannerman, long a prominent statesman and finally Prime Minister; Mr. James Bryce, author and politician, now Ambassador to the United States; William Watson, Lord Advocate and afterwards a judge of the Court of Appeal in London;

Sir Robert Giffen, long associated with the Board of Trade ; Sir Andrew Crombie Ramsay, the geologist ; Sir William Ramsay, who has extended the bounds of knowledge in Chemistry ; Sir Joseph Dalton Hooker, the veteran botanist ; James Hutchison Stirling, Robert Flint, and John Watson, widely known for their works in philosophy ; Robert Rainy, whose name is written in the ecclesiastical history of his time and country ; and Sir Archibald Alison, a famous soldier, who lost his right arm at the relief of Lucknow and led the Highland Brigade at Tel-el-Kebir.

Several attempts were made by the Government of Mr. Gladstone between 1880 and 1885 to pass a bill for the reform of the Scottish Universities, and afterwards by the Government of Lord Salisbury, and at length on 30th August, 1889, a second comprehensive Act for improving their endowment and organisation received the royal assent. This measure, either by its own direct provisions or by the action of the Commissioners under it, in whom great powers were vested, transferred the general management and administration from the senate to an enlarged University Court ; bestowed considerable additional endowments ; made payable to the University the class fees hitherto drawn by the professors, and the numerous and varied royal and parliamentary grants hitherto paid to individual members of senate, to whom definitely regulated salaries were now assigned ; introduced a stringent preliminary examination in Arts and Science, and numerous options in the selection of subjects for the degree of M.A. ; constituted for the first time a distinct faculty of Science ; and opened the University to women for the purpose of study and graduation. At first the Commissioners were embarrassed by the formidable possibility of claims for pensions under the old system, as the payment of pensions was now transferred from the Treasury to the individual Universities ; and they urged the Government to give further aid. Accordingly the Education and Local Taxation Account (Scotland) Act of 1892 provided an additional yearly sum of £30,000 for distribution among the Universities in a manner to be laid down by the Commissioners, who were now enabled to frame their ordinances for the allocation and regulation of finance.

Before 1889, apart from pensions which were paid by the Treasury, the annual amount of public money bestowed on the four Scottish Universities was £20,742, of which the University of Glasgow received £5,189 6s. 6d. Now the four Universities receive £72,000, the share allocated to Glasgow being £20,880. The outlays for pensions in 1906-07 amounted to £4,594 7s. 7d., but after allowing for this, the University has gained fully £11,000 a year under the Acts of 1889 and

THE VERY REV. ROBERT HERBERT STORY, D.D., LL.D.

Principal and Vice-Chancellor of the University of Glasgow

BORN 1835.   DIED 1907

392. The fees from professors' classes, and also from classes qualifying
for graduation though taught by lecturers, now form a fee fund, as it is
called, while the other endowments formerly attached to chairs are grouped
together under a salaries account. From these two sources the normal
salaries of professors are paid ; and in case the funds prove inadequate, the
salaries may suffer a deduction equal to a fourth of the normal amount,
but in no case is the salary to be reduced below £500, the general University fund being liable for a contribution to make up this minimum.
The professors have been relieved of all payments for assistants, and for
apparatus and equipment required to illustrate the teaching. The five
professors of Divinity, Ecclesiastical History, Biblical Criticism, Clinical
Surgery, and Clinical Medicine are outside the general arrangement, and
the class fees still belong to themselves, but assistants are provided for the
clinical professors in the same way as for others.

The Commissioners established from the funds at their disposal new
chairs of History and Pathology, and also founded a chair of Political
Economy, for which Mr. Andrew Stewart, merchant, Glasgow, provided
a capital fund of £15,000. Afterwards a chair of Geology, for which an
endowment of £15,000 was provided by the Carnegie Trustees, the Bellahouston Trustees, and others, was founded by the University Court in
903 ; and a chair of Mining, for which a sum of £16,500 was provided
by Mr. James S. Dixon, was likewise founded in 1907. Besides these
additional chairs, the teaching staff has under the system brought about by
the Act of 1889 been greatly reinforced by the institution of new lectureships, and by a marked increase in the number of Assistants, while the staff
of Examiners has also been greatly strengthened. Additional lecturers
have been employed in the temporary and somewhat inglorious summer
session in Arts, and in the holding of separate classes for women, but, apart
from these, lectureships have been established in French, German, Italian,
Arabic, Celtic, Education, British History, Electricity, Electrical Engineering, Physical Chemistry, Political Philosophy, Organic Chemistry,
Metallurgical Chemistry, Public International Law and International
Private Law (resulting from the splitting of the previous lectureship in
Public Law), General or Comparative Jurisprudence (also called Philosophy
of Law), Civil Law (no longer taught by the holder of the chair descended
from the professorship of Civil Law founded by Queen Anne), Mercantile
Law, Physics for Medical students, and Insanity.[1] The courses in all
these subjects count for graduation, and courses are given by lecturers on

[1] The lectureship in Insanity dates from 1880, but attendance was not made compulsory
till 1892. This lectureship was long held by Dr. David Yellowlees, and on his retirement
in 1905, he was succeeded by Landel Rose Oswald, M.B., C.M.

the Ear and on the Throat and Nose, which, though not yet made compulsory, are attended by almost all the medical students.

Among the many important tasks assigned to the Commissioners by the Act of 1889 not the least important was 'to enable each University to admit women to graduation in one or more faculties and to provide for their instruction.' Local circumstances influenced the arrangements actually made at the different Universities. In 1877 an Association for the Higher Education of Women was formed in Glasgow, at a meeting over which Principal Caird presided, and in 1883 the Association was incorporated as Queen Margaret College. Shortly afterwards Mrs. Elder, who took a warm interest in the movement, presented North Park House and grounds, on the banks of the Kelvin near the Botanic Gardens, to the New College, and there since 1884 its work has been carried on. A number of University professors took part in its teaching, as well as in its management, and from the opening of the College till her death in January, 1909, Miss Janet A. Galloway rendered unwearied and meritorious service as secretary. A Medical School for women was added to the organisation in 1890, and at first Queen Margaret College aimed at affiliation with the University in such manner that, while the College retained its separate existence and management, its teaching should qualify for graduation purposes. Negotiations for this end appeared to be nearing an adjustment in the course of the year 1891, but in February, 1892, the Commissioners issued a draft ordinance proposing to empower the University authorities to admit women to the ordinary classes or to institute separate classes for them. Upon this, the Council of Queen Margaret College changed their policy, and, instead of affiliation, proposed that North Park House and grounds, with the endowments of the College, should be made over to the University, which should itself undertake the arrangements for the instruction of women, it being stipulated that the buildings and grounds should be used for the University education of women exclusively, and that the funds made over should be kept apart. The Court resolved that it was desirable, in accordance with the power which the draft ordinance, if passed, would confer, to provide for the instruction of women mainly by instituting separate classes for them ; and they accordingly accepted the offer.

Under this arrangement Queen Margaret College was dissolved, and North Park House and grounds were made over to the University, along with an endowment of £25,482. Separate classes for women are maintained in many subjects, but in not a few, including all the honours classes, women are taught along with men ; and probably, as time passes and the presence of women in the University comes to be in accordance with use and wont, mixed classes may be more general. The number of women students in 1907-08 was 631, of whom about 60 were students of Medicine. Down to April, 1909, the degree of M.A. had been conferred on 439 women, the degree of B.Sc. on 15, the degrees of M.B. and C.M. on 16, the degrees of M.B. and Ch.B. on 117, and the degree of M.D. on 14. Miss Marion Gilchrist, who graduated with commendation in 1894 as M.B. and C.M., was the earliest woman graduate of the University ; while the earliest woman graduate in Arts was Miss Isabella Blacklock (now Mrs. Baxter), who obtained the degree of M.A. in 1895 ; and the earliest woman graduate in Science, Miss Ruth Pirret, who obtained the degree of B.Sc. in 1895. The number of women proceeding to graduation in Arts has shown a rapid increase, and at the graduation in April, 1908, no fewer than 53 obtained the degree of M.A. Of the women who have graduated in Medicine not a few have obtained public appointments, and the number of women graduates who have entered into marriage has been remarkable.

In dealing with the faculty of Arts the Commissioners introduced a stringent preliminary examination, each student being required to pass in English, Mathematics, Latin or Greek, and a fourth subject, which might be Latin or Greek, if not already taken, French, German, Italian, or Dynamics. They also set up a Joint Board of Examiners representing the four Universities, to supervise and control the examinations and maintain a uniform standard. The Commissioners retained seven as the number of subjects in the curriculum for the ordinary degree, but, instead of seven subjects fixed by predestination, they allowed the student under certain guiding principles to exercise his freewill in making the selection from a list of twenty-eight subjects, arranged in four departments. With a view to encourage graduation with honours they reduced the number of subjects for an honours degree to five, but, as candidates were required to attend two classes in each of their honours subjects, this brought the number of classes to an equality with those of students taking the ordinary degree. In the department of Language and Literature the Commissioners included Latin, Greek, English, French, German, Italian, Sanskrit, Hebrew, Arabic or Syriac, Celtic, and Modern Greek ; while under Mental Philosophy they included Logic and Metaphysics, Moral Philosophy, Political Economy, Education, and Philosophy of Law ; under Science, Mathematics, Natural Philosophy, Astronomy, Chemistry, Zoology, Botany, and Geology ; and under History and Law, History, Archaeology and Art, Constitutional Law and History, Roman Law, and Public Law.

Except that they established chairs of History and Political Economy at Glasgow, the Commissioners did not directly provide for the teaching of any new subjects, but left the University authorities to increase the teaching as they best might, and in several subjects qualifying courses have not yet been established.   The principal restrictions on the choice of subjects for the ordinary degree, in case qualifying courses were held, were that the student must take one subject from Latin or Greek, a second from English, a Modern Language, or History, a third from Logic or Moral Philosophy, and a fourth from Mathematics or Natural Philosophy; and that the remaining three subjects should be so arranged that every candidate for an ordinary degree should take both Latin and Greek, or both Logic and Moral Philosophy, or two subjects chosen from Mathematics, Natural Philosophy, and Chemistry.   The regulations were so drawn as to afford some inducement to students desiring afterwards to graduate in Medicine or Law to begin by taking a degree in Arts; and by making an appropriate selection the student might include so many of the early subjects of the medical course as to be exempted from a year of study in that faculty, or might bring into his course in Arts a number of subjects which would afterwards count towards graduation in Law.   Some guiding principles were also laid down for the selection of subjects for an honours curriculum, and the subjects were arranged in honours groups differing considerably from the departments for the ordinary degree.   The new regulations have stimulated the desire for honours, and the number who now graduate with honours is considerably greater than under the previous system.

Graduates in Arts of five years' standing, with honours of the first or second class in the appropriate group, may become candidates for the degree of Doctor of Philosophy (D.Phil.) or Doctor of Letters (D.Litt.), on presenting a thesis or published memoir or work embodying an original contribution to learning.   The degree of Doctor of Science (D.Sc.), open to those who have held for five years the degree of B.Sc. in Pure Science or Engineering, or the degree of M.B., may also be obtained by Masters of Arts of five years' standing who have graduated with first or second class honours in Mathematics and Natural Philosophy.   The thesis in this case must be a record of original research by the candidate.   These higher degrees are also open under certain conditions to research students. The Commissioners under the Act of 1889 made special regulations for admitting graduates or other qualified persons to special study and research, and authorised the conferring of the title of research fellow. Lord Kelvin showed his interest in the new system by becoming a research student and fellow when he resigned his professorship.

Of the new subjects which have been added, probably History is the most important.　Mr. Richard Lodge was the first professor, and when after five years he was transferred to Edinburgh, Mr. Dudley J. Medley, the present incumbent, was appointed.　From the first the class attracted a good following of students, and it now bids fair to rival the number in some of the long-established and traditional subjects of the Arts course. Political Economy, the other subject for which a chair was founded, and Mr. William Smart appointed professor in 1896, though not in its nature so universally interesting as History, has maintained a good hold on the attention of students.　In the important group of Modern Languages the students of French have far outnumbered those in any other subject.　A lectureship in this subject was instituted by the University Court in 1895, the first lecturer being Mr. Alfred Mercier, and in 1898 the present lecturer, Mr. Charles Martin, was appointed.　A lectureship in German was instituted in 1899, Dr. Alexander Tille being the first lecturer.　He was succeeded next year by Dr. George P. Thistlethwaite, and the present lecturer, Dr. Herbert Smith, was appointed in 1907.　The lectureship in Italian dates from 1902, when the present lecturer, Dr. Fernando Agnoletti, was appointed.　Women students have shown a proclivity for Modern Languages, and since the range of teaching has been extended so as to make it practicable, not a few have graduated with honours in this group.　There is also a lectureship in Celtic, Dr. George Henderson being the lecturer.

Chiefly to meet the needs of the many students in training for the teaching profession, the University instituted a lectureship on Education in 1894, which has been held successively by Dr. David Ross, rector of the Church of Scotland Training College ; Mr. John Adams, rector of the Free Church Training College, now professor of Education in the University of London ; Mr. John Clark, now clerk to the School Board of Glasgow ; and Mr. William Boyd, the present lecturer.　The lectureship on Education naturally suggests the relation of the University to the teaching profession.　It was in Glasgow that Mr. David Stow, beginning with Sunday Schools, went on to organise week day schools and afterwards Colleges for training teachers, the first of which was opened in 1836. Being heavily burdened with debt, a grant of £5,000 was obtained from the Government a few years later, on condition that the buildings and management should be transferred to the Church of Scotland.　Stow joined the Free Church and had to quit the College, but in a short time he was provided with better buildings for a Free Church Training College, and thus there have been in Glasgow two Normal Schools or Training Colleges side by side.　At first they stood quite apart from the University, but between 1860 and 1870 it became customary for students from the

Training Colleges to attend some classes at the University. In 1873 the Education Department recognised the practice, and freed such students from part of the usual attendance at the Training College ; and in 1877 agreed to defray three-fourths of the University fees of such students and of the cost of the books required for their classes.

The Parochial and Burgh Schoolmasters Act of 1861 formed another link of connection between the Universities and those preparing for the work of teaching. It withdrew the examination of teachers from Presbyteries, and empowered the University to appoint three professors from the faculty of Arts and three from the faculty of Divinity to be examiners of parochial schoolmasters. The school district associated with the University of Glasgow included the counties of Ayr, Argyle, Bute, Dumbarton, Dumfries, Kirkcudbright, Lanark, Renfrew, and Wigtown ; but the arrangement disappeared with the passing of the Education Act of 1872. A large number of Training College students—both men and women—came to attend the University, and a Local Committee representing the University, the Training Colleges, and the School Boards of Glasgow and Govan, supervised the arrangements for the training of these students some years before the Education Department organised the scheme of Provincial Committees. The work is now carried on through these Provincial Committees ; and there is a tendency to bring a larger number of graduates into the teaching profession, and also to bring students in training for that profession under the influence and instruction of the University during some part of their course, though they may not obtain a degree.

During the last forty or fifty years there has been a very great increase in the number of bursaries available for students, the faculties of Arts and Divinity being best supplied in this respect ; and an appreciable number of scholarships and fellowships have also been added. For the maintenance of these foundations many donors have presented or bequeathed to the University, or to outside boards and trustees, funds which in the aggregate amount to a very large sum. In 1863 there were about 80 bursaries, less than a fourth of which were awarded by competition, the rest being assigned by presentation ; now there are more than 450 bursaries, nearly nine-tenths of which are awarded by competition. In many cases, however, the competition is not free and open, but restricted by the terms of foundation to students of a specified description, or from a particular locality, or following a certain course of study. The placing of the management of bursaries in the hands of outside boards and trustees is probably intended to secure greater attention to such qualifications, or to the personal circumstances of candidates, but it embarrasses the award of bursaries in the gift of the University, for if these were assigned without waiting for awards by outside bodies it would frequently result in one candidate carrying off two or more bursaries awarded by different patrons acting independently and without knowledge of each other's doings. In 1898 the University Court, as empowered by the Commissioners under the Act of 1889, resolved to admit women students as well as men to open bursaries in Arts, Science, and Medicine which were in operation before 30th August, 1864. An enactment by the Commissioners that, in the examination for bursaries, English, Latin, Greek, and Mathematics should have double the marks assigned to other subjects—double the marks assigned to French and German, for instance—gave rise to much discussion, and has now been abolished.

On the resignation of Professor Jebb, Mr. George Gilbert Aimé Murray was appointed to the Greek chair in 1889. He held it for ten years, but for a time was laid aside by ill health, and the class was conducted during his enforced absence by Mr. George Macdonald, now Assistant Secretary in Edinburgh to the Scotch Education Department. Mr. John S. Phillimore, who had been professor of Greek since 1899, was transferred to the chair of Humanity on the retirement of Mr. Ramsay in 1906, and Mr. Gilbert Austin Davies became professor of Greek. Mr. Andrew Cecil Bradley succeeded Nichol as professor of English Language and Literature in 1889, and held the chair till his retiral in 1900. Mr. Walter A. Raleigh was the next incumbent, but being called to a similar chair at Oxford in 1904, the present professor, Mr. William Macneile Dixon, was appointed. After the death of Mr. Veitch in September, 1894, the Logic class was conducted for a year by Mr. Robert A. Duff, and in 1895 Professor Adamson exchanged the Logic chair at Aberdeen for that at Glasgow. He died prematurely in 1902, but during his brief tenure he gave an impulse to the policy of the faculty of Arts in the direction which it has since followed. He was succeeded by the present incumbent, Professor Robert Latta, who had previously held the chair of Moral Philosophy at Aberdeen. Professor Henry Jones was appointed to the Moral Philosophy chair at Glasgow in 1894; and in 1899 Professor Andrew Gray succeeded Lord Kelvin in the chair of Natural Philosophy.

The Commissioners under the Act of 1889 ordained that the winter session should extend to at least twenty weeks of teaching, and that the University Court should institute a summer session including at least ten weeks of teaching. The length of the winter session had been much curtailed since the eighteenth century, and had been appreciably shortened since the time of the Commissioners under the Act of 1858, who found that in the several Universities it extended from 23 to 25 weeks. There were few who considered a session with 20 weeks of teaching sufficient, and some were inclined to expect good results from the introduction of a summer session.   But the professors in Arts appointed before 1892 were under no obligation to teach during the summer session, few subjects were taught except Latin, Greek, and Mathematics, and settled arrangements were not announced till near the time when the session opened.   Only a moderate number of students attended, and there was little tendency to add other subjects to the list of those in which teaching was provided. Two summer sessions in appropriate classes were allowed to count as equivalent to a winter session ; but it was pointed out that two periods of ten weeks with a yawning gulf of well nigh a year between them did not afford a good course of training, and that, if students were occupied with other subjects in the winter session, the effect of the first summer's teaching in a given subject would be greatly weakened before they reached the second.

It was urged that any teaching given in summer should be an extension of what was given in winter and not a substitute for it, and that the whole teaching of the academic year in a given subject should, as far as possible, form an organic unity.   It was further alleged that the classes met too frequently, and that the meetings should be reduced in number, so as to give the students time and opportunity to assimilate the instruction afforded to them in lectures or otherwise, to engage to a greater extent in reading and research on their own initiative, and to cultivate a less receptive and more independent habit of mind.   Fault was found with the number of subjects which the ordinance of 1892 required students to include in their course, and with the educative value of some of the combinations which might be made in choosing a curriculum.   The discussion took new forms, and instead of questions regarding the merits or methods of a summer session, demands arose for considerable changes on the ordinance of 1892.

The Act of 1889 empowered the University Court to make new ordinances altering or revoking existing ones, but provided that such ordinances when framed by the Court must be sent to the Senate and the General Council for consideration, and afterwards to the University Courts of the other Universities.   They must finally be submitted for the approval of the King in Council, and be laid before Parliament, either House having a right to petition the King to withhold his assent from an ordinance as a whole or from any part of it.   Any of the other University Courts or any person directly affected by a new ordinance is authorised to notify dissent and make a representation to His Majesty in Council, while the King may refer the ordinance to the Scottish Uni-

MISS JANET A. GALLOWAY, LL.D.

Secretary of Queen Margaret College

versities Committee of the Privy Council, a new body created under the
Act of 1889, more or less resembling the Universities Committee of the
Privy Council established in 1877 to consider alterations of the ordinances
affecting the Universities of Oxford and Cambridge. Some who favoured
changes complained of the slow and cumbrous nature of this procedure,
but their objections were mainly theoretical, for it was not shown that in
actual practice the procedure required had prevented the passing of amending ordinances. Many important changes were made by the smaller and
less aggressive Courts under the Act of 1858, and the difference in procedure under the Act of 1889 is not really very great, consisting chiefly
in the necessity of laying new ordinances before Parliament, which has
not shown any disposition to hinder amendments by the University Courts,
and in the institution of a Scottish Universities Committee of the Privy
Council, which can hardly be more formidable than the Council itself, to
whose consideration ordinances have all along been subject.

With a view to altering the regulations for graduation in Arts, negotiations were carried on for some time with the other Universities, but in
the long run the University Court of Glasgow framed a separate ordinance
in December, 1907, which was approved by the King in Council on 5th
May, 1908. It provides for a single yearly session in Arts, beginning
within the first seven days of October, and divided into three terms, the
dates of which are to be fixed by the Senate and the University Court,
the same bodies having power to determine that attendance for two terms
may constitute a session. The curriculum for the ordinary degree now
consists of five or six subjects instead of seven, but candidates taking five
subjects must attend two of them for two sessions; while candidates taking
six subjects must attend one of them for two sessions, and two of their
other five subjects must be cognate and the classes in them must be
attended in separate sessions. A higher standard is required in the degree
examination in the case of subjects in which the student has to give two
sessions of attendance. Honours may be obtained by attending four
qualifying courses in two subjects of an honours group and two courses
appropriate to the ordinary degree; or a full curriculum may be constituted
by the prescribed attendance in two honours groups that have no subjects
in common, but if there be a subject in common the candidate must attend
one subject outside his honours groups.

It is laid down that the qualifying course for an ordinary degree shall
consist of 75 meetings of the class on separate days, with additional meetings for tutorial or other supplementary instruction; and a qualifying
course for honours, of 50 meetings on separate days during at least two
terms; while the Senate with the approval of the University Court may

sanction half courses of not less than 40 meetings in ordinary classes or 25 meetings in honours classes. The arrangement of subjects in departments for the ordinary degree and in groups for honours is nearly the same as in the ordinance of 1892, except that Sanskrit, Modern Greek, and Archæology—subjects for which teaching has not hitherto been provided—have been omitted from the departments, and Public Law has been split into Public International Law and International Private Law. The Senate, with the approval of the University Court, is authorised to modify the arrangement of subjects in departments and groups, and to regulate their classification as cognate, the order in which they are to be studied, and the standard of the examinations for the ordinary and honours degree. Proposed changes of this nature are to be communicated to the General Council, and any representations made by the Council within two months are to be considered by the Court before changes are approved. The curriculum extends to three sessions at least, two of which may be passed in another Scottish University ; and attendance given and examinations passed in Universities outside of Scotland, if recognised by the Court, may be accepted, but in that case the student must attend for two sessions at Glasgow and pass the degree examinations in the subjects attended there. Such is an outline of the provisions of an ordinance which will probably mark a new era in University reform from within. The extension of the session to 25 weeks falls short of the 30 weeks of teaching contemplated by the Commissioners under the Act of 1889, and only very slightly exceeds what the Commissioners under the Act of 1858, who made no enactment on the subject, found to be in operation. The reduction of the number of subjects of study and the frequency of meetings of classes must greatly influence the system of instruction in the faculty of Arts, and some expect good results from the division of the session into three terms.

The institution of a degree of Bachelor of Science in 1872 has already been described, and by and by a demand arose for a degree of Doctor of Science as well. After much discussion the University framed regulations for the conferring of this degree, and it was first granted in 1890. By ordinance No. 12 the Commissioners under the Act of 1889 laid down regulations for conferring the degrees of B.Sc. and D.Sc. in Pure Science in all the four Universities, while for degrees in Applied Science they issued separate ordinances for the individual Universities. Ordinance No. 23 authorised the University of Glasgow to confer the degrees of B.Sc. and D.Sc. in Engineering, and ordinance No. 134 authorised the granting of a degree of B.Sc. in Agriculture. The ordinances for degrees in Pure Science and in Engineering had both been in force for a short time before the Commissioners by ordinance No. 31, passed on 23rd November, 1893, constituted the faculty of Science. Afterwards an ordinance passed by the University Court in May, 1903, authorised the conferring of the degrees of B.Sc. and D.Sc. in Public Health, and a further ordinance of the Court passed in February, 1907, empowered the University to confer the degree of B.Sc. in Pharmacy. Science, which is the youngest of the faculties, can thus boast of a greater variety of degrees than any other, and while a considerable number of subjects are divided between it and the faculty of Medicine, Science is pre-eminently the faculty of laboratories and of practical teaching. The extension of practical work and methods has been the most marked feature in the development of the University during the last twenty years, and it now threatens to begin at the beginning, for the latest regulations provide for its being applied even in the preliminary examination. Further, in the faculties of Science and Medicine it has led to the erection of great, costly, and elaborately equipped laboratories, employing a large number of lecturers, demonstrators, and assistants, in addition to the professors of the various subjects.

A great laboratory for Physics, a subject for which the University had a reputation in the time of Dick, and reached its crowning fame in the time of Kelvin, has been provided in separate buildings, at a cost of £40,859, of which £20,000 has been contributed by Principal Story's equipment fund and the rest by the Carnegie Trustees. During the tenure of the present professor, Dr. Ludwig Becker, the equipment of the Observatory has been much improved, largely by means of grants from the Bellahouston Trustees. The ordinance regulating the degree of B.Sc. in Engineering made the provision of a laboratory essential, and for a time a small laboratory was fitted up in underground chambers in the substructure of the Bute Hall. The present professor, Dr. Archibald Barr, appointed in 1889, had long been putting forth efforts to secure better accommodation, and at length a great building elaborately equipped was opened in 1901, the cost amounting to £41,000, of which £12,500 was provided by the Bellahouston Trustees. Naval Architecture was but indifferently housed at the north-eastern entrance, in an edifice formed from the gateway and an adjoining portion of the old College in High Street, for the removal and re-erection of which Sir William Pearce provided the funds; but it has now been better accommodated in the rooms left vacant by the removal of Natural Philosophy to its new premises.

A Mining lectureship was instituted in 1902 upon an endowment provided by Mr. James S. Dixon of Bothwell, which was increased so as to allow of the foundation of a professorship in 1907. For this subject accommodation has been provided in a portion of the main buildings left vacant by transferring other subjects to larger premises. Mr. Charles Latham, who had been lecturer from the outset, was appointed to the chair on its foundation. Geology had been taught in the University long before the establishment of a separate chair, and in 1876 Mrs. Honyman Gillespie of Torbanehill endowed a lectureship in connection with the chair of Natural History; but it was felt that the subject deserved to stand on a better footing, and efforts to found a chair were repeatedly made. At length an endowment of £15,000 was procured from the Bellahouston Trustees, the Carnegie Trustees and others, and an ordinance instituting the chair of Geology was approved by the King in Council in August, 1903. Next year Dr. John Walter Gregory was appointed professor. This subject has been provided with classroom and laboratory accommodation in the same way as Mining.

In Chemistry, besides the general course of lectures and laboratory instruction by the professor, there have been for several years three subdivisions of the subject under the care of lecturers, namely, Physical Chemistry taught by Mr. Frederick Soddy, Organic Chemistry by Dr. T. S. Patterson, and Metallurgical Chemistry by Dr. Charles E. Fawsitt, with appropriate laboratory courses for the various subdivisions. A very large temporary laboratory for this department, costing more than £13,000, was opened towards the close of 1904. Professor Bayley Balfour, who held the chair of Botany from 1879 to 1885, introduced a class for practical work in 1881, and the present professor, Dr. Frederick Orpen Bower, long endeavoured to procure improved accommodation for his department. At length in 1901 handsome and commodious buildings on a separate site in University Avenue were opened. They include classrooms, laboratories, museum, and herbarium, and, with equipment, have cost fully £19,000, of which £6,000 was contributed by the Bellahouston Trustees, and £10,725 from the bequest by Mr. Charles Randolph —a munificent benefaction, amounting to fully £70,000, which has afforded aid to the University in many departments. Zoology, previously included in the chair of Natural History, has existed as a separate chair since 1903, a year after the present incumbent, Mr. John Graham Kerr, became professor. Its accommodation and equipment have been greatly improved within the last few years.

In the department of Anatomy the requirements have outgrown the accommodation oftener perhaps than in any other, and though the present professor, Dr. John Cleland, succeeded to the chair only seven years after the opening of the new University buildings, it was soon necessary to procure considerable extensions. These were at first of a temporary character, but through the liberality of the Trustees of the late Mr. James Brown Thomson, who in 1899 made a grant of £10,000, afterwards increased to £13,000, for the purpose, commodious premises, suitable to the needs of the department and in keeping with the architecture of the University, have been provided. In 1894 a separate lectureship on Embryology was instituted in connection with the Anatomy department, the first lecturer being Dr. John Yule Mackay, who was soon afterwards appointed to the chair of Anatomy in University College, Dundee, of which he is now Principal. Dr. James F. Gemmill has been lecturer since 1897, and the new buildings include a laboratory for instruction and research in Embryology. Dr. John Gray M'Kendrick, who held the chair of Physiology from 1876 to 1906, soon organised a laboratory well equipped for the times, but, with the larger number of students and increased emphasis laid on practical teaching, the premises became inadequate, and Physiology, along with Materia Medica, and Forensic Medicine and Public Health, has been accommodated in new buildings situated about half-way between the University and the Western Infirmary, on a slope overlooking the Kelvin. These buildings cost £57,259, of which £20,000 has been contributed by the Carnegie Trustees[1] and a like sum from Principal Story's equipment fund. Dr. Noël Paton has been professor of Physiology since 1906.

A lectureship in Physiological Chemistry has been founded under the will of the late Dr. Grieve of Glasgow, who left £8,000 available for the purpose, and Dr. Edward P. Cathcart has been lecturer since 1905. More recently a lectureship in Psychology has been founded, with Dr. H. J. Watt as incumbent. Dr. John Glaister, who was appointed to the chair of Forensic Medicine in 1898, equipped a laboratory for the teaching of Public Health in the premises then available, but the ample accommodation and equipment now provided are in keeping with the increased importance attached to this subject. As degrees in Public Health may be registered in the books of the General Medical Council, they might be regarded as belonging more appropriately to the faculty of Medicine, but Glasgow has followed the example of Edinburgh by instituting degrees in Public Health in relation to the faculty of Science rather than of Medicine. Apart from the adaptation of portions of the main buildings to the needs of departments recently placed there, the separate buildings now mentioned, with a laboratory for Operative Surgery, all erected within the last eight or nine years, have cost about £195,000, and probably no

[1] The building grants from the Carnegie Trustees mentioned here do not include items later than 30th September, 1907.

University within the same time has shown a more remarkable extension. But these great laboratories involve a heavy and abiding burden of outlays, and it was a wise intuition that prompted the Court in 1891, when the project for one of the larger laboratories was put forward, to express an opinion that funds should be raised not only to provide buildings but also endowments.

Mr. John O. Scott, London, and Mr. John J. Burnet, Glasgow, were joint architects for the Engineering and Botany buildings, while Mr. Burnet was architect for the Anatomy, Chemistry, and Surgery buildings.

The new buildings for Natural Philosophy, and for Physiology, Materia Medica, Forensic Medicine and Public Health, of which Mr. James Miller, Glasgow, was the Architect, were opened on 23rd April, 1907, by the Prince of Wales, who was accompanied by the Princess. Earlier in the day the freedom of the city was conferred on Their Royal Highnesses in St. Andrew's Halls, and on their reaching the University, where a great gathering had assembled in the Bute Hall, the honorary degree of LL.D. was conferred upon them by the Chancellor, Lord Kelvin ; and after this the opening ceremony took place. Since 1888 the University has twice been honoured by a visit from the reigning sovereign. On 14th May, 1903, the King and Queen paid a visit, halting their carriage in front of the main entrance, where a platform had been erected for the members of the University Court and Senate, and Principal Story on behalf of the University read a loyal and dutiful address of welcome. Queen Victoria, who had been received within the old College in 1849, drove to the new University on 24th August, 1888, and halted her carriage to receive an address at the main entrance, where a representative company had assembled.

The Commissioners under the Act of 1889 passed two general ordinances revising the regulations for the degrees of LL.B. and B.L., although they stated that they had some hesitation in continuing the latter degree. They raised the number of subjects in the curriculum for LL.B. to eight, including four courses of 80 lectures and four of forty lectures. Of the longer courses Civil Law and Constitutional Law and History are compulsory, while the student has the option of taking Law of Scotland or Law of England (if taught), and of selecting one subject from Conveyancing, Political Economy, and Mercantile Law. Of the shorter courses General or Comparative Jurisprudence and Public International Law are compulsory, and the other two may be chosen from International Private Law, Administrative Law, Forensic Medicine, or Political Economy if this last subject has not already been taken as a substitute for Conveyancing. The regulations for B.L. were reissued without any very far-reaching changes, but the ordinances for both degrees provide for the awarding of distinction to candidates who show exceptional merit in their examinations. The Commissioners raised the number of professors in the faculty of Law to four by including in it the chair of Political Economy founded in 1896, but the great enlargement in the teaching staff in Law witnessed within the last generation has taken place mainly by the institution of new lectureships, courses in the six qualifying subjects of Civil Law, Constitutional Law and History, General or Comparative Jurisprudence, Public International Law, International Private Law, and Mercantile Law, being conducted by five lecturers. A professorship in Civil Law was founded by Queen Anne in 1713, but by a sort of digressive evolution Scots Law came to be the principal subject taught from this chair, and since 1894 it has been the only subject.

A separate lectureship in Civil Law was founded that year, and after being held for a short time by Mr. Frederick P. Walton, Mr. James M. Irvine was appointed to it in November, 1894, and held the position till in 1907 he was chosen professor of Law at Aberdeen. Mr. Hugh R. Buchanan was the next lecturer, but he resigned in 1909, on being appointed Solicitor to the Caledonian Railway Company. Mr. Ure having resigned the lectureship in Constitutional Law and History, Mr. Robert T. Younger was appointed to it in 1889, and when he retired after five years of service, the present lecturer, Dr. William S. M'Kechnie, was appointed in 1894. Besides the ordinary course, which qualifies for graduation both in Arts and Law, Dr. M'Kechnie also conducts an honours course for students preparing for the degree of M.A. with honours in History. Mr. William Galbraith Miller, who had been lecturer on Public Law since 1878, continued to teach Public International Law and International Private Law, the two branches into which the subject was divided in 1894. He was also lecturer on General or Comparative Jurisprudence from 1893. After Mr. Miller's death, Mr. Archibald H. Charteris became in 1904 lecturer on the two former subjects, and Mr. James A. M'Callum was chosen as lecturer on Jurisprudence. In 1894 Mr. James Mackenzie was appointed to the lectureship on Mercantile Law then founded, and in 1900 was succeeded by Mr. William Shaw, while the present lecturer, Mr. Thomas G. Wright, was appointed in 1907. In 1905 a lectureship on Evidence and Procedure was instituted, and Mr. Robert Lamond appointed lecturer. The preponderance of lecturers over professors is more marked in the teaching staff in Law than in any other faculty ; but if lecturers conducting separate classes for women be taken into account, there are nearly as many lecturers conducting qualifying classes in the University as there are professors. It may be said that it matters little to a student who is taught by an efficient teacher whether that teacher be called a lecturer or a professor; but lecturers, who are shut out from the faculty, from the senate, and from direct representation in the University Court, have not an equal opportunity to obtain favourable conditions for their teaching.

The faculty of Divinity was little affected by the doings of the Commissioners, but they passed a general ordinance regulating the conferring of the honorary degrees of D.D. and LL.D. in all the Universities, adopting in the main the rules which had previously been observed at Glasgow. They prohibited the taking of any fee for an honorary degree, and put an end to a system under which Bachelors of Divinity of eight years' standing might proceed to the degree of D.D. by passing a higher examination in three of the six subjects required for the degree of B.D. They also provided that in conducting the examinations for B.D. two additional examiners appointed by the University Court should act along with the professors. In addition to the classes taught by the professors in the faculty of Divinity, students preparing for the ministry of the Church of Scotland have since 1895 been required to attend two short courses on Pastoral Theology delivered by lecturers appointed by the Home Mission Committee.

In 1901 Mr. Andrew Carnegie of Skibo and New York made over to a body of Trustees, of whom the Earl of Elgin is chairman, ten million dollars yielding an annual return of five per cent., directing that one half of the income should be applied to improving the Scottish Universities in Medicine and Science, increasing the facilities for acquiring a knowledge of History, Economics, English, and Modern Languages, with such other subjects relating to commercial or technical education as come within the scope of the University curriculum, the erection and maintenance of buildings, provision of equipment, and the endowment of professorships and lectureships and of scholarships for encouraging research; and that the other half, or such portion of it as may be requisite, should be applied to the payment in whole or in part of the class fees of students who are of Scottish birth or extraction or have been educated for two years in schools under the inspection of the Scottish Education Department. The Universities have been greatly aided by subventions under the first purpose of the Trust, and the fees of legions of students have been paid under the second. This payment of fees has been denounced by some on account of its alleged pauperising tendency. But before fees are paid by the Trust, students must have passed the preliminary examination appropriate to the course they are pursuing, which should afford reasonable evidence of their capacity as students; and considerable outlays for board and lodging, matriculation and examination fees, and miscellaneous expenses must

QUEEN MARGARET COLLEGE, GLASGOW

be defrayed from other sources. The Carnegie Trust has made things easier, not only for many students who otherwise would have been severely straitened, but for parents and friends who, but for this subvention, would have had to pinch and scrape to enable students to go through their University course. In this way many worthy people besides students have been benefited. Here and there a youth may be found of such exceptional force and efficacy as to earn the funds required for his academic education ; but in the main students must be supported by others, and if they are capable students, which to a great extent the preliminary examination guarantees, it is not easy to see why a benevolent rich man should not help them if he is willing. But in many cases students take advantage of the Carnegie Trust whose parents or relations might easily pay their fees, and in this case disapprobation should rather fall on the parents and relatives than on the students. The possibility of the Carnegie Trust, with its great financial resources, exercising, it might be unconsciously and unintentionally, an undue influence over the University administrators, and perhaps leading them into a policy they would not on its own merits approve, might conceivably involve greater risk than the payment of students' fees. Since the institution of the Trust there has been a general raising of class fees, which has borne rather hardly on those who still pay the dues for their classes.

On the 12th, 13th, 14th, and 15th days of June, 1901, celebrations were held to signalise the ninth jubilee of the University, and invitations were issued to representatives of Universities and Colleges all over the world, and of the chief learned societies in Europe and America, as well as to many men of literary, scientific, and professional distinction at home and abroad. The office-bearers of the University, the teaching staff, and many members of the General Council and students took part in the celebrations, and a numerous and most distinguished company gathered at Gilmorehill. The proceedings, which were carried through most auspiciously, included a religious service in the Cathedral ; a reception of delegates and presentation of addresses ; orations on James Watt, Adam Smith, and William Hunter ; a graduation ceremony in which a long roll of distinguished men received honorary degrees, and the degree of LL.D. was for the first time at Glasgow conferred on ladies ; and a banquet given by the City Corporation.

The Universities Act of 1889 continued the former members of the University Court, excepting the dean of faculties, made the Lord Provost of Glasgow an *ex officio* member, empowered the Lord Provost, Magistrates and Council of the City to return an assessor, and raised the number of assessors assigned to the General Council and the Senate to four each.

Towards the close of the year 1889 elections were held for the choice of the additional assessors, and the Council returned Mr. David Hannay (who had long acted as clerk to that body), Dr. Hector Clare Cameron, and Sir John Neilson Cuthbertson; while the Senate chose Professor Leishman, Professor Stewart, and Sheriff Berry. The Commissioners having declared that the new and enlarged Court, which was henceforth to be the chief ruling body in the University, had been duly constituted, the first meeting was held on 24th January, 1890. Besides the general work of administration, the new Court for some years had much to do in formulating or criticising and amending draft ordinances, and communicating with the Commissioners during their long drawn out tenure of office. Amid the pressure of other affairs time was found, however, for the consideration and revision of the arrangements adopted by the University for academic costume, a subject to which the General Council had invited attention. A deputation from that body, consisting of Professor M'Kendrick, the Rev. Dr. Donald Macleod, the Rev. David Hunter, B.D., Mr. James Aiken, M.A., and Mr. Archibald Craig, LL.B., Clerk to the Council, waited on the University Court, in April, 1891, exhibited designs and patterns of existing and proposed hoods for degrees, and were heard at length. Arrangements were made for conferring with the Senate, and after some time a number of improvements were adopted. Quite recently hoods were adopted for the degrees of D.Phil. and D.Litt., but there are as yet no hoods for the degrees of Ch.B. and Ch.M.

Besides *ex officio* members, and the assessors returned at the close of 1889, already mentioned, the enlarged Court has included the following assessors holding office for longer or shorter periods: Sir James King, Mr. Henry E. Gordon of Aikenhead, and Mr. William Lorimer, representing successive Chancellors; Lord Blythswood, Mr. Matthew P. Fraser, Dr. David Murray, Mr. Alex. Ure, M.P., Mr. Allan F. Baird, Mr. William Lorimer, and Sir John Ure Primrose, representing successive Rectors; Dr. James Colquhoun, Mr. Robert M. Mitchell, and Mr. Alexander Murray, representing the Town Council; the Rev. Dr. James W. King, David C. M'Vail, M.B., Sir James Bell, Sir William R. Copland, Dr. David Murray, Dr. John Hutchison, and the Rev. Dr. Smith, representing the General Council; and Professors Ramsay, Sir William T. Gairdner, Jack, Adamson, Young, Moir, Raleigh, Muir, Jones, Gray, and Sir Hector C. Cameron, representing the Senate.

In the new era introduced by the Act of 1889 the endowments of the University have been considerably improved, though additional funds might well be turned to good account, and there is some prospect that Government may be induced to make further provision. The teaching staff has been greatly strengthened, mostly by the addition of lecturers and assistants, whose remuneration, though still rather moderate, is much better than before 1889. A Students' Representative Council, which had existed as a voluntary association since 1886, obtained statutory recognition under the Act of 1889. A University Union was instituted in 1885, and shortly afterwards Dr. John M'Intyre of Odiham, Hants, presented a sum of £5,000 to erect a building containing a dining hall for students, a reading room, committee rooms, a debating hall, recreation rooms, and other accommodation. This building has been more than once enlarged, the latest addition having been opened in the autumn of 1908. Students' Societies of which there are many—professional, literary, philosophical, scientific, social, recreative, philanthropic, and political— are mostly affiliated to the Union and hold their meetings in it. A gymnasium, managed by a joint committee of professors and students, has been maintained since 1872 ; and the increased interest now taken in physical culture has led to the acquisition of fifteen acres at Anniesland, for the proper equipment of which as a recreation ground the greater part of the requisite £10,000 has been secured.

In Arts, though many more subjects are taught, there is considerable freedom of selection in making up the curriculum ; while under the regulations of 1908 fewer subjects are required for graduation, and the courses include fewer lectures spread over a longer session. After graduating at the end of the curriculum students are encouraged to continue academic or scientific pursuits, with the possibility of obtaining higher degrees ; and the provision made for special study and research within the University may help to bring to light and discipline workers and investigators destined to future advancement and distinction. More especially in Science and Medicine, greater stress is now laid on practical and experimental work and research, as the enormous laboratories recently erected bear monumental testimony. Searching, striving, and endeavouring, one generation of students rapidly follows another, and among office-bearers and teachers changes are also frequent. But, while members are ever coming and going, the University abides, and from the ability and faithfulness with which successive generations of her children render service to mankind in the many and varied positions to which they are called, she gathers fresh power and fame with the lapse of ages.

' The one remains, the many change and pass.'

CHAPTER V

THE MEDICAL SCHOOL

MONKS and clerics had for centuries the main share of medical and surgical practice, though the Jews, besides their eminence in usury, professed the healing art, and, but for their outcast and despised condition, might have cultivated it with better success. Some of the clergy found Physic more to their liking than Divinity, and came to be so much engrossed in the former that the rulers of the Church intervened to restrain them. In 1163 the Council of Tours prohibited the clergy from performing operations involving the shedding of blood, and henceforth such operations fell to the laity. But the profits of surgical practice were too great to be willingly let go, and the barber of the Monastery was sent to perform operations which the clergy were forbidden to undertake. Monastic discipline required that monks should be bled from time to time, and the barbers who opened their veins were accustomed to the shedding of blood, as well as to artistic tonsure of the crown, and the application of cold preparations to the shaven head as a remedy for various complaints.

Barbers were thus to some extent initiated into the work of surgeons, and by perseverance and practice, especially in times of war, the more capable of them became surgeons possessing such skill as the age afforded, and left off being barbers; but it was long before a strict and final distinction was drawn between the trade of barber and the profession of surgeon. Guilds and corporations were established, an incorporation of barber surgeons being founded in London in 1462 and in Edinburgh in 1505. These bodies usually embraced practitioners of the mixed art, and while they formed useful organisations for the regulation and defence of the affairs and interests of those concerned, they restricted the practice of members to the limited territory belonging to each corporation, caused their members to be looked upon as craftsmen, and hindered the rise of a distinct profession of surgery. The formal separation of the barbers from the surgeons did not take place in Edinburgh till 1719, nor in London till 1745.

In Paris, however, the surgeons formed a distinct College from the thirteenth century, the same century witnessing the foundation of the faculty of Medicine there, one of the earliest medical organisations within a University. A famous Medical School arose at Salerno in Italy in the 11th century, the first institution in which regular diplomas were granted after a prescribed course of study and examination ; and the University of Bologna was one of the earliest to take medical studies under its care. Contact with oriental life and learning through the Crusades brought the healing art in the west under the influence of the Arabs, who had procured translations of Hippocrates and Galen after the conquest of Alexandria, and had themselves made some improvements in Medicine. In England the authority of the clergy in reference to medical practice persisted for a very long time. An Act of 1511 provided that no person in the city of London or within seven miles of it should practise as a physician or surgeon until examined by the Bishop of London or by the Dean of St. Paul's, with the assistance of four Doctors of Physic in the case of candidates in Medicine, and other expert persons in that faculty in the case of candidates in Surgery. Even down to quite recent times the Archbishop of Canterbury exercised the power of granting the degree of Doctor of Medicine, and the Medical Act of 1858 authorised the registration of all such degrees granted before its passing.

From the first, Medicine might be looked upon as *licita facultas* in the University of Glasgow, but for a long time it underwent little development. In 1469 Andrew de Garleis, *Doctor in Medicinis*, was received to the bosom of the University, but there is no further trace of the man or his doings. William Manderstoun, who graduated as B.A. at Glasgow in 1506, is mentioned in 1525 as Licentiate in Medicine and Rector of the University of Paris. Five years later he appears as Doctor of Medicine and Rector of the University of St. Andrews. From an inscription on one of his books—'*Robertus Gra[yme], Medicinae amator, praeceptori suo Vilelmo Manderstō, Appoloniae artis professori peritissimo*'—it would appear that he taught Medicine. The Pope's bull of 1494 founding the University of Aberdeen provided that the staff of higher teachers should include a Doctor of Medicine to give instruction in that faculty, and Medicine was taught for some time after the opening. The book of Discipline shows that the reformers designed that Medicine should be taught in a five years' course at St. Andrews, but not at Glasgow or Aberdeen. In 1536 an Englishman named Andrew Boorde, who had been a Carthusian monk, a wanderer about Europe, and latterly a physician, studied and practised Medicine 'in a little University or study named Glasgow.' It appears from his account that the services of a physician were then much in request, and that the University recognised Medicine as worthy of countenance and support. Boorde says he came into contact with many of the nobles and clergy, and had access to the house of Arran (afterwards the Regent Arran) and to the royal home of James V. He describes the condition of the people in the town and country parts of the Lowlands as not unprosperous or uncomfortable, and says the men were hardy, strong, well-favoured, and skilled in music; but he blames them for being much addicted to boasting and dissembling. Yet Boorde himself boasts of dissembling successfully to the Scots.

Glasgow is believed to have had a population of 4,500 or 5,000 in 1560, and about 7,000 at the close of the 16th century. The whole area then covered by the city could not have been great, and from its central portions a very short walk would have brought one into the open country, while within the town itself many of the houses had gardens attached to them. There were no great factories, furnaces, or chemical or other works to vitiate the atmosphere. On the other hand, the houses were to a great extent built of wood, covered with thatch, poorly supplied with windows, and closely piled together, at least in the dark and narrow wynds which diverged from the main streets. Heaps of dung and other impurities were allowed to accumulate beside the dwellings, and even down to the end of the 18th century there was no underground drainage to carry away foul liquids, but only surface gutters or 'syvers,' very imperfect in their action. Water for household use was largely obtained from wells which must often have been contaminated. Probably Glasgow was not in a worse sanitary condition than other towns of the period, but besides diseases now prevalent, it suffered from others which have long since disappeared. The plague frequently visited the city and claimed many victims, and leprosy was so persistent that a hospital for lepers was long maintained at the south end of the bridge over the Clyde. In such circumstances the city could not safely dispense with practitioners of the healing art, but the number of those who had any real skill was very limited. A few physicians and some surgeons, mostly barber-surgeons, made their appearance, and to induce them to settle in the city the Town Council began to grant them allowances. The remuneration did not always satisfy the recipients, one of whom was punished for railing against the 'hungerie toun of Glasgu.' Occasionally a physician or surgeon trained abroad returned to Scotland, but within the country itself there was hardly any means of acquiring a training except by the long and not very effective process of apprenticeship. The public suffered not only from disease but also from the perilous treatment followed by ignorant pretenders, resident or itinerant, who entered upon practice.

In view of these evils the Kirk Session in 1598 urged the Town Council to take action so as to distinguish between skilled and unskilled practitioners, and to exclude the latter from practice. In April of next year the Council appointed three Bailies, three city ministers, and three University officers, namely, Principal Sharpe, Blaise Laurie, one of the regents, and John Blackburn, dean of faculty, with other men skilled in the art, to examine for the future those who practised in the town. This body of examiners, most of whom were probably but indifferently qualified, could hardly have got to work when they were superseded by a new authority created by the crown. Just before this, there had come to Glasgow a Scotsman named Peter Lowe, who had practised surgery on the continent for more than twenty years in peace and war, who styled himself 'Doctor in the facultie of Chirurgerie in Paris,' and claimed to have been 'ordinary Chyrurgeon to the French King and Navarre.' Upon his return from the continent he published at London a work on the *Spanish Sickness*, and another of a more extended and elaborate nature on *Chirurgerie*, and having chosen Glasgow as the scene of his future activity, he seems to have felt that his attainments and previous record would entitle him to stand at the head of his profession. It is not certain whether he had prompted the Kirk Session, but he found means to convey some kind of representation to King James VI.

The King, probably nowise unwilling to appear as a patron of learning and a lawgiver to professors of the healing art, when it cost him nothing, granted in November, 1599, letters under the privy seal empowering Peter Lowe and Robert Hamilton, 'professoure of medecine, and their successouris, indwelleris of our citie of Glasgow,' to examine and try all who professed or practised the Art of Surgery, to license, 'according to the airt and knowledge that they sal be fund wordie to exercise,' those whom they judged fit, and to exclude the unqualified from practice, with power to fine those who proved contumacious. The visitors, as Lowe and Hamilton were styled, were appointed to report to the city magistrates on cases of death by accident, violence, or poison, and empowered to exclude from the practice of medicine all who could not produce the testimonial of a famous University where medicine was taught ; and also, with the assistance of William Spang, an apothecary in Glasgow, to regulate the sale of drugs, especially of poisons. These extensive powers of licensing practitioners were not confined to the city, but extended to the baronies of

Glasgow, Renfrew, and Dumbarton, and the sheriffdoms of Clydesdale, Renfrew, Lanark, Kyle, Carrick, Ayr, and Cunningham.

The creation of this new body—the Faculty of Physicians and Surgeons, as it subsequently came to be called, a body whose constitution and means of maintaining a continuous and permanent existence were not at first very clearly defined—was an important event for the University, and to some extent limited its powers, which under the original Constitution extended to every legitimate faculty. Now, however, the examination and licensing of surgeons was committed to the new body. More than two centuries after, when medicine had long been taught in the University, and a chair of Surgery had also been founded, the faculty of Physicians and Surgeons procured legal decisions that, without examination and license by them, neither a University degree in medicine nor in surgery entitled the holder to practise Surgery within the territory of the Faculty.

The Faculty of Physicians and Surgeons gradually developed some organisation and made their influence felt in the city, and, after having procured a favourable decision from the Lords of Council and Session, they obtained in 1635 signet letters from Charles I. confirming the privileges conferred by his father, and charging the magistrates within their territory to assist and defend the visitor, Mr. James Hamilton, his brethren, and their successors in executing the functions committed to them. Shortly before this, about 1630, a movement had been begun to collect subscriptions for improving and enlarging the buildings of the University, erecting a new library and furnishing it with books. The foundation of additional chairs was not one of the directly avowed objects of the movement, but it was soon realised that University extension must involve extension of the teaching staff, and within a few years a chair of Medicine, a chair of Humanity, and a second chair of Divinity were founded. Other circumstances besides the successful lawsuit and signet letters of the Faculty of Physicians and Surgeons excited public attention at this time, and may have impressed the rulers of the University with a sense of the importance of Medicine.

In 1630 efforts were made to procure from Charles I. authority to incorporate a College of Physicians in Edinburgh, a proposal to which his father had been favourably inclined in 1617. Charles referred the subject to the Privy Council, but no further action was taken. In 1636 Dr. William Gordon, the Professor of Medicine at King's College, Aberdeen, applied to the Privy Council for authority to receive dead bodies for dissection, and was permitted to receive the bodies of criminals who had been executed, or of the poor who died in hospitals or without friends who might raise objections. Somehow a stimulus to action was felt at Glasgow, and at a meeting 'for advancement of learning' within the College, held in the Bishop's castle on 25th October, 1637, with the Bishop present as Chancellor of the University, along with Principal Strang, Zachary Boyd, and a number of regents, ministers and others, Robert Mayne, who had been a regent for two years, was elected and admitted 'to be ane professor of medicine within the said Colledge, to teache ane publict lecture of medicine in the said Colledge once or twyse ewerie weik, except in the ordiner tyme of vacance,' for which he was to receive a yearly stipend of 400 marks.   Mayne's tombstone in the High Churchyard credits him with greatness as a philosopher, orator, poet, and physician, but Byron's caution against believing epitaphs may fitly be remembered.   In the University records Mayne is once styled doctor, and he seems to have been admitted to the Faculty of Physicians and Surgeons in virtue of a University degree in medicine, but it is not known where he studied or graduated.   In September, 1642, a Commission of Visitation from the General Assembly found that the profession of Medicine was not necessary for the College in all time coming, but allowed Mayne to continue as professor during his life.   They also delegated to certain persons power to regulate the times, matter, and manner of teaching in connection with the profession of Medicine 'during the tyme of Dr. Maine, in whose persoune allenerlie that professioune is established.'   Robert Baillie, writing in 1643, records that 'Dr. Maine on the Fridays afternoon and other dyetts hath very elegant discourses on the choycest Physic questions.' Early in 1646 Mayne died, and the chair died with him, before it could have had much practical influence on medical education, but something was gained, inasmuch as from this time, notwithstanding the action of the Commission from the Assembly, a chair of Medicine was regarded as part of the rightful equipment of the University.   The year of Mayne's death witnessed a virulent and fatal outbreak of plague in Glasgow—surely a very inopportune time for abolishing the study of medicine.

In 1664 a Royal Commission reported on the condition and needs of the University.   They recalled the greater variety of teaching and graduation before the Reformation, and the founding of several short-lived chairs after that event ; and declared that the University had still the power to create, not only Masters of Arts, but also Doctors and Bachelors in other faculties.   They deemed it necessary that provision should be made for the maintenance of additional Professors which the University formerly had, and by the erection and foundation ought to have, but could not possibly have at that time for want of revenue ; and among these necessary chairs they included Medicine.   The plan of establishing a College of Physicians at Edinburgh had the countenance of Cromwell, and a year or

2 H

two before his death a charter was drafted, but disputes arose and he died leaving the project unaccomplished.   The College was actually founded in 1681 by a charter of Charles II., obtained mainly through the exertions of Sir Robert Sibbald.

In 1672 the Scots Parliament had granted ratification 'in favours of the present chirurgians, apothecaries, and barbours within the said burgh of Glasgow' of the letter of gift by James VI. passed under the privy seal in 1599.   It was a further sign of the times that there had recently been a notable increase in the number of Scotsmen who obtained degrees in Medicine from foreign Universities, of whom Dr. Matthew Brisbane, rector of Glasgow University in 1677 and again from 1679 to 1681, and Dr. Gilbert Rule,[1] who became principal of Edinburgh University, may be taken as examples.   In such circumstances it is not surprising that, when the Revolution brought more settled times and better opportunities of progress, the rulers of the University at Glasgow should again bethink themselves of Medicine.   When Principal Dunlop was sent to London by his colleagues in 1691 to plead with the king for aid to the University, he was instructed to carry with him the report of the Commission of 1664 as evidence of the needs of the institution, among which was included the revival of the suppressed chair of Medicine.   Two or three years after this a royal grant of £300, destined mostly to the gradual extinction of debts, was obtained, and in 1698 a larger grant from the archbishopric of Glasgow.

The establishment of a chair in Medicine soon came to be suggested, if not pressed, from the outside.   In September, 1703, Samuel Benion, a student of Medicine from England, applied to be examined with a view to obtain the degree of M.D.   The University meeting, considering that, from want of funds, there was no ordinary Professor of Medicine, resolved to appoint Robert Sinclair, Professor of Mathematics, who held the degree of M.D., to be Professor extraordinary of Medicine for the occasion, and to associate with him two physicians from the town as assessors, with a view to the due and regular conduct of the examination.   Accordingly, Thomas Kennedy and George Thomson, both of whom held the Degree of M.D. from Leyden, were appointed assessors.   Benion solved a medical case propounded to him, and was also examined on the several parts of Medicine by Sinclair and the two assessors, who recommended that Benion 'should be graduate Doctor of Medicine, since he had undergone due and sufficient tryals by a College of Physicians, and had behaved himself well therein.'   A Latin diploma was drawn up, and a few days

[1] Sir Alexander Grant states that Rule was a regent in the University of Glasgow, but I have not found his name as such in the records.

later read over to the meeting before being delivered to Benion, upon whom it conferred '*absolutam potestatem legendi, docendi, consultandi, scribendi, in cathedram doctoralem ascendendi, omnes denique tam theoriae quam praxeos actus exercendi hic et ubique terrarum quos Medicinae Doctores exercere solent,*' and assigned to him all the privileges and pre-rogatives usually granted to Doctors of Medicine.

At the end of 1711 Robert Houstoun, surgeon, who sometime before had applied for the degree of M.D., insisted on being admitted to examina-tion, and the Faculty of the University, considering they might still need Professors of Medicine, determined to invite some physicians in the city to assist at the examination.   Dr. Johnstoun, who graduated as M.D. at Utrecht in 1709, and Dr. Montgomerie, whose place of graduation has not been ascertained, were appointed to examine, and a medical case and an aphorism of Hippocrates were propounded to the candidate, which he solved satisfactorily.   He was then examined on the several parts of Medicine by the two physicians, with the Dean of Faculty, James Brown, one of the city ministers, as a sort of lay assessor.   They reported that he had acquitted himself well, and it was unanimously resolved that 'the said Mr. Houstoun be promoted to the degree of doctorat in Medicine.'   Such applications had now come to be looked upon as usual and needing regula-tion for the future, and in January, 1712, the Faculty enacted that each candidate for the degree of M.D. should pay a fee of £10 sterling, one-half of which was appropriated to the Library and the other to the ex-aminers ; and that he should also give twenty shillings to the servants. It was further laid down that the candidate should print a thesis on some medical subject, and defend it *sine praesidio*, before graduation.

Already means of teaching botany had been provided.   On 4th July, 1704, the Faculty resolved that, for the amenity of the College and for the instruction of students in a knowledge of Botany, some portion of the great garden should be improved and converted into a Physic Garden. On 17th September following, John Marshall, a surgeon in the city, who is believed to have studied at Paris, was appointed to be keeper of the Botanic Garden, or Physic Garden, as it was then called, and to give instruc-tion in Botany to students who applied to him, £20 sterling being assigned as his salary, with a further allowance for a gardener to work under his direction.   In 1708 Queen Anne, among a number of other grants, allo-cated a sum of £30 a year to the Professor of Botany.   Marshall continued to teach Botany till his death in 1719 ; and from this small beginning in 1704 till the early years of the 19th century the University continued to possess a Botanic Garden within its own grounds, though possibly not on the same site during the whole period.

The time was at length judged ripe for founding chairs of Medicine and Law, and on 16th November, 1712, the Faculty—after setting forth that the professions of Law and Medicine had long been neglected in the University to its great prejudice, that the Visitation of 1664 declared it necessary that they should be revived, that their revival would greatly promote the advantage and honour of the institution, that several persons of quality had expressed their wish to see the chairs re-established, and that the rector, Sir John Maxwell, had pronounced in favour of their being re-established, and, if possible, endowed from funds derived from King William's grant—resolved that the professions of Law and Medicine should be revived, and the subjects taught as soon as possible by Professors with fit qualifications ; and that the Queen should be petitioned to allocate funds for the purpose from the portion of King William's grant originally appropriated to the extinction of debts, these debts being now cleared or nearly so. The Queen granted the petition, and in December, 1713, assigned £40 a year as a salary to the Professor of Medicine, and £90 as a salary to the Professor of Law. It is notable that the first appointment to the chair of Medicine was made, not by the crown, as in all subsequent instances, but by the faculty. That body met on 1st June, 1714, and 'having good and satisfying information that Dr. John Johnstoun in Glasgow is a person well skilled in Medicine and very capable to teach the same, does therefore elect and present the said Dr. Johnstoun to be Professor of Medicine in this University.' Shortly afterwards the precedence of the Professor of Medicine was fixed as coming next after that of the Professor of Law, and that of the latter next after the Professor of Divinity, an arrangement stated to be in conformity with the practice of other Universities at home and abroad.

Probably Johnstoun did teach to some extent in the earlier part of his tenure of the chair, and, to make the training in Medicine more effective, a surgeon in the city was brought into the College to lecture on Anatomy. This must have been John Gordon, with whom Smollett passed his apprenticeship, and who in 1750 received the degree of M.D., as the minute which records his graduation sets forth that he was ' the first person who taught Anatomy in this University long ago with great applause and success.' Proposals were made to found a chair of Anatomy, and the lecturer was encouraged to hope that the appointment would fall to him, but a different course was pursued, and Thomas Brisbane, M.D., whose father, also a Doctor of Medicine, had been rector about forty years before, became the new Professor, and was admitted to office on 7th March, 1720. No account of the foundation of the chair of Anatomy—at first it was a dual chair of Anatomy and Botany—has been preserved, but Brisbane is believed to have been appointed by the crown, and it is significant that the chair arose just after the death in 1719 of John Marshall, who, in 1704, was appointed to have charge of the Physic Garden and to instruct students in Botany.   For some time Botany was regarded as the leading subject of the dual chair, perhaps out of deference to Brisbane, who had a rooted aversion to Anatomy and would not face the work of dissection.

In 1721 the Faculty laid down a vague regulation that Brisbane should give a course of Comparative Anatomy some time between 1st December and 1st May; but some of his colleagues encouraged or condoned Brisbane's disinclination to teach.   The medical students missed the instruction they had formerly received from Gordon, and having in vain applied to the new professor, they presented a petition to the faculty.   Consideration was postponed from time to time, and when some students waited on the faculty to make a representation, they were summarily dismissed by the principal.   Indeed the principal and the other friends of Brisbane appear to have thought that his case was proved to demonstration.   For the teaching of Anatomy it was necessary that there should be an operator (dissector); Brisbane's commission did not oblige him to operate; therefore he could not be obliged to teach Anatomy.   In 1727 the Commission of Visitation took a different view, and declared that 'Dr. Brisbane, present professor of Botany and Anatomy in the said University, is obliged to teach Anatomy as well as Botany.'   They ordained that he should begin to teach as soon as ten students entered; and, in case ten students did not enter by 1st November, he was to give weekly prelections on Anatomy till 15th May, from which date till 1st July he was to teach Botany if five students entered.   This is the earliest distinct notice of a summer session.   From the positive way in which the Commission laid down that it was Brisbane's duty to teach Anatomy as well as Botany, it seems probable that he had hitherto taught the latter subject to some extent.   However, he soon ceased from teaching Botany, and it is doubtful whether he ever began to teach Anatomy.

On 12th October, 1730, the faculty (with Dr. Brisbane and Dr. Johnstoun present in the meeting) allowed 'Mr. Jo. Paisley, Surgeon in Glasgow, to advertise in the Edinburgh newspapers and here in town that he is to teach Anatomy within the College this session.'   Paisley was a surgeon in good practice, yet zealous as a student, and he owned a considerable library of medical books.   On 21st December, 1730, Paisley having requested the use of the old Humanity classroom for the teaching of Anatomy, the faculty, being sensible that his teaching was very beneficial to the College, permitted him to keep the key of the room for that session.   On 28th October, 1731, Principal Campbell, Dr. Johnstoun.

Dr. Brisbane, Mr. Dunlop, and Mr. Dick were appointed a Committee to inspect the old Humanity classroom, and report what was proper to be done to render it a convenient place for making dissections and teaching Anatomy. Again, on 24th October, 1733, the faculty granted Paisley the use of the old Humanity classroom for the purpose of teaching Anatomy as formerly, and authorised him to keep the key for the session, and to advertise his teaching in the public prints. Thus far accommodation had been granted for only one session at a time, but in 1734 the faculty, considering the usefulness of having within the College lessons in Anatomy and other things subservient to Physic and Surgery, allowed Paisley, who as they themselves testified, had for some years ' successfully taught the same, the use of the old Humanity classroom and the key thereof during the faculty's pleasure.' From this point annual entries on the subject do not recur, but it is probable that Paisley had continued to teach the subject for ten years from 1730.

In December, 1740, Mr. John Love, a surgeon who just before this had removed from Greenock to Glasgow, applied for leave to teach Anatomy in a room in the College, and the faculty allowed him for the ensuing session the room formerly used for the purpose. In October, 1741, Dr. Robert Hamilton and John Crawford, surgeon, petitioned to be allowed to teach Anatomy and to dissect in the Anatomy room. Johnstoun and Brisbane being absent when the application was submitted, consideration was postponed till next meeting, at which they were both present, and the petition was granted for the session about to begin. By this time, without aid from Brisbane, some progress had been made with Anatomy and dissection, for the faculty themselves bore witness to the usefulness and success of Paisley's teaching, and after he ceased to teach other anatomists petitioned for leave to carry on the work.

Brisbane died on 27th March, 1742, and a few weeks afterwards Dr. Robert Hamilton, who had begun to teach the year before, was appointed to succeed. Perhaps by way of warning against such remissness as Brisbane had shown, Hamilton in his commission was described as ' professor and teacher of Botany and Anatomy,' and the words were repeated in the commission to his successor, Dr. Black. There was trouble in connection with the work of Practical Anatomy. In 1744 and again in 1745 the mob, incensed by some rumour or suspicion, swarmed about the College, forced open doors, broke windows, and did other damage. Again in May, 1748, the mob gathered ' without any provocation' as it is plaintively stated, and broke several windows; and a still more formidable attack was made in March of next year. Several of the rioters were arrested, and a committee appointed to confer with the Magistrates, after which the attacks appear to have ceased. Improvements were made on the accommodation for Anatomy, and in the autumn of 1746 Hamilton went to London to procure anatomical preparations and other requisites for teaching. In March, 1756, Hamilton was appointed to succeed Cullen as professor of Medicine, but he could scarcely have entered on his new duties, for he died on 15th May following.

While the teaching of Anatomy was thus creditably maintained, Johnstoun, who held the chair of Medicine, proved as inert a professor as Brisbane. But in the end of 1744 Dr. William Cullen settled in Glasgow and began to teach Medicine, to which he soon added Botany, Materia Medica, and Chemistry. The question soon arose whether the chair of Medicine should not be held by a man so able and efficient rather than by one who wore the insignia of a professor and neglected the duties. With a view to bring about this change, Cullen in August, 1749, had an interview with the Duke of Argyll, to whom he had previously been recommended, and the Duke agreed to use his influence. It appears that in October, 1749, Cullen and Johnstoun came to an understanding, and the minutes bear that next month Johnstoun had consented to demit office in favour of Dr. Cullen, if allowed to retain his College house for life. The University meeting considering 'of how great importance it is to have Medicine well taught in this University,' agreed to the condition about the house, provided Cullen were appointed as professor. Notwith- standing Argyll's efforts, fully a year elapsed before the matter was settled, but on 12th December, 1750, the King appointed Cullen to be professor of Medicine.

Cullen was born in 1710 at Hamilton, where his father was a lawyer. Betimes he was sent to Glasgow, attended some classes in the University, and was apprenticed to John Paisley, surgeon, before the latter had begun to teach Anatomy in the University. Having finished his early training at Glasgow, Cullen repaired to London, and went on a voyage to the West Indies on board a vessel of which his cousin was captain, having previously undergone an examination in Medicine and been complimented by his examiners. After his voyage he was some time in London with an apothecary, and made a particular study of Materia Medica. Return- ing to Scotland about the end of 1731, he spent two years in study and practice at Auchinlee in Shotts, but having inherited a small legacy, he determined to prosecute further study at the University of Edinburgh, where he spent the sessions of 1734-5 and 1735-6. If Brisbane and Johnstoun had been active and enterprising professors, there would have been an earlier and better development of the Medical School at Glasgow, for the opportunity was not wanting. But they turned opportunity to better account at Edinburgh, where the first Monro, after teaching some years in Surgeons' Hall, was received into the University, and other four professors joined with him in 1726.   Provision was thus made for teaching the main branches of Medicine as then understood, and preparing students for graduation, and the Edinburgh Medical School grew in strength and reputation.   Cullen shared the energy of the young and vigorous institution, pursued his studies resolutely, and took an active part in the work of the Medical Society which had been founded as an outlet for the eager and enquiring spirit of the students.

Cullen next began practice at Hamilton, where William Hunter, who had just finished his studies in Arts at Glasgow, engaged to be his apprentice, with a view to become his partner and deal with the surgery cases ; but after one session at Edinburgh Hunter went to London, and having been a short time with Dr. William Smellie, was engaged by Dr. James Douglas to assist in dissection and act as tutor to his son.   Another partner was found for the surgical side of Cullen's practice, and he himself, still devoting part of his time to study, graduated as M.D. at Glasgow in 1740.   He kept an eye on that city, not only as affording prospects of wider practice, but opportunities for teaching medical subjects, an enterprise to which his past studies and experience, as well as the example of Hunter and Smellie in London and other acquaintances in Edinburgh, naturally prompted him.   On the death, early in 1742, of Dr. Brisbane, who had an extensive medical practice, Cullen was about to remove to Glasgow, but was dissuaded by the Duke of Hamilton, whose patronage he had enjoyed, and to whom his father had been factor.   Besides salary, the Duke promised that a chemical laboratory should be fitted up for him, and that he should have the superintendence of a botanic garden attached to Hamilton Palace.   The Duke fell into ill health, however, and Cullen, who attended him till his death next year, seeing no prospect of further advancement in Hamilton, came to Glasgow in the end of 1744.   From a letter of William Hunter's, dated in February, 1745, it appears that Cullen began teaching that winter.   Probably his first course in Medicine was given outside the University, but Johnstoun, though he could not be got to teach himself, seems to have acquiesced readily in Cullen's doing so, and in the winter of 1746 the latter began his first course of lectures on Medicine in the University, with a following of about twenty students, the attendance improving considerably in later sessions.   He wisely put aside Latin in favour of English for teaching purposes, and did not read his lectures on Medicine, though he had short notes, and sometimes gave out a sheet of manuscript notes to be circulated among his students and copied by them.   On this subject he declared

WILLIAM CULLEN, M.D.

WILLIAM CULLEN, M.D.

Professor of Medicine in the University of Glasgow

BORN 1710.   DIED 1790

From oil painting by William Cochrane in the Senate Room, University of Glasgow

that it would take too much time to write out his lectures, though written lectures might be more correct in diction and fluent in style; and that a familiar style would be more agreeable and more fitted to command attention than a formal one.   In these early lectures he gave the first draft of his views on a number of important questions in Medicine, afterwards more fully matured in his published works.

In the summer of 1748 Cullen began to lecture on Materia Medica and on Botany, neither of which branches had hitherto been adequately taught in distinct courses at Glasgow, excepting perhaps Botany in the time of Marshall.   In dealing with Botany, he lectured in Latin, probably owing to the formidable array of technical terms used in that subject. Whether or not this was wisely done, at all events it disproved the charge afterwards made against him that he chose to lecture in English because he did not know Latin.   In his course on Botany he gave an account of the principles on which the different systems of Botany had been founded, sketched the system of Tournefort, and then proceeded to explain that of Linnæus, first published in 1735.   The Botanic Garden formed in 1704 was still carried on, and occasional references to it occur.   In 1740 a lease was granted for seven years to John Paisley, surgeon, of a nursery at the foot of the College garden, under an obligation that he should erect a greenhouse within two years.   In 1741 a proposal was raised but not settled to turn the Physic Garden into a bowling green, and to assign a suitable part of the great garden for a Physic Garden.   In 1754 Hamilton and Cullen recommended that means should be taken to render the great garden more useful for the study of Botany, and that a good gardener should be procured, and probably some action may have followed.   The lectures on Materia Medica and Botany were repeated in the summer of 1749, and may have been continued longer, for a reference to Cullen's summer lectures occurs so late as 1754, the year in which he urged the improved arrangement of the gardens.   In the earlier courses on Botany and Materia Medica, Cullen was aided to some extent by John Carrick, a young surgeon who assisted Hamilton, the Professor of Anatomy, and was appointed to teach that subject during a short absence of the Professor in 1746, and again during the session of 1749-50 when the Professor suffered from ill health, Carrick himself dying prematurely in 1750.

The institution of teaching in the important subject of Chemistry was also owing to Cullen.   The project had doubtless been ripened by previous discussion, and on 5th January, 1747, Alexander Dunlop, who two or three years before had been appointed professor of Oriental Languages while acting as tutor at Geneva to the son of a nobleman, and had been excused for a session from entering on the duties of the chair, proposed that the teaching of 'Chemie' should be established in the University, and that the £30 saved from the salary of his chair between the death of his predecessor and his own admission to office, along with any further sum the University might grant, should be applied in purchasing the necessary apparatus, building furnaces, and making the needful preparations. On 28th January an estimate amounting to £52 was presented, and a fortnight later, Dr. Cullen and Mr. Carrick being present by request, gave their advice as to what would be requisite. The meeting then voted £30 saved from the chair of Oriental Languages and £20 (which seems to have been afterwards increased to £22) from the College revenue to be expended under the direction of Cullen and Carrick in providing equipment for the teaching of 'Chemie.' From an account kept by Cullen it appears that £136 was expended on the Chemistry Laboratory in 1747 and 1748. On 26th June, 1749, Cullen informed the faculty of the success of the project, and received their thanks for teaching the subject and illustrating his teaching constantly by the most useful and necessary chemical processes and experiments; and, as Cullen had expended a considerable additional amount on instruments, they acknowledged his personal right to dispose of them. An allowance of £20 was given to the lecturer in session 1749-50, and early in 1751 Cullen represented that the emoluments from Chemistry had been insufficient for instruments and materials, and asked whether the allowance of the previous year would be continued, and on what footing the lectureship would be for the future. Shortly afterwards the allowance of £20 was voted for that year, and it was determined to hold a meeting annually at the end of May to consider how the teaching of Chemistry had succeeded, and whether the encouragement from students had increased so as to make a grant unnecessary. After this the modest annual grant of £20 was regularly continued.

It was Carrick who began the first course of Chemistry, but after a few lectures he fell ill, and Cullen came forward to bear the undivided burden. At the outset he stated his regret at Carrick's indisposition, and told his students that he and Carrick did not profess to be great masters of the art, but, in the absence of such masters, were making an effort to supply students with the rudiments of a branch of knowledge so useful and necessary. At the opening of next session he printed and distributed to his students a plan of his course of lectures and experiments. Since 1726 Chemical lectures had been delivered in the University of Edinburgh by Dr. Andrew Plummer, but he confined himself mainly to an exposition of the preparation and chemical properties of medicines. Cullen, on the other hand, dealt with the subject as a branch of knowledge whose phenomena and laws were to be investigated and ascertained, and which had relations to other sciences, as well as arts and industries, and yet formed a wide and to a great extent unexplored science by itself. In his lectures he adopted a division into the general and particular doctrines of Chemistry, comprehending under the first the laws of combination and separation, and under the second the chemical history of bodies, which he arranged under the five classes of salts, inflammables, waters, earths, and metals. He added a view of the various properties of vegetable and animal substances, and ended with an account of the application of Chemistry to some of the more useful practical arts. In connection mainly with the first division of his lectures, he dealt at some length with the sources, transmission, and effects of heat, and made a number of researches and calculations, being the first to describe the boiling of ether on the reduction of pressure, and the lowering of temperature which accompanies the process.

As early as 1751 Cullen had some notion of removing to Edinburgh, and Lord Kames and other friends were ready to keep an eye on any opportunity that offered for his settling there. In 1755 Dr. Plummer, the Professor of Chemistry, having fallen into a hopeless illness, the Town Council appointed Cullen to be joint Professor of Chemistry while Plummer lived, and to succeed him in the chair upon his death. The path of entry to the new office was not altogether smooth, but Cullen accepted it, and began teaching in Edinburgh on 12th January, 1756. Though the way had been to some extent prepared for establishing a successful Medical School at Glasgow, and much more might have been done if Brisbane and Johnstoun had been energetic teachers, yet Cullen had done a great work. He had set agoing courses of instruction in Medicine, Materia Medica, Botany, and Chemistry, had drawn students to his classes in considerable numbers, had attracted the notice of professional and scientific men in the United Kingdom who took an interest in Medical education, and of not a few beyond its shores, and had greatly extended the reputation of the University. His achievements in Medicine rival those which Melville accomplished in Arts about 170 years before, and the University cannot but indulge a lingering regret that in both cases men whose labours and fame made so deep a mark on its history left it to pursue their career elsewhere.

The removal of Cullen was followed by a number of changes. Dr. Robert Hamilton being appointed to succeed him in the chair of Medicine, the chair of Anatomy and Botany was left vacant, and as Hamilton died in less than three months, the chair of Medicine was again left without an incumbent. By commissions issued by the Crown on 4th March,

1756, and 4th March, 1757, respectively, Dr. Joseph Black succeeded Hamilton, first in the professorship of Anatomy and Botany and next in that of Medicine; and in due course a commission was issued to Thomas Hamilton to fill the chair which Black had vacated, and, after delivering a Latin dissertation on the teeth, he was admitted to office on 14th April, 1757.

Black studied for about five years at Glasgow, first in Arts and afterwards in Medicine. He showed a special aptitude for Chemistry, and soon attracted the notice of Cullen, who sometimes in the course of his lectures rested his statements on the authority of his young pupil and assistant. Afterwards Black's extraordinary zeal and progress raised for a time an unbecoming jealousy in the mind of his master, and led the latter to be reticent about his experiments, but the two were soon fast friends again. The fuller opportunities of study afforded at Edinburgh induced Black to spend the latter part of his medical course there. He investigated by an elaborate series of experiments the relations of the caustic and mild alkalies, and the separation of 'fixed air' from various compounds, this 'fixed air,' which he was the first to discover, being subsequently called carbonic acid. He introduced into some of his processes quantitative as well as qualitative analysis. He embodied a portion of the results of his investigations in the thesis which he presented in 1754 for the degree of M.D. at Edinburgh—*De humore acido a cibis orto, et Magnesia alba*—and he again made use of this thesis as an inaugural dissertation before admission to the chair of Medicine at Glasgow in April, 1757. He held this chair for nine years, but, as might be expected from the previous bent of his studies, he made the greatest mark in Chemistry, the lectureship in which he held for ten years, along with the successive professorships. The usual annual grant for the lectureship was continued, and in June, 1757, he obtained an allowance of £40 for additional apparatus.

The accommodation for Chemistry soon proved inadequate for the increasing number of students who gathered round Black, and in May, 1763, a Committee reported that a new and complete laboratory should be built if the University funds would admit; and that the existing laboratory should be converted into a classroom for Mathematics. On 24th June following, the University meeting having adverted to the state of the funds, considered it safe and prudent to proceed with the building of a laboratory at an expense not exceeding £350, and authorised Black to have plans and estimates prepared. Shortly afterwards Leechman and Clow entered a long dissent against building the laboratory, doubting whether the funds could bear the strain; asserting that the existing laboratory was sufficient for necessary and useful purposes, that the lecturer on Chemistry was as well provided with the requirements for teaching as some of the professors, and that the expenses for Chemistry should not be unnecessarily raised, as the subject had no statutory foundation in the University; and pointing out that there were several professors with small salaries and some without houses, and that there were also public buildings still unfinished, as an instance of which they mentioned that the Library needed a stair. Principal Leechman further objected to the competency of passing the resolution at the meeting which adopted it, and reserved the right to bring the matter before the statutory visitors, the rector and dean.

To these reasons of dissent Black gave in a temperate but firm answer, acknowledging that the University had done much for the encouragement of Chemistry, but pointing out that the existing laboratory was by no means sufficient for all necessary and useful purposes. It was too small, and was damp and disagreeable, the floor never having been laid nor the walls plastered, so that students would be deterred from attending if the lectures were delivered there. The lecturer had to teach in another room while the processes were going on in the laboratory. It had appeared to the majority advisable to encourage the study of a science which was one of the most useful and solid, and was every day coming into greater esteem, but there appeared to be no particular necessity for troubling the rector, though all would value his advice and pay proper regard to it. Thomas Millar, Lord Advocate, who was rector at the time, was too clear-sighted and judicious to be misled by Leechman and Clow, and at a meeting on 2nd November, 1763, at which he presided, the minutes relating to the building of a new laboratory and fitting up the old one as a Mathematics classroom were read over in his presence, and received his approval. The work was to be set about with all convenient speed, the expense of the laboratory was limited to £350, and the conversion of the old laboratory was to be carried out with all proper economy, as recommended by the rector.

Black's great achievement at Glasgow was his discovery of latent heat, a discovery which belongs as much to the domain of Physics as of Chemistry. He found by experiment that when water in the state of ice is changed to the liquid condition it takes in a large amount of heat which cannot afterwards be demonstrated by the thermometer, and that before liquid water can be frozen into ice it must give out a large amount of heat which the thermometer does not demonstrate as previously existing in the water. He also found that in the case of water this latent heat, which in ordinary circumstances remained imperceptible, was about 143 or 144 degrees on the Fahrenheit thermometer ; and he made some progress in investigating the latent heat of other bodies besides water. He made further experiments on the amount of heat that passed into a state of latency when water is converted into steam, and followed up researches previously made by Cullen and others on the lowering of the boiling point of liquids by reducing the atmospheric pressure to which they are subjected. While these researches were in progress, James Watt, with whom Black and the other Professors frequently discussed their problems, was by patient and laborious effort devising means of harnessing steam to the wheels of industry.

Cullen having been transferred to another chair at Edinburgh, Black was appointed to succeed him as Professor of Chemistry, and on 27th May, 1766, he resigned his appointments at Glasgow. His colleagues bore witness to the ability and diligence which he had shown as Professor of Medicine, and the honour conferred upon the University by his great achievements in Chemistry. On 14th June he resigned the office of Clerk to the University meeting which he had held for four years, and received a unanimous vote of thanks for his faithful and gratuitous services. For some time before this there had been sharp divisions within the University regarding the management of academic affairs, and by Black's withdrawal the party which had previously been in the ascendant was reduced to a minority, and Leechman and his followers came into power. Professor Thomas Reid, who, at the age of fifty-five, attended Black's lectures on Chemistry, tells us that most of the medical students followed him to Edinburgh, so that for a time the Medical School at Glasgow must have suffered severely by his withdrawal.

In the lectureship on Chemistry, Black was succeeded by a young man who graduated as M.A. in 1756 under the name of John Robertson, but from some whim or another afterwards called himself Robison. He early showed a taste and capacity for physical science, and won the good opinion and friendship of Black and Watt. About the beginning of 1759 he entered the navy as a midshipman and continued in that position four years. This service led him to various foreign parts, and he was on duty in the boat in which Wolfe went to inspect some posts on the eve of the storming of Quebec, and brought back the story of the gallant general repeating aloud nearly the whole of Gray's *Elegy*, then recently published, and declaring he would rather be the author of that poem than conquer the French on the morrow. The discharged midshipman returned to Glasgow, and on 11th June, 1766, the University meeting, being well assured, from the particular conversations of many of its members with Dr. Black, of the abilities and fitness of Robison, appointed him lecturer on Chemistry.   When the laboratory with its equipment was taken over, some few appliances belonging to Black were purchased from him for £12s. 9s.   It was long the custom to reappoint lecturers annually, the working year running from 10th October to 10th June, and Robison, whose salary was £20 a year, was twice re-appointed.

In May, 1769, he informed the meeting that he was not to be in Glasgow next session, and therefore could not continue to teach Chemistry. Robison had secured an appointment as secretary to Admiral Knowles, then at the head of the Russian Admiralty, and after some years in the Russian service, he was appointed in 1774 to be professor of Natural Philosophy in Edinburgh University.   He published in 1797 *Proofs of a Conspiracy against all the Religions and Governments of Europe*, a work showing extraordinary credulity.

In June, 1769, the lectureship in Chemistry was assigned to a young medical graduate, Dr. William Irvine, who had for some years lectured on Materia Medica.   For Materia Medica a salary of £20 was allowed, and only £10 for Chemistry, probably owing to the combination of the lectureships and to there being considerable fees from students.   Irvine, who had been associated with Black in some of his experiments, taught a class in Materia Medica in 1765-66 by permission of the University, and it is recorded that he did so with success.   Having graduated as M.D. in 1756, he was appointed lecturer on Materia Medica, with a salary of £20, it being minuted that Professor Hamilton did not insist on his right to teach the subject.   It is not clear that between the time of Cullen and Irvine separate courses in Materia Medica were maintained, but the subject was regarded as within the encyclopædic scope of the chair of Anatomy and Botany, as Surgery and Midwifery continued to be for a much longer time.

It is sometimes asserted that the lectureship in Materia Medica was created for Irvine, who wished to be lecturer on Chemistry and was disappointed when the office was conferred on Robison, but it will be seen that Irvine lectured on Materia Medica a year before Robison's appointment to Chemistry, and probably the reason why Irvine was permitted rather than appointed to teach Materia Medica in 1765-66 was that he had not then obtained his degree.   The explanation of the origin of the lectureship seems to be simple enough.   Teaching in Materia Medica was wanted ; Professor Hamilton was too busy to give it ; and consequently a lecturer was appointed.   In May, 1779, there is a statement that the faculty considered a report by a Committee on a memorial given in by Professor Hamilton (who was then in poor health), and also a letter from Irvine, and decided that no one connected with the College had a right to teach Botany without Hamilton's permission; and that if a professor did not teach, any substitute nominated by him must have the approval of the faculty.   The subject is not fully explained, but it seems a fair inference that Irvine wished to add Botany to the list of subjects which he taught.   All accounts indicate that he acquitted himself well in the two lectureships on Materia Medica and Chemistry, which he held till cut off by a premature death in 1787.

Dr. Thomas Charles Hope succeeded Irvine in the two lectureships, and taught Chemistry till 1791.   In 1788, however, the faculty, calling to mind that it had long been intended to establish additional lectureships in Medicine, appointed Dr. Robert Cleghorn to be lecturer on Materia Medica, with a salary of £25, while Hope was re-appointed lecturer on Chemistry with a salary of £50.   Cleghorn was an Edinburgh graduate who settled to practise in Glasgow, and became one of the original managers of the Royal Infirmary and one of its two earliest physicians. In 1791, when Hope attained his full status as professor of Medicine, Cleghorn exchanged the lectureship on Materia Medica for that of Chemistry, and continued to teach the latter subject till a professorship was instituted 26 or 27 years later.   Dr. Richard Millar, who graduated as M.D. in 1789, succeeded Cleghorn as lecturer on Materia Medica and held the lectureship for 40 years, when a chair was founded, and he became professor of the subject for a year or two at the close of his career.   Millar was elected a physician in the Royal Infirmary in 1796, and continued in that office with little interruption till his death in 1833.

After Black's resignation, George III. in June, 1766, appointed Dr. Alexander Stevenson to the sole profession of Medicine, and he was admitted to office in September.   The son of a medical practitioner in Edinburgh, Stevenson graduated as M.D. at Glasgow in 1749, and he was also a member of the Royal College of Physicians of Edinburgh. Dr. John Moore describes him as

> ' In manners how soft, in apparel how trig !
> With a vast deal of physic contain'd in his wig !'

Yet it was rather an exacting position to hold the chair of Medicine after Cullen and Black.

Stevenson took an active part in promoting the foundation of the Royal Infirmary, a movement on behalf of which a number of other professors worked strenuously, notably Jardine, to whom the origin of the movement is attributed.   On 7th November, 1786, Stevenson informed the faculty that a subscription was in progress for the purpose of erecting an Infirmary in Glasgow, and suggested that they should consider what

JOSEPH BLACK, M.D.

Professor of Anatomy and Botany, 1756-1757, and of Medicine, 1757-1766

Lecturer on Chemistry, 1756-1766

BORN 1728.   DIED 1799

it was proper for them to do in furtherance of the project. On 19th December it was considered advisable to subscribe £500 to a project so beneficial in itself, and in which the interests of education and the success of the Medical School were so deeply concerned ; and to spread the payment over two years. This proposal was confirmed by a resolution formally adopted on 17th January, 1787, and on 11th April following, the Visitors gave their approval. Payment was not required quite so early as had been anticipated, but on 11th March, 1788, the principal was authorised to issue orders for payment of the money in three instalments. Members of the faculty were deputed on several occasions to attend meetings of subscribers, the principal, Professors Stevenson, Jardine, Reid, Millar, and Cumin being among the number. The Crown granted a site for the Infirmary on ground which had formerly belonged to the Bishop's Castle, and also issued a charter regulating the new institution. In September, 1791, when the draft of the royal charter was under discussion, the faculty were offered an option of the principal being named one of the managers *ex officio*, or of the faculty being empowered annually to elect a manager, and they chose the latter alternative. The professor of Anatomy and the professor of Medicine were included as managers *ex officiis*. Jardine was chosen as the first elected manager on 2nd January, 1793, and for many years he was re-appointed. The Infirmary was opened for patients towards the end of 1794, and more will be said afterwards of its relation to the Medical School.

Before the completion of the Infirmary, Stevenson had gone the way of all the earth. In July, 1789, he complained of having suffered from ill health for some years, and proposed that Dr. Thomas Charles Hope should be nominated his assistant, and that the faculty should unite with him in an application to the Government for the reversion of the professorship to Hope. Consideration of this proposal was deferred, but Stevenson did not defer taking action. At a meeting a week later he announced that, having previously consulted most of his colleagues and procured their approbation, he had made a request to the Government, and that Hope had now been appointed to be his assistant and successor, an arrangement with which the faculty expressed their satisfaction. Hope was a nephew of Stevenson's, and there is little doubt, the uncle's influence had been instrumental in bringing him to Glasgow as a lecturer in 1787, as it now was in procuring his swift appointment as assistant and successor, although the nephew soon displayed abilities which could not but command recognition. He was the son of John Hope, who graduated as M.D. at Glasgow in 1750, and afterwards became professor of Medicine and Botany at Edinburgh.

21

The younger Hope received the degree of M.D. at Edinburgh in 1787, just before his appointment as lecturer on Chemistry at Glasgow. The work by which he earned honourable mention in the history of science was his discovery of the special law which water obeys in reaching its maximum density 4 degrees Centigrade above the freezing point, a law which explains why ice floats, and why the surface layer of rivers, lakes, and other bodies of water is not directly cooled down till it is congealed into ice, but, on reaching this temperature of 4 degrees and acquiring its maximum density, sinks to a lower level, while warmer and lighter water from below rises to take its place, and in turn passes through the same process, so that the freezing of bodies of water is very much retarded, and bodies of considerable depth can hardly be reduced to a solid mass of ice. As Hope only attained his full status as professor of Medicine upon the death of Stevenson in May, 1791, and was transferred to the chair of Chemistry in Edinburgh in succession to Black in 1795, he is usually counted an Edinburgh professor. When he resigned in October, 1795, the faculty adopted a valedictory minute which is an echo, with only slight variation, of what was said when Black retired nearly thirty years before. Professor Jeffray offered to teach the class of Medicine till the next professor was admitted, but a similar offer by Dr. Cleghorn was preferred, which drew forth a dissent from Jeffray and some others.

On 27th January, 1796, the King issued a commission appointing Dr. Robert Freer, physician in Edinburgh, and member of the Royal College of Physicians there, to the chair of Medicine, which by some blunder was described as 'vacant by the death of Dr. T. C. Hope.' The new professor had had a somewhat chequered career, graduating as M.A. at Edinburgh in 1765, studying Medicine in Holland, acting as an army surgeon on the continent and in America, and being present at the battle of Bunker's Hill. In 1779 he obtained the degree of M.D. from King's College, Aberdeen, and he settled to practise Medicine in Edinburgh. He had a tall gaunt figure, and a countenance sedate and imperturbable except when he sang *Tullochgorum* at the Glasgow Medical Club. He is further said to have had a stereotyped series of questions for his patients. 'How are you to-day? Are you any better, or are you any worse, or are you much in the same way?'

After Black's short tenure of the chair of Anatomy and Botany, it fell in 1757 to Thomas Hamilton, a brother of Robert Hamilton, the successor of Brisbane, the two brothers belonging to a branch of the Hamiltons of Preston in Haddingtonshire, which produced some notable Covenanters, as well as distinguished professors. Thomas Hamilton had been some time in partnership with John Moore, surgeon, and when the degree of M.D. was conferred on the latter in 1772, Hamilton protested, apparently because the degree was conferred without examination and strict fulfilment of the regulations. At an earlier time Moore had described Hamilton as the leading spirit in the Hodge Podge Club:

> ' He who leads up the van is stout Thomas, the tall,
> Who can make us all laugh, though he laughs at us all;
> But *entre nous*, Tom, you and I, if you please,
> Must take care not to laugh ourselves out of our fees.'

Repairs and improvements in the Anatomy department are occasionally mentioned, and the number of students must have increased considerably during the second Hamilton's tenure. There was some trouble in March, 1776, when, in virtue of a general warrant from the Sheriff-Substitute, officers searched the College rooms for the body of a suicide; and Professors Baillie, Millar, and Reid were appointed to make a representation to the Sheriff-Substitute against the issue of such warrants, which were looked upon as involving possibilities of serious damage to the University. In 1740 the Faculty of Physicians and Surgeons resolved to fine any midwife practising within their territory unless previously examined and licensed by them; and in 1759 James Muir, surgeon in Glasgow, announced a course of lectures for the instruction of women in Midwifery. Some years later Hamilton made application for apparatus for teaching Midwifery, and a list of the articles required with an estimate of the cost having been submitted, permission was given on 10th June, 1768, to expend £80 on their purchase. At the same time Hamilton engaged to give a regular course on Midwifery every session.

In the summer of 1777 Hamilton was seized with palsy, and, on 10th October following, the faculty, at his own request, allowed him two months' leave of absence in the early part of the session. He never recovered completely, and in October, 1780, the faculty, knowing the precarious state of his health, allowed him to employ his son William as assistant in conducting the Anatomy class. This was only a step towards the end, and on 13th February, 1781, a letter from Professor Hamilton reminded the faculty of the breakdown in his health in 1777, from which he stated that he had recovered sufficiently to perform some part of his surgical work, but was hardly equal to the duties required as dissector and professor of Anatomy. He desired his colleagues to unite with him in a proper representation to the Crown to procure the professorship of Anatomy for his son William, who had passed a regular course of studies at the University of Glasgow, including Anatomy and Medicine, and next proceeded to Edinburgh, where he attended courses in Anatomy,

Botany, and the various departments of Medicine, afterwards studying three years under Dr. William Hunter in London, besides attending the ablest teachers there in the other branches of Medicine and Surgery. If the faculty agreed to the arrangement, Thomas Hamilton was prepared to resign his chair, retaining his College house, but on the understanding that William Hamilton would not claim a College house while his father possessed one. A week later the faculty agreed to the proposal, and unanimously resolved to recommend William Hamilton to the Secretary of State as most fit and qualified to succeed his father. The recommendation was effective, and on 8th March, 1781, William Hamilton was appointed professor of Anatomy and Botany; and, after reading an inaugural discourse on the Nature and Uses of the Absorbent Vessels, he was admitted to office on 10th April, 1781. The three Hamiltons who held this chair were shortlived, and William the most shortlived of the three, and probably the ablest and most active. Thomas Hamilton having died not long after his son's appointment, the son came into possession of a College house, and it is recorded that he used the parlour of it as a sort of dispensary for patients and pupils in Surgery. In 1784 Hamilton and Stevenson were put in charge of a collection of surgical instruments, left some time before for the benefit of the poor by Robert Luke, a merchant in the city. It was arranged that the articles in the collection were to be lent to any surgeon in Glasgow who had occasion for them, on his making a deposit in security for the loan. Probably it was with a view to distinguish and identify the various sets of instruments, that instructions were given in 1785 to procure from Hamilton an inventory of the surgical instruments belonging to the College. Botany seems to have received a considerable share of Hamilton's attention. He died on 13th March, 1790, before completing the thirty-second year of his age.

Six days after his death, James Towers, surgeon, who is said to have been a partner in William Hamilton's practice, of which Midwifery formed an important part, gave in a representation to the faculty, setting forth that, while officiating in the Royal Infirmary, Edinburgh, and during a recent stay in London, he had made use of special opportunities afforded him for the study of Midwifery, and proposed to give a course of instruction in that subject next winter in Glasgow. He solicited the patronage of the principal and professors, and asked to be allowed to lecture in the University. The request was granted for the ensuing year, and Towers was re-appointed lecturer from year to year till in 1815 he was made professor of Midwifery. At the outset of his career the Midwifery instruments belonging to the College were delivered to the custody of Towers, and the old Logic classroom was allotted as the place in which he was to lecture. In 1792 Towers pointed out that he had incurred considerable expense for instruments and preparations, and for a lying-in ward which he had opened and maintained for the more effective instruction of students of Midwifery ; and suggested that some remuneration should be assigned to him, upon which the faculty granted him an allowance of £25 a year from the fund conveyed a few years before by Dr. William Walton for a lectureship in Medicine. In 1794 when additional augmentations were being made to professors, Towers' salary, as well as that of the Lecturer on Materia Medica, was raised to £45, while that of the lecturer on Chemistry was raised from £50 to £70. By this time all the lecturers doubtless derived considerable sums from the fees paid by the students.

On 19th April, 1790, the king appointed James Jeffray, who graduated M.A. at Glasgow in 1778, and M.D. at Edinburgh in 1786, to be professor and teacher of Botany and Anatomy. He held the chair of Anatomy for 58 years, the longest tenure on record of any chair in the University, save one. Jeffray soon procured considerable improvements in the accommodation for his department. The dissecting room had hitherto been small and so imperfectly lighted that only one side of a subject could be turned to the light at once, the windows on one side requiring to be kept shut to prevent the interior from being in full view from the new court. What had formerly been the Materia Medica room was now added to the accommodation for Anatomy, the Clerk's chamber being converted into a room for Materia Medica, while a drain was made, and other improvements effected. In 1795 Jeffray was allowed the use of a garret above the Common Hall for a library, consisting chiefly of works on Anatomy and Surgery, which he had formed for the use of his students. Incidentally he mentioned that the public library was not yet open to students, and stated that many books which should be accessible to them were too expensive for themselves to purchase ; that the new library would be likely to help the progress of the rising Medical School ; and that the students, being keenly interested in the matter, had come forward with contributions.

Glimpses of Botany and of the Botanic Garden are found from time to time. In 1762 a site for a type foundry was granted in the little garden next the Physic garden, and in the same year an arrangement was made by which Alexander Adams, who kept the Physic garden for £6 a year, which was considered too little, was to have the College garden rent-free, on his keeping it in good order. It appears that the rent hitherto received was barely sufficient to pay the expense of maintenance, so that the arrangement seems to have been as beneficial to the College as to the gardener. For some time after this, accounts occur now and again for work in the

Physic garden and for tools, and in 1783 Robert Lang was appointed gardener, and it was part of his stated duties to take care of the Physic garden. In 1784, on the recommendation of Professor Hamilton, forty cart loads of manure were ordered for the Botanic Garden, and in 1787 further top-dressing and purchase of plants were authorised, while next year a small outlay for similar purposes and for extra work entailed on the gardener was sanctioned.

In 1789, it being considered that the Botanic Garden and work in the College Garden would afford sufficient employment for a gardener all the year round, the faculty engaged for the full services of Robert Lang, and fixed his emoluments at £17 a year, with the grass of the College Garden, valued at £8, an allowance of £1 for tools, and a house rent-free. Professor William Hamilton paid close attention to the Botanic Garden, and erected a conservatory in it at his own expense. By his will he provided that, in case of certain eventualities which did not occur, his Trustees should pay £200 to the University for the purpose of forming a Botanic Garden, showing that he did not think highly of the existing garden. The sum may seem small, but it is to be remembered that Hamilton contemplated the adaptation of some part of the College ground to the purposes of a Botanic Garden, not the purchase of new grounds. Hamilton further directed his Trustees to offer his apparatus, preparations, and conservatory to the faculty at a price to be fixed by arbitration, and in May, 1790, the faculty, without committing themselves to purchase, agreed to the appointment of valuators. After negotiating for about a year, parties failed to agree regarding the price, the faculty offering £243, and the Trustees insisting on £298. Hamilton's apparatus and preparations were removed, and Jeffray, his successor, purchased the hothouse.

For some time there is not much reference to the teaching of Botany, but the fact that in 1779, when Professor Thomas Hamilton had fallen into indifferent health, Dr. Robert Irvine showed a desire to begin teaching the subject, makes it seem probable that Hamilton had been in use to teach it. There is still extant a set of lectures delivered by Professor Hamilton, but it is not stated to what date they belong nor which of the Hamiltons delivered them. As Cullen taught Botany in the time of Robert Hamilton, and as the lectures bear internal evidence of belonging to a later date, there can hardly be a doubt that either Thomas or William Hamilton was the author. Jeffray seems to have taught Botany for some years at first, but before long he found it expedient to call in assistance. In May, 1799, he wrote from London that his business there would not permit him to return to Glasgow to open the Botany class by 1st June, as he had intended ; and proposed that Dr. Thomas Brown, who was well qualified and ready to begin, should conduct the Botany class till the professor's return.   The principal and Findlay were appointed to converse with Brown, and to advertise in the Glasgow newspapers the opening of the Botany class, if they found him ready to enter on teaching.   The Clerk was also instructed to enquire how long Jeffray requested leave of absence, and to say that his colleagues agreed to Brown teaching Botany, but wished to know what consideration Jeffray would allow him for performing that duty.   About a fortnight afterwards a letter in guarded terms from Jeffray was produced, stating that his stay in London would depend on the will of the Committee of the House of Commons by whom he had been summoned, and that he would settle matters with Brown.   In May, 1800, Jeffray sent a further letter regarding the arrangements for Botany, and the faculty declared their opinion that it would be for the advantage of the Medical School that Anatomy and Botany should be taught by different persons.   They therefore allowed Jeffray to employ Brown, with whose qualifications they were well satisfied, to teach Botany as long as it should seem expedient, and they agreed the more willingly because they understood Brown was to give lectures on Agriculture. They laid down a reservation that Brown should have no claim on the College funds for teaching the class ; and recalling that a few weeks before they had fixed the fee for each of the classes of Anatomy, Botany, and Theory and Practice of Medicine at three guineas, they now considered it inadvisable that the minimum fee for Botany should be so high, and fixed it at two guineas.

Dr. Brown, who conducted the Botany class for eight or nine years, graduated as M.D. at Edinburgh in 1798.   His grandfather and father had been prosperous surgeons, and he inherited Langside (which he sold in 1852, the year before his death) and Lanfine in Ayrshire, which passed to his daughter, his wife having been a sister of Jeffrey, editor of the *Edinburgh Review*.   He left a large collection of Minerals and Fossils to be given in equal portions to the Universities of Glasgow and Edinburgh, and in 1902, under the will of his daughter, a sum of £5,000 was bequeathed to the former University for Bursaries in Arts.

So much having been said of the teachers in the Faculty of Medicine down to the close of the eighteenth century, some account must now be given of the students, and the conditions of graduation and kindred matters.   Cullen began to teach Medicine in the University in 1746 to a class of about twenty students, a number which soon increased.   A class in Anatomy had been regularly conducted since 1730, and it had a fair following of students, though their number is nowhere stated exactly. Surgery was also taught from the Anatomy chair.   The class of Chemistry, which from the first was better attended than that of Medicine, dates from Cullen's advent, and classes in Materia Medica and Botany were also taught, and latterly a class in Midwifery as well. We must remember, too, that the same student would attend two or three classes simultaneously, and that some who attended Chemistry were not medical students. It is not probable that in Cullen's time the average number of medical students in all the classes would exceed 30 or 40. By the end of the century the number in Anatomy alone had risen to 115, and the average in that class for the eleven years preceding had been fully 83. The attendance on Anatomy, which then included a good deal of Surgery, was much more numerous than on any other class except perhaps Medicine, which included both practice and theory. It is stated that when Millar began to teach Materia Medica in 1791 his students numbered from 20 to 30, while in 1827 they had increased to between 80 and 90. On a moderate estimate, the number of medical students at the close of the eighteenth century may be set down as from about 175 to 200.

Apart from distinctly surgical degrees first granted in 1817, M.D. was the only degree in Medicine conferred by the University till 1865. During the fifty-five years from 1746 to 1800 the degree of M.D. was conferred on 250 individuals, an average of slightly over 4½ in the year, and 177 of these degrees were conferred in the last twenty-six years of the period, giving an annual average of nearly 7 for that portion of the time. The highest average occurs during the ten years of William Hamilton's professorship (1781 to 1790), when the degree was conferred in 89 cases, or an average of almost 9 in the year. But graduation, though it might be advantageous, was by no means necessary in those days. Society was less exacting, there were no Medical Acts, and though there might be particular localities where Medical or Surgical Corporations had a right to debar from practice those whose qualifications had not been tested and accredited in some way, yet there were many respectable practitioners who had never acquired any regular degree or diploma. Certificates of having studied for some years at a Medical School went a long way towards constituting a qualification, and even the medical departments of the public services, such as the Army and the Navy, were not very rigidly guarded. Those who applied for graduation had frequently been in general practice or in some branch of the public service for a number of years without holding a regular qualification from any Medical or Surgical authority.

In the eighteenth century there were no fixed periods for examination of candidates for the degree of M.D., and they were allowed to submit their certificates of attendance and to enter for examination at any time during the course of the academic year. In many cases the curriculum was made up of courses at more than one University, frequently no part of it had been taken at Glasgow, and it is evident that the great majority of those who studied at Glasgow did not graduate. Occasionally men who had been some years in practice, and who produced testimonials from two or more regularly qualified physicians, were taken on trial without strict evidence of having passed through any definite curriculum of study. Cases of this kind were never very numerous, as the organisation of the Medical School advanced they became less so, and from 1770 or earlier very few are found. The attendance was very seldom under two years, and on the average it would probably be more than three. Certificates of attendance at Edinburgh University were often produced, as well as from Hunter or other teachers in London, and not a few candidates had studied in Paris or elsewhere abroad. As there was no hospital at Glasgow till the end of the century, it was natural that attendance at a hospital should not form part of the requirements, but in a considerable number of cases the attendance of candidates at hospitals has been recorded, as if the University wished to countenance and encourage it. Till after the middle of the century there was occasional laxity in regard to examination, and even the presence of the candidate was sometimes dispensed with. In 1732 the University meeting laid down a regulation against conferring higher degrees in absence, excepting honorary degrees granted to candidates who had studied at Glasgow and been approved by the professors whose courses they had attended, or to candidates who produced certificates from professors in some protestant University in the respective faculties to which the degree belonged. The rule was not to apply, however, in the case of candidates for M.D. who produced the license of the College of Physicians of London; but in 1755 it was enacted that henceforth no degree in Medicine should be conferred in absence excepting honorary degrees, and no reservation was made in favour of the Royal College of Physicians, London.

If the candidate's attendance was deemed sufficient, he was examined apart on the various branches of Medicine by the two medical professors, the examination being no doubt conducted orally, and probably including a reference to specimens, preparations, and the like. If the student passed this part of the examination satisfactorily, the next step was to prescribe to him for solution a medical case and an Aphorism of Hippocrates. The medical case was a description in Latin of the symptoms of some ailment, and the candidate was required to diagnose it, and to furnish an account of the proper treatment. The solution of the case and a reasoned account of the meaning of the Aphorism were to be presented in Latin to a meeting of Senate over which the Dean of Faculty had the right to preside. Every member of the meeting was entitled to question the candidate, but probably most of the questioning was over when the previous ordeal before the two medical professors had been undergone. In theory the trials also included the preparation of a Latin thesis which had to be submitted to the Senate. Afterwards it was printed and a day fixed on which the candidate had to appear before a meeting of the *comitia* and defend his thesis *sine praesidio*. The *comitia* included the whole University—higher officers, professors, graduates, and students—but this disputation or defending of thesis before the *comitia* was in practice an optional part of the trials, and probably it seldom attracted a large audience. The trials usually lasted four or five days or longer, but occasionally they were disposed of in two or three ; and on their being passed successfully, diplomas were issued to the new graduates without waiting for any specific and formally appointed dates of graduation.

In 1748 it was resolved that no superior degree should be conferred upon any one who had not the degree of Master of Arts, and shortly afterwards it was laid down that every one who obtained the degree of Master of Arts as an antecedent to a higher degree should pay a fee of £3 for it. The next candidate who passed for M.D. was first created a Master of Arts, and then the degree of M.D. was conferred. A number of other cases were treated in the same way, but after the lapse of some time the regulation was often ignored. The subject was again discussed in 1766, and a Committee reported in favour of examining for the Arts degree all candidates for the degree of Doctor in any faculty, unless the higher degree were conferred *honoris causa*, or unless the candidate already possessed the degree in Arts. It was said that the degree of Doctor was more honourable and more important to society than that of Master, that some persons had lately been made Doctors who were ignorant of some common and necessary things in Arts, and that as the regulations for degrees in Arts at Glasgow had been made more severe than formerly and more severe than in any other University of Scotland, consistency pointed towards more severe regulations for the degree of Doctor. It was further argued that the diploma issued to Doctors bore that they were Masters of Arts, and it does not seem to have occurred to the academic authorities that the wording of a diploma could be changed. To have enforced the Committee's proposal strictly would have gone far to extinguish graduation in Medicine, but it was rendered less formidable when the Committee declared that it was not necessary to enact the proposal into a law, as every member of the Dean of Faculty's meeting had a right, if he thought fit, to examine in Arts any candidate for the degree of Doctor in any faculty, if the candidate were not already a Master of Arts. This absurd measure did not promote Arts studies, but it procured for a number of medical graduates an additional degree of M.A. which they did not wish and probably very seldom deserved. By and by reason prevailed, and medical degrees were conferred without this arbitrary accompaniment.

There had long been complaints that the conditions of graduation in Medicine in some of the Scottish Universities were not sufficiently strict, and that degrees were often conferred on the unskilful and undeserving. This was made an occasion for the wholesale disparagement of Scottish medical degrees, the just suffering for the unjust, and Scottish medical graduates in England, though many of them deservedly stood high in the profession, often felt the weight of the reproach. In 1774 Cullen and some others at Edinburgh drew up a memorial asking the intervention of the Government to regulate the granting of degrees in Medicine by the Scottish Universities. Cullen was then President of the Royal College of Physicians at Edinburgh, and that body had just elected the young Duke of Buccleuch to be an honorary member—not a very logical proceeding on the part of those who were contending against laxity in admitting to the medical profession. The Royal College of Physicians were bound by their charter to admit to membership candidates holding the degree of M.D. from a Scottish University, and they complained that they were sometimes obliged to admit members whose company they did not relish. The memorial set forth that the Universities of St. Andrews and Aberdeen gave degrees in Medicine in absence, and brought discredit on Scottish medical degrees, and that, though Glasgow did not give degrees in absence, it often gave degrees without requiring certificates of the candidate's previous attendance. The memorialists appear not to have been fully informed regarding the practice at Glasgow, for, though at an earlier time candidates were sometimes admitted without evidence of a regular course of study, by the time in question the attendance of students who wished to be examined for graduation was carefully ascertained. It is true that in a few instances degrees were conferred without examination, as in 1772 in the case of John Moore, a member of the Faculty of Physicians and Surgeons, who had long been one of the leading practitioners in Glasgow; and in 1784 in the case of Charles Combe, one of Dr. Hunter's English Trustees, described as a person of very extensive literature and distinguished abilities in many branches of Science, as well as in the different branches of Medicine.

The regulations proposed from Edinburgh did not aim at putting an end to the conferring of degrees in such cases, but expressly allowed it to continue; and indeed the opinions entertained at Glasgow were more strict, for the degree conferred on Moore called forth a protest from Professor Hamilton, who did not regard it as quite regular. The memorial proposed that the Universities should give no degrees in absence, excepting honorary degrees, conferred without fees on persons of rank and distinction, or who had given public specimens of their literature and medical knowledge; and further that, as regards candidates who presented themselves with a view to undergo a proper examination, none should be admitted unless they brought certificates of having resided two years at least in a University where Physic was regularly taught, and had applied themselves to all the branches of medical study. The memorial recommended that the Government should appoint a Visitation of the Scottish Universities in order to carry out the desired reform; or, if that were considered too troublesome, it was suggested that the Secretary of State for the Northern department might give his advice to the administrators of the Universities. The Duke of Buccleuch undertook to use his influence with the Government in favour of the proposed measures, but before doing so he forwarded the memorial to Adam Smith, who had been his tutor, in order to procure his opinion. Smith condemned the scheme outright, and probably hindered the Duke from bringing the memorial under the notice of the Government. In a long letter to Cullen, Smith gave frank and almost gleeful expression to his objections.

He considered the Scottish Universities to be as unexceptionable as any institutions of that kind, yet capable of considerable amendment, and looked upon a Visitation as the proper means of procuring improvement; but before applying for so arbitrary a tribunal he thought it desirable to know who were likely to be appointed, and what plan of reform they were to follow. He did not think the Government would resort to admonition or threatening or other irregular interference with the affairs of a body corporate. He regarded the proposed regulation that no one should be admitted to examination for medical degrees unless he had certificates of having studied two years at a University, as very unfair to private teachers, such as the Hunters, Hewson, Fordyce, and others. 'When a man has learned his lesson very well, it surely can be of little importance where or from whom he has learned it.' Smith traced the degradation of Universities in most parts of Europe to the large salaries frequently enjoyed by the professors, which rendered them independent of diligence and success in teaching; and to the great resort of students to such institutions in quest of bursaries and scholarships, or of admission to degrees and professions, whether the instruction received was valuable or not. These causes did not greatly affect the Scottish Universities, and at Edinburgh the salaries of the medical professors were insignificant, there were few or no bursaries, and their monopoly of degrees was broken in upon by all other Universities foreign and domestic. He required 'no other explication of its present acknowledged superiority over every other society of the same kind in Europe.'

To sign a certificate in favour of a man we knew little or nothing about could not be vindicated, but the most scrupulous men in the world sometimes did it from mere good nature and without interest of any kind. The title of Doctor might give some credit and authority to the man on whom it was bestowed, but in most cases persons who were trusted in matters of health had either some knowledge or some craft which would procure them nearly the same trust whether they had the title of Doctor or not. Persons applying for degrees in the irregular manner complained of were mostly surgeons or apothecaries who were in the habit of advising and prescribing, in other words, of practising as physicians, and who desired to be made Doctors more for the sake of increasing their fees than extending their practice. Degrees conferred even undeservedly upon such persons could do very little harm to the public. The University of St. Andrews brought ridicule and discredit upon itself by conferring a degree on one Green, a stage doctor, but in what respect did that hurt the public? Green continued a stage doctor as formerly, and probably never poisoned a single man more in consequence of his degree. The coppers thrown up to a stage doctor would never find their way into the pockets of a regular physician, and hence stage doctors did not excite the indignation of the Faculty as more reputable quacks did. 'Do not all the old women in the country practise physic without exciting murmur or complaint? And if here and there a graduated doctor should be as ignorant as an old woman, where can be the great harm? The beardless old woman indeed takes no fees ; the bearded one does, and it is this circumstance, I suspect, which exasperates his brethren so much against him.'

'There never was, and, I will venture to say, there never will be, a University from which a degree could give any tolerable security that the person upon whom it had been conferred was fit to practise physic.' The more strict Universities required students to reside at them for some time, and spend money among them. He believed the examination at Edinburgh was as good as at any other University in Europe ; but when a student had resided some years there, behaved dutifully to his professors, and regularly paid his fees, the University was disposed to be good natured when he came to examination. Several Edinburgh graduates, upon applying for a license to the College of Physicians in London had been recommended to continue their studies, and, from a particular knowledge of some of the cases, he was satisfied the decision was perfectly just, and that the candidates were really very ignorant of their profession.   A degree, though it might give some slender security for the science of a graduate, could give none 'for his good sense and discretion, qualities not discoverable by an academical examination.'   It was for the real advantage of Universities that, in order to attract students, they should depend, not on their privileges, but on their merit—on their ability to teach and diligence in teaching.

He argued that a degree conferred only upon students of a certain standing would have an effect upon science similar to that produced by other statutes of apprenticeship on arts and manufactures, which, assisted by additional corporation laws, had banished arts and manufactures from the greater part of towns corporate.   Such degrees, with other regulations of similar tendency, had banished almost all useful and solid education from the greater part of Universities.   Bad work and high prices had been the effect of the monopoly induced by the former; while quackery, imposture, and exorbitant fees had arisen from the latter.   The private interest of some poor Universities that sold their degrees to whoever would buy them, generally without residence, and frequently without examination, had partly remedied the inconvenience.   'Had the Universities of Oxford and Cambridge been able to maintain themselves in the exclusive privilege of graduating all the doctors who could practise in England, the price of feeling a pulse might by this time have risen from two and three guineas, the price which it has now happily arrived at, to double or triple that sum,' while English physicians would probably have been the most ignorant and quackish in the world.   That in every profession the fortune of every individual should depend as much as possible upon his merit, and as little as possible upon his privilege, was certainly for the interest of the public.   'The great success of quacks in England had been altogether owing to the real quackery of the regular physicians.   Our regular physicians in Scotland have little quackery, and no quack accordingly has ever made his fortune among us.   After all, this trade in degrees I acknowledge to be a most disgraceful trade to those who exercise it; and I am extremely sorry that it should be exercised by such respectable bodies as any of our Scotch Universities.   But as it serves as a corrective to what would soon grow up to be an intolerable nuisance—the exclusive and corporation spirit of all thriving professions and of all great Universities— I deny that it is hurtful to the public.'

There is a curious mixture of truth and error in Smith's arguments. He rightly conceives the public interest to be the chief consideration, but it is the public interest which requires that those who are to have the care of the health and the lives of their patients should undergo a suitable training to qualify them for duties so important and responsible. Even in cases where the physician may be unable to do direct and positive good, it may be important that he should know how to prevent harm. Discretion and good sense, though in some degree they may be regarded as natural gifts, are yet to a large extent products of education, and a man who has had a fair training under capable teachers, and has made reasonable use of it, must be greatly improved in knowledge and skill, and probably a good deal improved in sense and discretion as well. It may be sound policy to allow part of the curriculum to be taken outside the Universities ; but though the Edinburgh plan might be imperfect in that respect, this does not touch the vital question of requiring those who are to enter the medical profession to go through an adequate course of study and training, and to submit to an examination or examinations in order to test whether they have profited by their opportunities. It is also somewhat surprising that Smith, who had a strong regard for the wellbeing of the Scottish Universities, should not have been anxious to put an end to practices existing in some of them which he himself declared to be disgraceful.

Whether the memorial and the discussions connected with it had become known to the academic authorities at Glasgow is uncertain, but on 8th May, 1775, the Senate appointed Stevenson, Hamilton, Anderson, and Reid, with all the members who chose to join them, a Committee to propose rules for conferring degrees in Medicine. In October following they were allowed further time to bring in their report, and it does not appear that they ever did so. Again, in 1784 it was proposed to make public intimation in the newspapers of the regulations for graduation in Medicine, and Stevenson and Hamilton, with any others who chose to join them, were appointed to draw up an account of these regulations and to report. Their report, if ever they presented one, does not appear in the minutes, and, though a perusal of these may give a fair idea of the requirements, the eighteenth century closed without any detailed code of regulations being formally put on record.

At the end of the century the Medical School had a staff of six teachers —a professor of Medicine (who taught both the practice and the theory of Medicine, the latter including Physiology and Pathology), a professor of Anatomy (who taught a good deal of Surgery as well, and was also nominally professor of Botany), and lecturers on Chemistry, Materia Medica, Midwifery, and Botany. The medical students approached two hundred in number, and the opening of the Royal Infirmary marked a great advance in the opportunities of instruction available to them. The earliest record of a student having attended clinical lectures in the Infirmary occurs in the case of Robert Agnew, who graduated as M.D. in May, 1796. Notwithstanding the disadvantage of having inert professors in the early years of the Medical School, the University, which during the 18th century acquired a reputation in Philosophy, Mathematics, and Physics, also laid the foundation for Medicine becoming one of its chief studies. With little external aid or endowments, it had developed a Medical School, with a creditable organisation for the times, and continually undergoing extension and improvement, and had gained an assured position and reputation in Medicine, provided there were wise management for the future. It could number among its teachers men like Cullen and Black, Hope and Hamilton; and among its graduates, not only the leading local practitioners, such as Gordon and Moore, but men like William Smellie, who, after practising as an apothecary at Lanark, went to study Midwifery in London and Paris, and with a modest but well-founded confidence that he could improve the theory and practice, set up as a teacher in London, and acquired a solid and lasting reputation; and William Hunter, one of the foremost teachers and practitioners of his age, and also one of the most munificent benefactors of the University.

II. 1801–1858.

THE course in Natural History, for which a chair was founded by the King in 1807, with Lockhart Muirhead as professor, was not at first included in the curriculum of any faculty, but the Commissioners under the Act of 1858 brought it into the faculty of Medicine. The foundation of the chair has been elsewhere related, and it had important results, for the Court of Session decided that the professor of Natural History was a member of the University of Glasgow but not of the faculty or College, and seven other chairs afterwards founded by the Crown in various branches of Medicine were placed in the same category. The general administration of the academic property and revenue, and the patronage of chairs not in the gift of the Crown, were reserved to the principal and the thirteen professors whose chairs were founded before 1807, and professors holding chairs founded after that date were shut out from these privileges, and left to deal with regulations for degrees, the management of the Library, and some crumbs and fragments of other business. Muirhead was admitted as a University professor in December, 1808. Under his commission he had a salary of £100 from the Bishops' rents or other Crown rents or casualties in Scotland; and having pressed the faculty, he obtained in 1812 an annuity of £40 from the College funds, which was raised to £75 three years later. Besides holding the chair of Natural History, he continued to act as librarian and registrar of medical students till

WILLIAM HUNTER, M.D., F.R.S.

Founder of Hunterian Museum

BORN, 1718.   DIED 1783

After R. E. Pine, in the Hunterian Museum, University of Glasgow

October, 1827, when he resigned the latter offices, and he died on 25th July, 1829.

Muirhead's most notable work was his supervising the removal from London to Glasgow of the great Museum formed by William Hunter. In early life Hunter had gone through the usual course in languages and philosophy at Glasgow, and held a Foundation bursary. Subsequently he was apprenticed to Surgery with Cullen at Hamilton, and after one session in Medicine at Edinburgh, he repaired to London, where he was taken under the patronage of Dr. James Douglas. Hunter soon rose to wealth and eminence as a practitioner in Medicine and Obstetrics and teacher of Anatomy; and in recognition of his position as one of the 'most able Anatomists in Europe' the University in 1750 conferred on him the degree of M.D. Disappointed in his efforts to move the Government to aid in providing a School of Anatomy in London, he told his friend Cullen that he had a 'great inclination to do something considerable at Glasgow some time or another'; and, not without a touch of 'that last infirmity of noble minds,' declared that he was independent, and wished to do something that would not be forgotten when the few years he had to live were over. With great care and cost he collected in the course of years a Museum of such extent and value as have rarely been equalled by a private collection. The contents included zoological and mineral specimens, books, manuscripts, paintings, coins, and archæological relics, and what was of more importance in connection with a Medical School, an extensive Museum of anatomical preparations illustrating both healthy and diseased structures, part being obtained from his own researches or procured to illustrate his teaching, while part was contributed by former students on whom he had impressed a taste for his own pursuits. Hunter, who died on 30th March, 1783, directed that this great collection should ultimately be made over to the University of Glasgow, allowing it to remain in London for the use of his nephew, Dr. Matthew Baillie, and his partner in teaching Anatomy, William Cruikshank, for thirty years after his own death. He also bequeathed a sum of £8,000 to erect a building at Glasgow for the reception of the Museum, to maintain the collections in proper order, and to provide lectures, his aim being to make the Museum useful to the students of the University and the public in general.

Cruikshank died in 1800, and Baillie having retired from teaching Anatomy, arrangements were made for the removal of the Museum to Glasgow before the expiry of the thirty years. A handsome building was erected in the College garden from designs by William Stark, an able young architect who died a few years later, and with whom, according to

Scott, there died more genius than was left behind 'among the collected universality of Scottish architects.' For the heating arrangements of this building the faculty sought the advice of their old tenant and ally, the veteran James Watt, and it was freely given. In the summer of 1807 Muirhead went to London to superintend the packing and despatch of the contents of Hunter's Museum in Windmill Street. The cost of packing and removal amounted to about £1,100, besides an outlay of £330 for cleaning the pictures and repairing their frames. The other contents of the Museum were shipped to Glasgow, but the faculty were much exercised regarding the safe conveyance of the medals. At one time there was a proposal to bring them also by sea and to apply to the Government for the escort of a warship, but afterwards land carriage was deemed preferable. The jolting and vibration of the stage coach were held to render that mode of conveyance unsuitable, and finally it was decided to bring down the medals by wagon. Upon Baillie's advice, six trusty men, accustomed to the use of arms, were sent to London by sea, to return with the wagon and guard its treasures.

Muirhead's commission nominated him to be keeper of the Museum or repository of natural curiosities, and some interpreted this as a claim on the part of the Crown to appoint a keeper of the Hunterian Museum. The office might possibly have been given to Muirhead but for this sinister clause, which naturally led the faculty to make an independent choice, in order to demonstrate their right to make the appointment. Some wished further time to look out for a person qualified by training and acquirements for the post, but the majority resolved to proceed at once to elect a keeper at a salary of £60, who should give bond for £2,000, and be allowed to nominate an under-keeper at £30 a year, the faculty having a negative on the latter appointment. Both officials were to reside in the Museum. By a considerable majority James Pate, librarian of Stirling's Library, was appointed keeper, but he soon resigned, and in May, 1809, James Couper, son of the professor of Astronomy, was chosen to succeed. He was unable immediately to enter on his duties, and his father was asked to take charge of the Museum till his son's admission, and to assist the new keeper in making himself acquainted with the collections. Young Couper was admitted in October following, but he soon obtained leave of absence, and ere long his father became keeper, and held office apparently till the end of his life. Dr. William Couper, who succeeded Muirhead as professor of Natural History, was joint keeper, at a salary of £70 from the College funds, in his father's later years. The keeper now received a salary of £65 from the Hunterian funds. William Couper is said to have had considerable skill in Mineralogy. In 1856, the year before his death, Couper had fallen into ill health, and John Pringle Nichol lectured for him on Geology and Crystallography, Allen Thomson adding a few lectures on Fossil Zoology. Henry Darwin Rogers, an American naturalist, more conversant with Geology than Zoology, succeeded Couper in 1857, and held the chair for a comparatively short time, dying in 1866. During the 19th century, after Muirhead's time, the commission of the professor of Natural History usually nominated him to be keeper of the Museum or repository of natural curiosities, and the University authorities appointed him keeper of the Hunterian Museum after obtaining an acknowledgment that his commission did not entitle him to that office.

For a considerable time the charges made for the admission of visitors gave appreciable assistance in defraying expenses. On account of the removal of the Museum to Glasgow six years before the limit of time had expired, the accumulation of the funds left by Hunter was checked, and the outlay on buildings and on the removal and rearrangement of the collections went beyond what was expected, so that only a slender remnant was left to provide for a keeper and other expenses. In a print issued in 1877 it is stated that an annexed building was added to the Museum in 1838[1] to accommodate the anatomical preparations, the cost being defrayed from the Hunterian funds. By this time or shortly afterwards the funds derived from Hunter were exhausted. In 1844 a sum of £200 in excess of its own funds had been expended on the Museum. By October, 1846, this balance on the wrong side had risen to £863 8s. 4d., and unfortunately it did not stop there. About 1823, in consequence of an article which appeared in the press complaining of the state of the preparations, an examination was made, jars were refilled with new spirits to the value of £50 or £60, and the old spirits were filtered and redistilled.

In January, 1839, Dr. William Thomson of Edinburgh, afterwards professor of Medicine at Glasgow, inspected the anatomical collections of the Museum at the request of the Royal Commission then sitting, and prepared an elaborate report. The wet specimens were mostly crowded on thirteen or fourteen rows of shelves, the upper rows being accessible to view only by means of ladders, while doors of too heavy pattern, made of trellis work in wooden frames, further hindered inspection, and the preparations not being arranged in the order of the catalogue or any other definite order, it was difficult to see whether all articles were in their places. The dry specimens, mostly without labels, were almost all deposited in drawers in closed presses, an arrangement incompatible with proper exhibi-

---

[1] There is almost certainly a mistake here, for in 1839 Dr. Wm. Thomson inspected the collections, and reported that they were in a crowded state and much in need of extended accommodation.

tion and apt to lead to neglect. The custodians were aware of the defective condition of the collection, and anxious that means of remedy should promptly be found. Dr. Thomson declared that the anatomical preparations, though far from being in a state worthy of the memory of the donor or satisfactory to the members of the University, had sustained a much smaller amount of irreparable damage than was generally imagined by members of the medical profession. He recommended increased accommodation, and arrangement of the articles in accordance with the catalogue and in such manner as to facilitate inspection, renewal of suspension where needful, filling up of jars with spirits, and the cleaning of articles requiring it ; and that besides bearing labels with consecutive numbers, and with the markings entered in the catalogue, the preparations should have cards accompanying them to indicate their nature and the point or points they illustrated. The catalogue should be printed and made available as soon as possible ; and medical students and practitioners should have free access to the collection and be invited to contribute to its extension. There should be a quarterly inspection by curators, and the keeper should report to them the transactions of the preceding quarter, indicating what preparations had been injured or repaired, and whether there had been any additions. These proceedings should be regularly minuted, and a distinct account should be kept of the expense of the department. There should be a limit to the number of the preparations which a professor might borrow, and no professor should be allowed to circulate preparations through his class. A list ought to be made of delicate or rare articles which from their nature the keeper should be instructed not to lend out of the Museum. There should be a skilled assistant for repairing and maintaining the articles in the collection, and preparing any additional specimens which might be procured. As an indication of the outlay necessary for maintaining the anatomical preparations, Dr. Thomson mentioned that the annual expenditure for keeping the anatomical Museum of the Royal College of Surgeons at Edinburgh, which contained 7,000 specimens, was £265.

In some departments of the collection a considerable number of additions have been made, and it would not now be safe to conclude that an article placed in the Hunterian Museum belongs to the collection made by William Hunter.

Professor Jeffray, in the course of an exceptionally long tenure of a chair involving much work and responsibility, appears frequently on the academic scene. In 1800 he was appointed vice-rector by Sir Ilay Campbell. In January, 1801, the faculty authorised a loan to him of £400 for which he was to give bond ; and next year a loan to him and Mrs. Jeffray of £1,500 was authorised, for which he gave a bond over the lands of Craigendmuir and Cardowanmuir, and agreed that the interest should be paid out of the salary due to him by the College. This loan appears to have been repaid in 1830. Towards the end of 1821 Jeffray, without obtaining consent from the faculty, transformed some office houses attached to his official residence, and let the premises as a shop. The faculty objected, and though Jeffray promised to restore the shop to its former purpose, he made no haste to do so. On 20th December, 1821, the faculty peremptorily appointed that the shop should be shut by 3rd January, and appointed a Committee to see their order carried out, and if needful to take steps along with the College Law Agent to have the tenant summarily removed. Some years later Jeffray had an opportunity of making a reprisal. In 1832 he put forward a claim for £500 for improvements made by him upon his house about thirty years before. He had laid before the faculty a plan of the proposed improvements, and the faculty approved of his carrying them out, and, while declining to bear the expenses at the time, they agreed that if in future allowances were made for similar improvements on other houses, an allowance should be made to Jeffray also. Many years elapsed, but at length very large allowances were made to Davidson and Sandford, and, upon this, Jeffray raised his claim and threatened an action in the Court of Session. The Visitors gave their opinion that he was entitled to whatever sum he could show that he had expended on the faith of the agreement of 1800, and some time afterwards, in December, 1833, his colleagues compounded with him by making a payment of £200.

In the session of 1802-03 dissection and the means of supplying subjects for it gave rise to excitement and tumult, and in the end of January, 1803, a party of soldiers was retained for the protection of the College, for which an account of £27 was paid. Shortly after this a proposal to annex Anatomy rooms to the new buildings for the Hunterian Museum was thought to involve danger on account of the excitability of the mob, and the risk of their attacking the buildings and wrecking the contents. In October, 1803, there was a dispute between Jeffray and the faculty, the former insisting that the faculty should appoint some one recommended by him to be dissector to the class. The faculty, while willing to allow assistance, considered Jeffray's plan would transfer responsibility to some extent from the professor to the faculty, and regarded this as inexpedient and impracticable. The principal tried to mediate, but Jeffray declared that, if his plan were not accepted, he would not teach his class as formerly ; but, as the subject is not further mentioned in the minutes, probably he had not carried out his threat. The number of students of anatomy at this time was 91, and for some time afterwards it rapidly increased, owing largely to the war and the demands of the Army and Navy medical service. From 1809 to 1814 there were more than 200 students of Anatomy every year, and in 1813 the extraordinary number of 352 was reached. From 1824 to 1829 the annual number again exceeded 200. By 1835 it had fallen to 119, and for the next 12 years, when Jeffray's advanced age rendered him less active, the average was about 71, a larger number of students doubtless resorting to extra-mural teachers during this time. An effort was made to provide better accommodation for the rising number of students, and the additional buildings begun about 1810 included new Anatomy rooms. The dissecting rooms and Anatomical Museum were placed above an extension formerly erected to the Library, the floor of the dissecting room being covered with lead to secure the Library rooms below from danger of fire ; and, on the recommendation of Jeffray, considerable changes were made from the original plans in order to provide better lighting.

Students sometimes took part in resurrectionist work, and there were troubles in consequence. In April, 1813, on the proposal of Freer, the faculty enacted that, as the College had been in considerable danger from students being concerned in raising dead bodies for private dissection, for the future any student guilty of such misconduct should be expelled. Orders were given that this should be intimated in the medical classes at the commencement of every session. Further irregularities had probably occurred, for in December, 1815, the faculty ordered the intimation respecting dead bodies to be read in the medical classes. There were keen discussions regarding the means of supplying subjects for dissecting rooms, and the legal measures which should be enacted, and the criminal and revolting methods by which Burke and Hare supplied the Edinburgh dissectors with material intensified the public interest in the question. Warburton's Anatomy Bill for regulating the supply of bodies and the conditions under which dissection should be carried on, was several sessions under discussion before being finally passed in 1832. The Senate in 1829 adopted a minute calling for amendments on the bill, and copies were sent to Peel and Warburton, while shortly afterwards a petition was sent to the House of Lords. In April, 1830, a memorial drawn up by Jeffray and Burns, the two professors most interested in the matter, criticising the measure at considerable length, was forwarded to the Duke of Montrose, the Marquis of Lansdowne (rector of the University at the time), the Duke of Wellington, Peel, and Warburton.

The memorial recommended that the sale of bodies or the gratuitous disposal of unclaimed bodies should be made legal, as well as the transmission of bodies from place to place; deprecated the punishment of professors or authorised teachers for possession of a dead body, unless it could be shown that they had assisted at its exhumation; and argued against University professors appointed by the Crown being required to take out an annual license. It was urged that professors of Anatomy in Scottish Universities should have preference over others to a certain extent, else they would be worse off than before. If the supply came chiefly from hospitals, the surgeons of Glasgow had such influence with the Managers that they would procure most, if not the whole, of it, for private teachers belonging to their own Society. The hospital in Glasgow was not subservient to the University Medical School, but distinct from and opposed to it. By the articles of union the Scottish Universities were to continue for ever, and surely this implied the support and protection of the Government. From the difficulty of procuring subjects many students resorted to Paris, and, though their resort thither was not creditable to the Medical Schools of this country, it was preferable to having practitioners without anatomical knowledge, which was the foundation of skill and success in every branch of the profession. If the supply at Paris proved inadequate, or if hostilities between the two countries arose, very grave evils would follow as a consequence of uninstructed practitioners, and no hasty expedient could prevent it. The Anatomy Act of 1832 allayed the public apprehension and provided legal means for the supply of material necessary for the training of medical students in an essential part of their education. Notwithstanding the large number of students at Glasgow in the thirty years before the passing of the Act, and the troubles and excitement that frequently arose, it appears that there was hardly any other Medical School in the United Kingdom so well supplied with subjects as that of Glasgow, the abundant communication with Ireland partly accounting for this.

Jeffray's successful effort in 1795 to form a separate collection of books for medical students has already been mentioned, and additions to the collection were afterwards made. In 1818 Jeffray protested against the meagre allowance made for procuring books on medical subjects for the General Library. He stated that the medical professors and students had raised a sum of nearly £600 to purchase books which were then in the separate medical collection, and hinted that they might be willing to see the collection merged in the General Library, but it was long before this was carried out.

In 1827 when it was resolved to divide among all the medical professors the fees for M.D., half of which had previously been assigned to Jeffray and half to Freer, Jeffray was allowed to receive the full half during his incumbency. For the last ten or twelve years of his tenure, if not longer, Jeffray suffered from advanced age. In 1836 the Senate agreed that Dr. James Marshall, who had been his dissector and demonstrator for more than twenty years, should superintend and direct students of Practical Anatomy who did not attend the lectures on Anatomy, while Dr. James Jeffray, the Professor's son, should do the like for those who attended the lectures as well. The Commission which reported in 1830 stated that the number of students attending dissections was about a hundred, but the returns furnished did not show what fees they paid. Again the Commission of 1839, holding that, when assistants were allowed, it was the duty of those who sanctioned the arrangement to secure such conditions as would guard against the work being entrusted to men of doubtful qualifications, were disappointed because they could get no account of the pecuniary arrangements between the professor and the gentlemen appointed to assist him. In February, 1838, the faculty at his own request allowed Jeffray to employ his son to assist him occasionally in the work of teaching, and at the opening of next session the permission was renewed. After this he probably took little part in teaching. In May, 1840, the College gave a dinner in his honour on his completing fifty years of service. Having held the chair of Anatomy for nearly fifty-eight years, he died on 28th January, 1848, and his colleagues recorded their sense of his soundness of judgment, consistency of conduct, profound knowledge of his subject, zeal for its advancement, and happy talent of communicating information to his students ; and declared that he had added to the celebrity of the University and attracted numerous students from every quarter of the world. This last statement must have been more applicable before his powers felt the chilling touch of age than in his later years, when the number of students dwindled seriously.

After Jeffray came Allen Thomson, an eminent member of a family eminent in Medicine. His father, John Thomson, the son of a Paisley weaver, began the study of Medicine at Glasgow at the age of twenty-three, and afterwards completed his course at Edinburgh. Through Lord Lauderdale, whom he had previously assisted in his studies, Thomson was introduced to Dr. John Allen and the Holland House circle of politicians, to whom Allen was a sort of resident secretary, and by their influence a chair of Military Surgery was set up at Edinburgh and Thomson made professor. He resigned this chair in 1821, and ten years later advised the Government to create a chair of Pathology at Edinburgh, which was done and Thomson again made a professor. His eldest son, William, was professor of Medicine at Glasgow from 1841 to 1852, and is noticed in the account of that chair. Allen Thomson, his second son, named after Dr. Allen of the Holland House circle, graduated as M.D. at Edinburgh in 1830, was two years professor of Anatomy in Marischal College, Aberdeen, and six years professor of Physiology in Edinburgh University. On his transference to Glasgow, his ability and diligence soon enabled him to exert a notable influence both in the University and outside of it; while his work and reputation furthered the progress and credit of the Medical School. He was one of the editors of the seventh and eighth editions of Quain's Anatomy, and contributed to Todd's Cyclopaedia of Anatomy and Physiology, the latter work containing the results of important researches in Embryology with which his name is associated.

Much had happened since 1790, the date of Jeffray's appointment, and 1848, when Allen Thomson succeeded him, and among other things a chair of Botany had long been established, but the oblivious officials of the Home Office adhered to the old form, and made out a Commission appointing Thomson to be professor of Anatomy and Botany. On 3rd March, 1848, he delivered a Latin dissertation *De ratione nexus qui inter cerebri fabricam et animi facultates hominis animaliumque observatur*, and was admitted to office. The faculty purchased for £250 Jeffray's anatomical collection, which embraced 717 wet preparations, 252 dry, 39 in glass frames, 9 wax and plaster models, and 99 preparations of bones, including 10 human skeletons, 24 human skulls, 29 skeletons of animals, and 36 skulls of animals. A portion of the specimens were not in good condition, and a sum of £57 was expended on repairing them, of which Thomson paid the greater part. Thomson proposed to place some portion of Jeffray's collection in the Hunterian Museum, retaining in an apartment adjoining the Anatomy room such specimens as were fitted to illustrate lectures. With this teaching collection the professor wished to incorporate his own Anatomical preparations, and to add such preparations as might be made in the Anatomical department, except a few connected with researches in which he was engaged. Thomson's collection embraced 190 wet preparations, 77 dried vascular preparations, 30 wax and plaster models, 230 preparations of bones, including 38 human skeletons, 59 animal skeletons, and 58 animal skulls; and also comprehended a very large number of drawings and paintings illustrating Anatomical and Physiological subjects. In Anatomy the number of students rapidly increased after his appointment, being doubled, trebled, and almost quadrupled within the next twelve years, though it never reached the extraordinary total of 352 recorded under Jeffray in 1813. Notwithstanding the exacting duties of his chair, Thomson took a leading part in the administrative work of the University, and in 1851 was appointed Clerk of Senate, an office he held for a long time.

Robert Freer continued to act as professor of Medicine till he was eighty years of age, though it must have been with impaired efficiency in his later years.   In October, 1825, the faculty authorised Dr. Whitsone, a nephew of Freer's, to assist him in lecturing and in examining for graduation.   Whitsone conducted the class till Freer's death in April, 1827, and afterwards applied to the Senate for a certificate stating how long he had carried on the class, and giving their impression of the manner in which he had acquitted himself.   Having obtained this, he next claimed remuneration from the Senate, but they repudiated the claim, declaring that, though the faculty had allowed Freer to avail himself of Whitsone's assistance, the professor alone was responsible for the remuneration to be provided.   Whitsone's cupidity was not yet exhausted.   He applied for a share of the examination fees, on the ground of his having taken part in examining, but this application was also repelled.

On 29th May, 1827, the King issued a commission to Charles Badham, Fellow of the Royal College of Physicians, to be professor of Medicine, with all the fees, emoluments, and privileges belonging to the office. The Crown at the same time reserved power to appoint an additional professor to teach either the Theory or the Practice of Medicine, though both had been hitherto taught from the same chair.   To this salutary reservation the faculty demurred, declaring they did not understand it to imply a power on the part of the Crown to alter the constitution of the College, or to affect the rights of existing members or of Badham.   The new professor came down from London about the end of June, but could not be admitted for want of a quorum, and it was not till 3rd October that he was admitted.   After Freer's death the Senate arranged that the graduation fees, hitherto equally divided between the professors of Anatomy and Medicine, should be divided among all the medical professors, and that they all should take part in examining, but reserved to Jeffray a full half of the fees so long as he held the Anatomy chair. Badham contended that the royal warrant appointing him to the chair of Medicine conferred upon him every right, privilege, and emolument possessed by his predecessor, and claimed the same share of the graduation fees as had been given to Freer, desiring the Senate to reconsider their decision.   Having failed to move the Senate, he invoked the aid of the Royal Commission then sitting.   The Senate still adhered to their decision, pointing out that it was for the credit of the University that all the medical professors should examine for degrees, that during the lifetime of Freer they had been appointed to do so, and, except Burns, all of them had actually examined.   They also declared that the Senate had a right to appoint what fees should be paid for graduation, and how they should be disposed of ; and that they were not aware that the professor of Medicine was more interested in the study of Medicine than the other medical professors, a remark for which there was ample justification during Badham's incumbency. His claim to half the graduation fees failed, and he seems usually to have made haste to quit Glasgow at the end of the winter session, and to have been absent from the examinations for M.D.

There can be little doubt that Badham's influence was concerned in obtaining the degree of M.D., as it would seem for a kinsman of his own, in October, 1828, an occasion on which the Senate acted with greater remissness than in the case of any other medical degree conferred since the 18th century. It was reported that John Badham, who had been a student of Medicine five years and was described as very proficient, and who had attended the lectures in Botany in the University in the preceding summer, had returned for the purpose of becoming a candidate for graduation in Medicine. He was prevented from accomplishing his purpose, however, by severe illness which rendered it necessary that he should leave the country without delay, and, in the event of his recovery abroad, it would be of great importance to him to possess the degree of M.D. The Senate being satisfied from certificates laid before them of John Badham's qualifications, 'agreed unanimously to confer on him the honorary degree of Doctor in Medicine, without personal examination.'

On 11th December, 1832, Badham represented that the state of his health rendered him unable to give a course of lectures on the Theory of Medicine in addition to his course on the Practice of Medicine, and Harry Rainy was appointed to deal with the former branch of the subject. Rainy was re-appointed in April, 1833, when it was mentioned that a full course, meeting five days a week, would be given. In October, 1833, Badham, on account of the ill health of his son, sent a request for leave of absence for two months at the beginning of the session, leaving the faculty to appoint a substitute, but the faculty urged him to consider the great importance of his being present at the beginning of the session, and stated that if circumstances occurred during the session to render his absence unavoidable, they would adopt any practicable arrangements for his relief. Early in October, 1839, Badham wrote from Paris that, on account of ill health he must ask the faculty to dispense with his presence for the coming session, and to appoint a substitute. His colleagues requested him to send a medical certificate of his inability to discharge his duties as professor, and informed him that, if a substitute were appointed, he would be entitled to the whole of the fees paid by students. About the end of October medical certificates of Badham's inability were produced, and Rainy was appointed to lecture on Practice of Medicine and to receive all the fees, and a similar arrangement was made next year.

In this state of matters, Badham having been in the south of Europe since May, 1839, and the University having received no hint of his intended resignation, on 1st September, 1841, the Principal was startled by having a royal commission put into his hands, setting forth that the office of professor of Medicine was vacant by the resignation of Badham, and appointing Dr. William Thomson of Edinburgh to succeed him. Ignoring the University, Badham had sent his resignation to the Home Secretary, which was very irregular, and a worse irregularity remained behind, for a stipulation was introduced into the commission that the new professor should pay to Badham £300 a year during the life of the latter.   The Principal looked on the commission as so objectionable that he requested two Advocates, Mr. E. R. Sandford, and Mr. George Graham Bell, to give their opinion regarding its validity.   By 20th October the two Advocates had declared in favour of the validity of the commission, and the faculty, without putting the matter to a vote, agreed to sustain it, the new professor being admitted to office nine days afterwards.   The Principal thought the commission should not have been received, and gave in a vigorous protest, pointing out that the whole salary of the chair was £270, of which the College provided £220 and the Crown only £50, and alleging that Badham had been allowed to dispose of his professorship for a large and valuable consideration on the security of the Government. He recalled the decision of the Court of Session that resignations should be tendered to the faculty to be by them intimated to the Crown, and the regulation which empowered the principal and professors, with the rector and dean, to try professors for negligence or misconduct.   By a private and surreptitious resignation Badham had been relieved from responsibility to his academic superiors, and yet allowed to hold emoluments provided by them.   The Government had not only given official sanction in the commission to a discreditable pecuniary arrangement, they had also forgotten that a chair of Theory of Medicine had been founded in 1839, in conformity with the reservation in the commission granted to Badham, and they now reproduced with perfect and unmeaning accuracy the clause from Badham's commission reserving power to do what had already been done.

The new professor was a son of John Thomson, already mentioned as professor of Military Surgery and afterwards of Pathology at Edinburgh.   William Thomson studied Medicine at Edinburgh and Glasgow, as well as at Paris, Lyons, and other places abroad, and, as his course did not conform to the regulations of Edinburgh, he resorted to Marischal College, Aberdeen, for his degree of M.D.   Settling to practise at Edinburgh, he soon became a prominent member of the medical profession there, and was sent as a delegate to London in 1833 on behalf of the Royal College of Surgeons, and next year on behalf of the Royal College of Physicians and the University, to watch over proposals then being discussed in Parliament regarding medical legislation. At Edinburgh he acquired considerable experience in teaching, having lectured both on the Theory and Practice of Medicine, and done duty for his father in the work of the chair of Pathology. While careful and diligent in the duties of his chair, his activity was felt in many other directions. He was an *ex officio* director of the Royal Infirmary, and one of its physicians, delivering lectures in his turn, as the custom then was. He was also a director of the Asylum at Gartnavel, and in the winter of 1848-49, the post of physician-superintendent being suddenly left vacant at a time when a virulent outbreak of cholera occurred among the inmates, Professor Thomson came forward to carry on the work till a new superintendent could be appointed. The ravages of the disease were so fatal that more than forty inmates died while Thomson was in charge. Within the University Thomson was one of the chief administrators, and for a number of years he acted as Clerk to the faculty. While he held this post an extraordinary amount of work was thrown upon him in connection with the negotiations and legislation for the removal of the University from High Street to projected new buildings at Woodlands, an Act of Parliament being obtained in 1846, but the scheme falling through owing to the inability of the Railway Company to fulfil their engagements. He was also one of a Committee appointed in August, 1846, the members of which for a number of years assisted the Maitland Club in selecting and arranging the old records of the University printed in the *Munimenta*. A few months before this, in April, 1846, he had proposed to the faculty that the Deeds of Bursary and other foundations, with relative documents regulating the administration of funds left to the University, should be printed, as a tribute to the memory of benefactors and for convenience of reference. The faculty sanctioned the proposal, and appointed Fleming, Reid, and Thomson to see it carried out. In the midst of his beneficent activities symptoms of heart disease appeared, and Thomson died suddenly on 12th May, 1852, in the fiftieth year of his age.

He was succeeded by John Macfarlane, who graduated as M.D. at Glasgow in 1824, and not long afterwards was appointed surgeon to the Royal Infirmary. In 1832 he published a volume of Clinical Reports, which procured him some reputation, and he gradually acquired a considerable practice. He held the chair of Medicine for only ten years, retiring in 1862 owing to failing health, and dying in 1869. He does not count as one of the most prominent professors of Medicine, but his brothers and sister founded a medical Bursary bearing his name, which helps to perpetuate his memory.

In the year 1815 the Crown founded the two chairs of Midwifery and Surgery, and again in 1818 the two chairs of Botany and Chemistry. In 1815 the commissions issued to the first professors set forth that the King, considering it would be of importance in the education of youth and for the public advantage that a professor in the particular subject should be appointed in the University of Glasgow, and being desirous to give suitable encouragement to seminaries of learning, deemed it proper to erect a professorship accordingly. All the four new professors were reckoned to belong to the University but not to the College of Glasgow, and to be members of the Senate but not of the faculty or College meeting. For a long time it was usual to distinguish a professor in this position as a *regius* professor, though this was not a very logical use of the word, numbers of the College professors being also appointed by the Crown to chairs which the Crown had instituted. The chairs of Midwifery and Surgery were instituted and the first professors appointed by royal warrants dated from Carlton House on 31st July, 1815; but the original warrants in the case of Botany and Chemistry have not been recorded in the books of the Senate. Several restrictions suggested by the Court of Session's decision in the Muirhead case were very unguardedly introduced into the commissions of all the four professors. They were to have no right to examine for degrees in Medicine, to share in the fees paid by candidates, to participate in the funds or emoluments belonging to the College or University, or to interfere with the patrimonial rights of the other professors already established, or with the management of the funds vested in the College or University. It was also declared that they should not have right to vote in the election of a professor, or to exercise, in virtue of their appointment by the Crown, privileges as members of the College of Glasgow not otherwise belonging to them; but that they should be entitled to vote in the election of the Dean of Faculty, and to act as members of the University in cases not expressly excepted. In the case of Midwifery and Surgery a clause in the royal warrant reserved to the professor of Anatomy power to lecture on either of these subjects in the same manner as hitherto, or in whatever manner might be necessary for the proper treatment of his subject. A salary of £50 a year was granted from the Crown to each of the four new professors.

James Towers, who had long and successfully taught Midwifery as a lecturer, was appointed to be the first professor of the subject. On 6th May, 1817, on the proposal of Jeffray, the degree of C.M. was conferred on him and on Professor Burns. He did not long hold the chair, being succeeded by his son John Towers in 1820, the commission of the second Towers containing the same restrictions as were laid down in the case of his father.   On 8th December, 1828, John Towers had the double distinction of being created M.A. by the Senate and being appointed vice-rector by the poet Campbell.   Before the opening of session 1831-2 he had fallen into ill health, and he does not seem to have recovered sufficiently to resume teaching, the class being conducted by Professor Burns, assisted to some extent by his son Allan Burns.

Towers died in 1833, and on 16th October of that year the King issued a commission to Robert Lee, an obstetric physician and lecturer in London, who had graduated as M.D. at Edinburgh in 1814, to be professor of Midwifery.   His commission was not submitted to the Senate till 20th March, 1834, and he was not admitted to office till 30th April.   The restrictions inserted in his commission similar to those in the case of his two predecessors, may have interfered with his relish for the office ; at all events he was very slow to make his appearance at Glasgow, he seems never to have entered on teaching there, and he must have resigned office almost immediately after admission, for the commission to the next professor, William Cumin, is dated 16th July, 1834.

Cumin was a son of the professor of Oriental Languages, and graduated as M.A. at Glasgow in 1805 and M.D. in 1813.   For some time he was a surgeon in the Army, and afterwards professor of Botany in Anderson's College.   For the illustration of his lectures and the better instruction of his students he expended, shortly after his appointment to the Midwifery chair, about £200 in the purchase of preparations, drawings, casts, and models from Paris, London, and elsewhere, and of obstetrical apparatus and instruments.   The average number of students in his time was about eighty.   When he had conducted the class for about five years his health unfortunately gave way.   In October, 1839, he sent a letter informing his colleagues that he was about to repair to Clifton in the hope of being restored by its mild climate, and requesting them to permit Dr. James Wilson, who was 'for many years a successful private lecturer on Midwifery,' to conduct the class for next session, a proposal to which the Senate agreed.   In April, 1840, the Crown called for a return of professors whose duties were performed by assistants.   Cumin must have resigned soon after this, and he died in 1854.

The royal warrant appointing John MacMichan Pagan to be the next professor of Midwifery is dated 20th July, 1840.   On this occasion the sinister restrictions inserted in the commissions of previous professors were not repeated.   Having graduated as M.D. at Edinburgh in 1823, Pagan settled in Glasgow three or four years later, was for ten years lecturer on Medical Jurisprudence in Portland Street Medical School, and in the early months of 1840 lectured on the same subject in the University during the illness of Professor Cowan.   Sheriff Alison appointed him vice-rector in 1851, and when Lewis Gordon gave in his resignation as professor of Engineering in 1855, Pagan recommended the suppression of the chair—an illustration of the truth that no man is wise at all times. Pagan continued as professor of Midwifery till his death in 1868.

When the chair of Surgery was founded in July, 1815, a few weeks after the battle of Waterloo and the close of the great war, the advisers of the Crown were partly influenced by the needs of the Army and Navy, for the royal warrant founding the chair set forth that it would be for the public advantage that a professor of Surgery, particularly of that branch of it which relates to the wounds and diseases of the military and naval services, should be appointed in the University of Glasgow.   The first professor, John Burns, a son of the minister of the Barony, was educated at the Universities of Glasgow and Edinburgh, and obtained his first qualification from the Faculty of Physicians and Surgeons in 1796.   Soon afterwards he opened a private Medical School in which he taught Anatomy, Surgery, and for some time Midwifery ; and some years later he was taken into the staff of Anderson's College, and taught Anatomy and Surgery till he was made a professor in the University in 1815.   Upon being appointed surgeon to the Royal Infirmary, he began to give clinical lectures there in session 1797-98.   It is sometimes claimed that he was the earliest clinical teacher in that institution, but the statement in the minutes of Senate that Robert Agnew, who graduated as M.D. in May, 1796, had previously attended clinical lectures in the Royal Infirmary is inconsistent with this view.   Burns soon showed good ability as a teacher, and his work as an author commanded the respect of his contemporaries. His *Principles of Midwifery* went through ten editions, but a later and more elaborate work on the *Principles of Surgery*, though dealing with his own special subject, was not quite so successful.   His merits as a practitioner, professor, and author received numerous recognitions, and, among other distinctions, he was made a Fellow of the Royal Society and a Member of the Institute of France.

Burns was admitted to office on 3rd November, 1815, and soon attracted a large following of students.   The number attending his class fluctuated considerably, but his minimum would compare favourably with the maximum in some other classes.   For some years preceding 1830 the average number of students of Surgery was about 195, in 1833 there were 213, in 1834, 132, and in 1835, 143.   In 1839 or earlier he had begun to exercise his students in the performance of operations on the dead body.

Burns took an active part in the work of the Medical Faculty, although it appears that he did not examine for the degree of M.D. till after the death of Freer, when all the professors who examined were allowed to participate in the fees. It is generally believed that the Senate acted under the guidance of Burns when, in 1817, they resolved to grant degrees in Surgery, but the minutes do not show with whom the proposal originated. On 6th May following, the degree of C.M. was conferred for the first time, Professors Towers and Burns being the recipients, and the latter also obtained the degree of M.D. in 1828. When the Faculty of Physicians and Surgeons were contesting the validity of the degree of C.M. as a qualification to practise within their territory, Burns, along with Jeffray, Thomson, Hooker, and Towers protested against the fees for that degree, normally divided among the professors who examined for it, being used to defray the expenses of the lawsuit. The second Professor Towers having fallen into ill health, the Senate in October, 1831, approved of an arrangement by which Burns undertook to conduct the class for the ensuing session, receiving half the fees paid by students, while Towers retained the other half and the salary paid by the Crown. In November, 1832, the Senate requested Burns to conduct the Midwifery class for the ensuing session, Towers being still in poor health. Before the beginning of another session Towers had died, but there was no intimation of the appointment of a successor; and on 1st November, 1833, the Senate, considering themselves bound to provide for the teaching of Midwifery, requested Professor Burns and his son Allan to continue their valuable services in taking charge of the class. The arrangement was intimated to Lord Melbourne, who wrote approving of it as a temporary measure, and stating that he was very sensible of the attention of the Principal and Professors, but without telling them that on 16th October the King had issued a commission to Dr. Robert Lee to be professor.

Frequent attempts were made in Burns' time to pass through Parliament measures for regulating the medical profession, and his colleagues relied greatly on his advice and help in preparing memorials and representations, and concerting measures for defending the interests or securing the objects the University had in view. On an important occasion in 1845, when one of the numerous Medical Bills was under consideration in Parliament, Burns was requested to proceed to London to watch its progress, and was empowered to employ parliamentary agents to aid him in such action as he might think expedient. The Senate began with adverse criticism of certain clauses, but they appear soon to have become more hostile, and desired the rejection of the measure. Eventually the Bill was rejected or withdrawn, and the credit of this result was attributed in a considerable degree to the exertions of Burns. In January, 1847, Burns ventured to remind his colleagues that his expenses in London had amounted to £111 16s. 6d., and applied for repayment. The Senate appointed a Committee to consider the subject, and in August following requested him to sit to Mr. Graham Gilbert for his portrait, to be preserved in testimony of their high esteem for his personal and professional character, and their sense of his services to the University, and especially to the Medical School. The resolution was passed unanimously, but Professor James Thomson, who had not been present at the time, afterwards desired it to be recorded that, though he had the most friendly feelings towards Burns, and looked upon him as having greatly contributed to the advantage and fame of the University, he dissented from the resolution to pay for his portrait from funds under the management of the Senate, the application of which he considered to be so definitely fixed that they could not be applied to other purposes. The portrait was executed in due time and delivered to the University.

In 1849 Burns made over to the Senate a collection of casts, models, and preparations which had belonged to his son Allan, a promising young practitioner who had taken part for a time in conducting the Midwifery class, and had resigned a barren appointment as lecturer on Forensic Medicine, made after a chair had been founded and a professor appointed by the Crown, and who died prematurely in 1843. Though Burns was now five or six years beyond the allotted span of three score and ten, age had been less severe with him than with some younger men, yet his long, active, and useful career was nearing a tragic close. He was returning to Glasgow by the ill-fated steamer Orion, and on 18th June, 1850, the vessel was wrecked near Portpatrick, and he was one of the victims. His colleagues, deeply moved at the news of his death, declared that for many years he had been a bright ornament of the University by the exemplary and successful discharge of his immediate duties, as well as by the high reputation he attained, extending to every part of the civilised world, and raising that of the Medical School to which he belonged ; and that his zeal and humanity in professional work, his high-minded integrity, his kindly spirit and deportment had won the esteem and confidence of all.

James Adair Lawrie succeeded Burns as Professor of Surgery. Both his father and his grandfather had been ministers of Newmilns, and the poet Burns, albeit unused to the praying mood, after spending a night at the grandfather's manse, left a prayer in verse invoking manifold blessings on the whole family of Lawries. As a student young Lawrie held the Brisbane bursary, and after graduating as M.D. at Glasgow in 1822 he was some time in the service of the East India Company, and subsequently became Professor of Surgery in Anderson's College. His commission as professor in the University was dated 17th July, 1850, and after he had read a dissertation concerning the use of Chloroform in Surgery he was admitted to office on 18th September, 1850. Like his predecessor Burns, Lawrie was not active in asserting the claims of the regius professors against the faculty or College professors, but both Burns and Lawrie took a leading part in discussions regarding legislation for the medical profession. The Medical Act of 1858 assigned to the Universities of Glasgow and St. Andrews one representative in the General Medical Council, and Lawrie was nominated by the Senate of the former University on 26th October, and a few days later it was reported that the Senate of St. Andrews had concurred. Lawrie died at Bridge of Allan on 23rd November, 1859, at the comparatively early age of fifty-eight.

About 1808 Dr. Thomas Brown ceased to teach the Botany class, and for some years Professor Jeffray seems to have conducted it, but in May, 1816, the faculty agreed to a proposal of Jeffray's that Dr. Robert Graham should teach the class, and made the usual allowance of £20 for the purchase of plants to illustrate the teaching. Next year Graham was again appointed, and the allowance of £20 for plants was made to him. At that time a keen interest in Botany had been aroused, and a movement was in progress for the establishment of new Botanic Gardens on a public footing, to which the University contributed £2,000. Overtures had probably been made to the Government for the establishment of a chair of Botany, and on 3rd March, 1818, a commission from the Crown appointing Graham to be professor of that subject was produced. About a fortnight later he was admitted to office, the Senate asserting their right to appoint examiners for medical degrees, and appointing Graham accordingly, notwithstanding a restrictive clause in his commission. During his short tenure of the chair at Glasgow, Graham is said to have been much occupied with the laying out of the Botanic Gardens. In January, 1820, the Town Council of Edinburgh appointed him professor of Botany in their University; and as the Edinburgh Botanic Gardens were about to be transferred from Leith Walk, it fell to Graham to superintend the formation of new Gardens in Inverleith Row, where they still remain.

At a meeting on 27th April, 1820, a royal warrant was produced for William Jackson Hooker to be professor of Botany at Glasgow, and, as the time for beginning the lectures had arrived, his admission was carried through with unusual swiftness. He was appointed to read a Latin discourse *De Laudibus Botanicis*, which he seems to have composed extempore and read forthwith, and being allowed to take the oaths and sign the Confession of Faith afterwards, he was admitted there and then. Five days later the Senate marked their appreciation of the new professor's abilities by conferring on him the honorary degree of LL.D. Zealous and successful as Hooker was in teaching, for a considerable time he had a smaller following of students than the other professors in the faculty of Medicine. Till 1833 the average was about 65, but after that, probably owing to some change in the regulations, the number doubled. The salary from the Crown to the professor of Botany had been £50, but in 1826 the King raised it to £150 by appropriating to it £100 previously paid to the University under a gift of Queen Anne. In 1830 the average emoluments were set down as about £320 a year, but with the increase of students after 1833 a considerable improvement must have taken place. In 1827 when it was proposed to devote the fees received for the degree of C.M. to the defence of the graduates in Surgery against whom the Faculty of Physicians and Surgeons had raised an action, Hooker emphatically protested against withdrawing thirty guineas for this purpose from his income, which he declared did not then exceed £200 a year. He had expended more than this on professional pursuits, and if he continued to be a professor, it was because he thought it an honour to be connected with the medical professors, whose celebrity was as great throughout Britain and Europe as it was the envy of the sister University of Edinburgh. Botany did not, any more than Mathematics or Greek or Civil Law, form a part of the curriculum in Surgery ; but while he continued a member of the Society he would co-operate with his brethren in supporting the dignity of the Medical School, and, if need were, of the University. In 1831 he protested against admitting a candidate to examination for M.D. who had not attended a Botany class in a University ; and in 1834, along with Thomas Thomson and John Couper, he again objected to applying the fees for C.M. to defraying the expenses of the lawsuit. In December, 1838, the Senate, having previously recognised other courses held in the Medical Schools of London and Dublin, extended their recognition to Botany also. In February following, Hooker moved that this resolution, passed in his absence and without his knowledge, should be rescinded, and that he should receive compensation for pecuniary loss suffered by him in consequence of the admission of candidates who had attended the courses of Botany recently recognised. On 29th March, 1839, it was resolved that any change affecting the privileges of the chair of Botany should not be adopted except as part of a general measure for revising the medical curriculum.

The respite was brief, for next month a revised code of regulations for graduation in Medicine and Surgery was adopted, and Hooker entered another animated protest. He alleged that the measure now passed would diminish the number of students attending his class and reduce his income, and that Botany, which was required for the Army and Navy medical services, could not be effectively taught in the schools now placed on a level with chartered Universities, as they had no Botanic Gardens and there was no security for the competence of their teachers. In 1841 Hooker was appointed to be Director of the Botanic Gardens at Kew; and in October of that year a commission, dated 11th May preceding, was presented to the Senate, appointing John Hutton Balfour to be professor of Botany, and to have the oversight of the Botanic Garden. Hooker appears to have followed so far the example of Badham, and to have given in his resignation to the Government without informing the University. When Balfour's commission was produced, Fleming desired it marked that in his opinion the Senate, before receiving it, should have a formal resignation from Hooker. However, on 29th October, after reading a dissertation *De Plantis quae Strychnium praebunt*, Balfour was admitted. In October, 1843, he applied for a room in the College to accommodate his dried specimens, and a few days later desired to be allowed to occupy one of the College houses on paying rent for it, in order that he might be able to keep his plants within the College. The faculty, though they did not grant his request for a house, seem to have allowed him some accommodation. In 1845 Balfour was transferred to Edinburgh to succeed Graham, who died in August. As an example of the incidental benefit which the public have derived from professors of Botany taking their students into the country on excursions, it may be mentioned that shortly after this Balfour was instrumental in starting the controversy which ended in establishing a right of way on the part of the public from Blair Athole through Glen Tilt to Braemar.

The vacant chair was given to George Arnott Walker Arnott, a graduate in Arts of Edinburgh, who became an Advocate in 1821, but soon turned aside from the study of Law to that of Botany, to which he gave much time and attention. He was admitted to office in December, 1845, when he read a dissertation *De Sexibus Plantarum*, and afterwards pursued the even tenor of his way as professor till 1868. He was appointed vice-rector by the Duke of Argyll in 1855.

The year 1818 witnessed the establishment of a chair of Chemistry, as well as of Botany. Dr. Thomas Thomson was admitted professor on 17th March, in virtue of a presentation from the Crown, and as in the case of Graham, the Senate appointed him to be an examiner for degrees in Medicine and Surgery, notwithstanding a restrictive clause in his presentation. Thomson was worthy to stand at the head of the dynasty of professors of Chemistry. At the age of twenty-three he succeeded his brother as editor of the third edition of the *Encyclopædia Britannica*. He published a *System of Chemistry* in 1802, which went through numerous editions, and he was the author of a *History of Chemistry*, a *History of the Royal Society, Outlines of Mineralogy and Geology*, and various other works. While a medical student at Edinburgh, he came under the influence of Black, who inspired him with a strong and lasting zeal for Chemistry, and shortly after graduating as M.D. in 1799 he established a laboratory and began to teach Chemistry. About 1802 he invented the oxy-hydrogen blowpipe, and soon afterwards formed a numerical nomenclature of oxides to indicate the graduated ascent in the process of oxidation in the series of compounds formed by certain elements with oxygen. He also made a beginning with the use of symbols in Chemistry, the idea being taken up and further developed by Berzelius. Thomson was much impressed by Dalton's Atomic Theory which had been privately made known to him some years before, and in the third edition of his *System of Chemistry*, published in 1807, he expounded it with such clearness and force as to gain general acceptance for it. He discovered a number of chemical compounds, and made a comprehensive and elaborate series of experiments to determine the specific gravities of all the important gases then known.

Upon his appointment to the newly founded chair at Glasgow, besides teaching a class, which in the early years numbered 140 or 150, he applied himself with great ardour and diligence to research and investigation, and in 1825, the year in which he was appointed vice-rector by Brougham, he published an attempt to establish the first principles of Chemistry by experiment, and five or six years later his *History of Chemistry*. These works were very favourably received and drew the attention of those interested in Chemistry to Glasgow. Meantime the development of the subject and the increase in the number of students urgently called for better accommodation, and new buildings for the Chemistry department erected in Shuttle Street, at a short distance from the University, were opened in 1831. The edifice in Shuttle Street included a laboratory as well as classrooms, and Lord Kelvin and others have stated their belief that this was the earliest laboratory in the world for research in Chemistry and the instruction of University students in that science. This is rather unfair to Cullen and Black, in whose time there was a laboratory in the University in which good work was done, though the organisation might not be quite the same as in modern laboratories, and possibly the organisation in Thomson's might not be the same as in laboratories of the present day. Both Cullen and Black laid out appreciable sums of their own on laboratory equipment, and the latter, in the face of considerable opposition, persuaded his colleagues to expend £350 on a new laboratory. Cullen's laboratory existed more than eighty years, and Black's nearly seventy years, before Thomson's.

Like several other professors, Thomson continued in office for a number of years after age had made it desirable that he should retire. From session 1844-45 or perhaps from an earlier date he was assisted by his nephew and son-in-law, Dr. Robert Dundas Thomson, in carrying on the classes. In April, 1845, this gentleman requested from the Senate a certificate as to his attainments, and Dr. William Thomson and Dr. Balfour were appointed to draw it up. Possibly this was a strategy to disarm criticism, for the classes fell more and more under the care of the younger Thomson, and the Senate had themselves certified his efficiency. In November, 1848, a letter sent by Thomas Thomson to John Couper for communication to the Senate was submitted, stating that from age and infirmity the former was unable to conduct the Chemistry class for the coming session, and had gone to Nice to pass the winter; and that he recommended Dr. Robert D. Thomson to take charge of the class in his absence. The Senate after some delay declared that they felt called upon to express their surprise that Professor Thomson had not formally communicated with the Senate before leaving the country, and had delegated his duties to an assistant without obtaining consent. Being fully satisfied, however, that Dr. Robert D. Thomson was qualified to teach Chemistry, they accepted his services, and authorised him to teach the Chemistry class and the Laboratory for the coming session. Next session the professor having applied in a more regular manner, his nephew was authorised to conduct the class, and from this time the whole work of teaching Chemistry seems to have devolved upon him. Professor Thomson died on 29th June, 1852, and his colleagues recalled with pride the share taken by the University in the promotion of Science, especially of Chemistry, and the discoveries and advances made by those who had taught Chemistry at Glasgow, which reflected high honour on the institution to which they belonged.

Thomas Anderson, who graduated as M.D. at Edinburgh in 1841, succeeded Thomson as professor of Chemistry, being admitted to office in October, 1852. He held the chair for twenty-two years, dying on 2nd November, 1874.

Dr. Richard Millar taught Materia Medica in the University as a lecturer for forty years from 1791 to 1831, and in the latter year the Crown founded a chair and made him professor of the subject. The faculty of the College were singularly well affected to him, for, though other lectureships were held from year to year, in 1819 they appointed him to be lecturer for life, with a salary of £70, besides the class fees paid by students; reserved power to appoint another lecturer who should have right to the fees, if Millar should be incapacitated by old age or otherwise; and stipulated that if the Crown should appoint him professor, as had happened with other lecturers, his claim to the £70 from the College should cease. The number of students attending the Materia Medica class in Millar's later years was between 80 and 90. After Millar had been made a professor, the faculty, from regard for his diligence, ability, and exemplary conduct as lecturer for more than forty years, resolved to continue the £70 of salary during his time, but without incurring any obligation to do so in the case of his successor. In 1827 the Senate granted a certificate of their favourable opinion of Millar's character and qualifications as a practitioner and lecturer, upon his own application, apparently to enable him to combat some outside aspersions.

Age and illness soon cut short Millar's course as a professor, and the Senate had no regular intimation of his resignation till Dr. John Couper's commission to be his successor was submitted to them. Millar had resigned to the Home Secretary who forthwith filled up the vacancy, and when, in October, 1833, Couper's commission was produced, a letter from Millar to the principal was also read, explaining that ill health had obliged him to resign, and expressing regret for the irregularity in not communicating his resignation to the Senate, but pointing out that his intention to resign had long been known, and that Couper had announced himself as a candidate several months before. The Senate declared that the resignation should have been sent to them for communication to the Crown, and regretted that the Government had proceeded to an appointment in such circumstances; but as Millar's health made retirement necessary and the circumstances of the University required that the office should be promptly filled, they agreed to accept his letter to the principal as a resignation, and to proceed to the admission of Couper. Extracts of the minutes on the subject were ordered to be sent to the Home Secretary and to Lord Melbourne, with the expression of a hope that the Senate would receive an answer relieving them from the apprehension of being again called upon to perform a duty every way so painful. It does not appear that any assurance of the kind expected was ever received, and several other resignations of the same sort occurred before long.

The chair of Materia Medica had been founded without any endowment by the Government, and soon after his appointment Couper applied to the faculty of the College, as the body having the power of the academic purse, to make an allowance of £60 for providing apparatus, and to grant him a salary. The faculty agreed to the grant for apparatus, but resolutely refused a salary, alleging that the salary they had given to Millar had been conferred from personal regard and consideration for long service, and was expressly guarded against being treated as a precedent. The foundation by the Crown of a chair without endowments was a measure of such a dangerous and alarming aspect that they could not countenance it, or encourage the repetition of similar appointments. They hoped, however, that, on a proper representation to the Government, Couper might receive at least as good a salary as the other regius professors. Couper tried to move the faculty to reconsider, but in vain. In May, 1836, they re-affirmed their refusal of salary, expressing their willingness to consider an application Couper had made for a laboratory, if he presented it in a separate form without irrelevant and unreasonable accompaniments, and their desire that the chair should receive an adequate endowment from the Government. Couper had reminded the faculty of the large augmenta-tions they had voted to themselves, an argument that did not produce a favourable impression. They answered that the augmentations were uni-formly made in the form and under the authority prescribed by the consti-tution of the College, that none had taken place since 1817, and that those who received them did not follow lucrative professions distinct from their professorships. The last assertion was only partly accurate, for a number of members of the faculty held lucrative places in the Church along with their academic positions ; and if the faculty really regarded the foundation by the Crown of unendowed chairs as dangerous and alarming, it is strange that they made no sign of their apprehension in the case of Millar to whom they continued a salary, though they had previously passed a resolution not to do so.

In 1852 Couper dissented from the resolution to send a memorial to the Queen and the Lords of the Treasury in regard to the buildings, asserting that the evident object was to procure removal to a new site, and that this would involve serious evils, especially to the Medical School. When Couper died in 1855 he was described by his colleagues as one of the most eminent physicians in Glasgow, and a teacher whose expositions were comprehensive and lucid in an unusual degree. He was succeeded by John Alexander Easton, who graduated as M.D. at Glasgow in 1836, and taught Materia Medica in Anderson's College for fifteen years before being made professor of the same subject in the University. He held the chair till his death in 1865, and introduced a preparation known as Easton's syrup.

In 1839 Queen Victoria founded the two chairs of Forensic Medicine and Theory of Physic. The preamble of the royal warrants instituting these chairs followed the phraseology previously used in similar cases, and set forth that the sovereign considered it would be of importance in the education of youth and for the public advantage that a regius chair should be erected, and being desirous to give suitable encouragement to public seminaries of learning, in each case erected the regius chair accordingly. In appointing the professors the sinister restrictions introduced into too many previous commissions were this time avoided, and the new professors were declared to have all the rights and privileges which belonged to any other professor in the University. Both the royal warrants, dated from St. James's on 9th July, 1839, superscribed by the Queen and signed by Lord John Russell, were in one respect disappointing, as they provided no salary for the incumbents.

In 1832 the Senate had deliberated at great length on the propriety of instituting a lectureship on Medical Jurisprudence, otherwise called Forensic Medicine, and early next year a committee reported that, though there was a course of instruction at Edinburgh University, attendance upon it was optional, and that such a course was not required at any other University in Scotland, at Oxford, Cambridge, or Dublin, the College of Surgeons, London, the Apothecaries Company, Dublin, or for the East India Company's service ; while, on the other hand, the College of Surgeons, Edinburgh, required a course of three months, the Faculty of Physicians and Surgeons, Glasgow, one of six months, the Apothecaries Company, London, a course of forty-five lectures, and candidates for service in the Army and Navy were recommended to attend a course. No action was taken for some years, but when new regulations for graduation in Medicine and in Surgery were adopted in 1839, a course in Forensic Medicine was required in each case ; and on 29th April the Senate agreed to meet on 7th August to appoint a lecturer on that subject. When the Senate met on 7th August, though the Clerk had in his possession the royal warrant erecting a chair of Forensic Medicine and appointing a professor, and though Cumin and Nichol advised its production, the majority, led by the principal, ignored for a time the existence of the warrant, and elected Allan Burns, son of the professor of Surgery, to be lecturer on Forensic Medicine. When this abortive appointment had been made, the Clerk produced the two royal warrants founding the chairs of Medical Jurisprudence and Forensic Medicine (so the first chair was named in the warrant) and Theory of Physic ; and appointing Dr. Robert Cowan to be professor of the first subject, and Dr. Andrew Buchanan to be professor of the second. Consideration of the new appointments was deferred till 4th September, and special intimation was ordered to be sent to the rector, Sir James Graham, a prominent supporter of Sir Robert Peel.

On 4th September the Senate, while sustaining the commissions and resolving to admit the new professors, expressed their disappointment at the absence of a provision for salaries, an omission which they hoped would be supplied; and appointed the principal, Burns, and Fleming to prepare a memorial against the institution by the Crown of unendowed chairs, which was afterwards presented to Lord Melbourne by Sir James Graham.   In a letter to Lord Melbourne, Graham declared that, when the hereditary revenues of the Crown in Scotland were at the disposal of the sovereign, the royal bounty had provided liberally for the endowment of professorships (a statement more easily made than substantiated); and argued that if the royal prerogative were exercised in creating new professorships and selecting persons competent to instruct, it could not be intended to leave these instructors without endowment, and that, since the hereditary revenues of the Crown had been transferred to the public, Parliament would not refuse its aid if the sum required were really necessary for the better education of the students of Glasgow University. Melbourne replied that the memorial had been sent to the Home Secretary, that he might consider it along with the report of the Commissioners appointed to enquire into the state of the University.

Robert Cowan, the first professor of Forensic Medicine, graduated as M.D. at Glasgow in 1834, was for some time physician and afterwards surgeon in the Royal Infirmary, and, shortly before his appointment to the University chair, gave his thoughts to the Epidemiology and Vital Statistics of Glasgow, on which he published several papers.   Allan Burns thanked the Senate for the honour conferred upon him, but declined to be lecturer, seeing the Crown had founded a chair; but a further opportunity still awaited him, for unfortunately ill health compelled Cowan early in 1840 to intimate to the Senate that he was unable to teach.   Upon this, the Senate requested Allan Burns to conduct the class, but he again declined, and the work was taken up by Dr. Pagan, afterwards professor of Midwifery.   Cowan seems to have conducted the class in the early months of 1841, but in October of that year he died.

In December, 1841, Dr. Harry Rainy presented his commission as successor to Cowan.   It was countersigned by Sir James Graham, who had now become Home Secretary, and bore a postscript by three Lords of the Treasury authorising Rainy to be placed on the proper schedule at the established rate, though no sum was stated.   At the time of his admission the Senate were in trouble regarding the heavy costs consequent on the adverse decision of the House of Lords in the process between the University and the Faculty of Physicians and Surgeons, and Rainy, like a careful man, desired to have it minuted that he considered he was not personally liable, as he was appointed and admitted after the judgment of the House of Lords. Rainy, who held the chair till 1872, obtained his first qualification as a practitioner from the Faculty of Physicians and Surgeons, and graduated as M.D. in the University in 1833. Before this he had become a member of the teaching staff. In December, 1832, Badham, the valetudinarian professor of Medicine, represented that his health did not enable him, in addition to lecturing on Practice of Medicine, to conduct the course hitherto held on Theory or Institutes of Medicine, and was authorised to employ Rainy to lecture on the latter subject. This arrangement was renewed in 1833, and seems to have continued during the rest of Badham's time. Not only so, but towards the end Badham ceased to lecture on the Practice of Medicine, and in October, 1839, Rainy was appointed to conduct the class in that subject also. In 1852 the Earl of Eglinton appointed Rainy to be vice-rector. Next year Loudoniana and Rothseiana voted for Eglinton, while Glottiana and Transforthana voted for Tennyson, and Rainy being, according to the custom of the time, empowered to give the casting vote, declared for Eglinton. A thoughtful and active member possessing considerable influence among his colleagues, Rainy rendered valuable service to the University in combating and at length helping to secure the abolition of the sinister and exclusive authority which had too long been exercised by the faculty of the College. He took a kindly interest in medical students, and made over £1,500 to establish bursaries for their benefit.

The other subject in which a chair was founded in 1839, Theory of Physic or Institutes of Medicine, had long been taught from the chair of Medicine, though Badham was unequal to the task of teaching both the Practice and Theory, and Rainy was called in to teach the latter branch. In the commission granted to Badham the King declared that it might afterwards be found expedient that the two branches should be taught each by a separate professor, and reserved power to the Crown to name an additional professor for teaching either the Theory or the Practice of Physic. Queen Victoria acted on this reservation when in 1839 Dr. Andrew Buchanan was appointed professor of the Theory of Physic. He graduated as M.D. at Glasgow in 1822, and a few years afterwards was appointed professor of Materia Medica in Anderson's College, a post which he held till made a professor in the University. He was one of the first to investigate the phenomena of the coagulation of blood. On 21st March, 1849, Macaulay appointed him to be vice-rector, and about two years later he received the thanks of the Senate for his management of finance at a time when the pressure of the expenses of the unsuccessful action with the Faculty of Physicians and Surgeons was severely felt. For some time Buchanan had difficulty in finding adequate accommodation for his class, and he was an ally of Rainy's in the warfare against the faculty of the College. He continued in office till 1876, and towards the end of his tenure, having declined into the vale of years, he could not altogether escape the effects of age.

Till the nineteenth century no code of regulations for graduation in Medicine was put on record, though the measure was several times proposed, and resolutions were passed regarding particular points. The course of study and the examination to test the competence of candidates were regulated partly by use and wont and partly by express enactment. But in November, 1801, the Senate appointed Cumin, Jeffray, and Freer to enquire into the existing regulations for medical degrees, and to suggest what alterations might be advisable. They reported shortly afterwards, and on 30th March, 1802, the Senate enacted a code of regulations, specifying in detail the length of the curriculum, the courses to be attended, and the examinations to be passed. A curriculum of three years (or sessions of six months) was required, one year at least being in the University of Glasgow, while the remainder, if not in that University, had to be in some other University or Medical School of reputation. The candidate was required to produce evidence of having attended courses on Anatomy, Surgery, Chemistry, Pharmacy, Theory and Practice of Physic, Materia Medica, and Botany; and to undergo three examinations conducted in Latin by the medical professors, the first in Anatomy and Physiology, the second in Theory and Practice of Physic, and the third in Chemistry, Materia Medica, Pharmacy, and Botany. If the examiners reported favourably, the next step was to propound to the candidate an Aphorism of Hippocrates and a case of disease, on each of which he had to compose a Latin commentary to be read before the Senate on an appointed day. On that day he was also liable to be further questioned before the Senate on any branch of medical science. If he passed this ordeal successfully, he might graduate there and then, unless he had published a thesis. Candidates who published theses were required to defend them in the *Comitia*, which included the Senate, the students, and other members of the University. It was laid down that no thesis should be received if it contained illiberal reflections on the writings or lectures of any medical teachers or writers; and that the name of every medical student attending the University should be annually inscribed in the University album. A strictly defined minimum of three years of study had not hitherto been laid down, though for some time previously most candidates would not have fallen short of it. The requirement that at least one year must have been spent in the University of Glasgow was also a new one; but in most of the other points the regulations only expressed the previous practice, and it will presently be seen how subsequent regulations were gradually developed.   Though three examinations were prescribed, they were not separated by any appreciable intervals, but only formed three stages of one complex examination.   Orders were given that the new regulations for graduation in Medicine should be advertised in the *Glasgow Courier*, in one paper published at each of Edinburgh, Dublin, and Belfast, and in two London papers.

Having thus revised and put in order its own regulations, the University of Glasgow invited the University of Edinburgh to co-operate in an effort to bring the medical degrees of the other Scottish Universities to a reasonable standard of efficiency.   Members of the various Scottish Universities who repaired to Edinburgh to take part in the proceedings of the General Assembly of the national Church sometimes held meetings there to discuss matters affecting the Universities, and they had recently been in conference regarding the standing to be required of Arts students before admission to the Divinity classes.   In January, 1804, Freer proposed that the representatives of the Universities who met in Edinburgh at the time of the next General Assembly should consider measures for placing the degrees in Medicine of the different Universities on a more equal footing.   A representation was afterwards drawn up, setting forth that degrees in Medicine were conferred at St. Andrews and at the two Universities of Aberdeen without personal knowledge of the candidates, and without requiring them to attend courses of instruction at the institutions which conferred the degrees or elsewhere, these Universities relying solely on general certificates from persons at a distance.   As a consequence, medical degrees were sometimes conferred on the undeserving, which was detrimental to the health and safety of the lieges, unfair to those who, at a considerable sacrifice of time and money, went through a regular course in order to obtain a proper qualification, discreditable to the particular Universities concerned, and a possible source of injury to the reputation of the other Scottish Universities.

Though the Universities had no control over each other, and the abuse had now been incorporated with the interests of individuals and might be difficult to remedy, yet, if Edinburgh would heartily concur, a joint representation should be made setting forth the abuse and its consequences, and requesting the Universities concerned to make some improvements and bring their systems at least nearer to a just standard.   If the representation proved ineffective, it was suggested that Edinburgh and Glasgow should take means to make public their own regulations and practice in regard to graduation in Medicine, and the effort made, though without vail, to render the medical degrees of the other Scottish Universities honourable marks and evidence of a complete and regular medical education. Probably the other Universities would desire to prevent such a statement going forth to the public, and might be induced to make some reasonable improvements. It was not clear whether Edinburgh would concur, and if not, doubts were entertained whether Glasgow could with advantage bring forward the subject. The Faculty approved the proposals, and authorised their representatives, in case the subject were introduced when the conference took place at the time of the General Assembly, to support measures for promoting the end in view.

On the 18th and 19th of May, 1804, delegates of the various Universities met in Edinburgh, St. Andrews being represented by Dr. Arnott, Dr. Henry, and Dr. Hill; Glasgow by Principal Taylor and Jardine; King's College, Aberdeen, by Dr. Gerrard; and Edinburgh by Dr. Finlayson, Dr. Hope, and Principal Baird, the last named being in the chair. The co-operation of Edinburgh had been secured, and Dr. Hope introduced the subject, urging that the Universities, both from a regard for their own dignity and the health of their fellowmen, should be strictly cautious in conferring medical degrees. He then submitted draft regulations which, after discussion and modification, were sent to the different Universities for consideration. It was proposed that no person should be received as a candidate for M.D. unless he produced certificates of study at a celebrated University or Medical School during the full medical session of three several years, and of having attended during that period the courses of lectures on Anatomy, Chemistry, Materia Medica, Institutions of Medicine, Practice of Physic, and also Botany if a course in that subject were given; that evidence of good character and liberal education should be required; and that every candidate should be strictly examined in Latin in the various branches of medical science by the professor or professors of Medicine in the University from which the degree was sought, or, in the case of Universities which conferred the degree on the recommendation and attestation of two physicians, by the two physicians, who, in that case, must certify that they had examined the candidate and found him worthy of the degree. After consideration, the Faculty of the College of Glasgow approved the earlier portions of the proposed regulations, but disapproved of the degree being conferred on the recommendation and attestation of two physicians. The effort to raise the general standard of Scottish degrees in Medicine is the point of chief importance in this episode, as the regulations adopted at Glasgow in 1802 were more stringent than those now proposed for general adoption.

The subsequent evolution of the code of regulations for graduation in

Medicine may be briefly described. In 1812 attendance on a course in Midwifery was required, and also on a course in Surgery unless the candidate attended three sessions in Anatomy, but in 1817 a course in Surgery was made compulsory. In 1824 attendance for at least two years at a public hospital was prescribed, the two years being made up of two sessions of six months. The regulations of 1824 set forth that the three examinations which candidates must undergo before the medical Examiners, dealing, first, with Anatomy and Physiology, second, with Institutes and Practice of Physic, and, third, with Chemistry, Materia Medica and Pharmacy, were usually conducted in English, while the commentaries on the prescribed Aphorism and case must be in Latin, as also the thesis, if the candidate submitted one, and the answering before the Senate. In 1826 an important advance was made by lengthening the currciulum to four years; and in 1828 a Committee recommended that the Latin commentaries on the Aphorism of Hippocrates and the case of disease, having degenerated into mere forms, should be abolished, but that candidates should be required to show their knowledge of Latin by translating a passage from that language into English, as well as a passage from English into Latin, if desired. It was further recommended that every candidate should be required to write in English a dissertation on a medical case, and that, instead of the examination being broken up into three parts, there should be one general examination in Anatomy, Physiology, Chemistry, Pharmacy, and Practice of Physic.

In 1833 these proposals were adopted and embodied in the rules, candidates were ordered to be examined in Botany, and it was laid down that all the professors in the Medical Faculty should be examiners, that three examiners should be required to constitute a quorum, and that only those examiners who actually attended should share in the examination fees. Considerable improvements were made in 1839, when a course of three months in Forensic Medicine and at least six months in Practical Anatomy were prescribed, and it was ordered that candidates should be examined in all the subjects of the curriculum, provision being thus made for examination, not only in the new subject of Forensic Medicine, but also in Midwifery, which had been included in the curriculum from 1812, and in Surgery, included in the curriculum from 1817. Regulations designed to secure better attendance on the part of medical students and more efficient supervision of them were also passed in 1839, these regulations requiring the registration of all medical students at the University Library, and forbidding enrolment in any class after 1st December, except by special permission of the Senate. A bye-law of retrograde tendency was passed at the instigation of Pagan in 1853, and the best that can be said of it is that it appears to have been seldom put in practice. The board of medical examiners were empowered, when deemed desirable or expedient, to admit to examination candidates for medical and surgical degrees who had attended for three winter and three summer sessions, instead of the four winter sessions prescribed by the regulations, on condition that all such cases should be reported to the Senate before the candidates proceeded to graduation.

When the degree of C.M. was instituted in 1817, it was enacted that a curriculum of at least two sessions in a University should be required, one of the sessions being necessarily in the University of Glasgow, that the attendance should include two courses of Anatomy and Surgery, and one course on each of Materia Medica and Pharmacy, Chemistry, Institutions of Medicine, Practice of Medicine, Midwifery, and Principles and Practice of Surgery, together with at least twelve months' attendance at a public hospital; and that the candidate must undergo examination in all these subjects. For the degree in Surgery a fee of ten guineas was to be charged, eight of which were to be divided among the medical professors who examined for the degree, a fee of six shillings to the bedellus being also imposed. At the outset provision was made for conferring the degree of Bachelor of Surgery as well as Master, but the former degree was suffered to drop after 1822, being conferred in only seven cases. In 1826 the University increased the stringency of the regulations for the degree of C.M., and extended the curriculum to three years. In 1839 a curriculum of four years was enjoined, each year including at least two courses of six months, and every student being obliged to attend at least one year and take not fewer than three courses in the University of Glasgow. Students were required to attend for two years at a general hospital, devoting half of the time to Surgery and half to Medicine; and during their four years' curriculum to take courses of six months' extent in Anatomy, Surgery, Chemistry, Theory or Institutes of Medicine, Practice of Medicine, Midwifery, Materia Medica and Pharmacy, and Anatomical Dissections, with a course of three months in Forensic Medicine. Candidates were to be examined in all the subjects of the curriculum, to submit a thesis in English on a surgical subject, and to give evidence of a competent knowledge of Latin.

For a short time at the outset, the regulations for graduation in Surgery were in some respects in advance of the regulations for graduation in Medicine, inasmuch as candidates were required not only to attend courses in what were then considered all the standard subjects of medical and surgical education, but also to be examined in them all. The minimum curriculum of two years prescribed at the outset was doubtless too short.

2 M

but in 1826 it was extended to three sessions, and probably students had in practice attended that length of time from the first. The diploma issued to graduates in Surgery certified that they were duly qualified in Surgery, Obstetrics, and Pharmacy. In an Act passed in March, 1827 (George IV., Chap. 116, Sect. 12), for regulating vessels carrying passengers to foreign ports, the degree of C.M. from Glasgow was recognised by Parliament as qualifying the holder for employment as a surgeon. For the first ten years after its institution the degree of C.M. was in greater demand than the degree of M.D., 202 obtaining the former and 146 the latter. In the next ten years, however, the order was reversed, 197 students graduating as C.M., while 525 graduated as M.D., 258 of the M.D.'s belonging to the last three years.

Glasgow was the first University of the United Kingdom to introduce a distinct degree in Surgery. Its introduction is sometimes represented as a strategic measure, adopted in view of an adverse decision of the Court of Session regarding the rights of Doctors of Medicine to practise Surgery within the territory of the Faculty of Physicians and Surgeons. The two events were closely related in time, but it is probably a mistake to regard the legal decision as the sole motive or cause for instituting the degree. As elsewhere narrated a discussion had sprung up in regard to legislation for regulating the practice of Surgery in the United Kingdom, and in 1816 and the early months of 1817 the Senate were much exercised by a bill for that purpose which had been introduced into the House of Commons. It was immediately after this that the resolution to institute degrees in surgery was taken, and though the motives of the Senate are not disclosed in their minutes, probably the imminence of legislation and the lawsuit with the Faculty both tended to the adoption of the course actually followed. In his charter of 1599 James VI. had authorised the Corporation then called into existence to examine and try all practitioners of Surgery in Glasgow and the other defined districts in the West of Scotland, making no mention of exceptions on account of qualifications previously obtained, although, for the practice of Medicine, a testimonial from a famous University where Medicine was taught was declared sufficient. The Scottish Universities, with the exception of Aberdeen for a short time at the beginning of its career, did not take up Medicine or Surgery in earnest ; and the regulation that practitioners of Surgery in Glasgow and the West of Scotland should submit to examination by the Faculty of Physicians and Surgeons may have been quite sound in 1599 and for a long time afterwards. So far as equity was concerned, the question would have assumed an entirely new aspect when the University of Glasgow had developed a considerable eaching staff in Medicine, and conferred medical degrees only after a engthened curriculum and an examination probably more severe than that f the Faculty of Physicians and Surgeons, if the curriculum and examinaion had included Surgery.   From 1812 candidates for M.D. were reuired to attend a distinct course of Surgery, unless they attended three ourses of Anatomy, which as then taught included a good deal of Surgery ; nd from 1817 a course in Surgery formed a necessary part of the curriulum, though it was not made a definite subject of examination for M.D. ill 1839.   Viewing the question, not as a purely legal one, but as one of quity and commonsense, one must admit that the University degree of V.D. did not in 1815 completely fortify its possessor in the right to ractise Surgery.   It does not seem that the requirements in Surgery were nore stringent at Edinburgh than at Glasgow, and at St. Andrews and Lberdeen the standard for graduation in Medicine was more lax.

In the early years of the 19th century there was a marked increase in he number of candidates preparing for M.D., and the number of those rho obtained it from the Scottish Universities was also increasing at a otable rate.   Graduates in Medicine were afterwards settling to general ractice in Glasgow in such numbers as to alarm the Faculty of Physicians nd Surgeons, as they made no application for examination or license by hat body, and contended that the degree of M.D. conferred a right to ractise Surgery as well as Medicine.   In 1815 the Faculty raised an ction in the Court of Session against four Doctors of Medicine, holding heir degrees from the Universities of Glasgow, Edinburgh, St. Andrews, nd one of the Universities of Aberdeen, and acting as general practiioners in Glasgow, with a view to have them interdicted from practising urgery.   Towards the close of the year the Lord Ordinary decided that he defenders were all entitled to practise Medicine within the Faculty's erritory ; but that, in virtue of the power conferred upon the Faculty by reir original charter to examine all persons professing or using the art of urgery, no person could lawfully practise Surgery within that territory rithout submitting to examination by the Faculty.   An appeal was taken gainst this decision, but after three or four more years of argument and elay the original decision was confirmed.

This decision and the public discussion of legislative measures for gulating the practice of Surgery led the University to consider the lvisability of introducing graduation in Surgery as a distinct subject. 'he practice of Surgery demanded scientific training and skill as well as lat of Medicine.   Many of the requirements were indeed common to both, it so far as they differed, the University might quite as fitly train and attest actitioners of Surgery as of Medicine.   No other British University at that time granted degrees or diplomas in Surgery, but there was nothing in the nature of the case to prevent it.   Some continental Universities, including that of Bologna, granted a degree in Surgery, and the bull of Pope Nicholas V. provided for teaching and conferring degrees at Glasgow in any legitimate faculty.   The Senate considered that their charter entitled them to grant degrees in Surgery, and that there was ample provision for teaching everything requisite to qualify surgeons for the practice of their profession.   Influenced by such considerations, and guided, as is believed, by the advice of the new professor of Surgery, the Senate on 30th April, 1817, resolved to grant degrees or diplomas in Surgery, and the degree of C.M. which was instituted was soon in very considerable demand.

The success of the new degree kindled the hostility of the Faculty of Physicians and Surgeons, and in 1826, in the April of which the University had increased the stringency of the regulations for C.M. and extended the curriculum to three years, the Faculty raised a process in the Court of Session with the object of interdicting Masters in Surgery from practising within the territory of the Faculty.   On 3rd January, 1827, a representation was given in from the graduates against whom the action had been raised, pointing out that they had been served with a bill of suspension and interdict by the Faculty of Physicians and Surgeons to have them prohibited from practice as surgeons till they had been examined by that corporation and paid heavy fees to it ; and praying the Senate to intervene and relieve them from a demand so oppressive and so fatal to the degree of C.M. conferred by the University.   The Senate recognising the importance of the affair, asked the faculty of the College to supply the means of consulting counsel.   The faculty agreed to do so, and Mr. Graham, the College law agent, drew up a memorial for the opinion of counsel, which was submitted to three advocates—Sir James Moncrieff, Dean of the Faculty of Advocates, John Jardine, and Duncan Macfarlan, junior.   By the 1st March the answers of counsel were received, and the faculty or College meeting handed them over to the Senate, with an intimation that the College would incur no further expense in the matter.

The memorial cited passages from the Pope's bull of foundation and from the *Nova Erectio* of James VI., the latter of which expressed the King's will that the College of Glasgow should enjoy all the privileges and immunities granted by the Crown or in any other way to any of the academies in the kingdom, while the Pope's bull conferred immunities and privileges equal to those of Bologna and Paris, the most ancient and famous Universities, both of which had the right to confer and did actually confer diplomas in Surgery.   Besides degrees in Arts and honorary degrees, Glasgow had long conferred degrees in Medicine, and, since the recent

)undation by the Crown of the chair of Surgery, it had granted degrees r diplomas of proficiency in Surgery after a rigid examination and pro- uction of certificates of attendance on the required courses. The 1emorialists considered that these diplomas entitled the holders to practise urgery and Pharmacy unmolested within the bounds of the King's ominions. By the legislature they had been placed on a par with practi- oners holding their diplomas from the Colleges of Surgeons of London,)ublin, and Edinburgh, more particularly by the Act George IV., Chapter 16, entitled Act for regulating vessels carrying passengers to foreign orts, Section 12 of which enacted that no British ship having license to arry passengers, carrying fifty persons or upwards, including the master nd crew, should be cleared at any port of the United Kingdom unless such hip were provided with a surgeon, to continue during the whole voyage, nd who should produce to the officer of Customs at the port where the hip was cleared a certificate of his having passed his examinations at the urgeons Hall in London, or at the Royal College of Surgeons of Edin- urgh or Dublin, or before the Medical Faculty of the University of ilasgow.

Notwithstanding this, and notwithstanding that Surgery was *licita acultas*, and though these diplomas under the favour and protection of he legislature were received in every port of the United Kingdom, ttempts had been made to prevent the holders from practising in Glasgow, he seat of the institution which granted them, without submitting to irther examination and paying extravagant fees to a body styling them- ɛlves the Faculty of Physicians and Surgeons of Glasgow, originating in irtue of a charter or letters of gift from James VI. in 1599, and ratified y Parliament in 1672. The grant of 1599 set forth that great abuses had itherto existed and still continued from ignorant and unskilled persons busing the people under colour of chirurgeons, and conferred on the rantees the power of examining all persons professing or using the art of irgery within the bounds specified (embracing approximately the counties f Lanark, Renfrew, Ayr, and Dumbarton), and of licensing those whom ley found worthy. Reference was made to a decision of the Court of ession affirming the right of persons holding the degree of M.D. from cottish Universities to practise Medicine within the territory assigned to ie Faculty of Physicians and Surgeons; and it was contended that the rovision in reference to Surgery only authorised the Faculty to proceed yainst ignorant and unskilful persons practising Surgery, but gave them o right to interfere with practitioners who held regular certificates of roficiency. The claim of the Faculty to charge fees for examination and cense was also disputed, as not being provided for in their charter, and as being the subject of litigation at the time with some of their own licentiates, who after obtaining license objected to being amerced in freedom fines. It was further urged that the Faculty were not a corporation nor vested with corporate privileges, and therefore had no title to sue. Upon the Faculty raising a bill of suspension against four persons holding the diploma of C.M. from the University, the judge had passed a bill to try the question, but had refused interdict.

The three advocates to whom the memorial was submitted returned opinions favourable to the University. They held that the memorialists had a right, after examination, to grant diplomas of Master in Surgery, or bearing the testimonial of the University as to the qualification of the holders to practise Surgery; and that, according to the true construction of the charter of 1599 to the Medical Association styling themselves the Faculty of Physicians and Surgeons, and still more clearly according to the Act of ratification in 1672, the testimonial of any famous University superseded the necessity of any examination by the Faculty, and enabled the holder to practise any branch of the medical art, and particularly Surgery and Pharmacy, and that holders of the University diploma of C.M. were entitled to practise Surgery and Pharmacy without entering with the Faculty. Counsel considered that in cases where the Faculty could make out a right to examine they would be entitled to reasonable fees, but that their amount would be subject to the control of the Court of Session. The memorialists could not appear in their own name in the suspension, but counsel advised them to support one or more of the Masters in Surgery against whom the action was raised, and in this way the question might be as fully tried as if they were pursuers in an action of declarator.

On 5th March, 1827, the Senate considered the opinion of counsel and the resolution of the faculty of the College not to incur further expenses, and decided to take no further steps for the time, Jeffray and Burns dissenting. Shortly afterwards three of the Masters in Surgery who had been attacked sent a letter asking the support of the Senate. The question seems to have given rise to a sharp division of opinion among the members, and probably those favourable to supporting the graduates in Surgery had requested the presence and aid of the rector. On 19th April, 1827, Burns moved that the graduates should be supported. Eight having voted for and eight against the motion, Thomas Campbell, the poet, who was rector at the time, gave his casting vote in its favour. It was then moved by the principal, seconded by Jeffray, and acquiesced in by all the medical professors present, that the fees for C.M. should be appropriated to the purpose for that year, except a small portion assigned as fees to servants and for writing diplomas. Part of the fees for C.M. was divided among the medical professors and a smaller part appropriated to the Library, and Macgill dissented from the resolution so far as it involved withdrawal of funds from the Library. The question of funds was not yet settled, however, and on 24th April the rector Campbell read to the Senate two letters of a very controversial nature, the first of which was from Jeffray, Burns, Thomas Thomson, Hooker, and John Towers, and the second from Hooker individually. In reference to the decision of the preceding meeting to support the Masters of Surgery from funds normally appropriated to the Library and the medical professors, those who signed the first letter declared that they had been accused of mercenary motives in urging measures for the defence, and that they had been hurried into compliance with a proposed means of defence which, on reflection, they thought dangerous as a precedent and injurious in its immediate operation. Individual professors should not at their own expense have to maintain the general rights of the University. They now recalled their consent, and considered that the resolution should be carried out by means of the corporation funds. If the Senate would not maintain its resolution, they preferred to give in their own name what they judged proper, and in that case they would decline to receive any aid from the fees allotted to the Library. In the second letter, Hooker described himself as one of the least privileged of the medical professors, with an average income not above £200, from which it was hard that he should have to give thirty guineas to defend the rights of the University, especially as Botany formed no part of the surgical curriculum, any more than Mathematics or Greek or Civil Law.

On 30th April Burns moved that the defence of the Masters in Surgery should be at the expense of the Senate, but after considerable discussion this was negatived. The principal then moved and it was carried to defend Messrs. Macmillan, Marshall and Menzies, and to appropriate to the purpose the portion of the fees for C.M. which would otherwise have gone to the Library fund. After this the case proceeded slowly, and on 5th January, 1833, Mr. Andrew Mitchell, the law agent of the University, explained the situation, stating that John Hope, the dean of the Faculty of Advocates, had given his opinion that the rights of the University to grant degrees in Surgery could not be properly vindicated unless the University raised a process of declarator. Hope strongly advised that such a process should be raised and conjoined with the action then depending, and the Senate agreed to follow his advice. An action of declarator was accordingly raised, asking the Court to declare that the degree of C.M. qualified its possessor to practise Surgery within the territory claimed by the Faculty of Physicians and Surgeons. The two causes were conjoined, the University being called the pursuers, and the Faculty of Physicians and Surgeons defenders. In February, 1835, it was reported that the Court had given judgment in favour of the defenders, within whose territory Masters of Surgery were interdicted from practice ; and had awarded expenses to the amount of £532 11s. 8d., of which £219 8s. 10d. was charged directly against the University, and £313 2s. 10d. against the three surgeons who were the original defenders. Of the three, one was now dead, another had emigrated to America, and the third was a country practitioner in poor circumstances, so that the burden fell to be borne by the Senate.

The agents for the victors in the lawsuit threatened to extract the decree so as to compel immediate payment, and the Senate, in order to gain time, resolved to enter an appeal to the House of Lords, to be followed up or not as might afterwards be deemed advisable. It was also resolved to apply the whole fees for graduation in Surgery, excepting twenty-four shillings assigned to servants and for writing diplomas, towards the liquidation of the expenses. Shortly afterwards Thomas Thomson, Hooker, and John Couper vehemently objected to the Surgery fees being devoted to this purpose, alleging that Thomson did not approve the lawsuit, that Couper was a member of the Faculty of Physicians and Surgeons and actually opposed to the University at the time the process was begun, and that Hooker and Badham never took part in the action. They suggested that the fees of the professors who originated and carried on the action might be used, but objected to individuals being made to pay for measures of which they extremely disapproved ; and hoped the Senate would rescind the resolution, otherwise the three professors would resist by every means in their power. On 19th March, however, the meeting confirmed their decision, declaring that the power of granting degrees, appointing examiners, and fixing the amount and distribution of the fees, belonged exclusively to the Senate, that no individual member could claim the whole or any part of the fees for degrees in Surgery as a matter of right, that the granting of degrees in Surgery had increased the number of students, extended the reputation of the Medical School, and benefited the professors, that it was equitable to use the fees for degrees the validity of which had been questioned in defence of these degrees, and that the Senate would easily find within their own body a sufficient number of examiners qualified and willing to discharge the duty on the terms proposed. Shortly after this quietus had been administered to the three dissenting professors, a vote was taken, and on 8th April, 1835, the Senate resolved to proceed with the appeal in the House of Lords. Again the case moved slowly, and when in March, 1837, the Senate gave instructions concerning it, a note was made that Macgill, M'Turk, and Hooker gave no opinion on the subject. At first the judges of the House of Lords, especially the Chancellor Brougham, were impressed by the contention that the Faculty of Physicians and Surgeons were not a corporation and could not be entitled to maintain an action of this nature. The question depended mainly on the construction of the letter granted by James VI. in 1599, and was remitted to the Court of Session for the opinion of the whole of the judges. The Court of Session returned an opinion favourable to the Faculty of Physicians and Surgeons, and gently reminded the House of Lords that they had taken unnecessary trouble, as the Court of Session had previously given a full, minute, and comprehensive opinion on the very question which the House of Lords afterwards remitted to them.

In August, 1840, the House of Lords confirmed the decision of the Court of Session and dismissed the appeal. Costs amounting to £1,684 were awarded against the University, and as the Senate had no funds excepting the fees charged for certain degrees, and the funds of the Library, including certain small fees annually exacted from students, they were in evil case. In December, 1841, a sum of £350 in the hands of the Quaestor of the Library was ordered to be paid, and shortly afterwards, as the law agents on the other side were importunate, Mr. Andrew Mitchell, the law agent of the University, procured a bond for the remainder on the security of the estates, funds, and revenues of the University, to be paid off gradually as means were forthcoming from these sources. The books in the Library were pledged in security, and for many years considerable portions of the Library funds were diverted from their normal purpose to pay interest on the debt and gradually to reduce the principal. Among the rest, Government stock belonging to the Brand-Hollis mortification was sold for £156 7s. 2d., and used in part payment. By and by a fortunate discovery was made. It was found that the faculty of the College were much in debt to the Senate. The debt had been growing for about twenty years till the principal amounted to fully £800, and the interest to an almost equal sum. In April, 1851, Buchanan and Rainy proposed that the revenue derived from fees, after deducting sums necessary for the immediate exigencies of the University, should be applied to extinguish the residue of the debt. Under the guidance of Maconochie the Senate, however, resolved to extinguish the debt from the £800 of interest due by the faculty of the College, considering that, as the Library had been impignorated for payment of the costs in the action with the Faculty of Physicians and Surgeons, it was requisite that the funds collected under the authority of the Senate and hitherto employed in improving and extending the Library, should be used in its defence by discharging the debt on account of which it was at any time liable to be attached. Provision was also made for restoring the Brand-Hollis fund, which, with interest, amounted to £209 18s. 11d.

The University of Glasgow suffered rather severely and undeservedly for establishing a degree in Surgery and setting an example which was afterwards followed by the other Universities of the United Kingdom. There was no question of the sufficiency of the degree of C.M., but only of the preservation of a chartered monopoly in a particular district. Indeed the sufficiency of the C.M. degree was recognised by Parliament in the Act of 1827 already mentioned, and it was afterwards recognised by the Medical Act of 1858. The Judges of the law courts seem to have felt, however, that it was not for them to decide the case on equitable considerations in reference to the times and circumstances in which they lived, but that they were bound by the strict letter of the charter granted by James VI., which authorised the Faculty of Physicians and Surgeons within the area assigned to them to examine and license all practitioners of the art of Surgery, making no exception in favour of those who had already been examined and licensed by other competent authority. Previously the degree of C.M. had been conferred on about twenty candidates annually, but after the decision of the House of Lords it was not much in demand, and for the next twenty years the annual average was only about three. After 1858, however, and before the degree of M.B. was first granted in 1865, the degree of C.M. had risen to nearly its former average.

At the end of the 18th century there were nearly 200 medical students, but in a short time the number increased greatly. In 1826-27 there were 437, and for eleven years ending with 1836-37 the average was about 425, the highest number during the period being 486 in 1829-30, and the lowest 367 in 1832-33. For some time full statistics are not available, but there are indications that there was a falling off soon after 1840 and probably a still further decrease after 1850. In 1859-60, the first session in which a thorough and uniform system of matriculation was introduced, the number of medical students was 311.

In 1803 a first attempt was made to establish a register of medical students, to be kept by the librarian, who was to receive from the various professors and lecturers a return of the students attending their classes. Students were to pay a shilling to the librarian for keeping the list, the accuracy of which they were to have an opportunity of checking, and they might afterwards, on payment of five shillings, obtain a certificate on vellum showing what classes they had attended. In 1812 medical students were required to enrol with the librarian of the medical library, a separate collection, paying a fee of seven shillings for the winter session, with a further fee of three shillings and sixpence if they wished to borrow books in summer as well.   The medical library had been begun by Jeffray about 1795, when a garret was assigned for its reception, improvements on accommodation costing £35 in 1814 and £84 eleven years afterwards. In 1818 the Senate ordered a general register for all students to be kept at the library, each student paying a fee of six shillings, and the fees from medical students being devoted to the purchase of medical books.   Half the sums accruing to the library from medical and surgical degrees were ordered to be applied in the same way, Jeffray urging that the whole amount ought to be so spent, and hinting that the collection, which had cost the medical professors and students upwards of £600, might be merged in the general library.   This was not done, however, and in 1838 it was stated that there were more than 3,000 volumes in the medical library.   About the same time a number of medical graduates requested to be allowed the use of this separate collection, but their wishes do not seem to have been granted, and it was not till March, 1857, that graduates were admitted to the use of the general library.   The regulations for the registration of students at the library were frequently altered and not very consistently enforced, and in 1833 students who had paid library dues for four years were exempted from further payments, though their attendance might continue longer.   In 1843 the number of medical students who had enrolled at the University library was returned as 162, which shows that many must have exempted themselves.   The method of applying the library fees paid by medical students was not uniform, special resolutions on the subject being passed from time to time.   The diversion of the library fees from their normal use to the liquidation of the costs in the action with the Faculty of Physicians and Surgeons has already been mentioned.   In 1839 a rule requiring medical students to enrol not later than 1st December was passed, and it was reaffirmed in 1842.

Early in 1803 the Faculty, influenced by troubles with the townspeople in regard to Anatomy, enacted that in future no medical student should reside within the College.   The solitary medical student affected by the regulation had to remove immediately, a certificate being given that his removal was owing to the regulation just passed, and not to any objection to his conduct.

On 15th February, 1802, there appears in the minutes of the faculty the first mention of a society formed by medical students of the University, which afterwards came to be known as the Medico-Chirurgical Society. At the end of April estimates for fitting up two rooms for the accommodation of the Society were submitted, and on 11th May the faculty authorised an expenditure of £20 8s. 4d. for the purpose. In Edinburgh there had been such a society when Cullen was a student, and in 1789 a Medical Society was established at Aberdeen, which at that time had no fully organised Medical School, though it had a number of sanguine and capable young medical men and students. The society was late in making its appearance at Glasgow, and has had some intervals of latency, but it still subsists, more vigorous after the lapse of a century than in its days of youth.

In 1836 the Principal informed the faculty that William Armstrong and Dugald Blair, students of Anatomy, had contravened the statutes by publishing a periodical called *The Scalpel*, containing gross personalities and articles calculated to excite feelings dangerous to the security of the College. The Principal had admonished them, but they persisted in publishing the periodical. Armstrong, when called before the faculty, acknowledged himself responsible for the publication, hoped the second number would be considered less exceptionable than the first, and promised that no improper article should appear in any subsequent number. Blair declared he had no further concern in the publication than helping to procure subscribers. It is stated that the faculty, deeply sensible of the criminality of such conduct, and the pernicious effects likely to be produced by such a publication, were unanimously of opinion that it must be discontinued; but that they did not object to a literary or professional work free from the blemishes of *The Scalpel*, or under a different title. It is not probable that *The Scalpel*, whose name was part of its offence, had ventured to outlive this condemnation. Its brief existence is notable as the first attempt by the students to carry on a periodical.

The relations between the University and the Royal Infirmary claim some notice. Clinical teaching was begun in that hospital from its opening, one may say. In session 1795-96 or earlier such a course must have been given, for it is recorded that Robert Agnew, who presented himself as a candidate for M.D. in May, 1796, had attended Clinical lectures in the Royal Infirmary. But specific courses of clinical instruction were not given quite regularly even in the earlier years, and as time went on they became more intermittent, and afterwards ceased for a number of years. Students continued to attend the hospital as the University regulations required them to do, and they might observe the treatment of patients, and pick up instruction as well as they could, but it was only sometimes that regularly organised clinical teaching was provided, and courses of this nature did not form part of the compulsory curriculum. At the outset the Faculty of Physicians and Surgeons had claimed that the medical officers of the Infirmary should be drawn exclusively from their ranks, and had framed an elaborate code for regulating the duties of these officers. On the other hand, the University wished that some of its professors or lecturers should conduct courses of clinical instruction, and in the early stages, there being no professor of Surgery in the University till 1815, Clinical Medicine seems to have been chiefly contemplated.

In October, 1810, Freer submitted to the faculty of the College the report of a committee on clinical lectures, and the Principal, Jeffray, Richardson, and Jardine were appointed to converse on the subject with Cleghorn, the lecturer on Chemistry. A further report was received, but action was postponed, and the medical professors were recommended to consider what measures should be adopted. On 7th May, 1812, Richardson proposed that the faculty of the College should appoint two physicians from the medical professors and lecturers, to give courses of clinical instruction during the winter session, each of them acting for half the time; that attendance on at least one such course should in future be required from every candidate for graduation in Medicine; and that the managers of the Infirmary should be requested to permit the two physicians to treat such cases as the latter considered best adapted for the instruction of students who were pupils in the Infirmary, it being left to the managers to lay down such regulations as they considered proper. The proposal was approved, and the Principal, Richardson, Jardine, Jeffray, Freer, and Davidson were appointed a committee to make arrangements with the managers. On 10th June following, the committee on clinical lectures recommended the faculty of the College to appoint two physicians as proposed on 7th May. The recommendation was approved, and as Jeffray and Freer declared it would be inconvenient for them to give clinical lectures next session, Dr. Cleghorn and Dr. Millar were appointed to do so, each taking half of the session, from 1st November to 1st May. The proposal seems to have borne little fruit, and for some time there is not much reference to the subject in the University records. At the beginning of the session in October, 1821, and again on 1st November, 1822, the faculty granted to Dr. William Cumin the use of a room within the College for the purpose of giving lectures on Clinical Surgery. If Cumin were at the time a surgeon in the Infirmary (which is not stated), he might have been able to some extent to give in his lectures at the University guidance and instruction to students who attended cases under his treatment in the Infirmary, but clinical teaching at a time and place apart from the meeting of surgeon and students with the patients must have been subject to great disadvantages, and it seems to have been discontinued after the second session.

In October, 1824, the Senate unanimously resolved to represent to the managers of the Infirmary their earnest desire for the regular delivery of clinical lectures, both medical and surgical, agreeing that they should form part of the curriculum so long as they were delivered by professors or lecturers belonging to the University. Emphasis was laid on the importance of lectures on Clinical Surgery, about which it was understood that there might be more difficulty than with the other subject; and the Senate instructed the managers sent from the University to urge the great benefit which would accrue to the teaching of Surgery if the professor of that subject were allowed to illustrate the principles taught in the University by cases occurring in the hospital; and to point out that, if the subject were taught by the surgeons of the hospital, who were annually changing, it could not be admitted to the curriculum nor form part of a connected plan of education. There were lectures on Clinical Surgery in every other well constituted hospital, and the growing celebrity of the University Medical School, which could not fail to be gratifying to the citizens, should induce the managers to accede to a proposal beneficial to the School, creditable to the city, and likely to benefit the hospital by attracting more students to Glasgow. The Senate would not object to clinical lectures being delivered by hospital surgeons in summer or other time not interfering with the courses proposed by the University, but such courses would not form part of the curriculum. The Senate recalled that the College of Glasgow, as an institution and through its members, had promoted the establishment of the Infirmary, contributing largely to its funds at the outset, when it could have secured in the charter any privileges thought desirable for the Medical School. This last argument reads like a confession that the Senate had neglected their opportunity.

The minutes of Senate of 20th December, 1825, embody a long report by a Committee of the Managers of the Royal Infirmary. They had held a meeting with the Principal, Dr. Freer, and Professor Meikleham, as representing the University, and Drs. Robertson, Steel, and Panton, as representing the Faculty of Physicians and Surgeons, when the gentlemen representing the two learned bodies were heard at full length. The Committee reported that the importance of clinical lectures was universally admitted, that it was the duty of the Managers to facilitate by every proper means the introduction into the Infirmary of lectures both on Clinical Medicine and Clinical Surgery, that for some years after the erection of the Infirmary clinical lectures had occasionally been delivered, but that for several years they had been altogether discontinued. Students did not attend, as the clinical lectures were not made part of the curriculum, and the University would not make attendance imperative unless they had such a control of the nomination of the lecturer as would insure their confidence in his qualifications. On the other hand, the Faculty of Physicians and Surgeons considered this an unconstitutional interference with the rights of the Directors, an improper assumption of a jurisdiction which none but the medical members of the University were qualified to exercise, and injurious, in the first place, to the students, by precluding that diversity of illustration which would arise from a change of lecturers, and also to the Infirmary, since the permission of the professor of Surgery to interfere with the treatment of patients would be considered by the house surgeons as derogatory to their character and feelings, and would be a bar to any respectable person accepting the situation. The Committee thought that, if both learned bodies adhered to the ground they had taken up, there was no hope that clinical lectures would ever be properly instituted, and had tried to find some middle course which would give justice to both without conferring a preference on either.

The least objectionable plan seemed to be that the clinical course should extend to six months, divided into two periods, with two lecturers participating equally in the emoluments fixed by the Directors. One lecturer was to be appointed by the Directors for three months, while the other was to be recommended by the University for a like period. The University lecturer should attend during the period of the junior surgeon, and the senior surgeon, nominated by the Directors, for the other three months, the priority of time being matter of arrangement. The Committee expected that their views would be combated by the ingenuity of the medical Directors, but considered that their plan would have the advantage of dividing the patronage and emoluments equally, and securing that the junior surgeon would enjoy the benefit of the skill, science, and experience of an advanced practitioner, and that the students would benefit by variety of precept and demonstration from two lecturers.

On 22nd December, 1825, the Senate adopted with very little modification the proposals made by the Committee of Directors, claiming, however, that the University lecturer should give the first half of the six months' course each session. Before admission to examination candidates for graduation in Surgery were to be required to take two courses of three months in Clinical Surgery, and candidates for graduation in Medicine two similar courses in Clinical Medicine. Certificates from any clinical teacher in the Glasgow Infirmary, or any other hospital of proper standing where regular teaching was given, were to be accepted.

It seemed as if the University and the Infirmary were on the point of adopting a working arrangement, but the proposed scheme was vehemently opposed by the Faculty of Physicians and Surgeons. Upon the opening of the Infirmary they had claimed a monopoly of the medical and surgical appointments, settling that the physicians and surgeons of their own body were to act in rotation, each physician for six months and each surgeon for two months, surgeons who were in arrears with the payment of certain dues to the Faculty being disqualified from service in the hospital. They remonstrated strongly against the Managers electing particular physicians or surgeons to fill the posts. They must be filled by a system of rotation, else the Faculty predicted all manner of mischief. They further arrogated to themselves the framing of rules for the management of the medical and surgical staff in the hospital. Though this had been their former attitude, the Faculty now declared that it was the inalienable right of the Managers to appoint the medical officers of the Infirmary, and that Managers who could speak of dividing the patronage had no proper notion of their duties and responsibilities. They questioned the right of the University to grant degrees in Surgery, pointed to the pending lawsuit, hinting that it might be decided in their favour, and declared that they would take no part in the work of the hospital if the proposed monopoly, as they called it, were established.

There was some exaggeration in the allegations of the Faculty of Physicians and Surgeons, as well as inconsistency with their former proceedings. Dr. Burns, for whom it was desired to afford opportunity to teach Clinical Surgery, was a member of their own body. He had given clinical instruction in the Infirmary 'when they both were young together,' and with his long and varied subsequent experience and high reputation, neither the hospital nor the Faculty of Physicians and Surgeons need have looked with distrust or apprehension on his resuming clinical teaching. The proposals made by the University in 1812 were not rigid and inflexible, but admitted of mutual concession and adjustment, and in 1825 the University fell in with the scheme devised by the Infirmary Managers. Allowing University professors or lecturers to give half the teaching was described by the Faculty of Physicians and Surgeons as an obnoxious monopoly, though they themselves had previously claimed to fill all the medical and surgical posts with members of their own body. At a later time provision was made in the constitution of the Western Infirmary for University professors being allowed to give clinical instruction within it, and the institution has not suffered in consequence. It must be owned, however, that in the hostile relations that existed between the Senate and the Faculty of Physicians and Surgeons in 1825 and for a considerable time before and after, it was not easy for either body to be considerate.

In October, 1826, the Senate seemed to expect that arrangements would be made for teaching Clinical Surgery, but some years passed and nothing was done. In session 1829-30, however, the Managers introduced an arrangement under which a course in Clinical Medicine and one in Clinical Surgery were given each session by a physician and surgeon of the hospital annually appointed by the Managers, the fee charged admitting the students both to hospital practice and to clinical teaching. By and by all the physicians and surgeons of the hospital became clinical teachers in their several departments. It is to be regretted that the University did not make attendance on clinical teaching compulsory, but as attendance on hospital practice had long been compulsory, and students could not now gain admission to it without at the same time paying for clinical instruction, the evil may not have been so great as it looked.

Some interesting information regarding hospitals is given in a report of the faculty of Medicine presented to the Senate on 27th January, 1835, on the question of accepting attendance by candidates for M.D. on hospitals which contained fewer than eighty beds. It was stated that the London College of Surgeons recognised the City of Dublin Hospital, though it contained only 52 beds. The University of Edinburgh recognised another hospital in Dublin containing about thirty beds, and also accepted attendance on Mr. Syme's hospital in Edinburgh, though the number of beds did not exceed 25. In these and other cases the licensing bodies had been guided by the consideration that the hospitals in question were not general hospitals admitting all patients indiscriminately, but clinical hospitals selecting only such cases as were best adapted to medical education. The City of Dublin Hospital was established in 1832 entirely for clinical instruction, having six physicians who attended daily, besides four consulting physicians and surgeons for difficult cases. Each pupil had a case to manage, and three clinical lectures were delivered weekly. That winter the pupils numbered 70, and it was thus the greatest clinical school in Dublin, and much greater than any in Scotland. The clinical wards in Edinburgh, which alone were attended by students, did not contain 30 beds. It would be unjust to recognise the hospitals of Edinburgh and Glasgow and to reject the City of Dublin Hospital and other similar institutions. The Glasgow Infirmary was virtually closed to medical students who attended the University for only one year, as was the case with at least two-thirds of those who graduated at Glasgow, because no ticket was issued for a shorter period than two years. The faculty of Medicine, therefore, recommended the Senate to acknowledge all hospitals recognised by the London and Dublin Colleges of Surgeons, though containing fewer than eighty beds, these bodies having better means of knowing the merits of clinical establishments in their respective countries than those possessed by the University.   The Senate adopted the report and resolved accordingly.

It is somewhat surprising to find that about this time two-thirds of those who graduated at Glasgow studied there for only one year.   For the ten years ending with 1835, on the average about 45 candidates received the degree of Doctor of Medicine and 21 that of Master in Surgery ; and the number of medical students was fully 400.   But, if 44 of the 66 graduates attended for only one year in the University, it is clear that the other 22, even if they attended for a longer period than the normal curriculum, could not have made up the number of students to 400.   There must therefore have been a considerable number of medical students attending the University who did not graduate there.

For nearly half a century before the final passing of the Medical Act of 1858, unavailing attempts were from time to time made in Parliament to organise and regulate the medical profession.   A bill for improving medical, surgical, and veterinary science, and for regulating the practice of Physic was under consideration in 1810.   Again, in September, 1816, there was laid before the Senate a bill which the House of Commons had ordered to be printed, and which aimed at regulating the practice of Surgery throughout Great Britain and Ireland, and the Senate forwarded a memorial on the subject to the Government.   Early next year the proposed measure was further discussed, a letter regarding it having been received from the President of the Royal College of Surgeons, London. A further memorial was drawn up and copies sent to Members of Parliament, and on 25th March, 1817, the Senate requested Mr. Mundell, Solicitor, London, to watch the progress of the bill, to take the necessary steps to secure the rights of the University, and to advise whether it would be expedient to engage Counsel to appear before Parliament.   The interest of Kirkman Finlay, M.P. for the Glasgow Burghs, was invoked, communications, apparently on the same subject, were opened with the Faculty of Physicians and Surgeons, and it is significant that it was immediately after this that the Senate resolved to institute degrees in Surgery.

Discussion and agitation on the narrower question of regulating Practical Anatomy went on very keenly for a number of years, Jeffray, Burns, and Mackenzie, who became University lecturer on the Eye in 1828, taking an active part in the effort to secure a proper system, which was effected by the passing of the Anatomy Act in 1832.

In 1826 and again in 1833 the Senate petitioned Parliament that graduates in Medicine and Surgery of the University might be relieved from the restriction placed upon such of them as settled to practise in England and Wales by the Apothecaries Act of 1815, a restriction which seems to have been keenly felt by those subjected to it. The Act contained a clause, which passed unobserved by the Universities and other Corporations, and conferred a monopoly on the Apothecaries Company of London, empowering them to exclude from dispensing medicine all who had not complied with their regulations, including a servitude of five years, payment of considerable fees, and the passing of an examination which does not seem to have been the most formidable part of the requirements. It was only in the large towns that the practice of physicians, surgeons, and apothecaries was kept distinct, elsewhere it was usual and convenient for practitioners to furnish medicines to their patients, and the monopoly conferred on the apothecaries of dispensing medicines greatly hampered the practice of Scottish graduates in England and Wales.

In April, 1834, queries formulated by a Select Committee of the House of Commons on Medical Education were remitted by the Senate to the consideration of a Committee consisting of Jeffray, Burns, Thomas Thomson, Hooker, Badham, William Couper, and John Couper. On the last day of the month the draft answers of the Committee were presented, but they seem to have needed further adjustment, and next day the Committee, with the addition of the Principal and Fleming, were empowered to frame and transmit answers to the queries. Some attempt at legislation seems to have followed in 1836.

A bill was introduced into the House of Commons in 1841 by Mr. Warburton and Mr. Hawes, which aimed at the establishment of a system of registration for qualified practitioners, and of a permanent Board to control the Universities and Medical Corporations, the election of a representative body in each of the three divisions of the United Kingdom, and, apparently, confining to the three capitals the power of examining candidates and granting qualifications to practise. The scheme foreshadowed in a crude and imperfect form some of the provisions adopted in 1858, but a Committee of Senate reported adversely upon it, as tending to centralise authority in the capitals of the three kingdoms, and to injure the Medical Schools in other localities. They also announced that the true policy of Medical reform was to abolish the close system by which members or licentiates of particular corporations enjoyed an exclusive right to practise in particular localities, and to open the right to practise in all parts of the United Kingdom to all graduates and licentiates. The most essential requirement for such a uniform system was the adoption of a minimum course of education through which all candidates must pass in order to be eligible for any qualification to practise.

In February, 1842, the heads of a bill for regulating the medical profession were considered, along with a letter from the Home Secretary, Sir James Graham, and the measures proposed do not seem to have shown much consideration for the University of which Graham had been rector only a year or two before. A memorial on the subject drafted by Burns was approved. It set forth that apparently the powers of the Scottish Universities to confer degrees in Medicine and Surgery were to be taken away and transferred to Colleges of Physicians and Surgeons. Probably the University of Glasgow would be set aside, and the Faculty of Physicians and Surgeons empowered to grant licenses or degrees both in Surgery and Medicine, though it was not pretended that the Faculty had any advantages superior to the University or any more efficient curriculum. The University degrees in Medicine were valid over the greater part, if not over the whole, of the United Kingdom, and Parliament had recognised the power exercised by the University of granting a degree of C.M., enabling the holder to practise both as a surgeon and general practitioner everywhere, except where exclusive claims of local corporations or of the Apothecaries Company extended. It would be useless to continue the power of granting medical degrees if they were merely honorary, as in Divinity and Law. Would the public be best served by teachers appointed by the Crown, or by teachers undertaking instruction on their own authority and for decidedly lower fees? If there was no advantage in having teachers selected by authority, the keeping up of a Medical School in the University was no longer necessary. The Senate did not object to the improvement of examination and licensing in England if England were satisfied, but they did object to changes in Scotland which would render the degrees of Glasgow University nugatory. The memorial was forwarded to Graham, and a Committee was appointed to correspond with other Universities and public bodies. A great part of the difficulty seems to have arisen from the different circumstances of England and Scotland, in the former of which the Universities were then of little account in regard to medical education, which was mainly in the hands of other corporations, while in the latter, notwithstanding the respectable position occupied by such corporations, the Universities were the leading institutions, both as regards instruction and the granting of qualifications to practise.

In the spring of 1843 the subject was again under discussion and a petition to both Houses of Parliament was adopted. Next year the question seems to have slumbered, but in 1845 there was again much ado over a measure which proved abortive. In spring the Home Secretary once more introduced a bill. The Provost and Magistrates suggested a meeting with members of the University in reference to some points in the measure, but the Senate do not seem to have relished the overture. On 26th March, 1845, a Committee of Senate reported that they approved not only of the principles on which the bill was founded—uniformity of study and examination and equality of privilege in each grade of the profession—but also generally of its details. The obligation that University graduates should undergo an additional examination before acquiring a legal qualification to practise might be considered an infringement of the privileges of the University, but the Committee so far receded from the position formerly taken up that they were not inclined to contest the arrangement, which seemed to be a fundamental part of the bill, and believed that a joint board of examiners composed of the medical professors and the Royal Colleges of Physicians and Surgeons of Scotland could not be injurious to the University. They disapproved of the provision which made the occupant of one particular chair an *ex officio* member of the Council of Health, holding that the University should be allowed to select the fittest representative. They considered that the age of twenty-six fixed as the lowest for examination for qualification as a physician, and twenty-five for qualification as a surgeon, should be reduced to twenty-four. If the College of Physicians of England were empowered to hold special examinations for practitioners of the age of forty, the length of time they had previously been in practice should be specified, the number of candidates thus admitted should be subject to limitation, and similar powers should be conferred on the Universities. Scottish graduates and licentiates should, without further examination, be registered as qualified to practise Midwifery, that branch being included both in their curriculum and their examinations. The bill substituted the word 'Inceptor' for the word 'Bachelor' to designate the lower degree in Medicine, and strong objections were made to this word, as being neither intelligible nor acceptable. The stamp duty on the degree of M.D. was viewed as a fine imposed by the State on higher medical education, and its abolition was urged. A memorial to the Home Secretary was afterwards drawn up, instructions were given in regard to petitioning Parliament, and Burns was requested to proceed to London as soon as convenient to watch the progress of the bill, with power to employ Richardson and Connell, parliamentary agents, to aid in the measures deemed necessary. The disposition of the Senate seems to have passed from faint approval to decided hostility, and Burns was heartily congratulated on the ability which he had shown in opposition to the bill, and the large share which he had in the credit of preventing it from passing.

In May, 1849, the Faculty of Physicians and Surgeons requested the Senate to send representatives to confer with them with a view to arrange the terms of a proposed bill for medical reform so far as medical corporations in Scotland were concerned. The proposal in this form seems to have been dropped, but in December of the same year intimation was received that the Faculty of Physicians and Surgeons had given notice of their intention to promote a bill in Parliament for important changes respecting their body. A Committee of Senate conferred with representatives of the Faculty, and reported that they found no clause in the bill calling for opposition, that the bill would enlarge the privileges of the surgical graduates of the University and free them from some restrictions. The University might give their countenance to the bill as it then stood, but should watch its progress to guard against dangerous alterations. The measure as actually passed on 10th June, 1850, abolished the monopoly of surgical practice in the city of Glasgow and the counties of Lanark, Renfrew, Dumbarton, and Ayr so long enjoyed by practitioners licensed by the Faculty, and opened surgical practice in this district to the fellows, members, and licentiates of any other Corporation or Royal College authorised by law to grant licenses or diplomas in Surgery ; and, by way of compensation, declared that the fellows and licentiates of the Faculty should have the right to practise throughout the Queen's dominions wherever no exclusive privilege had been granted by competent authority to any other Corporation or Royal College.

In May, 1850, Burns called attention to a proposal by Mr. Syme of Edinburgh to withdraw from the Universities the power of granting degrees in Medicine carrying with them authority to practise, and a Committee was appointed to watch the development of the scheme, and to petition Parliament against it, if they saw fit. In March, 1853, the Senate discussed another medical reform bill which proposed to enact that all (excepting graduates of Oxford and Cambridge, whose exclusion was deemed indefensible, as these places were not seats of Medical Schools) who intended to practise Medicine in the United Kingdom should be examined and licensed by Boards to be established in London, Dublin, and Edinburgh. The Universities were to have so limited a representation on the new Boards that their interests would be overborne. Edinburgh alone of Scottish Universities was favourable to the plan, and its attitude was explained by its close connection with the Royal Colleges of Physicians and Surgeons there, from which half the governing body was to be selected. A great deputation to Palmerston in support of the bill had been organised, and Lawrie was asked to proceed to London to urge the adverse views of the Senate. The same year the University joined in opposing an effort made by the Royal College of Physicians of London to procure by charter power to confer the degree of Doctor of Medicine, which was considered a violation of the constitution of established Universities. Another bill introduced in 1854, whether by oversight or otherwise omitted the degree of C.M. from the list of qualifications to which recognition was to be granted. In March, 1856, a petition was adopted against the Medical Reform Bill of that time, and Lawrie was sent to London to enforce the objections entertained to it.

The incorporations of Medical and Surgical Colleges set themselves to procure the establishment of a uniform system of education and registration for physicians and surgeons, under which latter title general practitioners were to be included. Their plan was exclusive in not recognising the rights of University graduates, but in various other respects it was regarded as commendable. On the other hand, the Scottish Universities entered into conference with each other with a view to bring about a uniform system of medical graduation in Scotland, so regulated and so adapted to the practice and the circumstances of England as to remove the only reasonable objection hitherto urged from that quarter against Scottish medical graduates. Though not in accordance with claims previously made, it was now admitted that the right of Scottish medical graduates to practise in England was not clear ; but it was held that the new system would enable the Universities to claim legislative sanction for their graduates to exercise an unfettered right of practice in all parts of the Queen's dominions.

The main points in the plan agreed upon were that the Scottish Universities should grant the degrees of Bachelor and Doctor of Medicine, and that the degree of C.M. conferred for some time at Glasgow should be abandoned. Students proceeding to the degree of M.B. were to pass a preliminary examination in certain subjects in arts and philosophy, and the curriculum of study was to extend over four years, and to correspond as nearly as possible with that hitherto required for M.D. at Edinburgh. The professional examination was to consist of two distinct parts, the first dealing with the fundamental medical sciences, and the second with the practical branches. Students were to be required to study at least two years in a University, and one year in the University in which they desired to graduate, but the latter part of the rule was not to apply to Saint Andrews so long as there was no Medical School there. The degree of M.B. was to qualify for general practice in Medicine, Surgery, and Midwifery, and only those who obtained the degree of M.D. were to rank as physicians. For this latter degree a more extended preliminary examination, an additional course of at least two years' study beyond that required for M.B., and a further examination on the practical branches of Medicine were to be required. It was also proposed that each University might grant the degree of M.D. in not more than three instances annually to qualified practitioners of forty years or upwards, who had been fifteen years in general practice, though they might not have studied at any University. A register of Scottish graduates in practice was to be published yearly, and it was proposed to apply to Her Majesty to provide, in virtue of her power of visitation, such superintendence as would ensure the efficient working of the scheme. This plan was not followed out, however, for the Medical Corporations of the three kingdoms made overtures to the Scottish Universities to co-operate with them in a general plan of medical reform, and the Universities declared that they would willingly co-operate, on the understanding that equal rights to practise should be granted to graduates and to members of incorporated Colleges.

The goal, though near, was not yet reached, and in 1857 two medical bills were before Parliament, one introduced by Mr. Headlam and the other by Lord Elcho. The Senate unanimously adopted a petition to the House of Commons against the former and in favour of the latter, while Lawrie and Andrew Buchanan were sent to London to use their influence in support of the views of the University. Early next year a memorial to the Government on medical legislation was drawn up, and the Senate voted a sum of £26 10s. 7d. to print a pamphlet by Lawrie on the medical privileges of the University.

After the turmoil and contention of many years, an Act to regulate the qualifications of practitioners of Medicine and Surgery, and to enable those requiring medical aid to distinguish qualified from unqualified practitioners, was finally passed on 2nd August, 1858. It established a General Medical Council consisting of representatives of the Universities and Medical and Surgical Corporations of the United Kingdom, and of six persons nominated by the crown—four for England, one for Scotland, and one for Ireland. To this Council, constituted to some extent on home-rule principles, with branches for England, Scotland, and Ireland, was committed the power to register qualified practitioners. It was also laid down that bodies authorised to grant degrees or licenses should afford such information as the General Medical Council might require in reference to the course of study and examinations demanded of candidates, and that if the General Medical Council considered the course of study or the standard of examination defective, they might report accordingly to the Privy Council, the latter body being empowered to suspend the registration of qualifications granted by the licensing authority in question until its course of study and examinations were brought to a satisfactory standard.

It was enacted that every registered practitioner should be entitled to

THE CLOISTERS BETWEEN EAST AND WEST QUADRANGLES

practise, in any part of Her Majesty's dominions, Medicine or Surgery or both, according to the qualification or qualifications he possessed, and to recover reasonable charges for professional services, except in cases where a College of Physicians passed a bye-law forbidding fellows or members to sue in a court of law ; and that none but registered practitioners could validly grant certificates required under any Act of Parliament from members of the medical profession. A schedule annexed to the Act enumerated the qualifications in virtue of which the holders might be registered, and among them were 'Doctor or Bachelor or Licentiate of Medicine, or Master in Surgery, of any University of the United Kingdom.' Only a niggard representation was allowed to the Scottish Universities by the Medical Act of 1858. While one representative was allowed to each of Oxford and Cambridge, which at that time hardly had Medical Schools, and a similar representation to the College of Physicians and the College of Surgeons of Edinburgh, and the Faculty of Physicians and Surgeons of Glasgow, only two representatives were allotted to the whole of the Scottish Universities, one being assigned to the University of Edinburgh and the two Universities of Aberdeen, and one to the University of Glasgow and the University of Saint Andrews, it being provided that if the Universities in a group did not agree, each might nominate a candidate, the Queen in Council being left to determine which nominee should be the actual representative. Professor Lawrie was returned as the first representative of the Universities of Glasgow and Saint Andrews, and when he died towards the end of 1859, Allen Thomson succeeded and held office till 1877.

The year which witnessed the passing of the Medical Act also witnessed the passing of the Universities (Scotland) Act, a measure which directly effected a number of reforms, and appointed a body of Commissioners with very extensive powers, including power to regulate the course of study and the conditions of graduation in the various faculties. One of the most important changes made by the Act was the transference of the general administration from the Principal and the thirteen Faculty or College Professors, as they were called, to the Principal and the whole body of the Professors. The Professors of Medicine and Anatomy had previously been included in the general administrative body, but the other seven or eight Professors in the faculty of Medicine had been excluded from it, and thus prevented from receiving any salary from the University funds, and often from obtaining adequate accommodation or equipment for the teaching of their subjects.

III. 1858–1909

AT first the Commissioners under the Universities Act had been inclined to look with favour on the Universities conferring only one degree in Medicine as a qualification for all branches of the healing art, but questions that arose under the Medical Act moved them to another decision. The words 'medicine' and 'medical' were sometimes used in that Act in the restricted sense as applied to Physic, and sometimes in the more general sense as including Surgery and all departments of Medicine ; but Section xxxi. provided that 'Every person registered under this Act shall be entitled, according to his qualification or qualifications to practise Medicine or Surgery, or Medicine and Surgery, as the case may be, in any part of Her Majesty's dominions.' Some authorities employing practitioners requiring a knowledge of both Medicine and Surgery were perplexed how to interpret this clause, and the Poor Law Board, to which memorials had been addressed by the Universities of Edinburgh, Glasgow, and Aberdeen, the Colleges of Physicians and Surgeons of Edinburgh, the Faculty of Physicians and Surgeons of Glasgow, the Royal College of Surgeons of Ireland, and the University of London, requested the General Medical Council to say how far the degrees and licenses of these bodies were evidence that the persons holding them were properly qualified in either or both branches of the profession. On 10th August, 1859, the General Medical Council, after hearing a report from a Committee on the subject, resolved that the Universities and Corporations in question were legally qualified to grant degrees or licenses in Medicine or Surgery, or in both, that their curricula required an education on all the important branches of the profession, and that a perfect equality of privileges among their graduates and licentiates, according to their several qualifications, should be maintained throughout the United Kingdom. It being thus left doubtful whether a University degree in Medicine sufficiently guaranteed the legal right to practise Surgery, the Commissioners under the Universities Act, who, in regulating graduation in Medicine, dealt first with the University of Edinburgh, were convinced of the soundness of the Edinburgh Senate's contention that the University should exercise its right to grant degrees in Surgery—a right exercised by the University of Glasgow and by the continental Universities most distinguished for their Medical Schools.

The Commissioners accordingly drew up Ordinances for graduation in Medicine and Surgery at Edinburgh, providing for the granting of the degree of Bachelor of Medicine (M.B.) (which had been introduced at

King's College, Aberdeen, in 1852) and also for the degree of Master in Surgery (C.M.)—both degrees being conferred on the same curriculum and examinations, and the candidate having the option of taking M.B. without C.M., but not of taking C.M. without M.B. The degree of M.D. was to be obtained only after the candidate had reached the age of twenty-four, and had attended a hospital or been engaged in practice for at least two years after obtaining the degree of M.B., and further had passed a somewhat higher preliminary examination than for M.B.

No objection was taken to the introduction of the degree of M.B., and in other respects the Ordinances only placed the University of Edinburgh in the position formerly occupied by the University of Glasgow, and had it not been for the action previously taken by Glasgow, it is not likely that the granting of degrees in Surgery in the other Universities could have been vindicated. Now came the tug of war, for the Royal Colleges of Physicians and Surgeons of Edinburgh, the Faculty of Physicians and Surgeons of Glasgow, and the Royal College of Surgeons of England petitioned the Queen in Council to withhold her approval from the ordinances for graduation in Medicine and Surgery at Edinburgh. The petitions were referred to the Commissioners with instructions to hear the petitioners by counsel. On 2nd July, 1860, the petitioners' counsel were heard—Mr. Maitland and Mr. Alexander Robertson for the Royal College of Physicians of Edinburgh, Mr. Young and Mr. Dove Wilson for the Royal College of Surgeons of Edinburgh, Mr. Gifford for the Faculty of Physicians and Surgeons of Glasgow, and Mr. Lee for the Royal College of Surgeons of England. Mr. Macfarlane and Mr. Millar were then heard as counsel for the University of Edinburgh in support of the ordinances, and counsel for the petitioners were offered an opportunity of reply, but did not avail themselves of it.

The Commissioners gave little weight to the contention that the University of Edinburgh had no power to grant the degree of Master in Surgery, holding that the University had an inherent power to grant degrees in any department in which it gave a full course of instruction. They pointed out that the Medical Act distinctly provided for the registration of anyone holding the degree of Master in Surgery from a University of the United Kingdom ; and argued that, though Glasgow was the only University which conferred that degree at the date when the Medical Act was passed, the institution of the degree by other Universities was clearly contemplated and provided for. Some of the petitioners laid stress on clause xix. of the Medical Act which empowered two or more of the Universities and Medical and Surgical Corporations, with the sanction and under the direction of the General Medical Council, to unite or

co-operate in conducting the examinations required for registrable qualifications.   They contended that the University had the choice of either
confining itself to Medicine, or, by co-operating with the Royal College
of Surgeons, of conferring a legitimate double qualification, but had not
by itself the right to grant registrable qualifications both in Medicine and
Surgery.   The Commissioners held that clause xix. was merely permissive, and that as it sanctioned the co-operation of two or more bodies,
thus allowing three bodies to unite, it could not be the intention of the
legislature to confine the co-operation to that of one Medical and one
Surgical body.   In fact two Universities, two Medical Corporations, or
two Surgical Corporations were left free to co-operate just as much as one
Medical and one Surgical Corporation.   The University of Glasgow conferred the degree of Doctor of Medicine, and at the time when the Medical
Act passed it was the only University of the United Kingdom which
conferred the degree of Master in Surgery.   As the Medical Act provided
for the registration of both these degrees, Parliament must evidently have
contemplated the registration of a qualification both in Medicine and
Surgery from one University.   Counsel did not venture to assert that
graduates under the new ordinances would not have the requisite knowledge and skill for efficient practice, but they contended that there should
be a higher preliminary examination and a more extended period of study
for a University degree than for a license from a Corporation, and that no
degree should be conferred till the candidate had reached the age of twenty-
four.   Whatever merits such proposals might have in the abstract, counsel
admitted that their enforcement would seriously diminish the number of
University degrees, and would induce nearly all those intending to become
general practitioners, instead of graduating at the University, to take the
license of the Corporations.   The Commissioners were unwilling to adopt
such prohibitive measures and to close the Universities to the great body
of medical students who sought admission.

    The Commissioners made what they described as a large and liberal
provision for the recognition of extra-mural teachers, and they also laid
down that there should be additional examiners besides the Professors to
conduct the professional examinations, but some of the petitioners were
still dissatisfied.   One of the petitions urged that the non-professorial
examiners should constitute at least three-fourths of the Examining Board,
and should be nominated by the Royal Colleges of Edinburgh and the
Faculty of Physicians and Surgeons of Glasgow.   The Commissioners
would go no further, however, as they did not conceive 'that it would be
for the public advantage that the University should so far abdicate its
functions as to confer its degrees on persons who have never studied within

its walls, at the bidding of a Board of Examiners in whose appointment it has had no share.'

Though vanquished before the Commissioners, the petitioners were ready to argue still, and it seems that, reinforced by the Royal College of Surgeons of Ireland, they again urged their objections before a Committee of the Privy Council, but with no better success than previously. At length on 4th February, 1861, the two ordinances for graduation in Medicine and Surgery at Edinburgh were approved by the Queen in Council and came into force. The way being thus cleared, an ordinance regulating graduation at Glasgow, and another regulating graduation at Aberdeen, with provisions essentially similar to those laid down for Edinburgh, were approved by the Queen in Council on 26th June, 1861.

Ordinance No. 15, which regulated graduation at Glasgow, prescribed a curriculum of four years for the degree of M.B., during which the student was required to attend a course of a hundred lectures on each of Anatomy, Chemistry, Materia Medica and Pharmacy, Physiology, Practice of Medicine, Surgery, Midwifery and Diseases of Women and Children, and Pathology (a three months' course of lectures on Pathological Anatomy, with a supplemental course of Practice of Medicine or Clinical Medicine, being allowed as a substitute for the last); as well as a course of Practical Anatomy for six months, of Practical Chemistry for three months, and of compounding and dispensing drugs by apprenticeship or otherwise for three months; and a course of at least fifty meetings on each of the three subjects of Medical Jurisprudence, Botany, and Zoology. Attendance for at least two years on the medical and surgical practice of a general hospital was prescribed, as well as attendance on a course of Clinical Medicine for six months and of Clinical Surgery for the same period. It was further laid down that the student should have six months' attendance on the out-practice of a hospital, or the practice of a dispensary or of a physician or surgeon; and three months' attendance at a Midwifery Hospital, or a certificate from a registered medical practitioner of attendance on six cases of labour. The ordinance made no change on the length of the curriculum, and in the main confirmed previous usage. The requirement of two years' attendance at a hospital remained as before, but the strict enforcement of attendance on distinct courses of clinical instruction was new, as was also the requirement of a separate course on Zoology and on Pathology, though the latter subject had long been taught as a branch of Institutes of Medicine.

Candidates for graduation were required to attend at least one year in the University of Glasgow, and a second year either in the same place or in another University entitled to grant the degree of M.D. The University, whilst accepting as part of the curriculum attendance in certain extra-academic Medical Schools outside of Glasgow, had probably been unreasonably strict in excluding extra-academic teaching in Glasgow itself. The Commissioners now empowered the University Court to recognise private teachers under whom students might take four of the required lecture courses on condition of their paying fees of as great an amount as the University Professors were authorised to charge.

The degree of M.B. might be taken by itself or in combination with the degree of C.M., but the University was not empowered to give the degree of C.M. separately as it had hitherto done.   The degree of M.D. was to be conferred only on those who had been engaged in further hospital attendance or in practice for at least two years after obtaining the degree of Bachelor of Medicine, who had reached the age of twenty-four, and complied with somewhat higher requirements in regard to preliminary examination.   For M.B. the subjects of preliminary examination to be passed before entering on the curriculum were English, Latin, Arithmetic, Elementary Mathematics, Elementary Mechanics; while two further subjects were required before admission to a professional examination, any two out of Greek, French, German, Higher Mathematics, Natural Philosophy, Natural History, Logic, or Moral Philosophy, being allowed. The candidate for M.D. was required, not later than three years from the time of graduating as M.B., to pass in Greek, Logic or Moral Philosophy, and one or other of French, German, Higher Mathematics, Natural Philosophy, or Natural History.   The subjects of preliminary examination were rather numerous, and higher proficiency in fewer subjects would have been preferable.

For the degrees of M.B. and C.M. three professional examinations were prescribed.   The first, in Chemistry, Botany and Elementary Anatomy, might be taken at the end of the second year; the second, in Advanced Anatomy, Zoology with Comparative Anatomy, Physiology, and Surgery, at the end of the third year; and the third, in Materia Medica, General Pathology, Practice of Medicine, Clinical Medicine, Clinical Surgery, Midwifery, and Medical Jurisprudence, at the end of the curriculum.   Students could not be admitted to any of the three examinations till attendance on the prescribed subjects had been completed, nor to the later examinations till the earlier ones had been passed; but they were allowed to take the first and second examinations together at the end of the third year, or all three examinations at the end of the fourth year.   It was provided that, besides the Professors, three other fit persons should be appointed by the University Court to conduct the professional examinations, these examiners being fellows of the Royal College of

Physicians of Edinburgh, the Royal College of Surgeons of Edinburgh, and the Faculty of Physicians and Surgeons of Glasgow, or otherwise possessed of qualifications deemed satisfactory by the University Court. Each of the three examiners was to receive £80 a year for his services.

The Universities Act provided that Ordinances made by the Commissioners might be altered or revoked by the University Court, with the consent of the Chancellor and the approval of the Queen in Council; and under this provision a number of amendments were made from time to time. In 1868 Physiology was transferred to the second professional examination and Surgery to the third. In 1875 the Court was empowered to appoint not fewer than six persons specially qualified to examine in the subjects of the medical curriculum, instead of the three originally authorised, and to apportion among them the £240 provided by the Treasury. The normal period for which examiners might hold office was fixed at four years, and no limitation was laid down as to the medical or surgical authorities from whom their qualifications were derived. In 1877 it was provided that there should be four professional examinations—the first in Chemistry, Botany, and Natural History; the second in Anatomy and Physiology; the third in Regional Anatomy, Pathology, Materia Medica and Pharmacy; and the fourth in Surgery, Clinical Surgery, Medicine, Clinical Medicine, Therapeutics, Midwifery, and Medical Jurisprudence. It was further laid down that the examinations should include Practical Chemistry and Practical Anatomy, as well as Histology and Practical Physiology, and that the examination in Surgery should include Operative Surgery. The times at which students might enter for each of the four examinations were also defined. In 1878 it was enacted that students should attend a class of Practical Materia Medica in a University or recognised School of Medicine or under a recognised teacher. The requirement that candidates for M.D. should pass the additional preliminary subjects within three years of their graduating as M.B. was now abolished; and in 1880 Natural History was removed from the list of preliminary subjects for M.D. At the same time the Court was authorised 'in special circumstances' to reappoint an examiner who had held office for the four years fixed in 1875 as the normal tenure. In 1881 it was made compulsory for all candidates to take the degree of Master in Surgery along with the degree of Bachelor of Medicine, a change in which Edinburgh and Aberdeen soon afterwards followed the example of Glasgow; while a further alteration made in 1883 required candidates for the double degree to pay five guineas when entering for each of the four professional examinations, and another change made in 1885 regulated the time when students might be admitted to the second professional examination. In

1885 Pathology was transferred from the third to the final examination. Finally in 1889 the requirements in Practical Midwifery were made more stringent, and a new Universities Act having been passed in that year, new Commissioners and new Ordinances followed.

Important changes were sometimes made in matters not regulated by Ordinance. In 1868, acting on a recommendation by the Scottish branch of the General Medical Council, the faculty of Medicine, as authorised by the Senate, laid down a rule that every candidate for a degree in Medicine or Surgery should be required to produce a certificate from a public institution where Vaccination is practised that he has been instructed in that subject. In 1876, on the proposal of Dr. Simpson, it was resolved to institute a Qualification in Public Health, open to registered medical practitioners who had attended special courses on Public Health and Analytical Chemistry and passed prescribed examinations. It was arranged that courses of instruction should be given in the ensuing session. By and by a Diploma in Public Health was conferred, instead of a Qualification, as it was at first called. Medical authorities in other parts of the country also introduced Diplomas or Degrees in Public Health, and they came to be regarded as of greater importance both in relation to registration and to public appointments. The sufficiency of an examination for the Diploma in Public Health held at Glasgow in October, 1889, was afterwards discussed in the General Medical Council, and the papers on the subject may be read in their Minutes. Additional examiners besides the six provided for in 1875 were introduced, and, as the needful remuneration came from the University funds, no change of Ordinance was required. In 1884 the Court resolved that in future there should be a separate examiner for each of Chemistry and Materia Medica, instead of one examiner acting in both subjects, and in 1886 separate examiners were similarly provided in Botany and Zoology. Further additions to the number of examiners have since been made.

The Commissioners under the Act of 1858 made some additions from new parliamentary grants to the salaries of the less remunerative chairs, and at the end of 1861 they estimated the whole emoluments of the chair of Medicine at £410, of Anatomy at £750, of Natural History at £300, of Surgery at £320, of Midwifery at £230, of Chemistry at £620, of Botany at £400, of Materia Medica at £270, of Institutes of Medicine at £310, and of Forensic Medicine at £210. They also allotted from parliamentary grants £200 for the salaries of two assistants in Chemistry, and £50 for the salary of an assistant in Materia Medica and Forensic Medicine. In 1868 power was obtained to appoint a separate assistant in each subject, and divide the remuneration between them. For the pur-

NEW MEDICAL BUILDINGS AND SOUTH FRONT OF UNIVERSITY

pose of defraying class expenses the Commissioners assigned from the University funds £200 annually to Anatomy, £70 to Chemistry, £50 to Materia Medica, and £35 to Forensic Medicine.   The somewhat modest emoluments then received by professors depended to a great extent on the fees paid by students, and as the number of students during the period of the Commissioners was rather limited, the emoluments were correspondingly restricted.   For about ten years the number of students showed little advance, but afterwards there was a marked increase, which improved the income from fees, while in several cases new regulations requiring students to attend practical classes had a similar effect.   In 1860 the number of medical students was 311 ; and in 1865, 272 ; while from 1867 to 1871 the annual average was 330 ; from 1872 to 1876, 381 ; from 1877 to 1881, 551 ; from 1882 to 1886, 692 ; and from 1887 to 1891, 802, the highest number being recorded in 1891, when there were 820.

After the passing of the new Ordinance in 1861, it required four years for students to go through the curriculum and obtain the degree of Bachelor of Medicine, so that this new degree was not conferred till 1865, and thus far, many candidates who had begun their course under the old regulations continued to graduate as M.D. without taking any prior degree ; but the number of new Doctors of Medicine fell very considerably when it became necessary first to obtain the degree of Bachelor of Medicine and comply with the other requirements.   The degree of C.M. came again into favour, and was taken by the great majority of those who obtained the degree of M.B. before 1881, when it was made compulsory on graduands to take both degrees together.   For the thirty years from 1862 to 1891 the degree of M.D. was conferred on 687 individuals, an annual average of 22.9 ; the degree of C.M. on 1,794 individuals, an annual average of 59.8 ; and the degree of M.B. on 1,772 individuals, an annual average of 65.6.[1]

The extension of accommodation and increase in the teaching staff in a number of subjects common to the faculties of Medicine and Science have been mentioned in the account of the rapid growth of the latter, but some further notes must be added regarding the chairs and the teaching staff in the faculty of Medicine.   John Young, who graduated as M.D. at Edinburgh in 1857, and was some time engaged in the medical service of an Asylum and afterwards in the Geological Survey, succeeded Rogers in 1866 as professor of Natural History.   Shortly after his appointment Dr. Young had, like Lockhart Muirhead, to superintend the removal of the Hunterian Museum, and there was much to be done, though this time

[1] The number of years for this degree (first granted in 1865) is only 27, as compared with 30 in the other cases.

2 O

the distance was only from the east to the west end of Glasgow. From 1876, when the Honyman Gillespie lectureship in Geology was founded, he also held that post, with an additional income of about £200 a year. His keen and versatile powers wrestled with many problems. He taught classes in Zoology and Geology, he was keeper of the Hunterian Museum, and he busied himself in the work of general administration; but, alert and aggressive as he was, greater concentration would have enabled him to accomplish more valuable and enduring work. Towards the end his health gave way, and for some of the later sessions the Zoology class was conducted by James Rankin, B.Sc., M.B., C.M. Dr. Young, who had been appointed one of the Senate's representatives in the University Court in 1899, resigned his chair in 1902, and died on 13th December of that year. Mr. John Graham Kerr, M.A., was next appointed to the chair of Natural History under an arrangement by which almost immediately afterwards the subject was divided, Mr. Kerr continuing as professor of Zoology, while in 1904 Dr. Gregory became professor of Geology.

During the tenure of John Ferguson, M.A., LL.D., who succeeded Anderson as professor of Chemistry in 1874, the work of the department and the teaching staff have much increased. Chemistry being a standard subject, not only in Medicine, but for the first Science examination for the degree of B.Sc. in Pure Science, Agriculture, Engineering, Mining, and Pharmacy, as well as a possible subject of the final examination for B.Sc. in Pure Science, a necessary subject in the final examination for B.Sc. in Pharmacy, and a possible subject for the degree of M.A.—there is hardly any limit to the scope and ramifications of the teaching. Professor Ferguson was Convener of the Board of Examiners in Science before the faculty of Science was constituted, and may be said to have presided over the nascent stages of the development of that faculty. It is also to be remembered that Sir William Ramsay was a student of Glasgow, and for several years a member of the teaching staff in the Chemistry department.

The new regulations for graduation in Medicine which came into force in 1892 brought a short course in the kindred subject of Physics into the early part of the medical curriculum. This course was first taught by Magnus Maclean, D.Sc. In 1899 he became a professor at the Technical College, and Lord Kelvin retired from the chair of Natural Philosophy. Since then the class of Physics has usually been taught by a lecturer, but sometimes Professor Gray has himself conducted it. The present lecturer is James G. Gray, D.Sc.

After the death of Mr. Arnott in 1868, Alexander Dickson, who graduated as M.D. at Edinburgh in 1860, was appointed professor of Botany, and held the chair for eleven years, when he was transferred to Edinburgh, on the retirement of Dr. John Hutton Balfour, who thirty-four years before had been similarly transferred. Dr. Isaac Bayley Balfour, a son of the veteran professor at Edinburgh, then succeeded to the chair at Glasgow, and upon his being appointed Sherardian professor of Botany at Oxford in 1884, the present professor, Frederick Orpen Bower, Sc.D., was appointed early in 1885. Professor Bayley Balfour was the first to establish a class of Practical Botany at Glasgow, and the teaching and equipment have since undergone extensive development. Commodious and well equipped new buildings for the Botany department were opened in 1901 by Sir Joseph D. Hooker, who gave some interesting particulars regarding his father's means and methods of teaching Botany at Glasgow, and of his Botanical excursions in the olden days when there were no railways, cycles, or motors.

John Cleland, M.D., D.Sc., F.R.S., professor of Anatomy from 1877 to 1909, in the later years of his tenure was in a sense the senior member of the teaching staff, having been demonstrator of Anatomy at Glasgow under Dr. Allen Thomson from 1861 to 1863. He then became professor of Anatomy and Physiology at Queen's College, Galway, where he continued till in 1877 he was appointed to succeed Thomson in the chair of Anatomy at Glasgow. The great extension of accommodation provided from funds given by the Trustees of the late Mr. James Brown Thomson has already been mentioned, as well as the institution of a lectureship on Embryology. More recently a lectureship in Applied Anatomy has been established, with Robert Kennedy, D.Sc., M.D., as lecturer.

Notwithstanding advanced age, Dr. Andrew Buchanan held the chair of Institutes of Medicine till 1876, when he retired. The professorship was afterwards held for thirty years by John Gray M'Kendrick, M.D., F.R.S., under whom the teaching and equipment were greatly extended; and, on his retirement in 1906, Dr. Noël Paton, who had been for seventeen years superintendent of the Research Laboratory of the Royal College of Physicians in Edinburgh, was appointed. The appointment fell at a time which enabled the new professor to make his influence felt in the equipment and organisation of the commodious new premises in which Physiology is now housed.

No provision was made within the University for the teaching of Pathology as an independent subject for some years after the new regulations of 1861 came into force, but in 1870 Joseph Coats, who graduated as M.B. in 1867 and M.D. in 1870, was appointed lecturer on Pathological Anatomy, being regarded, however, as an assistant to Professor Andrew Buchanan, whose right to teach this delegated subject was reserved. This arrangement was continued till the opening of the

Western Infirmary in 1874, when Dr. Coats became Pathologist to that institution, and though ceasing to be an official University lecturer, conducted classes which almost all the medical students attended.   In 1890 a committee of the General Council discussed the question of establishing a chair in Pathology, and the Council recommended the Court to take steps for its institution.   This desirable object was not immediately realised, but Dr Coats was appointed University lecturer on the subject from November, 1890, and in November, 1893, the chair was at length founded by an Ordinance of the Commissioners under the Act of 1889.   The patronage is vested in seven curators, of whom four are appointed by the University Court and three by the Directors of the Western Infirmary. Classroom and laboratory accommodation, for which the University pays a considerable rent, is provided at the Infirmary, and, the professor being also pathologist to the latter institution, its materials are fully available for teaching purposes.   In 1894 Dr. Coats, who had taught Pathology for nearly a quarter of a century and produced a textbook on the subject, was appointed first incumbent of the new chair.   Preferment came rather late, for, though Dr. Coats was not advanced in age, his health had given way. A long voyage to the Antipodes failed to re-establish it, and the class was for some time conducted by Lewis Robertson Sutherland, M.B., C.M. Professor Coats died on 24th January, 1899, and Dr. Robert Muir, the present professor, having been appointed to the chair at Glasgow, Sutherland succeeded him in the chair which he vacated at University College, Dundee.   In the professional examination Pathology seems, till 1873, to have been included under Institutes of Medicine or Practice of Medicine, but in that year a separate paper on Pathology was introduced.

John Black Cowan, who succeeded Easton in the chair of Materia Medica in 1865, was the son of Robert Cowan, the first professor of Medical Jurisprudence, and graduated as M.D. at Glasgow in 1851.   After acting as a Civil Surgeon in the Army in the Crimea, he returned to Glasgow, and lectured at Anderson's College—first on Medical Jurisprudence and afterwards on Practice of Medicine.   Infirm health induced him to resign his professorship in 1880, when the Senate conferred upon him the honorary degree of LL.D., and he died at Largs in July, 1896. After Cowan's resignation, Matthew Charteris, who graduated as M.D. at Edinburgh in 1863, held the chair till June, 1897, when he died.   He had been professor of Medicine in Anderson's College from 1876 to 1880, and having published a work on Practice of Medicine which went through many editions, he was perhaps more widely known in that subject than in Materia Medica, though his efforts to find a remedy for sea-sickness attracted considerable notice.   For some time about 1884-85, during an illness of the professor, the Materia Medica classes were conducted by Dr. Alexander Napier. Ralph Stockman, who graduated at Edinburgh as M.B. and C.M. in 1882, and M.D. in 1886, has been professor since 1897. Ample accommodation and equipment have been provided for this department in the new Medical Buildings opened in 1907. For a number of years Dr. Stockman has also been one of the Physicians of the Western Infirmary, and his clinical classes have attracted a large following of students.

The veteran Harry Rainy, who retired from the chair of Medical Jurisprudence in 1872 and died in 1876, gave £1,500 to the University to establish bursaries for medical students. He was succeeded by Pierce Adolphus Simpson, a licentiate of the two Royal Colleges of Edinburgh, who also graduated as M.D. at St. Andrews in 1861. For several years before his appointment to the University chair, Dr. Simpson had been professor of the same subject in Anderson's College. During the last four or five years of his tenure, Simpson's health was so much impaired that he was unable to take any great part in the teaching, and the class was carried on, first by Dr. Donald Munro, who acted as his assistant for twenty-three years, and afterwards by Gavin M'Callum, M.B., C.M., and Hugh Galt, M.B., C.M., in succession. Simpson resigned his chair early in 1898, and dying on 11th August, 1900, left a type-written will. An ensuing lawsuit settled that testamentary writings expressed in such characters are valid. Dr. John Glaister was next appointed to the chair, and during his tenure, not only the department of Forensic Medicine, but also that of Public Health has been reorganised, degrees in Public Health have been introduced, and large and well-equipped laboratories and other accommodation provided.

After the death of Pagan in May, 1868, William Leishman, who graduated as M.D. at Glasgow in 1855 and was some time professor of Medical Jurisprudence in Anderson's College, was appointed to the chair of Midwifery. He had a considerable reputation in his own subject, and was the author of a *System of Midwifery* which passed through several editions. For a long time he was dean of the faculty of Medicine, from 1889 to 1893 he was a member of the University Court, and from 1886 to 1893 he represented the University in the General Medical Council. In the midst of a career of active and decided usefulness, failing health compelled him to resign in 1893, and he died on 18th February, 1894. Dr. Murdoch Cameron, who had been assistant to Leishman from 1885 onwards, and had carried on the work of the class for some time during the illness of the latter, was appointed professor of Midwifery in 1894. After the opening of the Western Infirmary a number of beds were placed in charge of the professor of Midwifery to enable him to give clinical instruction in cases appropriate to his department. In 1883 Dr. Leishman also instituted a separate summer course in Gynaecology.

After the death of Lawrie there were some rather unusual proceedings with a view to guide—or, as some thought, to misguide—the Home Secretary in regard to the next appointment to the chair of Surgery, and, as they were noticed in the newspapers, they made some considerable stir at the time. On 16th January, 1860, the two Members of Parliament for the City of Glasgow, Mr. Walter Buchanan and Mr. Robert Dalglish, sent out a circular to medical practitioners in Glasgow and the neighbourhood, stating that they believed the candidates for the vacant chair were Drs. Corbett, Fleming, Lyon, Macleod, E. Watson, and George Buchanan —all of Glasgow, and Drs. Edwards and Lister of Edinburgh ; and asking the practitioners to return on a paper (which need not be signed) the name of the candidate they considered best qualified for the post ; after which Messrs. Buchanan and Dalglish would decide which candidate they would recommend to Sir George Cornwall Lewis, the Home Secretary, for appointment. The list was a notable one, in respect that out of the eight candidates named, three actually came to hold the position of professor of Surgery, or some branch of it, in the University ; but the Senate did not relish the proceedings, and solemnly protested against the patronage of chairs being exercised under the pressure of sectional or local interests, or in any other way than by the unbiassed judgment of Her Majesty's responsible advisers. On 28th January, 1860, the Queen issued a commission to ' Joseph Lister, Esqr.,' to be professor of Surgery. Lister graduated as M.B. of London in 1852, and soon afterwards became House Surgeon to Syme at Edinburgh, whose daughter he married in 1856, and about the same time became a lecturer on Surgery in Edinburgh. He was admitted to office as professor at Glasgow on 9th March, 1860, after reading a Latin dissertation *De Arte Chirurgica Recte Erudienda*.

It was unfortunate that for some time Lister did not obtain an appointment in the Royal Infirmary to enable him to apply his unrivalled skill and ability to the treatment of surgical cases and the teaching of Clinical Surgery. The Commissioners under the Act of 1858 requested the faculty of Medicine to send a statement of the existing arrangements for clinical teaching in Medicine and Surgery, and to suggest means of improving it. The faculty considered that it would be better to establish a permanent connection between the existing chairs and a public hospital than to institute separate clinical professorships ; and that any recommendation by the Commissioners would carry great weight, especially if it were understood that, in the event of the Infirmary Managers absolutely refusing accommodation for clinical instruction in connection with the University, the Commissioners would be prepared to aid in establishing a University clinical hospital. This well-meant communication from the Commissioners did not lead to any permanent result, but in about two years from the time he became professor, Lister secured an appointment in the Royal Infirmary.

A writer in the *Glasgow Herald* of 6th April, 1907, describes his work there, pointing out that in those days 'chronic surgical cases were treated in the present central block of the Infirmary, which then was the fever hospital of Glasgow. When fever was sparse the patients were accommodated in the upper wards of that block, and the chronic surgical cases were treated in the lower wards. If fever increased, ward after ward was emptied of surgical cases until the whole block was occupied with fever patients. As the epidemic declined the wards, beginning with the lowest, were again utilised for surgical work. In these circumstances it is little wonder that blood poisoning and hospital gangrene were of frequent occurrence. . . . That septicaemia and hospital gangrene were due to infection no one could possibly doubt. What was the material of the infection and how did it operate? Surgeons everywhere endeavoured to solve these questions, Professor Lister most earnestly of all. And he looked everywhere for guidance in his enquiry. About that time Pasteur, the great French chemist, had been consulted by wine makers in Paris as to the occasional malfermentation of the juice of the grape. . . . After much consideration and many experiments, Pasteur came to the conclusion that the cause of fermentation was only in a secondary sense chemical, that primarily it was vital, and that when the fermentation of the grape juice went wrong it was due to the presence of foreign living germs which were introduced from the atmosphere, or by uncleanness of one kind or other in the vats or from the hands of the workers. After great labour Pasteur established conclusively that the causation was particulate, and that the particles were minute living organisms. It flashed into Professor Lister's mind that septicaemia and hospital gangrene were likewise due to living germs which fell into the open wound from the air, or were conveyed into it by unclean hands, unclean instruments, or unclean dressings. He repeated many of Pasteur's experiments and made many original investigations into the living germs floating in the air, and in the winter session of 1865-6 he applied solutions of probable germicides to the surfaces of wounds—solutions of certain salts of metals. The success of these, however, was not very apparent; but in the spring of 1866 Professor Lister became aware of certain experiments conducted at Carlisle for the disinfection of drains by an acid then known only to a few chemical experts —carbolic acid—and in May of that year in the Royal Infirmary he employed solutions of this acid to destroy germs that might in any manner be conveyed into a wound.   At first the solutions were strong ; gradually he found that he could reduce their strength, and that up to a certain degree of reduction the results became better and better, and before the end of the year the outcome of his work was such as to convince every observer that a revolution in surgical procedure and surgical possibilities had begun.'

The writer then narrates that Syme in Edinburgh gave Lister's method a trial, while in the great hospitals of London and other parts of England his work was ignored or derided, but in Germany it was appreciated at its true value and further improvements were made.   At length, mainly through the influence of Professor Tyndal, Lister's views came to be generally adopted in England.   'Since then antiseptic or aseptic surgery has been universally adopted.   Prior to Lister's discovery operative surgery was extremely restricted.   It dealt mainly with the surface of the body and with the limbs. . . .   Now the abdomen and the cranium are opened with practically no risk of septic inflammation occurring.   Modern surgery had its birth in Professor Lister's wards in the Royal Infirmary in 1866.'   It may be added that, as it was some years before his system was generally adopted, and Lister resigned his chair at Glasgow in 1869, and removed first to Edinburgh and afterwards to London, the connection of the University and City of Glasgow with this great revolution in surgical practice is not always sufficiently recognised.   The University conferred the degree of LL.D. on Lister in 1879, and in 1907, when the office of Chancellor became vacant through the death of Lord Kelvin, he would have been nominated for that high office, with small risk of any rival candidate appearing, had not his advanced age and the state of his health induced him to decline the offer.   He was made a baronet in 1883, and raised to the peerage as Baron Lister in 1897.

George Husband Baird Macleod, the next professor of Surgery, graduated as M.D. at Glasgow in 1853, acted as surgeon in the General Hospital in the Camp before Sebastopol, and was some time professor of Surgery in Anderson's College.   While holding the University chair he taught very large classes, alike in Systematic, Clinical, and Operative Surgery, and had also a very extensive practice.   After the foundation of clinical chairs, questions arose regarding the province and standing of the new professors in reference to those of the professors of Medicine and Surgery.   In 1878 Macleod appealed to the University Court against a decision of the Senate, and the Court found that Professors Macleod and Gairdner were equally

LORD LISTER, M.B., F.R.C.S.
P.C., O.M., LL.D., F.R.S.
Professor of Surgery, 1860-1869

entitled along with Professors Buchanan and M'Call Anderson to have the lists of their clinical students printed in the class catalogues of the University; and expressed an opinion that the professors of systematic Surgery and Medicine are, by virtue of their inherent rights as such professors, and without any other or further recognition, on a par with the professors of Clinical Surgery and Clinical Medicine as regards clinical teaching. In 1887 Dr. Macleod was knighted, and he died in 1892. As a memorial, Lady Macleod in 1895 instituted a gold medal, with the intention that it should be annually awarded to the most distinguished student in the Surgery class.

William Macewen, who graduated as M.B. and C.M. at Glasgow in 1869, and M.D. three years later, and whose work in Surgery in the Royal Infirmary had made him widely known, was appointed in succession to Macleod. Some time afterwards proposals were made which would have reduced the accommodation and facilities for clinical teaching hitherto afforded to the professor of Surgery in the Western Infirmary, but after conference between representatives of the University and the Infirmary, the previous arrangement was continued. Professor Macewen soon procured the erection of new premises for Operative Surgery—of a temporary character at first, but soon replaced by a permanent building which cost upwards of £9,000. In 1902 he was created a knight, and learned and professional societies at home and abroad have admitted him to membership or conferred other distinctions.

William Tennant Gairdner, who graduated as M.D. at Edinburgh in 1845, and was afterwards a physician in the Royal Infirmary there, and for ten years a lecturer on Practice of Medicine and Clinical Medicine, was peculiarly well fitted by his previous training for the chair of Medicine at Glasgow to which he was appointed in 1862, and which he held for thirty-eight years. From 1863 to 1872 he was Chief Medical Officer of Glasgow, and had a great share in organising the public health system of the city. He was devoted to his own profession but by no means limited to it, and his interest in all manner of subjects, his wide range of knowledge, his long and varied experience, and his scrupulous fairness of view made him a teacher not readily to be equalled. Created a K.C.B. in 1898, he was a member of the University Court for a number of years, and in 1893 he succeeded Leishman as representative of the University in the General Medical Council. Sir William Gairdner retired from his chair in 1900, and died on 28th June, 1907. He was succeeded in the professorship of Medicine by Dr. Thomas M'Call Anderson, who had been professor of Clinical Medicine since 1874. Sir Thomas Anderson, who had been knighted in 1905, died on 25th January, 1908; and Dr. Samson

Gemmell, who had followed him as professor of Clinical Medicine, then succeeded him in the chair of Practice of Medicine.

The scheme for procuring new buildings for the University included the provision of a hospital conveniently situated for the clinical instruction of medical students and in which the professors should have a right to give such instruction. In the early stages there was only one fund, but it was understood that a certain portion of it would be allocated to the hospital. In 1871, however, it was resolved to make a separate appeal for subscriptions to the Infirmary, and the response was liberal. The University expended nearly £30,000 in procuring about eleven acres for the site and grounds of the Infirmary, and in October, 1874, a general meeting of subscribers adopted a constitution for it, under which a Board of Managers was elected. Both in the deed conveying the lands and in the constitution of the Infirmary it is laid down that reasonable provision shall be made within it for clinical instruction by such professors as the University authorities may from time to time appoint—the Managers being left free to elect the medical officers of the institution and to appoint other clinical teachers besides the professors. The Western Infirmary was not ready for several years after the University classes were transferred to Gilmorehill, and medical students had still to attend clinical courses at the Royal Infirmary, being conveyed to the University at the close of their clinical classes in omnibuses provided at the cost of the Senate. By this time the Royal Infirmary had become more accessible, the professors of Surgery and Medicine and the two newly appointed professors of Clinical Surgery and Clinical Medicine holding positions within it, which they relinquished in order to begin clinical teaching in the Western Infirmary when it was opened in November, 1874. At the outset the wards contained about 200 beds for patients, but by subsequent additions this accommodation has been more than doubled, and there are now 543 beds.

In 1851 a number of medical students made a representation to the Senate in favour of instituting professorships of Clinical Medicine and Clinical Surgery, and six years later Professors Lawrie and Allen Thomson were authorised to apply to the Trustees of the Ferguson fund for a grant to secure a ward or wards in the Royal Infirmary for clinical teaching in connection with the University, but both proposals were fruitless. In 1861 the faculty of Medicine were rather averse to the founding of clinical chairs. At the time when the Western Infirmary was nearing completion interest in the proposal to found clinical chairs was somehow revived, and a capital fund of £2,500 having been offered for the endowment of each of the twin chairs of Clinical Surgery and Clinical Medicine, deeds for their foundation were drawn up by the Senate and executed in May, 1874.

These deeds did not confer any monopoly of clinical teaching on the new professors, the right of the professors of Surgery and Medicine to give such instruction being expressly reserved, and no restriction being placed on clinical teaching by the physicians and surgeons of the Infirmary, though not professors at all.   The patronage of the new chairs was assigned to the University Court, and the University provided no further emoluments beyond the income of the capital funds.[1]   Though this income is supplemented by the fees paid by clinical students, the clinical chairs have the most modest emoluments of any in the University.

As already mentioned, the two professors of Clinical Medicine have been promoted in succession to the chair of Medicine.   As yet no appointment has been made to the vacancy caused by the transfer of Dr. Samson Gemmell.

In 1874 George Buchanan, who became a Licentiate of the Royal College of Surgeons of Edinburgh in 1849, and graduated as M.D. at St. Andrews in the same year, was appointed to the new chair of Clinical Surgery.   He had been a surgeon in the Crimea, was for some time surgeon and lecturer on Clinical Surgery in the Royal Infirmary, and from 1860 to 1874 was professor of Surgery in Anderson's College.   Advanced age and failing health induced Dr. Buchanan to resign in 1900.   The present professor, Sir Hector Clare Cameron, M.D., who had long been a surgeon and clinical teacher in the Western Infirmary, and from 1889 one of the General Council's representatives in the University Court, was then appointed.

A new Ordinance for graduation in Medicine, passed in 1892 by the Commissioners under the Act of 1889, extended the curriculum to five years, in keeping with changes made about the same date in other Universities and Medical Schools.   The minimum hospital attendance was raised to three years, and short courses, to consist largely of practical instruction, have been prescribed in Mental Diseases, Fevers, and Ophthalmology.   Attendance on Post-mortem Examinations is also required, and students are recommended to attend short practical courses on Diseases of Children, the Ear, the Throat and Nose, and the Skin, and the great majority do so.   The tendency in Medicine is to render the curriculum more practical, and one of the questions frequently discussed is how to distribute the students over the wide field for clinical study afforded by the various city hospitals.   Women students, comparatively few in number as yet, have taken their clinical instruction in the Royal Infirmary, but the great majority of the men attend the Western Infirmary, which,

[1] For a number of years the University has provided salaries to assistants who aid the professors in the work of clinical teaching.

on account of nearness to the University, is much more convenient, while the Victoria Infirmary has been very little utilised. It may be doubted whether any plan of distribution which limits its view to the Western and the Royal Infirmaries will be fully effective; but even without further change, the opportunities for clinical work enjoyed by Glasgow students are probably more ample than in some of the other foremost Medical Schools of the country.

INDEX

CORRIGENDA.

Page 18, line 15, *for* 'acting as regent,' *read* 'acting as dean.'
Page 78, line 28, *for* 'Earl of Stair,' *read* 'Viscount Stair.'
Page 456, line 8, *for* 'right arm,' *read* 'left arm.'

GLASGOW : PRINTED AT THE UNIVERSITY PRESS BY ROBERT MACLEHOSE AND CO. LTD.

ImTheStory.com

Personalized Classic Books in many genre's

Unique gift for kids, partners, friends, colleagues

Customize:

- Character Names

- Upload your own front/back cover images (optional)

- Inscribe a personal message/dedication on the

  inside page (optional)

Customize many titles Including
- Alice in Wonderland
- Romeo and Juliet
- The Wizard of Oz
- A Christmas Carol
- Dracula
- Dr. Jekyll & Mr. Hyde
- And more...

Lightning Source UK Ltd.
Milton Keynes UK
UKOW031802260313

208237UK00018B/743/P